ID984644

BROKERS OF CULTURE

Brokers of Culture

ITALIAN JESUITS IN THE AMERICAN WEST,
1848–1919

Gerald McKevitt

STANFORD UNIVERSITY PRESS

STANFORD, CALIFORNIA 2007

Stanford University Press
Stanford, California
©2007 by the Board of Trustees of the
Leland Stanford Junior University. All rights reserved.

Printed in the United States of America on acid-free, archival-quality paper

Library of Congress Cataloging-in-Publication Data
McKevitt, Gerald.
    Italian Jesuits in the American West, 1848–1919 / Gerald McKevitt.
    p.   cm.
    Includes bibliographical references and index.
    ISBN-13: 978-0-8047-5357-9 (cloth : alk. paper)
    1. Jesuits — Missions — United States — History. 2. Jesuits — West (U.S) —
History. 3. Jesuits — Italy — History. I. Title.
    BV2290.M35 2007
    271'.53078 — dc22   2006019061

Original Printing 2007

Typeset by BookMatters in 10/12.5 Sabon

For Patty and Tim,
Janice, Karen,
Barbara and Mike,
and Carol

Contents

CONTENTS

Illustrations

Preface

The dusty clutter of an old attic sparked my first thoughts about this book. As a seminary student in the 1960s, I lived in an antiquated Victorian building perched on a leafy hillside above Los Gatos, a small town on the edge of California's Santa Clara Valley. The seminary, an elaborate wooden pile replete with false quoins and mansard roof, had been erected in 1888 amid vineyards and olive groves by Jesuit émigrés driven from Italy during national unification. My curiosity was piqued by those atypical refugees and by the gingerbread edifice they left behind. When not occupied with Latin study, meditation, and handball, I explored their ancient structure — from its dark, labyrinthine basement to its lofty turret, below which spread, in springtime, a pink-and-white quilt of blossoming orchards. Already in the sixties, that landscape was changing as plum and apricot groves gave way to high rise technology centers and the Santa Clara Valley metamorphosed into Silicon Valley. The old seminary alone seemed constant.

It was not the view from the tower that most fascinated this twenty-four-year-old, however, but rather the building's fourth-floor attic. A vast chamber crouched under the roof, it had served as *dormitorium* or common sleeping room for novices of the nineteenth century. By the 1960s, the iron bedsteads had long since disappeared. In their place, the debris of a discarded past littered the plank floor: cracking portraits of no-longer-fashionable saints; scrapped Victorian furniture; religious canvases consigned to oblivion by a shifting aesthetic; and steamer trunks inscribed with the names of long-departed Jesuits. Who had once slumbered in that odd space? I mused. What had prompted the immigrant Jesuits' flight from Italy to Gold Rush California? What sort of life had they transplanted to the Los Gatos hillside?

The questions remained largely unresolved when I moved on a few years later, but they resurfaced in 1975. After completing doctoral studies in the history of the American West at UCLA, I began teaching at Santa Clara University. Founded in 1851, that institution, too, had been brought into existence by displaced Italians. In the process of researching the school's history for a book subsequently published by Stanford University Press, I learned that the Jesuit immigrants had not confined their work to California. Itinerant missionaries circulated among Native Americans in the Pacific Northwest, erecting sturdy missions that still serve as functioning churches and historical monuments. In the Southwest, adobe school houses, churches, and a printing press testified to widespread community-building by Neapolitan missionaries. From Montana to Texas, from the Pacific Coast to the high plains of Wyoming — the émigrés left footprints. In light of my research in educational history, the queries once prompted by the ghosts of the seminary attic evolved. What mark did these Italian clerics make on the cultural and religious life of the West? What were the distinctive qualities that typified their status as immigrants? And how did their national genesis mold their encounter with a multifaceted and ethnically diverse frontier Catholicism? Thus, a new research project was born, resulting in this book about Jesuits that is also a book about America.

That these clerical refugees warranted study seemed evident from the works of other scholars who either ignored the Italians or made only passing mention of them. Most intriguing was a reference by the historian Howard R. Lamar in his presidential address to the Western Historical Association in 1986. Listing topics that awaited scholarly scrutiny, Lamar challenged researchers to give more attention to both the religious and the intellectual history of the West. "The frontier and the West . . . had their full share of ideologues and theorists," he argued. But "I believe we have omitted covering several crucial groups of westerners who not only played a role in resolving . . . seemingly incompatible versions of the western mind, but who, in the process, created ideas, concepts, institutions, and even lifestyles that we call genuinely western." In his tally of overlooked westerners, Lamar cited the Jesuits who are the subject of this volume. "European-born Jesuit fathers dreamed of a new civilized Catholic Indian substate" in the Pacific Northwest, and "in a quiet, almost invisible way, determined teacher-priests established the tradition of Catholic higher learning at Santa Clara College in gold rush California."[1]

Stirred by Lamar's appraisals, which situated the Jesuits in broad context, I was further drawn to the Italians because their multiple projects embodied many of the major themes of western development — education, immigration, gender, religion, and minority relations. Additionally, their story braided together two linked phenomena, religion and immigration, that historians tend to treat separately. Although studies of globalization and transnational migration have multiplied in recent decades, for example, the role of religion in that process has received scant scholarly notice. In the case of the Jesuits, the correlation between religion and migration was essential, not only in understanding their own experience but also in explaining how they affected others. One of the reasons why the Italian missionaries were accepted by Native Americans, for instance, was their nationality. Because they were not regarded by the tribes as Americans, they were not held accountable for repressive United States policy.

And what about the connection between religion and multiculturalism? Despite our contemporary passion for ethnicity, historians have yet to fully explore how specific European newcomers to the United States interacted with older, established ethnic communities, particularly Hispanics and Native Americans, two groups with whom the Italian missionaries were closely tied for decades.[2]

Thus, the case of the expatriate Italians provided a novel entrée into the topic of immigration. Although an enduring theme of American historiography, migration has never ceased to offer new questions for scholarly analysis. Historians have for generations fruitfully studied the ways in which America refashioned new arrivals, but in an era of globalization, counter agency has become equally significant: How have outsiders molded and propelled American society in new directions? As the writer Jeremy Eichler has said, nineteenth-century America was "a country reaching both inward and outward in its quest to forge a national cultural identity, yearning to be free of Europe's shadow but seeking its counsel in finding that freedom."[3]

The relationship between European Jesuits and American Catholics revealed a similar exchange. When the Italian clergy introduced old world religious notions to congregations in the United States, for instance, they usually met acceptance rather than rejection. Why were alien ways readily embraced? One reason was that heterogeneous American congregations interpreted the supranational and centralized practices offered by the European priests as a means of transcending the restrictive confines of ethnicity.[4] Of a German Jesuit who toiled among fractured immigrant populations in the nineteenth-century Midwest, a historian wrote: "He gave them a Catholic sense and determination where before they were separate and dissonant."[5] Much the same could be said of Italian Jesuits in the Far West.

If Italy brought novelty to America, the reverse was also true. Research on the Jesuits underscores another issue central to immigration studies: the impact of receiving countries upon sending nations. As students of contemporary migration have demonstrated, once neophytes become adjusted to a new environment, they channel money, ideas, and other cultural innovations to their former homeland. Jesuit exiles of the nineteenth century did the same thing. While importing the traditions of Italy into the United States, they transmitted new world concepts and practices back to the old world. They exemplified the transnational character of American Catholicism, which the historian John T. McGreevy has aptly described as "an international set of ideas, people, and institutions circling back and forth across the Atlantic, the Pacific . . . and up and down the American continent."[6]

Furthermore, the study of the Jesuit saga offers an opportunity to restore some equilibrium to the history of the American frontier. The frequent lament of students of church history has been that the story of the churches in the trans-Mississippi West remains a lonely *terra incognita*. "All that most of us know and learn about American religion keeps us firmly moored in an east-to-west framework," the historian Laurie F. Maffly-Kipp argues. "The farther west we go, the less important the religious events seem to become, in part because the vast majority of us know much less about them."[7]

Patricia Nelson Limerick and other proponents of the "New Western history" have advanced the study of previously ignored subjects and populations, including religious figures and their institutions. Nonetheless, much is yet to be learned. For instance, although Christian missionization of Native Americans has been a consistently productive research topic, both Indian adaptation and resistance to proselytization — issues explored in this book — have left many questions hanging. In their ideological encounter with native peoples, how did missionaries attempt to effect conversions? What practical strategies and methodologies were employed in soul-saving, where did they come from, and why did they succeed or capsize?

A final consideration that propelled the project is a desire to bring some balance to the writing of history about the Jesuits. In recent decades, researchers have gravitated to the earlier period of the order's sixteenth-century origins. While this emphasis has resulted in many ground-breaking studies, it has also created the impression that this era stood as an archetype for all subsequent Jesuit history. But as John W. O'Malley, author of the exemplary *The First Jesuits*, has cautioned, the Society of Jesus is best understood by looking beyond its founding moment and early documents. We cannot presume that "the ship sails through the sea of history without being touched by it." Instead, scholars must grasp how the organization existed and changed in different historical epochs. "If we want to understand such a body," he has advised, "we must at some point descend to the lived and continuing experience and then try to discover and weigh its impact."[8]

For the nineteenth century, the lacuna is especially stark. Although some deeply informative monographs on European Jesuit history have appeared in recent years, what has been written about the society's early activity in the United States has often been disappointing or incomplete.[9] Impediments to research on Jesuit topics that scholars once lamented — the order's secrecy about its internal affairs, its defensiveness, and the inaccessibility of its archives — no longer exist. The mystique that surrounded the group from its founding era, however, dies hard, and we are left with an impression of lifeless, impersonal characters who occupied a parallel universe separate from the rest of the human race. In the words of Frances Trollope, author of the Victorian novel *Father Eustace: A Tale of the Jesuits*, human nature was "not quite the same . . . for Jesuits as for other people." A century later, the writer Luigi Barzini used a mechanical metaphor to stereotype them: "All Jesuits were interchangeable cogwheels in a vast machine; they spoke all languages and could fit in anywhere." The historian David J. O'Brien put it more deftly: "The works of the Jesuits are all around us, yet they themselves remain elusive." The task of the contemporary church historian, therefore, is to explore both the public and the private lives of the Jesuits as well as to situate their story in its larger social and cultural context. This book attempts to do both.[10]

Writing about the uprooted Italian clergy of the nineteenth-century is sparse. In 1968, Andrew F. Rolle drew upon the careers of the Jesuit refugees to effectively make his interpretive point about the unique features of Italian immigration in the West in *The Immigrant Upraised: Italian Adventurers and Colonists in an Expanding America*. Full-length biographies of a few individuals have been published, although they often are uncritical and aimed at a popular readership. And cursory analyses of the most influential among the expatriates have appeared in standard biographical dictionaries. Those who have drawn the most scholarly notice, as several masters' theses and doctoral dissertations attest, were the ones who undertook missionary careers among western Indians.[11] Editions of the letters of several Italian missionaries have found their way into print because of the rich ethnographic data they contain.[12] Until the present volume, however, there has been no comprehensive study of the entire group and no analysis of the implications that national difference had for missionary work.

It has taken forty years to answer the questions I originally posed in the attic. In the interval, I have accumulated many debts in research trips in the United States and Europe. Although I cannot list all of my benefactors, I wish especially to acknowledge the guidance provided by the staff of Rome's Archivum Romanum Societatis Iesu, the chief depository of documentation on Jesuit history. For the hospitality and assistance of Filippo Iappelli during an intense month of research in Naples in the Archivo della Provincia Neapolitana della Compagnia del Gesù, I remain deeply grateful. Similar kindnesses were extended by the staff of the Archivo della Provincia Torinese della Compagnia del Gesù, then housed at Villa San Maurizio near Turin. Michele Casassa of Turin's Istituto Sociale aided my investigation by supplying the California Jesuit Province with photocopies of hundreds of useful documents under his care. Closer to home, Thomas A. Marshall, Daniel J. Peterson, and Silvano P. Votto of the Archives of the California Jesuit Province graciously responded to my every request for assistance during many years of archival digging. I am grateful to Thomas H. Clancy for the liberal access he provided during two visits to the collections of the New Orleans Province of the Society of Jesus at Loyola University. During research on Jesuit history in the Pacific Northwest, I enjoyed the help of the late Wilfred P. Schoenberg of the Jesuit Oregon Province Archives at Gonzaga University, a tradition sustained by his able successor, David Kingma. Others to whom I am indebted include Michael J. Kotlanger of the University of San Francisco; Paul Totah of St. Ignatius College Preparatory in San Francisco; Nancy Merz and William B. Faherty of the Jesuit Missouri Province Archives, St. Louis; the librarians of the Special Collections Division at Georgetown University; and the staff of the Marquette University Archives. Anne McMahan, who directs the Santa Clara University Archives, and Elwood Mills of the university's media services gave generous assistance in ways too many to count.

Support for research was provided by several groups, beginning with the Bannan Institute of Santa Clara University, which aided both the initial and final stages of the project. Don Dodson, the university's provost for academic affairs, supplied a grant for indexing the book. I wish to acknowledge assistance tendered by the Irvine Foundation for my study of the encounter between Jesuit missionaries and Native American and Hispanic communities. The Woodstock Theological Center at Georgetown University offered a splendid place to work and write during a sabbatical year, as did the Jesuit communities at Gonzaga University and at Fairfield University. While I was at Fairfield, Gerhard Bowering of the Department of Religious Studies at Yale University facilitated my work in New Haven. To Howard R. Lamar, Andrew Rolle, and David Weber, who once wrote letters of support to accompany my requests for grants, I offer sincere if belated appreciation.

Like all books, this one is the result of collaboration with many scholars who offered insight and good company along the way. I had the fortune of receiving guidance from colleagues who read, in whole or in part, early drafts of the book and rendered wise feedback, especially Wilkie W. K. Au, Jeffrey M. Burns, Michael E. Engh, George F. Giacomini, Jr., Patrick J. Howell, Michael C. McCarthy, Alfred E. Naucke, Robert C. Senkewicz, Thomas J. Steele, and Nancy Unger. I am grateful to Anne M. Butler for expert editorial counsel and for her research on the religious history of the West, which supplied me with a title for this volume. A deep personal debt is also owed to many Jesuit friends, especially James E. Flynn, William H. Muller, and Mario J. Prietto, who patiently sustained the project by words of encouragement over many years. *A tutti, grazie dal cuore.*

BROKERS OF CULTURE

1 Introduction

> Of all the religious orders, the Jesuits have been the most
> slandered and the most praised, the most studied, and yet
> the most difficult to be understood. . . . We love them, or
> we hate them, cordially and decidedly.
>
> — Protestant essayist, 1855[1]

In 1908, Augustus D. Splivalo of San Francisco penned a memoir about his school days at Santa Clara College, the small institution from which he had graduated fifty years earlier. Looking back on his collegiate experience, the lawyer and state legislator marveled at the diversity that had characterized his California alma mater in the 1850s. Students "were of all ages and nationalities and opposite creeds," he recalled, and yet they forged a congenial community out of variety. "Whether native or Eastern, Mexican or South American, English, French or Italians, Catholic or Protestant, Jew or Gentile, they were Santa Clara boys." Living in a state whose population was 39 percent foreign-born, Splivalo had acquired social skills and personal connections that were of inestimable worth at his mixed institution.[2]

Santa Clara College, mirroring the heterogeneity of Gold Rush California, had sprung into existence in 1851 as a crossroads culture. Its students were an omnium gatherum from around the world (Splivalo himself was born in Italy and emigrated to California with his parents). Its professors were also foreigners — émigré Jesuits hurled from Italy during the revolution of 1848. These stateless refugees had transformed a decaying California mission into Santa Clara College, a nineteenth-century version of globalization. The school's curriculum, as well as its faculty and student body, straddled cultures. Trained in Latin and Greek and classical culture, the Jesuits transplanted a European educational model into California soil. But by offering instruction in bookkeeping, physics, and mineralogy, they accommodated western interests. Since the Italians, like many of their students, were not native speakers of English, they recruited Americans to teach Shakespeare and Washington Irving, poetry and rhetoric. Undimmed by the dislocation of foreignness, the refugee clerics propelled their students into American life at an institution that was essentially multicultural.

Although the fact was lost on Splivalo, his school was a metaphor for a reality that extended beyond California. During the nineteenth century, a cadre of less than four hundred Jesuit expatriates planted dozens of institutions serving a diverse clientele across the western landscape. By century's end, cosmopolitan colleges had arisen not only in Santa Clara but also in San Francisco, Spokane, Denver, and Seattle. In Washington, Italian missionaries fluent in multiple native languages introduced European religion and American farming to the Yakima and Okanagan tribes. On reservations in Montana and Idaho, they ran boarding schools aimed at assimilating Flathead, Blackfeet, and Coeur d'Alene youths into mainstream culture. Circuit-riding priests imparted the sacraments to a farrago of nationalities in mining settlements across mountainous Colorado. In New Mexico, Italian Jesuits ministered to Hispanic Catholics by building churches, publishing books and newspapers, and running schools in both the public and private sectors.

That there was urgent need for clergy capable of coping with the ethnic and linguistic potpourri of frontier American was the frequent complaint of church leaders. Joseph P. Machebeuf, retiring Catholic bishop of Colorado, Utah, and Wyoming territories, identified this need when he searched for an episcopal successor in 1887. Machebeuf favored a candidate named Nicholas C. Matz because he was well liked by both the priests and people of the region. "Born in Europe, but identified with America since his early years, he will understand how to deal with the French, the Italian, and other European priests," Machebeuf wrote. "And he has the advantage of knowing English, French, German and sufficient Spanish to treat with the Mexicans."[3]

As Machebeuf proclaimed, an accommodating clergy was a prerequisite for building the church in a new and heterogeneous society. For this reason, most missionaries, men and women alike, moved regularly amid a medley of cultures and a babel of tongues, ministering to Native Americans one day, to European immigrants the next, and to Anglo-Americans another time.[4] "Whether planned or not," the historian Anne M. Butler has written, "missionaries bridged between communities, serving as mediators in the overlapping social dynamics." These encounters inevitably induced friction, interchange, compromise, and malleability. "People came into contact with languages, customs, and values they had not known. Some they accepted; some they rejected. Either way, the process influenced religious practice as well as secular life. This brokering of cultures constituted a major element in Catholic communities in the West, and the result brought both difficulty and understanding to group relations."[5]

The Jesuits were readied by both nationality and religious tradition to link cultures. Among Italians, this inclination was bound to behaviors associated with national character. Coming from a society that valued the *arte de arran-*

giarsi, the skill of making do and coping with the unexpected, the refugees possessed a high tolerance for ambiguity. Their fluid behavior — prizing cooperation over confrontation, appropriation and absorption over resistance — followed the popular maxim *Una mano lava l'altra* ("One hand washes the other"). In a polyglot frontier mapped by racial conflict and suffused with a culture of confrontation and conquest, these adaptive tendencies served a useful purpose. That they were priests gave them added clout among America's hybridized Catholic population. That they were Jesuits facilitated cultural bridge-building.

The First Jesuits

Founded by St. Ignatius of Loyola in the mid-sixteenth century, the Jesuits resembled older orders of the Catholic church in many essential features. Like its precursors, the Society of Jesus admitted some men as candidates for ordination; others joined as brothers, full members of the institute, who were not trained to become priests. Hence the latter were called "brothers," not "fathers." As with other groups, Jesuits took the three customary vows of poverty, chastity, and obedience in imitation of aspects of Christ's life. Poverty was embraced in response to Jesus' challenge to the rich young man: "If you would be perfect, go, sell what you have, and give it to the poor." The vow was also seen as a pathway to spiritual freedom. There is "no purer and more fruitful life . . . than that most sheltered from the pestilence which is love of money," Jesuit documents declared, and therefore one should "love poverty as a mother." They did not commit to a life of utter destitution, however, but to simplicity and detachment — often described as "apostolic poverty," meaning that it was accommodated to the needs of particular ministries.[6]

Although its *Constitutions* declared that the order's "manner of living is ordinary," members inevitably differed on what that meant. Nineteenth-century Italian Jesuits inclined toward a strict interpretation, as was clear from the impression their asceticism made on John Henry Newman, when he visited them in Rome in 1847. "They have no enjoyment of life," he said, recalling an encounter with his Jesuit confessor, Giuseppe Repetti, on a cold winter evening. "I find myself in a cheerless room, door and window not shutting close — no fire of course — a miserable bed — however perfectly clean, and he reading." "What has he to look forward to in life?" the visitor wondered. "Nothing; nothing is there to support him but the thought of the next world."[7] A similar determination to remain free of dependence upon material comforts was part of the ideology brought by many Italian clergy to nineteenth-century America.

For Jesuits, as for other religious, the vow of chastity proscribed marriage, physical intimacy, and exclusive relationships. Although Protestant critics stressed the restrictive aspects of the vow, Jesuits themselves understood it as liberating them for greater service to God and community. Virginity implied a life that was chaste in every regard and invulnerable to scandal or gossip, which accounts for the strict precautions taken by Jesuits in their interactions with others. Unlike modern observers for whom the psychological value of celibacy is suspect, nineteenth-century Jesuits accepted it as an ideal without question, concurring with Ignatius, who wrote in the order's *Constitutions* that "the vow of chastity does not require explanation since it is evident how perfectly it should be preserved."[8] This uncomplicated view, coupled with a clerical fear of the opposite sex, meant that relations between Jesuits and women were tightly circumscribed during much of the order's history.

Through their vow of obedience, Jesuits made themselves available for whatever ministry their superiors assigned them. Embraced in imitation of Jesus who sought to do God's will, obedience also functioned as a way of preserving the cohesiveness of a highly mobile and dispersive organization. A hallmark of the order, Jesuit obedience became a source of caricature by outsiders who focused on Ignatius' metaphorical references to "blind obedience" and to placing oneself "like a cadaver" in the hands of superiors. As a character in one of Frances Trollope's Victorian novels declared, there was no "limit to the obedience of a Jesuit." In reality, as we shall see, the founder provided a system of checks and balances obliging authorities to consult and discuss before rendering decisions. Nonetheless, throughout the order's history, the vow gave Jesuits great flexibility in meeting the shifting needs of an expanding church.[9]

In other ways, the first Jesuits broke the mold of custom by cultivating a disposition to mediate between cultures. Shaped by the Renaissance world in which their Society arose, humanistic priests took on education as a major ministry, something no earlier Catholic order had done in such a significant way. Influenced by the classical rhetoric of Greece and Rome, Loyola's followers were dedicated to the principle of measured accommodation in all their activities, an orientation enlivened by a spirituality centered on God's adaptation to the human race for the sake of salvation. The leitmotif of every Jesuit activity, from the first school in sixteenth-century Spain to the Indian missions of nineteenth-century Oregon, was the same: to adapt all things to "the circumstances of persons, times, and places."[10] Equally central to the order's self-definition was its embrace of secular culture. As a corollary to educational work, the Society of Jesus engaged in all spheres of human activity — as theologians, philosophers, astronomers, physicists, cartographers, agriculturalists, artists, architects, and playwrights. This unconventional approach to soul-saving enabled Jesuits to mediate between religion and a wide variety of persons and cultures. It also invested them with power in both the ecclesiastical and secular realms. And with power came enemies and controversy, two features that marked Jesuit history from its very beginning.

Another source of strength (and vulnerability) was the order's universality. Since its founding moment, the Jesuit institute, like the expansionist Europe of its day, drew members from all over the world. It was likewise global in its activities. Their *Constitutions* admonished Jesuits to embrace mobility for the sake of the Gospel, "to be ready at any hour to go to some or other parts of the world where they may be sent." This dispersive trait was reinforced by a special fourth vow of obedience to the pope. Taken by selected Jesuits outstanding in virtue and learning, the vow committed them "to go anywhere His Holiness will order, either among the faithful or the infidels . . . [for] the welfare of the Christian religion." Accordingly, adaptive missionaries labored as astronomers and Confucian scholars in China and as linguists in Vietnam.[11] To support their evangelical projects, early Jesuits invested in the silk trade in Japan, served as diplomats in Portugal, and grew sugar on slave plantations in Brazil and tobacco in colonial Virginia.

As a result of these far-flung activities, Jesuits were disposed to think and act globally. Their interconnected multinational communities engaged a "great diversity of persons throughout a variety of regions," as their *Constitutions* urged. In an effort to understand alien cultures, Jesuits adopted a type of cultural relativism that complemented their ad hoc approach of "using some means at one time and others at another."[12] Innovation and a cosmopolitan outlook served them well in missionary countries. But it alienated rulers dedicated to enhancing the sovereignty of newly emerging nation-states. In the late eighteenth century, the Jesuits' transnational organization contributed to their suppression as a religious order. Purged first in Portugal in 1759, they were subsequently disbanded throughout the world by a papacy pressured into action by European monarchs bent on curtailing ecclesiastical leverage over their national churches.

Rehabilitated by papal decree in 1814, the reemerged Society had lost much of its original flexibility and verve during the near half-century of its repression. In the absence of a living tradition upon which to rebuild, the resurrected order relearned its manner of proceeding from books. Brought low by the trauma of dissolution, it was cautious and conservative. Nevertheless, the Society managed to retain some of its instinctive tolerance for cultural difference — in part because it quickly resumed a global missionary thrust. Imbued still with an adaptive mind-set, Jesuits of nineteenth-century Italy were primed by both cultural and religious ideology to engage American diversity.

Italian Jesuit Émigrés

Although better educated than the average frontiersman, the refugee clergy resembled many of their American contemporaries. The sons of merchants, shopkeepers, civil officials, lawyers, and other professionals, the Italians sprang largely from middle-class soil. Many of them had rural roots. The Indian missionary Giuseppe Cataldo came from a prosperous farm family in Sicily, while the parents of his contemporary Giuseppe Chianale were landless *contadini*, or peasants. The father of Giuseppe Sasia, a Piedmontese missionary, earned his living as a poor railroad worker. Although most of the Jesuits were from the bourgeoisie, a few belonged to the Italian nobility. Some were related to high church officials, including the Oregon missionaries Gregorio Gazzoli and Filiberto Tornielli, whose uncles were popes. In short, the Jesuits drew recruits from all strata of Italian society.

A common denominator among those who became priests was that their families valued education. Many had been drawn to religious life by the example of Jesuit teachers; others attended diocesan seminaries before signing up. Rich or poor, high-born or common, they were all well-schooled prior to joining the Jesuits — in part because the order itself placed a high priority on academic qualification for trainees studying to become priests. Different expectations, however, were applied to the Jesuit brothers, a few of whom were illiterate. Charged with managing the physical plant at a college or mission, a brother typically performed humble domestic chores and manual labor, exhibiting "the virtues befitting his vocation," summarized by a nineteenth-century Jesuit as a "spirit of devotion [that] went hand in hand with his spirit of labor."[13]

Their motives for entering religion varied. But the vast majority ascribed their decision simply to a sense of being called and to a desire to place their lives at the service of lofty ideals. Twenty-four-year-old Michele Accolti, Oregon missionary and founder of the order's California Mission, was enrolled in a pontifical academy in Rome when he set off to become a Jesuit in 1831. After making the *Spiritual Exercises*, a form of Jesuit retreat, he applied for admittance, saying he felt strongly drawn to God, to religious life, and to apostolic service. Some youths, looking for ways to satisfy their idealistic selves, responded to the allure of a missionary career in Indian America. Opportunities for escape and advancement lured others — a few as early as age sixteen. The possibility of pursuing those goals in a community rather than as solitary diocesan priests intensified the attraction.

Individuals who enlisted as brothers, although usually older, were drawn to Jesuit life for the same reasons as potential priests: apostolic zeal, a sense of adventure, and a quest for a more meaningful existence. John Donnegan, an Irishman who became a Jesuit at the age of forty-eight, recounted why he joined the Italian Jesuits as a brother in the Pacific Northwest. His motives mirrored those of many men with experience of the world. "I became wealthy" in the gold mines of Montana, "rich, but not happy," he said. Seizing the chance to draw upon a clean slate, "I sold my farm and my goods," and entered the Society. "I have nothing any more, [but] I am always happy."[14]

Jesuits who emigrated to the United States found ample opportunity to test their dedication. Their nomadic life started with a grueling trip across the Atlantic, undertaken with the certainty that they would never see home again and ended with uncertainty about the future. Although orphaned away from their familiar past, the vast majority of the expatriates lived out their lives as Jesuits. Nevertheless, emigration from a hierarchical and authoritarian society to a pluralistic and democratic one tested their readiness to adapt all things to "the circumstances of persons, times, and places." But the experience of hardship and expatriation also produced qualities of maturity, endurance, and flexibility that enabled them to tolerate the challenges that came with uprooting.

For most migrants, acclimatization started on the East Coast. There priests found work in schools and churches run by their American brethren while seminarians resumed studies cut short by revolution in Europe. Young men bent more readily than did their elders, some of whom were dismayed at American nonchalance regarding Jesuit rules. Convinced that religious life as practiced in Italy stood as a global paradigm, migrants believed laissez-faire American Jesuits were too much men of the world. The Americans also seemed enmeshed in running rural parishes when they should have busied themselves with care of the nation's expanding urban population. Taking advantage of their leverage with European church authorities, the refugees prompted a series of reforms that profoundly transformed the way Jesuits lived in the United States.

The Italians' eastern sojourn shaped their subsequent missionary work in the West. In Massachusetts, Maryland, and Virginia they acquired the apparatus of assimilation. They mastered the language and became acquainted with the mores of their adopted homeland. The experience of teaching at Georgetown College and the College of the Holy Cross charted their path. Stumbling into unfamiliar territory, the missionaries often groped eastward for help when they raised up colleges of their own in California and New Mexico. Their western institutions would be essentially autonomous and based on Italian models. The East continued, however, to supply the expatriate educators with ideas, counsel, and personnel. Thus, in the religious as in the secular world of nineteenth-century America, the east-west cultural divide was never as wide as geography made it appear.

Jesuits were drawn west by many of the same possibilities that lured thousands of other migrants in the aftermath of the Mexican War. In the vast territories acquired by the United States in 1848, a developing community offered fresh opportunities. Clergymen and teachers responded as enthusiastically to new possibilities as investors, farmers, miners, and ranchers did. From California, its population swollen by an international influx of gold seekers, Catholic bishops appealed to the outside world for missionaries to staff churches and open schools for both newly landed immigrants and resident Spanish-speakers. Similar summons issued from Santa Fe, where a largely Hispanic population had for several generations during Mexican rule operated without benefit of clergy. In the Pacific Northwest, missionaries warned that their mission to Native Americans would collapse if reinforcements were not forthcoming.

The first Jesuits to respond to these entreaties were Piedmontese from northern Italy. Perched on the edge of extinction at home, the dispersed clergy saw in the American West an opportunity to reinvent themselves. Consequently, in 1854 the *piemontesi* adopted California and the Pacific Northwest as permanent mission fields. Twelve years later, Neapolitan Jesuits, who had fled home when the Italian upheaval spread to the Kingdom of the Two Sicilies, took up missionary work in New Mexico. Arriving with little more than a can-do attitude and a sense of adventure, these expatriates shaped frontier culture by founding Indian missions, hospitals, churches, presses, and colleges that blended American and European antecedents.

In the Pacific Northwest, the Italians' linguistic skills and their ambiguous national allegiance gave them entrée among many tribes not receptive to American missionaries. Their encounter with native peoples demonstrated that the brokering of cultures was a reciprocal affair. Through a process of subtle manipulation, cooperation, and resistance, there evolved a native Catholicism that merged Euro-Christian doctrines with traditional beliefs and practices.[15] When the dream of creating a Christian utopia in the midst of the indigenous world proved illusory, the Jesuits became school masters, underscoring the role of education and religion in the encounter between Indians and whites. The missionaries' industrial boarding schools manifested features that set them apart from other schools for Native Americans. They also sparked the fires of jealousy and sectarian conflict. The priests' success in winning federal funds from Congress for their institutions during the Grant Administration eventually precipitated a backlash that ended government support of church schools on a national level. And more. It produced a reinterpretation of the first amendment of the U.S. Constitution that strengthened the wall of separation between church and state.

The Italians made their greatest impact as teachers. Of the nearly four hundred priests who fled Italy between 1848 and 1919, the vast majority spent all or part of their careers in the classroom. In 1902, for example, 30 of the

FIGURE 1. Jesuit faculty of Las Vegas College, New Mexico, together with writers of the influential Spanish-language newspaper *La Revista Católica*, 1886. Third from right in the front row is white-haired Salvatore Personè, a jovial Neapolitan whom contemporaries dubbed "George Washington" because of his resemblance to the first president. Courtesy Jesuitica Collection of Regis University

108 Jesuits working in the Neapolitans' New Mexico-Colorado Mission were concentrated in Denver's College of the Sacred Heart.[16] As founders of five institutions of higher learning, the Italians participated in what contemporary churchmen described as "the great battle" for cultural hegemony of the American frontier. "If Western society is left destitute of seminaries of a decidedly Protestant character," warned Yale professor Noah Porter in 1852, "the Jesuits will occupy the field."[17] The only remedy to the Catholic invasion was "to preoccupy the ground with colleges and schools" before Jesuit institutions sprouted "in the unformed society of the West." "Let them have the privilege of possessing the seats of education in the West," another alarmist in the East cautioned, "and we may give up all efforts to reproduce in the West what Puritanism has gained here."[18]

Denominational rivalry unleashed a remarkable proliferation of church-related colleges in the United States, transforming the nation into what one scholar dubbed "the land of colleges."[19] Nowhere was that competition more apparent than in the West, which provided a vast and fresh arena for missionary zeal. According to one study, sectarian rivalries yielded a fervor for educational supremacy among the churches of California to a degree evidenced on no other American frontier.[20] From the foundations laid by the immigrant clergy there arose numerous preparatory schools and five institutions of higher learning that exist today: Santa Clara University and the University of San Francisco in California, Gonzaga University and Seattle University in Washington, and Regis University in Colorado.

Catholics vied with both Protestants and one another to plant their standard in virgin terrain. "The banners of St. Benedict are now unfolded in the middle of the United States on the great Mississippi River," boasted Abbot Wimmer, founder of the American Benedictines, in 1857 when his men opened a monastery in Minnesota. "The stream of immigration is tending westward. We must follow it. . . . We must seize the opportunity and spread." The desire to surpass rivals was not limited to male religious. In 1841, Sister Louis de Gonzague of the Sisters of Notre Dame in Ohio rejoiced at the news that members of her congregation were sailing from Belgium to Oregon. The reason: Notre Dame was catapulting even farther west "than where the Religious of the Sacred Heart have gone."[21] Jesuits were not above using pious subterfuge to block competition. Under the pious pretext of avoiding "any danger of misunderstandings so prejudicial to the cause of our dear Lord," missionary Michele Accolti pressured church officials to prevent the Picpus Fathers, a rival French congregation, from establishing themselves in northern California.[22] In a region without established precedents, the struggle for supremacy in debates over property titles and jurisdictions found religious congregations and bishops frequently at odds.

It was dread of Protestantism that drove Neapolitan Jesuits to scatter their institutions throughout the length and breadth of the desert Southwest. Although relatively latecomers to the region, beginning in 1867 the Italians speedily established themselves among New Mexico's Hispanic and immigrant populations. They extended their sway into neighboring Colorado, Arizona, and Texas. Determined to prevent the absorption of Hispanic civilization by Anglo-American Protestant culture, the priests engaged in a delicate balancing act. They embraced the region's Mexican heritage by promoting time-honored celebrations such as Holy Week and Corpus Christi and other public rituals and collective devotions. But the Jesuits also altered customs they judged unorthodox, reshaping them according to normative European practice. They thus reformed the Feast of Santiago, a popular Southwestern holiday that was customarily celebrated with horse races, rooster pulls, and cock fights, by inserting a solemn high mass and special sermon into the festivities.[23] Through a tangled mix of accommodation, coercion, and subtle redefinition, the Italians standardized local practice while paradoxically preserving it.

Other factors, too, were involved in that exchange. For years, the Jesuits and other Catholics opposed to public education successfully blocked the emergence of a state school system in New Mexico. This flaunting of priestly power angered Anglo-Americans, but it gratified natives because it promoted the use of Spanish in the classroom and thereby preserved aspects of traditional culture. The Neapolitans' Spanish-language newspaper, *La Revista Católica*, molded public opinion throughout the Southwest on a host of combustible issues at a time when Anglo-American and Hispanic viewpoints competed for ascendancy. Through their advocacy of cultural pluralism, the Jesuits emerged as insiders within indigenous Southwestern communities.

Wherever they went, the émigrés were torn between two conflicting desires. On the one hand, they sought to adhere to European conventions in all their undertakings. On the other, they sought to adapt to the exigencies of American culture. As Americanizers, the Jesuits advanced the assimilation of the populations whom they served — Native Americans, Hispanics, and European immigrants — into mainstream society. Their schools, for example, operated as fulcrums, facilitating the transition of young *californios* and *nuevomexicanos* from pre- to post-conquest culture in the years after the Mexican War. And for European immigrants, the Jesuit colleges filled much the same function as the Catholic parish, a mediating force between old and new cultures. Missionaries in the Pacific Northwest, recognizing the coming domination of the region by Anglo-Americans, assumed a similar role vis-à-vis Native Americans. They instructed their Indian converts in farming and irrigation techniques while also tutoring them in the Catholic catechism. In the process of facilitating the assimilation of their hybrid flocks into the new American order, the Italians themselves entered the American mainstream.

Even so, the Italians bucked against aspects of Americanization that they found objectionable. Offended by the secular character of state education, they struggled against public schools in the United States as vigorously as they had in Italy. Victims of anti-clerical government in Europe, the Jesuits appreciated American religious freedom, if not church-state separation. Their relations with Protestants ran the gamut from friendly to downright hostile. As ministers to varied ethnic communities, they favored assimilation but not co-option. Advocates of distinctiveness within community, the Italian Jesuits functioned, therefore, neither exclusively as Americanizers or as Europeanizers, but as brokers of multiple cultures.

Like all refugees who move from their own culture to an alien one, the Jesuits carried their European legacy with them. In the clerical world of Italy, men and women were assigned separate spheres of activity and contact between them was assiduously monitored. St. Ignatius, founder of the Society of Jesus, had devoted much attention to women and relied on them for support in the order's early years. So chastened was he, however, by charges of undue familiarity and other difficulties that his *Constitutions* ordered Jesuits not to "take charge of religious women or any other women." Although that ruling proved to be highly elastic, for much of their history Jesuits betrayed the same prejudices against women that prevailed in European society at large.[24]

But in the United States, Italian émigrés encountered a bewildering array of behaviors that challenged old assumptions. For example, gender-based divisions of labor that applied in Europe did not apply in Indian America. Among some matriarchal tribes, husbands were economically subservient to their wives. And women in Anglo-American culture enjoyed greater social mobility than they did in Italy. As a result, Jesuits came daily into greater contact with females. In the Pacific Northwest, nuns and sisters even toiled as partners with the clergy in running schools for Native American children. To forestall temptation, scandal, and false accusations in laissez-faire America, Jesuit authorities erected a firewall of regulations between the sexes. But on the western frontier, that barrier was frequently put to the test.

The importing of Italian religious customs was less controversial. Wherever they went in frontier America — in the Hispanic Southwest, in the Native American world of the Northwest, or in urbanized California — the Jesuits fostered distinctively Italian forms of piety. Their lodestar in matters spiritual was Rome. Intent on avoiding the homogenization of their religion in Protestant America and on conserving what was distinctive about Catholicism, they hastened the Romanization of American culture in their colleges, missions, parishes, and publications. In pursuing these objectives, they were one with other contemporary churchmen who believed, in the words of historian R. Laurence Moore, that some ways of becoming American were incompatible with remaining Catholic.[25]

In their promotion of Roman usages, the Jesuits insisted on the universality of Catholic culture. Eschewing notions of American exceptionalism, they were counted among churchmen who promoted — to borrow a phrase from the scholar Peter R. D'Agostino — "the profound connectedness of European and American Catholic peoples, ideas, practices and institutions."[26] That they were successful in imparting this ideology to ethnically diverse congregations underscores an argument made by another historian. In the melting pot mix that was America, Colleen McDannell has suggested, Catholics embraced the transnational feature of their religion. Why? Because that connectedness enabled them to enjoy both "the familiarity of ethnic traditions . . . and the universality of the supernatural." Standardized religious practices not only provided spiritual satisfaction, they also brought relief from the age-old tensions between nationalities.[27]

Like other immigrants, the Italians faced opposition, not only from nativists, but from within their own ranks. The tension between adherence to European norms and adaptation to American mores brought inevitable conflict among Jesuits. As increasing numbers of Americans joined the order in the West, resentment of European domination festered among native-born clergy. Opponents were not strictly divided along national lines, however, since some of the most vocal advocates of assimilation were Italians.

By the end of the nineteenth century, Jesuits butted heads on many things — the way they should live in America, how seminarians should be trained, what ministries they should undertake, how they should relate with women. In their colleges, members of the Society debated the merits of the classical curriculum. Should the time-honored emphasis on Latin and Greek be retained — or should it be jettisoned in favor of a more utilitarian course of studies that better suited American interests? Traditionalists, cheered on by superiors in Europe, argued for the status quo; many Americans fought for reform. As western demographics shifted at the end of the century, the Jesuits also argued over which populations should receive the bulk of their attention. The diverse student body with whom Augustus Splivalo had studied at Santa Clara College in the 1850s was replaced fifty years later by mostly Anglo- and Irish Americans. Like California, the Pacific Northwest and the Southwest too were increasingly dominated by Anglo Americans. Italian missionaries, who had earlier ministered primarily to immigrants, Native Americans, and Hispanics, were challenged by co-workers who argued that influential Anglo-American populations should benefit from their ministry as well.

With the new century, internecine struggles for power between so-called Americanizers and Europeanizers intensified. As Jesuit operations in the West steadily moved from reliance on Europe to being independent American entities, ethnic conflict among the clergy as well as natural evolution eventually led to a severance of ties with Italy. Piedmontese jurisdiction on the West Coast folded in 1909. Ten years later, Neapolitan administration of Jesuit operations in the Southwest ceased. In the seventy-some years in which they dominated their Society's operations in the West, however, the Italians had contributed unique features to the cultural, intellectual, and religious life of the region. In the process, they themselves were changed and Americanized.

2 *"Out with the Jesuits"*

BECOMING REFUGEES

Take the first passerby and ask him, "What are the
Jesuits?" He will at once reply: "Counter-revolution."
— Jules Michelet, *Les Jesuites*, 1843[1]

On the evening of March 28, 1848, Jan Roothaan, the Dutch-born
superior general of the Society of Jesus, received an urgent message at his
headquarters on Rome's Piazza del Gesù. Written by Pope Pius IX, the letter was hand-delivered by Cardinal Castruccio Castracane, an official of the
papal government. Its news, exploding in the night air like a thunder clap,
was exceedingly unwelcome. The pope informed the Jesuit that he could no
longer guarantee the safety of the members of his order living in the city. He
left to Roothaan what course of action the superior general should take to
side-step bloody violence.[2]

As both churchmen recognized, many forces contributed to the cloudburst
that had engulfed papal Rome and now began to rush toward dramatic resolution. Opposition to the Society of Jesus had been brewing for decades,
the culmination of a host of complaints, some of recent origin and others of
long-standing inception. What neither the cardinal nor the Jesuit superior
general could foresee, however, was that the Roman disaster of 1848 would
have far-reaching, even global significance. Before the hurricane of anti-
clerical fury spent itself, Jesuits from Italy would be dispersed to six continents. In the nations that took them in, particularly in the United States, the
deposed religious would emerge as a significant force in the evolution of
Roman Catholicism in their new homelands. Even in uncharted regions of
the American frontier, the form and direction of religion would be directly
traceable to church-state tensions in nineteenth-century Europe and to the
chain of irreversible events that precipitated the Jesuits' expulsion from Italy.

The steps leading to dispersal were as dramatic as they were unpredictable.
In the months preceding the pope's communiqué to Roothaan, Rome had
echoed with the sound of protesters howling derision at Jesuits. Easily recognized in their black cassocks, priests no longer dared appear in public by
early 1848. During carnival season, a belligerent rabble had rallied nightly

in the torch-lit piazza fronting the Society's Roman College to stage mock religious ceremonies and scream threats at the clergy walled inside. Frequent late-night harassment and fear for their students' safety finally forced the Jesuits to close the school. Protesters had pelted the door of Roothaan's residence at the Gesù with stones while threatening still worse violence if the occupants did not vacate the city.

Unrest was not confined to the Papal States. Reports pouring into Rome from the Kingdom of Piedmont-Sardinia in the north were even more ominous. In mid-March, King Carlo Alberto, capitulating to the demands of a revolutionary parliament, ordered the seizure of all institutions of the Society and the banishment of its many members from the realm. His desk cluttered with requests for help, Roothaan penned a hasty letter on 25 March, "Every day is critical and menacing here."[3] Three days later, Cardinal Castracane appeared in his office with the announcement that Rome had become ungovernable. Rapidly sinking into the hands of revolutionaries, the city was no longer safe for Jesuits.

Pius IX's missive called for immediate action. Having lived for several weeks with the possibility of flight, Roothaan now bowed to the inevitable. After a hastily convened conference with his staff, the Jesuit leader informed the pope of his decision and began preparations that night for the evacuation of himself and 350 other Jesuits from Rome. The next morning Roothaan trudged the corridor connecting his residence with the adjoining church of the Gesù. After kneeling for a long time at the tomb of St. Ignatius, founder of the order, he descended into the vault under the massive Baroque temple for a few moments of final reflection before the resting place of his interred predecessors with whom he shared responsibility for governing the Society. That afternoon, disguised in a black wig and wearing the cassock of an ordinary parish priest, the twenty-first general superior of the Society of Jesus waved good-bye to the handful of his staff that remained and quietly slipped out of the city in a carriage provided by Lord Clifford, an English supporter. Before boarding the vessel that would carry him into exile in Marseilles, the sixty-two-year-old priest told friends he expected never to see Rome again.[4]

To Roothaan and his contemporaries, the crisis of 1848 recalled the darkest pages of Jesuit history. Seventy-five years earlier, a storm of anti-clericalism unleashed in Portugal by the government of the Marquis of Pombal had roared across Europe and swept the Society of Jesus into oblivion. Except for a small remnant of survivors in Russia and Prussia, the entire order — once 23,000 men strong — was suppressed by papal mandate in 1773. Although the Society was re-established in 1814, recovery was slow because the forces that had engulfed it in the eighteenth century continued to buffet it. "Old calumnies, decked out in new colors, are scattered broadcast among the people," Roothaan lamented in 1839, "with word and writing, in book, pamphlet, and periodical, flooding the world like a deluge, they daily defame and vilify us." Within a decade, a tide of antipathy once again threatened to submerge the order. As the general observed in 1848, the similarity between his experience and that of his eighteenth-century predecessors was disconcertingly similar. "The same happens in many places that once took place under Pombal, with this difference however that then it was the work of one tyrant while now there are thousands."[5]

That the Society endured the recurring assaults of the nineteenth century testified to its powers of survival. Although the order experienced remarkable growth under Roothaan's leadership, it did so under trying circumstances. Barely reconstituted in Europe in 1814, it was banished from St. Petersburg in 1815, and from the entire Russian realm and Belgium three years later. Revolution drove Jesuits from Spain in 1820, from France in 1830, from several Italian states in 1831, and from Portugal in 1834. The following year, they again fled Spain after a mob savagely massacred fifteen members in Madrid. The only country in South America that offered safe haven to Jesuits after 1842 was Brazil. "There is no place in the world wherein we are not the target for the poisoned shafts of our enemies," an anxious Roothaan declared in a circular letter to Jesuits in 1847. "To such an extent have the minds of the people been embittered in our regard" that we seem "not human, but the monstrous exhalations from the depths of Hell. What the future may bring, He alone can tell who knows all things." A bitter religious civil war that ousted 274 men from Switzerland that same year portended still worse. The flight of Roothaan and other Jesuits from Rome in 1848 was part of a general European dispersal that left half the Jesuits in the world in exile within the space of a year. The second half of the century witnessed still more expulsions: from Spain once more in 1868, Italy again in 1870, Germany in 1872, and France in 1880.[6]

Thus, the century that endowed much of Europe with the beginnings of constitutional democracy was not gentle to Jesuits. Nor was it kinder to other religious congregations. In the course of the nineteenth century, Franciscans, once ten thousand strong in Spain, shrank to a few hundred members. The Augustinian Hermits, who had earlier possessed nearly fifty monasteries in Portugal, evaporated. Dominicans were suppressed throughout Europe and Latin America again and again. It was ironic, a historian observed, that the "suppression of religious orders, especially the Jesuits, and confiscation of their goods were even more characteristic of the era of constitutional Liberalism than of the era of 'enlightened despotism'" that had preceded it.[7]

How did the Jesuits provoke such universal enmity? That question puzzled John Henry Newman, who mingled regularly with them when he lived in Rome following his conversion to Catholicism. "Plodding, methodical, unromantic Jesuits," the Englishman described them in a letter to his sister in 1847. "It quite astonishes me how little the Jesuits are understood or estimated generally. I respect them exceedingly, and love individuals of them much," he declared. "They are a really hardworking, self sacrificing body of men — but they have little or nothing of the talents that the world gives them credit for." "They certainly have clever men among them . . . but tact, shrewdness, worldly wisdom, sagacity, all of those talents for which they are celebrated in the world they have very little of. They are continually making false moves, by not seeing whom they have to deal with. . . ."

More troubling, the Jesuits manifested "a deep suspicion to *change*, with a perfect incapacity to create any thing *positive* for the wants of the times." Their conservatism, Newman explained, made them "unpopular in the extreme and the butt of journalists." They are "considered the enemies of all improvements and advance." "It is most difficult to say what will become of the Jesuits," he mused. "I cannot understand a body with such vitality in them, so flourishing internally, so increasing in numbers, breaking up — yet the cry against them in Italy is great — they are identified with the antinational party in the thoughts of people."[8]

The roots of the Jesuit predilection for the status quo remarked upon by Newman were bound to broader events. In large part, the traumas sustained by the order in the nineteenth century reflected the challenge religion itself faced in finding a *modus vivendi* with forces set in motion by the Enlightenment and the French Revolution. Unwilling or unable to accept the political and social transformations of the post-revolutionary era, the Society and the Catholic Church at large found themselves in open conflict with the dechristianized modern state. The two powers disagreed on everything. When secular governments attempted to extend their control over activities that had for centuries been the domain of religion — marriage, public charity, and education — church and state found themselves in a face-off. The violent upheaval that attended that struggle in many European countries frequently called into question the existence of not only Jesuits, but even the papacy and the church itself.

In Italy the disestablishment of religion was complicated by the temporal power of the papacy. There, in addition to separating the functions of the state from those of the church, reformers sought to mold the diverse kingdoms of the Italian peninsula into a single entity. That amalgamation was fraught with special difficulties, however, because of the existence of the Holy See. "To advocate the independence and unification of Italy," one historian has said, "or even to demand significant reforms within the existing states entailed a confrontation with the papacy." Pope Gregory XVI and his successor, Pius IX, made it clear that they would never sacrifice the existence of the Papal States on the altar of Italian political consolidation. In consequence, the Italian *Risorgimento* became, first and foremost "an anti-

Catholic movement." Promoted by Italy's network of Masonic lodges and secret societies, opposition to the church was its "most important unifying principle." And the *Risorgimento*'s most obvious targets were the temporal power of the papacy, the powerful Roman curia, and the Society of Jesus.[9]

There were many reasons why Italy's patriots directed their hottest fury against *i gesuiti*. The memory of the suppression was a factor in the anti-Jesuit movement in Italy as it was in the rest of Europe. Popular belief in the anathemas hurled against the order in the eighteenth century continued to fester, keeping fresh the memory of that confrontation. Like a wound that refused to heal, it left the Society a vulnerable target of Italian anti-clericalism. The power of the restored Society provided still more motives for resentment. In the eyes of many Italians, the black-robed priests symbolized the clergy in general; in particular, they also represented the church's resistance to the winds of change sweeping through Europe in the nineteenth century. As a contemporary Piedmontese writer summarized, Italy heaped its "hatred and revenge" upon Jesuits because they were "the priests of priests."[10]

The order's conservatism was another incentive for attack. Resistant to innovations embraced by the modern world, Jesuits themselves often supplied the rocks hurled at them by their enemies. "To friend and foe" alike, the Society of Jesus symbolized the values of ante-1789 Europe, a historian has said. "Born during one of the great transitional periods of European history, the Renaissance," the order was "reborn during still another important era of change, that of the democratic and industrial revolutions of the nineteenth century." Adaptation was not achieved with equal ease in each case. To most Jesuits, the wave of democratic values unleashed by the French Revolution challenged the peace and stability of established political order. Those innovations also undermined the very foundations upon which Christian culture rested. Most Jesuits (there were exceptions) opposed in principle, if not in practice, Italian unification, representative government, freedom of conscience and of the press, state control of education, and the granting of political rights to religious dissenters.[11]

Forced to choose between buttressing an old order that was crumbling or joining the creation of a new world of democratic freedom, the Society clutched the familiar. As a consequence, its members appeared to European liberals as "the enemies of all improvements and advance," as Newman had noted. Indeed, their staunch refusal to reconcile religion and modernity made them "the only cloud in an otherwise clear sky." "The Jesuits and their friends wonder that the modern State abhors them," added Prince Hohenlohe, a Catholic member of the German Reichstag in 1872. "And yet the Society has taken upon itself to make war on the modern State."[12]

The Jesuits were in many ways victims of their own history. Founded in 1540, "fresh and unhampered by memories of the medieval world," in the words of one scholar, the Society "embraced the predilection of the modern world for the literary traditions of Greece and Rome," and it "placed these traditions at the service of the Church." "Flexible and even revolutionary" in the way they reexamined everything conventional, the early Jesuits retained only "what promoted their pastoral aims and main tasks" in preaching, teaching, and advancing the spiritual life. But the spontaneity, sureness, "and above all, freedom from the past with which the Society moved into the sixteenth century," did not characterize its nineteenth-century reincarnation.[13]

Shaken by the experience of suppression, the Society accepted variety reluctantly following its revival in 1814. "Filled with recollections of a world of national monarchies and accustomed to the intimate association of altar and crown," wrote the historian William Bangert, the Jesuits found adjustment to the nineteenth century "a painful, anxious, and uneasy experience." The cruelties visited upon them and the church in the name of the fresh freedoms promoted by totalitarian democracies deepened their distrust and made adaptation even more difficult. Unable to discern the spiritual values of the revolutionary era, most Jesuits instead "looked back with nostalgia to the old regime." "There is a touch of irony," Bangert concluded, "in the wistful looking back of these men toward a royal kind of government, which only shortly before had done them to death."[14]

Jesuits and the Educational Debate

Few issues so aggravated the conflict between the new democratic ideology and the stasis of the Society of Jesus than education. The anti-Jesuit rampage in Italy was, as it had been earlier in France, in large part a battle for control of the classroom. And just as educational hegemony had helped precipitate the original smothering of the Society, so too it provoked the expulsion of Jesuits from many European states in the nineteenth century.

The Society's origins were intimately yoked to teaching. "This was an order that acquired power with far less political planning than is commonly assumed, chiefly through education and schooling," according to one scholar, "the very means that would have seemed preposterous and childish before and without the historical example of the Jesuits." An unpopular ministry among other sixteenth-century religious orders, the Society with its unprecedented commitment to education met the church's need for clergy trained in a systematic and effective manner in order to face the challenge posed by the Reformation.[15] Within a century Jesuit schools stretched across the continent.

By 1679, France boasted eighty-three colleges, and Italy had even more. Tuition-free and subsidized by royal governments, they made the Jesuits a potent force in European culture. That ascendancy began to waiver in the late eighteenth century, however, with the emergence of new branches of scientific learning and with innovations in humanistic studies. The Jesuit emphasis on Latin and Greek gradually morphed into a formalized variety of classicism that resisted deviation and invited critique.[16] As one authority observed, in some countries the Society's tentacular hold on schooling "turned into a kind of tyranny when the educational principles of the order became antiquated."[17] The resulting conflict had contributed to the Society's downfall in 1773. Educational issues continued to raise difficulties after the order's resurrection.

The struggle over schooling, like the church-state conflict over other matters, was intensified by the French Revolution and the novel purposes it gave to the classroom. As movements toward national unity and democracy gained momentum, schools were enlisted to hasten the unification and democratization of society. General literacy emerged as a required complement of nascent democracy. The industrial revolution and advancing scientific thought also marshaled the forces of education to their needs. Hungry for trained technicians and a more literate work force, industrial democracy revolutionized the academy. It cast aside the classics and the humanities and imposed instead more pragmatic schooling that emphasized science, modern languages, and specialized vocational training.

The assault on entrenched educational values did not pass unchallenged. By attempting to replace the church and private associations as society's chief educator, the modern state precipitated a struggle between the secular and the spiritual worlds that traumatized Europe throughout the nineteenth century. Secularists insisted on society's right to tax-supported, state-controlled, undenominational schooling, starting even at the most elementary levels. Conversely, defenders of traditional schooling — including the Jesuits — complained that such a system abused and exploited individual and parental rights. Failure to resolve the educational dispute contributed to the wars that divided France, Switzerland, Italy, and Holland at mid-century.

The tug-of-war for influence over youthful minds and hearts was especially sharp in Italy, where illiteracy was widespread. According to a survey completed in 1871, 72 percent of the citizens of the recently forged Italian kingdom could neither read nor write. In most parts of the country, access to higher education hinged on religious affiliation. Only Florence allowed non-Catholics to attend the local university. Reformers, noting the deplorable state of training, never tired of pointing out that schools in almost all Italian states were run by Jesuits and other religious. Although recent studies show that papal Rome enjoyed the highest rate of schooling in Italy and perhaps in all of Europe, the peninsula's overall low literacy became powerful ammunition in the arsenal of those who sought to dismantle ecclesiastical control of education. "Such facts cry vengeance against the clergy," a contemporary critic concluded, because they have "shamefully betrayed" their responsibility.[18] A more hotly debated issue than illiteracy, however, was religious instruction. According to the liberal politicians who ruled the nation after 1870, the aim of elementary education was "to 'make Italians,' and Italians who would be patriotic and free from clerical domination."[19]

Strongholds of humanistic formation, the Society's colleges were similarly targeted for destruction because they seemed to resist modern learning, especially in the sciences and modern languages. By their critics' account, the Jesuits offered too much religion and too little practical training. One of their most influential antagonists, Count Camillo di Cavour, later prime minister of Savoy, wrote in 1844: "Woe to the country, woe to the class that should confide to them the exclusive education of youth! But for fortunate circumstances, which destroy in a man the lessons of his childhood, they would make in a century a bastard and brutalized race."[20]

Aware of this critique, the Society had attempted to adapt its teaching to the needs of the contemporary world by reworking its famous *Ratio studiorum* (Plan of Studies). That comprehensive charter, first issued in 1599, had for over two hundred years defined the distinctive curricula and methods of Jesuit pedagogy. Revised during Roothaan's generalate, the reformed code of 1832 gave greater emphasis to vernacular languages, mathematics, history, geography, modern philosophy, and natural science. By 1840, the Society's colleges in Naples, for example, highlighted these subjects both in their curriculum and at the *saggi*, or public exhibitions, that wrapped up the academic year. The new-found appreciation for Italian prose moved one patriotic Neapolitan Jesuit to boast that the work of Dante "is on hand every day in our schools."[21] But opponents dismissed these innovations as being too little and too late. Despite the embrace of up-to-date subject matter, the promotion of the humanities, religion, and strict discipline remained hallmarks of the Jesuit studies. Consequently, even though the order's reforms were moderately successful in accommodating to the new needs of the times, they failed entirely to blunt the hostility of enemies bent on destroying the Jesuit educational network.

If liberals faulted the Jesuit curriculum, they were even more frustrated by the widespread political power wielded by the clergy. The Society's schools, favored recipients of royal patronage and popular with the middle and upper classes, overshadowed public institutions in many countries, as in the Kingdom of Savoy, where they dominated the state educational system. As a result, advocates of secular schooling considered the Jesuit system not merely outmoded, but intolerable because it was so potently entrenched.

Nor was antipathy limited to radicals and anti-Catholics. University students in Turin, Padua, Pavia, Pisa, Bologna, and even in the Papal States

FIGURE 2. "By Their Fruits You Will Know Them," a caricature of a Jesuit classroom, 1849. Opposition to the Jesuits' educational system was a factor in their expulsion from Italy and other European states in the nineteenth century. Courtesy Istituto per la Storia del Risorgimento Italiano, Rome

vociferously protested the order's influence. The Society also managed to alienate the clergy. The founding of Jesuit colleges in Salerno and Benevento, for instance, had signaled an end to a system of private schooling offered by local priests, thereby depriving them of a customary source of income. Thus, despite its successes, the Jesuit educational system generated a wide spectrum of opposition among both the liberal laity and the diocesan clergy.[22]

The beginning of the anti-Jesuit movement in Italy was interlaced with events in France, the most potent source of Jesuit opposition in Europe. Within a decade of its reestablishment, the Society there had became entangled in a long, drawn-out struggle over freedom of education. Hostile to the state's attempt to monopolize and secularize schooling, French Jesuits resisted change and precipitated a reaction that led ultimately to their expulsion from the country. In 1828, all eight colleges of the Society were closed. Two years later, the revolution that swept Charles X from the throne ushered in a parliamentary system in which anti-clerical and middle classes forces predominated. With this further rupture of the crown and altar alliance, insurgents attacked the Jesuit novitiate in Paris, forcing its shutdown and the flight of seminarians from the country.[23]

The 1830 revolution in France immediately touched off a succession of small uprisings up and down the Italian peninsula. Eager to strike a blow against the governing Roman Curia, anti-clerical secret societies led revolts that swept through four-fifths of the Papal States. In their wake, Jesuit colleges in Ferrara, Bologna, Forli, Fano, Spoleto, and Modena locked their doors. Although peace was restored after Austrian troops came to the rescue of the beleaguered papal government, the rebellions of 1830–31 had long-term significance. They whetted the Italian appetite for national consolidation and political reform. They also exposed the depth of public antipathy to the Society of Jesus. The fact that Austria relied on the order to run schools in its Italian protectorates linked the Jesuits with the forces of reaction and foreign oppression in the minds of many Italian patriots.[24]

Nothing so dramatically identified the Society as the great enemy of Italy, however, as the publications of the liberal Turinese priest Vincenzo Gioberti. He is "the great writer against the Jesuits," Newman wrote in 1847, and he "is doing them a great deal of harm." Although his chief objective was to rally the princes of Italy to purge the peninsula of foreign domination, Gioberti could not disguise the depth of his dislike for Loyola's followers. "I hate the Jesuits," he once declared, "as Hannibal hated the Romans." Embittered by Jesuit Carlo Curci's harsh condemnation of his writings, the sensitive cleric leashed a broad attack on the Society in 1847 with his five-volume study *Il Gesuita Moderno* (The Modern Jesuit). Resurrecting many of the old charges that had precipitated the eighteenth-century eclipse of the order, he accused the Jesuits of seeking to dominate the church by any and all means. He also charged them with promoting a system of education that fostered hypocrisy and destroyed freedom. Incapable of either embracing democracy or breaking with the outdated political systems of absolute power, the Jesuits were, he concluded, the single most important obstacle to the rebirth of Italy. Everything pointed to a new downfall of the order.[25]

Gioberti's tour de force provoked a great uproar among his readership. Capitalizing on long-standing suspicion of the Society, his powerful polemic played a major role in persuading Italian political leaders and the general public to turn against the Jesuits. Nowhere did Gioberti's writings find a more sympathetic ear than in his homeland, the Kingdom of Piedmont-Sardinia. Greatly swayed by events in neighboring France, this "unusually conservative, closed, and even static society," as one authority described the realm, was transformed by an outburst of liberal reaction in the 1840s. The kingdom, containing one-fifth of Italy's population, was destined to play a leading role in the *Risorgimento*. It was also the first Italian state to uproot Jesuits from its national life.[26]

Until 1848, the Society of Jesus had enjoyed perhaps greater influence in Piedmont than in any other part of Italy. That preeminence, however, engendered distrust and dislike among a wide cross-section of society. The order's large membership; its central role in the nation's educational system (which especially antagonized its great rival, the University of Turin); its alleged collusion with Austria, Piedmont's hated enemy; and its close ties with the monarchy made Jesuits the most conspicuous target of the anti-clericalism that swept through the country at mid-century. "Those who are in power do not love us," Antonio Bresciani, head of the Turin Jesuit Province, reported in 1843. That opposition was not restricted to political leaders, as a Genoese priest reminded Roothaan in 1847: "We are detested by a large part of the clergy." Joined to these long-simmering accusations was Gioberti's critique, which portrayed the Society as the major deterrent to the reform of Italian society.[27]

The tidal wave of anti-clericalism that attended Piedmont's rush toward revolution soon engulfed the Society. By 1846, animosity toward the order had become critical. "Perhaps at no time since its restoration has there ever been so much obstinately impugned" to us, Bresciani warned stewards in Rome. By the end of the following year, as the nation's political crisis deepened, the pace of protest accelerated. "Our situation here is constantly getting worse," a priest reported after demonstrators staged protests in front of the Jesuit house in Genoa. Death threats prompted Francesco Pellico, Bresciani's successor as provincial, to notify his Roman superiors that the Jesuits might have to abandon the city. As control of Genoa and other centers in both Piedmont and Sardinia slipped from government hands, royal troops could no longer be counted on for protection. When revolution finally erupted in 1848, shouts hurled at the windows of the Jesuit college in Cagliari echoed in all the major cities of the realm: "Out with the Jesuits" and "Long Live Gioberti."[28]

Under attack everywhere, the Jesuits placed their final hope in the ruling house of Savoy, whose head, Carlo Alberto, had always promoted and defended the order (and whose ancestor, Carlo Emmanuele I, had surrendered his crown and become a Jesuit). "As long as the king lives, the Society cannot be destroyed," Bresciani declared.[29] With events hastily moving beyond his control, however, the monarch concluded that in order to preserve the dynasty and the peace of the kingdom, concessions had to be made to the popular will. Therefore, in March 1848, Carlo Alberto accepted constitutional democracy and declared war against much-hated Austria. Ignoring personal appeals from the Jesuit provincial, the king banished all foreign-born Jesuits from the kingdom and ordered all the others to immediately vacate their residences. With their colleges and residences seized by the government, over four hundred Jesuits, along with hundreds of other proscribed religious, prepared to depart the realm.

The emergency called for quick action under chaotic circumstances. Although many clergy sought refuge with family and friends, others were without food and shelter. Arranging for the sick and elderly was especially difficult, because no hospital or public institution, especially in Turin, dared give refuge to a Jesuit. So harsh was the ill treatment given them that even Gioberti condemned the excesses.[30]

Escape from the country was a nightmare for the retreating clergy, who were harassed even as they fled. To dodge detection, the refugees exchanged their black robes for less conspicuous lay attire supplied by sympathetic students. In their dash for freedom they "donned all sorts of odd disguises," the Jesuit philosopher Giuseppe Bayma recalled, and they made their way, as best they could, "through the infuriated mob, whose cries of 'Down with the Jesuits,' 'Death to the Jesuits' resounded on all sides." Four frightened scholastics, including eighteen-year-old Luigi Varsi, later president of California's Santa Clara College, tried to make their way from Turin to Genoa. But they were spotted by a band of rowdies in a public park where they were awaiting transportation. Pursued, they skittered away at the last minute in a hail of rocks by flagging down an empty carriage. Others fled Turin on foot, hiking through the mountains to safe refuge beyond the borders of the kingdom.[31]

Opposition was more violent on the island of Sardinia than elsewhere, according to contemporary accounts. A ragtag group of scholastics attempting to pass from the island to the mainland was halted by government officials at the port of Cagliari and imprisoned on board a ship for a month before finally being permitted to depart. Strict enforcement of the governmental decree suppressing the Jesuits succeeded in driving a large number of men from the order. Parliament's official abolition, on 25 August 1848, confronted Jesuits with a dilemma, demanding that they leave their homeland or leave the order. Separation from the Society could be accomplished in one of two ways: either by abandoning religious life altogether and becoming a lay person, or by accepting secularization, that is, by joining the diocesan clergy. Many young Sardinian Jesuits, cut off from their superiors on the mainland who might provide counsel regarding the best course of action, were unsure what to do. Believing that the government *obliged* secularization and fearing that non-compliance would bring punishment to themselves or to their families, almost everyone accepted disaffiliation. Thus it was that seventy-nine Jesuits exited the order. Forty of them, mostly scholastics and brothers, including eighteen-year-old Luigi Varsi, subsequently retracted secularization, however, by opting for exile. Among those who eventually found their way with Varsi to the United States were Giuseppe Caredda and Nicola Congiato, later prominent missionaries in California.[32]

Paulo Ponziglione, a scholastic teaching in Genoa, recorded the story of his flight, which typified the experience of many Piedmontese Jesuits. "Times were very hard for us," he recalled of the days preceding the revolution.

"Almost every night furious mobs would parade in front of our college, shouting 'Death to the Jesuits.'" Although they managed to keep the boarding school in operation, the faculty feared the rabble "would break in and massacre us all." Living in constant dread of what the next day might bring, they faced their greatest crisis on the night of 28 February 1848, when an angry crowd of two thousand collected in front of the college. When protesters began pounding a battering ram against the large portal leading into the courtyard, the Jesuits implemented a plan of escape laid out several days earlier. Dividing their students into small groups, they led them through an abandoned tunnel, away from the college and into the city. Once free, pupils and professors fled to the safety of private homes.

Ponziglione and two companions remained behind to guard the college. Their three-hour siege ended around midnight, when troops arrived. Dispersing the mob, the soldiers took command of the institution but arrested Ponziglione and his colleagues. They, along with sixteen other priests captured the same night, were marched to the waterfront and imprisoned in the hold of a frigate anchored in Genoa harbor. After confining them for three days, authorities ordered their expulsion from the country. Handed tickets and passports, they were transferred to a steamer bound toward the Papal States.

Attacked along the way, Ponziglione finally reached Rome, where he was granted sanctuary. However, five months after his arrival, that city too erupted in revolution. After being hastily ordained a priest in the Jesuit novitiate of San Andrea, the Piedmontese Jesuit backed his bags and once again took to the open road. Blocked from remaining in Italy, he and his companions booked passage on a ship bound for America.[33]

Revolution and Restoration

The fate of Ponziglione and other Jesuits in the Papal States was closely connected to the crisis that engulfed the papacy at mid-century. The ascent of Pius IX to the papal throne in 1846 had been heralded with high expectations. The fifty-four-year-old churchman, eager to dampen the political tensions that had surged during the rule of his predecessor Gregory XVI, gave every evidence of a willingness to modernize the inefficient and arbitrary administration of the papal territory. When he bestowed amnesty upon thousands of prisoners soon after his election and granted a constitution to the state, Pius was greeted with wild enthusiasm.[34] It seemed for a time that a pope had arisen who, in the words of one historian, "was destined to set the seal on the unification of Italy, to reconcile and satisfy unitarian and anti-Austrian aspirations, and at the same time to manifest his devotion to the religion of his forebears and to the ideal of representative government." Some nationalists even looked to Pius as potential president of a republic that would include all the peoples of Italy.[35]

Those expectations were dashed, however, by the pope's refusal to lend his name to revolution. When he made it clear in April 1848 that he would not make war on Catholic Austria and drive its troops from Italy, Pius IX's position became ever more problematic. Economic crisis intensified the discontent of the Roman crowds and made them easy prey for political agitators. Critics, who had at first blamed the Jesuits and the Roman Curia for the pope's resistance to change, now began to openly attack the pontiff himself. With the assassination of the papal prime minister, Pellegrino Rossi, the pope's position, like that of Rome itself, become unmanageable. Increasingly on the defensive, he found himself de facto prisoner in his own house. Shortly after a mob stormed the Quirinal palace, Pius fled the city, and the revolutionary party grabbed control of the capital and proclaimed a republic. Disguised in the cassock of an ordinary priest, he took refuge to the south in Gaeta under protection of King Ferdinando of Naples. The pope's flight from Rome followed by eight months Roothaan's departure from the city.[36]

Even before the pope took flight, attacks on monasteries and other religious houses had become regular features of life in the uneasy city. Jesuits appearing in public were met with threats of violence. In mid-March 1848, the pope, learning that the civil guard was debating whether or not to protect Jesuits, had recommended a lock-down of the Roman College. When that failed to staunch the daily drip of opposition, Roothaan closed the Society's remaining seven houses in the city, and he and most of the 350 Jesuits still remaining in Rome packed their bags and departed.[37]

What to do about the order's younger members was especially problematic. Roothaan, unsure what the future held and recognizing that extraordinary times called for extraordinary measures, adapted tradition to the moment. In the belief that scholastics might be better provided for during the travels that lay ahead if they became priests, he permitted the early ordination of many trainees. Eleven seminarians, including Nicola Congiato and Carlo Messea, future American missionaries, were secretly ordained in Turin on 13 March 1848, in a private home where their provincial, Francesco Pellico, was in hiding. At least twenty-five students of theology attending the Roman College in 1848 (one of which was Ponziglione) were also made priests before slipping into exile abroad; others were hastily ordained when they crossed the border into France. Decked out incognito, Jean Baptiste Miege, then a fourth-year theology student from Savoy, was one of those who escaped Rome by traveling to volunteer for the Indian missions in the United States.[38]

Many of these men had not completed the study of theology, usually a req-

FIGURE 3. During carnival season, 1848, torch-bearing demonstrators gathered nightly before the Roman College, hurling threats at the Jesuits. This Italian caricature, "The Finger of God Is Here," ca. 1849, depicts the Jesuits' flight from Rome following the closing of the *collegio*. After their departure, the institution became a barracks for troops and later a technical school. Courtesy Istituto per la Storia del Risorgimento Italiano, Rome

uisite for priesthood. Santo Traverso, age twenty-six, had barely spent eight years in the order. Although Antonio Maraschi had studied at a diocesan seminary before becoming a Jesuit, this California missionary-to-be had been in the order but seven years and had made no theology studies as a Jesuit when he was ordained in 1848. His contemporary Luigi Testa, who would likewise spend the rest of his life in California, had joined only six years before he became a priest. Ugo Molza was ordained in Rome in the middle of his first year of theology studies, on the eve of sailing for the United States.[39]

According to one account, the only Jesuit identified as such who was allowed by republican authorities to remain in Rome was Giovanni Antonio Grassi, a former president of Georgetown College and a U.S. citizen.[40] Others lingered surreptitiously. Walter Tempest, a visiting English priest, described what life was like in the papal capital in 1849 during the period of the republic. Although attacks on the clergy were less in evidence in Rome than in the countryside, existence was precarious nonetheless. Because Jesuit letters into and out of the city were apt to be intercepted, Tempest's dispatch was probably hand-carried by a third party to its destination in London. He wrote: "Rome is now inundated with the scum of Italy and other nations and not a priest to be seen about the streets. Several of the Society are in prison. . . . It is feared many are now murdered. It is not a pleasant sojourn at this moment here, I can assure you. No one is now allowed to leave the town. . . . We are surrounded by barricades."[41]

Simultaneous with the outbreaks in Rome and Piedmont-Sardinia, Jesuits in other parts of the peninsula were driven from their posts in 1848. Not long after Ferdinando II of the Kingdom of the Two Sicilies reluctantly conceded a constitution in his realm, anti-Jesuit riots broke out in Naples and Palermo. Although no lives were lost, 114 Jesuits either went underground, fled to nearby Malta, or took refuge abroad. But as revolution spread, it became ever more difficult to find states willing to grant sanctuary to Jesuits. Within the space of as many months, eight provinces of the Society were disbanded (Turin, Rome, Sicily, Naples, Venice, Hungary, Austria, and Galicia). More than eighty colleges and residences were closed, and two thousand Jesuits expelled.[42]

The storm of 1848 proved of short duration. The collapse of one revolutionary government after another the following year paved the way for the reestablishment of conservative regimes throughout Italy. Pope Pius IX returned to Rome in mid-April 1849, after France and Austria intervened by sending troops to restore order in the Papal States. Only Piedmont-Sardinia — which to conservative Europe seemed "a hotbed of revolution and a menace to the peace of the continent" — maintained its proscription of religious orders. With papal restoration, Jesuits who had taken shelter abroad in 1848 reappeared in Italy. Roothaan once again took up residence in the Gesù in May 1849, and within a year the Society had regained all its colleges and houses in Italy.[43]

Those who came back soon reported that conditions were, in the words of one Jesuit, "even better now than before." Carmelo Papalo, a Neapolitan scholastic who had spent nearly three years abroad at Georgetown College, was struck by the "flourishing circumstances" that greeted him when his steamer glided into the bay of Naples in September 1851. "What an imposing scene!! What a sublime scene!!," he enthused in a letter to American confrères. The Jesuit college in the city — bursting with an enrollment of "more than 1,000 day scholars and 100 boarders" — was in "far better condition than it was before our dispersion." Requests for Jesuit workers were pouring in from "almost all the bishops and cities of the kingdom," and the number of men wanting to join the order was so great that "there is no more room" in the novitiate. "The Sicilian Province is in good condition," he summarized, and "the Roman Province goes on quite well."[44]

Although the experience was short-lived, the Jesuits did enjoy a resurgence of acceptance following the revolution's collapse. The cause of their popularity is not difficult to discern. The traumatic tumult of 1848 had not only tempered the anti-Jesuit feelings of many conservative politicians and churchmen, but it had led them to look upon Jesuits as allies in restoring the established order of church and state. Ferdinando II of Naples, for example, informed Roothaan that his sympathy for the Society had been strengthened by the suffering it had endured at the hands of revolutionaries. Although insufficient personnel stymied compliance, according to one report, the king even "insisted that the Society should take all the colleges and lyceums of his kingdom."[45] Pius IX, who had earlier offered lukewarm support, also showed increased respect for the order after 1848. Piedmont's attack on religious orders had heightened his conviction that the *Risorgimento* was fundamentally anti-Catholic. It has also undermined whatever sympathy he might have had for the liberal cause. In the Jesuits he found allies who shared those convictions as well as his belief that preservation of the temporal power of the papacy was integral to preserving the church's spiritual independence. Thus, "favored by the conservative reaction following the crisis of 1848," the historian Roger Aubert wrote, "the progress of the Society was even more rapid than before."[46]

Their standing in ecclesiastical circles had been upgraded, but Jesuits still faced formidable problems. The solidified authority that its conservatism bestowed upon it darkened the ominous image of the Society in the eyes of Italian liberals and revolutionaries. Tales of subterranean Jesuit malfeasance, promoted in popular novels, circulated everywhere after the restoration. "There is no doubt that the Jesuits are the real men in Rome," Newman had observed when he arrived in the city in 1846. "They are the prominent men."[47]

Jesuits themselves, however, were less confident of their standing after the restoration. "It is not courtly to be a warm friend of the Society," a highly placed member of the order confided to a colleague in England in 1854. The Society "is *very frequently* a subject of unfavorable remarks in the Vatican even in the presence of the Holy Father." And Pius IX "is undoubtedly upright and desirous of God's greater glory," but he was "educated in prejudices against the Society," the priest concluded. "We must not too often or too confidently rely on him as a last resource." According to a papal biographer, Jesuits were "very far indeed from running either religious or political policy" of the Holy See. Nonetheless, they did bask in the sunshine of renewed acclaim after the pope's return from Gaeta. "With the development of the Neo-ultramontane movement, and of his own policy of centralisation, it was really inevitable that he should turn to the Society whose very *raison d'être* was the defense of the authority of the Holy See."[48]

One of the chief vehicles of Jesuit influence was the journal *La Civiltà Cattolica*, which first appeared in 1850. It was the brainchild of the writer Carlo Curci, who viewed it as a platform from which to challenge liberal and revolutionary ideas issuing from Piedmont. The publication had been founded at the insistence of Pius IX over the objections of Superior General Roothaan, who feared its appearance would plunge the Society into political controversy and thereby compromise its freedom of action. Roothaan's concerns were not groundless. Although Curci attempted to navigate editorial opinion between the Scylla of democracy and the Charybdis of absolutism, *Civiltà Cattolica* made fresh foes for the Jesuits. On the one hand, it alienated liberals by writing about excesses committed in the name of the revolution and by challenging the notions of freedom of the press, liberty of conscience, and educational freedom. It warned that idolization of the centralized modern state menaced the rights of the individual, the family, and the church. Additionally, the periodical outraged Italian nationalists. *Civiltà*'s leading political writer, Luigi Taparelli, convinced that the unification of Italy would undermine the prestige of the Holy See, maintained that national individuality could be attained without going to the extreme of independence from the papacy.[49]

On the other hand, *Civiltà* antagonized conservatives, including the king. When the editors announced they would uphold the principle of authority without however preferring one form of government to another, Ferdinando II perceived a threat to his own political absolutism. The monarch banned the journal's distribution in the Kingdom of the Two Sicilies. If that was not enough, Curci also alienated the pope, his one-time patron. When the editor suggested in 1863 that the doctrine of toleration might be desirable in certain concrete circumstances, Pius IX fired him. Henceforth the journal came under tighter Vatican scrutiny and control.[50]

Thus, despite its professed respect for all legitimate forms of government, *Civiltà Cattolica* managed to alienate all factions. According to one authority, the journal "failed to capture with any degree of perception the positive values in the spirit of freedom." In addition, it "made the serious mistake, in an attitude both negative and inflexible, of tending to identify the Christian order with the old regime."[51] The controversial periodical enjoyed a wide circulation and it effectively defended traditional values, but *Civiltà* reinforced the Society's reputation as the enemy of progress. By asserting that liberalism was tainted with heterodoxy and hence incompatible with true religion, it also helped assure that the Italian *Risorgimento* "was left to the anticlericals, with corresponding disadvantages for both church and state."[52]

The Final Push

The decisive onslaught that drove the Jesuits from their last remaining stronghold was inaugurated by a new outburst of political uprisings in 1859. With the launching of Cavour's campaign to unite all of Italy under

Piedmont's liberal monarchy, most of the Papal States quickly tumbled before the northern kingdom's ever-expanding revolution. As its hegemony spread throughout the peninsula, the Piedmontese government introduced anti-Catholic legislation into regions freshly incorporated into the new nation. Laws were passed secularizing the state, the church was stripped of its control of education, ancient convents and monasteries were taken over by the state, and, as one historian observed, "the suppression of religious bodies became general, not to say universal." In all, some 334 religious congregations, with about 5,500 members, were suppressed. About two-thirds of all men and women in religious communities were expelled from the kingdom, the majority of them nuns. Piedmont-Sardinia outlawed Jesuits in 1855. And as the northern revolution advanced southward, they were expelled in 1859 from the Romagna, the duchies of Modena and Parma, and Tuscany. When Umbria and the Marches fell under the Piedmontese mantle the following year, they were driven from those regions as well.[53]

To the south, in the Kingdom of the Two Sicilies, Jesuits fled the advancing army of Giuseppe Garibaldi — "that name which is never uttered by an exiled Italian Jesuit," one priest declared, "without a thrill of horror." After Sicily and Naples joined the red shirts, the revolutionary government banished all religious orders, whom it associated with the discredited Bourbon monarchy. By late 1860, a total of fifty-six institutions had been confiscated in the Jesuit provinces of Italy and placed under state control. Caught in an ever-tightening vice, many Jesuits — this time, from both north and south — took refuge in the Papal States.[54] Although Pius IX's little kingdom had shrunk by 1860 to the city of Rome and its immediate environs, it offered the only remaining sanctuary in Italy for members of the proscribed order. As long as the papacy retained its secular authority, the pope's domain provided safe haven for Jesuits expelled by revolutions in unfriendly states and kingdoms in the peninsula. Thus Jesuits from all over Italy continued to flow into the city, either to study or to teach. The Neapolitans opened a novitiate at nearby Castelgondolfo following their dispersal in 1860.

But with the final collapse of Rome a decade later, their papal asylum vanished, thus obliging the vast majority of Jesuits to abandon Italy entirely. With the outbreak of the Franco-Prussian War in 1870, France recalled its garrison from Rome, leaving the city open to attack from the armies of united Italy. The last assault came on 20 September, as the combined forces of Garibaldi and Piedmont broke through the Porta Pia. When Piedmont annexed Rome a few days later, Pope Pius IX refused to recognize the new kingdom or to surrender the temporal power of the papacy. Abandoning his headquarters in the Quirinal palace, he crossed the Tiber and became a self-proclaimed "prisoner of the Vatican."

The seeing off of the Jesuits was more incremental and less dramatic than that of the pope. With the collapse of Rome, Italian troops immediately occupied many religious houses in the capital, including a wing of the Gesù, headquarters of the Jesuit superior general. Additional portions of the building were walled off in succeeding months until eventually four-fifths of the sprawling complex had been commandeered for government use.

Fresh harassments seemed reminiscent of the worst days of 1847–48. Ruffians disrupted religious services in the Gesù church and paraded the streets by day and by night shouting the old canards "Death to the Priests" and "Down with the Jesuits." The Society's schools and libraries had been confiscated by the new state immediately after Piedmont's annexation of the city. The Roman College served as a barracks for soldiers and later as a technical school. Although a few scholastics were permitted to continue their philosophy and theology studies in small rooms left to them, the majority of the Jesuit students resumed their studies abroad. The only faculty member allowed in the appropriated college itself was the astronomer Angelo Secchi, whom the government allowed to continue research in the observatory. To outside observers, it seemed that the Jesuits were finished. "It is not impossible," concluded the *New York Times* in 1872, "that the centenary of their suppression may witness the issue of another Papal decree, which is more likely than the last to be final."[55]

The ultimate blow against the order fell in May 1873, when parliament ordered the abolition of all religious orders and the transfer of their properties to the state. Eventually over 4,000 religious houses were suppressed. For this reason, even today many official buildings in Italy — schools, prisons, hospitals — occupy former monasteries or convents. The superiors general of religious congregations headquartered in Rome were allowed to remain in the city. There was, however, one exception: the Jesuit general was evicted. Thus, Pieter Beckx, the fifty-eight-year-old Belgian priest who had succeeded Jan Roothaan upon the latter's death in 1853, retraced his predecessor's footsteps into exile.

On 30 October 1873, Beckx assembled his staff for the last time in the Gesù. A participant recorded that the rooms, which had for two hundred years housed the Jesuit curia, "were mostly empty, and the floor strewn with torn up papers." In the great stillness permeating the silent, wide corridors, "the splashing of the garden fountain sounded louder than usual." After an emotional farewell to his staff, Beckx traveled by train north into exile in the rural village of Fiesole, a short distance from Florence. Although he hoped that his banishment might be as short-lived as Roothaan's, the months lengthened into years. A hostile government obliged him to govern the Society from the isolated monastery of San Girolamo for the rest of his life. In fact, the Jesuit curia remained confined in Fiesole for twenty-two years, long after Beckx himself had died.[56]

Some priests, even after the formal dissolution of the Society in Italy, operated covertly. By wearing the garb of diocesan clergy and side-stepping government scrutiny, they remained active throughout the revolutionary era.
Twenty years after the uprising of 1848, sixty-five men were still working
in Piedmont and Sardinia, "as far as the circumstances of the times permit,"
as one man put it. All of them were priests or veteran brothers; none were
scholastics. Several of them had accepted offers from sympathetic bishops
to teach in diocesan seminaries; others lived in private homes with relatives
or with associates. Some cities were friendlier to Jesuits than others.
Although in 1848 no hospitals or public institutions in Turin would admit
sick or elderly Jesuits, members of the order found refuge in less hostile locations such as Remo and Chieri.[57]

Conditions were no better in the *Mezzogiorno* to the south. Forty-one of
Sicily's two hundred Jesuits stayed on the island after the revolution, some
of them through the intercession of relatives who served in the provisional
government. Fifteen Jesuits, a remnant of the Naples Province's 340 members, lingered under cover in Naples. These holdouts, most of them native-
born, lived with their kin and toiled clandestinely. According to a report published in England in 1867, about eighty priests remained in the Kingdom of
the Two Sicilies. Functioning as "private priests," they were described as
"cautiously working in such religious duties as occasion offers." However,
the account continued, "they are obliged to be very careful, as they are liable
at any moment to be hurried off to a loathsome prison, . . . a fate that has
befallen some of them."[58] Public preaching was assiduously avoided, and no
Jesuit dared publish anything that might draw notice. After the police
intercepted a missive sent by the provincial to one of his men, even the
exchange of correspondence among confidants became infrequent.
Henceforth, letters were sent through third persons, an inconvenience that
made it difficult for superiors to keep in touch with personnel. "We vacil-
late," the Neapolitan Provincial Davide Palomba summed up in 1871, "between hope and fear." [59]

What impact did persecution have on individual Jesuits? One can only
imagine what rejection meant to them, although surviving accounts suggest
that their most immediate response was terror. Assaulted by armed bands
threatening "insult and outrage, if not death itself" — as they themselves put
it — instinctive fear overrode all feelings. Nor were the émigrés immune from
roller-coaster extremes of emotion. Once safety had been attained, fright
mutated to anger at the injustice of it all, as exemplified by a refugee who
fumed that he and his fellows had been "persecuted like cornered wolves."[60]
In time, rage usually gave way to grief over what had been lost. Many
refugees absorbed the experience of rejection by sublimating it into Gospel
categories that made sense of nonsense. Thus, Giuseppe Bayma, who fled

Piedmont in 1848, confided to friends that he was "proud of being deemed worthy to suffer something for the name of Jesus."[61] Rejecting the temptation to regard the world with a misanthropic eye, most embraced a belief in the redemptive value of self-donation. A glimpse into that interior landscape was provided decades later when an acquaintance asked Antonio Ravalli, a missionary in the Pacific Northwest for over forty years, if he ever yearned to revisit his family and the land of his birth. "Yes, and I could have had that pleasure," he replied, "but then the sacrifice would not have been complete." The old man had paid a price for self-abandonment, however. He suddenly lowered his head, broke into tears, and sobbed like a child.[62]

With entire provinces driven from the country and no prospect of immediate return in view, a prolonged winter of exile settled upon the Jesuits of Italy. To Beckx and to the leaders of the dispersed provinces, the crisis posed many questions and offered few answers. Safe refuge had to be found for several thousand men displaced by revolution. But where could they go? Providing for the education of younger members of the order with as little interruption as possible became a top priority. But how would their travel and schooling be paid for? All assets had been confiscated by the government. As Jesuit Italy sank into darkness, these were some of the difficulties with which the order would continue to wrestle for the remainder of the century. "What can we do?," one provincial said rhetorically. "We live at a time when events occur so swiftly and on such a vast scale that history provides no equivalent. Where will we go and where will these extraordinary times take us?," he wondered. "The mind is lost in a thousand speculations. We would like to know what lies ahead, but God determines our destiny; and what that may be, we shall know only if we live long enough to see it."[63]

3 *"Instant Despatch"*

THE IDEOLOGY OF EMIGRATION

"Here I am, at last, an Englishman, after having been a
Spaniard and a Frenchman."

— Jesuit Santo Schiffini, 1880[1]

Pressed to remove quickly, Jesuits seeking safe haven made choices similar to those of millions of other displaced Europeans in that turbulent century. Many of them relocated several times, ricocheting from one refuge to the next, before reaching a final destination. And, when possible, they made short-distance moves within Italy before taking the more drastic and final step of moving abroad. Thus numerous Piedmontese clerics fled south to the Papal States after their banishment from the Kingdom of Piedmont-Sardinia in 1848. Uprooted again by the Italian invasion of Rome, some subsequently sought refuge in the Kingdom of the Two Sicilies. It was only after national unification and their eviction from the entire peninsula that they fled to neighboring European nations and later to America. To be sure, not every Jesuit followed this sequence of repeated removals, but many emigrated more than once in the course of their lifetime.

What was the outcome of this frequent uprooting? In some cases, it proved the truth of the cautionary proverb *Albero spesso trapiantato mai di frutti è caricato* ("A tree that is often transplanted is never loaded with fruit"). The trauma of multiple dislocation fostered instability and restlessness among vagabond Jesuits. Some, like Giuseppe Bixio, brother of Nino Bixio, the famous Piedmontese revolutionary, became rolling stones, incapable of lingering long anywhere. Mesmerized by motion, that ever-outward Jesuit passed his entire career on the go, working first in Maryland, then in California, Virginia, and Washington, D.C. Upon returning to the West Coast, he next headed to Australia before finally coming to rest in California, where he spent the last years of his gypsy life.

But for many more expatriates — perhaps because they were young and malleable — the willingness to uproot themselves and move wherever revealed a passion for possibility and experimentation. Travel elicited the best from them. It induced an indifference to material comforts and a capacity for itinerancy that made any place seem habitable, traits useful for future circuit-riders in missionary lands. The experience of living in several countries proved another advantage when they finally settled in the United States. Removals rehearsed again and again relativized the exiles' understanding of culture and fostered a new-found tolerance for differences that enabled them to accommodate the jumble of traditions they met in multicultural America.

Superiors initially tried, however, to avoid sending seminarians to multiple locations, preferring to keep them together for the sake of morale and continuity in schooling. When doing so proved impossible, they compromised by consolidating novices in one place, humanities students in another, and philosophers and theologians in still another locale. The extensive European network of Jesuit residences to which men could be sent facilitated that complex implementation. Bowing to the inevitable, Sicilian Jesuit scholastics, for example, scattered to Ireland, Spain, France, Belgium, and England. Dismayed at the prospect of splitting up classmates and scattering them about, Pietro Fontana, their leader during 1857–59, voiced a frustration felt by all the Italian provincials when he lamented, "All Europe has been invaded by Sicilian Jesuits."[2]

Thus it was that many young Jesuits spent their years of training on the move, passing through countries as though through revolving doors. Italian religious who had taken refuge in the Austrian Tyrol after their expulsion in 1870 were uprooted a few years later. Fleeing across the border in shifting disguises, they trudged into France, according to a bemused observer, "dressed in every conceivable fashion."[3] Before he reached the United States, twenty-seven-year-old Giuseppe Marra lived in five different countries. His fellow Neapolitan, Vito Carrozzini, resided in six locales in thirteen years — Italy, Spain, Cuba, Puerto Rico, France, and the United States. Santo Schiffini was studying theology in France when the Third Republic dissolved the Society, thereby obliging him to flee to a seminary on the island of Jersey in the English Channel. He described his landing in a letter to his brother. "So, then, here I am, at last, an Englishman, after having been a Spaniard and a Frenchman," he exclaimed. "It can hardly be that the government will drive us out of this place."[4]

Few Jesuits were as frequently torn up and replanted as the Sicilian Carmelo Polino. Having entered the novitiate in Naples, in 1859, at the age of fifteen, he launched his odyssey a few months later, after revolution broke out, traveling with classmates to Ireland. He completed his humanities course in France, studied philosophy in Spain, taught for five years in the Philippines, returned to study theology in Spain, but was again forced by revolution to go back to France. Finally ordained a priest in Toulouse in 1875, Polino then embarked for the United States, where he completed his formation in Maryland before teaching philosophy at Woodstock College. Fluent in Spanish, he was summoned to New Mexico ten years later to join the staff of the *La Revista Católica*, the Jesuits' Spanish language newspaper. Only death four years later prevented Polino from still one more move — a return to Naples to teach philosophy. When he died, three words in his obituary recapitulated his otherwise unextraordinary life: "He traveled much."[5]

Some Jesuits journeyed not at all. Novices of the Roman Province, who had temporarily returned to their homes when revolution erupted in 1848, were swept up in the excitement of the times and left the order. By a Jesuit chronicler's account, "A few of them later took a part, even a very active part, in the revolution."[6] Other scholastics, faced with the prospect of separation from family and homeland, also departed the Jesuits. Still others were dismissed from the order by superiors who recognized the Society could no longer adequately provide for them in the molten times in which they were mired.

Departures from the Society dramatically shrank the ranks of the younger, non-ordained group. At the time of the 1848 dispersion, sixty members of the Roman Province, most of them scholastics, suddenly became ex-Jesuits. During the same upheaval, the 226-member Venice Province saw one-fourth of its men exit religious life. The Turinese, Neapolitan, and Sicilian provinces each lost approximately one-third of their coadjutor brothers. The ranks of the Neapolitan scholastics were devastated, plunging from a high of 128 in 1861 to just thirteen in 1877. The Sicilians bade good-bye to two-thirds of their seminarians in roughly the same period. Before Piedmont-Sardinia erupted in revolution in 1848, the Turin Province had boasted 151 scholastics. Ten years later, its members deported and dispersed abroad, the province retained merely thirty-one.[7]

Still, the survival rate of those who weathered the trials of revolution and deportation was surprisingly high. Although it meant separation from family and exile, many men elected to remain Jesuits by emigrating. About 40 percent of the scholastics of the Turin Province, who were deported in 1848, spent the remainder of their lives as Jesuits — an elevated figure by modern standards. Perseverance among Neapolitan seminarians who survived the dispersal of 1860 was even greater — nearly 60 percent.[8] Some individuals manifested a rock-ribbed determination to hang on. The Neapolitan brother Rafael Vezza was sent home after the order's dispersal to live with his family and await better times. Bent on remaining a Jesuit, he repeatedly petitioned for assignment abroad, which was finally granted in 1864, when he was sent to assist in the establishment of the Neapolitan mission in New Mexico. Giuseppe Cataldo, a man of prodigious energy and determination, was typical of many scholastics who remained Jesuits. After eight years of routine seminary education, his career took a dramatic turn-about in 1860, when Garibaldi occupied Sicily. When the provisional government began its

FIGURE 4. Sketch of Jesuits preparing to leave Italy in 1848 as their arch-enemy
Vincenzo Gioberti (in top hat on far left) feigns tears at their hasty departure.
Gioberti's writings were a key influence in persuading political leaders and the
Italian public to turn against the order. In the background, a steamship stands
at the ready to ferry the Jesuits into exile. Courtesy Istituto per la Storia del
Risorgimento Italiano, Rome

campaign to eradicate Jesuit influence on the island, young Cataldo had to
chose between leaving the Jesuits or leaving Sicily. Revealing a tenacity and
toughness of character that would later become his trademark, Cataldo
brushed aside parental pleas and chose exile. He fled first to Belgium and then
to America, where he became a famous missionary and founder of Gonzaga
College (today's University) in Washington.[9]

Finding safe asylum for Cataldo and those who wished to carry on challenged the order's resourcefulness. As is often the case with persons hastily
evicted from their homeland, options were limited. Since all Jesuit institutions in Italy were eventually closed and their occupants banished, clinging
to *la terra vecchia* was not possible for most men. Some priests stayed behind,
working under cover, but scholastics had to resume studies abroad. Their
emigration became even more urgent after 1866, when the government
passed a law making seminarians subject to military conscription. Hence, the
first objective of those in charge was to whisk them out of the country as soon
as possible so that their schooling would suffer as little interruption as possible. The international character of the order, which had houses in most
countries of the world, facilitated such transfers, as did the utility of Latin
as a lingua franca in all seminaries.

Because their resources had been seized by a hostile government, most provinces had to borrow money to pay traveling expenses. During the early exportations, this meant that costly long-distance emigration for the majority was out of the question. The lingering impecuniousness of the Neapolitan Province delayed for years the posting of men to new assignments. In 1871, the consultors, a small circle of priests who served as official advisers to the provincial, reported that they had insufficient funds to either send men to better locations or support them once they got there. Even after the province had established a mission in New Mexico "as a refuge, especially for our young men," it often could not afford to pay their passage. It cost 2,000 francs to send men to New Mexico, the consultors reported, but neither the mission nor the province was "in any condition to spend that kind of money." Consequently, they decided "for now, no one moves from where he is."[10]

Among the European countries to which the fugitives fled, nearby France provided a convenient first choice for French-speaking *piemontesi*. When revolution began in 1848, the Turin Province had 113 younger members for whom lodging had to be found. Although France itself was in political turmoil — the king had fallen in February and a republic was proclaimed a month later — Jesuits for a time enjoyed full liberty in the general confusion that ensued. For several years thereafter, French training centers provided ready refuge for scholastics studying philosophy and theology. After the closure of the novitiate of San Andrea al Quirinale in Rome, the Roman Jesuits established a novitiate-in-exile in Avignon. By 1852, the Turin Province had set up a novitiate, scholasticate, and provincial headquarters across the Italian border in the principality of Monaco. In Corsica they maintained two residences where they carried on a pastoral ministry.[11]

Although the Italians slipped into France as displaced persons, their Roman connection gave them authority in church circles. Indeed, Roman professors of theology and philosophy quickly made their presence felt in every European country to which they journeyed, although that impact was often controversial. The refugees of 1848 left a permanent impression on the seminary of the French Jesuits at Vals, in southeastern France. Theologians Giovanni Battista Franzelin and Carlo Passaglia immediately took sides in a brewing controversy between the Vals faculty and authorities in Rome over the French professorate's promotion of ontologism, a philosophic theory concerning the origin of ideas and how knowledge of God is attained. Its advocates implied that humans possessed an intuitive grasp of the deity, a proposition that seemed to Roman neo-Thomists perilously close to pantheism. In 1849, the visiting Italians relayed their misgivings to officials in Rome. These objections, coupled with the French provincial's mismanagement of the dispute, precipitated an investigation of the Vals system, the sacking of the provincial, and the removal of the offending ontologists to other institutions. Thus, even in exile, the Italians were a power to be reckoned with and their arrival a mixed blessing, as church leaders in the United States would soon discover.[12]

The Italians had staged an academic coup d'état at Vals, but elsewhere in France they themselves were the victims of rebellion. Frequent fluctuations of government made that country an undependable asylum, because priests — French as well as foreign — were periodically sent packing by anti-clerical regimes. Scholastic Luigi Sabetti, for example, had been a student of philosophy when Garibaldi's invasion of Naples forced him into hiding. After a month of wandering about, the peripatetic seminarian made his way to Vals to resume studies. Émigrés who came later, however, were ousted from even that sanctuary during the Franco-Prussian War. For many Italians, therefore, itinerancy became a way of life — with contradictory outcomes. The repeated uprooting thwarted continuity in academic training. But it also fostered fluency in multiple languages and an ability to adapt to new cultures, skills that were of paramount utility for missionaries-to-be.[13]

Ireland provided a more stable shelter to the novices of the Neapolitan and Sicilian provinces. So, too, did Spain, except during periods when the government banished Jesuits from the realm. "Our Neapolitan Jesuits have left Spain," an Italian superior lamented in 1873. "Please God they can stay in France." In peaceful times, the Iberian peninsula was attractive because of the historic bond between the Kingdom of the Two Sicilies and Bourbon Spain. Convinced that Spain offered the best religious training then available in Europe, the Neapolitans sent many of their young men there for schooling. After missionary work was inaugurated in the United States, clergy who needed to master Spanish in preparation for careers in New Mexico found Spain a convenient staging ground.[14]

Although expatriate leaders preferred to keep seminarians within Europe, priests were sent wherever work could be found. For this reason, large numbers of Italian exiles became foreign missionaries. The Roman Jesuits adopted Brazil and British Honduras as mission fields. The Piedmontese sent personnel to Corsica, California, the Pacific Northwest, Alaska, and Jamaica. A missionary project in New Mexico and Colorado drew Neapolitans. Still others worked in Europe. Venetian Jesuits started green careers in Albania and Illyria-Dalmatia. Turkey and the Aegean islands drew Sicilians, who founded a school in Constantinople. Fugitives from Sicily also found haven in neighboring Malta, where they established a novitiate and school. Corsica welcomed French-speaking priests from the Turin Province, including Giuseppe Giorda, who eventually became a North American missionary. France's recently conquered colony in Algeria provided temporary employment for others. In the aftermath of the *Risorgimento*, there was hardly a missionary country in the world that had not by century's end benefited from the diaspora of Italian Jesuits.

England, too, served as a sanctuary for Jesuits, as it had for liberals and nationalists persecuted during periods of conservative ascendancy in Italy. Jan Roothaan, the Jesuit superior general, had briefly found asylum there after his proscription in Italy. Even Pius IX made diplomatic overtures to see if he might be given refuge in London if forced to leave Rome. By 1848, twenty-five Jesuits were resettled in various houses of the Society in England. They included two of the most prominent members of the Roman College faculty: the mathematician Giovanni Battista Pianciani and the astronomer Francesco De Vico, renowned for his research on comets. Giovanni Perrone, author of a widely used compendium of theology, *Praelectiones Theologicae*, began teaching in English seminaries, as did Carlo Passaglia, a professor of dogma, who subsequently became embroiled in the battle over ontologism at Vals. G. B. Franzelin, later a cardinal and papal theologian, landed in London after a difficult escape from Rome, flanked by the scripture scholar Francesco Saverio Patrizi.[15]

Although an impressive lot, most of the Italians did not linger long in England. Antipathy toward Catholics — especially Jesuits, who were, as one writer put it, "objects of suspicion, fear and hatred" to the average Englishman — favored a short visit. Encompassed by a hostile environment, the refugees kept a low public profile.[16] Although they located in the countryside to avoid drawing unfriendly notice, their coming was interpreted by some Englishmen as a plot to subjugate the realm to Roman Catholicism. The charge reached fever pitch after 1850, when Pope Pius IX reestablished the Roman Catholic hierarchy in England, an innocuous action that nevertheless provoked an explosion of public outrage. To Protestant alarmists, this restoration of regular church structures in England exposed the murky fingerprints of Roothaan "and his companions in the *Collegio Romano*." Since the foreigners were present in England when the new dioceses were delineated, critics charged, it was "highly probable" that they had masterminded the innovation. The novelist Catherine Sinclair voiced the common hysteria: "Roman principles are as out of place in an English drawing-room as an Italian organ-boy would be in a palace," but "the true Italian school of morality is now about to raise its head in Great Britain." [17]

In these circumstances, the Jesuits of England welcomed their ejected brethren with ambivalent emotions. Englishmen familiar with Italian mores would be "indulgent" toward the visitors, William Cobb, the English provincial advised Roothaan, but they would not receive a warm embrace. That prediction proved true. "Ours [Jesuits] were very coldly received in England," an American acquaintance of the Italians reported later. "It is just like them. They are all like bulldogs," he wrote with ill-concealed schadenfreude.[18] The problem solved itself, however, when the castaways received word from Roothaan that they had been offered refuge in America. Later that year, twenty-one of the theologians set off for New York.[19]

Expatriation to America

The transfer of the Roman College Jesuits to United States in 1848 marked the beginning of a steady emigration. For the next seventy years, especially during times of greatest political turmoil in Italy, nearly four hundred Italian Jesuits claimed the United States as their adopted homeland. Although they streamed in from all regions of the Italian peninsula, the vast majority were members of the Turin Province in the north and the Neapolitan Province in the south. By 1879, over half of the Piedmontese and nearly a fourth of the Neapolitan Jesuits resided in the United States.[20]

Several factors made this nation an appealing destination. Not the least of its appeals was the possibility of resuming academic careers in a cordial milieu. "A good number will go to America," reported Silvio Pellico, brother of the Turinese provincial, because the Society has "colleges in the United States, where they are admired and liked even by the Protestants, who consider them educated and useful citizens."[21] As anti-clericalism drove Jesuits from Italy and the other European states where they had taken refuge, religious freedom made the United States a preferred sanctuary. It was paradoxical, of course, that the principle of separation of church and state — which the Society had vigorously opposed in Italy — made America an enticing alternative. The irony of that ideological juxtaposition was not, however, immediately apparent to the deracinated clergy. It was only with the passing of time that these most orthodox of churchmen would come to acknowledge the practical advantages of the American system.

If the Italians were eager to embrace the New World, Americans were eager to receive them. Between 1840 and 1850, the nation's Catholic population had grown from 650,000 to 1,750,000 — and by 1860, it doubled again. As a result, the church experienced a shortage of clergy. Half of the Catholics in the nation "do not have any priests," Bishop Simon Bruté of Illinois reported in 1836. A New York Jesuit voiced the same concern twenty-five years later. We are "obliged to leave undone a great deal" of what we wish to accomplish, and to "do imperfectly" even what we attempt, he said. Our colleges are "by no means sufficient to meet the wants of the country [and] too numerous for our limited supply of professors."[22]

In the absence of native-born pastors, church leaders competed with one another to acquire the services of the immigrants. The expulsion of German-speaking Jesuits from Switzerland, in 1847, prompted Ignace Brocard, the provincial of the Maryland Province, to propose that they join the Society in America. Teachers were particularly welcome. When some of the Swiss planted their feet in New York the following year, President John Larkin of St. John's College was euphoric: "I managed to get a brother from them and even a father." When an Italian provincial inquired in 1848 if his Maryland counterpart could accommodate some of his men, Ignace Brocard's immediate response was to list specific jobs for which personnel were needed. "America is open to you, perhaps the only home left us in this world," Father Joseph Keller of Maryland told European Jesuits after the fall of papal Rome in 1870. "We are looking for a large accession to our numbers."[23]

The presence of several Italian members of the Society already in the United States inspired others to emigrate. Like other immigrants, Jesuits were drawn to destinations where previously transplanted compatriots could assure them of hospitality and support. Even before the *Risorgimento* made Italy unwelcome to churchmen, over a dozen Italians had emigrated to America as missionaries. Their successful integration into the country emboldened others to seek asylum when Italy began expelling religious orders. One of the earliest was Giovanni Antonio Grassi, who, after arriving in 1810, became one of the most respected Catholic churchmen in the country. Superior of all Jesuits in the United States and president of the fledgling Georgetown College, Grassi returned to Italy seven years later, but he continued to mold events in America. To correct erroneous European impressions of the church there, in 1818 he published a book, *Notizie varie sullo stato attuale della Repubblica degli Stati Uniti di America* (A Report on the Present State of the Republic of the United States of America). He also wielded authority in the Society of Jesus as Italian Assistant to the Jesuit superior general during the critical 1840s, when many of his countrymen sought asylum in America.[24]

Other Italians had emigrated in the period preceding the *Risorgimento*. Stefano Gabaria, a priest from Rome, arrived in 1834, along with Andrea Mazzella, a Neapolitan brother, who spent most of his career in the Midwest among the Potowatami and Kickapoo tribes. During a recruiting trip to Italy in 1845, James Ryder, a former president of Georgetown College, had netted three Roman and five Neapolitan volunteers. The gaggle included Angelo Paresce, who later held key jobs in the Maryland Jesuit world as director of novices, provincial, and co-founder of Woodstock College.[25]

The trickle of expatriates drafted by Ryder swelled into a stream when revolution descended upon Italy. In 1848, the Naples Province sent a cluster of seminarians to complete their training in America, initiating a practice that persisted for decades. That same year, Roman College students and professors, who had taken asylum in England, crossed the Atlantic, their way having been paved by the high-profile Jesuit astronomer Francesco De Vico. The priest, provided with transportation and letters of introduction by the U.S. Ambassador to England, George Bancroft, arrived in Washington, D.C. Warmly received by scientists and civic officials, including President James K. Polk, De Vico decided to make America his home when Georgetown College offered him the directorship of its observatory. So enthusiastic was De Vico that he wrote to his Roman College colleagues uncomfortably lodged in England, urging them to join him. He even offered to personally accompany them to the United States. Struck down with typhoid, however, the forty-three-year-old scientist died in London on 15 November 1848. He was, a companion lamented, like Moses, who expired before he could bring his people into the promised land. And like the ancient Israelites, the Romans continued on without their leader.[26]

Disembarking in New York, the Italian refugees were met by James Ryder, who conducted them to Washington, D.C., and to an enthusiastic reception at Georgetown College. Although accustomed to integrating displaced Europeans into their ranks, the Americans were impressed by this scholarly delegation from Rome, the hub of the nineteenth-century Catholic universe. The group was comprised of "venerable fathers" with "silvery locks" and seminarians with "the ruddy looks of youth," Bernard A. Maguire, an American Jesuit, orated with sanctimonious seriousness during welcoming ceremonies. There was Giovanni Perrone, the well-known theologian; Felice Sopranis, the former rector of the Roman College; the mathematician Francesco Provenzali; and the astronomer Angelo Secchi, heralded internationally for his spectral classifications of the stars.

The party also included younger men who were destined for high office in the church: Salvatore Tongiorgi, philosopher and later critic of neo-Thomism; Giuseppe Brunengo, who became a writer for the influential journal *Civiltà Cattolica*; Torquato Armellini, later Secretary of the Society of Jesus; Ugo Molza who became rector of the Roman College; and Antonio Maraschi, founder of the University of San Francisco. "We cannot . . . receive you in magnificent colleges such as you have left," Maguire declared, but "no edict of tyranny can reach you" within the walls of our institutions. "I congratulate our country upon your arrival," he concluded, "and am almost tempted to cry out, O *felix culpa!*, O happy frenzy of deluded Italy that has borne such precious fruit for America."[27]

Despite the embroidery in Maguire's pious polemic, there was also a measure of truth. The arrival of the exiles from Rome was propitious for Georgetown College, whose faculty was immediately strengthened by the acquisition of eminent scholars. Their coming would also have far-reaching consequences for American Catholicism, an outcome still hidden from the purview of both the immigrants and their self-congratulatory hosts since the Roman College assembly of 1848 was merely a vanguard. In the decades that followed, several hundred more Italian Jesuits set out across the Atlantic to assume new careers on the American frontier.

Traveling Strategically

The manner in which the Jesuits emigrated to their new home owed much to their spiritual orientation, especially to their order's high estimation of mobility. When Ignatius of Loyola established the Society of Jesus in the sixteenth century, he set no limits on the place or circumstances of its undertakings. Unlike the members of older, monastic congregations, his followers saw themselves as pilgrims committed to an itinerant ministry. "We should always be ready, at any hour," wrote the founder, "to go to some or other parts of the world." Travel for the sake of the Gospel was the "first characteristic of our Institute" and indeed its very "end and aim," he declared. Jesuits should therefore not seek "to reside in or to be sent to one place rather than to another."[28] Jerónimo Nadal, an early authority on the order's *Constitutions*, further developed this inclination for the open road. The Society had several types of permanent residences, such as colleges and seminaries, he said, but its "most characteristic dwelling" was wherever people stood in spiritual need. Nadal encapsulated the order's dedication to ministry-on-the-move in an axiom: "The world is our house."[29]

The Jesuits had created not only an ideology of travel but practical procedures for journeying strategically. In the sixteenth century they published *Regulae Peregrinorum* (Rules for those who travel), a series of short spiritual exhortations to guide members on pilgrimage. Men who undertook more extensive voyages followed the *Regulae eorum qui in Missionibus Versantur* (Rules for those on missions), a list of twenty-seven general dos and don'ts regarding the exercise of their ministries.[30] Like the general rules of the Society, these local directives were adapted to changing times and circumstances, and they left much to the discretion of the traveler. With the passing of time, individual provinces drew up regional guidelines that spelled out in greater detail the steps to be followed when on the road. The 1873 edition of the "Custom Book of the Maryland Province" outlined with great specificity a protocol for leaving one assignment and going to the next. It prescribed methods for calculating expenses, how much luggage a priest could take (one trunk and a small valise), and how many books (a breviary, a compendium of moral theology, and "certain little books for private devotion").[31]

These dictates evolved over several centuries, as did the nature of Jesuit peripateticism itself. When the order founded institutions requiring long-term commitment of personnel, mobility was necessarily restricted. Convinced that education offered a unique opportunity for rendering service, Ignatius had approved the founding of thirty-nine colleges for lay students before his death in 1556. By the time the Society was suppressed two hundred years later, it ran over seven hundred colleges, most of them in Europe.[32] Jesuits still dedicated themselves to mobile ministries such as foreign missions and itinerant preaching, but Ignatius' commitment to education inevitably brought with it stability and permanence.

Although reconstructed Jesuits of the nineteenth century often experienced themselves more as victims than as adventurous pilgrims, they still prized mobility. Indeed, the metaphor of wayfarer had special applicability as national upheavals sent thousands into exile. During Jan Roothaan's generalate, missionaries poured forth from Europe into Asia, Africa, and the Americas in record numbers. Seminary training aimed at encouraging obedient acceptance of whatever assignments were given. Novices, for example, were instructed to halt a task without skipping a beat when a new one was assigned. As one scholar has summarized, "If one novice was talking to another during a recreation period, at the first vibration of the bell signaling its end, he would cease talking, in the middle of a word or sentence if that is where he found himself, smile, and silently take up whatever task followed." Additionally, trainees were sent on pilgrimage as a way of instilling in them the values of the order and testing their qualifications. "These practices were a rehearsal writ small for welcoming larger assignments."[33] As the English Jesuit Gerard Manley Hopkins once explained to his mother, "Ours can never be an abiding city nor any one of us know what a day may bring forth; and it is our pride to be ready for instant despatch."[34]

As a result, an ideology that valued mobility shaped the *mentalité* of the Italian émigrés and the way they journeyed. It also differentiated their experience from that of other emigrants. Codes of conduct for successful journeying, the product of three centuries of trial-and-error learning, eased the cleric's trip and spared him some of the trials that roiled more typical refugees. Moreover, the ascetic principles of religious life bestowed high purpose and meaning to what otherwise was a trying experience. The Jesuit exaltation of travel provided categories for coping not only with the discomforts of transoceanic travel, but also with exile itself. In sum, travel for the sake of ministry was elevated to a virtue.

This did not mean that Jesuits suffered any less from displacement than other refugees did. Nor did all of them succeed in integrating the order's lofty standard into their own lives. The transformation of travel into a spiritual adventure presupposed certain dispositions on the part of participants, dispositions that not everyone was able to attain. It required detachment regarding one's place of work and living conditions, ready availability for service, and adaptability. Some persons met the test; others did not. But how they coped with dislocation and the way they traveled sheds light on central aspects of the immigrant experience.

"It is especially important that the man being sent should learn from his superiors the scope of his mission and the result intended," a rule directed. "If possible, he will take care to get this in writing." Accordingly, every Jesuit met with his superior to lay the groundwork for a successful trip. In the 1840s, missionaries departing Italy for the United States conferred with the superior general of the order himself. A stickler for detail, Roothaan laid out guidelines for their trajectory, expectations regarding behavior, and indications of what to anticipate in America. Fortunate for history, he required that Jesuits send him detailed accounts of whatever they encountered throughout the course of their hegira.[35]

Since few travelers sailed directly for America, stopovers en route from Europe were used to advantage. Gregorio Gazzoli, who headed an expedition to the Rocky Mountain Mission in 1846, wrote to Roothaan from Paris that he and his companions were busy gathering "useful and necessary" supplies for the remainder of their journey. He reported the purchase of "a small number of books of absolute necessity, among which the most expensive was a copy of the [Jesuit] Institute, then some theological things — but with great economy, being careful to keep an eye on both our needs and on our budget." A community of nuns in Paris had given them "a generous gift of liturgical vestments." "After spending a few francs more," he concluded, "we have everything needed to outfit a little chapel." The missionaries took advantage of their French sojourn to acquire skills needed in America. Two brothers were "working diligently, one learning the carpenter's craft, another that of a mason." Gazzoli and another priest passed their days learning English. We are, he assured the ever-vigilant Roothaan, not "wasting our time."[36]

Treks within Europe tested their readiness for the transatlantic crossing. In Paris, Gazzoli recalled an advisory that cautioned: "If anyone becomes so ill that he cannot proceed, and it is not advisable for the rest to delay there," the sick person should proceed no farther. Nor should the weak advance. The voyage of Gazzoli and his party across the Mediterranean from France to Italy had been difficult. They traveled in "great fear," he said, "because of a sea storm which did not let up until we had almost entered the port" of Marseilles. The ordeal convinced him that one member of the group, a priest named Ballerini, was unfit for missionary life. Having shown "excessive natural timidity when faced with the littlest difficulties," Ballerini was sent back to Italy.[37]

The lavish preparations that engaged Gazzoli in 1846 were not possible a few years later, when Italy started expelling Jesuits by the hundreds. Unplanned flight became the norm, although deportees tried to follow protocol insofar as circumstances permitted. Like Gazzoli, they paused in several countries as they worked their way toward ports of embarkation, benefiting from the Society's internationality, which proffered hospitality in cities along their route. In this, they resembled other emigrants who erected networks of support among relatives and neighbors to garner aid on the way to their new homeland.[38]

The Jesuit travel code required that they journey modestly. They "will take care," a rule advised, "so far as possible, to preach the Gospel as poor men." In the sixteenth century, this had meant missionaries trudged on foot "if the superior judges them able to do so." They should not "tire themselves out," however, and they were urged to "be moderate regarding both the travel itself and other hardships." Roothaan, whose dedication to simplicity banished curtains and all forms of decoration from his room, insisted that travelers take "such lodging as the poor could go to," as long as it did not impede the work itself. [39] Guided by these directives, the first missionaries who traveled from Europe to the Rocky Mountain Mission on vessels of trade had the barest of accommodations. Later in the century, Jesuit political refugees traveled as second-class passengers on vessels built to transport immigrants across the Atlantic. In 1873, when Filippo Rappagliosi and his companions crossed from Liverpool to New York on an English ship, they enjoyed the comfort of "a nice cabin with four beds." "You wouldn't believe you are at sea," he wrote, "but on land in a real palace with rooms and salons furnished like the best first class rooms of a railroad station. Right now, for example, I'm writing in a superb salon with sofa, carpets, mirrors, piano, stoves."[40]

Most Jesuits eschewed luxury, not only because it was incompatible with religious poverty but because they could not afford it. Neapolitans suffered the greatest economic constraints. Unlike the Piedmontese and Roman Jesuits who fled after 1848, castaways from *Il Regno* had no one to whom they might turn for assistance. When the former Kingdom of the Two Sicilies started evicting Jesuits, earlier havens such as the Papal States had already dissolved, along with any remaining economic resources that might have buoyed the Neapolitans in their flight. Even the superior general, driven from Rome in 1873, could offer them little more than moral succor. Provincial Davide Palomba, who presided over the Neapolitan dispersal, told his companions that they would have to fend for themselves. "I do not have a single extra speck [*grano*], especially now that I am reorganizing the province," he told Donato Gasparri in 1869 when he asked for money to bring men to New Mexico. If Gasparri himself could not find the funds, the provincial warned, "you can sing a requiem for the Mission." "I am sorry to say this, but that's the way it is. . . . I cannot do the impossible, and I do not have the gift of miracles." A travel fund, sustained by monies raised by exiles in America, was eventually established in Paris, but whenever its reserves dried up, travel ceased.[41]

Like many nineteenth-century immigrants, Jesuits left Europe with the expectation that their departure was final. Upon boarding a ship that would carry him to America, one twenty-year-old Neapolitan reflected, it was "our last look at Europe, where we spent our childhood, where we learned to come to know God. . . . Perhaps for the last time we were looking at those shores."[42] Another missionary, writing a hasty valedictory to friends, suddenly realized: "I am now writing to them perhaps for the last time from this old world."[43] Religious asceticism of the day cautioned against excessive emotional attachments, but, as memoirs reveal, separation from one's family was inevitably painful.

Every detail of a farewell was impressed indelibly in the traveler's memory. Young Carmelo Giordano, who left Naples for America in 1885, took ship in haste, leaving behind a heart-broken parent. "My Mother accompanied me to the stage, crying 'Good-bye! I will never see you anymore!'" No less poignant was the plight of those denied adieus. Paulo Ponziglione and his companions, who were chased from Genoa by rioters, set off for America with the clothes on their back. Political unrest kept some refugees from returning home, even for a rushed good-bye. Lorenzo Palladino left for a missionary career in Oregon in 1863 after living in exile in Monaco. "Up to now I have not told our parents your new destination," his brother Sebastiano wrote to him from Genoa, "but as soon as they know, I want to hope they will be consoled by it." Despite "the enormous distance" that was about to separate them, Sebastiano concluded: "Give us news about yourself sometimes." What Lorenzo felt about his abrupt exodus is revealed by that tattered letter, still preserved among his sparse possessions when he died decades later, a palpable reminder of his sacrifice.[44]

To take the edge off sorrow, Jesuits elevated leave-taking into a religious ritual. When possible, missionaries were feted by their communities with ceremonies that simultaneously encouraged the traveler and gave public support to his decision to emigrate. Such farewells also infused meaning into the odyssey and the new life that lay ahead. Giuseppe Giorda's exit from Bertinoro, Italy, in 1858 was transformed into a civic send-off. When the popular priest announced his decision to abandon a seminary teaching post in order to become an Indian missionary, "news of his departure caused an uproar," a contemporary recounted. On the day Giorda took leave, "priests and canons accompanied him for a distance from the city."[45]

Letter-writing played a similar role in the rite of separation. From comrades sprinkled throughout Europe, departing missionary Lorenzo Palladino received notes expressing "sorrow at not being able to be part of that beautiful group" that walked him to his ship. In lieu of embraces, friends offered congratulations and a promise of prayers. Even after missionaries left for America, superiors urged that their separation "be in some degree compensated for by the interchange of suitable letters" between those staying at home and those in "bitter exile."[46]

If deportation provoked resentment and sorrow, religion offered recompense. "The ministry of propagating the Gospel of Jesus Christ and the Catholic Faith, even in remote regions," Roothaan reminded Jesuits in 1833, was "truly noble and most in keeping with our vocation." The Society's promotion of missionary careers as "a gift from God," was transformative when coupled with youthful idealism.[47] Many young men, longing to spring into spiritual combat, found an opportunity to do so when exile was imposed upon them. Indeed, as modern studies have shown, when a traveler is young and teeming with lofty aspirations, migration can be embraced as "a life adventure." As the case of the Italian religious demonstrates, no period in life is better fitted for such an experience.[48]

Not a few Jesuits left Europe fired with romantic expectations. "You can imagine the desire we have to be with our much-longed-for Indians as soon as possible," one missionary wrote from Paris on the eve of his departure for the Pacific Northwest.[49] "The moment so ardently desired, the moment for us to embark for our dear mission finally arrived," another said. Although he dreaded travel on the high seas, the Jesuit was consoled to think of St. Paul, "who undertook even more voyages." "The only thing that pains me is the great distance that separates me from my destination. I wish I had wings to go there in an instant."[50] Passion for missionary life was not restricted to the young. When forty-year-old Santo Lattanzi received word that his application had been accepted, he immediately shared the news with friends. "To tell the truth, I don't know what I am writing," he said, "so great is the excitement that I feel at having just now glanced at Father Provincial's letter."[51] Like many missionaries thrilled at the prospect of starting for America, he had sublimated the painful aspects of travel into religious idealism.

No matter what adventures, real or imagined, awaited at journey's end, few emigrants savored the trip across the Atlantic. "The ordeal of the voyage separated the two worlds of Europe and America," wrote the scholar Jonathan Raban, "in much the same way as Purgatory separates Hell and Heaven."[52] The Jesuits attempted to ease the journey by trying to assure that no one traveled by himself. Companionship provided benefits lost to the solitary wayfarer, especially when illness struck or language sputtered. The fact that seminarians migrated in company, usually flanked by a priest, provided additional security that the single immigrant might envy.

Crossing solo invited disaster. When nineteen-year-old Beniamino Tovani cruised from Naples in 1885 with the aim of joining the Society in New Mexico, he boarded the wrong vessel. Instead of arriving at an American port, he ended up in Vera Cruz, Mexico. Undeterred, the young adventurer "worked and begged his way with difficulty and delay to the Land of Liberty," arriving in Colorado six months later.[53] It comes as no surprise, therefore, to learn that Maryland superior Joseph Keller prohibited three newly arrived Jesuit brothers — proverbial innocents abroad, none of whom knew English — from crossing the continent by themselves. Fearing that "alone they would not be able to travel without ending up at the North Pole instead of New Mexico," he sent them with a priest who had mastered a bit of the language.[54]

One of the worst features of the trans-Atlantic voyage was its long duration. When Gregorio Mengarini sailed from Italy to Philadelphia in 1840, his ship was blown off course by a hurricane. What had been expected to take three weeks instead took eight. As cupboards emptied and provisions failed, the crew battled starvation by fishing for dolphins and sea turtles and by soliciting bread from a passing ship. After 1848, when the majority of Italian Jesuits emigrated, the crossing had become quicker but still varied enormously, depending on the season and type of vessel. The twenty-one Roman College theologians who sailed from England to New York in 1848 made the voyage in eighteen days, but another group departing from Antwerp that same year took three times as long. By the 1860s, vessels powered by wind were replaced with steamers, which were soon carrying 90 percent of America's immigrant traffic and doing it in half the time. By the turn of the century, European immigrants uniformly ran the Atlantic in less than a week.[55]

Despite technological improvements, rough weather made torture of any trip. Thirty-four-year-old Jesuit Giacomo Diamare described a terrifying storm at sea in 1873 in which "waves reached up to the sky like mountains." Seawater swept over the shuddering ship, making it impossible to remain seated or even to lie in bed. "No one who has not actually experienced it can imagine what all this is like," he wrote.[56] Rare was the traveler who did not succumb to seasickness induced by the perpetual rolling of the sea. Tossed about like dice in a cup, Gregorio Mengarini's companion became so ill that he spent most of the trip incapacitated. "Spitting of blood was of daily occurrence," Mengarini reported, and "the poor father did not have one good day during the fifty-six days of travel." "He vomited two and three times daily, and of the twenty-four hours that constitute a day, he passed twenty-two in bed."[57] Salvatore Personè never forgot his passage of the North Atlantic in the winter of 1871. Bouncing through rough seas amid "immense blocks of ice, some of which were taller than our ship," the travelers suffered from severe illness. "Brother Pandolfi and I spent thirteen days in bed," he said, "and he even a few more, without any food except a cup of broth or lemonade now and then."[58]

Some passengers did not survive the pilgrimage. Joseph Keller, a Bavarian Jesuit, lost his traveling companion during a tempest at sea in 1869, and Keller himself was badly injured when an overturned table knocked him unconscious and pinned him to the floor. Three years later, Vincenzo Novelli and his shipmates encountered a killer storm two days before reaching New York. The missionaries feared their quaking ship would break up. "For most of the trip, I stayed in the cabin because I felt so ill," Novelli recalled. "Waves splashed into the cabin, . . . and a member of the crew was swept over board and could not be rescued."[59]

Death plagued some crossings. The missionary Pietro Zerbinatti became so sick that he feared he "would be the second person buried at sea" from his ship, "a little girl having died on the fifth day" of the voyage. The Jesuit survived, but he drowned in a Montana river two years later. When two brothers named Carrozzini traveled from Spain to Puerto Rico in 1863, their ship stopped in Cuba because the younger of the pair turned seriously ill. He expired in Havana a few days later, leaving his grieving brother to travel on alone.[60]

If the trek cracked some voyagers open to new experience, others merely cracked. Men whose psychological readiness for exile had not been sufficiently tested suffered the most. When Giuseppe Giorda emigrated in 1858, he was joined by a Jesuit brother who, according to one report, "went crazy on shipboard." In New York, Giorda, not yet conversant in English, experienced "immense trouble" in trying to find his way to a Jesuit dwelling "with this poor lunatic."[61] During an epoch in which travel was prescribed as a cure-all for neurosis, some Jesuits booked passage in seeking relief from psychic distress. "Maybe the trip will be the best remedy against the scrupulosity," Maryland provincial Angelo Paresce said upon learning that a troubled Neapolitan was about to emigrate to the United States. On second thought, he added more sagely, "I fear that the change of customs, along with everything else that one naturally has to undergo when one comes to this country for the first time," would leave the man more unhinged.[62]

Although the rules for travel urged the pilgrims to offer themselves "spontaneously for what is more difficult, more humble, more disagreeable," the discomforts of prolonged time on the ocean tested their patience. Weeks of motion sickness, crowded quarters, poor food, and boredom prompted complaints, and it magnified tension even among friends. Although religious life urged forbearance in adversity, lapses in charity were keenly noticed. Published accounts of crossings are piously silent about conflict, but private correspondence reveals a darker tale. The Oregon missions were still suffering the "baneful effects" of friction that had arisen among travelers a decade earlier, a missionary reported in 1854. As a result of discord among the refugee clergy, several Jesuit brothers left the order. So unpleasant was the ordeal of oceanic transit that some men resolved never to take to the sea again. Summoned to an important meeting in Naples, missionary Carlo Pinto of New Mexico begged off because he could not countenance "a long trip" and "so many days of wretched existence in a boat."[63]

To cope with the trials of travel, Jesuits inevitably turned to religion. "They should all recite together the litanies . . . at the start of each day's journey, and they should not neglect prayer and the usual examens," a precept advised travelers. Since the ability to transcend inconveniences was an essential element of the immigrant's identity as a pilgrim, another regulation counseled the cultivation of "a strong desire to be tested by the need and lack of bodily necessities." Neither the conventions of religion nor male stoicism encouraged whining. Indeed, spiritual purpose gave clergy incentive to tol-

FIGURE 5. The Jesuits' flight from Italy was part of a general dispersal that pushed half of the order's global membership into exile within the space of a year. This 1872 cartoon, entitled "Jesuits Tossed Out and Taken In," appeared in *La Raspa*, a journal published in Rome after the fall of the Papal States. It depicts the Jesuit superior general, Pieter Beckx, and seminarians who found temporary refuge in Austria after their expulsion from Prussia. The Jesuits appear benign but they bear serpent tails. Author's collection

erate tribulations. "Divine Providence guides us," Pietro Zerbinatti declared, on the eve of his leave-taking in 1843. Even though we are "strangers" and "inexperienced" in the ways of travel, he added, "we are pupils surrendered to the tutelage of an exceedingly good Father." Like Zerbinatti, men slated for missionary work interpreted their discomforts as a school of preparation for hardships hereafter. The ability to put up with the privations of ocean travel would stand them in good stead, they reasoned, when they began life among Indians. Hence Gregorio Mengarini's matter-of-fact remark after a difficult passage to America: "the voyage by sea was precisely what was fitting for two missionaries."[64]

Familiar routines provided continuity between a solid past and a molten future. When Jesuits and Sisters of Notre Dame de Namur sailed together from Antwerp to Oregon in 1844, they carried liturgical vessels, prayer books, and pictures to facilitate the transplanting of European devotions in Indian country. On the high seas in May, the missionaries celebrated the last day of the month in honor of the Virgin Mary, just as they would have done at home.

Their floating chapel, replete with candlesticks and portable piano, so closely replicated the chapel of their mother house in Belgium that some of the sisters grew nostalgic.[65] Momentarily suspended between two worlds, the castaways found comfort in the recitation of common prayers, which salvaged a sense of community with those left behind in Europe while at the same time readying them for what awaited on American shores. As we shall see, religious devotions would also serve a mediating function in the Jesuits' missionary work in the American Far West, both consolidating community among diverse ethnic groups and easing their process of Americanization.

For practical reasons, the amount of time dedicated to formal religious exercises on the transatlantic voyage was not great. "As for spiritual things during the trip, we have to content ourselves with whatever and how much one can do," Italian provincial Giovanni Battista Ponte advised Lorenzo Palladino on the eve of his sailing. In a play on words that linked prayer and sea sickness, Ponte recommend short, spontaneous prayers (*giaculatorie*), "excellent little pills to comfort the stomach," when nausea stuck. Uneven seas meant the Catholic mass, which was not celebrated with regularity lest wine be spilled, was sometimes replaced with prayer services. One Sunday, the captain of Filippo Rappagliosi's ship gave one of the Jesuits permission to preach to the Catholics on board. "Even the Protestants gathered for this Sunday service," recorded the priest, taken aback by the bonhomie and tolerance accorded his company.[66] For Italians who had never stepped beyond the walls of papal Rome, the voyage became a crash course in diversity. The transatlantic crossing provided the Jesuits with first-ever meetings with Protestants as well as encounters with fellow emigrants who, like themselves, were on their way to a new life. En route to New York in 1874, Father Alessandro Diomedi marveled that the Sunday mass he celebrated in his ship's large salon was attended by "five hundred persons of different nations — Irish, French, Italians, Germans, Alsatians."[67] Thus it was that the sea voyage introduced the priests to the ethnically and religiously mixed world that awaited them at journey's end.

Coming to Terms with America

Landfall etched itself indelibly in the memory of the Jesuits, as it did for millions of immigrants. "Land, land!," a jubilant Rappagliosi exclaimed with a catch in his throat when his steamer drew within sight of Long Island on 23 November 1873. With only seventy miles to go, the vexations of a long voyage fell away. "This morning three huge whales came dancing alongside and sort of gave us a welcome," he continued. "This a day of celebration for everyone. The trip was a bit difficult, but today all that is forgotten." Donato

Gasparri expressed similar sentiments when the morning sun unveiled the New York horizon. The spectacle of the high seas had been quite grand, he declared, but the first glimpse of the new continent at New York was "something enchanting." "Beautiful in itself, it was even more beautiful after so many days without the sight of any land."[68]

But arrival in port brought with it an experience dreaded by all immigrants — encounter with customs officials. At their point of entry, travelers were subject to hours of examination by port authorities charged with determining if they met medical and legal requirements. Ill health could result in detention or even deportation. "Poor Jorio . . . is terrified of being tossed out because of those eyes of his that are always inflamed," Giuseppe Marra said of a friend who had accompanied him to New York. Unlike millions of immigrants who disembarked with no one to assist them, the Jesuits had instant allies. They were usually met at the pier by brethren who shepherded them through the red tape of customs and then conducted them home when the last knot had been untangled. Newcomers invariably commented upon this quayside reception in letters to friends and family in Europe. Francesco Tomassini and his companions, who arrived in New York in 1875, reported delight at finding Jesuits from a local college "waiting for us on the dock." "They really helped us in everything with an incredible kindness."[69]

Equally memorable was arrival in a Jesuit house for the first time. While still at sea, Rappagliosi took comfort in the thought that "in New York we will rest well among our brethren in the College of St. Francis Xavier. Even in the new world I will find our Society and embrace other brothers in religion." Stepping through the college's portal not only mapped the end of a difficult voyage, it brought definitive closure to persecution. Immigrants described in exuberant detail the hospitality they received from empathetic American hosts. But more than relief was involved. That emotional encounter in which strangeness and familiarity fused transformed the travelers from aliens into friends. To the end of his days, Giovanni Pinasco recalled the "wonderful charity" he had received from Jesuits in multiple nations during the frequent uprootings of his youth. "This brotherly attention to an utter stranger," he said, "bound him more tenderly and strongly to the Society of Jesus than would a month's retreat."[70]

Landfall also enabled the wayfarers to renew friendships with displaced European classmates. Paulo Ponziglione recorded his arrival in New York in 1848 after "a very stormy crossing, lasting forty-eight days." One of the first people he met was a Jesuit with whom he had been imprisoned months before in the dark hold of the frigate *San Michele* in Genoa harbor. "That very day I went to Fordham," said Ponziglione, "and God alone knows the joy I experienced when arriving at that College."[71]

One of the refugee's first duties was to compose a narrative of his venture for stewards in Europe. These accounts were crafted to impress as well as inform. Reproduced and distributed to members of the dispersed provinces, they preserved communication among separated colleagues. Like notes in a bottle, they also offered practical information to future sojourners, as Giacomo Diamare indicated when he told the superior general in 1873: I am "telling you all this for the benefit of those who will next have to make the same voyage." Jan Roothaan insisted on highly detailed reports, as he reminded Gregorio Mengarini when he failed to put to pen to paper immediately after disembarking. "I had intended to pass over everything in silence," Mengarini replied, in a hasty mea culpa from Georgetown, "because it is over now." "But I know your reverence does not want short letters." Roothaan admonished another missionary, Michele Accolti, for his "long silence" after a trek to Oregon. The chastened Jesuit responded with a twenty-eight-page chronicle of his expedition, a rich store of information not only for his supervisor but also for the historian.[72]

With fresh eyes, the fugitives recorded their reactions to the United States. They "had a very vague idea of the country they were coming to," an American Jesuit said. "They fully expected to find Indians and wild beasts even around New York." Like other immigrants, the Jesuits idealized the unfamiliar, magnifying the new world's positive features and disparaging the old country that had rejected them. Few Europeans were as uncritical of the United States as the Jesuit astronomer Francesco De Vico, whose celebrity won him a warm reception even at the White House. "The new world delights and pleases me," he rhapsodized to a friend in Europe, "infinitely more than the old."[73]

The Jesuits frequently invoked Biblical imagery that placed exile in a religious context. Relieved to be "far away from Italy and especially from the seven hills of Babylon," Giovanni Battista Pianciani was comforted to find himself in the United States, "the most peaceful and safe place possible." Wayfarer Michele S. Tomei compared his American sanctuary to Noah's ark, noting there was "a very noticeable difference" between the biblical refuge and his own asylum. Once the survivors had entered Noah's vessel, the door to the ark was sealed, and no one else was admitted. By contrast, America's portals remained wide open. "Not only is no one excluded, but they extend both hands in welcome to those who want to enter." In St. Louis, Francesco de Maria was fascinated to discover at least thirty religious denominations, each of which exercised its creed without governmental interference. The priest attended a public gala at the city's Jesuit college on the Fourth of July that contrasted with civic events in Italy. "It is beautiful," he marveled, "to see at that banquet persons of every sect treating us in a very friendly manner."[74]

The Jesuits penned many of the same first impressions as any traveler encountering novelty. Donato Gasparri found New York "enormous, rich, and commercial to an extraordinary degree." Neapolitans visiting New

York's St. Xavier College in 1889 told friends in Europe, "This is a palace!" Less smitten, Ugo Molza thought New York was "not very clean and uncouth." "There are stores more beautiful and as a group much more grand than in Europe," but American architecture lacked the magnificence to which he was accustomed.[75]

The refugees soon dispersed to destinations where, depending on their language skills and training, jobs awaited. Exiles from the Roman College and others who came in the wake of the revolutions of 1848 remained in the East. Incorporated into the Maryland Jesuit Province, which at that time extended into the New England and mid-Atlantic states, they took positions as teachers and pastors of immigrant parishes. The Piedmontese followed a similar pattern until 1854, when they adopted California and the Pacific Northwest as mission fields. The majority of the Neapolitans, who began arriving in 1867, were still in studies and thus enrolled in American seminaries to complete their education before taking up missionary work in New Mexico. The upshot was that most of the Italians, like many other immigrants, eased their adjustment to the United States by spending a couple of years on the East Coast before trekking west.

The first stop for the immigrants of 1848, and for many who followed in their footsteps, was Georgetown College, in the nation's capital. There the Italians began to familiarize themselves with a new language and customs. In their eyes, the college disclosed features both familiar and foreign. Its location pleased Europeans because it afforded ready access to both city and country, a feature believed ideal for a Jesuit college. This placement enabled the faculty to exercise their ministry among an urban population, and it gave students an elevated location that was both healthy and spiritually uplifting. The expansive layout of the college, however, contrasted uncomfortably with European establishments, which usually occupied a single compound. Georgetown College "consists of many separated buildings," a puzzled Italian observed. There were quarters for boarding students, several Jesuit lodgings, an observatory separate from other classroom buildings, and various other structures. This distribution meant that American Jesuits lived differently from their European confrères, as evidenced, for example, by their unrestricted comings and goings from one place to the next.[76]

Living in Georgetown gave the immigrants the opportunity to explore Washington. The émigrés of 1848 visited the Capitol, which twenty-seven-year-old Ugo Molza praised as "a magnificent building," especially the rotunda, because it evoked monuments in Rome. He admired the "dignified" proceedings of the Senate but was less enchanted by the "tremendous noise" on the floor of the House, where speakers could "barely be heard" over the din. In America the Italians discovered a society disconcertingly more democratic than the one they had left behind.[77]

Accustomed to the pomp of papal Rome, Molza was struck by the simplicity of American ceremonies. He bristled, however, at the ordinary citizen's easy access to civic officials, something he witnessed first hand in 1849 when he attended a New Year's levee at the White House. Except for uniformed generals and ambassadors, none of the *prominenti* wore "extravagant" attire, "not even . . . the ladies." President James Polk bore "no badge of honor" differentiating him from others in the milling crowd. "I took the president for one of the ushers, and passed by without even greeting him," Molza said; "but then recognizing my mistake, I spun round to shake his hand." To his amazement, there was a banquet that evening "for whomever wished to attend."[78]

A few months later, the Georgetown Jesuits took their guests to the inauguration of newly elected President Zachary Taylor. "Our Italians seemed much struck with the quiet and orderly conduct of the immense crowd," an American observed. The president, whom Molza had met earlier at the college, was "an elderly man with rather coarse features, but with a courteous manner." Taylor rode to the inaugural ceremony in a "most ordinary carriage," pulled by four horses whose only ornamentation was "a few tricolored ribbons, like coachmen use in Italy on the feast of Saint Anthony." The lone coachman guiding the carriage wore no livery, and the president "bore no badge of distinction." Attentive to decorative detail, Molza noted that the diplomatic corps on the inaugural platform were seated on "plain benches" and on two simple chairs bereft of damask drapery. [79] The contrast between the austerity of that inauguration and the formality of European celebration was striking. In subsequent years, when the expatriates established colleges and parishes of their own, they transplanted the rococo rites and rituals of their homeland to a Western tableau.

A differing interpretation of the United States was drawn by the Neapolitan Jesuit, Donato Gasparri. When the newcomer passed through Georgetown in 1867, he too was much taken by American public ritual, in his case an event at the Jesuits' Holy Trinity church on the anniversary of the pastor's ordination. Unlike Italy, where public displays of religion were now taboo, here large crowds flocked to the celebration, and students from the college "took a very interesting part in the function." Supplied with arms by the federal government, the college's military drill company marched to the church and chaperoned the honoree's carriage back to campus after the service ended. "This custom might find admirers in Europe, even among our opponents," Gasparri said. But "if such a thing was done there," our critics would accuse us of "flaunting our pride and arrogance." To him, the celebration at Holy Trinity Church epitomized "the freedom which is guaranteed by the laws of this country."[80]

The contrast between the two immigrants' responses to the United States was instructive. Although it was impossible to predict reactions, to some extent their varying perceptions reflected different personalities and regional mentalities. Ugo Molza, a Roman, was a theologian whose life experience centered in the clerical capital. Donato Gasparri, the twice-uprooted Neapolitan, came to America after years of exile in France and Spain. But their differing first impressions represented more. One man critically measured all things America against a Roman standard; the other, while holding Italy in counterpoint, saw in the new nation features worthy of emulation.

In their polarity, the two symbolized hundreds of Italian clerics who followed them to the United States. Like Gasparri, the admirer of religious liberty, most of the exiles assumed the coloring of their new environment, evidencing a capacity to adapt traditions to an unfamiliar place among an unfamiliar people. Others, as represented by Molza, were stirred by less-commendable aspects of American life. These differences in first impressions, although seemingly minor, were to have far-reaching consequences, prefiguring the ideological outlooks that sometimes pitted European and American Jesuits against one another. Unable to shake entrenched notions, Molza and those who saw themselves as upholders of Jesuit and Catholic orthodoxy sought not merely to identify American transgressions but to correct them. Some of their reforms were progressive, as we shall see. Others, which ignored that some American problems required American solutions, were not.

4 *"Witnesses to Shortcomings"*

REFORMING JESUIT AMERICA

Never did I think I would see the Society in such trouble.

— Jesuit Benedetto Sestini, 1859[1]

Stepping ashore, the refugees were greeted enthusiastically by their fellow religious, beginning with the first wave in 1848 and continuing into succeeding decades. "Thanks be to God and Garibaldi," exclaimed Joseph Keller of Baltimore in 1873, grateful that the Italians had made America their destination.[2] Their arrival strengthened the Catholic Church at a crucial time in its development when priests were badly needed. But the Europeans' vision of how the church and the Society of Jesus should operate also provoked confrontation. As a result, the émigrés came to face antipathy not only from anti-Catholic nativists but also from their own confrères. Blind-sided by the challenges that the refugees brought in their wake, some Americans even resolved to admit no more foreigners to their company.

The initial reaction to the immigrant clerics, however, was optimistic if not euphoric. The high esteem in which local Catholics held the Europeans and the benefits they were expected to bring to the church were summarized by a New York priest, John Larkin. The outsiders would supply a welcome corrective to American provincialism, he predicted in 1848. The present state of the persecuted Society of Jesus in Europe was "a very painful one, . . . but many advantages will accrue from it." Contact with Jesuits from abroad would have a broadening effect on the order in America, Larkin believed. "The different provinces will be acquainted with one another, learn to appreciate what is good and solid, [and] local prejudice will be done away with. The ideas of many, confined within too narrow a circle, will be enlarged. They will learn there are more ways of doing a thing, and doing it well."[3]

But before Larkin's rosy forecast could be realized, work had to be found for the new arrivals, to restore confidence to egos shattered by exile and guarantee them a place in the new society. However, the inability of some immigrants to master English thwarted easy placement. "For the last four years I have been carrying a cross which now *no one* is willing to shoulder even for one year!," groused Maryland provincial Angelo Paresce in 1855, after failing to find a job for fifty-one-year-old Felice Cicaterri, the former rector of a college in Verona. Unable to breach the language barrier, the unhappy priest was restricted to teaching Latin to a handful of novices, which left him feeling "useless." A year later, however, a corner had been turned. "I have a piece of news for you." "Fr. Cicaterri is practicing music for holy week with the ladies of St. John's choir!," chuckled Paresce to a friend, amused that his countryman had found a ministry to women that he would not have attempted in Italy.[4]

A few immigrants were entirely ineffectual. Francesco Di Maria, a forty-seven-year-old Neapolitan priest with an itch for novelty, left Maryland to work in a parish in Missouri. But he was no more competent there than he had been in the East. He is "very fond of the ministry," a co-worker observed, but "not very successful" at it. "As a professor of philosophy he is in great repute, deservedly, I believe, but it is almost impossible to pin him to his chain; he must be moving."[5]

Most of the expatriates found jobs at Jesuit colleges. Reliance on Latin as the language of instruction in philosophy and theology courses eased their transition from one culture to another. No institution profited as much from the refugee influx as Georgetown College, which had relied on recruits from abroad since its founding sixty years earlier. Two of the brightest lights among the Roman exiles were the astronomers Benedetto Sestini and Pietro Angelo Secchi, both of whom resumed their research work in the college observatory. Although Secchi lingered in America for only a short time, Sestini reigned for years as the school's top scientist. His sunspot research, published by the United States Naval Observatory, was supported by contracts with the federal government. Equally accomplished in mathematics, Sestini also brought recognition to the college through a series of widely used mathematics textbooks.[6]

These reinforcements, joined by Jesuits from Switzerland, inflated the Georgetown faculty from sixteen to twenty-two professors in the space of three years. Classes in German and Hebrew suddenly made their debut, while chemistry and physics began to be offered every year. Advances in the curriculum, accompanied by a jump in the size of the student body, sparked an upswing in the fortunes of the growing institution, whose enrollment spiraled from a trifling 136 pupils in 1849 to over three hundred a decade later. This burst of progress prompted the college to publish a printed catalogue during the 1850–51 academic year. "For the first time," a university historian wrote, "the detailed blueprint of the studies provided at Georgetown was presented to the public in a readable and attractive form."[7]

All Jesuit schools on the East Coast profited from the coming of the displaced academics. The College of the Holy Cross in Massachusetts reported that philosophy students were "well pleased with Father Sopranis," who surmounted his ignorance of English by lecturing in Latin.[8] The Italian philosopher-theologian Nicola Russo became the first published professor at Boston College. A leader in the revival of Thomism in the United States, Russo authored a two-volume *Summa philosophica iuxta scholasticorum principia*, which was adopted as a text in many American seminaries.[9] Eventually, twenty-one of the Italians became presidents of American colleges, most of them in the West. Russo served as the seventh president of Boston College, and President Antonio Ciampi, praised by American contemporaries as "one of the brilliant and most popular" of the Italians, completed three terms at the College of the Holy Cross and another at Baltimore's Loyola College.[10]

Several of the exiles who emigrated at an early age were particularly adept at hitching their star to a new culture. As president of Loyola College, the accommodating Ciampi scrapped practices deemed unsuited for American students (such as daily recitation of the rosary), while championing others that some churchmen opposed (dancing the waltz). In an era when Catholics and Protestants vied in hurling insults at one another, Ciampi was ecumenical, encouraging, for example, one of his female converts to accompany her non-Catholic husband to his church, "for the sake of association and to hear the eloquence of the preacher."[11] Varsi's swift acculturation evoked praise from Americans, too. His scientific lectures in Boston, "delivered in an interesting style and illustrated with costly apparatus procured at his desire," were, they said, "perhaps the best until then given on those subjects in the province."[12]

So many exiles skittered off to pastoral work, however, that the Maryland provincial, Angelo Paresce, carped they were abandoning the classroom for the pulpit. "They barely begin to babble a bit of English," he grumbled, "and they become attracted to ministries and want nothing more to do with teaching." In preferring the freedom of parish life to the regimen of an academic career, the Italians were not alone. American Jesuits had a long tradition of running rural churches, a tradition they were reluctant to let go of.[13]

In the seventeenth century, circuit-riding priests had established a network of missions in Maryland's rural counties. Driven by a desire to win acceptance and assimilation in British North America, Jesuits had financed their religious work through trading and operating farms that were supported by a slave work force. Their eight plantations, the center of Catholic religious life in colonial Maryland, gradually morphed into stable parishes. Although their reliance on bonded workers ended in 1838, the planter-priests continued to say mass, till their fields, and run farms far into the nineteenth century. From Georgetown College, Jesuits also cared for congregations in rural Virginia, while pastors from St. Mary's parish in Alexandria fanned out to missions in eastern Virginia. Similar networks developed in Pennsylvania and Maine, where by mid-century the Jesuits ran eight churches and thirty-three mission stations.[14] Although the Americans' penchant for country parishes would soon emerge as a point of contention between native and foreign Jesuits, that ministry was temporarily beefed up by the arrival of priests from abroad. Most of the refugee clergy, however, were drawn to ethnically diverse urban churches because of their fluency in multiple languages.

So dependent had the American Jesuits become on their European brethren that the return of some Italians to Rome following the 1849 papal restoration plunged Georgetown College into crisis. Maryland's Ignace Brocard protested that one "can judge what difficulty this recall puts us in," when the Jesuit provincial of Rome began retrieving his men at the end of the academic year. "We will do all we can to carry out his orders," Brocard said, in letters brimming with frustration, "but to send back *all* of his priests and scholastics will be impossible for us." Brocard lobbied for the superior general's intervention, insisting that experienced European hands were indispensable for laying a solid foundation for the reestablished Society in the United States. Felice Sopranis, for example, whom the president of Holy Cross had once regarded as unemployable, had become "indispensable for the tertianship," a training program for newly ordained priests. Two others, Torquato Armellini and Felice Ciampi, had so progressed in their mastery of English that they were now "very useful to us"; it was "absolutely essential" that the mathematician Giovanni Battista Pianciani remain in American "until other help arrives."[15]

Brandishing every weapon in his meager arsenal, Brocard claimed that the well-being of Georgetown College had global implications. The school was providing an English tutor for the son of the French ambassador, he wrote, adding "We also have very good relations with the ambassadors of Russia, Mexico, Chile, New Grenada." If diminished manpower forced the Jesuits to abandon the care of these notables, he hinted darkly, the reputation of the Society in the diplomats' home countries might suffer. Others, too, joined the chorus of protest. When Rome sought to reclaim the astronomer Benedetto Sestini, an angry James A. Ward of Loyola College in Philadelphia howled: "What on earth are we to do, if the very person taken away is one for whom we can find no substitute?" Sestini and his countrymen had to stay put "so that our College may stay afloat." Besides, he snapped, "we have freely spent nearly twenty thousand dollars" caring for them.[16]

Some Italians were themselves dismayed at the prospect of leaving. Charmed by what they had discovered in America and skittish of revisiting Italy, they sought to linger. An anxious Giovanni Battista Pianciani voiced "extreme repugnance" at the prospect of a hasty return to Rome. In a letter to the superior general, he confided news that "I have told no one here." One of his brothers, a man once very dedicated to the pope, had enlisted in the nationalist movement. In addition, he learned from French newspapers that another relative had joined the resistance, fought against the papal restoration, and now languished in prison. Expecting any day to hear that one of his kin had been executed by a firing squad, the mortified Pianciani dreaded repatriation. A month later, however, he did a sudden about-face. The tabloids upon which he relied for intelligence about his relatives had exaggerated their plight, he concluded, and so, with *l'onore di famiglia* restored, he announced a cheery willingness to sail home.[17]

Other exiles, doubting the stability of Italy's new government, preferred to pitch their tents in America. Ignazio Ciampi, a twenty-two-year-old seminarian, volunteered to stay put in order to convert the country's "immense number of Protestants of every denomination." Exile had likewise fired Benedetto Sestini's sense of mission. Distressed by the unconventionality of American Catholicism, this watchdog of orthodoxy announced himself ready to spend the rest of his life in the United States in hopes of setting things right.[18]

But the majority of the fugitives of 1848 soon exited across the Atlantic. By 1854, the number of Italians in the Maryland Province dropped from thirty-two to a mere half dozen.[19] The vacancy created by the departing Romans was soon filled, however, with a fresh wave of asylum seekers. When the northerly Kingdom of Piedmont-Sardinia started ejecting clergy in the 1850s, Jesuits began arriving in even larger numbers. Unlike the Romans, for whom the doors of Italy had (briefly) reopened, the Piedmontese found themselves permanent exiles. And few years later, after southern Italy became absorbed into the newly unified secular state, scores of deported Neapolitan Jesuits too made the United States their home. Although both the *piemontesi* and the *neapolitani* would soon establish missions in the Far West, in the interval between deportation and re-emigration to the frontier, they, like their Roman predecessors, left their mark on the Jesuit world of the East Coast.

How did the immigrants regard their adopted home? Not every exile was as uncritical of the United States as Francesco De Vico, whom Roothaan once accused of looking at the United States through rose-colored glasses. Others, by-the-book traditionalists who cringed at the American lifestyle, soon made their presence felt. Dismayed by what they encountered, the émigrés exerted a corrective influence on American Jesuit culture that was disproportionate both to their numbers and to the length of their stay in the country. Their reports to Jan Roothaan (whom many refugees knew personally) and to his successor, Pieter Beckx, detailed dark impressions of America. Their accounts colored the superior general's view of Jesuit life and shaped his decisions regarding the order's activities there.

The immigrants' mal de terre was ascribable in part to the inevitable disruptions that afflicted exile. But their critique also exposed a deeply held conviction that religious life in Italy shone as a paradigm for the rest of the world.

Since the sixteenth century, the Roman houses had been viewed as the embodiment of Jesuit tradition and the gold standard against which all other institutions were measured. St. Ignatius had spent most of his career in the city, and many of the order's first establishments, including its headquarters in the Gesù, flourished there. Seminarians from around the world came to receive their formation at the *Collegio Romano*, "that great and blessed Roman nursery," as contemporary churchmen lauded it. From that "great generator of men" was launched — as from a Trojan horse — a phalanx of priests ready to "to overrun and conquer the wicked world." An English Jesuit put it more gently, calling the Roman College the Society's "central home, this vast palace of faith and piety."[20]

It was not just Jesuits who held an elevated estimation of all things Roman. Belief in the normative stature of the Eternal City spread like ripples from a tossed stone throughout the Catholic world during the centralizing papacy of Pius IX. In 1855, the pope informed the American hierarchy of his plan to found the American College as a seminary for the training of priests in Rome. "We strongly desire . . . [that] you should set up, here in this venerable City of Ours, your own College for clerics from your own nation," Pius IX told the bishops. "Imbued in Rome with devotion and good habits, drinking deep of pure doctrine from the very fountainhead, [they] will be able, when they return home, competently to fulfill the offices of pastor, preacher, or teacher."[21]

Accordingly, American Jesuits had for years sent their most promising seminarians to Rome to drink in the spirit of the Society at its Olympian spring. For this reason James Ryder, later president of Georgetown College, and other Maryland scholastics had been dispatched to Italy for training in the 1820s. Similar benefits were expected to flow in reverse when the Roman College exiles of 1848 arrived in the United States. "Shaking off the dust of their feet upon the continent of Europe," an American priest said, the faculty of the *Collegio* will "work as no other body in the church can work for converting this country to the Faith."[22]

Loss and Gain

In a short time, however, both native-born and immigrant Jesuits began to reevaluate the advantages of compounding cultures. The hosts soon found themselves outnumbered by their guests, as at Georgetown College, where, by 1849, nearly 70 percent of personnel were Europeans, expatriates not only from Italy but from France and Switzerland as well.[23] That the immigrants did not instantly shed the customs of their homelands and embrace the American way of life rankled local Jesuits. "When will they learn to lay aside their notions," griped a New York priest, "and take up the ways and customs and languages of those whom they live with?"[24]

For their part, refugees found Americans clueless about Jesuit tradition and unfailingly convinced of the superiority of their way of doing things. "I noticed various little things that cause me some concern for the future," Ignace Brocard wrote in 1849, soon after the first Roman castaways settled into Georgetown. The conventions to which our Italian guests are accustomed, he sighed, "will require some adjusting." Thus, as Europeans and Americans became better acquainted, lofty first impressions yielded to more critical reappraisals and finally, in some cases, to mutual incomprehension.[25]

Events outside the walls of religious communities heightened the tensions generated within by national differences. During the Know Nothing movement of the 1850s, American writers and politicians riveted their attack on the Catholic church and on foreigners by targeting clergy. Stories of villainous priests and nuns saturated the pages of sulfurous novels bearing such titles as *Danger in the Dark: A Tale of Intrigue and Priestcraft*. When hostility turned violent, Charles Stonestreet, Jesuit provincial of Maryland in 1852–58, forbade his subjects to wear clerical garb in public. Fearing assaults on foreign priests, he even took it upon himself in 1852 to hide the identity of Irish and German Jesuits by disguising their names in the province catalogue. "Without consulting the feeling of his victims," said a contemporary, he transformed "O'Toole" to "Toall" and "Walch" to "Wolch"; "O'Callaghan" became "Calligan" and "Bauermeister," "Barrister." Stonestreet's fears were not groundless. In 1854, a Know Nothing crowd in Maine tarred and feathered John Bapst, a Swiss Jesuit.[26]

In this superheated atmosphere, Jesuits grew acutely aware of ethnic identification. Whenever the time drew near for the appointment of a new provincial, factions formed along national lines. In 1854, Italians endorsed Angelo Paresce; Germans backed Burchard Villiger; and Americans favored one of their own. James A. Ward, a native, told Superior General Beckx that he should keep the Know Nothing threat in mind when making his choice. An imprudent appointment could "lead to worse things" in the "particularly dangerous . . . present state of this republic." Paresce and Villiger were sensible and "well versed in our rules," Ward advised, "but they are not Americans, nor are they very well acquainted with the American spirit."[27] Nevertheless, Villiger, a well-acculturated Swiss, got the job.

European critics conveyed their impressions of the fractious American scene to gatekeepers abroad. The Jesuit system of governance required a steady flow of data from the rank-and-file to keep decision-makers as fully informed as possible. Thus, individuals freely offered counsel whenever they deemed necessary. From the multinational communities of Maryland, letters packed with observations, suggestions, opinions, and complaints streamed across the Atlantic to Europe. The picture they painted of religious life in the United States was not an endearing one: American Jesuits were too much men of the world. Acknowledging no separation between the secular and sacred realms, they slighted their religious duties and spent too much time in the company of lay people. Georgetown College, home to both seminarians and secular students, blurred the distinction between clergy and laity. Scholastics were so immersed in the life of the college that both their intellectual and their spiritual formation suffered, and the faculty's absorption in secular business compromised their ability to sustain the regular routines of a religious community. The Georgetown arrangement was so bizarre, one Italian claimed, that it defied description.

It is not an urban institution because it has a vineyard and adjacent small farm, and it is located outside the city. It is not rural, considering it has a library, museum, and even a footpath in the woods, which is daily visited and traversed at random by both the learned and unlearned alike — by men, women, and children, as it pleases them. . . . I do not think anything more anomalous could be found under the sun.[28]

Georgetown's unconventional arrangement convinced newcomers that the place was not well-suited for serious study. Crowded living conditions, unconventional pedagogy, a poorly stocked library, and a host of other limitations conspired to make some of the 1848 refugees yearn for the regularity of Rome. When the opportunity to return to Europe arose, therefore, most of the Italians announced they were "ready to leave as soon as possible."[29]

Insouciant disregard of codes of religious decorum presented itself daily. Traditional protocol required a Jesuit to travel with a companion whenever he left his residence, a usage that Americans found impractical and detrimental to effective ministry. They similarly ignored the rule prohibiting late night visits outside the house except to attend to the sick or dying. And the frequency with which Americans socialized with women dismayed the Italians. When he attended the ceremonial laying of a cornerstone of a new church in Georgetown, the Roman priest Ugo Molza found it unseemly that lesser bottoms shared seats on the stage with the clergy. Accustomed to a hierarchical community in which priests occupied top rung on the social ladder, the Jesuit was ill at ease in the socially fluid world of America. Students from the college and women guests were out of place on the dais, he grumbled. Benedetto Sestini was similarly scandalized when several Georgetown priests, including the provincial, attended a wedding reception marred by an unseemly exposure of female flesh. They "found themselves in the midst of a crowd of women . . . naked from the head to halfway down the chest and on the shoulders." The clergy "stayed until midnight and enjoyed the beautiful view," Sestini waspishly noted. "I confess, I would rather die than find myself in such an ugly situation."[30]

FIGURE 6. Few Italian Jesuit exiles were as
critical of religious life in the United States
as the astronomer-mathematician Benedetto
Sestini, who taught at Georgetown College.
Founder of *The Messenger of the Sacred Heart*,
a highly popular religious magazine with wide
circulation in America and abroad, Sestini
became a founding faculty member of Woodstock College. Courtesy Maryland Jesuit
Province Archive, Georgetown University

The American mode of living was further tainted by too much independence and too much individualism. The Europeans acknowledged the
blessings that religious liberty bestowed on their church, agreeing with
Georgetown's one-time president, Giovanni Grassi, that "here, at last, the
Catholic religion is not persecuted by public authority; here she enjoys
peace." But they resisted the transference of notions of political freedom to
religious life. As a French missionary put it, "The spirit of independence in
this country does not mesh well with the spirit of the Society." Superior
General Jan Roothaan concurred, declaring that the American passion for
unrestrained personal liberty was for a religious order "like a second original sin." The ease with which American Jesuits gadded about, for example,
startled outsiders accustomed to a more monastic existence. When the aca-

demic year at Georgetown came to a close, the Jesuit community moved en masse to the country for the customary summer "villa" or vacation. Expecting all would enjoy the holiday together, the Italians were stunned when the Americans struck out on their own, some of them relaxing at the beach while others headed for private destinations. As a result, the vacationers were soon winnowed down to Italians who had been left behind.[31]

However, some of the Neapolitans who arrived in the 1860s reveled in the fresh and heady liberty that American life offered. The sudden lifting of conventional restraints was especially enticing to idiosyncratic personalities like Francesco Gubitosi, who relished diversions forbidden in Italy. To fellow Jesuits, Americans and Europeans alike, the thirty-year-old priest seemed on a perpetual holiday of *dolce far niente* as he gobbled up new experiences. "He goes visiting in town without any permission and without any companion," complained his rector at Holy Cross College. "He often goes a gunning. . . . The other day he came upon two such animals as he had never seen before." Having killed a groundhog, he "picked up the beast, wrapped it in his handkerchief, and carried it home in triumph."[32]

The similarly unbridled comportment of another Neapolitan led his partners to conclude he was as useless "in our difficult missions of Maine" as he had been earlier in Massachusetts. Eugenio Vetromile "has got a piano and a harp, a revolver and a gun, without any permission whatever that I know of," wrote his superior, "although the use and even the keeping of such articles are strictly interdicted." "He dresses himself and behaves as to fully deserve the appellation which was given to him in Boston: *the dandy priest*." For Neapolitans, who had received "a more restricted training" in Italy, the theologian Camillo Mazzella concluded, the liberties granted them in America were downright "dangerous."[33]

Some refugees burst free in more dramatic fashion. After two years in the United States, Almerico Zappone, a Neapolitan scholastic studying theology at Georgetown, decided he no longer wished to be a Jesuit, an about-face that reinforced the conviction that American laxity jeopardized the vocations of the young and compromised the work of the Society. The circumstance of his exodus in 1847 and subsequent marriage was reported by Peter Verhagen, the Jesuit provincial of Maryland. "One of our young Italian scholastics, Mr. Zappone, broke the rope about six weeks ago and succeeded in realizing the ardent wish of his heart," Verhagen said. He was determined "to be free and to live in a free and independent country."

He left us . . . for Alexandria [Virginia]. There he went to board in an old Catholic widow's house. I foretold that his exit from the College would soon end in a comedy. I was right. Mr. Zappone got a wife; for on last Saturday, he was yoked to the old widow. Only think of such a folly! A young man of 24 years wedded to a tanned and withered granny of 64.[34]

Europeans questioned the American commitment to isolated parish work. Unlike diocesan clergy, who often lived alone, Jesuits typically resided in communities and toiled in tandem in a shared enterprise as educators, preachers, and spiritual directors. Before their dispersal, twenty-six priests and brothers in the Jesuit church in Naples had taught, preached, and ministered to an urban population of over seven thousand persons. In 1847, the Roman College had housed a community of 151 Jesuits. Primarily engaged in teaching, they also conducted liturgies, heard confessions, led spiritual retreats, and directed sodalities (organizations for lay men and women that promoted devotion and piety). The typical European community further defined itself through a daily round of communal activities: rising and retiring at fixed times, personal prayer, liturgies and devotional exercises, recreation and meals.[35]

In the United States, however, every Jesuit seemed to cultivate his own garden. Missionaries were so scattered about in tiny rural rectories that the customary lifestyle was impossible to observe fully — or was simply ignored. For this reason, Benedetto Sestini declared the country parishes of the Maryland Jesuits were "foreign to our Institute" and "a plague on this province." "God knows how many misfortunes have occurred," he mused, because of the lack of discipline and irregularity that prevailed in these outposts.[36] Even Bishop John Hughes of New York agreed that parishes squandered Jesuit personnel. "If they wish to live out of their community," the prelate said bluntly, "let them become secular priests."[37]

That the Maryland Jesuits had lost their punch is a judgment with which historians have concurred. Devoted to their country churches and crops, they failed to grasp that the vital hub of American Catholicism had shifted from Maryland's backwater counties to flourishing cities such as Baltimore, Philadelphia, and Bardstown.

Once the spiritual centers of Catholicism, these farms had become run-down reminders of a vanished past; as their farms deteriorated, the Jesuits became more covetous about the monetary value of these estates; pastoral lethargy settled in as the Jesuits bickered over ownership and control of the farms. While they worried about their farms, time passed them by and the Sulpicians took over the leadership role among the American clergy.[38]

European superiors had long urged retreat from the countryside, but their caveats were quietly ignored. Pleading for more time, Americans argued that only a gradual pullback would enable them to find suitable diocesan clergy to replace departing Jesuits. Once disentangled from parochial duties, they promised to assign more men to traditional ministries such as "establishing schools in the large cities" and preaching retreats.[39]

Meanwhile, little changed. In 1854, John McElroy, founder of Boston College and a strong proponent of school work, complained to Rome

about the corrosive effect parish administration had had on the order's educational ministry. "The missions in Maryland have retarded the progress of
our Society very much," he said. They have "prevented us from having colleges, by this time, in all our large cities," where Jesuits could touch the lives
of far more Catholics than they could by tilling gardens in the countryside.
A greater harvest would be had by using the colleges as bases for pastoral
work. The chief impediment to reform, McElroy believed, was the provincial, Charles Stonestreet, who was "very partial to our country missions,
rather than colleges." We need an examiner here, he concluded, to investigate and set things right.[40]

Five years later, after no improvements had been made, Father General
Pieter Beckx responded by sending an official visitor to the United States. An
administrative official and personal emissary of the superior general, the visitor came not merely to inspect but also to implement reform if that was called
for. "Maryland always gives me much to reflect on," Beckx confided to the
visitor on the eve of his departure from Europe. "Many things are amiss."[41]

The person chosen to set things right was Felice Sopranis, a member of
the consortium of Roman expatriates who had fled to the States in 1848.
After a brief stint at Boston College, he returned to Rome following the
restoration of papal government and was serving as provincial of the
Roman Province when summoned back to America. According to Beckx's
directive, Sopranis was to review Jesuit undertakings not only in the
Maryland Province, but throughout the country. In light of his European
experience and his acquaintance with the United States, Sopranis seemed ide-
ally suited to redeem Jesuit America. His inspection tour, which carried him
from Canada to California, began in New York on 25 October 1859, and
ended nearly four years later.[42]

On the East Coast, Sopranis was assisted by the Georgetown astronomer
and mathematician Benedetto Sestini, a long-time observer of the American
scene. Fluent in English and Italian, the scientist was also familiar with the
Society of Jesus in Europe and in its American incarnation. Few individuals,
however, were more critical of Jesuit life in the United States. In a series of
lengthy confidential letters written at the visitor's request, Sestini tallied the
changes that had occurred in the province since Sopranis's return to Europe.
As the visitor's official éminence grise, he proposed a slate of reforms.

"Never did I think I would see the Society in such trouble," Sestini began,
re-sounding alarms he had raised in previous letters to Rome. The education
given to American scholastics was woefully deficient because of the absence
of well-trained professors. Their spiritual formation was no better, as evidenced by the fact that too much license and too little discipline had
resulted in the loss of many young vocations. The arrival of European Jesuits
in 1848 had resulted in the opening of a tertianship program for new priests

and in the inauguration of "the first real novitiate." But the order's future in America also demanded a good, common seminary where priests-to-be could be properly educated and "well trained in the spirit" of the Society.[43]

Sestini grieved the Marylanders' commitment to parishes as a distraction incompatible with the cultivation of solid values. "Remove the parishes," he predicted, "and you will thereby remove a well spring of discord with the bishops and a source of jealousy between us and the diocesan clergy." He lamented the "irregularity of religious discipline" among his American brethren, dismissing claims that "the circumstances of the country" required granting "greater freedom" here than was allowed Jesuits elsewhere in the world. But he warned that any attempt to implement reforms would meet stiff resistance: Americans instinctively closed their ears to any improvement proposed by a foreigner. They had such an inflated notion of their own country "that they feel a supreme scorn toward all others, England excepted." American parochialism was worsened by a string of bad habits: too much newspaper reading, too much gabbing, too little study, and excessive contact with the lay public.[44]

The problems facing American Jesuits were formidable, Sestini concluded, but not insurmountable. Providence had permitted the dispersal of himself and the other Italian Jesuits in 1848 for a purpose. They had been placed here "as witnesses to shortcomings," he told Sopranis. Therefore, it was their solemn duty to exercise their "good influence" in order that "thought can finally be given to correction."[45]

Sopranis spent a year visiting institutions on the East Coast. When his tour ended in 1860, he issued a series of directives, which, according to one historian's summary, aimed at reforming Jesuit domestic life by imposing a tautly regulated regimen. Superiors, particularly presidents of the colleges, were instructed to review the *Constitutions* and Rules of the Society, and to "apply them gently but efficaciously." The imposition of a daily order in every community became de rigeur. No one should be allowed to rise from bed whenever he wished or to perform spiritual exercises at his own discretion. Meals should be taken in silence, if common reading was not supplied. Newspaper reading was restricted to superiors and those who he decided had a legitimate reason to peruse them. Everyone should be home before nightfall, except priests engaged in essential ministry. No Jesuit should venture out alone in the evening, although, he conceded, there were some pastoral circumstances when this could not be avoided.[46]

When Beckx issued marching orders to Sopranis, he had empowered him to withdraw workers from projects judged unsuccessful or irregular. Accordingly, the visitor closed six parochial missions and transferred several parishes to diocesan control. Although unable to effect a complete retreat from rural churches, Sopranis did facilitate a major shift in priorities. Once unfettered to the countryside, he reasoned, Jesuits would be freer for educational and pastoral work in the bustling modern cities of the East.[47]

Sopranis wrestled with the vexing matter of leadership, an issue that had for years perturbed both American and European Jesuits, although for different reasons. Since the restoration of the Society in the United States, the highest offices in the Maryland Province had been staffed by foreigners. Only one native-born priest had been appointed provincial between 1840 and 1877, a pattern that Americans resented. "It seemed a kind of reflection on the men of the province," one Marylander observed, "that for so many years none of them were chosen to rule it."[48] No one was more sensitive to the delicate position of outsiders than Burchard Villiger, the accommodating provincial from German-speaking Switzerland. "Would that we had an American provincial in this region!," he told Beckx, repeating Sestini's charge that Americans showed "a natural repugnance toward everything foreign."[49] Most Europeans agreed, however, that few Americans were qualified to govern in the true spirit of the Society. Consequently, at the close of Sopranis's visit in 1859, another European, the Neapolitan Angelo Paresce, was named to head the Maryland Province.

With Paresce's appointment and with the promulgation of Sopranis's decrees, Italian agency moved toward its apogee. Within a decade of their arrival in 1848, the Europeans had already transformed American Jesuit life. Strengthened by an influx of immigrant clergy, the Society was now better able to meet the needs of a mushrooming Catholic population. Its schools, especially Georgetown College, had benefited from the acquisition of teachers and from the redirecting of energies from parish work to the classroom. The improvement was immediate, a Georgetown Jesuit attested, thanks to "the great benefit and successes" that "the arrival of numerous missionaries from different orders and of other religious has brought to us."[50]

But the coming of the Europeans was a mixed blessing. Although they gave a boost to urban educational work, their understanding of the order's traditions clashed with the practices of their American counterparts. National differences precipitated strife between outsiders and natives regarding the way their vocation was to be lived in the United States. A Jesuit official in Missouri, William S. Murphy, reflecting on conflicts that erupted in the Midwest after the arrival of displaced Europeans, spoke for many English speakers when he wrote in 1855, "We are every day more and more resolved to invite no foreign aid." Most Jesuit leaders conceded that the struggling order in the United States needed reform, but few of them believed that a strict imposition of foreign customs was the solution.[51] Protest was pointless, however, because, as events subsequently demonstrated, the Society of Jesus, like the American Catholic Church itself, would increasingly conform to a European model.

Of all the reforms introduced by Europeans, however, the greatest was yet to come: the restructuring of clerical education. The Italians' crowning achievement was the founding in 1869 of Woodstock College, Maryland, a national seminary for the cultivation of Jesuit priests. Americans could now pursue the same course of studies in philosophy and theology that was standard in Europe, thus pulling them into the intellectual orbit of the Catholic Church and the Society of Jesus worldwide.

Removed from All Dangers and Distractions

The low quality of seminary training in America was one of the few issues on which Catholic and Protestant church leaders agreed. At a time when science seemed to be undermining the Christian message and the relevance of faith, churches required ministers who could mediate the Gospel to the modern world. "The crude public performances of incompetent young preachers" were no longer acceptable, insisted Charles W. Eliot, president of Harvard. Instead of the isolated denominational seminaries that had suffice in the past, Eliot proposed that ecclesiastics undergo "theological education at universities or other centers of diversified intellectual activity." Similar concerns animated Catholics. After Archbishop Gaetano Bedini of Italy visited the United States in 1853, he left with the sad impression that "the most outstanding priest is the one that has built the most churches and begun the most institutions." What the country needed, he argued, were priests with "a wider, more complete and more solid education."[52]

No aspect of religious life in America was more lamented by European Jesuits than the dismal state of seminary studies. "With the exception of some fathers who have been to Rome," a French priest wrote, "hardly any have been trained according to the rules of our Institute."[53] In 1840, when Stefano Gabaria, a Piedmontese priest who had been appointed superior of scholastics at Georgetown College, began delivering Latin exhortations to his students, he met a wall of resistance — not just from seminarians but also from priests who were not fluent in the ecclesiastical patois. Three years later, Georgetown's president, James Curley, built an expensive astronomical observatory on campus, only to find out when it was done that he had misinterpreted a letter from Roothaan in elegant Latin forbidding the project.[54]

Poor training commenced in the novitiate, the two-year period when candidates were introduced to Jesuit life. Once admitted, trainees received a slapdash preparation, a shortcoming that no one denied but none could correct. Benedetto Sestini believed that most American Jesuits had never made a real novitiate, never truly studied, never even laid eyes on a well-ordered and disciplined religious community. "It is not an exaggeration to say," he told Roothaan, that the vine-dressers who labor at the Jesuit farms of Macao and Santa Sabina in Rome "more closely resemble properly formed men of the Society than do some of the missionaries that we have scattered about the countryside here."[55]

John McElroy, an Irishman who entered the order in 1806, recalled his introduction to religious life at Georgetown College. "I entered the Society as lay brother, [and was soon] employed as clerk, procurator, assistant cook, gardener, prefect, teacher of writing, arithmetic, etc. In these duties was I occupied during the two years of novitiate." Even after deciding to become a priest, McElroy was granted little time to prepare himself. "I was promised time to study, it is true, but as yet it has not arrived."[56] A generation later, this was still common practice. Personnel shortages meant seminarians were frequently pulled from study and put to work. The seminaries had become mere appendages of colleges for whom the preparation of trainee Jesuits ranked low on the list of institutional priorities.

Theological study was further compromised by its limited scope. An American predilection for polemics and apologetics mandated that priests be equipped, as one Jesuit expressed it, "to meet the objections and errors rampant in the country."[57] This meant that speculative analysis was subordinated to the nitty-gritty, especially to preparing for debate with Protestant adversaries on controversial issues of the day. As a result, American Jesuits remained ignorant of theological trends and traditions beyond their shores. In this milieu, preaching was prized above all else; as the Sulpician Archbishop of Baltimore, Ambrose Maréchal, said in 1826, "The grand object that the good of religion in this country demands that you have principally under your eyes, is sacred eloquence." Proficiency in the pulpit was "infinitely more important," he shrugged, than mastering "the learned words of our most celebrated theologians."[58]

Pressure to supply clergy for a soaring Catholic population intensified the temptation to cut study short and to ordain men to the priesthood with undue haste. There were never enough pastors to meet new needs spawned by the arrival of immigrants from abroad and by westward expansion. In this context, the freshly restored Society of Jesus, like an adolescent incapable of self-restraint, found it difficult to resist taking on more commitments than it could manage. "Our colleges, by no means sufficient to meet the wants of the country, were still too numerous for our limited supply of professors," a Maryland Jesuit said in 1863. "Hence our own studies were abridged and confined to what was strictly necessary in order that we might the sooner be employed in teaching."[59]

Although an inpouring of foreign clergy upgraded schooling, the most radical innovation came in 1860. Visitor Felice Sopranis, acting on instructions from the superior general, ordered the creation of a common seminary to which all scholastics in the United States would come for philosophical and theological study. Only individuals whose health or ability would be better served by completing a short course in their home province or mission were exempted from attending. By pooling resources and faculty, Sopranis aimed at bettering the quality of instruction and bringing it into alignment with normative Jesuit practice. The seminary whose creation he prompted consequently emerged as the order's flagship for training priests and, in one scholar's view, "the nation's most influential Catholic seminary." Through its graduates the institution molded Catholic life across the country for decades to come.[60]

Wasting no time, Sopranis had immediately launched a temporary program at Boston College, then located in the downtown section of the city. But the seminary did not remain there long, because the visitor had his eye fixed on a location removed from the distractions of an urban environment, something the superior general himself had ordered.[61] The search for a final location fell to Angelo Paresce, the Neapolitan provincial of the Maryland Jesuits. Upon assuming office, he reeled off the pros and cons of various options in several letters to superior general Pieter Beckx. To Maryland Jesuits who insisted the seminary remain on a college campus, Paresce was unbending. That Georgetown College offered many advantages (a splendid observatory, a magnificent library, and healthy surroundings), he readily agreed, but even if it were nudged to a quiet periphery of the campus, the scholasticate would still be too accessible to the public. In short, no college could ever provide the "discipline, recollection, [and] application to study that are required to train our scholastics."[62] In his dogged insistence upon separation, Paresce concurred with a growing number of contemporary educators who believed that crowded living arrangements, economic miseries, crime, and bad sanitation made the modern industrial city a poor place to train the young.

Accordingly, Paresce settled instead on a 245-acre farm in Maryland's bucolic Patapsco Valley, twenty-five miles west of Baltimore, near the village of Woodstock. Thus it was that the Jesuit siege mentality combined with an American anti-urban bias to place the seminary in a secluded forest. The property, which was purchased in 1866 for $4,500, boasted all the advantages its planners dreamed of.[63] Atop a sunny hill overlooking a stream, the wooded acreage, reported Paresce, was "in the country far from our other houses and colleges in a healthy location." In this sylvan setting, the seminarians would be freed from the burden of acting as prefect and other competing labors while pursing their sole responsibility, the study of philosophy and theology.[64] The institution was named Woodstock College.

When authorities decreed that the new seminary should arise far from a large metropolis, they departed from the Society's earlier preference for urban settings. However, with the outbreak of national revolutions, many major cities, including Rome itself, had become too perilous. When political unrest on a global scale hurled thousands of Jesuits into exile, caution and discretion became the new watchwords. "We should take great care to leave nothing exposed which can in any way furnish our adversaries with matter for calumny, or with a specious pretext for increasing their opposition," Roothaan had warned in 1845. "One can hardly believe how watchful our enemies are, even of our most ordinary actions."[65] In this uneasy milieu, Jesuits groped for safe surroundings in which to school trainees. At odds with the world, they espoused a religious asceticism that reflected their alienation from the age.

The beleaguered outlook that European expatriates brought to the United States found its counterpart in fears that Americans held about their own country. During the worst years of the Know Nothing movement, Catholic clergy kept a low profile in the hope of skirting nativist assault. Seminaries, a conspicuous focus of public scrutiny, exercised special caution, which was one of the reasons why Paresce objected to planting a program in Boston. During the Civil War, for example, superiors advised Jesuits to keep mum about the conflict lest they provoke offence and fan the flames of anti-Catholicism. And it did not help that an Italian Jesuit was arrested for the assassination of Abraham Lincoln. Mistaken for John Wilkes Booth, to whom he bore a resemblance, Giovanni Guida was detained by authorities. Although he was released, news of his arrest fed a widespread rumor that Jesuits had participated in the murder of the president.[66]

In this troubled context, the site selected for the new seminary at Woodstock beckoned as a *cordon sanitaire*. Buffered by deep woods and stretching fields, it shielded seminarians, in Paresce's words, "from every danger and distraction." In that safe haven, they would be free to wear religious garb without fear of recrimination and to peruse their books without diversion. Nearby hamlets provided opportunities to teach catechism and to preach "without being exposed to the dangers of the city." Like a self-contained military citadel, Woodstock College "provided every advantage that will promote orderliness [and] regular discipline."[67]

Flight to the countryside was also rooted in new American attitudes about clerical education. Since the sixteenth-century Council of Trent, Catholics had believed that training should occur within the context of existing institutions. For diocesan seminarians it had been the local cathedral, which was engaged in a host of activities of which the instruction of trainees was only one component. For members of religious orders such as the Jesuits, preparation had taken place at a local college or university located in the heart of a city in the midst of a Catholic community. But the growth of the church in the United States led to the emergence of a novel type of seminary. After 1850, small, local institutions no longer met the needs of a church that experienced massive immigration and climbing numbers of candidates for the priesthood. To consolidate resources and to provide more specialized formation, there developed the free-standing seminary, an institution that existed independent of and apart from other ecclesiastical operations.

This innovative academy was similar to other so-called total institutions of the period — penitentiaries and asylums for orphans and insane persons. In accord with current social theory, the care of prisoners, orphans, and the sick was best removed from local and familial settings and assigned to specialized establishments dedicated to providing for large numbers. Hence the free-standing seminary, like contemporary prisons, hospitals, and asylums, was devoted solely to one purpose: the training of large numbers of clergy. And, as one scholar has said, the new institution, unlike its Tridentine predecessor, forged a milieu in which seminarians and their priest-professors pursued a life divorced from other activities. With few exceptions, detachment was bolstered by a physical setting apart from an urban neighborhood.[68]

Woodstock College was one such place. A self-quarantined retreat whose sole raison d'être was clerical formation, it was not only armored against the distractions of the outside world, but supplied most of its own needs. Fields of crops, orchards, gardens, a vineyard, herds of cattle, barns, a slaughter house, carpenters' shops, laundry, and a hot-house for the cultivation of plants — all testified to institutional independence, as did a baseball field, tennis courts, and a network of walking paths that offered opportunities for healthy exercise. In 1876, the college opened St. Inigoe's Villa in southern Maryland, a get-away where the scholastics could take summer vacation in an environment as marooned and highly controlled as the seminary itself. Woodstock even created its own cemetery. The custodians of this vast enterprise were a staff of nearly thirty Jesuit brothers who performed the duties of cook, gardener, vintner, cattleman, carpenter, butcher, blacksmith, plumber, laundryman, tailor, shoemaker, night watchman, nurse, janitor, printer, and porter. As the historian John L. Ciani has observed in his study of the institution, "Whatever the brothers could not do was brought in for the scholastics: the dentist came to them."[69]

From the printshop issued a flood of textbooks. These included volumes in theology, philosophy, science, and mathematics, as well as catechisms, programs, and student theses. In 1872, the college began publishing *Woodstock Letters*, a periodical dedicated to news about Jesuit undertakings worldwide. The Woodstock press also produced *Messenger of the Sacred Heart*, a popular religious magazine with wide circulation. Founded at Georgetown in 1866 by Benedetto Sestini, the journal transferred to Woodstock when its editor joined the seminary faculty.

Because of the priority given to instruction in the natural sciences,

Paresce began assembling a physics cabinet and natural history museum through purchases in Europe even before the college opened its doors. Carlo Piccirillo, a theologian with a passion for natural history, augmented the collection by soliciting donations of mineral and biological specimens from missionaries and Woodstock graduates around the world. The seminary took advantage of its bridge to the American West. Some objects were obtained through barter, as when Piccirillo acquired ninety bird nests (130 pounds worth) from a priest in the Southwest. "With each nest is a card indicating the genus and species of the bird," explained the donor, who in return received a subscription to Woodstock imprints for the Jesuit college in New Mexico.[70]

The institution's leafy seclusion did not, however, gladden its occupants. "Cut off from every temptation to distraction or dissipation of mind," Woodstock provided "a noble home for the exclusive use of studies," one Jesuit allowed, but its isolation was depressing. "As far as his sight could reach, trees were ever in view." When a student "mounted to the top of the house, he would find still more and denser trees, and more far-reaching to the North and West."[71] "If any sound breaks the stillness," another inmate wrote, "it is the wonted snorting of the locomotive, as it turns a corner close by, and thundering with the cars through the valley below is lost again round another bend: *sic transit gloria mundi.*"[72] The place was as remote as the deserts of ancient Egypt. Jesuit wags contemplated posting over the main gate the warning that had startled Virgil and Dante on their descent into Hades: "Abandon all hope, you who enter here."[73]

Woodstock's confinement weighed on the faculty. A classic response to the place was coined by Domenico Pantanella, a thirty-eight-year-old Neapolitan philosopher who arrived there after teaching at the lively Georgetown campus. Woodstock offered its inmates two options, he quipped: "*Aut studium aut suicidium*" ("Either study or suicide"). "We live as exiles from our fatherland in a deserted place," Pantanella told friends in Italy.[74] "Everyone soon regretted the choice," Camillo Mazzella, the school's dean, admitted; "but now that it is done, it cannot be undone."[75]

The Roman College Replicated

Every detail of Woodstock's creation bore the imprint of Italy, from conception to design, from construction to daily operation. The visitor Felice Sopranis, acting on instructions from Rome, had mandated its erection. Angelo Paresce, from his headquarters in Baltimore, oversaw its founding, and when his term as provincial ended, he became its first rector. Benedetto Sestini, who transferred from Georgetown to Woodstock to teach mathe-

FIGURE 7. Of all the reforms introduced by the European Jesuits, none was more far-reaching than their restructuring of American seminary education at Woodstock College. In this 1873 photograph, the Neapolitan priest Domenico Pantanella (far left) supervises the landscaping of the grounds, designed *all'italiana*. Courtesy Jesuitica Collection of Regis University

matics and science, supervised much of the construction, because, in the words of an ironic contemporary, the seminary's requirements lay "outside the experience of the ordinary architect." Its chapel was fashioned in "the Italian style," which mandated the importing of holy remains from Italy: under the high altar rested the "waxen body of a Roman soldier whose relics are encased in the body." The library and science museum were handsomely frescoed by the versatile Sestini. Domenico Pantanella, a philosopher whose gifts lay in the practical realm, supervised the landscaping of the green park surrounding the college. Its centerpiece was a parterre designed "to reproduce the form of the plaza of St. Peter's in Rome." Even the workmen at the seminary were Italians, poor immigrants from New York whose destitution had moved Paresce to offer them employment.[76]

As early as 1862, Paresce approached dispersed Neapolitans in Europe about staffing the scholasticate. The American climate, customs, and diet would exact "a not inconsiderable sacrifice," he warned, but the presence of other Italian expatriates would "make their coming considerably easier." Besides, they "are not coming to live in the wilderness." They will discover here "a nation and a people that is highly civilized," a religious community that "observes religious poverty, but is still comfortable," a decent library, and well-equipped scientific laboratories containing "the best instruments from Paris." "There is work for all," he continued, especially for men who are "young, have a good attitude, are secure" in their vocation and "ready to adapt."[77] In 1867, Paresce finalized a compact with Neapolitans who agreed to teach at Woodstock. In exchange, the Maryland Jesuits committed to educate the scholastics of the exiled province free of charge. With that consensus, Paresce acquired *en bloc* a cadre of experienced faculty, and the Neapolitans secured asylum for their younger men, who, after finishing their studies and learning English, would take up work in the West.

Thus it was that Woodstock College became for many Neapolitans a stepping stone to their mission in distant New Mexico, which was launched that same year. The seminary played a similar role for Piedmontese exiles on the Pacific Coast. Although they did not regularly supply Woodstock with teachers, the northerners did send scholastics to Maryland for training because, as one Jesuit observed, mastery in English could more easily be secured there than in Italy, "and good English was more and more demanded at Santa Clara and San Francisco."[78] Thus, Woodstock functioned as a fulcrum between Europe and the frontier, a place of transition where missionaries-to-be perfected the skills they would need as mediators of cultures in the West.

When Woodstock's founders assembled in 1869 to ceremonially open the new seminary, six of the ten professors were Italian. Italians so dominated the place that Pantanella once told the Neapolitan provincial: "Your reverence cannot have colleges in Italy, but console yourself with the one that is in America."[79] Even as they gathered, the armies of united Italy were preparing their final assault on Rome, marking an end to the Papal States and the final expulsion of Jesuits from the new nation. Displacement left its mark on the seminary staff. Almost every member of the first faculty had been touched by revolution and exile, and many of them were long remembered for the ways in which the aftershocks had molded their character. The philosopher Carmelo Polino, for example, impressed upon students that the *Risorgimento* had "cured him forever of any sympathy he might have had with the republican form of government and made him a staunch defender of absolutism."[80]

The most distinguished of the scholarly émigrés, thirty-six-year-old Camillo Mazzella, was equally unable to shake entrenched ideas borne from Italy. Although he soon became an American citizen, the hefty theologian remained suspicious of the tainted atmosphere of his new homeland. A veritable Niagara of opinions about the United States, he informed the Jesuit superior general that American culture was permeated with "materialism, naturalism, rationalism," and "indifferentism," errors which even tainted the clergy. Some American Jesuits, for instance, advocated the separation of church and state. Others failed to comprehend "why the Pope does not allow Protestant churches to be built in Rome." Mazzella was skeptical of Angelo

Paresce and others of his countrymen who had accommodated to life in the United States. Believing "everything here was better than in Italy or Naples," such men had become, he chided, "more American than the Americans."[81]

It was not to the United States, therefore, that Mazzella turned for guidance in crafting Woodstock's curriculum. When the college opened, the dean announced that it would model itself on the Roman College, intending that the seminary would embrace both the pedagogical methods and the intellectual content of Roman training. Accordingly, the philosophy program ballooned into a comprehensive three-year course, and the theology curriculum to four; both sequences were based on the unitary neo-scholastic system that was currently being adopted abroad. So faithfully did Mazzella and his associates replicate the Roman prototype that their work drew praise from Archbishop Francesco Satolli, Apostolic Delegate to the United States, when he visited the seminary. "The inmates of Woodstock," he declared, "though far distant from the Holy See, are imbued with the same doctrine, the same spirit which are fostered in the Eternal City."[82]

One of the ways in which Woodstock mirrored the Collegio Romano was through its embrace of scholasticism as developed by St. Thomas Aquinas. The rediscovery of Thomistic thought in the early nineteenth century had sparked an intellectual revolution in Europe, and Mazzella and his colleagues — some of whom had been instrumental in promoting the revival in Italy — worked to introduce that tradition into the United States. In that endeavor they were strikingly successful. Their role in standardizing philosophical and theological instruction under the Thomistic banner testified to their ability to transform themselves from marginal castaways to major players in the American church. Thus, the transplanted Italians of Woodstock — Mazzella, De Augustinis, Sabetti, Russo, Brandi, and others — authored treatises that disseminated Thomism across the United States. By the 1890s, that prototype was flourishing even in distant Montana, where seminarians at St. Ignatius Mission pored over Thomistic textbooks and manuals authored at Woodstock.[83]

The school's impact did not end with intellectual formation. By supporting Pope Leo XIII's campaign to restore the tradition of St. Thomas to a place of honor in Catholic institutions, the Woodstock scholars enhanced devotion to the Holy See. For neo-Thomists, the defense of Catholic truth and papal power were inextricably yoked. As the scholar John L. Ciani has said, the founders of Woodstock "were not just exiles living in a foreign land and recreating a universal and static church as a substitute for home." They were, like their countrymen who became western missionaries, "agents of a centralizing ecclesiastical authority desirous of universal and trans-Atlantic unity and uniformity in a threatening period of religious and political upheaval."[84]

Although the faculty won international celebrity for their part in bringing American Catholicism into conformity with the universal church, they were not masters of original thought. The common threads running through their writings were unswerving dedication to scholasticism, suspicion of modern ideas, and unshakable defense of ecclesiastical authority. "He never claimed any originality," a confrère said of Luigi Sabetti, whose manual on moral theology, *Compendium Theologiae Moralis*, was printed in thirteen editions and adopted throughout the Catholic world. "I do not mean originality of principles for that would be a very dangerous claim for any theologian to make; but even originality of treatment." Parrot-like, Sabetti simply adapted the principles of previous scholars "to changed circumstances of time and place."[85] Nor was creativity the trademark of his associates. Teacher Emilio De Augustinis shunned "the dangerous gift of originality in theology," wrote Patrick J. Dooley, a tongue-in-cheek chronicler of early Woodstock, "for originality bordered too closely on the precipice of heresy to suit his mind." The theologian Salvatore Brandi, a disciple of Mazzella, plowed a similarly straight path. Although he was a popular lecturer, the iron maxim "error has no right to exist" guided his teaching, preaching, and writing, and "guarded him from slipshod or faulty utterance."[86]

In reverence for what he perceived as Catholic tradition, Mazzella set a commanding example. "A big man, physically and intellectually," the lordly Neapolitan "looked like a tower of orthodoxy," Dooley said, "always following in the footsteps of approved leaders." Although his publications flew off the shelf as fast as they were printed, Mazella's writing was largely derivative, as was the work of other neo-Thomists on the faculty.[87] The dean himself summed up his approach to theology in his Latin textbook *Praelectiones de scholastico-dogmaticae de virtutibus*, a scholastic survey of Christian virtues that was published at Woodstock in 1871. The aim of his exposition was *nova non docere* ("to teach nothing new").[88]

Mazzella's theological reading of the contemporary world was disclosed in another volume, entitled *De Religione et Ecclesia* ("Religion and the Church"). Reprinted in at least five editions, the last of which was published in Rome, this thick tome found ready reception in seminaries in Europe and the United States. According to Ciani, Mazzella's teaching centered on the argument that "there is one true religion which all men are held to confess and embrace." This assertion was news to seminarians reared on the American principles of religious liberty and tolerance. He wrote: "Not only individuals, but society itself, must profess the true religion. Therefore, civil society itself must embrace religion revealed by God and must be subjected by means of infallible authority in these areas in those things which pertain to religion."[89] Giving only grudging acceptance to American practice, Mazzella differed with liberal bishops who maintained that religious liberty and separation of church and state, as practiced in the United States, offered the ideal environment for the Catholic Church.

He also collided with Jesuits educated in the pre-Woodstock era. "Both as patriots and as Christians," Georgetown President Bernard A. Maguire said in a 1870 commencement, "we should feel it our duty to oppose the establishment on the soil of our common country of a State religion, were it our own or any other." The principles of religious liberty and the independence of church and state "we affirm and maintain, and shall ever affirm and maintain." Such opinions were anathema to conservative spokesmen like Mazzella and Brandi. Theologians who disagreed were marginalized and eventually silenced.[90]

Why did Americans unquestioningly accept a theology that contradicted principles upon which they had been raised and that darkly critiqued their own culture? The youthfulness of the seminarians (most were in their late teens or twenties) was certainly a factor, but social forces were also at work. An attractive feature of the Woodstock system was "its solid logic, its clever argumentation and its consistent, universal and eternal character," according to one appraisal. Rather than dispute with Protestants in the old controversialist mode, Woodstock's theologians proclaimed unabashedly not only that Catholics were different, but that they were intellectually and spiritually superior to their opponents.[91]

Moreover, for members of a church subject to frequent public ridicule, the recovery of Catholicism's intellectual tradition was a welcome antidote. Equally appealing was the knowledge that teachings promulgated at Woodstock reflected the centralizing of Catholic seminary education worldwide. The scholasticate gloried in constant reminders that it was part of an exciting global phenomenon — from the news reports that arrived daily from every corner of the Catholic world for publication in the *Woodstock Letters* to the accolades bestowed upon the faculty from the highest authorities in the church. In the classrooms of Woodstock, eminent professors imparted to American priests-to-be "a theology of universal and unchanging significance which did not make exceptions for one country or another, but held a general rule for the whole world."[92]

In addition, the first generation of Woodstock students saw themselves as actors in a historic drama that placed them on center stage of the Society's worldwide enterprise. Graduates who recorded their recollections of the seminary during its founding era viewed their years there with intense pride. The near-celebrity status of their European mentors contributed to their conviction that those seminary days were a privileged time. That belief was fortified by the sequestered scholasticate's highly controlled environment, which precluded the possibility of comparing Woodstock with anything outside the Catholic intellectual ghetto. Consequently, while Jesuits lamented the *rustico* isolation of the college, they did not decry its theology.

Although Woodstock was forever molded by its founding faculty, most of the Italians departed when new opportunities arose. After winning international repute by his promotion of scholasticism, Mazzella was recalled to Rome to teach in 1878. Named a cardinal by Pope Leo XIII eight years later, he continued to influence American Catholicism through his high office in the Roman curia, where he supervised seminary education worldwide. After Mazzella was promoted to the cardinalate, Woodstock's Emilio De Augustinis succeeded him as professor at the Roman College. Another papal summons repatriated Salvatore Brandi to Rome in 1891. After sixteen years in America, he became a writer for *Civiltà Cattolica* and adviser to the Vatican on American affairs. Other Neapolitans professors — Pantanella, Schiffini, and Degni — became missionaries in New Mexico. By 1884, six of Woodstock's founding faculty had departed from Maryland, and with their leave-taking, Neapolitan domination of the place dwindled.

There was no crusade to replace the departing Neapolitans. The theologian Carlo Piccirillo, a Roman, claimed that their "harshness and severity" had so alienated American students that there was no desire to import surrogates. But there were other reasons why Neapolitan dominance faded, the chief being that the Naples Province had diverted most of its personnel to its Southwestern mission. Moreover, Woodstock's leaden reliance on foreigners had become an embarrassment. "It does not look well for our Society in America to be depending so much and so long on Europe for professors," observed Nicola Congiato, the Piedmontese superior of the California Mission. "The Society is no longer in its infancy here," and therefore native teachers should begin supplanting the Europeans.[93]

Substitutes for the Neapolitans were not easily found — in part because they had not aligned others to take their place. According to Piccirillo, Woodstock's founders had "formed a deeply rooted opinion" that no Americans should be allowed to teach at the seminary, especially in theology.[94] Conversely, native Jesuits, repelled by the seminary's woeful isolation, bucked at assignment there; as a consequence, years passed before American professors eclipsed the foreigners. It was not until 1904, thirty-five years after Woodstock's founding, that all of its nineteen faculty, save one, belonged to the Maryland–New York Province. In the interval, a more cosmopolitan staff began to form with the arrival of Jesuits from Germany, Switzerland, France, and Ireland. These outsiders were more acceptable to the student body than the Neapolitans had been. The German theologian Friderick Brambring, who arrived in 1883, for example, was welcomed not only for his erudition but also because his generous treatment of intellectual adversaries was more palatable to Americans than the disdainful dismissals of Mazzella and De Augustinis had been. "Logic and sound principle, not sneers," a student recorded, "was his mode of refutation."[95]

Despite shifts in faculty, the scholasticate did not abandon its program of standardization. Widely acclaimed as the academic flagship of the Society of Jesus in America, Woodstock championed the neo-scholastic tradition and Roman-style training, and because of this, drew a large student body. By 1886, the college enrolled 168 philosophers and theologians. At the time of its thirty-fifth anniversary, 552 alumni had been ordained priests, disseminating across America the theology they had learned at Woodstock. Luigi Sabetti boasted that his class in moral theology enrolling 67 seminarians constituted the largest congregation of Jesuit students in the world.[96]

Admired for its faithful implementation of Roman ecclesiastical policy, Woodstock emerged by the 1890s as the intellectual center of American Catholic ultramontanism. The faculty were internationally renowned, as evidenced by the Roman appointments of its professors, the wide circulation of their textbooks, and the frequency with which its experts were consulted by scholars and the episcopal hierarchy. When the bishops of the United States met in Baltimore in plenary council in 1884, Antonio Sabetti rejoiced that four of the seven Jesuits invited as theological advisers came from Woodstock. What a "spectacle and embarrassment for old Europe," he gloated.[97]

American Jesuits acknowledged the benefits they had derived from Woodstock's founders. "Maryland owes its life to Naples," Joseph Keller, the Maryland provincial, once declared. "God alone can repay the province of Naples for all that it has done for Maryland. Without Naples we would still be doing our ABC's." European mentors had generated Americans who were better educated and more deeply schooled in the traditions of the Society than ever before. From the ranks of Woodstock alumni came the next generation of leaders in the United States.[98] The seminary's trickle-down influence was not limited to religion, however; its elevated academic status set the standard in a variety of non-theological subjects. "What course of mathematics [is] followed at Woodstock?," a teacher in Maryland asked in 1883. "I shall have to get some new books in algebra, geometry, and trigonometry. . . . [and] it would be better for me to procure the same as you use at Woodstock."[99]

In assessing the institution's significance, there was much to applaud. When an early chronicler claimed that there was "no more decisive turning point in the story of Jesuit development in America" than the opening of Woodstock College, he was not far from the truth, although the long-term fallout was more problematic than he realized.[100] The seminary's European faculty transformed the way theology was taught to Americans. What students learned was a vast improvement over the indiscriminate schooling of the previous era, when seminaries were moored to college campuses. By upgrading the caliber of instruction, Woodstock professionalized the clergy, thereby launching a tradition of theological reflection and scholarship that endured for over a century. From its classrooms there later emerged some of the most prominent theologians of the twentieth-century, including John Courtney Murray and Gustave Weigel, Americans whose views guided the Second Vatican Council.[101]

But Woodstock's early impress was not entirely benign. It did not benefit the colleges that had opposed its creation. President Bernard A. Maguire complained that Georgetown "suffered for some time" after the scholasticate took flight, because the college was obliged to hire lay teachers and prefects to replace the departing Jesuits. Thirty years later, then-President Joseph Havens Richards bitterly condemned Woodstock's creation as "a grave error of policy." "Professors and students were transported to a semi-wilderness, remote from libraries, from contact with the learned world, and from all those stimulating influences which affect intellectual life in large centres of population and culture." Stripped of its best faculty, Georgetown failed to become a major theological base. Left to compete with nearby Catholic University, founded in 1889 as a graduate school of theology, its program was whittled down, Richards lamented, "to a place of inferiority by the fact of the division of our resources."[102]

As Richards intimated, Woodstock's segregation bore fruit its founders never foresaw. Although seclusion liberated seminarians from the distractions of a college campus, it also posed serious drawbacks. In the pre-Woodstock era, the education of priests had taken place in close proximity to the communities that they eventually served. Disregarding lofty questions of speculative theology, training had centered almost exclusively on meeting the Protestant challenge and grappling with the practical religious and moral issues of the day. The neo-scholastic system inaugurated at Woodstock was more academically rigorous, but its excessively speculative orientation meant that important areas of theological inquiry — scripture, history, and patristics — were neglected. And by shielding students from engagement with the outside environment, the scholasticate thwarted their understanding of the very society to which they were being sent.

Woodstock's physical seclusion mirrored and abetted its intellectual isolation. Its European-born faculty, reared from an early age in a clerical subculture and victims of revolution, regarded the non-Catholic world as error-ridden and rife with threat. As an upshot of their self-imposed estrangement, they lived as if in a bubble, perilously ignorant of modern philosophy, science, and culture. Guided by the increasingly centralizing power of Rome, Catholic seminary education in the United States was marred by an unwillingness to reflect positively on secular culture and on the American Catholic experience. Shackled to a blinkered interpretation of the Thomistic tradition, it suffered, in the words of one historian, from "the virtually complete absence of any attempt to venture beyond the approved interpretations of the standard authors." As a consequence, Woodstock College, like most late-nineteenth century Catholic seminaries, spawned a static system of instruction, "frozen in a mold that was universally believed to have been fixed at the Council of Trent."[103]

Woodstock's intellectual disengagement from the world, which paralleled the isolation of the church itself, thus had long-run import for Catholic theology. As the scholar Gerald A. McCool has observed, the disdain of Catholic philosophers and theologians for modernity prevented the church from dealing effectively with the challenges posed by modern exegesis and historical method when these were applied to theological questions. As a result, they could not appreciate "the genuine questions with which modern historical science and modern philosophy confronted the church at the time of the modernist crisis." Thus, for all the benefits it brought to American Catholicism, the institution's heritage was for many years mixed.[104]

Woodstock's hand reached across the continent. Piedmontese Jesuits in the Far West, lacking cash to open good institutions of their own, looked instead to Maryland to train their scholastics. Thus, the cautious and critical mentality that shaped theological training in the East was extended westward. Woodstock provided more than academic and spiritual preparation to frontier clergy. Jesuits destined for the Rocky Mountain Mission also received their instruction in practical skills that aided their work among Native Americans. As soon as Alessandro Diomedi set foot in the United States in 1874, for example, he rushed to Woodstock to master the printer's trade before hurrying off to the Indian missions. Thus prepared, he founded the St. Ignatius Mission press in Montana, which published scores of dictionaries and grammars of native languages. Giuseppe Marra, future editor of *La Revista Católica*, likewise learned the publisher's art at Woodstock.

The seminary's imprint on frontier life did not end with the ordination of its graduates. Once they had emigrated west, missionary priests found the *Woodstock Letters* an effective instrument for publicizing their work and for winning fresh recruits for Oregon, Alaska, California, and New Mexico missions. And just as Georgetown College stood as an early exemplar of American education for expatriate Jesuits in the West, so too Woodstock became a fixed reference in matters philosophical and theological. Accordingly, when missionaries later opened their own houses of study in the California and Rocky Mountain missions, Maryland's seminary provided the textbooks, manuals, and curricular prototype.

The bond between Woodstock College and New Mexico was particularly tight. Not only did the seminary provide a "continual subsidy" to operations in the West, as one professor recounted, it also supplied personnel. Even building design was transferred from East to West. When Domenico Pantanella founded Regis College in Denver, Woodstock served as a template for both its architecture and its curriculum. As the *Woodstock Letters*

proudly reported, students of philosophy in Colorado "follow the same order of exercises as Woodstock, and use Schiffini as their textbook." From
Maryland, Neapolitan seminary professors also supervised operations in
New Mexico, advising superiors in both Albuquerque and Naples how best
to govern that challenging mission. Camillo Mazzella was twice summoned
from the classroom and sent west as official visitor to unravel crises in the
governance of the Southwest.[105]

The ideal of a sequestered seminary, established first in Maryland, was
replicated by Jesuits across the United States. As missionaries advanced westward, penury compelled them to return temporarily to the old practice of
locating scholasticates on college campuses. But the detached Woodstock
model eventually caught up with them and they warmly embraced it. The
Piedmontese in California, for example, had for over thirty years trained their
Jesuits-to-be at Santa Clara College. Once the number of applicants became
sufficiently large, however, the seminary was relocated from the "hubbub of
a boarding school" to a bucolic site near the village of Los Gatos, California.
On an unpeopled hillside amid vineyards and olive groves, Jesuit trainees
lived in splendid solitude, cocooned in a protected subculture — just like their
confrères at Woodstock College. "There we will be in wilderness," wrote a
credulous seminarian, "a long way from other dwellings [in] a real earthly
paradise."[106]

5 *"Attracted Toward Remote Lands"*

BECOMING WESTERN MISSIONARIES

It is but natural that those who shall have picked up a little
English should be drafted off to Bombay or to California.
— Jesuit William S. Murphy, St. Louis, 1855[1]

One of the abiding images of American history is that of the overland
traveler who, eager to attain riches in the West, set off from home ill-prepared
for a wilderness journey. Although most adventurers survived such ordeals,
there is truth in the stereotype of greenhorns who trekked ad-hoc fashion,
knowing little of camp life or the kind of society that awaited them in distant Oregon or New Mexico. Although they went West confident, for them
life became a lottery in which neither winners nor losers could be anticipated
at the onset. As one historian has said, "None of those who traveled to
California had any inkling of what was in store for them."[2]

Bernard J. Reid, who emigrated from St. Louis to the gold fields of California in 1849, typified the fortune seekers. Enraptured by travel reports of
the explorer John C. Frémont that "gave me a strong desire to see for myself
the interesting countries he described," Reid had no idea how to realize his
dream and get to Eldorado. "Without giving up my position some weeks in
advance," the twenty-six-year-old surveyor recalled, "I could not well have
given the necessary attention to the selection of a company to travel with,
and [to] procuring the means of transportation and the necessary equipment
for such a journey." Reid consequently put his faith in the "Pioneer Line,"
a wagon train that advertised it would convey two hundred passengers across
the plains in fifty-five days. Plagued by mismanagement, cholera, scurvy, and
death, his adventure metamorphosed into "a long, dreadful dream." Compounding his trials, Reid proved an unlucky gold miner. Hopes of amassing
a fortune dashed, the impecunious young man found a job teaching English
at Santa Clara College, a startup school recently opened by Italian Jesuits.
A few months later, after paying off his debts, Reid booked passage home,
leaving behind "the privations of a long and weary exile."[3]

Reid's Jesuit colleagues at Santa Clara College, by contrast, made their
east-west journey in comparative ease. Relying on systems developed dur-

ing three centuries of missionary travel, they crossed and recrossed the continent relatively well-informed about both trip and destination — just as they had traversed the Atlantic. While they were never freed from the perils of western migration, the émigrés amassed a storehouse of knowledge through frequent letter-writing that helped assure them safe passage to the West. Reports published in the *Woodstock Letters* and other epistolary exchanges enabled them to get a grasp on their eventual home even before it was actually at hand. Moreover, while Reid and other gold seekers participated in what one scholar has labeled "a migration of strangers," the missionaries journeyed collaboratively, in the company of familiars.[4]

Once they had arrived in San Francisco, Spokane, or Santa Fe, the weight of tradition also determined how Jesuits settled in. Their first instinct was to recreate familiar forms of education, parish organization, and Indian evangelization that had been pioneered by missionary predecessors around the world. Additionally, in times of crisis, the Jesuits turned to the East or to Europe for counsel, financial assistance, and personnel — although never with equal success. No less important, they relied on religious ideology and on their corporate ésprit de corps for motivation in coping with the trials of dislocation. Consequently, even when sober experience dampened a romantic faith in the future and youthful fantasies failed to materialize, their attitudes rarely turned sour.

The Western Missions

The Jesuits' choice of destination was the result not of happenstance, but of careful design. Their way west had been charted by forerunners who had emigrated from Europe to the Pacific Northwest a decade before the *Risorgimento* drove the majority of Italian clerics into exile. That vanguard worked among Native Americans in a jurisdiction called the Rocky Mountain Mission, a dominion embracing the modern states of Oregon, Washington, Montana, and Idaho. Led by the Belgian missionary Pierre-Jean De Smet, pioneer Jesuits had cleared the way by erecting a series of outposts among the tribes, whose progress was publicized through an unending flow of reports calculated to draw more volunteers into the field.[5]

Numbered among those precursors were several Italians. Roman-born Gregorio Mengarini's linguistic ability made him a pivotal player in the establishment of the Jesuits' first outpost, St. Mary's Mission, among the Flatheads in Montana's Bitterroot Valley in 1841. Three years later, De Smet enlisted five additional helpers from Europe, including three young Italians who would play roles in both white and Native American communities on the West Coast over the next forty years. Michele Accolti, an outgoing and convivial priest from Bari, began his career as business agent for the Rocky Mountain Mission at its headquarters on the Willamette River in Oregon Country. Antonio Ravalli, an architect from Ferrara, was assigned to the Flathead mission at St. Mary's. Giovanni Nobili, a naive but hardworking Roman, found his calling by launching a fresh mission in isolated New Caledonia in today's British Columbia.

Since none of these pioneers had extensive prior experience of aboriginal peoples, they looked abroad for guidance in running their enterprise. They relied especially on books they had read about the order's so-called Paraguay Reductions. Established in the seventeenth century among the Guaraní and other South America tribes, those missions had been one of the crowning accomplishments of the old Society. De Smet records that he carried with him to Montana a copy of *Cristianesimo felice*, an eighteenth-century study of the reductions written by the Italian historian Lodovico Antonio Muratori. "Nothing," he said, "appeared to us more beautiful than the Narrative of Muratori." Hoping to effect a "rebirth of the beautiful days of Paraguay" in the Rocky Mountains, we made this book "our vade mecum."[6]

The Paraguayan precedent prompted the Jesuits to hasten conversions by shielding their native converts "from all contaminating influence," De Smet wrote, "not only from the corruption of the age, but from what the gospel calls the world." The missionaries thus aimed at isolating the Flatheads from the pernicious example of white settlers. We will exercise "caution against all immediate intercourse" with them, he said, "even with the workmen, whom necessity compels us to employ, for though these are not wicked, still they are far from possessing the qualities necessary to serve as models to men who are humble enough to think they are more or less perfect, in proportion as their conduct corresponds with that of the Whites." In a village neatly laid out on the pattern of Paraguay, De Smet continued, "we shall confine them to the knowledge of their own language, erect schools among them, and teach them reading, writing, arithmetic, and singing." In order to free the tribe from incessant warfare resulting from reliance on hunting, the Jesuits hoped to draw the Flatheads from a foraging economy to a self-supporting, agrarian life centered around the mission. This same gestalt emerged at other settlements that were founded in quick succession, including Sacred Heart Mission among the Coeur d'Alenes and St. Ignatius Mission amid the Kalispels.[7]

The newly restored Society of Jesus, relying on the missionaries' optimistic reports, entertained high hopes for the Rocky Mountain Mission. Three months after the first band of religious set up their tents in the Bitterroot Valley, De Smet expansively announced: "The Flathead nation has been converted." According to the founder's shining vision, "It would be easy to make this tribe a model for other tribes, the seed of 200,000 Christians, who would be as fervent as were the converted Indians of Paraguay."[8]

Within a decade, this utopian vision had shattered. Blackfeet incursions into Flathead country produced instability and constant fear of attack. Confronted with disease and epidemic, the tribes became disillusioned with the priests' power; and missionaries made mistakes resulting from their blissful ignorance of native culture. Instead of conversion, there was schism; instead of religious enthusiasm, the Flatheads came to regard the missionaries with stony indifference. As a result, ten years after its founding, the Jesuits withdrew from St. Mary's Mission. The situation was hardly better elsewhere in the Northwest, where white settlers and gold seekers further undermined priestly authority. Despite his extraordinary status among the natives, De Smet seemed increasingly unable to govern effectively the enterprise he had founded. Having written himself into a corner with copious predictions of success, he was abruptly yanked from missionary work in 1849. Summoned back to St. Louis by the superior general, a dejected De Smet was assigned to raise funds and recruit personnel for the missions.[9]

So forlorn was the condition of the Rocky Mountain Mission by 1851 that some missionaries expected its eminent collapse. St. Mary's was gone, and "the others will follow it soon," Nobili prophesied; "it is unavoidable." "The missions of the mountains are coming to an end." Dismayed by pessimistic field reports, Roothaan agreed: "It seems the idea of renewing the miracles of Paraguay amid those mountains was a Utopia. . . . I don't see how these missions can be kept up. . . . Where should we get the necessary men and resources!"[10] Making matters worse, a fresh blow from another quarter nudged the Rocky Mountain Mission still deeper into crisis — the discovery of gold in California.

The California mining boom and the subsequent drain of resources southward struck every village, mining camp, and Indian mission in the Pacific Northwest. "The work of planting and rearing churches has been . . . retarded," an alarmed Protestant minister reported in 1850, "by the facility with which every occasion of fluctuation in California produces a corresponding effect in Oregon." Spiraling operational costs soon swamped Jesuit operations with debt, threatening their very survival. Unlike the reductions of ancient Paraguay, which had relied on governmental support, the Oregon outposts depended solely on Jesuit resources, which proved insufficient for the task at hand. We have amassed "great debts," Nobili observed, and our institutions "receive little from Europe." Business agent Michele Accolti, whose fervor for missionary work had begun to wane after five years of setbacks, grew more and more discouraged over the prospect of native evangelization. What instead provoked his intense curiosity was California, from which he received a flow of letters requesting priests for a mounting Catholic population.[11]

A voracious consumer of information from the new mecca, Accolti decided the Jesuits might more profitably shift their energies southward. Tidings from the gold fields, he exclaimed, "surpasses all imagination." Never one to tiptoe through life, Accolti, seized with relentless single-mindedness, ignited a one-man campaign to begin a fresh ministry there. "All that glitters is not gold," he admitted, but "I think we ought not to show ourselves indifferent" to a place that "will not fail to offer considerable advantages." The solution to the Rocky Mountain Mission's "poverty and misery," he argued, lay in the wealth of California. Worn down by Accolti's drumbeat insistence, his superiors finally cleared him to sail south to investigate options. With Giovanni Nobili as traveling companion, Accolti hitched a ride on a brig carrying lumber from Oregon to San Francisco, where he stepped down the gangplank on 8 December 1849.[12]

That visit provided the material from which the two Jesuits would construct a fresh missionary enterprise. While Nobili toiled in parishes in San Francisco and San Jose, Accolti cantered about scouting the possibility of opening a college. Although summoned back to the Northwest to head the Rocky Mountain Mission in 1850, Accolti retained California uppermost in his thoughts. Henceforth, he used his lately won authority to promote a permanent Jesuit presence in the south, bombarding superiors with galloping-style letters in which he presciently proclaimed the coming greatness of California.

A chance to realize his obsession appeared when a new bishop arrived in Monterey to take command of California's escalating Catholic community. Bishop José Sadoc Alemany saw the Jesuits as partial solution to one of his most taxing problems: too few hands on deck. Alemany had only twenty-one priests to staff twenty-six churches and to minister to an estimated forty thousand Catholics among the state's suddenly swollen population. Alarmed at the paucity of pastors and at California's "most miserable condition in regard to education," Alemany turned to Giovanni Nobili. In 1851, the bishop offered Nobili the adobe buildings of Mission Santa Clara, an eighteenth-century Franciscan outpost located at the southern end of San Francisco Bay, where, he proposed, the Jesuits would operate a parish and school. At Accolti's urging, Nobili accepted the bid and set about transforming the former mission into a schoolhouse that he expansively named Santa Clara College. Fifteen months after arriving through the Golden Gate, Accolti had achieved his objective of gaining a Jesuit foothold in California.[13]

With students packing the classrooms, Nobili struggled to find faculty for his Gold Rush institution. "There are not yet enough teachers in the school to give it the solid reputation that it should have," observed James Alexander Forbes, an early trustee, since clergy were few in number and lay instructors such as Bernard J. Reid soon found more rewarding employment. Without more Jesuits, Forbes said, "the advancement of pupils in the various branches of education" would remain at the primary level, and the future appeared precarious. "I fear that Father Nobili will have to quit the field, if you do not send him some fathers to aid him in the school," he warned Accolti. The Jesuits sent appeals for help to members of their order around the world, but no volunteers stepped forward.[14] Seeing that the letter-writing campaign to win faculty was going nowhere, Accolti lit on another stratagem. Recalled to Europe in 1853 to participate in the election of a new Jesuit superior general, he used the occasion to filibuster on behalf of his college in California. "You can accomplish more in one conversation," he observed, "than with a hundred letters."[15]

In Italy, Accolti conferred in 1854 with Pieter Beckx, the order's new head, and with Alessandro Giuseppe Ponza, provincial of the dispersed Turin Province. Moved by Accolti's Pied Piper appeal, the two leaders recognized that the American West offered fresh purpose to Jesuits ejected from Italy. Accordingly they agreed that the members of the Turin Province in exile would adopt California and the Rocky Mountain Mission as their mission realm.[16] As soon as that decision was made, Ponza dispatched several priests already in the United States to San Francisco. From the East, Antonio Maraschi, Carlo Messea, and Luigi Masnata caught ship in 1855. They were soon joined by Nicola Congiato and Giuseppe Caredda, and other expatriates who eagerly embraced the opportunity that America offered. After years of exile and dependence upon the support of strangers, the emigrants recognized that the West meant freedom. Now it was they who would select their ministries, they who would choose their lifestyle, and they who would control their destinies.

In the years that followed, additional *piemontesi* converged on the Pacific Coast from scattered points of diaspora. Their coming transformed the fledgling schools in California — Santa Clara College and San Francisco's St. Ignatius College, which was founded in 1855 — into prominent educational institutions. The displaced religious also infused new life into the Society's Indian mission in the Pacific Northwest. The Piedmontese Jesuits still maintained houses in Europe, principally in Corsica and Monaco, beyond the reach of enemies in Italy, but the main focus of their energy now shifted toward the United States. "The Province of Turin chiefly exercises its zeal" in California, they reported in 1862, and "the most important" of its projects was the College of Santa Clara. For the next fifty-five years, both California and the Pacific Northwest functioned as vital extensions of the exiled organization of the Piedmontese Jesuits.[17]

Thirteen years after Accolti persuaded the northern Italians to adopt the West Coast, Jesuits from Il Regno, the region south of Rome formerly ruled by Bourbon Spain and France, took up work in the Southwest. Once again, a frontier bishop played a key role in the decision to emigrate. In 1851, Jean

FIGURE 8. Early Jesuit outposts in the Pacific Northwest aimed at replicating the order's so-called Paraguay Reductions, established in seventeenth-century South America. This drawing by missionary Nicole Point depicts the first of those outposts, St. Mary's Mission, planted among the Flathead tribe of Montana in 1841. When the utopian vision of Paraguay collapsed, the Jesuits, reinforced by recruits from Italy, developed more effective strategies for converting the tribes. Courtesy Jesuit Missouri Province Archives, St. Louis, Missouri, De Smetiana IX C9 1a–1b

Baptiste Lamy of Santa Fe assumed spiritual responsibility for another portion of the region seized by the United States after the Mexican War. At the time of his nomination, a dozen priests ministered to approximately sixty-eight thousand Catholics dispersed over a territory as ample as Lamy's native France. Following the lead of Alemany and other bishops, he searched widely to find volunteers for his diocese, eventually persuading Sisters of Loretto from Kentucky and Christian Brothers from France to establish schools in New Mexico.[18]

Lamy also enlisted refugee Jesuits. Traveling to Rome on church business in 1866, he laid the needs of his diocese before the Jesuit superior general, Pieter Beckx, and Francesco Ferrante, head of Neapolitan Province in exile. Ferrante, eager to find employment for the three hundred forty displaced men in his charge, most of whom were already living abroad, offered Lamy five volunteers. Drawn chiefly from the ranks of forty Neapolitans exiled in Spain,

they were conveniently fluent in Spanish.[19] Donato M. Gasparri was working in Valencia and two others were employed in a seminary in Tortosa —
Father Raffaele Bianchi, a professor of philosophy, and Brother Raffaele La
Vezza, a carpenter. Another conscript, Brother Prisco Caso, trained as a cook
and gardener, was still living underground in Naples. Livio Vigilante, the fifth
recruit, was teaching at the College of the Holy Cross in Massachusetts.

In 1867, Lamy, the Neapolitan Jesuits, and a coterie of missionaries sailed
from Europe for the United States. Vigilante, the only English speaker among
the Neapolitans, who was named superior of the Jesuit group, met them in
New York when they disembarked. Wasting no time, the bishop and his
twenty-four companions began their traverse across the plains. "After a long,
difficult, and dangerous trip," Gasparri said, in understatement, the missionaries straggled into Santa Fe on 15 August 1867.[20] Their arrival inaugurated a half-century of Neapolitan missionary work. Soon additional émigrés who were dispersed throughout Europe and the United States crossed
the Santa Fe Trail in order to join their countrymen as school teachers, circuit riders, newspaper publishers, and pastors to both Spanish speakers and
Anglo parvenus. Theirs was an undertaking punctuated by adversity from
start to finish, however, and, as we shall see, the trial of coping with conflicting cultures, a harsh environment, and grinding poverty drove not a few
of them home.

The West's Reliance on the East

Founding missions was one thing; sustaining operations through a
steady enlistment of recruits and funding was quite another. While authorities in Europe might agree on the worthiness of undertakings in far-off New
Mexico, California, or Oregon, individual Jesuits had to be coaxed to go
there. Moreover, in an era of unlimited need when church leaders competed
for personnel, Jesuit officials on the Atlantic seaboard were loath to surrender
valued workers to frontier enterprises. Indeed, in some cases, they even resisted the uprooting of deported Italians from their colleges and parishes for
the sake of missionary projects.

Thus when Piedmontese authorities sought to extract their men from post-
ings in the eastern United States for work in California, they bumped up
against a wall of opposition. In 1854, the little academic community of St.
Joseph's College in Bardstown, Kentucky, was distressed to learn that its
Italian president, Nicola Congiato, had been appointed superior of the
California Mission. Although Easterners could not block his exodus, they did
fight to keep Congiato from taking other clergy with him. Compounding tensions, soon after he landed in California the new superior lost one of his most

valued helpers when forty-four-year-old Giovanni Nobili, the first president of Santa Clara College, contracted tetanus and died. The casualty left the institution leaderless.

Like other westerners in crisis, the Californians sought relief from Baltimore, Boston, and beyond. Anxious to find a president for Santa Clara College, Congiato appealed in 1856 to Charles Stonestreet, head of the Maryland Jesuits, pleading, "Your Reverence only can save me." "This College enjoys a very high reputation," he wrote, "and we must use every exertion to sustain it." In order to secure a president to replace the fallen Nobili, Congiato proposed a trade. Giuseppe Bixio, a Piedmontese Jesuit who was "always sighing after Maryland," would be released from California to resume pastoral work in the East. In exchange, Antonio Ciampi, a former president of the College of the Holy Cross, would come West to superintend Santa Clara. Stonestreet angrily retorted that this was not an even trade. Accusing Congiato of "Italian trickery," he refused to surrender the much-valued Ciampi. Instead, Stonestreet shrewdly exploited the crisis by ridding himself of an ineffectual Italian named Felice Cicaterri, for whom no employment could be found in Maryland. Thus it was that the hapless Cicaterri became the school's president.[21]

A few years later, when Luigi Varsi, a chemistry teacher at Boston College, was summoned to join his countrymen in the West, partners in Boston fought the attempt "to kidnap Fr. Varsi away."[22] The eastern Jesuits, who had invested heavily in the young man and had subsidized his graduate studies at the University of Paris in the expectation that he would eventually join the faculty at Woodstock, labored to retain the popular Italian. They lost the tug-of-war, however, and Varsi took ship for San Francisco.

Prejudice against missionary work colored the struggle over staffing. If forced to cede individuals to the frontier, eastern authorities preferred to yield men of minor talent (such as Cicaterri) whose services they could do without. Let the useless ones trudge off to foreign lands, argued William S. Murphy, a Jesuit official in Missouri: "It is but natural that those who shall have picked up a little English should be drafted off to Bombay or to California."[23] Inhabitants of the developed portion of the nation found it difficult to take the West seriously. Pierre-Jean De Smet of St. Louis, learning of Accolti's aspirations for Santa Clara College, joked to a friend:

The question is, from whence will Fathers, Professors and brothers come? Fr. Accolti invites them from the United States. As there is nothing in the country but precious dust and lumps (of which, by the way, he personally does not possess a single particle), he says that the Fathers should bring along all the necessary college paraphernalia, [such] as books, slates, pencils, steel quills, paper. . . . He even suggests to have the college framed in New York or in some other sea port, thinking there would be a great saving in that. The college with all its furniture and men, the kitchen with all its pots and pans, to be shipped on board of a Mammoth Steamer, bound by Cape Horn to San Francisco. Does this not beat all former speculations on California? . . . And do you feel any inclination to be the President of the Gold Dust College?[24]

The most protracted squabbles erupted in the Southwest, where jurisdictional boundaries became blurred beyond distinction. A triangle of three officials — the superior of the mission, the provincial of Naples, and the Maryland provincial — vied for authority over precious personnel. The Italian superior of the Southwest Mission frequently found it impossible to extract his men from Maryland, because American provincials refused to let them go, especially if they performed valued services in Worcester, Boston, or Washington, D.C. When Donato Gasparri tried to retrieve for New Mexico some Neapolitans stationed in Maryland, Joseph Keller spurned their release. Moreover, he ordered any would-be missionaries in his jurisdiction to obtain explicit permission from their provincial in Europe before they were snatched up and transported to the western wilderness. "I am sending no one to the Mission without orders from you," he bluntly informed Davide Palomba, his counterpart in Naples.[25]

The Maryland Province was especially unwilling to relinquish the outstanding teachers it had won from Naples. When the Neapolitans-in-exile attempted to transfer Woodstock's Salvatore Brandi to the Southwest, Provincial Robert Fulton of Maryland abruptly stopped the switch. Attempts to draft talented Giuseppe Marra, a professor of philosophy at the College of the Holy Cross, for missionary labor were also rebuffed. "Everyone wants to have this Father," Mazzella observed, and so for the time being, he counseled his stymied countrymen in New Mexico to forget about Marra, because it was impossible "to pluck him out of the hands of this provincial." The eastern Jesuits' unwillingness to manumit good teachers grated upon western missionaries, whose schools suffered prolonged birth pangs due to lack of staff. "There at Woodstock," Luigi Gentile of New Mexico once griped, "they imagine that this Mission . . . only needs missionary circuit-riders."[26]

Competition for laborers was complicated by the Neapolitans' dependency on their American confrères. When leaders of the dispersed province had met difficulty communicating with their men in distant New Mexico, the Marylanders had stepped into the breach and guided operations there. While the Europeans were grateful for rescue, this tripartite relationship clouded the lines of command of the mission superior, as Donato Gasparri found out soon after he took office in Santa Fe. You exercise "a certain authority" over our men in New Mexico, Neapolitan provincial Davide Palomba bluntly reminded him, but so too does Maryland. Therefore, do not become bellicose when contending with the Americans for men. Palomba confessed that his ability to govern was compromised by reliance on

Maryland. "What kind of a decision" can I make in these awkward circumstances?, he asked rhetorically. "I will do the same as Solomon."[27]

Then there was the financial tie. Naples remained economically beholden to Maryland for the education of its scholastics at Woodstock College until the close of the nineteenth century. Maryland also furnished the indigent province with income in the form of stipends offered by the Catholic faithful for masses said in America. "Maryland merits our profound gratitude," Pantanella summarized, "and we should not precipitously act in such a way as to give them grounds for annoyance."[28]

Their eastern connection also served the frontier missions by training workers. An internship in Massachusetts or Maryland, for instance, gave immigrants an interval in which to adjust to life in America, temper their idealism, and discover if they really wanted a missionary career. It also gave gatekeepers time to assess an individual's aptitude for that vocation. It was while teaching in Maryland that Carmelo Polino, a Neapolitan, demonstrated he was not cut out for missionary work. He is passionate about the academic life, Camillo Mazzella reported to superiors, but he "has no inclination for the Mission," where "he would be one of the most unhappy and useless" of men.[29]

Failure to take advantage of an eastern apprenticeship harmed some careers. Pasquale Tosi's poor grasp of American culture, according to an American co-worker, caused him to later make decisions that plunged him into conflict with natives and damaged Jesuit operations in Alaska. This washout was due "in great measure," Francis Barnum believed, to Tosi's "ignorance of American ways and his reluctance to adopt means which were new to him."

[Tosi] was sent directly to the Indian missions without ever having any chance to learn the least thing about the spirit and customs of America, or of visiting any of the principal cities of the United States, or of getting acquainted with our people. He had no regard for English which he considered as not worth learning, so he never succeeded in being able to speak it with any facility nor could he drive any profit from English books.[30]

Italians who founded colleges in the West — at Santa Clara, San Francisco, Las Vegas, Spokane, and Seattle — benefited greatly from teaching in Jesuit schools in the developed East. Armed with experience of American education, they were more confident when the time came to launch institutions of their own on the frontier. Antonio Maraschi's classroom work at Georgetown and Holy Cross colleges stood him in good stead when he later founded St. Ignatius College in San Francisco. Las Vegas College benefited from Giuseppe Marra's apprenticeship at the College of the Holy Cross. During their eastern sojourn, the refugee educators also developed a network of personal contacts upon whom they could rely for advice when problems developed in the hinterland. In many cases, initiation led to imitation. Describing himself as "young and inexperienced," thirty-eight-year-old Nicola Congiato sought Charles Stonestreet's advice about not only how to get to California, but also how to do his job when he landed there. Another missionary petitioned colleagues in Maryland to send him "a copy of the by-laws of St. John's Literary Institution," when the time came to draw up legal documents for institutions in California. As a consequence, the earliest catalogues of the California colleges copied almost verbatim statements of purpose and policy from the bulletins of sister institutions in Georgetown and Boston.[31]

The eastern umbilical brought economic advantages. From their established confrères, the immigrants sought funds for travel and guidance on how to make money when they reached their destination. When Enrico Imoda departed from Maryland for California in 1866, Angelo Paresce urged him to "begin thinking about the future" immediately by building a financial base for Piedmontese operations there. Buy property now, he advised, just as the first Jesuits had done when they came to Maryland. If investment in real estate was begun early, the Italians would, as California developed, eventually receive "enough rental income to maintain almost a small province."[32]

If there was a benefit, there was also a downside, however, to spending time in the East. Refugees who accommodated to life in the developed portion of the country were sometimes unwilling afterward to uproot themselves and emigrate anew. If Jesuit leaders in the Atlantic states were loath to surrender talented Europeans to missionary work, some immigrants were themselves slow to commit to a queasy hereafter in the West. As one missionary said, Jesuits who settled in at Woodstock College manifested an aversion to New Mexico. "Among our Neapolitans who are in Maryland, I do not see any who want to go there," Domenico Pantanella added. "The academic life that we have lived for so many years is so different from the apostolic life there!! An old tree does not bend easily."[33]

The prospect of a hardscrabble existence also discouraged some Italians from leaving Europe. Having read published accounts of life in New Mexico, they chose to stay put in their hiding holes at home. In 1855, the head of the Jesuits in the Midwest railed that the Turin Province's adoption of California was frustrating his efforts to bring *piemontesi* even to settled St. Louis. "Men do not want to come to Missouri from Turin for they fear they might be exiled to California." A Piedmontese Jesuit brother named Barbero was so petrified that he might be invited to the missions that he chose instead to leave the Society. The ostensible reason for departing was to take care of his elderly mother, a contemporary confided, but the real reason was "he did not feel like going to California."[34]

Those most indisposed to go were Neapolitans — not because they were less zealous than their countrymen, but because of the challenges posed by the Southwest. After the founding of the New Mexico Mission, Angelo Paresce had cheerily predicted that recruitment of workers would be a snap. "It is certainly easier for you to send your men to New Mexico," he wrote to Neapolitan provincial Davide Palomba, "than it is for the Turin provincial to send his men to California." Paresce was soon proved wrong, however. The following year, when Palomba tried to assign two Jesuits to New Mexico, the provincial of Maryland told him that "neither the one or the other seems inclined to leave, especially Father Guida, who would be very useful, [but] who won't even hear of it." In a mutinous mood, some individuals were so averse to emigrating that they refused marching orders outright. In 1879, Carlo Ferrari, a steely-willed priest at Woodstock, reminded his provincial that although superiors had the right to assign him, it was not the Society's custom to "order a subject to the missions."[35]

Professors at Woodstock College were outspokenly averse to moving to New Mexico. In 1882, a rumor circulated among the faculty that all Neapolitans would be soon withdrawn from the seminary and sent to Santa Fe. This intelligence — unfounded, as it turned out — angered the head of the Maryland Province and caused an uproar among the faculty. The theologian Luigi Sabetti claimed that associates referred to the Neapolitans as *professori vendutti* ("professors for sale"). Paralyzed with apprehension that any day now they "might be teaching somewhere else," the Neapolitans were, he wailed, in an insufferable situation. We live in constant worry that "at the slightest nod" we might be whisked off to New Mexico, he added. Terrified at the prospect, Sabetti and two other Neapolitans, Carlo Piccirillo and Nicola Russo, found an escape hatch: they switched their membership from the Neapolitan to the Maryland province to avoid being uprooted and replanted in alien terrain.[36]

Why this reticence? In 1873, Davide Palomba, the Neapolitan leader, explained that there were two basic reasons why his countrymen "do not feel called to that type of life." It was not the blazing heat or scorched deserts of New Mexico that kept them at home, he said, but rather the prospect of an existence that was "half-nomadic and totally apostolic." Features that nineteenth-century Jesuits considered essential for religious life were missing in America: a stable ministry and a reliable, fixed routine. In addition, they were repelled by the prospect of existing in near-solitude with only one other Jesuit for companionship in such sinkholes as San Luis, Conejos, and Pueblo in far-off Colorado.[37] Such restrictive arrangements lacked the support and work guaranteed by a traditional community. Divorced from their accustomed urban reality, Neapolitans regarded a missionary career in the rural Southwest as more suited to diocesan priests than to Jesuits.

They stayed home for other reasons, too. Although few would admit it, some of the Neapolitans shrank from the physical deprivations of frontier life. Giuseppe Marra once described a conversation with an Italian scholastic in New York, whom he hoped would volunteer for New Mexico. "From what he said to me, I gather that he does not want to be sent to the Mission," Marra conceded wistfully. "After having seen these marvels" of Manhattan, "it is not surprising." Pretexts for resisting assignment were many and varied. Forty-eight-year-old F. M. Lopinto, happily settled at New York's Fordham College, claimed he lacked the energy to begin "rushing across those vast plains on horseback or on foot." "I came to a new country, where they spoke two languages hitherto unknown to me. For several years I was unable to do more than babble like a baby. . . . To go now to another place and to begin a third" does not appeal to me, he concluded. "Let's forget it."[38]

Some foot-draggers pleaded incompetence. One reluctant religious thought New Mexico was not the place for him because his health was poor and he was "not virtuous enough" to sustain the privations of the place. Another fellow, Camillo Capilupi, when asked if he was willing to leave Maryland and go west, replied "frankly and freely" that he longed instead to return to Europe. The thought of never again seeing Naples filled him with "repugnance." He wouldn't be very "useful" in New Mexico anyway, Capilupi added, because he was shy and not very good at languages. Suspecting these reasons might not satisfy, he appended a final consideration: his throat was not well.[39]

The woeful isolation of the region horrified not a few. The theologian Luigi Sabetti dreaded going to "a mission as far from Woodstock as Naples is from Berlin," and where he would again have "to learn a new language and new customs." Besides, frontier ministries were a waste of time since there was greater need elsewhere. "Something should be done for the Italians who are arriving here by the millions," he said. "In my opinion, half of our men who are in New Mexico should take up work among the Italians of New York, Boston, Philadelphia, Chicago, Pittsburgh."[40]

The donkey-like refusal of brethren to find worth in their work riled men posted along the Rio Grande. People have "the most extravagant, and sometimes even ridiculous notions about New Mexico," groaned a scholastic. They believe that missionaries have "to bid farewell to civilization and to civilized life; to lead a life devoid of comfort and full of miseries of all kinds; to enter upon an existence as far removed, morally, from life in the East as New Mexico is distant, geographically." This rationale seemed baseless to those in the field — who failed to recognize that they themselves had unwittingly contributed to the corrosive image through their inflated reports of difficulties overcome by missionary derring-do. He could imagine the excuses easterners gave for not joining him, wrote F. X. Maffei from New Mexico: "There's nothing to do, there are no ministries, those who come die of starvation." The truth is, he concluded sarcastically, they preferred a cosseted existence in Maryland's "magnificent houses and colleges."[41]

No one struck out for Albuquerque or Santa Fe against his will, although superiors did sometimes twist the arm of individuals who clung to home. When the Naples Province started its mission in the Southwest, Palomba wrote to Gasparri, then in Spain, to inquire if he was willing to join the founding expedition. "Do you feel you are able spiritually and physically to accept this assignment?," he asked. "Pray over it and let me know." Jesuits, by their vow of obedience, made themselves available for any kind of work. In practice, however, most missionaries were culled from those who stepped forward to request a specific destination. "I agree completely with your reverence that it is not necessary to send anyone there who does not go cheerfully," Mazzella said of the Southwest in 1878. "The chief difficulty up to now has been the absence of this willingness." As the superior of the mission, Rafaelo Baldassare pointed out that all the brothers in New Mexico "were ordered here and with grand promises" that were never fulfilled. And yet authorities conceded it was undesirable "to put those poor fellows" who were already there "in an impossible situation" by failing to send them help. "We are here like a platoon of soldiers on the front waiting for reinforcements," wrote an unhappy Jesuit from Las Vegas in 1883. "And if it should happen that the reinforcements do not arrive, what will we do? Die on the field or surrender?"[42]

Desperate to shore up operations, provincials cajoled individuals into stepping forward. When seminarian Ianario Lezzi balked at accepting a teaching job in Las Vegas, Mazzella advised patience. If you treat him sweetly, he told the provincial, and do not talk about a "permanent assignment," but rather suggest a few years in the classroom, I think you could convince him. Mazzella suggested a similar stratagem to persuade Domenico Pantanella to leave Woodstock to become the mission's bookkeeper. Ask him "if he himself feels like going for one year," Mazzella urged. The stratagem worked. Pantanella "wants nothing more than to be left at peace in his job as professor," a friend said, but he is a good religious and would not refuse an assignment given him by superiors. Thus, after prolonged resistance, Pantanella emigrated west, where he enjoyed a fruitful career.[43]

But Carlo Ferrari, his contemporary, was a foot-dragger. Pressed to offer himself, this priest, whom companions found "insufferable," all but refused to leave Woodstock College, forcing superiors to command his relocation. "If you say, 'I want you to go,'" he told his provincial, "I certainly will do it." A few months later, Ferrari, gritting his teeth, was on the road to Santa Fe. Although he remained a westerner, Ferrari, after fifteen years of quarreling with fellow Jesuits, finally resigned from the order. Lobbying usually resulted in a change of heart, followed by a productive lifework; but sometimes it did not.[44]

To stragglers who pleaded illness as justification for staying put, superiors touted the hygienic advantages of frontier life. According to medical opinion of the day, a switch of scenery was a panacea for poor health second only to alcohol. The nineteenth-century traveler Francis Parkman discovered that salubrity drew nearly all the emigrants that he met on the Oregon Trail. In fact, many over-landers, Jesuits included, left home hoping that a switch of environment would induce well-being.

Thus it was that some of the most effective missionaries began their careers as health-seekers. When young Giuseppe Marra became incapacitated by headaches, his rector at Woodstock decided "the best solution is to have him break off his studies for a year or two and send him to Mexico." "The trip, the change of climate, the work, etc. are certain to do him a great deal of good." Giuseppe Montenarelli, who suffered from anxiety, was also shipped west for relief. "I will send him to [New] Mexico before he has a break-down," wrote Joseph Keller. "Better a live dog than a dead lion." The palliative of travel seemed a last resort for a depressed coadjutor brother whose inability to speak English had rendered him mute. "The only remedy I can suggest is to send him to New Mexico," Paresce said. "The trip and change of climate are certain to restore his health, while being among a community composed entirely of Italians will dissipate his melancholy and restore his spirits."[45]

Why They Went

If the prospect of frontier life spooked timid souls, others rushed to embrace a missionary calling. Like millions of other immigrants, clerics who went west were drawn by varied incentives — improvement of health, the thrill of travel, romantic expectations about converting Indians, a chance to start over. What a Methodist minister once said of applications for his church's missions in Oregon also described Catholic clergy: "Religious motives are probably united with others in inducing them to offer themselves." For some, missionary work was a "call of the wild," one Jesuit said, not unlike the romantic summons to adventure that drove young men by the thousands into the West. "It was a vocation, an invitation to a career."[46]

Among Jesuits, religious motivation was paramount. They had enlisted in an organization that idealized the promotion of the common good rather than individual convenience and had embraced a way of life that prized mobility and availability. The upshot was that many individuals stepped forward for whatever undertaking was asked of them, including the young Italian who left Europe because Santa Clara College needed a piano player. When President Cicaterri sought someone who could perform well enough to give lessons (thus saving the college the $8,000 it expended annually for a lay instructor), Angelo Affranchino seemed perfect for the job. A student

FIGURE 9. Jesuit missionaries, accompanied by cats and a dog, dining in a tent en route to Montana in 1841. Pencil sketch by the Jesuit artist Nicole Point, a member of the expedition. Courtesy Jesuit Missouri Province Archives, St. Louis, Missouri, De Smetiana IX C9 34

in England, he was "an excellent scholastic," his provincial said, and he "strongly desires the missions." Although eye trouble limited his study to a few hours a day, Affranchino made productive use of his free time in America by giving instruction in piano in California, where he taught for the next twenty years.[47]

Affranchino's choice testified to the effectiveness of years of training that emphasized self-donation for the sake of the Gospel. Luigi Parodi recalled the circumstance of his going to the Rocky Mountain Mission in 1878. The thirty-two-year-old was concluding theological studies in France when his provincial, Giovanni Battista Ponte, arrived to discuss his first assignment. Dropping by Parodi's room one day, he asked: "Did you ever feel a vocation for the Rocky Mountain Mission?" "No, Father," the young man replied, "but I will be glad to go, if you send me." Ponte replied, "Alright, then you will start next April with some other fathers." Thus Parodi began a peripatetic career, "turning up here and there," a historian observed, first in the Pacific Northwest and then in Alaska, "like a character in a Dickens' novel."[48]

Most volunteers had some knowledge of missionary life before they signed up. Like Protestants who discovered their vocations in the pages of the New

York *Christian Advocate*, Jesuits were drawn to their lifework through religious propaganda, especially the large body of personal accounts penned by men in the field. Labeled "edifying letters" (*lettere edificanti*), these lively if inflated descriptions of missionary adventure were published and republished in every language and every country where Jesuits could be found. The stirring effect of personal testimonials, especially when flaming with religious enthusiasm, cannot be overestimated. Gregorio Mengarini stated that he was "deeply moved" by epistles from America that were read aloud in the refectory of the Roman College when he was a student of theology. By another's account, the "beautiful letters" sent from the Pacific Northwest by Filippo Rappagliosi "wrought a deep impress on the minds and hearts of his Jesuit brothers in Rome." Superiors in the Society fostered the writing of missionary dispatches because they paved the way for vocations.[49] To Jesuits displaced from their ancestral lands after revolution descended upon Italy, these letters were like messages in a bottle, offering hope and new careers across the sea.

The Society's glorification of foreign evangelization inflamed Europeans with a desire to convert Native Americans. French scholastic Joseph Tréca expressed the attitude of many of his comrades when he said that he selected the Rocky Mountain Mission in preference to other missions primarily because it had "the greatest need." Idealism was sometimes joined to highly unrealistic expectations — a few young men boldly announced a willingness to embrace martyrdom. "I feel myself more and more attracted toward those remote lands," a volunteer wrote from England, "that I might devote all my energies . . . for the salvation of those poor Indians." Two just-ordained priests from Naples, Alessandro Leone and Pasquale Tomassini, went to the Southwest for the same reason. Although they knew little about the life and culture of Native Americans, the pair were fired with missionary zeal. They "long for the Navajos," their provincial informed Mission Superior Gasparri, and he urged him to try and satisfy their youthful dreams and ideals.[50]

Jesuit operations in the West that focused on the conversion of native peoples enjoyed an advantage in drawing entrants. Some men responded without skipping a beat when given the chance to emigrate. Twenty-three-year-old Carmelo Giordano, a novice brother who had joined the order only six months earlier, volunteered for the Rocky Mountain Mission in 1885 upon hearing a stirring lecture by Giuseppe Cataldo. In a dramatic before-and-after moment, "I offered myself for the missions. Fr. Cataldo took my name, put it in his diary, and gave a fine conference to the whole community about the Indians." A few months later, they set off for America. Equally swift was the decision made by Luigi Roccati who was studying theology at Chieri, Italy, when he met Georges de la Motte, a recruiter from the Northwest. "He wanted anyone willing to come," Roccati reminisced, "and I was kind of crazy, so I looked at him, and said, 'I'm ready.'" Twenty-four hours later, Roccati, bidding a hasty goodbye to his family, departed for the Far West, where he spent the rest of his life as a missionary.[51]

Some individuals fought to reach their goal. It took Urbano Grassi six years to fulfill his dream of evangelizing Native Americans. Sidetracked in St. Louis and California, Grassi finally appealed to the Jesuit superior general to hasten his posting to the Rocky Mountain Mission. "I would like to receive this letter from you as soon as possible," he insisted, "within two months, if possible, starting from today." Men like Grassi were ecstatic when word of their appointment finally appeared in the mail, convinced that prayers had been answered. "I don't know what sufferings the Lord has prepared for me," Mengarini said, as he readied for departure, but "this is precisely the mission to which God has been calling me right from the beginning." Vito Tromby, a member of the Naples Province, suffered from epilepsy, a condition that for years barred ordination. "He took a vow that if God cured him, he would volunteer for the missions," his provincial recorded. "The fact is, that he was ordained and has insisted on fulfilling the vow." Tromby was a good catch for New Mexico, superiors concluded, because "he is young and virtuous."[52]

A few enlisters were so inflamed with zeal that they scurried to fill the ranks of fallen friends. The sudden death in Montana in 1878 of Filippo Rappagliosi, member of a prominent Roman family, caused a sensation in Rome when a rumor circulated that he had been poisoned in America by a Protestant minister. "They wrote me that he had died," a shocked superior general is alleged to have said, "but they did not write that they had killed him." Although the gossip proved groundless, the young priest's death inspired at least three Italians — Filippo Canestrelli, Pietro Paulo Prando, and Giuseppe Damiani — to take his place by volunteering for the Rocky Mountain Mission.[53]

Political unrest lent added weight to piety in shaping a vocation. Not only Italians, but many other Europeans experienced both the attraction of missionary life and the impossibility of remaining in their homelands because of persecution. Giuseppe Cataldo, one of the most effective propagandists of the Rocky Mountain Mission, arrived in France in search of volunteers in 1885, a time when relations between the French government and the Catholic Church had not yet recovered from one of their periodic lows. Facing a wobbly status during the Third Republic, many youths elected to pursue careers abroad after hearing Cataldo's appeal. Political unrest in Germany also produced volunteers. In Belgium, England, and Holland, Cataldo met German Catholics, both Jesuit and lay, who had taken refuge abroad during Bismarck's *Kulturkampf* and sought new opportunities in the United States.

Orthodoxy — or the lack of it — propelled still others. Giuseppe Bayma's combustible theological views led superiors to conclude that his attempts to integrate scholasticism and modern scientific theory would never make it past ecclesiastical censors. Feeling his career had come to a dead end in Europe, they urged him to emigrate. "He goes willingly to California," the Turinese provincial advised the superior general, "but he feels strongly the humiliation of not being able to publish his controversial philosophy manuscript. However, Bayma possessed such a "good foundation of true virtue" that he would sacrifice "everything to God," included his unrealized scholarly projects. Filippo Canestrelli, who did pioneering work on Native American linguistics, once confided that one of his reasons for volunteering for the Rocky Mountain missions was his unorthodox opinions on philosophy and theology. Opposed to the revival of scholasticism, he and sympathetic colleagues had made themselves personae non gratae in Rome. Canestrelli summed up the result: "Pope Leo XIII took the broom and swept them all out." Europe lost a failed philosopher, but the Rocky Mountain Mission gained a talented linguist.[54]

Not every enlistee proved a fit soldier. Angelo Paresce, whom experience taught to exercise caution in assigning individuals to New Mexico, sketched out the prerequisites for a good inductee. Missionary work required Jesuits who were easy-going, adaptable, hard-working, and had some experience of the world, he wrote in a series of letters to Provincial Davide Palomba. They should be persons of good judgment, neither overbearing nor small-minded. "Do not send someone who, in the old days in Naples, we used to call madonnelle," a term roughly equivalent to a "prissy, pious type." "Persons like that impede progress here" because "they suffer and they make those with whom they live suffer." "Eloquent preaching or an elegant style" was not required, but priests should at least be able to speak effectively. Finally, they ought to "come here willingly and with the idea of making a sacrifice for God."[55]

Poorly educated and unsophisticated Jesuit brothers presented a special case. "They cannot learn the language," Paresce maintained. When they show up in America, they are usually "reduced almost to being deaf mutes in the midst of a foreign people." "Exposure to the change of food, climate, customs is a heavy trial" for excitable personalities, he warned. "So, if your reverence has a brother who is easy-going, loves to work and comes here willingly, send him right along." "Otherwise, it was better not to send him and run the danger of paying out the cost of a trip to America and then a return trip to Europe," when things don't work out and he wants to go home.[56]

Despite the caveats, superiors who were desperate for workers sometimes admitted candidates without sufficient screening. Cataldo grew dissatisfied with the Germans whom he had accepted for the Rocky Mountain Mission.

"The brothers we have received as novices from Germany are almost all good, a few excellent," he said in 1893. However, "it is not so with the scholastics and the fathers, none of whom are good, some are mediocre, and a few are more a hindrance than a help." A few Jesuits, disenchanted with frontier life, soon skittered home. Victor Garrand, a Frenchman, returned to Europe after he discovered that working with Native Americans was not his forte. He "doesn't indicate the slightest inclination toward or love of these poor Indians," griped a companion. Antonio Ravalli moved from working with natives to working with whites for the same reason. And Richard Whyte, a volunteer from Maryland who taught English in California, was repatriated because, as Congiato put it, he "doesn't like living with Italians."[57]

Some Jesuits were problems wherever they were posted. Gregorio Leggio shuffled back and forth between a variety of occupations in a variety of places, giving scant satisfaction in any of them. He has made "not a few enemies" in Colorado, a colleague observed, "above all, among the women." Biaggio Schiffini, a calamity in the classrooms of Woodstock and Fordham colleges, finally ended up in New Mexico. "Outside of philosophy," Marra sighed, "I do not know what he can do; or better, what he would do willingly." Troubled and troublesome, Carlo Ferrari caused so much turmoil that he was eventually dismissed from the order. "It is difficult," Marra said, "to find a person more eccentric."[58]

The vast majority of the missionaries persevered in their chosen career. A survey of sixty scholastics belonging to the Rocky Mountain Mission in 1895 revealed that 80 percent of them — a high percentage by modern standards — lived out their lives as Jesuits. Among American-born recruits, approximately 25 percent eventually left the order. The dropout rate among Europeans was only 13 percent. The reasons for the difference are not self-evident. Perhaps the trauma of persecution and deportation that most of the Europeans had known in their early years produced qualities of maturity, endurance, and adaptability that enabled them to better tolerate the vicissitudes of missionary existence.[59]

Getting There

Whatever path the future took, missionaries resembled other male travelers to the West in beginning their overland march with an intense sense of adventure. Like frontier soldiers and gold-seekers, they manifested curiosity about the novelties they encountered, and they too were impelled by a desire to describe what they saw along the way. In letters written to friends and family back home, a cataract of words and images poured forth from well-used pens. For men previously confined to a cloistered life in Europe, the trip was the experience of a lifetime. And the novelty of the venture inevitably burned itself into the traveler's memory for the remainder of his days, finding a permanent record in his obituary when he died decades later.[60]

Most Jesuits traveled in clusters, with the senior in religion or the one with the best command of English acting as superior. "Being a foreigner, not knowing a word of English, [and] not used to this country, I was liable to get into some trouble," the Piedmontese priest, Paulo Ponziglione, wrote of his march from New York to St. Louis. The solitary traveler was, therefore, relieved to link up with an American Jesuit who was traversing the same route. When Joseph Keller sent three inexperienced Jesuit brothers to the Southwest in 1871, he insisted they journey in the company of a priest who had some familiarity with English. "Alone, they would not be able to travel," he reasoned, "without ending up at the North Pole instead of New Mexico."[61]

The trip across the plains was arduous, notwithstanding its sublime novelty. It tested the emigrant's ability to tolerate not merely the physical inconveniences, but also the unrelieved tension of living with companions from whom there was no dodging. In 1844, a gaggle of missionaries who reached St. Louis too late to join the wagon caravan that annually departed for the Rocky Mountains were sidetracked until the following season. Finally on their way the next spring, the band plodded laboriously for several weeks without benefit of a guide. Beset by obstacles and internal squabbling, the Jesuits arrived at Fort Hall, Idaho, where one of their number, a young priest named Soderini, left the company. At odds with his confrères, he returned to Italy and left the Jesuits.[62]

In the pre-railroad era, clergy destined for California journeyed by sea. James Bouchard, who went to San Francisco by way of Panama, described his 1861 voyage from New York in "an old tub" improbably dubbed *Champion*. "Like a bottle, she was always rolling about, and so great were her heavings and tossings that walking, standing, or even sitting was next to impossible." Bouchard reacted with humor to hazards posed by the rolling ocean: "Sick as I was, I could not help but laugh at the misery of my companions, when I looked around and saw almost all, like myself, vomiting, groaning, and making grimaces as if they had the cholera or some other terrible disease." The following year, Antonio Cichi shuttled the same route by steamer, enjoying "consistently good weather all the way to San Francisco." However, his ship stopped en route off the coast of Mexico to rescue survivors from a vessel that had gone down in the Pacific. For two days, the steamer "scoured the country from north to south, collecting the poor victims . . . who were found in the nearby woods, naked and without food."[63]

Although California was the final destination of many missionaries, it was a mere intermission for others. Travelers headed for Indian missions in the

Pacific Northwest benefited from the rest and reunion with friends that the stopover provided. "I came in close contact with the last remnants of the California Indians," recalled Giuseppe Cataldo about his sojourn at Santa Clara College. "That knowledge was very useful to me in after years, for the direction of the Indian missions in the Northwest." It was at Santa Clara, a friend recorded, "that he first felt attracted toward the Indians, being filled with pity on seeing the hopeless state to which the remnant of the 'Mission Indians' had been reduced by circumstances. He saw them come often to the College for temporal as well as spiritual relief." California also afforded an opportunity to gain linguistic skills. "I began to study the Flathead language," Cataldo said, "under the direction of the great linguist" Gregorio Mengarini, who had written a grammar and dictionary of the language.[64]

Other missionaries, their gaze riveted on Indian country, could not escape California fast enough. Giuseppe Caruana and Giacomo Vanzini, worn down by their trip from Europe, paused at Santa Clara College to recover and to study English. Upon awaking one morning, however, Caruana was alarmed to discover that his companion had struck out alone for the Rocky Mountains. Fearing that he himself might remain bottled up in a California classroom, Caruana rushed a telegram to Vancouver, ordering Vanzini to halt and await his arrival so they could proceed in tandem to the Indian missions without further delay.[65]

The completion of the cross-country rail line in 1869 opened a novel chapter in western travel. Passage across the plains became quicker and cushier when sleeping cars were introduced in the 1870s. Giuseppe Bayma rode from New York to San Francisco to become president of St. Ignatius College during the first year of transcontinental travel. The trip "lasted seven days only and has been delightful," he said. "No food was to be had in the trains, but we stopped three times a day for twenty minutes, and could take a good breakfast, dinner, and supper, at convenient hours."[66] Filippo Rappagliosi, who rode by rail as far as Wyoming in 1873, rhapsodized about American transportation. "Every wagon has two stoves, a little room for necessities, drinking water, water to wash with," he wrote, and the speed was "truly extraordinary." "My expectation has been exceeded and I became open mouthed like a peasant from the countryside who comes to Rome for the first time."[67]

Delighted as he was by seeing a new world, Rappagliosi strove to put his experiences into a religious context. Reflecting on the poverty of the Indian camp to which his comfortable train rocketed, he wrote: "Comforts, dear parents, are over for me, and this is the last time progress will pay me its compliments. . . . Where I'm going, there are no cars and . . . everything moves slowly." The missionary-in-the-making intuitively sought to remain indifferent to the sleek machine that made travel smooth, knowing that the existence that awaited him at journey's end would be radically different. It was paradoxical that he saw things so clearly because, a few years later, the thirty-six-year-old Rappagliosi died alone in a crude wilderness cabin, far from the amenities of train travel and modern progress.[68]

After reaching Cody, Wyoming, by steam, Rappagliosi completed the remainder of his two-thousand-mile march to Montana by horse power. Traveling in winter, he progressed first by sleigh and then by stage, alternating back and forth between the two means, depending on the depth of the snow, but always "traveling day and night without interruption." Halting solely to replace horses or vehicle, only once did he rest in a hotel bed; other nights he slept amid snow drifts in a tent warmed by a radiant bonfire.[69]

Missionaries bound for outposts in the Southwest recorded similar experiences. Rafaelo Baldassare's crossing by stagecoach and wagon in 1874 took four months. Such treks were "not disastrous, one traveler said, but they were "a bit long."[70] Four years later, Jesuits who took the train as far as Colorado cryptically described the final 140 miles by carriage as "a novel experience." Accustomed to straw mattresses, the greenhorns spent sleepless nights on hard ground until members of a Mexican caravan offered buffalo robes to cushion their insomnia. It was not until 1879 — the year the Atchison, Topeka and Santa Fe Railroad line was extended to Las Vegas, New Mexico — that missionaries could go the entire distance from East to West by train.[71]

Like most overlanders, Jesuit diarists detailed the splendors of the western landscape. Since the vast majority of them traveled in a period before America's sectional differences had yielded to nationalizing tendencies and before the West had become like the rest of America, their accounts zeroed in on the idiosyncrasies of local environments. Mengarini, one of the first Italians to traverse the plains, recalled a tornado so strong that it uprooted trees and pummeled the travelers with hail "the size of a goose egg." Prairie dogs, "immense herds of buffaloes," and "a village of rattlesnakes" were equally original. Traveling by locomotive in 1869, Giuseppe Bayma, the priest-architect, highlighted the technological novelties he saw. Of all the sights along the way, he was most dazzled by the "wonderful" timber tunnel built to shield the line from winter snow as it crossed the Sierra Nevada mountains. "Nothing I have seen can be compared." The trip gave the Italian his first close contact with Americans. They "are supposed to be very rash," Bayma told friends, "yet we found them prudent and cautious enough all along the line we followed."[72]

The salient characteristic that all travelers commented on was America's unimaginable distances. After weeks of travel by horseback, Mengarini marveled that his destination was "still over a thousand miles away." Railroads would soon shrink the vast spaces, but since westerners depended on horses into the twentieth century, missionaries retained for decades an abiding sense of remoteness. After arriving in Montana, Rappagliosi tried to describe the region's geography. As he explained, a visit to Giuseppe Guidi, a contemporary from Rome who was stationed in Colville, Washington, took ten or eleven days' travel, an undertaking too laborious to attempt more than once a year. "We saw nothing but vast plain and towering mountains" as we plodded on horseback from St. Mary's to St. Ignatius Mission, and for two days we rode "without meeting anyone, except two wolves which stopped at a distance to stare at us." He concluded: "This gives you an idea of how vast our territory is; but, in fact, it's only a little corner of America."[73]

When seminarians Balthasar Feusi and Charles Mackin rode from Woodstock to Spokane by railroad in 1886, Mackin recorded his impressions. Vignettes of frontier life glimpsed from the window of his speeding car made the deepest imprint. He was shocked by the spectacle of a Negro hanged in effigy at a Montana station, a sight that made the two Jesuits wonder what sort of society awaited at the end of the line. And was the mayhem within the train typical of frontier life? Swaying to and fro, as if about to lurch off the track, their car "was crowded with people, many of whom rowdy cowboys returning from Chicago." The cowboys' steady consumption of alcohol, Mackin recorded, "made the car pretty lively all through Dakota." The revelers "were very generous in their offerings" of liquor to the two abstaining seminarians, who wore lay attire. When the locomotive rolled into Bozeman, Montana, it was encircled by "a number of men on horseback and on foot with their guns fixed at the train." They were informed that a labor strike was under way. The two wide-eyed seminarians, having refused the cowboys' offer of drink, were suspected of being scabs, and word of their presence on the train had been telegraphed ahead to the mounted vigilantes. When Mackin and Feusi did not exit at Bozeman, the train was allowed to proceed peacefully to Spokane.[74]

Unpacking in the West, missionaries began to confront the reality of their new life, an experience eased by the succor given by those already there. "After a trip of about eighteen days from France, I have arrived safe and sound at Albuquerque," Carlo Personè recounted. "It was 10:30 at night when I set foot for the first time in the room of dear Fr. Gasparri. I will leave it to you to imagine the joy we both felt at that moment." But the pleasure of reunion with old friends inevitably yielded to homesickness and to the trials of adapting to a novel environment. "The newcomers find everything disagreeable in the beginning, they speak ill of everything, criticize everything," said California superior Congiato, "and you need not a little patience with them." "Little by little," however, "they return to good sense and to a more spiritual outlook."[75]

Neophytes in the Southwest, both Jesuit and lay, experienced a profound culture shock. "Had I been set down upon some other planet," wrote Harriet

Benham, an American who arrived in 1900, "the country, the people and their customs would, probably, not have been stranger to me than those of New Mexico." Although less distressed than Benham, Jesuits too were initially mystified by the locale. Indeed, the mission's founders were almost undone by the obstacles they encountered in launching the enterprise. Within a year of their arrival, one of them had died and another fled to the East. Gasparri, frustrated by his inability to get along with Mission Superior Vigilante, wrote in desperation: "I absolutely cannot stay here any longer." The clash of personalities was made more burdensome by the Southwest's "isolation and privations." "There are four of us living in Conejos," missionary F. X. Maffei said in 1873, in a two-room adobe house with one table for all of us. It was difficult to write because our students do homework here, and they are "coming and going and chattering incessantly." To greenhorns, New Mexico seemed a land of countless "curiosities." "When the rains began," an American scholastic recorded, the mud-bricks of Las Vegas College gave little shelter because the best-roofed part of the house was reserved for the sick. "The others wrapped themselves in blankets and tried to sleep, sitting in their chairs."[76]

Gold Rush California offered a different set of challenges. "Whether it should be called a villa, a brothel, or Babylon, I am at a loss to determine," Michele Accolti summed up his *prima vista* impression of San Francisco. Neither letters nor newspaper reports had readied the well-traveled Jesuit for the tumult he met upon stepping ashore in 1849. He stood bolted to the busy waterfront in open-mouthed amazement at the "disorder, the brawling, the open immorality, and the reign of crime, which . . . brazen-faced, triumphed on a soil not yet brought under the sway of human laws." Although convinced that San Francisco was "the leading commercial place of California and soon will be such of the entire world," he feared the city was not "well suited for a college in view of the ebb and flow which prevails there." (The Jesuits changed their mind five years later, founding St. Ignatius College on the city's main street). Abandoning San Francisco, Accolti and his companion Giovanni Nobili instead opened their school in the bucolic countryside of Mission Santa Clara.[77]

By the 1860s, El Dorado's youthful exuberance had morphed into mature adulthood. Europeans gazed pop-eyed at the city's stunning material achievements, the fast pace of life, and the advanced state of technology that buoyed the transformation. Arriving in San Francisco in 1869, Giuseppe Bayma was struck by the great number of prefabricated buildings. "Very many splendid houses in town are of lumber, though a traveler would certainly mistake them for stone structures." The advantage was that they could be constructed *prestissimo* and with little outlay of capital. In a land of temporary arrangements, these sturdy edifices were "safer in case of earthquakes" and could

FIGURE 10. "I have found things much worse than I had ever imagined," one stunned Jesuit wrote on his arrival in the Southwest in 1869. "The great city of Santa Fe is nothing more than a small group of adobes." This photo shows a narrow, dirt street in Santa Fe, with San Miguel Church in the background, ca. 1880. Courtesy Denver Public Library, Western History Collection, J. L. Clinton, Z-4119

be "removed from place to place with little trouble and expense." Such operations piqued Bayma's curiosity, because he was about to build a three-story dormitory for St. Ignatius College.

I have already seen four or five houses traveling through the streets of San Francisco. . . . These Americans do even more than that. They raise a house (whether of bricks or lumber) with its inhabitants by fourteen or fifteen feet in the air, and then building a new story under it; a thing which is being done just now near our College and under our eyes. Decidedly, this is the land of progress.[78]

The Rocky Mountain Mission evoked a similar adrenaline rush from Europeans brimming with romantic stereotypes. Indeed, if there is one feature that differentiated Jesuit travel accounts from those of other men it was the optimism and affirmative regard with which they described encounters with Indians. Never the enemy or alien, the native was consistently imagined as prospective friend. "At last I had what I had always desired, and had come so far to find," a just-arrived French priest wrote. "How many times I complacently stopped to gaze on the white tents in the valley, and the fires kindled at the decline of day." For the rest of his life, Carmelo Giordano remembered the moment when he stepped through the door of the church at St. Ignatius Mission, Montana, and was "surprised to see Indians squatting on floors." The majestic liturgical celebrations of Christmas and Easter warmed him with speechless delight.[79]

Giuseppe Cataldo's eureka moment came during a meeting with the Spokanes in 1866. Riding through the mountains from the Coeur d'Alene mission, his party neared the Spokane River, whereupon their native guide ordered the Jesuits to dismount and remain behind while he approached the river bank alone. Once there, the leader animatedly called back to the Jesuits, "Come and see." "We went, and for the first time saw those grand, beautiful falls of the Spokane River," Cataldo recalled. "I was amazed at the aesthetic taste of the Indian, that he should so appreciate the beauty of the falls." Filippo Rappagliosi's expectations were confounded when he arrived at St. Mary's Mission in 1874. The young Roman was not prepared for the affection with which the Flatheads welcomed him into their camp. "I was especially impressed by a good old woman, who is the wife of the chief of the tribe. She took both my hands and greeted me from the heart," he wrote. "I will always remember that beautiful moment."[80]

Accustomed to *naifs*, veteran missionaries worked closely with beginners as *ciceroni*, or guides, instructing them in the realities of missionary life. In accord with the Jesuit penchant for careful planning, apprentices were immediately put to work learning the native tongue. They were usually not allowed to visit a tribe until the new idiom had been grooved into them. Starters engaged in ministry with experienced hands, who simultaneously tested their mettle and guided their first steps. Learning to ride for great distances was an essential early lesson. "I was not only tired, but really exhausted, and wounded," Cataldo moaned after his first forty-mile trek. "I could neither eat supper nor rest at night." The next morning, my companion "helped me to get on horseback, because I could not do it alone by myself, being sore all over."[81]

Adapting to native cuisine was also a trial. Even Cataldo, the most resilient of missionaries, hesitated to eat some foods. Offered a morsel of dried salmon after baptizing his first native child, Cataldo swallowed the fish with the greatest difficulty. In subsequent years, the Sicilian taught other greenhorns to adapt to native culinary culture. Pasquale Tosi was so upset at sight of food preparation on his first outing with Cataldo that he "offered his services to be our cook." But when he saw the large number of hungry children huddled around the fire, he resigned, accepting Cataldo's wise counsel: "The best is to eat what the Indians cook no matter how dirty."[82]

The fare provided at mission headquarters, however, was less strange than that served in the Indian camps. "The food is much better than what I'd expected," Rappagliosi said in 1874. "We have all kinds of meat, but most frequently pork and beef. We have cows that give good milk, and even hens, which provide eggs when young and soup when old." The *giardino*, or garden, at St. Mary's Mission provided potatoes and carrots — "better even than those in Belgium." As for fish, he continued, "we are the luckiest men in the world. . . . The Indians bring them often. If you could see how beautiful they are! Truly, you've never seen the likes in any fish market" in Rome.[83]

Rappagliosi's determination to view every experience affirmatively was telling. While intent on reassuring his relatives that he was secure in his missionary vocation, the Italian's description of himself and his co-workers as the world's "luckiest men" expressed an affirmative vision of the world and his role in it. That outlook was not the fruit of accident, but of assiduous training and of a positive ideology that encouraged adventure for the sake of the Gospel. Despite rough-and-tumble circumstances, these atypical westerners discovered possibilities in their novel environment, and they seized with both hands the opportunities it offered. After all, the missions of America had opened doors to a future that had been abruptly closed and cut short by *la miseria* of tumultuous Italy. Although living in a borrowed culture, they no longer had to rely on the charity of others for safety, survival, and meaningful labor. The missions, colleges, and parishes of the missions of the Rocky Mountains, California, and New Mexico were theirs to fashion and theirs to administer on their own terms.[84]

For clergy who ventured West, life did indeed become an adventure. The experienced missionary Angelo Paresce voiced this optimism in a letter to Davide Palomba in 1869. Seeking to ease the Neapolitan's worry about Jesuit work in New Mexico, Paresce, the seasoned administrator, assured his European counterpart that the undertaking had a great destiny, despite missionary worries "about how little they've been able to accomplish up to now." "All these things will disappear in a few years," he reassured Palomba. "Someone who hasn't been in America for a few years cannot have any idea of the speed with which things progress in this country." "My dear Father," he concluded, "one must keep one's eye on the future."[85]

6 "Methods Adopted by Us"

THE ART OF INDIAN CONVERSION

I must say, with grief, that the conversion of these Indians
is difficult.

— Jesuit Pedro Barceló, 1881[1]

No destination sparked more enthusiasm among Jesuits than Indian country. "All of my life," wrote the diarist Nicole Point, "I have felt my heart throb at the very sound of the word, 'America.'" The young Frenchman, who penned those words while en route to the United States in 1835, voiced a sentiment shared by many nineteenth-century Europeans who hankered for missionary careers. Felix Barbelin, another Frenchman, was so eager to proselytize, his sister recorded, that "he used to practice leaping over chairs, that he might be able to spring clear the ditches in America, whither he was always desirous of going." Steeped since childhood in exotic accounts of aboriginal life found in the works of Chateaubriand and other romantic writers, Europeans were further inspired to emigrate by their religious formation. Visits by recruiters and a steady stream of literature about missionary life produced a fascination with the frontier that reaped a bountiful harvest of ardent volunteers for the United States.[2] Among the male religious orders engaged in ministry to Native Americans, none provided more conscripts than the Society of Jesus.

The Jesuits' most popular goal was the Rocky Mountain Mission in the Pacific Northwest. So intoxicating was the allure of converting Indians that men from a wider spectrum of countries volunteered for duty there than at any other Jesuit enterprise in the West. By 1895, the Mission's work force numbered 160 Jesuit priests, brothers, and scholastics. Nearly 50 percent of these were Italians or Americans. Another 40 percent came from France, Germany, Ireland, and Holland. Additional volunteers emigrated from Belgium, Switzerland, Prussia, Malta, Corsica, Scotland, Spain, and Canada.[3]

This heterogeneity gave the Jesuits a jump in winning acceptance from native peoples. As scholars have observed, the Indians were "happily spared the experience of receiving Catholicism at the start from any single ethnic psychology — an Irish, French, Italian, or German Catholicism." Arriving in the

United States at a time when the identification between Americanism and Protestantism was almost complete, the European Jesuits enjoyed an advantage that escaped Protestant missionaries. Since Native Americans did not view them as Americans, they were not held accountable for repressive United States policy. Unburdened by an American background, European clergy were less inclined to meld the goals of civilization and Christianity, a mistake that undermined Oregon's early Methodist mission, for instance. "As Protestants never failed to point out," one historian wrote, the Jesuits had great appeal to the Indian because they had "ambiguous national allegiances."[4]

The benefits of ethnic diversity were not immediately apparent, however, and initial attempts at evangelization faltered. As the natives' quick acceptance of Christianity yielded to indifference and even hostility, early Jesuit enthusiasm gave way to discouragement. The Rocky Mountain Mission suffered from over-extension, inexperience, insufficient personnel, and internal squabbling. Many workers were "broken and prostrate from age, from work and from illness," Mission Superior Congiato reported in 1858, while others had become demoralized. A mounting influx of white settlers into Indian country led missionaries to complain that natives no longer listened to them. Despite the Rocky Mountain Mission's auspicious beginning, by the 1860s only two establishments were still functioning — Sacred Heart and St. Ignatius — of the six that had been in operation a decade earlier.[5]

The distressed enterprise gradually set itself aright, however, with an influx of fresh missionaries from Europe. Michele Accolti's success in 1854 in persuading the Jesuits of the Turin Province to adopt the Rocky Mountains and California missions marked a turning point. Although the impact was not immediately felt, that decision placed the fledgling operation on stronger footing and guaranteed permanency. The appointment in 1862 of the capable Giuseppe Giorda as superior, a position that he held for nearly fifteen years, signaled another turnabout. From a low of fifteen missionaries, when he took office, the enterprise boasted fifteen priests and twelve brothers six years later. With the reopening of St. Mary's Mission, twenty-seven Jesuits ran six major missions among the Coeur d'Alenes, Flatheads, Nez Percés, Blackfeet, Colvilles, and Pend d'Oreilles. Circuit riders from these epicenters fanned out to a vast network of chapels and way stations spread across an immense territory.[6]

Fortified by volunteers from Europe, the mission nudged eastward across the Rockies into the lands of the Blackfeet, Crows, Gros Ventres, and Assiniboins. Although Superior General Beckx cautioned the missionaries not to spread themselves thin, Giorda optimistically predicted in 1870 that before long a separate and independent mission would arise, and "the new one in the East will be more glorious" than its predecessor in the West. By century's end, the Jesuits had lifted their banner in Montana, Washington,

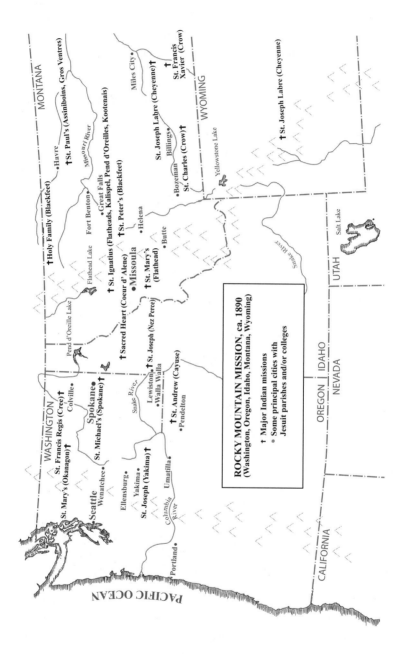

FIGURE 11. Map of Rocky Mountain Mission, ca. 1890

Oregon, Idaho, Wyoming, and the Territory of Alaska. Besides ministering to whites of all nationalities, the missionaries worked among seventeen different tribes in a dozen missions serving approximately 25,000 Native Americans.[7] Numbers alone did not tell the whole story, however. While some tribes embraced the new religion with relative ease, others became only nominally Christian or stood apart entirely. Thus, Jesuit Alessandro Diomedi, reflecting on "the methods adopted by us," concluded that "the conversion and civilization of the Indians" was a complex process and "no small undertaking."[8]

What was the Jesuit modus operandi for bridging the cultural chasm? Despite its singular importance in facilitating that encounter, the strategy constructed for dismantling native resistance to the Christian message and for establishing effective connections has not drawn much attention from historians. And yet, that process, so complex and varied despite its apparent simplicity, was the fulcrum upon which all else turned. Drawing on an extensive evangelical arsenal, the Jesuits focused almost exclusively on rudiments in the first decades: catechetical instruction, teaching of prayers, and the conferral of baptism and other sacraments. When tribal life later succumbed to Anglo-American cultural hegemony, the priests, convinced that the main hope of Christianization lay in the education of youth, undertook classroom work on a large scale. Throughout these shifts in program, a host of factors shaped the way missionaries won converts.

A paramount influence was classroom experience. All of the Jesuits had been educators before taking up missionary careers. Point had taught at the French *collège* of Fribourg, Switzerland, prior to serving as rector-president of a frontier school in Louisiana. Missionaries Ravalli, Grassi, and Prando instructed students in Italy. De Smet had trained both Native Americans and whites in Missouri. Giorda and Canestrelli were former seminary professors. Prando taught in Monaco, and Cataldo taught in Jesuit colleges in Sicily and California before joining the Rocky Mountain Mission. Pedagogical practices that the missionaries introduced to their Native American converts reenacted classroom techniques commonly employed in Jesuit schools of the nineteenth century. These included reliance upon repetition and competition to promote learning of Christian teachings and the rewarding of superior performance with prizes and awards.

The Jesuit art of conversion was profoundly molded by principles and techniques developed since the sixteenth century in the Society's world-wide missionary network. As historians have pointed out, the Jesuits were more accommodating than most Christian missionaries of their day. In their dealings with Indians, for instance, the priests of the Pacific Northwest adapted to native usages whenever possible, as earlier confrères had done when encountering the native peoples of Asia and South America. Although those adjustments appear limited by modern standards, by nineteenth-century norms they represented an innovative approach to proselytization.

The encounter between Jesuit and native disclosed unexpected points of convergence that facilitated evangelization. In those cultural interstices, the two parties found a channel, however narrow, for dialogue. Unlike Protestant clergy, who drew upon American conventions, the priests relied on European traditions, especially on devotions popular in their homeland. The piety of southern Europe, with its emphasis on an activist deity and communal worship, and its conception of a world brimming with miraculous forces and supernatural beings, complemented Indian belief. "Italian popular religion was a complex system of magical practices inherited from a pre-Christian past," one historian has written, "and sustained through centuries of co-existence with Christianity." Imbued with that culture, the Italian missionaries were, surprisingly, predisposed to tolerate many Native American expressions of spirituality.[9]

As a consequence, two religious systems — Indian and Christian — often overlapped and intermingled in the Northwest, not unlike the blending of pre-Christian and Christian notions that had occurred in Italy many centuries earlier. Despite the linguistic and cultural gulf that separated them, the two parties shared enough beliefs and practices to find common ground. What one historian has said about the relationship between Jesuits and Indians in eighteenth-century Canada is applicable to the nineteenth-century Pacific Northwest: "the Indians were not as far from the Christian invaders in religious belief as they seemed to be in practice (or ritual), which partially explains the success of the European missions as well as their failures." What the Jesuits were able (or unable) to accomplish, therefore, was profoundly determined by tribal tradition. As historians are only now beginning to appreciate, native custom and native involvement in the proselytization process shaped missionary outcomes.[10]

If the cultural encounter revealed similarities, it also revealed glaring contrasts. One of these was mutual incomprehension about gender roles. According to missionaries, the position of women in tribal culture — which shifted from region to region — played a crucial role in determining native response to the Gospel in the Pacific Northwest. Among the greatest impediments to the conversion of buffalo hunters was the subservient status of females. To the Crows and Blackfeet, "the woman is a real slave," who could be bought and sold, a priest recounted. She did most of the work, except hunting game and guarding horses, which were the responsibility of men.[11]

Missionary censure of this arrangement rendered women sympathetic to the Christian message, but it alienated their male relatives. "It is not good for women to carry these heavy loads," Prando told a group of Crow women. "I will teach your men, and I will push them to work." At this reproof, "the women were glad," he reported, but his bold interference in tribal custom did not please their husbands. As one native scoffed to a missionary, "Are you a woman? You work!" Hence Father Joseph Joset's conclusion: "There is one of the greatest obstacles" to the "conversion . . . and civilization" of these tribes; men were not willing to become industrious and to farm.[12]

Equally upsetting to patriarchal Europeans were the "haughty and independent" women of the fishing tribes along the Columbia River and Kettle Falls. "In less than six weeks," Joset reported, men of the Colvilles "were able to lay in their entire winter's supply of salmon," after which they had "nothing to do all year." Women cured the salmon and harvested berries and roots, all of which belonged exclusively to them. "If the husband exhausted his wife's patience or pilfered her food, she'd kick him out, without further ado." This prevented a husband from "gambling away his wife's property," the priest conceded. But it thwarted the missionary's attempt to establish "the custom of the wife's role being subordinate to that of her husband." More ideal from a European perspective was the division of labor among small game hunters such as the Coeur d'Alenes. Husband and wife shared "their labor and fatigue," the Jesuit noted with evident satisfaction, and as a result their married life "more closely resembled that of Christian couples."[13]

Confronted with these cultural differences, missionaries immediately grasped that the deciphering of native languages was a fundamental first step toward proselytization. The priest who could engage in dialogue was the priest who was most effective. It helped that linguistic skill had been a principle upon which Jesuit missionary tradition placed a high priority. St. Ignatius of Loyola, the founder of the order, had urged his followers to learn the idioms of the countries to which they were sent. Paul Le Jeune, a seventeenth-century Jesuit who served among the Montagnais of New France, stated the case for language-learning most succinctly in 1633, when, quoting St. Paul, he declared, "Faith enters by the ear."[14]

To be sure, not all Christian missionaries accepted the axiom. Some Protestant ministers refused to learn native languages. In schools established by the Methodist missionary Jason Lee in the 1830s in Oregon's Willamette Valley, natives were forbidden to speak their own tongue. Similarly, Methodists in Oklahoma, led by John Jasper Methvin, faced with a multiplicity of Indian languages in a small geographic region and convinced that Christianity could not be authentically expressed in any form but English, made no attempt to use Kiowa and other native tongues in their teaching. That language served as a key to the minds and hearts of a people, and to their culture, however, was a truism recognized by all effective missionaries. "For purposes of civilization, and especially of Christianization," said Congregational minister Stephen R. Riggs, who lived among the Sioux, knowing Indian languages was "indispensable."[15]

The Paraguayan paradigm, with its emphasis on isolation and linguistic competence, further shaped the Jesuit program. "We shall confine them [the Flatheads] to the knowledge of their own language," De Smet wrote. This meant that missionaries poured more energy into unraveling Salish than they did to mastering English — which few of them knew when they landed in America. Urbano Grassi asserted this same priority when he instructed new arrivals to speedily learn the Blackfeet tongue "so that we may at once break the barrier that language imposes before us in the conversion of these people."[16] This did not mean, however, that all Jesuits were good linguists. It is doubtful that De Smet or Point ever spoke a native idiom. Both relied instead on interpreters or communicated in French, the second language of some Native Americans and the principal language of most *métis* who worked for the Hudson's Bay Company. Thus the linguistic skills of the Indians came to the missionaries' rescue, especially in the early period while the priests were still learning native languages.

Most of the Jesuits could express themselves in one or more native tongues. "All our Fathers speak the Flathead" language, Joseph Joset, missionary to the Coeur d'Alenes, reported in 1871, although he did not characterize the level of competency attained by them. The Blackfeet were impressed by Pietro Paulo Prando's fluency. Kootenai was the specialty of Filippo Canestrelli. Contemporaries judged John Post of Luxembourg "remarkably proficient" in Kalispel, an appraisal borne out by the use modern scholars of linguistics have made of his writings. Mengarini, Canestrelli, Post, and Antonio Morvillo authored useful dictionaries and grammars of Northwest Indian languages. A few of the missionaries were multilingual. Giorda's "great talent for languages" was evidenced by his familiarity with the idioms of the Blackfeet, Nez Percés, Flathead, Yakima, Kootenai, and Gros Ventres tribes. Urbano Grassi was allegedly conversant in an equal number. Eduardo Griva, the "premier Jesuit linguist among the Salish tribes," managed to communicate — although certainly not with anything approximating equal grace — in twelve indigenous languages. Cataldo, one of the most accomplished native-language speakers, knew ten.[17]

Mengarini was the most gifted linguist among the first Jesuits, selected for missionary work because of his facility in languages. His method for acquiring Salish entailed total immersion. As Giuseppe Cataldo, one of his students, put it, "The best way to learn the Indian language was to go live in the Indian camp," a principle imposed on Mengarini himself by necessity. He once joined the tribe on their summer buffalo hunt, although he returned convinced that such travels were fruitless. The products of Mengarini's research were a vocabulary list that bloomed into a manuscript dictionary and, later, a study of the rudimentary rules and principles of the Salishan language that emerged as the first grammar of that tongue.[18]

The usefulness of his dictionary is clear from a report written in 1844. Commenting on the arrival of a missionary greenhorn at St. Mary's, Mengarini observed: "I have never seen another man apply himself so diligently in learning another language as Father De Vos. He has stolen my dictionary and God knows when he will return it." Passed for many years from hand to hand, the manuscript was finally published in 1877–79 as *A Dictionary of the Kalispel or Flat-head Indian Language*. And in 1861, Cramoisy Press of New York published Mengarini's *Salish or Flat-head Grammar*. The quality of the priest's scholarship reflected the standards of linguistic study of his day. His Salish grammar, for example, was not only written in Latin, but used the classical language as a framework for analysis of the native tongue. Shortcomings notwithstanding, the missionaries contributed to our understanding of Indian languages, preserving, in some instances, data that might otherwise have been lost.[19]

Once they arrived in an untrodden locale, other Jesuits, too, began composing word lists, dictionaries, and grammars to be used by their successors. These works were subsequently published by presses erected at St. Ignatius Mission and at other outposts in the Northwest. Morvillo's Nez Percé grammar, though cast in a Latin mold, was significant because it was among the earliest primers of the language. Giorda and Mengarini's works were standard references for the Kalispel language until a modern grammar appeared in 1940. The value of missionary publications has been confirmed by the fruitful use modern scholars have made of them. Herman K. Haeberlin discovered in Giorda's Kalispel dictionary "much material" for his study of Salish systems of reduplication. Linguistic scholar Gladys Reichard's research on Coeur d'Alene grammar drew on the earliest work of Giorda and Mengarini. Their writings also aided Haeberlin and Franz Boas in establishing the close relationship between Kalispel and Salish dialects. The priest's scholarship aided research on the origin of Salish. Perhaps the greatest testimony to Canestrelli's Kootenai grammar was its republication by Franz Boas, then the dominant figure in American Indian linguistics, in 1927.[20]

Their European ancestry colored every Jesuit undertaking, including language learning. The priests had studied classical and European languages before becoming missionaries, and they had also taught them. Although Native American idioms were strikingly different from those of the Indo-European family, and although the Jesuits' linguistic training was, from a modern viewpoint, limited in its technical aspect, the missionaries' old world experience did facilitate their study of the vernaculars of the new. The international composition of the order in the Pacific Northwest had important linguistic implications. Most of the missionaries were from small nations, and since childhood they had been exposed to a multiplicity of tongues. As Europeans, they were usually not intimidated by the prospect of learning an alien speech, but recognized it as a necessity of life, as, for example, when they resided in international houses of study during their years of preparation. The breadth of that experience freed them from the psychological barriers that impede effective mastery of new languages. It is significant that twenty-three of the twenty-six Jesuit linguists whose papers constitute the Northwest Indian Language Collection of Gonzaga University were foreign born.[21]

The Jesuits' European origins had other consequences. Many of them came to the Northwest knowing little or no English. Indeed, Italian so dominated conversation in the Jesuit community at Sacred Heart Mission that Father Luigi Parodi thought he was back in Italy when he visited there. Not a few recently arrived missionaries were obliged, simultaneously, to learn both English and an indigenous patois. In 1874, Filippo Rappagliosi recorded that his chief occupation was "studying two languages at once — English and Kalispel," a dilemma that provided urgent incentive for mastering the native dialect. Unable to speak with Native Americans in English, the missionary was compelled to master the aboriginal language as soon as possible. In some instances, priority was given to acquiring the Indian language. "As I expected to spend all my life amongst savages," the Belgian William Claessens recalled, "I did not pay much attention to English." Filippo Canestrelli, a professor at the Roman College, emigrated to America in 1878. Upon reaching Fort Colville, he dashed off a note to Cataldo announcing his safe arrival and his assumption that English was the first language he should learn. The riposte shot back from Cataldo: "No. Kalispel." A decade later, Canestrelli still did not know much English, but he had authored thirteen publications in Kalispel.[22]

One of the first tasks to which missionaries applied their new learning was rendering prayers and the catechism, a question-and-answer summary of the elemental tenets and principles of Catholicism, into the local argot. This was standard missionary custom, although putting it into practice was not evenly done. "We were no sooner settled" at St. Mary's, Mengarini wrote, "than Fr. De Smet, together with some Indians who knew a little French, began translating our prayers into Flathead." Cataldo followed the same protocol when he launched his work among the Nez Percés thirty-seven years later. He started by teaching morning and evening prayers, and "then I began singing, and they all joined in." After several weeks of instruction, the first baptisms were conferred.[23]

Indians, who, like the Jesuits, believed that the supernatural world could be communicated with, affirmed the potency of prayer. They were convinced, as were the priests, that beings from the spiritual realm sometimes manifested themselves to mortals in visions. As native leaders testified, one of the reasons why they invited the Black Robes to come among them was to learn their invocations and thereby acquire Christian power. "The Flatheads are fond of praying," De Smet said admiringly. "In the fort as well as in the camp, and when we are on the road, we never failed to assemble morning and evening to say the prayers in common, and to sing some canticles of praise of God." In addition, missionaries and natives shared a belief in the value of confessing sin and performing acts of penance. "A kind of [public] confession had been introduced among the Flatheads long before our arrival," Mengarini observed, and, as a result, "private confession such as we practice was easy for the Flatheads." Three years after the founding of St. Mary's, he said, "confession has so taken root among them that it is more necessary to hold them back than to spur them on, and their delicacy of conscience approaches scrupulosity."[24]

In many instances, the missionaries first taught the children of a tribe, particularly if adults were not yet receptive. In 1867, when Cataldo arrived among the Nez Percés, many of them rebuffed his overtures, but "they were willing that the children should learn." Five years later, when he returned, the priest was taken aback at discovering they had in the interval mastered the basic prayers and songs. Upon inquiring how this had happened, a chief replied: "Didn't you teach our children?" In Cataldo's absence, the young people "went all around" the Nez Percés camps communicating to their elders what they had learned from the missionary.[25]

De Smet devised a procedure for teaching prayers that shifted initiative to the natives. Youngsters were arranged in a circle and each person repeated a single line, so that by reciting it, phrase by phrase, the entire invocation, could be heard and memorized. This method, which reflected the influence of the *Spiritual Exercises* of St. Ignatius, which recommended repetition of a prayer mantra as a method of meditation, freed busy missionaries for other duties. Family members assisted one another in memorizing prayers and commandments and quizzing one another on their progress. The recitation of prayers in common and the singing of hymns quickly became part of the converts' daily routine at St. Mary's. De Smet wrote: "Every morning they assembled around the Missionary's lodge and more than three-fourths of them without any shelter than the sky, after having recited their prayers, listened to an instruction, proceeded and followed by hymns. At daybreak and sunset the bell was tolled three times for the Angelic Salutation [Angelus prayer]."[26] Devotions sometimes persisted into the night. "After the regular evening prayer, they will assemble in their tents to pray or sing canticles," an approving De Smet explained. "These pious exercises will frequently be prolonged till a late hour; and if any wake during the night, they begin to pray." The passing of time did not dampen their fervor. "With regard to prayers," Giuseppe Caruana said, "the Indians are accustomed to say their morning and evening prayers in common with a loud voice directed by a leader called head-prayer and head-singer. So they do also when they pray at home far from the church, and at the sound of the bell for the Angelus you would see them in groups kneeling down, bare-headed, saying loudly the Angelus answering to a leader in each group."[27]

When teaching the catechism, Europe once again supplied the model. "I taught the children catechism by a method commonly followed in Rome," Mengarini recorded. After they had memorized "several hundred questions and answers," a public contest was announced. "On the appointed day, all the competitors, none of whom must be over thirteen years of age, arrange themselves in two lines in the church. The first proposes a question to be answered by the opponent, and so all along the line, each in turn answering or proposing a question. Whoever misses, loses his chance for the prizes."[28] Boys who triumphed in Mengarini's Sunday afternoon "catechism bees" received arrows. "The wish to see their children distinguish themselves has attracted almost the whole colony to catechism," said De Smet. "None of the chiefs who have children fail to be there; and there is not less emulation among the parents than among the children themselves."[29]

Missionary pedagogy relied on the good example of outstanding converts to draw others into the fold. By focusing on high-profile persons and promoting them as models, the Jesuits advanced the Christian cause while making use of existing community structures. Chiefs and elders, whose function in native society probably reminded the priests of the patriarchy of rural Italy, played a central role. According to Mengarini, "from the beginning, the missionaries directed all their efforts toward encouraging submission to tribal leaders, making clear to the latter their obligation to watch over the conduct of their citizens, and expounding upon the power of these chiefs before the citizens."[30]

When Prando tried to promote monogamy among the Blackfeet, he concentrated first on tribal leaders. "If, as it ordinarily happens, subjects follow the example of their chief, I had reason to hope that all the Indians would soon abandon polygamy," he said ingenuously. And when instructing the tribe on Christian fundamentals, "I kept a constant watch on the movements of the chief, White Calf, to see if he would prove himself a fit candidate for baptism." In the performance of rituals, the spotlight also fell on the leader. Inviting the people to reenact the drama of Christ's Passion, Prando orchestrated a procession in which a large cross was solemnly conveyed to the summit of a little hill near the camp. "The part of our Lord I assigned to the chief, while I acted as Simon of Cyrene." Another time, he led a delegation of Crow chiefs from Montana to see the advanced Jesuit missions in Washington and to visit Spokane's Gonzaga College. The purpose was "to give them some idea of the work of our Fathers among the people of their color," an official recounted, "and so dispose them to accept our work and to help us among their people."[31]

FIGURE 12. Jesuit strategy encouraged chiefs and high-profile persons to stand as models for other members of the tribe. This photograph, probably taken at St. Francis Xavier Mission, Montana, in 1888, depicts Giuseppe Cataldo, seated, with his hand resting on the shoulder of an unidentified chief, possibly Busy Wolf, a Crow. Also pictured (from left to right) are Bishop J. B. Brondel and, standing, Jesuits Giuseppe Bandini and Pietro Paulo Prando. Courtesy Jesuit Oregon Province Archives, Gonzaga University, 147-2-01a

Despite their reliance on tribal leaders, Catholic missionaries, unlike Protestants, did not train native clergy. A Jesuit writing in 1897 ascribed this failure to two causes. In the early period, the Indians' so-called uncivilized condition prevented them from receiving the education necessary for ordination. In subsequent years, he claimed, the federal government's treatment of Native Americans as children and the stifling of their independence frustrated the emergence of individuals capable of assuming the priestly function.[32] The Jesuits did, however, train prominent women and men as catechists. The most famous of these was Black Elk, the Lakota Sioux mystic-turned-Catholic who assisted Jesuit missionaries in South Dakota, but there were many others. During the 1870s, John Wapato, an influential Chelan chief, assisted Grassi with baptisms and marriages. A cluster of twelve men and twelve women, members of Our Lady's Sodality, aided the priests at St. Mary's Mission (Omak) by teaching catechism, assisting at religious ceremonies, and caring for the sick and needy. When thirty Indian children received the sacrament of confirmation at Sacred Heart Mission, Chief Seltice and his wife Mary Julia stood beside them as sponsors.[33]

Among tribes without Christian headmen, other individuals known as "church chiefs" filled this role. At St. Ignatius Mission, these authorities carried the banner of the Sacred Heart during Good Friday processions. It was also customary, a Jesuit reported, "for the chief to stand near the rear of the church during services, not only to keep order but also to flip dark scowls at those leaving Mass" early.[34] When Cataldo launched his work among the Nez Percés in 1872, he first instructed twenty-five ancillaries whom he judged "best fitted" for baptism. "Then I asked them to assist in instructing the others . . . until I had baptized 100 in all." According one historian, this methodology provided "continuity of organization, leadership, and culture" among Catholic Indians "that was conspicuously absent among the Presbyterians."[35]

Fondness for music forged another bond between Native Americans and European missionaries. In Italian society the prominence of music, which had come to full flower in the eighteenth century, was frequently commented upon by outsiders. "Hardly has one crossed the Alps," a visitor observed, "before music appears quite spontaneously. The violin, the harp, and singing stop you in the streets. The further one advances into Italy, the closer to perfection the music. Even the service in village churches sounds much like a concert." Jesuits were gratified to learn that Indians shared their delight in song. "It is amazing how these natives love music," Mengarini wrote from the Flathead mission. "Both the young people and the small children have an admirable facility and quickness for learning whatever they are taught." Tunes were employed to entice a guardian spirit, who, Mengarini recorded, "would reveal his presence by singing with them." Like magic, music unstopped the ears of the most reluctant congregation, exemplified by several Nez Percé families who lived near St. Mary's, but never entered the church. "But when the music began, they often came to hear it, which provided a good opportunity for them to hear the instruction that is given during a sung mass."[36]

Having ascertained the centrality of singing in tribal life, priests translated Christian liturgical music into Salish. Mengarini wrote a funeral dirge by joining Christian concepts about death to a traditional Flathead lamentation. For evening prayer, he composed three songs in Salish, two based on scores of his own composition and a third lifted from a French melody. Popular Italian tunes were transposed into the native tongue. In 1875, for example, for a Christmas celebration at St. Peter's Mission, Filippo Rappagliosi translated an ancient holiday hymn, "Tu scendi dalle stelle o Re del cielo," into the Blackfeet idiom.[37] As early as 1845, Mengarini trained a small band of Indian boys, whose instruments included a clarinet, flute, two accordions, a tambourine, piccolo, cymbals, and a bass-drum. The ensemble performed a mass score that Mengarini had lugged with him from Italy. "We played to notes," he said, because "Indians have excellent eyes and ears." "They have learned (who would have believed it?) to sing the 'Gloria,' the 'Credo,' and everything else, and they sing it in plain chant," Rappagliosi rhapsodized. Over a century later, these "Bitterroot Valley songs" were still sung among the tribe.[38]

Music was not confined to worship services. Unlike Methodist missionaries, who declared in 1841 that singing "occupied only a secondary place in teaching" religion, in Jesuit catechetical instruction, melody resounded.[39] Adept at improvisation, Prando composed a tune in the language of the Crows to impart Christian lessons. "Setting together the words I knew, I made a hymn, and now the hymn is popular in two camps. They have a great desire to learn it by heart and to sing it according to the tune of *Iste Confessor*," a Gregorian chant. Describing his work among the Blackfeet, Prando said, "Their great love of song . . . aids me in teaching the prayers and truths of religion." In his campaign to uproot polygamy, the priest composed a chant. "They soon learned to sing it, especially the young squaws who were much pleased with the doctrine of one wife . . . When an Indian who had a wife came to see a squaw to get her for his second wife, the young squaw would sing for him the hymn about the Indian in hell with his three wives."[40]

Catholic evangelization placed great value on visual representation. Recognizing the didactic power of art, European Jesuits of earlier centuries had decorated hundreds of churches with paintings and sculpture in the Baroque style to quicken the faith of congregations. Images had also occupied center stage in the campaign to convert the peoples of Africa, Asia, and the Americas. Missionaries in the Pacific Northwest quickly discovered that one of the best methods for expounding Christian dogma and moral principles to illiterate peoples was through pictorial representation. As Joset explained, "the natives are very fond of images," which compensates "for our ignorance of the language, which one can come to know only after a good many years." Pictures "impress better in their minds the mysteries of our religion," Prando added, raising "their mind from the material that they see, to the above, that they do not see."[41]

Missionaries gave religious pictures to persons who made progress in learning. These charismatic images are "preserved with great care," De Smet declared, and they "are great stimulants, not only to the study of their catechism but also the practice of piety." On special occasions, as at a baptism ceremony at St. Mary's, priest and people artfully festooned floor and ceiling of the chapel with grass mats and garlands of greenery and flowers. "On a canopy was inscribed the holy name of Jesus. Among the ornaments they placed a picture of the Blessed Virgin over the tabernacle; and on the door of the tabernacle a representation of the heart of Jesus."[42]

Perhaps the most dramatic visual representations were the simple but effective paintings of Nicole Point. The French Jesuit's "arsenal of communication skills" enabled him, as one historian said, "to enter into some of the central meanings" of native culture. Convinced that the Flatheads "learned more quickly through their eyes than through their ears," wrote Point himself, "I made a great effort to speak to them through pictures." "This method of instruction had noticeable advantages. While the truths entered their souls through their eyes, the great virtues were infused into their hearts. The inspiration for these drawings came, for the most part, from the great religious ceremonies enacted before them and from the noble actions of their great men."[43]

An Italian priest who visited the Pacific Northwest saw art as a metaphor for the difference between Catholic and Protestant proselytization. The Catholic system was simpler and more realistically adapted to native intellectual capacities, he claimed. Protestants made "gross errors" by talking to Indians "as though they had been raised in secondary schools or in colleges, . . . and aspire to teach them to read the thrice-holy book from which they must receive their faith." Catholics, by contrast, were "content to teach them the truths of the faith that are purely and absolutely necessary."

The Indian's recollection of people and places is admirable; he never forgets a place or a person, once he has seen the former or met the latter. . . . From there springs his ability to retain spiritual ideas with the aid of material objects, and whence, also, the wisdom of the missionaries who would try to teach him by means of the images most apt to strike his imagination and to imprint the things thus represented on his memory . . . [44]

Reliance upon art took varied forms. To theatrically enhance catechism lessons imparted to children, teachers of religion relied on *fantoccini*, or puppets, that they had known during childhood in Europe. When electricity reached the reservations, the magic lantern joined the missionary repertoire. In 1895, on the patronal feast of Sacred Heart Mission, a Jesuit diarist recorded, members of the Coeur d'Alenes gathered in a schoolroom, "the men squatting on one side of the screen, the women on the other." Father Caruana effectively lectured on slides covering four topics: devotion to the Sacred Heart, the history of a gambler, the history of a drunkard, and then a pictorial review of the catechism. The performance "struck the Indians very much," the writer concluded, and the images were worth "several sermons."[45]

The Jesuits were fortunate in having several artists in their ranks. Antonio Ravalli, trained in the traditional arts of Europe, designed the imposing church at Sacred Heart Mission among the Coeur d'Alenes of Idaho. Today a national historic monument, this structure was modeled on the Baroque church of the Gesù in Rome, although it was constructed of crude timbers

FIGURE 13. The church at Sacred Heart Mission among the Coeur
d'Alene tribe. Designed by missionary Antonio Ravalli, the structure
symbolized the Jesuits' penchant for brokering different cultures. Built
western-style, of crude timbers and adobe, the church was modeled
on the Jesuits' baroque church of the Gesù in Rome. Once the center
of missionary activity over a broad area, it remains the oldest building
in Idaho. Courtesy Jesuit Oregon Province Archives, F. W. Gilbert,
167-1-01a

and adobe. Its columned portico, sunburst façade, and interior walls were covered with *scagliala*, plaster work designed to imitate veined marble. As one
scholar has suggested, the still-standing mission is "a perfect and fascinating
amalgam of Roman Jesuit architecture and mid-nineteenth-century, boom-
town American building." A versatile craftsman, Ravalli carved candlesticks,

wainscoting, moldings, statues, and a type of crucifix with movable arms that was used in reenactments of Christ's Passion on Good Friday.[46] When not peeling potatoes and washing dishes, Giuseppe Carignano, a Jesuit cook, decorated churches across the Northwest. His crowning achievement was a series of frescoes painted for Montana's St. Ignatius Mission church, which was designated a national monument in 1973. That *capolavoro* provided illustration for countless sermons to congregations, both Indian and white, throughout the nineteenth century.

Transnational Devotionalism

As in art, so too in religious ritual, the missionaries attempted to bridge the cultural gap between themselves and their converts. As the historian James Axtell has written, Catholic Christianity appealed to Native Americans as "a religion of the liturgy, of colorful and effective ceremony, based on daily habits of prayer and worship." Embracing the human emotions, it "resembled native religious observances in color, drama, and participation and appealed to the Indians' practical intelligence." When, for example, Mengarini sought to give the Flatheads "an idea of the ecclesiastical ceremonies that are used in the Catholic Church," he borrowed from vivid Roman archetypes. In order to promote the Forty Hours devotion, in which the Italian faithful honored the Eucharist, he fashioned a throne out of white muslin and two red handkerchiefs, "a rather decent monstrance" carved from "a piece of wood covered with gold leaf," and candles composed of buffalo fat. Thus prepared, "on Easter Sunday I was able to reproduce in miniature the spectacle presented in the Roman College during the Forty Hours devotion."[47] These Italian ceremonials elicited a lively response because they appealed to the native psyche, with its yearning for the supernatural and its delight in the pageantry of grand processions. Thus, Catholicism's rich symbolism and elaborate liturgical expressions mirrored many features of Native American piety. As one historian has surmised, "it must have been easy for Indians to see the cross, the saints, and the prayers of the Black Robe as at least similar to the charms and bundles, the spirits and prayers of their traditional religion."[48]

Cataldo let no opportunity pass to incorporate fire and flame into the liturgy, a practice that complemented the Indian aesthetic as well as his own. He had an "Italian appreciation of many candles in church," a colleague claimed, his behavior following the adage *ad ogni santo la sua torcia* ("to every saint his torch"). In his native Sicily, thousands of candles and lanterns transformed the normally dark cathedral into a radiant palace from the Thousand and One Nights on the feast of Saint Rosalia. Cataldo replicated these spectacles in modest wooden chapels throughout the Indian world. He ordered sacristans to " 'lit everything,' meaning *all* the candles" — almost the only slip he made in English, a contemporary observed — whenever large crowds assembled for services.[49]

This fusion and mixing of traditions served multiple purposes. Flamboyant ceremonials sought not only to attract and edify native worshipers, but also to remind them that they belonged to a community of believers stretching far beyond the limits of the local village. This centralizing dynamic in Italian devotionalism has been examined by historian Donald Weinstein, who distinguishes between the cult of saints in northern and southern Europe. The prototypical holy persons selected for veneration in Germany and the Low Counties, he argues, were political figures, great prelates and princes. The saints of the Mediterranean world, by contrast, were typically wonder-workers who were intimately engaged in the miraculous and the supernatural. Southern European hagiology, influenced by the papacy, also showed a preference for saints who both symbolized and furthered church unity.[50]

It was this transnational and centralized devotionalism that the Jesuits of Italy brought to native settlements of the Pacific Northwest. Through the use of shared symbols — processions, benediction, high mass, music, patron saints — the missionaries labored to integrate Native American congregations into a global supernatural community. Thus sermons and rituals frequently aimed at drawing parallels between the Indians' experience and the experience of Christians elsewhere. When, for example, Cataldo preached to tribes assembled at Sacred Heart Mission in 1895, he suggested that their painful loss of land due to federal allotment policy had spiritual antecedents. "This morning Fr. Cataldo delivered an eloquent sermon to the Indians," a companion recorded, "alluding to Ireland and St. Patrick, [and] how the land of this good people was taken away, and how it nevertheless always kept our Holy Faith."[51]

A series of festivities, celebrated with all the pomp and ceremony that a mission's modest circumstances allowed, followed seasonal rhythms. Native American communities entered into the Catholic liturgical cycle, beginning with the four weeks of Advent, which culminated with mass on Christmas Eve. At midnight, across the Northwest congregations assembled in the square before the church, where, as in Italy, bonfires lent drama to the event, casting "a truly fairy effect over the deep snow," in the words of an observer. Among the Nez Percés catechized by Cataldo, this ceremony was called "Allakki" (With fire). It, too, melded indigenous and European cultural elements.

The Indians gather around it in a broken circle, and form a fascinating scene, while the ruddy light of the bonfire plays on their bronze countenances and gay apparel. Some of the chief men, by turns, address the crowd eloquently on the feast commemorated and [on] the various significations of the bonfire. . . . The speeches being ended, all proceed to the church, where prayers, a sermon, and benediction of the Most Holy Sacrament follow.[52]

"The people is coming with candles." Thus a priest at Sacred Heart Mission described the Christmas Eve procession, a spectacle of reverence and wonder. The land was wrapped in winter darkness, and a gossamer of fluttering candles cast a glow across the snowy landscape, producing a "beautiful sight." In a line, the worshipers "two by two, left their camp singing, chiefs, soldiers, men and women towards the church." After a customary address by the head chief at the darkened door, the congregation entered singing "Adeste Fideles," advancing to the crib of the infant Jesus, where they deposited offerings of candles or coins and sang Indian hymns. At the high altar, "splendidly illuminated with over 200 lights," mass was celebrated with "the Indians singing from beginning to end." The pageant concluded with a firing of guns back in the Indian camp (as had been done during high points in the mass), which explained the feast's title, "Firing of Arms."[53]

The Christmas celebration at De Smet Mission continued for days, culminating with a ceremonial hand-shaking on New Year. After mass, a Jesuit recorded in 1898, "all the Indians went from the front of the church to the front door of the fathers' dwelling house to shake hands with the fathers, who were there waiting for that purpose, as prearranged with Chief Seltice." Forming "an interminable long line," the people passed by, "beginning with the chiefs, followed by the militia, then all the men followed by the women." Valedictories concluded, they "continued their way homeward through the big gate opposite our dwelling house."[54]

Spring brought a fresh round of holy days, the capstone of which was Easter, a celebration that coincided with the buffalo hunt. The stirring high point of the season was a dramatic reenactment of Christ's death, burial, and resurrection. Drawing on a devotion popular in southern Europe since the Middle Ages, this ceremony too drew on Indian and Italian traditions. The wooden corpus used in the enactment had been carved by Ravalli with removable arms, so that the crucified Jesus could be realistically laid out as if dead when borne in procession. At St. Ignatius Mission, the pageant began on Good Friday evening, when the people circled around bonfires in preparation for a grand outdoor procession. Inside the chapel, whose sanctuary had been transformed by green trees and scaffolding into a Mount Calvary, the body of the crucified Christ was removed from the cross and placed on a bier. Preceded by the instruments of crucifixion — nails and crown of thorns — the life-size figure was conveyed in solemn procession to the village cemetery for symbolic burial. Meanwhile, the keening congregation intoned a Flathead death chant adapted by Canestrelli. "Everyone mourned, as is the custom during these days," a priest recorded, with wailing and other expressions of sorrow.[55]

Other pious practices flowered during the spring. These included devotions to St. Joseph, one of the most popular saints in Italy. Venerated as the patriarchal protector and defender of Christians, a statue of San Giuseppe adorned the chapel of every Indian mission, college, and parish founded by Italians in the West. Joseph's name was affixed to the most improbable objects — from a silver mine in Colorado to a boat in Alaska. The saint's intercession guided even the weather. When a spring shower threatened to dampen the Indian school boys' picnic at St. Ignatius Mission, a grateful D'Aste recorded: "It rained some of the morning, but through St. Joseph's intercession, it stopped raining until they came back." Conversely, when a downpour rescued the mission's wheat crop from drought, the diarist jubilantly recorded: "Rain last night and today. Vivat St. Joseph!"[56]

The practice of dedicating the month of March to Joseph, inaugurated in Rome in 1810, was widely promoted by Jesuits. At Idaho's Sacred Heart Mission, on the nightly vigil before the feast on March 19, bonfires were lit and services held in the church before the illumined altar of the saint. The congregation heard speeches by their chiefs and a sermon by Cataldo, after which the priest distributed, first to Chief Seltice and then to the congregation, "March blossoms in honor of St. Joseph." These "blossoms," small pieces of paper inscribed with votive offerings, were deposited before the saint's statue, where they remained until the end of the month. On the saint's day proper, Native American Catholics celebrated the Sicilian practice known as St. Joseph's Table. According to custom, particular foods — notably oranges and lemons — were arranged in colorful display and then distributed to recipients. A ceremonial honoring the patriarch, Joseph Joset, on his namesake's day in 1891, illustrated the conflation of Italian and Native American customs. Staged in the school hall of Sacred Heart Mission before a large audience, the event began with an address by Chief Seltice, who then ritually "laid an orange on the table in front of the Father."

Chief Edward then followed in an address and an orange. Then all sang a hymn to St. Joseph, one of Father Giorda's compositions. The men then filed up and next the women each making an offering in turn. Most of the offerings consisted of oranges. One presented chewing gum; several gave eggs; one donated a little whistle; another gave a lead pencil; and a number laid down nickel dimes. When this solemn presentation had ended, Father Joset rose and made a speech in Indian.[57]

In May, communities honored the Virgin Mary. Although the practice of dedicating the month to Mary had a long history, its diffusion throughout Italy in the late eighteenth century began with the publication of a devotional book by the Jesuit theologian Alfonso Muzzarelli. Entitled *Il mese di Maggio* (The Month of May), this slender volume appeared in over 150 editions in the nineteenth century. Its aim was the sanctification of the life of the ordinary Christian through a series of ordinary actions. Each day during May, participants recited a sequence of prayers, hymns, and reflections and performed acts of virtue plucked from a series of *fioretti spirituali* ("spiritual blossoms"). These *fioretti*, like those honoring St. Joseph, committed the devotee to good deeds such as visiting the sick; performing acts of self-denial; setting aside part of a meal for a poor person; making fifteen minutes of mental prayer; and so forth. Inscribed on small bits of colored paper, the "blossoms" were later presented as a bouquet at a shrine to Mary, in whose honor the deeds had been done. Popular in Italy, the devotion was promoted in the United States by the Jesuit exiles — Salvatore Personè, who translated Muzzarelli's work for distribution in New Mexico, and Lorenzo Palladino — whose version, entitled *May Blossoms*, enjoyed wide use by Indian and white congregations in the Pacific Northwest.[58]

"We have begun, even here, the month of Mary," Rappagliosi wrote from St. Ignatius Mission, Montana, in 1875. "The method we observe is that proposed by Fr. Muzzarelli" and "our functions do not fall short of your Gesù, or the other churches of Rome," Giuseppe Caruana told friends in Italy. The Coeur d'Alenes gather in the church before "a beautiful painting of the Blessed Virgin, . . . an excellent copy of the Madonna in San Carlo in Corso," in Rome. "There is a distribution of acts of virtue to be practiced the next day, the ejaculations and flowerets, just as they are in Fr. Muzzarelli's book." The Roman custom of adorning an image of the Madonna with gifts quickly surfaced in Indian America. Offerings common in Italy ("gold and silver, precious stones and gems") were substituted in the Northwest with "trinkets of every kind." Accordingly, the Madonna of St. Ignatius Mission, Rappagliosi reported, wore "on her breast a beautiful necklace of shells, and many strings of glass beads of various colors with contrasting big wolf teeth, a bear's claw, and other niceties."[59]

One of the year's grandest celebrations was the feast of Corpus Christi, a June event honoring Christ in the eucharist. Universal in Europe since the fourteenth century, the holiday culminated with public veneration of the host in a promenade that twisted its way from church to village to open countryside. First introduced among the Flatheads, the spectacle appealed in part because it coincided with the annual summer rendezvous to harvest the roots of wild plants. For bands of Spokanes, Coeur d'Alenes, Colvilles, Kalispels, and tribes that lived separately much of the year, these lengthy rallies provided opportunity for games, trading, visiting relatives, and other communal festivities. When the U.S. government began to prohibit native ceremonials and pow-wows, Corpus Christi became even more attractive as a substitute ritual, further testimony to Indian adeptness at refashioning feasts to suit tribal needs.[60]

The celebration unfolded in early summer, when pink-petaled bitterroot and blue-blossomed camas painted the landscape. Two weeks prior to the

FIGURE 14. Corpus Christi procession by the Coeur d'Alene tribe at Sacred Heart Mission, Idaho, sometime after 1900. Such transnational devotions advanced the standardization of Catholic devotional life among worshipers throughout the West. On the hill stands a boarding school for native children. Courtesy Jesuit Oregon Province Archives, Gonzaga University, 146-3-01

event, caravans of 100, 200, or 300 people from "the four winds," as one Jesuit put it, streamed to the nearest mission and pitched their tents around the church. The grand climax at the Colville agency was a solemn display of the Blessed Sacrament. In preparation for the cavalcade, men of the Kalispel tribe "made a long alley, planting on both sides small pine trees from the church door down [across] the prairie, forming a semi-circle at the end to turn back." In 1877 over two thousand three hundred people participated in a half-mile queue, "walking two by two about three feet apart from each other singing hymns, reciting the beads." Men on horseback periodically fired their guns into the air in celebratory volleys as the parade advanced from one station to the next while the devout venerated the sacrament and preachers and chiefs exhorted the people. The march, which often took an hour to complete, meandered through an arbored pathway over a carpet of flowers scattered by children to several alfresco altars festooned with blossoms. For this reason, some tribes dubbed Corpus Christi "the Feast of the Flowers" or "Flower Days."[61]

At summer's end, missions celebrated the Rogation Days. An ancient Catholic rite involving prayers aimed at securing a good harvest, this celebration assumed greater significance after once-nomadic tribes became sedentary agriculturalists. "We walk in procession to the top of the hill above the church yard, singing the litanies," recorded a diarist at St. Francis Regis Mission in 1893. "We blessed all the land all around that God may be pleased to bless our crops, and the crops of all our neighbors." The Lord "was asked to bless the crops on which the little self-sustaining colony depended for its sustenance; his people on such days prayed to Him to shield from evil their beautiful valley."[62]

The Principle of Cultural Insertion

If ritual was central to the Catholic art of conversion, providing health care was an integral backdrop to preaching the Gospel. "In caring for the bodies of the poor Indians," Cataldo observed, one "also does good for their souls." Among the four hundred Flatheads with whom Mengarini lived, he wrote that not fifty could be found who did not suffer from some kind of chronic illness. "It is absolutely necessary that a missionary have some knowledge of medicine," Mengarini believed, because the natives would not abandon their recourse to traditional guardian spirits "if they are not convinced that the missionaries are much more practitioners of medicine than they." "Indians associate the priesthood with medicine," Point added. "He who is a specialist in medicine enjoys the attributes of the priest, the miracle worker, and the prophet."[63]

Mengarini, Ravalli, and Gazzoli, all of whom had studied homeopathic medicine in Italy, were summoned to treat illnesses. "One of the Fathers each morning visits the sick," De Smet wrote from St. Mary's, "to furnish them with medicines, and give them such assistance as their wants may require." Vaccinations supplied by the missionaries in the 1850s enabled the Kalispels to escape an epidemic that struck down tribes north of the Columbia River. Other Jesuits were trained in the field by Ravalli, a practitioner of medicine of all sorts, including surgery. In addition to studying folk medicine, priests became skilled in native herbalism.[64] Prando, for example, developed a liniment from Indian herbs that was used to treat syphilitic ulcers. Called *Isteumate*, a term derived from the sobriquet bestowed on the bespectacled Jesuit by the Crow ("Iron Eyes"), this popular medication enhanced Prando's reputation among the people.[65]

As epidemic diseases swept through tribes confined on reservations, the dual role of missionary and healer assumed even greater significance. "To be a missionary and at the same time a doctor (insofar as one is able) is something of great importance," said Prando, who carried both medical kit and breviary wherever he trudged. Although most agencies were served by health care professionals, cuts in federal appropriations sometimes left Indian communities without doctors. "We are quite in a fix at present," wrote Sanctus Filippi from the Colville reservation in 1889; "there is no more physician here, for the office has been suppressed last summer, and the Indians, naturally enough, flock to the Fathers for medicines." As medical care improved, the missionary's role as healer declined, although some natives still sought therapy. "Of course, we know that Indians as a rule are averse to taking medicines from agency doctors," a priest explained in 1890; "in spite of all that we can do, Indians will insist to be treated by the Fathers." "It is the Blackrobe who has changed our lives and who is our only true friend," the Blackfeet chief Painted Red claimed; "only he is concerned about our souls and our bodies."[66]

One reason why the tribes sought medical advice from Jesuits was that they were frequently in touch with them. "We live in the Indian lodges and are with them day and night," a priest reported from a Blackfeet camp in 1876. "Humanly speaking, this enterprise is a difficult undertaking [but] we have no other way to get close to them, except to travel among them with our tent, to live with them, and to follow them in their nomadic life." Wrapping the culture around them like a blanket, they tried to quilt themselves into the native lifestyle. Although this ad hoc strategy was imperfect, it left nothing to chance. For example, the Jesuits, unlike many frontier males, were clean-shaven. Whiskers provided welcome protection from winter cold, Rappagliosi explained, but we "do not wear beards because not only do the Indians not grow them, but they cannot. It's their practice to remove the beard, hair by hair, scarcely before it sprouts on the chin."[67]

In their effort to interweave their lives with the tribes', missionaries were always on the go, riding from one encampment to the next, in perpetual motion. From St. Regis Mission in Washington, three priests regularly visited fourteen outposts in a stretch of country running 110 miles along the Columbia River. A rancher in the Yakima Valley recalled seeing Jesuit Jean Raiberti making his rounds: "I often met him on the road, astride the old white horse which was his mount for so many years, repeating the rosary, oblivious of his surroundings."[68]

Living among the people required acceptance of the vagaries of Native American diet, housing, and sleeping. "Our food was no better than that of the Indian, if as good," Cataldo said of his first missionary posting; "indeed it was worse." A white settler described frequent encounters with the priest Giuseppe Caruana in both Coeur d'Alene and Okanagan country. He was "alone in the Indian camps, subsisting on Indian food." "Once at We-nat-sha when I offered him provisions, he refused on the ground that, in order to hold his influence with them, he must live as the Indians did." Another time, the rancher met Urbano Grassi, plodding on horseback "into the mountains, valleys and canyons, wherever Indians were camped. Like Father Caruana, he lived in their wigwams and ate their food."[69] Grassi's determination to merge with native culture was remarkable. When the missionary died in 1890, companions found in his room on the Umatilla reservation private notes that illuminated corners of a life unseen by even his closest companions. Written in imperfect English, the papers included a resolution "never to avoid the sufferings which insects that infest every Indian dwelling in abundance, would inflict on him."[70]

Jesuits claimed that living close to the bone had its compensations. Augustin Laure, one of Cataldo's French recruits, described his visit to the Yakama reservation in 1891. "On my last trip I spend the nights in the Indian tents, which were open on the top to let the smoke escape. It is good, after the telling of stories, to fall asleep to the noise of the wind; but towards nightfall the fires go out and one might as well be outside; besides, one could have the pleasure of counting the stars."[71]

As frontier conditions dissolved toward century's end, the practice of dwelling in the Indian camps faded. Circuit riders still hopscotched from one rural community to the next, but the free roaming life of both missionary and Indian melted away with the creation of reservations. As they shifted their apostolic emphasis to the running of reservation schools for native children, fewer and fewer Jesuits lived peppered about the countryside. But the principle of cultural insertion remained operative. In the 1890s, under the leadership of Giuseppe Cataldo, the Rocky Mountain Mission established immersion-type seminaries on reservations at Sacred Heart Mission, Idaho, and at St. Ignatius Mission, Montana. The rationale was that priests-in-training should rub elbows with native people from the inception of their careers. The best way to do this, they believed, was to pitch their tents in the heart of Indian country.

This willingness to adapt, within limits, to tribal customs, dress, and mentality benefited the Jesuits. "The rules of the Society allowed its men in the missions to merge themselves into their environment" in a variety of ways, one scholar affirmed, of which "adopting the native language was the most important." Prando, a master at conforming his routine to native etiquette, described a stratagem once used to placate a Blackfeet band whom he had offended by delaying his response to their invitation to visit. Knowing the great esteem they attached to the calumet, he purchased "the biggest pipe I could procure" and ten pounds of tobacco. "The stem was about three feet long, so that the smoker would require the assistance of someone to light it for him." The savvy priest correctly surmised that sharing the pipe with his hosts would erase resentments. "As soon as the Indians see me, they'll gather round me, and comment on my big pipe, and grow envious of the desire of getting a puff from it. As soon as I let them have their smoke, we'll all be friends again."[72]

Protestant missionaries usually did not employ the conversion strategies used by the priests. Ministers, charged with the responsibility of feeding and clothing their families and educating their children, could not afford to travel about the country. Jesuits, however, were acceptable to Native Americans because they were unencumbered by families or by individual property. Both Protestant and Catholic missionaries who worked among the Nez Percés proscribed polygamy and premarital sex; but, as scholars have pointed out, Catholics were less concerned about shamanism, "long hair, or attendance at aboriginal ceremonies, and stated publicly that aboriginal clothing was attractive."[73]

Frequent contact gave some missionaries extraordinary clout. When Pietro Bandini called upon bands of Kootenai on the Flathead reservation in 1885, he was sought out for his counsel on a variety of issues, including the tribe's negotiation over a right-of-way with the Northern Pacific Railroad. "I listened *pro tribunali coram populo* to everyone" (that is, in open court before all the people), he recounted, "adjusting questions of matrimony, clarifying certain doubts and giving them practical instructions on how to take care of themselves during the raging of the typhus." Individuals "reserved their major problems for a time when they could speak privately with the priest." In some cases, these exchanges produced relationships characterized by Jesuit paternalism and native codependency. More astute pastors were reluctant to offer opinions on nonreligious matters, conceding that occupation of the middle ground between cultures was precarious. When officials in Washington, D.C., sought Cataldo's intercession in negotiating a treaty with the Nez Percés in 1876, he refused. "I have promised to these Indians several times never to speak to them about making their reservation smaller," he said. "And I would lose a great deal of my authority, if I were to busy myself with them about such matters."[74]

If Jesuits reshaped Indian culture through years of intimate interchange, natives also molded the missionaries. A lifetime of day-to-day contact led some Europeans to prefer the Indian manner of living to their own, illustrating that cultural brokering was a two-way exchange. Of Gregorio Gazzoli, for instance, other Jesuits claimed that when absent from the Coeur d'Alenes he was "like a fish out of water." After Adrian Hoecken died in 1897, contemporaries said he was "to the end, an admirer of the Indians, even retaining in some degree, their manner of talking and their forms of expression." Cataldo's preference for natives was legendary. In 1907, when transferred from working with the Nez Percés in Idaho to a new assignment in California, the Sicilian wrote: "I shall never forget the Indians, . . . though bodily far from" their camps. "I hope, though, to die with the Indians." Caruana contrasted the "religious fervor" of the Indians to the "indifference of the white and half-breed Catholic population." "If I did not love the poor Indians with all my heart," he once confided to a friend, "I would long ago have asked superiors to send me somewhere else."[75]

The most effective Jesuits were those whose affection for people overrode

the cultural chasm that separated the races. Some individuals could not sur-
mount that divide. Lorenzo Palladino and Antonio Ravalli, poor linguists
and partial to whites, were considered prejudiced by fellow Jesuits. Palladino
"sometimes speaks favorably of Indians," Cataldo complained, but "he holds
strong opinions against them." Although a proficient architect and physician, Ravalli himself confessed that he did not understand tribal people. They
seemed *misteri ambulanti* ("walking mysteries"), incomprehensible beings
who from infancy worked "at hiding their feelings." Missionaries more
adaptive and skilled in native tongues knew this was not the case. "The
common belief that the Indian is stoical, stolid, or sullen is altogether erroneous," wrote the missionary Giovanni Boschi. "They are really a merry people, good natured, and jocular, usually ready to laugh at a joke with a simple mirth that reminds one of children." In Cataldo's eyes, the Coeur
d'Alenes were neither mysterious nor uncommunicative, but rather "very
sensitive and affectionate."[76]

What did they admire in tribal life? Boschi esteemed "fidelity to friends —
so intense that intimates "would literally give their lives for each other." The
respect that Indians showed "one another in their assemblies" and their self-
control impressed the priest, as did their custom of "adhering closely to the
truth in conversation." When a curious inquirer asked Cataldo if the Coeur
d'Alenes were as "cruel and heartless" as people alleged, the missionary
replied that "when angry, they are liable to commit cruel acts," but they are
easily appeased "if treated with kindness and taken by reason." "They are
less cruel than the Germans have been," he added tartly, "and less cruel than
the English are now in Egypt, India, [and] Ireland." In an era when many
Americans disdained aboriginal people as intellectual inferiors, Boschi
praised their intelligence. "The Indian has the mind of a child in the body
of an adult," he said, "and by this I mean that it is a mind in many respects
unused and absolutely without training as regards all matters which have to
do with civilized life."

This does not imply that the Indian is intellectually feeble; for when the young Indian
is separated from his tribe and is brought up in association with white people, and
so has an opportunity to have his mind trained to civilized modes of thinking and
to imbibe civilized ideas, he is found to be not less intelligent than the average white.
The difference in mind means merely that the Indian, like every other human being,
receives his knowledge and his mental training from his surroundings.[77]

Indian appraisals of missionaries are more difficult to uncover in the
absence of written testimony. To be sure, not every native felt affection for
the Black Robes, but some left positive assessments in interviews conducted in the early twentieth century. "All the people liked Father Damiani,"
a native woman at Holy Family Mission recalled. "He used to go down and

visit all the Indians at their homes. . . . [and] the Indians felt free to visit the priests and sisters at the Mission." "Cataldo is my friend, he is a good man," Chief Joseph of the Nez Percés stated, "all my people love him." Popular priests received emblematic Indian names, a sign that they had been accorded a degree of acceptance by the tribe.[78] Imoda became Akspinnin, "Cleft-Cheek"; Grassi was "Left-Handed Man"; and Rappagliosi's aquiline profile prompted the Blackfeet to name him Iskiskesi, "Eagle Nose." Natives of the Bitterroot Valley called blond-haired D'Aste "Chipapa," a word used to describe a sorrel horse. The lean and resilient Cataldo became "Dried Salmon" among the Kalispel and "Thrice Broken" among the Nez Percés, in admiring recognition of the courage with which he bore three bone fractures during his career.[79]

The Jesuits felt themselves regarded with affection. "The respect and love" which the people bear for the Black Robes "has no limits in the affectionate hearts of the good Indians," Caruana maintained. This was true "not only of these fervent Coeur d'Alenes, but of all the other Indians, even those who are not baptized yet." The priests felt "welcomed and sincerely esteemed" by non-Christian tribes, he said, "and they could go safely where other white people would jeopardize their property and even their lives, as in the time of war." Of popular Geronimo D'Aste, contemporaries said, "all know him and are full of veneration and love for him." Fellow Jesuits also observed the respect accorded the Alsace-Lorraine priest John Sifton, who toiled among the Arapaho of Wyoming. "Owing to the fact that he knows the Indian language perfectly and . . . can live like an Indian himself," a co-worker reported, "he has won the hearts of the Indians, young and old, to such an extent that he can do almost anything with them."[80]

Although they made many converts, the Jesuits were not universally successful; nor was their method of evangelization easily implemented. "I must say, with grief," Barceló wrote in 1881, "that the conversion of these Indians is difficult." The priests frequently contrasted the welcome they got from tribes on the western side of the Rocky Mountains with the chilly reception they received farther east. Contact had begun earlier on the western slope, in an era before white settlement and federal supervision had transformed tribal life, thus enabling the missionaries to wield stronger leverage. By 1900, Jesuits had baptized most of the occupants of the Flathead reservation — Flatheads, Pend d'Oreilles, and Kootenais. Although the degree of religious commitment varied among native people, as it did among whites, the missionaries believed some tribes were exemplary. They were, for instance, unstinting in their praise of the "practical Christianity" of the Coeur d'Alenes, as an official of the BCIM reported in 1907. And the federated tribes of the Colville reservation were, in the eyes of the priests, second only to the Coeur d'Alenes.[81]

The ability of Jesuits to make inroads among the tribes of the eastern slope was more problematic. Overextension by the Rocky Mountain Mission and a lack of adept personnel partly explained their struggle for acceptance by the Blackfeet, Gros Ventres, Assiniboins, and Crows. These tribes were "very slow and backward in giving ear to the instructions of the Fathers," a missionary conceded in 1897. While the response of young people was promising, "whether we shall ever be able to bring the grown people to the faith is not certain." Despite Prando's apparent effectiveness with the Blackfeet, his campaign to introduce Christianity remained, according to one analysis, "a complex mixture of resistance, accommodation, and assimilation rather than a simple conversion of Indians to white man's medicine."[82] In fact, the reshaping of culture was never a simple process; it was a highly intricate and inevitably composite undertaking, even when it seemed, on the surface, successful.

An array of factors — some the fault of the missionary, others beyond his control — frustrated evangelization. Shoddy federal administration of many reservations and the social disintegration that attended forced relocation raised formidable barriers. When Pedro Barcelò visited the Blackfeet in 1889, he found them receptive, but they were distracted by dwindling food supplies. After listening patiently to the priest's appeal, a chief declared "that I should not speak any longer on the matter, that they were starving, that the government should issue rations and provide them with farming implements." This "answer was somewhat rough," the missionary conceded, but it was "pretty reasonable in the present circumstances." "To speak to a starving people about the way to heaven without doing anything to relieve their pressing necessities is simply provoking." Jesuit Aloysius Van der Velden met similar objections when he approached the Cheyenne. The people "liked priests very much," he claimed, but the government's failure to supply rations hindered their responsiveness to his message. When a missionary enters their lodges, "their first word is 'Priest, give us something to eat. We are all very hungry. We cannot listen now; we are too hungry.'" "Really, these are good Indians," he concluded, but "a hungry belly has no ears."[83]

Government policies that redefined how Indians existed obliged the Jesuits to rethink the way they interacted with them. Geronimo D'Aste, who had begun his ministry among the Flatheads in 1869, believed that effectiveness was still possible three decades later, but "not like it was in earlier times." Confined to reservations and their lives reshaped by allotment, natives were isolated from the mission church by large tracts of land, he reported in 1902. Because the tribe no longer journeyed to the mission for solemn feast days, priests were obliged to go to them, constantly traveling about the reservation. The amount of good a missionary could accomplish in such circumstances, Damiani added, was "almost nil."[84]

The shifting conditions of tribal life prompted creative strategies. By 1880, when the tribes became fenced in on reservations and the governmental juggernaut of assimilation gained full steam, Jesuits inaugurated a different approach to evangelization: the education of Indian children. Thus it was that missionaries moved from a program that was largely European in concept and execution to one that was more American. They now became partners with the federal government in an ambitious program of native assimilation. The Jesuits took up schooling because they saw it as the most effective way of Christianizing Indians while simultaneously advancing their material welfare. As one missionary put it, Indian nature is such that parents "cannot deny their children anything they ask." Properly schooled children, therefore, could "do more for their parents through their good example and with a few good words than the missionary can accomplish with many sermons."[85] The building of schools did not mean that earlier forms of the art of conversion were jettisoned, however. They continued to characterize the Jesuit approach to pastoral work, but now they were also applied to the classroom.

7 *"Habits of Industry and Useful Toil"*

NATIVE AMERICAN EDUCATION

It was a strange business, this going to school.
— D'Arcy McNickle, 1929[1]

Few names are more identified with Catholic schooling in the United States than the Society of Jesus. As one historian has said, "the most persuasive European influence on American Catholic higher education was Jesuit."[2] A facet of the order's educational activity that has been overlooked, however, is its teaching of Native Americans. During the nineteenth and early twentieth centuries, Jesuits, like many other religious bodies, made a concerted effort not only to evangelize the native peoples of the Far West, but also to hasten their assimilation into American culture through education.

Jesuit classrooms dotted the western landscape. The Society operated schools in Kansas for boys and girls of the Osage and Potowatami tribes until their removal to Indian Territory in Oklahoma in the 1870s. In the Dakotas, Jesuits worked among various Sioux bands, establishing schools on the Rosebud and Pine Ridge reservations. Farther west, they founded an extensive educational network in the Rocky Mountain Mission that by 1896 reported an enrollment of a thousand Indians in fifteen schools. A hallmark of those institutions was their location in the heart of Indian country. In this they differed from most boarding schools, which were deliberately situated off-reservation to hasten Native American absorption of white culture. Another trademark of Jesuit institutions in their heyday was their reliance on federal funds, a corollary of church-state cooperation that characterized the administration of United States Indian affairs in the 1880s and 1890s. Governmental support enabled the schools to flourish, but it also had far-reaching significance for both church and state.[3]

Native American schooling emerged as a correlative to the order's missionary activity. Unlike Protestant missionaries, for whom church and school marched hand in hand, Catholics initially focused on religious conversion. "Our aim has been to make Christians of the Indians," said Joseph Joset, an early Jesuit missionary. Spiritual enlightenment took priority over all other forms of instruction. "When I arrived in the Mountains in 1844," he recalled, "there was never a question of teaching school — nothing but catechism, catechism endlessly." Since reading and writing were not mandatory for church membership, the priests concentrated instruction on Christian prayer and the basic tenets of Catholic theology. To this end, Indians who assisted missionaries as catechists learned European languages. "The Blackrobe Joset had taught me to read and to write," recorded Chief Michael of the Kettles, adding "he has also taught me French."[4]

Although Jesuits were less inclined than Protestants to fuse the goals of civilization and Christianity, they did endeavor, as spokesman Lorenzo Palladino put it, to promote "habits of industry and useful toil" among native peoples. Believing that economic stability and subsistence were the foundation of a truly human existence, they gave instruction in the trades — carpentry, animal husbandry, and farming. The aim was to guarantee their converts a more reliable food supply than was provided by nomadic hunting. Conversion was achieved by preaching the Gospel, a missionary stated, but also by "the preaching of *example*," which "we did from the start." "Our little garden and every year increasing farm was an object lesson to them."[5]

Many priests also inaugurated small boarding schools for boys who sought to acquire useful skills. "From the beginning of this mission," reported the Blackfeet missionary Camillo Imoda, we "have been keeping Indian children in our house boarding, clothing, and teaching them at our own expense." The same occurred at other outposts. "Our students do a little bit of everything," wrote Giuseppe Giorda of St. Ignatius, "wash dishes in the kitchen, prepare the refectory, split and carry wood, clean the rooms, etc. They do carpentry work and like it; they work in the fields when the seasons allows, and some are learning to drive the oxen," an especially favored exercise.[6] Joset said that the early training program for the Coeur d'Alenes shunned academic schooling. "It was thought more advisable to train them to habits of industry, to love of labor," he explained. Therefore, a farm was started where everyone could be employed. A small number of boys from eight to twelve were boarded, and were employed in all the works of farming and building. All were assiduously taught the principles of Christian religion.[7] "Experience proved the plan to be correct," Joset concluded. When the boys grew up and left school, "they started small farms, and, of course, received encouragement; others, witnessing how they had always plenty of food, imitated them. . . . Now all are farming more or less according to their means. By selling grain, they are able to purchase their necessaries."[8]

Missionaries imparted the ABCs, but on an informal and irregular basis. Their school at the Blackfeet agency in Montana was typical. It has "but one teacher and about a dozen pupils, mostly children of employees," a priest recounted, "because the Indians are nearly always away hunting. And it is only when they come to get their annuities that the teacher is able to muster a larger number for a few days." Lack of resources prevented anything more ambitious. Writing from the Nez Percé agency in Idaho in 1874, Giuseppe Cataldo said: "I have now more than fifty pupils in my Sunday school, of whom about 20 receive some literary instruction from me whenever I have leisure to do so, namely, whenever I am here." He was unable to open "a school properly speaking for want of means."[9]

The first step toward more organized instruction was prompted by a request from the Flathead reservation in Montana in 1863. The U.S. government had agreed by treaty to provide teachers, a blacksmith, a carpenter, and other helpers to the confederated Flatheads, Pend d'Oreilles, and Kootenais. Responsibility for the project was offered to the Jesuits of nearby St. Ignatius Mission. The invitation was a sufficiently significant break with past practice that the superior of the Rocky Mountain Mission, Giuseppe Giorda, requested clearance from Rome. "I would have no difficulty . . . if a few of the fathers busy themselves teaching school to youngsters," Superior General Pieter Beckx replied, as long as instruction is adapted to their "condition and to the place." Revealing how little European stewards understood missionary work, he added that teaching might be "a very useful occupation" for priests at times when they "have nothing else to do."[10]

Consequently, in 1864, Jesuits and Sisters of Charity of Providence started a day school for boys and girls, which broadened the following year into a boarding school. Other programs combining practical training and elemental instruction followed elsewhere. A school for Blackfeet children opened at St. Peter's Mission, Montana in 1874. Four years later, the Jesuits launched a boys' school at Idaho's Sacred Heart Mission and at St. Francis Regis Mission in Washington, where Sisters of Providence were already running a facility for girls. By 1879, the Rocky Mountain Mission operated thirteen schools in the Pacific Northwest.

What prompted the shift from an almost exclusive focus on catechetical and sacramental ministry to formal teaching? In part, it reflected a maturing conviction that the tribes' fate rested with the young. "It is hard to convert the old Indians," Prando reported from Crow territory in 1890, because they are always hankering "back to the olden times." Children, by contrast, were more open to white culture and religion. Another impetus was the rapid inundation of Indian country by white farmers and miners. According to Joset, the newcomers — "Protestant and mostly adorers of the god of the dollar and in general full of hatred for the poor Indians" — forced reversals in native life that made cultural assimilation inevitable. The gradual advance of the railroad across the Pacific Northwest brought still more outsiders. Like other reform-minded white persons of the era, most missionaries believed it was impossible for the tribes to remaining aloof from the alien culture that now surrounded them on all sides. Thus they prescribed industrial schools as an antidote to annihilation. The goal of these institutions, said the Jesuit writer Palladino, was "to enable the Indian to make a living and become self-supporting."[11] Prando doubted the Blackfeet could survive without mastering the trades.

The Blackfeet are sunk in want and misery, and, in my opinion, they will have trouble in getting through this winter without dying of hunger. Furthermore, I am persuaded, that the mission among them will not succeed, if we confine ourselves solely to spiritual ministrations. These poor people need beyond all to be trained and encouraged to agricultural labors: they themselves now admit the necessity of this, and are anxious to receive instruction.[12]

Some tribal leaders, persuaded that education was pivotal to their children's future, requested teachers. "The Indians begin to be aware of the benefit of schools," Giuseppe Cataldo reported in 1878, "and are very anxious to have their children instructed," especially the Kalispels and Pend d'Oreilles. According to Joset, the Coeur d'Alenes, too, "hoped that having yielded to the Whites a larger tract of very good land, they would get schools in return." For this reason, Chief Seltice wrote to President Grant in 1873 asking for Jesuit instructors. "Our good morals come from our Christian teaching," he said, "and therefore, we wish to stick to that teaching and have our children educated according to it. First of all, we want schools and Catholic schools for boys and girls separate [sic]."[13] Painted Red, a Blackfeet chief friendly with the Jesuits, speaking to a tribal gathering at St. Ignatius Mission in 1884, elaborated on the rationale: "The Blackrobe [Jesuit] comes and shouts out to us: 'My sons, cultivate the land, put up fences, learn the white man's language, teach your children how to read and write so that they can face the white man and be able to keep their lands.' I have seen that this is true, that this is the only way to save our land."[14]

The rush to the school house revealed a crucial transition in federal Indian policy. American reformers, arguing that the rapid disappearance of tribal lands meant that Native Americans could no longer follow their nomadic way of life, began to champion a fresh approach that would prepare them for coexistence with whites. Thus it was that the government became dedicated to the principle of assimilation through education. Who best to run the schools? Beginning in 1869 during the Grant administration, the government started making contracts with religious denominations, first Quakers and then other churches, not only to maintain schools for natives and to teach them farming and trades, but also to administer reservations themselves. Thus was launched the so-called Peace Policy, "the most extensive and prolonged attempt in United States history," according to one scholar, "at cooperation between the churches and the federal government."[15]

Despite the Catholic Church's long engagement in Indian affairs, the Peace Policy began as a Protestant program. Excluded from membership on the Board of Indian Commissioners, Catholics were also barred from ministering to Native Americans on many reservations where they had been active for decades. Expecting that their previous ministry guaranteed them access to thirty-eight agencies, they instead received only seven from the all-Protestant board. Methodists, who had done little missionary work heretofore, got fourteen, Quakers ten, Presbyterians nine, with the remainder going to other Protestant groups. Although the Jesuits were eventually given authority at the Flathead reservation, other tribes with many Catholic members — the Nez Percé, Yakima, and Blackfeet — fell under the Protestant mantle. With the stroke of a pen, some eighty thousand Catholic Native Americans in the Northwest were assigned to the religious care of new denominations. Catholics received another setback in 1875, when the government prohibited missionary activity on agencies consigned to other churches. Therefore, when the Jesuit Pietro Paulo Prando visited the reservation of the Blackfeet, which had been given to Methodists, he was summarily ejected.[16]

In an era of fierce sectarian rivalry, the exclusion of Catholics from participation in the Peace Policy had far-reaching implications. Because Protestants now controlled most Indian reservations, it was they who received the bulk of the federal monies appropriated for educating tribal children in the so-called contract schools. The Protestant bias of the Peace Policy, however, spurred Catholics into action. Denied seats on the Board of Indian Commissioners and turned away from Indian agencies with which they had long been affiliated, Catholic leaders began to aggressively promote their own interests.

A key step in that reorganization was the founding in 1879 of the Bureau of Catholic Indian Missions (BCIM) in Washington, D.C. Created to centralize the church's missionary work and to lobby on its behalf with the national government, the bureau launched a whirlwind of activity. It raised money from private sources in support of Indian education, its chief benefactors being Katharine Drexel and her two sisters, Elizabeth and Louise, daughters of the wealthy Philadelphia financier Francis A. Drexel. In 1891, Katharine founded a religious congregation, the Sisters of the Blessed Sacrament for Indians and Colored People, which further advanced the cause.

The heiress-turned-sister dispersed millions of dollars to cash-strapped Indian schools across western America, including those run by the Jesuits' Rocky Mountain Mission. Drexel dollars paid for brick school houses, chapels, dormitories, livestock, teachers' salaries, and transportation to bring volunteers to the missions. From a convent in Pennsylvania, the shrewd businesswoman purchased land, supervised building plans, and negotiated insurance rates with missionaries who lobbied for her support. The converse of the stereotypical nun as submissive subordinate, she was a hard bargainer, once informing Giuseppe Cataldo that she would donate $15,000 to his construction project only "provided that certain agreements were fulfilled." And when Montana's Pietro Bandini temporarily diverted $3,056 that had been stipulated for a new school house to pay pressing bills, Mother Katharine made clear her displeasure, writing in large script across his letter of apology — "This is not fair."[17]

Because Drexel's largesse alone could not cover the cost of Indian education, the BCIM fought for federal funding for the schools. Its greatest achievement was in persuading Congress and the Indian Office to let Catholics participate in the contract school system, whereby it annually issued per capita allotments for training native children. As a result, Catholic missionaries, who had been more or less reluctant bystanders during earlier years, emerged in the 1880s as major participants in the program. Federal aid to boarding schools assisted by the BCIM grew from $54,000 in 1883 to $394,533 six years later. By 1886, there were fifty institutions for Native Americans in the United States supported jointly by the government and by religious societies. Thirty-eight of them, with 2,068 pupils, were under Catholic control and twelve, with 500 enrollees, were under Protestant. Alarmed at "Roman aggressiveness" in procuring national assistance for their schools, Protestant leaders warned of the church's "growing power with the government in Washington."[18]

The contract school system opened a wide world of possibility for the Rocky Mountain Mission. Emboldened by the prospect of outside support, Giuseppe Cataldo, then superior, envisioned schools in every mission operated by Jesuits in the Pacific Northwest. Once obliged to turn away applicants for lack of space, the schools now experienced unprecedented enrollments. The influx of federal funds helped inaugurate an era of autumnal achievement in the Rocky Mountain Mission. "Missions extended from the Yakimas, Umatillas, and Nez Percés over to the Cheyenne, Assiniboines, and Crows," one scholar has written. "Schools and churches became large modern buildings." By 1895, the Rocky Mountain Mission operated eighteen federally subsidized schools for 1,318 Native Americans. Over a third of all the 3,613 native children enrolled in Catholic mission schools in the United States attended Jesuit establishments in the Pacific Northwest. While public funding was not the sole cause of that expansion, it contributed mightily to the enlargement of the Catholic educational network.[19]

The transformative power of federal dollars was exemplified by the mushroom growth of St. Ignatius Mission. Described in 1874 by a government inspector as "an extensive establishment [with] a large church, large school house, mills, residences, barns, gardens," the mission had three to four hundred acres under cultivation, "with large herds of horses and cattle and farming implements of all kinds." The number of juveniles enrolled in its schools remained trifling, however. Although it boasted a boarding institution for girls, run by the Sisters of Charity of Providence, and a small day school, the mission was able to school only five or six boys because it lacked a dormitory. Two years later, St. Ignatius received its first federal contract. Congress allotted $108 a year for forty pupils, an appropriation that was ratcheted up to seventy-five scholars in 1884, and later to one hundred and fifty.[20]

A mightier windfall arrived in 1885, when Congress voted an appropriation of $2,000 "to found and to organize at St. Ignatius a first class industrial and mechanical boarding school." According to BCIM director John Mullan, the act was momentous because it meant St. Ignatius would "not only rival Carlisle" but would convince Congress that this type of institution could be successful right in the heart of the Indian country. "We want St. Ignatius in the future to be a model mechanical and industrial boarding school to which Congress and the U.S. Indian Department may be able to point as a type and a pattern to be followed by all other Indian schools in the states and territories." If St. Ignatius succeeded, Mullan predicted, we "can point Congress to it next year as a visible voucher to aid our efforts at doing the same thing at Coeur d'Alene." Students would be taught to work in leather, wood, and iron "in workshops to be specially constructed and . . . fully supplied with all the necessary tools, materials, supplies to such ends, and with a first class mechanic in charge." Eager to implement the long-dreamed-of project, the Jesuit superior Lorenzo Palladino was ecstatic: "What was an airy nothing is now being shaped into objective reality."[21]

The trial run did not disappoint. By 1890, Congress had increased the St. Ignatius contract to $150 per year, for three hundred boys and girls. The appeal of the Indian Office to "save the papoose" was being carried out at St. Ignatius Mission in exemplary fashion, the *Sacred Heart Messenger* glowingly reported. The nation's "Indian problem" was fast nearing solution. In addition to nearly two hundred and fifty older boarders, the mission housed fifty-four smaller children, mostly orphans, in a kindergarten run by the Ursuline nuns. "Away from the wigwam and from Indian customs," the journal stated, these children would grow up as "real and true, little Americans."[22]

The Jesuits agreed with the Indian Office that boarding institutions were preferable to day schools. "It is the experience of the department," Secretary of the Interior Carl Schurz told Congress in 1879, "that mere day schools, however well conducted, do not withdraw the children sufficiently from the influence, habits, and traditions of their home life, and produce for this reason but a . . . limited effect." The Jesuit Giuseppe Cataldo was equally disdainful of day schools, dismissing them as "mere humbug." They were "of little use for Indian children as it is difficult to get them to attend," Palladino

FIGURE 15. With the Rocky Mountains as backdrop, students and teachers gather in 1878 for a formal photograph at St. Ignatius Mission, Montana, which had recently been awarded its first federal contract for educating Indian children. One of the most extensive Jesuit operations in the Northwest, the establishment included boarding schools for boys and girls, carpenter shops, barns, cow sheds, lumber and grist mills, and residences for priests and sisters. Courtesy Jesuit Oregon Province Archives, Gonzaga University, 114-4-08c

agreed, "and those that are prevailed upon to attend, generally attend but very irregularly." Among tribes still dedicated to the pursuit of game, "most of the day scholars are obliged to go with their parents on the semi-annual buffalo hunt, and consequently much time is lost" to study. For nomadic youngsters, "even mere attendance is practically impossible," Palladino concluded. "How can the Indian go to school and live, or live and go to school, as long as his daily living depends upon that which he may catch day by day?"[23]

Conversely, residential schools offered advantages to missionaries intent on transforming native culture. According to the Jesuit Leopold Van Gorp, boarders who had been uprooted from their home environment and were "constantly under the eye of the teacher" assimilated more swiftly. "These children are severed away from their lodges and brought to school," added Prando, "where they will lose the tracts of Indian mythology and foolish traditions that the old women are telling to their children during the cold nights of winter, and in the mountain breeze in summer, filling up their brains with wild imaginations and stories. So the very fact of having the children out of their lodges is a great step towards civilization and religion." Palladino agreed that the boarding school was "in the fullest possible way, the substitute for the home and the parent."[24]

Although Jesuits shared the government's belief in the superiority of residential programs, they disagreed with policymakers about where to put them. Ever since Richard Henry Pratt had founded the Carlisle Indian School in Pennsylvania in 1879, the Indian Office had favored moving young people to schools as "remote from reservations" as possible. Only in that way could they escape the negative impact of tribal life. Once relocated, students would be "free from the great pull-down of the camp," wrote Commissioner Morgan, and "able to mingle with the civilized people that surround them." For this reason, Carlisle shone as an ideal for the over two dozen industrial boarding schools distributed across the United States. It was designed, in the words of one historian, "to transform the Indians by placing them in direct contact with American society," in places where they "could be shorn of their cultural heritage." By the turn of the century, nearly 18,000 of the 21,568 Native Americans attending school were in residential institutions. And fully a third of the boarders lived in off-reservation locales.[25]

Most native people, however, abominated removal. "There exists a widespread aversion among the Indians in the West, against Carlisle and sending their children there," a priest reported." "During my short stay at St. Paul's Mission," Cataldo wrote in 1890, "three large boys came from the woods at the Little Rockies to the Mission, saying that they had hid themselves in the woods for a few days to avoid to be sent by force to the Carlisle school."[26] Jesuits instead advocated educating children in Indian country in places close enough to gratify parents yet sufficiently detached to provide a break from the home environment.

"To wrest the children from the parents and carry them thousands of miles away to train them . . . is a process as unnatural as it is cruel," Lorenzo Palladino maintained. It will inevitably "alienate them from their own blood and country." By contrast, schools planted on reservations imposed "no unbearable separation" of child from parent. Families "can see their children daily, at church, in the class-room, at play, at work, in the shop, or in the field." Boarding institutions near home held other advantages for teachers. Besides being cheaper to run, the schools were better able to adapt training in farming and stock-raising to the peculiarities of the local environment. Reservation schools brought "civilization and the uncivilized face to face," argued Leopold Van Gorp, by providing "an example and incentive, not to the children only but to the whole tribe." St. Ignatius Mission "affords a clear proof of this."

Here the grown-up Indians, men and women, can be seen striving to follow as best they can the examples of industrious civilized life daily set before them. . . . Their dairies, their meadows, their fields, their kitchen gardens, their little strawberry patches and orchards, are all so many and unquestionable proofs of what we state, since many of the old people were never given any direct instruction in all such matters. Their practical knowledge about many of these points was acquired by them simply from what they saw others do.[27]

Indians held more complex views, and they were never of one mind. Some parents, eager that their children learn skills required for survival in a rapidly changing world, petitioned the missionaries to open institutions. Others, although they liked the priests, were torn. "When there is question of giving their children to school," Prando said, "they cannot resolve themselves to part from them." Far more dismissed the idea outright. "One of the great difficulties to be contended with in the boys' school," wrote an agent on the Flathead reservation, "is the fact that the parents are not willing to leave their sons long enough under instruction to give them a proper training." Because of their usefulness "in herding stock or working about home, the boys are taken from school . . . when they attain a certain age."[28] A priest confirmed, "to tear the child away from his parent is like inflicting a deep wound in the Indian's heart." Nor were youngsters themselves yearning to enroll. "It is no little sacrifice for the Indian child to be deprived for an entire year of his pony and saddle." As a reservation official in Montana attested, "This love for a roaming, lazy life, makes it at all times hard to get a boy or girl of ordinary school age to resign himself or herself to the confinement of a boarding school."[29]

Education of female children elicited even more resistance. "We want our boys educated," declared Arlee, chief of the Flatheads in 1876, "but not our girls." Missionaries insisted on training both genders, however, arguing that the shared experience of boarding school life would enable them to find partners of similar background when they married. "You must educate both sexes in order that the one shall support the other," Palladino said, so that "they may go out into battle against barbarism hand in hand."[30]

But strict separation by gender was enforced in school. A French Christian Brother who taught boys at a Jesuit institution recorded amazement at the extreme steps taken by his Ursuline co-workers to circumvent males. The nuns cooked meals for the boys, but laid the food out on tables before the pupils entered the dining room to avoid contact with them. "Once I took my boys on a walk up the canyon, unaware that the nuns had the girls there," another brother recalled. "Our coming was not expected and it created quite a panic among the nuns supervising. Sisters and girls turned around, faced to the cliff, while we filed along." He ascribed this odd behavior to the Ursulines' semi-cloistered lifestyle and contrasted it with the less "standoffish" approach of Franciscan sisters on the Umatilla reservation.[31]

Accustomed to the casual fraternization of camp life, students, too, were puzzled by segregation. "The girls and boys couldn't play together," some Blackfeet recalled, and "you were not allowed to look at the boys." "When you went to church you were separated, the boys on one side, the girls on the other side. You could not mingle with each other or sit together." Dissociation also offended U.S. Indian Commissioner Thomas J. Morgan, who in 1892 warned that the separation of genders in "these monastic schools" was "a serious defect." Despite pressure from the Indian Office to integrate the sexes, Catholics held their ground. The classrooms of St. Labre Mission school in Montana were not merged until 1922, an unwelcome reform in the eyes of an Ursuline teacher, who claimed desegregation placed the Cheyenne girls at a disadvantage. "After the boys joined them in the classroom, they would not recite aloud even once during the nine months I taught them."[32]

The Abiding Quest for Teachers

Industrial boarding schools required a heavy investment in personnel. Although priests taught some academic subjects, the number of them engaged in classroom work at a given mission was never large. Instead, they devoted the bulk of their time to administration and to sacramental ministry, which necessitated frequent absences from the school. Those who exercised the most consistent influence over male scholars were Jesuit brothers. "They helped by their daily example, to illustrate the principle that men should do manual labor, and not leave it all to women to do," a priest recounted. "The men would marvel as they watched the brothers cooking and washing, as well as plowing, hoeing, building barns, etc. Their toil, in effect, was a public service."[33]

Often ignored by historians, these non-ordained religious played vital, if unpublicized, roles in the day-to-day operation of Indian schools. Since the majority of the brothers came from Italy, Ireland, and the United States, they were as ethnically diverse as the priests. And they entered the order for many of the same reasons — a desire to "do God's work," a sense of adventure, and a quest for a more meaningful life. But they often took up careers in religion at an older age. Moreover, the brothers frequently had less education than did the seminarians but more work experience. For example, John Dunningham, a forty-eight-year-old Irishman, had been a wealthy Montana gold miner and rancher before he commenced his new life as Jesuit cook and chicken farmer. Some men, like the Italian Michele Campopiano, who spoke French and Kalispel, were fluent in several useful tongues, whereas Brother Benevento Priotto garbled Italian, Indian, and English in the same sentence.[34]

These brothers — artisans, bakers, carpenters, mechanics, tailors, farmers, and tradesmen before entering religious life — were well suited to the needs of the industrial schools. So essential was their contribution to successful operation that superiors lamented they never had enough. "A good brother . . . would be the resurrection of our mission," sighed the superior of St. Mary's Mission, Washington. "Much more could be done here if we had one." As BCIM inspector, John Mullan, reported,

[They] teach the boys the details and mysteries of steam machinery, and instruct them how to plow the ground, how to plant the seed, and how to reap their own harvest; how to repair their own harness and wagons, and how to clean and to harness their own teams and repair their own wagons and farming utensils and tools, and how to use the same, and how to feed their own stock and how to prepare food for the same.[35]

Musicians, too, were highly prized. "I would like to attract the attention of all the Crows and their children to our school," said a Montana missionary, and the way to do it was to make music. At St. Paul's Mission, a German brother, Nicholas Fox, tripled as gardener, postman, and bandmaster. "He is not a Bach, nor a Schumann, Wagner, [or] Beethoven," a partner stated, "but he has plenty of music in his system." "I do not see how we could have carried on along that line without him." When not conducting the band or plowing fields, brothers joined in outdoor sports thereby establishing a rapport with the boys not attained by priests.[36]

Lacking Jesuit personnel, the missionaries sought outside help. Brothers of Christian Instruction (also known as the De Lamennais Brothers), who had been deported from France by an anti-clerical government, began teaching in Jesuit schools in 1905. Lay instructors further augmented the staff. The one hundred and forty apprentices enrolled at St. Xavier's Mission in Montana were taught by three priests, eight sisters, and seven lay instructors. "We have now a carpenter, a shoemaker, a blacksmith, a painter, three farmers, all hired hands," Cataldo reported in from Sacred Heart Mission in 1889. At St. Paul's Mission, "all the discipline and teaching has to be left in the hands of lay persons," said Superior Damiani.[37]

The schools were hard pressed, however, to secure laity willing to work for low wages on remote reservations. "I have been looking for a lay teacher for our Indian boys for three months and could find none," a Montana missionary wrote to the BCIM in Washington, D.C. "Please find a good Catholic lay teacher and send him immediately."[38] Terms of employment, encapsulated in a job description for St. Paul's Mission, were such as to discourage all but the most idealistic applicant. "He should be a gentleman, a good practical Catholic, able to keep boys in order and teach them the elementary school branches. . . . Out of school time he has to be day and night with the boys, keeping them in order and working with them [doing] ordinary work or playing with them. . . . He should not be married [and] should have good health."[39]

It is not surprising that some hires fell short of the mark. The superior of St. Ignatius Mission was dismayed at a new teacher, who appeared sight unseen to teach music. "He is an old man of 72," exclaimed the distraught priest. He "cannot play piano because cripple, clarinet because he has no teeth."[40] Other instructors gave satisfaction, but moved on when new jobs were offered. One of these was Louis Riel, leader of the *métis*, people of mixed Indian and French-Canadian ancestry in western Canada. After two years' teaching at St. Peter's Mission, Riel returned in 1885 to Saskatchewan, where he guided a rebellion that resulted in his execution for treason.

Women religious who ran orphanages, kindergartens, and schools for girls were a powerful asset. By 1890, the number of Jesuits involved in educational and missionary work in the Rocky Mountain Mission totaled only thirty-eight men: eighteen priests, twelve brothers, and eight scholastics. The number of women assisting them — sixty Ursuline nuns and fourteen Sisters of Providence — far outran both the brothers and priests.[41] Their presence testified to the growing reliance of the Catholic Church on congregations of women not only to sustain Indian missions, but also to staff the nation's network of parochial schools.

If a residential school is to enjoy "any good repute among Indians," Giuseppe Giorda maintained, it had to be run by religious women. Camillo Imoda made the same assertion, when he laid plans to expand operations at St. Peter's Mission. "To make it a success, it should be a boarding school directed by four sisters." Although no effort was spared in recruiting them, these atypical westerners coped with challenges of every sort-living in primitive housing; nursing the sick; performing domestic chores for the students and Jesuits; coping with the isolation of frontier living; and trying to maintain their financial independence. "We are beginning the year '93 without a cent of money in the treasury," an Ursuline nun reported from Montana. Despite "the monotony of our quiet lives," said another sister in Idaho, "the difficulties we meet are hard to imagine."[42]

In 1864, Sisters of Charity of Providence, a cloistered community from Montreal, Canada, opened a day school for girls at St. Ignatius Mission, which rapidly evolved into a residential institution. A similar establishment thrived at St. Regis Mission, where the sisters preceded the Jesuits by five years. Still another flourished at Sacred Heart Mission, Idaho, where a high school and commercial course for girls were sustained by a dairy and vegetable garden. So great was his need for teachers that the Jesuit Stephen de Rougé founded a community, the Lady Missionaries of St. Mary's Mission, to staff a school on Washington's Colville reservation. In 1884, six Ursuline nuns from Ohio emigrated to Montana to open a school at St. Labre's Mission on the Cheyenne reservation. Led by Mother Mary Amadeus Dunne, these women, popularly known in the Northwest as Lady Black Robes, soon had a thousand children under their care in schools among the Crows, Gros Ventres, Assiniboines, Blackfeet, and the confederated tribes on the Flathead reservation.

The relationship between the women and their Jesuit partners was a complicated one. On the one hand, the dictates of religious decorum stifled fraternization. As Giuseppe Giorda, superior of the Rocky Mountain Mission, observed, "proximity and familiarity between monks and nuns has never looked good" (*"non ha mai portato buon odore"*). And yet their joint labor threw them into daily contact, the consequence of which was both high mutual regard and conflict. "The self-sacrifice of these good sisters" was most impressive, an admiring priest said of the Ursuline nuns at St. Ignatius Mission. "A dozen of them wash, feed, clothe (and make the clothes), teach, do everything for 125 helpless youngsters, besides washing and mending for the 90 boys and the community of the mission school." For their part, Ursulines lavished praise upon their Jesuit confrères. Regarding the friendly and benevolent priest Pedro Barcelò, a nun at St. Labre's Mission in Montana stated, "He was grandly kind to us, and did all in his power to assist us." He "worked in the garden, helped at the mowing of the day, the digging of the cellar, the well, [and] chopped the wood, etc., etc. and then, what spiritual help!"[43]

Sometimes, however, relations between the sexes took on the characteristics of a family feud. Overworked women religious felt put upon by the priests. "Our novitiate table is piled up with work that must be finished before Christmas," Mother Amadeus Dunne of Montana fumed in 1884. There were Jesuit cassocks and shirts to be made; stockings to be knitted and darned; "and all their clothes even pants and coats to be put in order. We have to wash, bake and mend for the Jesuit household." "They believe in the law of compensation," she sighed. "We take much, so much must be given."[44]

Women felt unappreciated by male colleagues. Experts at self-advertisement, the Jesuits were slow to acknowledge the achievements of others, a failing that gave offense to associates. Mother Amadeus railed to Joseph A. Stephan, head of the BCIM in Washington, D.C., that when Cataldo and other priests toured the East lecturing on the Montana missions, they "never mention the Ursulines." "The Jesuits have reaped no small part of the benefit derived from the labors" of others, Stephan agreed, but when it came to publicizing Catholic schooling of Native Americans, they credited no one but themselves.[45]

More serious were struggles over social power, provoked by priestly interference in the running of convents and schools. "It is contrary to our way of conducting Indian missions to have the management in the hands of the

FIGURE 16. Women religious ran orphanages, kindergartens, and girls' schools at many missions administered by Jesuits. In this 1892 photograph, Gros Ventres and Piegan students at St. Peter's Mission demonstrate their accomplishments in sewing, leatherwork, drawing, needle-point, knitting, and music. They are joined by Ursuline teachers, including Mother Amadeus Dunne, founder of the Ursuline missions in Montana (seated on left). Courtesy Jesuit Oregon Province Archives, Gonzaga University, 106-01a

sisters," a Jesuit once stated. "Father Cataldo insists that the Fathers have the management." So inflamed were feelings on this issue that another Rocky Mountain superior, Georges De la Motte, had to admonish his men in Wyoming to mind their own business, an intervention that testified to the women's skill in subverting male power. The Jesuit superior should deal only with the Sisters of St. Francis's superior, De la Motte ordered, and he should never issue a direct order to the women. The leader of the sisters "must be allowed to run her community and school as she pleases." Jesuits might make suggestions, but it had to be done in such manner that the sister "feels she is free, that her authority is entire."[46]

In their struggle for autonomy, women resented being kept in the dark about finances. In 1904, Cataldo obtained the services of the Sisters of St. Joseph from Philadelphia to sustain the mission school at Slickpoo, Idaho. Although the work of both the Jesuits and the sisters was funded by the

BCIM, the patriarchal Sicilian maintained exclusive control over the budget. Cataldo never disclosed to the women the amount of financial support they received from the Bureau — a deception that his more enlightened successor found embarrassing, particularly since the sister superior was "an excellent manager."[47]

Learning to Be White

Whether schools were run by men or women religious, all parties agreed their primary purpose was "to enable the Indian to make a living and become self-supporting." Disregarding native traditions that valued communal ownership of land and hunting, missionaries joined the government in its campaign to transform Indians into independent farmers. To this end, their institutions, like those run by the Indian Office, created a two-tiered program that offered both academic and industrial instruction. If a scholar remained in class for a sufficient length of time, he received the rough equivalent of an eighth grade education. "A plain, common, English education, spelling, reading and writing, with the rudiments of arithmetic," Lorenzo Palladino summarized, "will be for the Indian at large book-learning enough for all purposes of his civilized life and social intercourse." "These Indians want their children trained well, not only in reading, writing," but in "necessary industries" such as "husbandry, farming, stock-raising and the like, since these are . . . the most suited to his actual needs." "What our children will do after leaving school is impossible to say," a Montana missionary conceded. But we hope "the training they receive in the trades and in farming will enable them, when they have obtained the proper age, to earn their livelihood in these vocations."[48]

This curriculum reflected assimilationist federal policy in every detail. "While proper attention is paid to book learning and to the moral and religious training of the pupils," an Indian Office official wrote approvingly of St. Ignatius Mission, "especial attention is paid to teaching them industrial pursuits." The agent Peter Ronan reported: "In addition to the usual branches taught in school — reading, writing, arithmetic, grammar, music, and geography — the girls are taught housekeeping, such as washing, ironing, sewing, dairy work, cooking, and general household duties."

In the boys' school the pupils are taught black smithing, carpentering, work in saw and grist mills, running shingle-machines, farming work, gardening, teaming, and all general farming work, tailoring, shoe-making, saddlery and harness, painting, and all work incident to the institution. The art of printing is also taught in a neat little printing office, where dictionaries of the Kalispel language, the Gospels, and innumerable pamphlets and circulars have been neatly printed.[49]

Classroom instruction was rudimentary. The youngest learners studied elementary subjects — reading, geography, history, penmanship, and arithmetic. Drawing on European practice, Jesuit teachers relied on melody to aid in the memorization of multiplication tables, just as they once had employed tunes to teach the catechism. "They sing their tables every day," a missionary reported, "from twice one to twelve times twelve." In addition to the usual secondary school subjects, students received instruction in vocal and instrumental music and even stenography.[50]

The girls' school at Sacred Heart Mission pursued an equally ethnocentric curriculum. Besides regular classroom subjects, Sisters of Providence instructed pupils "in all the requirements of household duties." Apprentices mastered "general housewifery" — cooking, laundry, dairy work, and "cutting and fitting plain and fancy needlework." The girls sew their own garments, a teacher reported, and they "do all the repairing on the boys' clothing." As part of their transformation into Victorian homemakers, "painting and drawing and those branches common in convent schools are also taught here." Each girl maintained her own garden plot, a sister said, and "owing to the number of stock in our dairy farm, each pupil has the advantage of learning how to make butter" and how to perform "all such work as concerns the dairy."[51]

Mastery of English received top priority, although proficiency varied from reservation to reservation. According to one estimate, by 1880 approximately one-fourth of the Flatheads could read and write the English language, but other students trudged to school knowing only their native tongue. As late as 1909, a missionary at the Holy Family school for the Blackfeet reported that about half "of our new students do not yet understand English at all."[52] When a government delegation led by Secretary of the Interior Carl Schurz inspected St. Ignatius Mission in 1883, the visitors were surprised to discover that scholars were instructed in both English and Flathead — a workable option since many teachers were bilingual. A missionary at St. Xavier Mission stated that English was used in the classroom, for the most part, but "we limit ourselves to encouraging" the youngest children "with little rewards, or prizes, to express themselves in English, if they can."[53]

The Jesuits resisted government pressure to jettison the use of native languages. Although this controversial feature distinguished their schools from others, they insisted on teaching religion and prayers in the students' own tongue. Thus the priests promoted assimilation while at the same time preserving some elements of native culture — just as they did in their ethnic parishes. Every Sunday, boys at Sacred Heart Mission studied the catechism in English, Kalispel, or Nez Percé. Native leaders expected as much. "If you can't learn the Indian language, go back to Montreal," a chief at St. Ignatius Mission admonished Sisters of Providence at St. Ignatius Mission in 1866. Otherwise, "you are no good to us here." Reliance on native tongues (except for religious services) gradually faded, however, as national guidelines increasingly determined curricula. In 1880, the Indian Bureau threatened a cessation of government funding to any school that failed to offer English instruction in all subjects. "A mastery of idiomatic English is particularly essential," declared Commissioner Morgan, for teachers charged with "breaking up the use of Indian dialects and the substitution therefore of the English language."[54]

Although easier to command than to enforce, federal mandates posed a challenge to teachers who themselves labored under a linguistic handicap. That English was not the first language of the Jesuits did not escape the notice of government inspectors. The boys' school at St. Ignatius Mission was of "greatest interest," Secretary of the Interior Carl Schurz remarked, after a visit in 1883. The English spoken by two instructors from Italy was "frightfully fractured." Even worse, the teachers had contaminated the speech of their pupils. "All the boys read well, although with a strange singsong, I might say Italian intonation." When an inspector from the Indian office repeated the complaint ("Fathers Bandini and Crimont speak very broken English"), a BCIM official warned the missionaries, "all employees shall be able to speak the English language fluently."[55]

But there were limits to their ability to comply. After an agent at the Colville reservation deplored that Brother D'Agostino was "not sufficiently versed in English to constitute him an efficient teacher," the BCIM rallied to the school's defense. Teaching boys to become industrious farmers or mechanics does not require language mastery, wrote director J. B. Brouillet. "A dumb man can give it as well and as usefully as the best talker." Nonetheless, their linguistic handicap consumed the Jesuits. "Without English, we are perfectly useless in this country," said Giuseppe Cataldo. "We old timers make even Indian kids laugh when we misuse English." The arrival at St. Ignatius Mission of a fresh recruit from France caused Italian-born Geronomo D'Aste to raise his eyebrows: "He can scarcely talk English," the priest mused, and yet "he comes to be prefect of the boys."[56]

As a consequence of the practice of enrolling adherents from a variety of tribes in a single institution, the typical student body was as mixed as the teaching staff. The school at Sacred Heart Mission, for example, enrolled children from the Coeur d'Alene, Nez Percé, Kalispel, Spokane, and Umatilla tribes. The classrooms of St. Ignatius Mission were equally heterogeneous, its schools brimming with young people from the Flathead, Kootenai, Nez Percé, Cheyenne, Lower Pend d'Oreille, Piegan, Upper Pend d'Oreille, Cree, Blackfeet, Colville, and Spokane tribes. This blending of nations was not solely the fruit of expediency. When fifty Piegan Blackfeet children joined the melting pot at St. Ignatius, the Jesuits welcomed them, not only because they thereby avoided capital outlay for a separate school for the Piegans, but also because the neophytes would benefit from contact with the more acculturated Flatheads. Even when a separate school was erected for them a few years later at St. Paul's Mission, Cataldo worked to persuade Piegans to attend school with Gros Ventres at St. Peter's Mission. The two tribes had been "enemies in the old times," he argued, and hence it would be beneficial "to persuade them to have their children together and to all be children of God." "This may seem strange in the beginning to the Indians," he admitted, "but if we insist and repeatedly tell them same, they will finally come to understand the reasonableness of living together in harmony."[57]

The mission schools also enrolled *métis* pupils, whom Father Damiani of St. Peter's Mission once described as "those poor half-breed children related with different Indian tribes who are around this mission." In his view, "they are in a very miserable condition and worse [off] than Indians," but they "would like to have their children in the school with the Indians." All of the *métis* at St. Ignatius spoke English and had already received some instruction, a priest observed, and hence they "could better understand the advantages of education." Although students with mixed ancestry found adaptation to school life less traumatic than did their full-blood classmates, they suffered because of insecurity about their identity. The novelist D'Arcy McNickle, son of a *métis* mother and a white father, recalled his difficult childhood spent as a tyro at St. Ignatius Mission. "As 'breeds' we could not turn for reassurance to an Indian tradition and certainly not to the white community."[58]

Unlike off-reservation schools that were created exclusively for Native Americans, Catholic institutions admitted white pupils. The rationale for integrated education was both theoretical and practical. With the allotment of many reservation lands at the end of the century, the white population of the Pacific Northwest soared. By 1902, an agent from Washington's Yakama reservation wrote that because there were "so many white people renting land on the reservation," it was necessary to create schools for them. "Many Whites from the settlements surrounding the reservation avail themselves of the chance to have their children educated in the same school alongside of the Indian pupils," said a missionary at Sacred Heart Mission, Idaho. By 1890, ten of the sixty-seven boys in attendance at the school were whites, who, through their tuition, helped subsidize the education of native classmates.[59] According to one priest, the St. Joseph's school at Attanam, Washington, was "supported by white children as day scholars," although their number was restricted because priority was given to Indians. When eighteen white children applied for admission to the school at Sacred Heart Mission in 1884, they were turned down, Pasquale Tosi said. "Only a few are permitted and the best, and this is needed to make the Indian boys speak English."[60]

The primary motive for mingling races, however, was to prepare students to live in an integrated society. This principle flowed from Cataldo's conviction that natives and non-natives should learn to co-exist and that significant benefits accrued to each by so doing. It pleased Giuseppe Caruana, therefore, that "many whites from the settlements surrounding the reservation avail themselves of the chance to have their children educated in the same school alongside of the Indian pupils."[61]

There was, however, an exception to the integrationist policy. In 1889, Giuseppe Damiani stirred a hornets' nest among Jesuits when he split the school at St. Peter's Mission, creating one division for Blackfeet boys and another for non-natives, claiming that an exception was required in this case because of unique circumstances. "The other missions are in Indian country," he argued, "but this one is in white territory," where "the white element is increasing daily while the Indians decrease." The objection that we Jesuit are here primarily for the Indians does not hold in this case, since we're surrounded by whites whose "poor kids" should be cared for. "I was opposed to it from the beginning," Mission Superior Cataldo complained, but "to comply with the wishes of the bishop, I let it be done."[62] Despite the Jesuit's vision of an integrated multiethnic society, segregation of the type seen at St. Peter's Mission would be the pattern of the future.

As the government's insistence on English made clear, the schools were expected to transform their Indian charges into model Americans. The Jesuits additionally sought to make them good Catholics through catechetical instruction, the sacraments, and a lively ceremonial life — the same elements utilized in their parishes and colleges. The great feasts of the liturgical cycle were still woven into the rhythms of tribal life. These events were celebrated with great pomp by the entire community, whose members trooped to the mission from the four corners of the reservation. As in their schools for white youngsters, the priests employed holidays for pedagogical purposes, highlighting the meaning of a church festival or the values exemplified by the life of a saint by staging festive celebrations.

Students joined in the grand processions that marked the celebration of Good Friday, Holy Thursday, Easter Sunday, Corpus Christi, Christmas, and rogation days. The month of Mary, with its participatory exercises and pageants, was inaugurated with a ceremony involving the entire tribe. "The children of the schools and the Indians betook themselves processionally with the banners of their respective sodalities to the church," a priest at St. Ignatius Mission wrote, "where a special altar with flowers has been erected in honor of the Blessed Virgin Mary." Scholars harvested "spiritual blossoms," acts of virtue, which they had performed during the month in honor of the saint, inscribed on small slips of paper. Devotion to the Sacred Heart of Jesus was imparted to Cheyenne academicians by "granting a half-holiday on the first Friday [of every month] to convince the boys that it was a great day of the month." In addition to elaborate liturgical ceremonies, Christmas was marked by the decoration of a Christmas tree, an appearance by Santa Claus, and presentation of gifts to the students.[63]

Just as religious feast days prompted religious assimilation, civic holidays (celebrated at government command) furthered the Indians' cultural and political integration. "Special attention is paid in government schools to the inculcation of patriotism," declared Indian Commissioner Morgan. "The Indian pupils are taught they are Americans, that the government is their friend, that the flag is their flag, that the one great duty resting on them is loyalty to the government." Every year on 8 February, contract schools observed Indian Citizenship Day, or Franchise Day, a holiday created especially for Indian schools. The event must have evoked an ironic response from participants, since it commemorated the enactment of the 1887 Dawes Act, which had mandated the end of the reservation system. The celebration urged them to join the white man's march of progress by accepting the values of private property and citizenship. St. Ignatius Mission solemnized Thanksgiving with a "first class dinner in the refectory with the traditional turkeys" and elaborate entertainment. Washington's Birthday prompted the printing of special programs proclaiming the day's events — plays, declamations, singing in boys school, girls school, and kindergarten. At every celebration, a missionary said, "the boy's band plays a few national airs during recreation."[64]

Missionaries sought to cultivate academic achievement through techniques that blended Jesuit and Native American customs. Superior performance was fostered by emulation, competition, and the bestowal of awards — the same system employed in Jesuit colleges worldwide. Used earlier in the Pacific Northwest to teach Indians the catechism, rewards now served to stimulate scholastic proficiency. These devices assumed special importance in the training of Native American youngsters, a priest explained, because their tender years and their culture rendered them "doubly children." "They need these things essentially," and "they must be kept interested all the time."[65] The time-honored Jesuit system of "monthly places," whereby grades and class standings were publicly announced at the end of every month, served to reward both scholarly accomplishment and good conduct. Enrollees at St. Ignatius receiving a grade of "very good" in at least one branch of studies and in diligence marched to the office of the superior to receive special congratulations and a prize.[66]

As a means of engaging the local community in the educational process, tribal leaders as well as teachers evaluated learners at semester's end. Accordingly, pupils at Sacred Heart Mission were formally interviewed by a board of examiners composed of the faculty; Seltice, the head chief; and "a large number of the most prominent members of the tribe." Recreation daily mingled features from both native and white worlds. The boys played baseball, but they also engaged in familiar sports. "A few apples are put up as a prize for the winners at marksmanship," a missionary reported. "Here they rush for the bows and arrows to gain the apple suspended by a string seventy-five feet distant. Without waiting for a command, a shower of arrows reach the object so accurately that at times no vestige of the apple remains."[67]

FIGURE 17. By 1895, over a third of all Indian children attending Catholic mission schools in the United States were enrolled in Jesuit institutions in the Pacific Northwest. In this photograph, members of the Blackfeet tribe pose before the school building at St. Paul's Mission, Montana; women are seated in front; men, including two Jesuits, stand. Courtesy Jesuit Oregon Province Archives, Gonzaga University, 149-1-11a

The annual exhibition at year's end unfurled the usual repertoire of academic performances — student recitations, songs, dialogues, speeches, skits, and musical interludes rendered by the boys' band. In early years, a preference was shown for selections from Italian opera. Commencement provided an occasion for showcasing the school to the assembled tribal chiefs, parents, and dignitaries from native and white communities. "Our boys had a nice entertainment," a missionary reported at closing ceremonies at St. Ignatius Mission, "and premiums were given to them who distinguished themselves." The prizes were calculated to gratify the young scholars — bridles, whips, and spurs, on some occasions; and spoons, knives, and belts at other times.[68]

Native Resistance to Enculturation

Notwithstanding the missionaries' attempt to keep them content, many students scorned the boarding school experience. Although their parents smiled on education, they spurned the confinement and conformity that it demanded. Dismay at the trauma of deculturation exploded into acts of rebellion, homesickness, withdrawal, and fear — the same forms of rejection seen in schools run by Protestant missionaries and by the government. The unhappiness recorded by one youngster at St. Paul's Mission typified the ordeal experienced by students during their first weeks at school. "I was not a very good mixer and sort of kept out of everybody's way," a boarder recalled. "I did work well," but "was very secretive [and] kept much to myself, absolutely dominated by fear and loneliness." In his autobiographical novel *The Surrounded*, D'Arcy McNickle described returning as an adult to the St. Ignatius Mission school, which he had attended as a boy: "These visits to the church awakened old images that lay in the beginning of life. They were disturbing, half fearful. . . . One lived in the perpetual tyranny of the life-everlasting. . . . It was inexplicable, the dread which had been instilled into the mind of the child never quite disappeared from the mind of the grown man."[69]

Resistance took many forms. In 1896, a fifteen-year-old boy torched his dormitory, an offense for which he was tried, convicted, and jailed.[70] Obliged for the first time in their lives to mix with members of other tribes, some youngsters experienced depression, while others behaved aggressively toward classmates. The most common signal of discontent was desertion, a phenomenon common in Native American boarding schools.

The location of missionary schools, while offering many advantages, enabled unhappy boarders to slip away with relative ease. "The Indian camps are quite near our convent," recorded a nun at St. Labre's, and "hence it is with difficulty that we keep our Indian children." The construction of a tribal dance house near the school in 1888 intensified the temptation to escape. The villagers "are making a constant use of it," a priest lamented, "and as long as our larger children are hearing the drum, it is hard to prevent them from running away." In other cases, however, the close proximity of the Indian camp lessened the desire to flee. The Sacred Heart school may have had fewer fugitives not only because of the Coeur d'Alenes' esteem for education, but also because the nearness of the tribal community resulted in less homesickness. Boarders "are visited by their parents every Sunday," a missionary reported, which aids considerably in helping them to forget the length of the year."[71] Students who came from greater distances were, of course, deprived of that comfort.

Permitting scholars to return home for summer vacation presented a disciplinary challenge. After a summer "in the woods," as one sister put it, "the freedom from control of two months is evident in their conduct." This obliged us "to take the upper hand." "A good part of the disciplinary work must be recommenced. Their response to correction is not good."[72] On the other hand, a school's placement near the community enabled older boys to assist parents with chores. In 1886, Lorenzo Palladino, of St. Ignatius Mission, wrote to Lusk of the BCIM seeking permission to release students from the classroom for this purpose.

In the spring when the seedling season begins and in summer during the harvest, I have permitted some of the larger pupils, when their old people, either by age, weak health, or inexperience, would happen to be unable to do the work by themselves, to go and help them put in a little crop and gather it in. . . . I cannot believe it to be against the intention of the Government to allow this.[73]

Lusk consented, as long as the students were visited "at least once a week by one of the Fathers of the Mission in order to see that they are legitimately employed." This arrangement was, he claimed, "infinitely superior" to the outing system employed at Carlisle and other off-reservation boarding schools, "whereby many of the pupils . . . are regularly apprenticed out among the neighboring farmers." Despite its liberal work program, runaways were as numerous at St. Ignatius as at any mission school.[74]

The ease with which adherents flew the coop gave them leverage with their overseers. As a nun at St. Labre's reported, "We are often obliged to give our pupils permission to go home to prevent running away." After seven girls fled the school at Sacred Heart Mission, instructors sought to entice them to return by altering the daily grind. "Considering their disinclination for study and their love of manual work, we have decided to give them a half-day of sewing, . . . reserving the afternoon for regular class work." The device did not work, however, since some students "took to the woods," escaping through a dormitory window "when all seemed to be asleep."[75]

Dissidents learned to play one school off against another. Some Indians "complain that in our schools children 'pray too much,'" a Jesuit said. Another priest griped that teachers at a nearby government school poached disciples by showing "that they will have greater liberties" with them than with us.[76] According to Prando, Piegan children, upon hearing of the freedoms enjoyed by boys attending the agency school at Fort Shaw, sulked because the Jesuits "herd them like sheep." We make them "kneel down praying; but in the other schools, the boys play with the girls." When two girls ran away from St. Francis Regis Mission, officials recorded: "They have gone to the Okanagan school, attracted by the freedom which is said to prevail there."[77]

Natives' evaluations of the educational experience varied. Some graduates voiced gratitude for the time spent in school. "They were the happiest days of my life," one reminisced. "They took care of the children," another said. "You had three good meals a day and a clean place to sleep." Pupils appreciated the security that school provided, as during the disastrous winter of 1883–84, when hundreds of Blackfeet died of starvation. "The few children that managed to escape this catastrophe," a tribal historian wrote, "were students either at St. Peter's Mission or at St. Ignatius." On the other hand, the large number of fugitives testified to the resentment that others felt about the restrictions imposed upon them by assimilation.[78]

With the passage of time, the schools claimed some successes. According to one native chronicler, youngsters who studied at the schools of St. Peter's, Holy Family, and St. Ignatius missions "provided the Blackfeet with intelligent leadership," which was a great asset, considering the level of Indian education at the time. Schooling also enabled tribes to cope with threats posed by white culture. When Seltice, leader of the Coeur d'Alenes, traveled to Washington, D.C., in 1887, he was flanked by a mission school student. The chief wanted "to have somebody on whom he may trust entirely," Father Grassi said, so that he might grasp "what is said to him and vice versa."[79]

The schools at St. Ignatius Mission contributed to the high literacy rate among the Flathead. According to an agency report, about one thousand natives out of a total reservation population of 1,621 could speak English by 1900. A few graduates went on to college and to professional careers. One of these was Pascal Sherman, an Okanagan Indian, who credited the "substantial and practical" schooling he received at St. Mary's Mission on the Colville reservation with preparing him well for doctoral studies at Catholic University. Although Jesuits themselves sometimes discounted the effectiveness of their schools, they did believe that many Native Americans remained active in the church because of their educational experiences. As an official at St. Xavier Mission, Montana, observed in 1906, there were "many Catholic Indians" in the Lodge Grass district, "many of whom are devoted old school boys."[80] While many native religious traditions perished in the enculturation process, Indians themselves maneuvered the spiritual transition without abandoning their past. "To dismiss all native Christians as acculturated, anachronistic traces of religious colonialism," the scholar James Treat has written, "is to miss innumerable demonstrations of their insightful historical and social analysis, their complex sophisticated religious creativity, and their powerful devotion to personal and communal survival."[81]

The apex of the boarding school era was the last two decades of the nineteenth century, when enrollments spiked, prompting many white observers to heap praise on the institutions. In 1883, a government report claimed the school at St. Ignatius Mission did "more for Indians than anything we have yet seen."[82] Inspector E. D. Bannister told the secretary of the interior five years later that the mission ran "the best equipped and the most *intelligently* conducted school in the Indian services. . . . The buildings are all spacious and commodious, including the printing office, tailor, shoe, tinsmith, harness, carpenter, and blacksmith shops, and all are in perfect sanitary condition." His tribute to Leopold Van Gorp, superior of the mission, was unstinting. The priest's "culture and education" and his "remarkable administrative abilities, . . . coupled with his thorough knowledge of the Indian character, make him the peer of any man engaged in educational work in the Indian services."[83]

The industrial school's success, however, became the cause of its undoing. The rapid expansion of the Catholic school network unleashed a backlash that terminated government support. As the historians Robert H. Keller, Jr., and Francis Paul Prucha have shown, aggressive promotion of church institutions, coupled with escalating support for public education, eventually brought the contract system to a close. In the 1880s, when Catholic establishments began receiving two-thirds of the government funds, it became apparent to many Protestants (who had earlier championed church-state cooperation) that the time had come to reevaluate their constitutional principles. With the rise of the American Protective Association, anti-Catholic feeling intensified and federal support of sectarian schools exploded into a national political issue. With the appointment of Thomas J. Morgan as commissioner of Indian affairs in 1889, the battle was joined. No admirer of the Catholic Church, which he denounced as "an alien transplant from the Tiber," Morgan condemned the "Jesuitical cunning" that had led to federal support for Catholic institutions. Under his direction, the funding of church-operated schools was curtailed and, by 1900, suspended.[84]

Catholic missionaries, led by the BCIM, reacted by turning to private charities for support. The Jesuit school system in the Pacific Northwest had, nonetheless, been dealt a severe blow from which it never fully recovered. After the tap of federal dollars ceased to flow, some institutions shut their doors. Others, including the industrial school at St. Ignatius, Montana, struggled to ride out the crisis. Whatever tomorrow might hold, a Jesuit wrote in 1901, "for the finances of these schools we now depend entirely on Divine Providence."[85] In the years that followed, public schools replaced missionary institutions as the chief educators of Native American children.

From a Jesuit viewpoint, the experiment in church-state cooperation had been a two-edged sword. Federal financing had enabled the clergy to school native children on a scale that would have been inconceivable in an earlier generation. The academic advance made by many tribes was in large part attributable to the combined efforts of the Rocky Mountain Mission and the U.S. Indian Office. But accomplishment came at a price. Increasingly viewed as agencies of forced assimilation and as business operations, the schools drove a wedge between priest and people. The Flatheads of St. Ignatius Mission were becoming antagonistic, Jesuits said, because we seem riveted "only on making money."[86] Herds of cattle, horses, and sheep and vast acreage developed to support their educational establishments provoked criticism not only from Native Americans but also from white farmers, with whom the missionaries competed for sales. However, having hitched themselves to dependence on farm income to sustain the schools, the Jesuits could not unyoke themselves from the consequences.

Thus the new emphasis on generating income prompted painful soul-searching. Many missionaries regretted that their days were swallowed up by administrative paperwork, while others moaned that running schools, ranches, grist mills, farms, and lumber mills left little time for pastoral ministry. For this reason, the closure of the boys' school on the Umatilla Mission in 1902 was greeted with relief by the missionary Georges de la Motte. "The measure frees the father from what was slavery, and allows him to devote more time to visiting the reservation, a thing which was considerably neglected in the four or five previous years."[87]

Although most missionaries lamented the decline of boarding schools, Giuseppe Damiani glimpsed a silver lining behind the dark cloud of vanished federal funding. Our schools have become "nothing more than institutions of charity," he declared. "In order to give the poor people — which is what the majority are — a chance to give their children a Christian education, we have to reduce tuition as low as possible." But doing so requires that we support our work by becoming livestock and grain merchants. "I see the hand of the Lord" in the withdrawal of government aid. "We have deviated not a little from the example" set by our first missionaries in caring primarily for the Indians' spiritual welfare. "It used to be that all of our attention centered on the conversion of the Indians, but now, it seems to me, that we are trying to do nothing but open schools." Operations had grown so large and so numerous that "all the discipline and teaching has to be left in the hands of lay persons." While still favoring an educational apostolate, Damiani questioned the utility of trying to maintain boarding institutions. Schooling is "a good and beautiful thing for young people," he concluded, but with some tribes it "amounts for nothing because upon leaving they live just as their Indian parents do."[88]

Other Jesuits grieved that many scholars abandoned Christianity after graduating. Writing several years later, missionary Louis Taelman agreed with Damiani. "The closing of the boarding school" at St. Xavier Mission "will benefit and augment our ministry among the Crows," he wrote in 1921. "They will be more satisfied and in consequence, better disposed to us. In their frame of mind, the boarding school gets the blame for all the school children that have died in the past," he said. "All things considered, the closing of the boarding school was a wise and opportune, nay more, a necessary decision."[89]

Nevertheless, the missionaries remained on the reservations. Despite the loss of several establishments to fire, they continued to run schools, but on a more modest scale. That those outposts survived at all testified to the persistence of both the Jesuits and their Indian supporters. "A large portion of the budget for these schools came from tribal funds," one historian has observed, "and Indians were vehement defenders of sectarian schools threatened by closure." But the institutions never again occupied the role they played in their heyday, when church and state conspired to assimilate the Native Americans through the unique experiment known as the contract school system. "Our present conditions are not quite as brilliant" as they once were, a priest at Sacred Heart Mission wrote regretfully in 1912. Classrooms once infused with apprentices now housed a mere handful: "To date we have only about one dozen pupils."[90] The golden age of Jesuit schooling of Native Americans had ended. With the closure of one school house after another, the missionaries increasingly redirected their focus to pastoral activity, the very work that had launched the Rocky Mountain Mission, albeit in a very different environment, half a century earlier.

8 *"The Darkest Part of the U.S.A."*

THE SOUTHWEST

In our preaching we did not lose sight of the aim of
our mission, which was to reform the customs of that
demoralized place.

— Jesuit Francesco Tomassini, 1880[1]

In 1874, the Methodist minister Thomas Harwood reported to church headquarters in New York on the progress of his missionary work in New Mexico. Advancement was slow, he said, because most people were Catholics. Second, the country was being "stirred from center to circumference" by "banished Jesuits from other countries." "They come here in flocks," he sulked, "like blackbirds to a corn field." "Jesuitical intrigue" thwarted every attempt to "break the silent slumbers of a sleeping people."[2]

Although Harwood was preoccupied with the Jesuit presence in New Mexico, scholars writing later have tended to overlook it. The history of the Catholic Church in the Southwest has instead long been dominated by the commanding figure of Archbishop Jean Baptiste Lamy. Fictionalized in Willa Cather's novel *Death Comes for the Archbishop* and eulogized in Paul Horgan's award-winning biography *Lamy of Santa Fe*, the French-born cleric is associated with the Europeanization of the region's Hispanic American church and with the clash of cultures that erupted when he tried to impose nineteenth-century French norms and practices upon its indigenous religious system. Although resisted at times, the reforms advanced by Lamy and his ancillaries had a lasting effect. As Horgan pointed out, even the French-styled churches that Lamy erected served as "reminders of France," shaping "the whole material character" of the Catholic Southwest, just as "his French clergy were affecting its spiritual life."[3]

More recent studies have underscored Lamy's desire to Americanize his frontier diocese during the years of transition from Hispanic to Anglo cultural hegemony.[4] Having spent ten years in missionary work in Ohio and Kentucky before he moved to the Far West, he had developed a sympathy with American ideas and ideals that he brought with him to New Mexico. "If his Romanesque-styled cathedral in Santa Fe suggested that Lamy

178

wished to Europeanize his diocese," one historian concluded, "there is other convincing evidence that his stronger desire was to bring the Catholic Church of the Southwest within the physical and psychological boundaries of the American Catholic Church." "Making matters worse," in the view of other scholars, "the bishops and the new French clergy they recruited often did not understand or respect their Mexican parishioners and their traditions."[5]

This focus on French and American influences has enriched our understanding of the area's cultural heritage. But it has also diverted scholarly attention from the role played by other ethnic groups, including the Italian Jesuits, in forging a multifaceted Southwestern Catholicism in the half-century following acquisition by the United States. By concentrating on Lamy and his French confrères, scholars have failed to recognize that the region's religious history manifests, in the words of one study, a "kaleidoscope of development" that blended a medley of impulses that produced "a unique regional Catholicism, mosaic in nature."[6]

Nineteenth-century New Mexico's cultural mosaic did indeed contain a variety of pieces. The work of Jesuits from the order's Neapolitan Province in the Southwest confirms that the region's Catholic culture was molded not only by Hispanic, French, and American values, but also by Italian initiatives. The Neapolitans' cross-cultural activity bore the stamp of their national origin from its very inception. Donato Gasparri and his fellow Italians — like Lamy and his French contemporaries — brought with them the religious conventions of their homeland and impressed them upon local Hispanic American congregations. For a half-century, they imparted Italian notions throughout the Southwest through their parishes, schools, colleges, and publishing house, thus advancing the Italianization of the church there as they did elsewhere in the West.

The devotions and policies promoted by the Neapolitans may have been less disruptive of local custom, however, than were the innovations of their French counterparts, although the difference was one of degree rather than of kind. Several factors account for the variance. Although the Italians, too, promoted institutional Catholicism, they and their Hispanic congregations both drew on a shared cultural heritage that valued patriarchy, community, and Mediterranean folk religion. Each consortium, moreover, favored a devotional style that was celebratory, penitential, and centered on potent intercessor saints. Lengthy Spanish domination had left indelible traces in Italy, particularly in Naples and the Kingdom of the Two Sicilies, as it had in the Southwest.[7]

Additionally, the Neapolitans appear to have taken a more tolerant attitude toward human fallibility than did the French clergy, whose outlook was shaped by Jansenism and by notions of Gallic cultural superiority. This is not to say that the two religious groups did not get along. Good relations and cooperation on many levels characterized the relationship between the Italians and Bishop Lamy and his French priests. Although the Jesuits clashed with J. B. Salpointe, Lamy's French-born successor, over jurisdictional matters, they were particularly friendly with Joseph P. Machebeuf, who invited them to run schools and parishes in his Denver diocese. Indeed, the immigrant European clergy, facing similar challenges in the Southwest, had more in common than separated them; nevertheless, their differences were not insignificant.

From the very start, the Italians, like their French counterparts, perceived the Southwest through European eyes. When Donato Gasparri penned his first report about the country in 1869, he highlighted features that distinguished it from the world of his readers in Italy, warning potential missionaries that they would discover there much that was novel. Lacking water, agriculture took unfamiliar forms. "Irrigation is necessary for all farming," he wrote, and "the populated areas are usually found along the rivers, of which the principal one is the . . . Rio Grande." Unlike Italy, where piazzas embraced magnificent urban churches and palaces of marble, in New Mexico the humble and "irregular" plazas were lined with houses "poorly designed and built of *terrones* or blocks of earth cut from the ground and mortared with mud." Frontier culture mirrored frontier architecture. "There is as little education as there is urbanization and commerce." New schools were being opened, but "professional studies are unheard of. . . . Very little is grown or manufactured in the Territory for lack of training and especially for lack of energy. . . . Everything comes from the States."[8]

New Mexico seemed to stretch on endlessly. Riding on rutted washboard trails is "our principal fatigue, . . . and travel in these new lands is much more dangerous than in Italy," a missionary wrote. "It's rare that I spend two days in a row in my own house," another reported from southern Colorado. "Almost all week I am out galloping from village to village in order to preach, say Mass, administer the sacraments." For many years, traversing by horse through deserts of mesquite and prickly-pear cactus was the chief method of transport. "In Europe, it would seem strange to maintain a stall of four horses," he continued, "but here four are often not enough. . . . I remember in Naples when we had to go fifty miles, we prepared again and again" before setting out. But here, "the only preparation to be done is to put the bridle and saddle on a good animal, and off you go."[9]

The most serious affliction was a dearth of workers. Some prospective recruits were so terrified by what they heard about the Southwest that they refused to emigrate. "Can't you send us some men?" superiors in New Mexico cried repeatedly to leaders in Europe, who replied that their hands were tied because they lacked travel money. Once, after Gasparri had ingratiatingly expressed confidence in Provincial Davide Palomba's ability to help the mission, Palomba retorted sharply: "I don't need encouragement. What I do need is many thousand French francs," because there are men here whom I would like to send to you in America.[10]

Some missionaries were nearly undone by hardships, confirming a later writer's description of the arid Southwest as "too strong, too indomitable for most people."[11] "I have found things much worse than I had ever imagined or supposed," one stunned Jesuit exclaimed in 1869. "The great city of Santa Fe itself is nothing more than a small group of adobe houses." From Las Vegas, another lamented that his squalid dwelling of dirt had no connection to comfort. The house was capped with a flat roof that rendered its occupants vulnerable during the wet season, with the best-protected portion of the hovel reserved for the sick; meanwhile, rain water drizzled down on the healthy, who "wrapped themselves in blankets and tried to sleep, sitting in their chairs." Even the normally resilient Gasparri, whom co-workers would later dub "the man of the hour under any conditions," became so depressed by afflictions that he confided to a friend, "I absolutely cannot stay here any longer."[12]

Conditions had improved by the 1880s, but expatriates still carped that their pleas for help went unheard. "Colorado and New Mexico are no longer as they once were, places to strike fear among some of our Jesuits," Luigi Gentile asserted in 1881. The railroads, which were speedily transforming the country, relieved missionaries of much of the travail of circuit-riding. By the turn of the century, superiors extolled the relative ease of trans-Atlantic travel and assured prospective recruits that they could return to Italy after a few years' service in the Southwest. Nonetheless, need still outstripped supply, driving Gentile to protest that we are "like a voice crying in the desert." You Europeans "have little interest in us."[13]

Adding insult to injury, some conscripts proved incompetent. In 1884, authorities in Naples conceded they had been remiss in sending troublesome men to the Southwest Mission and promised to exercise greater care in the future. Nevertheless, twenty years later an official proposed that a particularly difficult brother be sent to America as punishment for wrongdoing, an idea that was finally rejected only because "no one would want to have him." Jesuits in the East were equally stingy with personnel. "They make gifts to us of persons like him," Gentile once griped about an "almost useless" American apprentice, "while retaining our best men in the service of their own provinces." A frustrated Giuseppe Marra contrasted the superiority of volunteers sent to the Rocky Mountain Mission with those who appeared in the Southwest. "We are the only ones who, when we manage to get someone, really get the worst," he sighed. In this place "useful men [are] rare."[14]

Jesuits were not the only ones who found it difficult to entice more hands to come on deck. In 1864, the general conference of the Methodist Church grieved there was "not one Protestant minister engaged in preaching the Gospel among the 90,000 Mexicans and Americans in New Mexico." The reason was that leaders "were unable to find anyone able to preach in Spanish whom they considered competent and trustworthy." Another twenty years passed before Thomas Harwood and his Methodist comrades were able to establish their first Spanish-speaking outpost in what one minister described as "this long-neglected, benighted southwest corner of our republic, shut out from the civilized world." A Congregationalist clergyman summed up his situation in 1910: "The key word to the past year's work is 'struggle.'" "It has been a struggle to get men to fill pastorates, a struggle to get money to pay them, a struggle to get members for church and congregation — a hard, unrelenting struggle. . . . I see no future for this church for a long time to come but *struggle, struggle, struggle.*"[15]

Compounding the challenge was the fact that the Southwest, molded by centuries of Spanish colonization, remained largely Hispanic in culture and population. At the conclusion of the Mexican War in 1848, when the United States acquired the coming states of New Mexico, Arizona, California, Utah, Nevada, and parts of Wyoming and Colorado, the sprawling domain contained approximately 100,000 Anglo-Americans, most of them in Texas. There were an additional 150,000 inhabitants of Spanish, Mexican, Native American, and African American extraction. Although post-conquest emigration boosted the population, by 1850 New Mexico Territory claimed only about 60,000 inhabitants, of whom fewer than 10 percent were Anglos.[16]

An insufficiency of pastors to serve this population had been a problem since the late eighteenth century. Mission secularization and the departure of Spanish Franciscans after Mexican independence in 1821 had shifted the religious welfare of the Southwest to the secular clergy. But a host of problems, both national and local, rendered the church incapable of providing care in many communities. New Mexico fared better than other provinces, but customary ecclesiastical services were wanting even there. As Antonio José Martínez, a public-spirited priest of Taos, observed, poor *nuevomexicanos* "buried their dead without proper ceremonies, neglected to have their children baptized by a priest, and many couples lived together without being married because they had no money with which to pay for the wedding." And yet, a vibrant folk Catholicism thrived. Despite a scarcity of *curas* in many villages, religious practice centered on devotional dramas, prayers, processions, hymns, and local art. The most influential organization was not the parish, but the *cofradía*, or religious confraternity. "Together with the celebration of religious festivals," according to one historian, it "nurtured the religion of the people and helped them to maintain their identity as a people once they became part of the United States."[17]

When French-born Jean Baptiste Lamy planted his feet in Santa Fe as bishop in 1851, he was staggered to find his vast diocese contained only fifteen priests, six of whom were old or inactive, "incapable or unworthy." Faith remained central in the lives of Spanish-speaking Catholics, but the laity had mobilized their own forms of worship. Despite Lamy's skill at drawing new clergy from abroad, church ministrations long remained inadequate. Accustomed to communities run by priests, Neapolitan Jesuits who arrived in Conejos, Colorado, in 1872, described their three thousand parishioners as "nearly abandoned" in religious matters. And they worshiped in a church that resembled "a cave or stable rather than a house of prayer."[18]

Isolation shaped the way the Europeans viewed the inhabitants of the Southwest. "The people profess Catholicism," one Jesuit said, "but their practice of religion is mixed with superstitions that must be eradicated bit by bit." "I would never finish if I named all their talismans or amulets," which they believed could preserve them from "the evil influence of certain objects and persons," another added, or "the charms and remedies attributed to certain things or persons." For example, "a man with a wound never allows a pregnant or sick woman to enter his house. They are convinced that the mere sight of such a person will cause the wound to become worse and infect the whole body."[19] Some priests ascribed these deficiencies to a "terrible lack of education, which withers and dries up the good seeds of virtue." A more perceptive Jesuit understood that the southwesterners had responded impressively to adverse circumstances: "The character of the New Mexicans is the same as one would expect from any people who lived for years separated from any center of civil and moral instruction and almost exclusively occupied in pastoral activity . . . . Indeed, it is a wonder how they were able to preserve the faith and religious fervor, though it is mixed with some superstition."[20] Other clergy, too, detected perseverance under trying circumstances. Giuseppe Marra, drawing on many years' experience, considered the Mexicans of the Southwest to be "almost naturally religious." "The people have a wonderful attachment to the Catholic religion," wrote another Jesuit, who worked among Mexicans in Los Angeles in 1870. Although "their morals are anything but conformable to their belief, . . . their faith is as strong as that of the Irish."[21]

While promoting religious renewal, the priests resisted the corrosion of traditional values by non-Hispanics. As historians have frequently observed, most Americans "had little regard for traditional Hispano customs or for the indigenous Indian cultures of the region." The stereotype drawn by the journalist Rufus B. Sage in 1846 was typical of the omnipotent arrogance of many arrivistes. New Mexico, he sourly reported, was a charmless place. "Superstition and bigotry are universal, all, both old and young, being tied down to the disgusting formalities of a religion that manifests itself in little else than senseless pride and unmeaning ceremony." The Congregationalist minister Jacob Miles Ashley joined in the dark refrain. "Their priests are blind leaders of the blind. . . . In spiritual matters we are in the darkest part of the U.S.A."[22]

The Jesuits, matching the Americans' bias with prejudice of their own, made fighting Protestantism a main focus of their ministry. *Gli americani*, while exhibiting "many attractive social qualities," were usually Protestant, religiously indifferent, or materialistic, they claimed. And expanding American hegemony "increased the corruption and diminished the religious feeling and piety which was the chief ornament of the New Mexicans." According to Father Salvatore Personè, the new arrivals set an appalling example: "The American, by nature a speculator and risk-taker, works and earns like a horse, and spends like an ass; but he always has something more to spend. The Mexican, although lacking this skill, wants to imitate the newcomers but ends up skinned, like the crow that tried to adorn itself with peacock feathers." Few actions more dramatically laid bare the Neapolitans' determination to outreach the competition than Jesuit Francesco Tomassini's boast that during a mission in Peña Blanca, "we tore up five Protestant bibles and consigned them to the fire."[23]

When they tramped into New Mexico in 1867, it was not immediately apparent to the Neapolitan missionaries how to meet these challenges. Although appointed to "one of the best parishes in the diocese," in Bernalillo, north of Albuquerque along the Rio Grande, the neophytes soon regretted their assignment. "After taking over the parish," Gasparri said, "our lives, at least as far as our duties were concerned, were no different than those of other parish priests. In Bernalillo we remained available to anyone asking for confession or for help with their sick at all the parts of the parish. In addition, we fulfilled our responsibility of visiting the outlying plazas at least once a month to celebrate mass."[24]

Gasparri's observation that the Jesuits' duties were "no different than those of other parish priests" betrayed anxiety about the nature of their work — an unease that lingered for decades. In part, the hesitation stemmed from the Society's historic reluctance to staff parishes. Viewed as the domain of the diocesan clergy, pastorates were seen as incompatible with the Jesuit vow of poverty and the ideal of mobility. Moreover, the Italians, relying on Lamy's invitation to help train clergy, trudged to New Mexico expecting to exercise their accustomed ministries and to live in regular religious communities, not in companionless isolation. When we came here, authorities promised we would be doing the work of rural priests "in civilized countries," observed Baldassare in 1876. Since that did not happen, "it was a real mistake to have accepted this mission." Unlike the diocesan clergy, who often lived alone in parishes, the Jesuits typically resided together in communities, where they engaged in shared activities that reflected their work as educators, preachers, and spiritual directors. Before their exile, for example, twenty-six priests and brothers in the Jesuit church in Naples served an urban population of over seven thousand persons. In addition to its external ministries, the typical Jesuit community defined itself through a daily schedule of internal activities: private prayer at fixed times, liturgy and devotional exercises, community talks, and meals in common.[25]

The American frontier threatened the time-honored lifestyle of many religious orders. When German Benedictines established themselves in the United States in the 1850s, they faced the dilemma of preserving their monastic customs or serving the needs of the church in a changeable borderland. Instead of following the conventional, cloistered life of a monastery with its fixed routines, the monks found themselves drawn outward into a busy world of parishes, missions, and schools, which obliged them to temporarily set aside their former ways until a more settled society could be established. In the meantime, however, many Benedictines, like the Jesuits, worried that their strength would be dissipated by parish work.[26]

Although they had never lived as monks in monasteries, the Jesuits learned that their accustomed style of living was unthinkable in New Mexico. Unable to start a mission among the Navajo (the reservation was instead assigned to Protestants), they found themselves stuck in tiny outposts where they were confined to parish work, which they described as "not very desirable because it was not very Jesuit." In those modest, rural *plazas*, or villages, which embraced hundreds of square miles and whose maintenance demanded constant travel, the émigrés faced circumstances unlike any they had known in Italy. Without religious communities of "regular observance," the mission's fate was "very problematic," Baldassare cautioned. "Until we begin setting ourselves to educating youngsters, which is only possible in some central Mexican place, we will end up doing very little."[27] Twenty years later, the missionaries were still searching for projects "more appropriate to the Society." "The Mission has too many houses, certainly more than it can properly attend to according to its Institute," Giuseppe Marra wrote in 1888. "So many small residences are not calculated to foster religious life," and "a spirit of individualism creeps into our ranks [so] that we are no longer what we should be to serve God and his church. My superiors in Italy are constantly urging on me to withdraw from these numerous scattered residences."[28]

And yet, parish work ballooned with each passing year. What made it tolerable were the opportunities for a broader ministry that growth promised. The first step in this direction occurred in 1868, when the missionaries transferred from Bernalillo to Albuquerque. Here they staffed two churches and founded a novitiate, a grammar school, and a printing press. From this base,

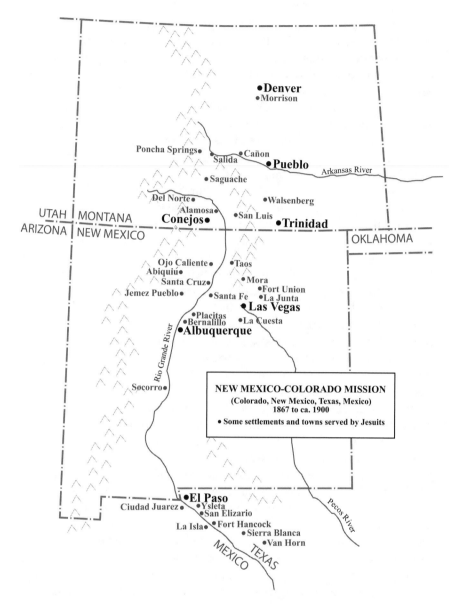

FIGURE 18. Map: New Mexico–Colorado Mission, 1867 to ca. 1900

the Neapolitans extended operations into the Rio Grande Valley, where most of the region's population was clustered. By catapulting northward into Colorado and southward into Texas, they aimed to develop more diversified projects.

After 1871, new foundations followed in quick succession, thus creating the impression of Jesuit ubiquity — "from center to circumference," as Thomas Harwood put it. Expansion northward from the mother house in Albuquerque began with a parish in Conejos, a settlement of about three thousand people in Colorado's San Luis Valley. For the next fifty years Jesuits ministered to the largely Hispanic population of the town and its twenty-nine neighboring farm hamlets and immigrant mining camps. In 1872, in the rising manufacturing center of Pueblo to the north, they accepted a parish that served the city and another network of rural missions. With the founding in 1873 of a parish in La Junta (today's Watrous), a New Mexico city planted at the confluence of the Mora and Sapelló rivers, the Jesuits assumed responsibility for a grammar school and dozens of dependent chapels in the surrounding countryside.[29]

Within a year, they had also set up shop in Las Vegas, New Mexico, some forty miles east of Santa Fe. A strategically located transshipment hub on the Santa Fe Trail, Las Vegas was expected to become even more vital when the transcontinental line reached the Southwest. It was here that the Italians established Las Vegas College and relocated their publishing house, the Revista Católica Press, after it was flooded out in Albuquerque. In 1875, the Neapolitans added to their list Trinidad, a city in Colorado that by century's end embraced two urban churches and twenty-four outlying chapels distributed over 4,800 square miles. With the move to Trinidad, the Southwest Mission's thirty-five Jesuits, their numbers augmented by the arrival of new recruits from Europe, were engaged in variety of activities — running parishes, preaching parish missions, teaching, and publishing.

An even greater shift occurred in 1879, when the Neapolitans launched a parish in Colorado's chief city, Denver, where they subsequently inaugurated the College of the Sacred Heart. Two years later, they entered the emerging city of El Paso, Texas. Consequently, by 1906, the Southwest Mission staffed nineteen parishes in New Mexico, Colorado, Texas, and one in Mexico itself. In addition to their parishes, the Jesuits attended to 121 mission stations serving 78,420 Catholics. To their ongoing regret, however, these posts remained small and tucked away, leaving their solitary managers perpetually in doubt about the worth of their labor.[30]

The administration of widely dispersed mission stations posed a puzzle. How to respond to the spiritual needs of the dozens of far-flung ranching and farming communities sprinkled for hundreds of miles along the Rio Grande and its tributaries? From Conejos, Colorado, for example, the missionaries served about seven thousand persons scattered in dozens of outlying hamlets. "This number would seem exceedingly small in our established European countries," a missionary told friends, "but if you consider the circumstances prevailing in this place, you would see that it is immense." Those responsible for the most distant congregations spent more days away from the central residence than in it, prompting one priest to observe, "a missionary's greatest fatigue is travel."[31]

Committed to scores of dispersed settlements, most of which had been without pastors for years, the Neapolitans early on developed a strategy that made maximum use of their limited work force and rendered travel more efficient. Different priests were assigned to each side of the Rio Grande River, thus avoiding the inconvenience of repeated crossings of its broad waters. The missionaries also adapted both their manner of living and their ministry to frontier conditions. Writing in the third person, Gasparri described how he scooped up scattered settlers for services as he hoofed from one lonely outpost to another. Upon arriving in a plaza, he would signal his arrival either by ringing the church bells three times or by some other means. (Another Jesuit, appearing in a settlement without a bell, fired a rifle shot into the air.)[32] As Gasparri explained, "This system proved successful . . . After visiting one plaza, he could continue visiting neighboring ones in much the same way without having to return home. He thereby saved time and energy, even though, on the other hand, staying away from home for six or seven days on visits like this proved to be arduous."[33]

Circuit-riders lived in perpetual motion. Since farm families "are scattered here and there, we ourselves are obliged to run about a lot if we want to visit them," Salvatore Personè wrote. "We say mass in private houses, except in two places where there are small chapels. This necessity of going from house to house causes very great fatigue and causes us to lose a good deal of time." "It is rare that I spend two days in a row in my own house," another missionary, Pasquale Tomassini, said. "Almost all week, I am out galloping from village to village in order to preach, say mass, administer the sacraments. And let me state frankly, that living alone, as I live, a great distance of two days from any other priest, is very unpleasant." Tomassini's immense parish in La Junta stretched 75 miles into the desert in one direction and 120 in another, with scores of ranches and villages that were "few and far between." In order to visit his dispersed flock, he was constantly on horseback. When one of us returns home, Tomassini recounted, the other takes off.[34]

This system of rotating visits took more permanent form in subsequent years. Like their Jesuit compatriots in the Pacific Northwest, the Neapolitans created hubs out of which circuit-riders issued on weekly rounds and to which they returned to take up more or less regular community life when traveling was done. These residences were established in centrally located cities such as Albuquerque and Las Vegas in New Mexico; El Paso in Texas; and Conejos, Pueblo, Trinidad, and Denver in Colorado. With this system in place, expatriates struck a compromise between the idiosyncratic requirements of missionary work in the Southwest and their own desire to salvage some semblance of the life they had known in Europe.

Centering their living in key locales solved one problem, but finding work suited to their corporate character continued to perplex them. The Neapolitans soon discovered, however, a way to jump-start their work that both capitalized on their previous training and met the religious needs of their congregations. They began giving popular or parish missions. An itinerant activity that originated in sixteenth-century Europe during the Catholic Counter-Reformation, the mission had become a powerful means of reviving religion in the years of chaos following the French Revolution. Comparable to the Protestant revival meeting, the parish mission sought to "bring back the lost sheep, convert the sinner, and built up the local church," as one historian has observed. "An extraordinary event," it achieved those objectives by intense and dramatic preaching and by increased reception of the sacraments.[35]

Italian Jesuits had played a pivotal role in systematizing *le missioni popolari*, particularly the seventeenth-century Roman orator Paolo Segneri. Loosely based on the *Spiritual Exercises* of St. Ignatius, the practice was adapted to the needs of both urban and rural congregations. In 1830 alone, Jesuits of the Neapolitan Province gave no fewer than 579 missions. After the political upheaval of 1848, the practice became even more widespread, since the Jesuits, ejected from their metropolitan colleges and churches and obliged to maintain a low profile, were freer to give them. Outlawed priests skittered into the Italian countryside, where they delivered the popular exercises in inconspicuous parishes run by diocesan clergy. Although the institution's diffusion throughout the nineteenth century meant that revivalism was no longer the exclusive work of the Society of Jesus, Jesuits continued to regard it as one of their primary tasks. Steeped in that tradition, exiled Neapolitans recognized the mission's suitability for the settlements of New Mexico, where Christian life seemed nearly extinguished by generations of neglect and isolation. But there were differences. In Italy, the undertaking had been connected with Jesuit colleges, whereas in the Southwest priests operated out of rural parishes. Second, when preaching to Hispanic congregations, the Italians tailored their missions to the customs and traditions of the region.[36]

The revival usually began and ended on a feast day, taking advantage of large crowds and special fanfare — banners, sacred images, special costumes — that enlivened Southwestern holidays. The missionaries' arrival in a village (they generally traveled in pairs) was dramatically announced by ringing church bells and by their formal reception by the local priest and people in the town square. The mission, which lasted from eight to fifteen or even twenty days, depending on the needs of the place, commenced with morning mass and a sermon, which were succeeded by other spiritual exercises in the late afternoon or evening. Two series of conferences or meditations were delivered daily, each by a different homilist. It was not uncommon in Italy for preachers to arouse religious fervor by using dramatic stratagems — bearing a statue of the dead Christ in penitential procession in the town square to provoke repentance, clutching a skull or bones when preaching on death, or displaying images of the Madonna to accentuate the importance of purity and divine mercy. Similar stratagems flowered in the Southwest. "Many times," an observer wrote, "the earnest exhortations of the preacher were interrupted by the tears and groans of the hearers."[37]

On the final day, missionaries sought to make a lasting impression on their congregations with a lavish closing pageant. The service included special music, general communion, a farewell sermon that stressed the importance of persevering in good intentions made during the revival, and a papal blessing. A festive parade led to the erection of a large cross in a prominent public place to serve as a reminder of the mission. Before leaving the village, the Neapolitans distributed prayer books to sustain religious fervor. Sodalities and confraternities were founded or renewed to consolidate the good results after the preachers had departed.

The first Jesuit mission in New Mexico took place in 1867, in Santa Fe. Gasparri's account suggests that it followed standard Italian procedures. Begun with a three-day retreat for children on the Feast of the Immaculate Conception on 8 December, it ended about two weeks later on Christmas Day. "This system was adopted for subsequent missions," Gasparri reported, and its success led to invitations to repeat the experience in other places. "Because of what happened in Santa Fe we found ourselves able to accomplish more in our own parishes, and we decided to try something special in each one of them."[38]

Previously unknown in New Mexico, the popular mission proved powerful. As one scholar has pointed out, it was well suited to areas boasting few churches, still fewer priests, and congregations that had "long been without the consolations of the word and sacraments." The Italians' earlier sojourn in Spain stood them in good stead in New Mexico. They "spoke Spanish fluently," a native of Las Vegas once said of the Neapolitans. "I still remember Father Donato Gasparri, for he was the most eloquent speaker I had ever heard. Even my father had never heard such preaching."[39]

A series of revivals given during Lent of 1874 drew crowds of people to the villages of San Miguel, San José, and Las Vegas. Participants, barefoot and poor, who had been separated from the church for years returned to received the sacraments. In the process, congregations long characterized by diversity and independence were exposed to the unifying and centralizing impetus of nineteenth-century Catholicism. Catechetical instruction drew upon doctrines shared by all Catholics, and the bestowal of a papal blessing at the end of a mission symbolized the loyalty of all church members to the pope.[40] "It was clearly a great success," declared Gasparri. "The mission was something new in these areas, and, thank God, it could not have worked better [although] much still remains to be done because of the people's days under former authorities and because of the prejudice and coldness with which the foreign clergy were received."[41]

Missions delivered in Mora and in Taos helped mend a long-standing rift between Bishop Lamy and followers of the popular Mexican priest Antonio José Martínez. After clashing with the French bishop over his controversial religious reforms, Martínez had resigned as pastor of Taos, but when he reclaimed the parish without episcopal approval, Lamy eventually excommunicated him. This drastic act alienated large numbers of *Taoseños*, some of whom remained estranged from the church even after Martínez's death in 1867. The following year, Donato Gasparri was invited to give two-week missions. The report that he sent to superiors in Europe after the event, although self-congratulatory, is valuable for its first-hand account of the reconciliation of the warring factions.

God blessed the preaching, the private conferences, and the other efforts such that very soon even the schismatics — including Martínez's own family, who were among the first — came forward to be reconciled, receive the sacraments and, what was most difficult and important to do, validated their marriages. . . . The schismatics were almost all reconciled, their schismatic chapel was closed, and Father Lucero, who had been running it, promised to retire.[42]

Success such as this enhanced the reputation of the Jesuits and led to requests that they remain as permanent pastors in many villages and pueblos. The revivals also proved an effective vehicle for arousing interest in schools run either by the Jesuits or by the religious women who worked with them.[43]

Transnational Religion

If popular missions gave the Neapolitans opportunity to shape the spiritual life of the Southwest, so too did parish administration. Like the French clergy, the Jesuits sought to bring their long-marooned congregations in line with the universal church. This was primarily done by introducing them to the religious practices and theological values found elsewhere in nineteenth-century Catholicism. Many of the new devotions were of Roman origin — novenas, blessed altars, stations of the cross, benediction, the rosary, devotion to the Sacred Heart and to the Immaculate Conception. The Neapolitans additionally highlighted the mass, Marian devotion, the cult of the saints, processions, the veneration of relics, and other public displays of religiosity familiar to Hispanic Catholics. The Jesuits sought to regularize these activities where they had degenerated into unconventional forms during years of feeble ecclesiastical control. In the process of standardizing devotional life, they promoted an Italian type of piety, which one scholar has compared to other forms as "more indulgent, occasionally more superficial but also more human and popular."[44] Gasparri described how he took advantage of the opportunity offered by a mission in Santa Fe in 1867 to substitute new notions for old.

> We sought to promote devotion to Mary, to saying the rosary, to the scapulars of Carmel and of the Immaculate Conception, to the Holy Guardian Angel, and, among the very young, to Saint Aloysius Gonzaga and to Blessed Mariana de Paredes, of whom little was known of the former and nothing of the latter. Through these devotions we have also seen some success eradicating superstitious and foolish practices.[45]

The Marian May devotion imported from Italy met with ready reception, dispersing quickly. "Once settled in Albuquerque," Gasparri recalled, "we thought of introducing the devotional practice of the Month of Mary as May drew near in order to make the Jesuits known and to encourage the people to fulfill their religious obligations." Throughout the month, two priests alternated weeks of preaching. "In the afternoons we said the rosary and used sermons, litanies, orations, and hymns from Father Muzzarelli's book." Although these practices were often associated with the individual, dedication of the month of May to Mary combined both private and group activities. "I translated Muzzarelli," Salvatore Personè said, "and in our oratory in Las Vegas a choir of twenty persons sings the litanies and reads the meditations outlined in the classic prayer book." Within a short time, this devotion was celebrated in all the Jesuit schools and churches throughout the Southwest.[46]

Among the practices promoted by the Neapolitans, dedication to the Sacred Heart of Jesus ranked among the highest. An ancient if largely ignored cult for many centuries, it took familiar form around 1600 and speedily became one of the most popular of all Catholic pieties in the latter half of the nineteenth century. This emergence was in part traceable to Jesuits who had embraced the devotion during the period of their suppression. A major force in its diffusion was Benedetto Sestini's periodical, *Messenger of the Sacred Heart*, founded to combat the forces of darkness that he saw menacing Christian civilization. Focusing on Jesus' love for humankind, the devotion invited devotees to make reparation for the indifference and hostility of the contemporary world toward religion and the Catholic Church.

Devotion to the Sacred Heart was closely connected to support of Pope Pius IX, who achieved near-cult status among the faithful. With the collapse of the temporal authority of the papacy following Italian unification, promoters emphasized the pope's moral and spiritual authority, linking love of the suffering Christ to loyalty to the church and its aggrieved leader. As one scholar said, in the siege mentality that ruled conservative thought after the implosion of the temporal authority of the papacy, ultramontane piety flowered, making the pope "the nerve center of the Mystical Body and the principal focus of the Sacred Heart."[47] Every mission given by Jesuits in every corner of the Southwest concluded with a papal blessing, and religious processions that had long echoed with cries of "Viva la santísima cruz de Jesús Cristo," now resounded with "Viva la Iglesia" and "Viva Pio Nono."[48]

This new devotion, coupled with the declaration of papal infallibility, had contributed to the remarkable centralization of the Catholic Church in the nineteenth century. A newly imported clergy made sure the Southwest was not isolated from this transformation. For generations, New Mexican *fiestas* honoring the Madonna and local saints had centered on parades and other open-air ceremonials coordinated by lay associations. The Jesuits, like their French counterparts, infused clerical oversight into these festivals by relocating them within the church and under priestly control. The people of La Cuesta (today's Villanueva), New Mexico, had long celebrated Holy Week in the town plaza with a performance of the *Paso de las tres caídas*, a dramatic enactment of the Three Falls of Jesus on the way to Calvary. In 1880, Father Francesco Tomassini recorded that although the square had been decorated for the event, "a strong wind and dust storm quickly convinced the people that the *paso* could not take place in the plaza." "It was my good luck," he rejoiced, that the performance was instead staged in the church.[49]

Roman guidelines increasingly shaped all rites and rituals. When a new church was dedicated to the Sacred Heart in La Junta, New Mexico, in 1874, Pasquale Tomassini insisted that the blessing of the cornerstone be done "according to the ceremonials prescribed in the Roman ritual." Clerical clout was amplified by the founding of parish-based sodalities and confraternities in whose every activity the priest emerged as a high-profile figure. Accordingly, when 350 parishioners in Las Vegas were inducted into the confraternity of Our Lady, they received membership scapulars "from the hands of the worthy pastor, Father Carlo Personè."[50]

The Italians, like the French clergy, promoted ecclesiastical conformity by sanitizing and sacralizing rituals that they judged tainted by profane influences. Prior to the coming of the Jesuits, the people of Conejos had celebrated the Feast of Our Lady of Guadalupe on 12 December by carrying a statue of Mary in procession through the towns and villages of the spreading parish. When the Neapolitans discovered that "Our Lady would be put in a corner or attended by some old women while the people would go to a *fandango*," they resolved to eliminate the rowdy dance parties. Henceforth, they announced, Our Lady would "visit the plazas accompanied by a priest who would say mass in the different towns." This abrupt break with custom drove some people "into a rage," a Jesuit noted. But eventually "almost all of the people came to the conclusion that the Fathers were justified in their action of eliminating the *fandangos*." As a consequence, "the feast was carried on in a satisfactory manner and for us was a victory." A similar transformation marked the Feast of Santiago, or St. James the Greater, who was honored as the apostle of Spain and patron of warriors and horsemen. Formerly acclaimed on 25 July with horse races, rooster pulls, and cockfights, the day was sanctified, no doubt to the roosters' relief, by the Jesuits, who inserted a solemn high mass and a special sermon into the festivities.[51]

The Italians never lost sight of the ultimate aim of their preaching — "the reform of the customs of this demoralized region," as Francesco Tomassini described it. But in the process of introducing variation, they inclined toward incrementalism and compromise. Recognizing that the umbilical between themselves and the people was popular religion, they were scrupulous not to sever that integral connection in their quest for standardization and the eradication of unorthodox notions. What was said of Salvatore Personè after fifty years of missionary work could be said of most of the Neapolitan clergy. "He did not merely destroy," an associate wrote. "In the place of celebrations that were demoralizing, he substituted others which were more magnificent but innocent, and which attracted and pleased his people no less."[52]

The impulse to accommodate to idiosyncratic customs was made easier by the fact that many Southwestern religious practices reminded the Italians of popular piety in *la patria*. Both traditions exulted the graphic, the theatrical, and the emotive, and both appealed to the world of the senses through symbol and rite. These actions included music, communal singing, candles, vestments, incense, pyrotechnic processions, and other public manifestations of faith. Villagers in New Mexico, like their counterparts in rural Italy, staged dramatic passion plays during Holy Week in which large mobile statues took the roles of Christ and Mary. The Feast of Corpus Christi, a day of highest solemnity for New Mexicans, mirrored rituals associated with the same celebration in Naples. "The crowd of people gathered in the church is extraordinary, " Salvatore Personè reported from Conejos in 1874. Led by a cavalcade of mounted horsemen, the entourage snaked its way through the town, pausing at a series of six outdoor altars or shrines, just as in Italy. What was novel was the *velorio del santo*, a prolonged litany of prayers of thanksgiving and petition. Unlike churchgoers in Naples, New Mexicans maintained an all-night vigil, which consisted primarily of singing that commenced shortly after sunset and persisted until dawn.[53]

Sensitive to cultural differences, the Europeans sought both to conform and to reform. For example, when a Jesuit purchased an elaborate, Italian-style Christmas crêche from Naples in 1877, he penned specific instructions about which pieces were appropriate for southern Colorado. Offerings presented to the Christ Child by the shepherd figures, he told his agent, should be close to nature, such as animals and fruit. Human figurines should be about a palm-and-a-quarter high, with hands, feet, and face of clay; and they should wear real clothing. Characters unique to Naples, however, should not be sent — tavern keepers, railroad signalmen, or riders to hounds. "Such things," he insisted, "would be exceedingly odd here."[54]

The folk religions of both New Mexico and Italy blended elements approved by church authorities with so-called occult practices. Additionally, each displayed a predilection for splintering devotions — especially those related to the Virgin Mary and to Christ — into the widest possible array of functions and regional forms. As one scholar has explained, "Italian Catholics don't really venerate simply 'Mary' under some particular title"; rather, they expand their devotions into an array of practices suited to different locales and purposes.[55]

In the Southwest, the Neapolitans found an abundance of Marian pieties that gave devotion a local name, rivaling what they had known at home. The saint was honored as Nuestra Señora de los Angeles, Nuestra Señora de la Anunciación, Nuestra Señora de Atocha, Nuestra Señora de Begona, Nuestra Señora del Camino, Nuestra Señora de las Candelarias, Nuestra Señora del Carmen, Nuestra Señora de la Conquistadora, Nuestra Señora de los Dolores, El Corazón del Nuestra Señora de los Dolores, Nuestra Señora de Guadalupe, Nuestra Señora de la Manga, Nuestra Señora del Patrocinio, Nuestra Señora de la Piedad, Nuestra Señora del Pueblito de Querétaro, Nuestra Señora Refugio de Pecadores, Nuestra Señora de San Juan de los Lagos, Nuestra Señora del Socorro, Nuestra Señora de la Soledad, Nuestra Señora de Talpa, and Nuestra Señora de Valvanera. To these established Marian devotions, the Neapolitan melded still more, including the Italian practice of dedicating to Mary the month of May.[56]

Some devotions were welcomed for their novelty. Others, including those that incorporated song, were approved because they married the new and the familiar. The rosary, usually performed elsewhere as a private devotion, was recited in common in the Southwest, either in the church or while walking in procession through the streets. To this old practice, and to many others, the Neapolitans added melody. According to Pasquale Tomassini, it was Salvatore Personè who first introduced parishioners to the chanted rosary. "This practice of singing the rosary, which delights and pleases the people, is employed not only during missions, but every Sunday in every parish run by Jesuits," Personè himself related. "Half of our work in organizing a mission," is the chanting of hymns by the entire community — young and old, men and women. "Everything the Mexicans know" about their religion, he stated, "is summed up in these songs."[57]

Theatrically compelling Italian devotions complemented the New Mexican love of procession, active participation, and elaborate fanfare. Celebration of the Feast of Our Lady of Guadalupe had been "a triumph" in Conejos, Salvatore Personè boasted to friends in Italy in 1872. Brothers Tadeo and Ansalone labored for two-and-a-half months to transform the sanctuary into a Neapolitan-style grotto, "decorated with an apparatus erected over the altar in our Italian fashion." The procession that filed through town included two hundred men on horseback, a territorial senator carrying the flag, and riders "armed with pistols from which from time to time six successive shots were fired." Next came children carrying colored flags, a processional cross, men, women, a gorgeously vested priest, and finally the statue of Our Lady, surrounded by a throng of people who discharged fireworks. As clergy working in southern Arizona reported, liturgy in this country must be staged "with all possible ceremony."[58]

If some innovations met acceptance, others provoked resistance. When Riccardo Di Palma attempted to replace a time-honored statue of St. Anthony — a rough, homemade carving decorated with hair fashioned from the tail of a horse — with a newer one of European style, parishioners rebelled. They refused outright to shoulder the imported statue in procession when the time arrived for its official installation. "We can't carry that San Antonio," the priest was told. "We no like gringo saint. We want our own *santito*." Like the French clergy, the Neapolitans disparaged regional folk art, preferring instead plaster saints imported from Europe. In the 1870s, the Jesuits of Albuquerque collected money from parishioners to replace the *bultos*, or gesso-covered statues of cottonwood root, that had long adorned the chapel of San Felipe Neri. The native figures were tossed away to any donor who would accept them.[59]

Toward members of the "Cofradía del Nuestro Padre Jesús Nazareno," popularly known as the *penitentes*, the Jesuits showed uneasy tolerance. For generations these brotherhoods had met the religious needs of Hispanic Catholics by filling the void carved by the absence of priests and by providing mutual aid and other services to their communities. The image of them that became fixed in the Anglo American mind, however, fastened on their spectacular penitential rites — cross-bearing, simulated crucifixions, and public flagellations. Although these rituals appalled Anglo Americans, they did not appear outlandish to the Jesuits, who had known penitential processions in both Italy and in Spain.[60]

Consequently, although the Neapolitans treated the *penitentes* with patient condescension, they appear to have been more tolerant than the French clergy. Not bound by the restraints imposed by Lamy on the brotherhood's activities in the diocese of Santa Fe, the Italians maintained relations with them for half a century in southern Colorado. Indeed, according to one study, the Neapolitans sought to cooperate with and reconcile *penitentes* to the

FIGURE 19. *Penitentes* near San Mateo, New Mexico, perform one of their rites, a simulated crucifixion, in this 1888 photograph by Charles Lummis. The Neapolitans gradually curtailed the influence of the controversial religious brotherhoods by creating rival ceremonials and by redirecting their activities. Courtesy The Autry National Center/Southwest Museum, Los Angeles, N. 22541

church rather than denounce them as Lamy, his predecessor Zubiría of Durango, and his successor Salpointe had done in New Mexico. Writing from Conejos, Salvatore Personè reported that the confraternity's gatherings in their *morada*, or private chapel, were semi-secret, but the "priest can attend the meetings whenever he wishes, and he knows everything that is done and said there." The Jesuit admired the brothers' sincerity. These "poor simple people . . . count on buying heaven with such indiscretions, and maybe they do because they do it in good faith." Some of their customs appeared extreme, however, even to Personè. "The things they do during Holy Week" — especially their emulation of the crucifixion, in which one of the *hermanos* was tied hands and feet to a cross — were "unbelievable." Informed (erroneously, as events later proved) that a *penitente* in a neighboring parish had died during the ordeal, he concluded, "we are gradually working to end these abuses."[61]

The Neapolitans developed strategies for incrementally curtailing the potency of the *cofradía*, one of which was to offer competing rituals. For example, they may have introduced their Conejos parishioners to the Buena Muerte confraternity, a devotion dedicated to preparing oneself for a "happy death," as a means of drawing people from analogous rituals in the *morada*. Another way of redirecting *penitente* activity was to infiltrate the *morada* by working closely with its members and by providing religious services for them. Some participants may be guilty of fanaticism, the missionary Carlo Pinto reasoned, but they "certainly have good intentions," and they honor an "inviolable rule" that obliges them to annually confess their sins to the priest. Besides, the Jesuits were reluctant to interfere overtly in the rites of the *morada* because, as Pinto explained, the leading *hermanos* were too politically powerful in the local community to be challenged head on. Thus, he shrugged, "we can only guide them indirectly."[62]

In communities dominated by Anglo Americans, however, the priests cast a more critical eye on the *penitentes*. As agents of assimilation, they feared their extravagant penances set a disturbing example to uncomprehending non-Hispanic Catholics and scandalized Protestants. In consequence, as the American population of New Mexico grew, the Italians and other European clergy increasingly found the *penitentes* an embarrassment. Why? Because their rites, like other elements of Southwestern popular culture — elaborate saints' days, passion plays, and primitive art — offended the Victorian sensibilities of the newcomers. Thus, the editors of *La Revista Católica* pleaded with the brotherhoods to exercise prudence in performing penances. Now that outsiders were entering the Southwest in greater numbers, a priest worried, "there will be great dishonor to the religion" that the *penitentes* profess "if they are seen naked and bloody on plains and mountains." The *Revista* further worried that the rituals would exacerbate prejudice against Hispanics and Catholics and block plans for statehood. "Men who only seek pretexts for mobilizing public opinion against the Catholic Church . . . [will attribute] to the entire Catholic population in this land that which is only the effect of the aberrations of a few Mexicans who make their whole religion consist of these practices."[63]

As American censure of the so-called "barbarous practices" mounted, the Neapolitans distanced themselves from them. In 1884, after the Albuquerque *Morning Journal* claimed that "the members of this strange order acknowledge the utmost obedience to the authority of the Jesuit order," Salvatore Personè protested. A decade earlier, the missionary had advocated patience in dealing with the *moradas*, but now he censured both the *Journal* and the *hermanos*. Six years later, however, the *Revista* was again pleading for tolerance and understanding. And it faulted critics for failing to situate the flagellants within the Christian tradition of "mortification and penance." "Why, when speaking of the flagellants," editors asked, "can you not distinguish between use and abuse? And why do you condemn en masse all of the flagellants, past and present, without distinguishing the good from the bad?"[64]

Ferdinand Troy, an Eastern European Jesuit who arrived in the Southwest in 1893 and gained firsthand knowledge of the *penitentes*, defended them, offering a novel interpretation of their purpose. "I am inclined to believe that it is rather a dramatic society, combining charitable motives and some religious practices," he suggested. "My opinion is based on the fact that in some localities on Christmas Day, they have a religious play called 'Los Pastores' or 'Los Reyes Magos' or 'Adán y Eva.' Why not . . . have a religious drama in the Holy Week?" Such a celebration, he mused, would "supply the need of regular religious ceremonies in the absence of the priest."[65]

Hispanics seem to have reacted positively to the Jesuit reformers. In part, their acceptance reflected a welcome end to spiritual isolation and a desire to reconnect to the church. In addition, the Neapolitans offered something new: a devotionalism that accented the experience of personal conversion. The highly popular parish mission not only personalized faith, it provided a foundation for belief beyond the communal activity of folk religion. It helped that the Italians achieved these objectives through the promotion of dramatic, graphic, and emotive rituals that complemented local antecedents. The religious transition that occurred in the post-conquest Southwest, therefore, was not only the fruit of a Hispanic penchant for syncretism. It also resulted from the Neapolitans' instinct for both flexibility and enculturation. Their ability to bend to local customs — while simultaneously pursuing standardization in essential matters — legitimized them in the eyes of Hispanic Catholics.[66]

Appraisals of the Jesuits by their contemporaries are not easily come by in the absence of written testimonials. In estimating the people's estimation of the Neapolitans, the historian can only offer conjectures based on minimal information. Certainly in the beginning, the "foreign clergy" were received, in Gasparri's words, with "prejudice and coldness." That suspicion slowly yielded to acceptance, however, is suggested by the nicknames the New Mexicans subsequently bestowed on favorite priests. White-haired Salvatore Personè, a man of sunny aspect and perennially pleasant personality, became "the Vanisher of Sadness." "He can make you cheerful," one woman said, "by simply looking at you." People christened Luigi Gentile "the Man of God," and nimble Donato Gasparri was "the Walking Encyclopedia." What contemporaries said of Alessandro Leone — the "preacher who thrills his audience" — when he died after forty-three years of missionary work could be applied to many of the Neapolitans who entered into the Hispanic world: "Although an Italian by birth, Father Leone was a Mexican at heart."[67]

There were pragmatic as well as personal reasons why these outsiders found favor among *nuevomexicanos*. "We honor the teachers of [the] sublime lessons" of our Catholic faith, Rafael Romero, a territorial legislator, once told an applauding crowd at the Jesuit school in Las Vegas. But we are also grateful to the Jesuits for "their commitment to and solicitude for the education of youth."[68] In addition to facilitating Hispanic assimilation, the Italians aggressively championed Hispanic culture. This was evidenced not only by their promotion of schools, but by their support of traditional village and town life that was rapidly succumbing to Anglo-American pressures. As the Jesuit scholar Thomas J. Steele has observed, the Neapolitans' practice of constructing new chapels in plazas across the Southwest was effective. "A chapel in their own community was a source of enormous pride to the people and symbol not only of religious devotion but also of social cohesion, since the care and maintenance, as well as the initial construction, was shared among the *vecinos* (residents). Even . . . today, most communities still maintain their chapels, virtually all of which were initially built under the Jesuit administration."[69]

New Mexico's tolerance of ecclesiastical reforms is further explained by Catholicism's tendency to offer a substitute symbolic language while simultaneously adapting the cultural heritage with which people identified. With the advent of Anglo Americans in greater numbers, the ancestral world of the Southwest was plunged into a transformation that threatened Hispanics with a loss of self. Thus the church emerged in the Southwest (as in Hispanic California) as an institution with which people could identify in an era of upheaval. Despite the jarring new emphasis on standardization, the Italian clergy did endorse many aspects of popular Catholicism — "the key matrix of all Hispanic cultures," as many scholars have insisted. In short, the missionary approach provided coherence between the past and the future. What one historian has written about post-conquest California also applied to the Southwest. During the years of transition from Mexican to American rule, the native Hispanic "found it easier to retain his identity as a Catholic than as a miner, rancher, voter, or naturalized citizen." Forced to integrate into an alien and often antagonistic political and economic system, Hispanics ultimately viewed the church not solely as an instrument of coercive transition but as a force for stability and continuity in troubled times.[70]

Instruction in Many Modes

Education was another Jesuit project calibrated to bring the Southwest into conformity with the broader world. "The people here . . . are ignorant," Michael Hughes, an American Jesuit, wrote from New Mexico, "and their ignorance is the cause of all their miseries." No opportunity was lost, therefore, to promote schooling — even devotional practices that aroused interest in study. The Confraternity of Christian Mothers, for instance, a prayer group which the Jesuits established in their parishes for the "sanctification of families," had as one of its principal aims "the Christian education of children."[71] While laboring to reform parish life, the priests recognized that schools were, as Raffaele Baldassare said, the most promising "means of instructing this poor people, so unlearned and superstitious." "Until we begin to commit ourselves to educating youngsters — which is only possible in some central Mexican place — we will end up accomplishing very little. If students in grammar school were taught the rudiments of piety and religion, along with reading and writing, certain superstitious and silly ideas would gradually be dispelled."[72]

But educational progress in the Southwest was unhurried. Twenty-five years after U.S. acquisition, New Mexico possessed a sparse forty-four primary schools, only five of which were public. Although the Territory contained 29,312 school-age children in 1870, the number who frequented school, public or private, was a tiny 5,114. Two decades later, more than one-third of the 154,000 residents of New Mexico remained illiterate.[73] This apparent lack of interest in schooling had several explanations, one of which was the natives' conviction that public establishments were rife with prejudice. According to one assessment, some of the schools were worthy "educational institutions for the betterment of the people," but others were patently anti-Catholic and anti-Hispanic.

Their procedure was to blacken Catholicism in the eyes of simple folk. The old canards about the evil secret lives of priests and nuns, the adoration of images, and other such lies were broadcast in print and by word of mouth in rural settlements. . . . What these sects did effect too well was to confuse souls; they took away the Faith of many and left them, not Protestants, but infidels and scoffers.[74]

New Mexicans, arguing that the majority of the population was Spanish-speaking and Catholic, sought instruction in their own language and religion. Thus the church opened as many parochial schools as its resources would allow, relying on the Sisters of Loretto, the Sisters of Charity, the Christian Brothers, and the Jesuits for teachers.

Led by Bishop Lamy, in 1863 New Mexican Catholics championed legislation that allowed religious to teach in public schools. The Neapolitans, accustomed to the loose boundary between the public and private realms in Italy, plunged into the campaign, which was so successful that they soon dominated education. By 1873, the Jesuits were running bilingual schools in Bernalillo, Albuquerque, Las Vegas, Santa Fe, and in hamlets in the upper Rio Grande Valley. Public schools in at least five New Mexican counties were staffed by Jesuits and other religious congregations; the omnicompetent Donato Gasparri even served as superintendent of schools for Bernalillo County.[75] Instruction was bilingual, but not with equal emphasis, as one priest revealed in 1874, when the Neapolitans were offered the administration of the county school of Conejos, Colorado. "We could not accept since we had nobody to teach English," he explained. "Thus our ignorance of this language deprives us of a great means of guiding and instructing this poor people so unlearned and superstitious."[76]

As elsewhere in the West, Jesuit school masters worked hand in hand with congregations of women religious. Although it is difficult to discern the relationship between the two, a memoir left by Sister Blandina Segale, a Sister of Charity, sheds some light on their interaction. In a world of strictly defined gender roles, she moved with remarkable ease among all levels of frontier society — teaching children, nursing the sick, protesting lynching, ministering to prostitutes and criminals, engaged in fund-raising and building construction. In 1880, when the Jesuits asked the Sisters of Charity to start a day school in Albuquerque, it was Segale who negotiated a contract with the priests, a potentially difficult undertaking that typically left nuns feeling exploited. Raised in an Italian American family, she was the right person, however, to deal with the Neapolitan clergy. "It was agreed that the Jesuits would build a house for the Sisters, furnish it, and give them the deed in fee simple," Segale reported with satisfaction. "The Sisters were to support themselves. All spiritual needs were to be rendered by the Jesuits." "It is a pleasure," she concluded, "to work with the S.J.'s."[77]

The control of public education by Catholic priests and sisters outraged citizens bent on modernizing New Mexico. This opposition was led by the territorial secretary, William G. Ritch, described as "a vigorous Protestant with a strong distrust of the Catholic religion," and by Governor Samuel B. Axtell, whose hatred of Gasparri exceeded even Ritch's antipathy. Intent on breaking the Catholic near-franchise on public schooling, the pair translated loathing into action in 1878. When the Jesuits petitioned the territorial legislature to legally incorporate the Society of Jesus as an educational institution, Ritch and Axtell tried to steer the U.S. Congress to reject the so-called Jesuit Act. The "Neapolitan adventurers" were not fit to teach, Ritch charged, because they favored "the retention of the Spanish language in preference to the language of the country." The schools of New Mexico should be controlled by Americans, Axtell added, not outsiders from France or Italy.[78]

But the Americanizers had grasped a nettle. They could not trump the Catholic opposition, and the Jesuit Act passed. Anchored by popular public opinion, clerical leverage over schooling therefore continued for decades, as did the controversy it engendered. Opponents charged that the disagreement spawned "a legacy of bitterness that seriously retarded the growth of the public school system in New Mexico for many years." Catholics countered that they acted by default, filling an educational void that territorial authorities were for decades unable or unwilling to fill.[79]

In 1875, the Neapolitans founded their own academy in Las Vegas, New Mexico. "Many of the Mexicans . . . started asking us to open a school," Gasparri said, because it would obviate "the dangers that many youngsters of wealthy families encounter who are sent east to study." Education in the

States taught men to become bankers and businessmen, the *Revista* argued, but these careers were inappropriate in New Mexico's economy; besides, few students returned to help New Mexico once they graduated. Schooling at home would help prepare the territory "for the next wave of immigrants," who were expected to appear when the railroad tethered the Southwest to the rest of the Union. Although enthusiastic supporters of transportation, the Jesuits believed the rail line would bring both woe and weal to the people of the region. The great majority of the new arrivals would be "either Protestants or persons of no religion," they reasoned, and hence the local population needed to prepare for the transformation.[80]

Although it was placed in the territory's second largest city, the project was difficult to launch. "Giving birth to a school in this country," a missionary wrote, "is a lengthy undertaking and difficult beyond belief." Nonetheless, by the end of its first year, in 1878, Las Vegas College enrolled 130 day students and boarders. Six seminarians studied Latin there, but the majority of the pupils received elementary and secondary instruction in geography, history, mathematics, English, Spanish, bookkeeping, and music. "This number is really something if you consider the circumstances of the place," Salvatore Personè assured friends in Europe. "To have 130 students in Naples is nothing, but for Las Vegas it's a lot."[81]

The modest operation, like the church-controlled public school system, thrived because instruction was bilingual. For this reason, it siphoned adherents not only from the Southwest, but also from Mexico. According to one story, perhaps apocryphal, young Francisco Madero, later president of the Republic, journeyed north to master English. Spanish speakers in the Southwest — like their counterparts in post-conquest California — viewed education as a required means of adapting to the Anglo-American culture that dominated their homelands in the wake of the Mexican War. People recognize the "sheer necessity of learning English, which is so essential here for trade with the Americans of the United States," a teacher said. Therefore, "the Spanish people make great and protracted sacrifices to send their boys to schools where it is taught." English, another priest reported, is "more important than any other academic subject."[82]

Las Vegas College, like all Jesuit schools in the West, was a single-sex institution. Even in public schools overseen by the priests, boys and girls were separated. When Camillo Mazzella of Woodstock College paid an official visit to Albuquerque in 1875, he condemned the "abuse" of gathering school girls in the courtyard where boys played games before Sunday catechism. "Ridiculous and dangerous," coeducation of young people would, Gasparri opined, "remove any brakes to contain the passions of the human heart, . . . add fuel to the fire," and "stoke the flame" of illegitimate amour. Instructors, too, were segregated by sex. The Neapolitans, cheered on by like-minded par-

FIGURE 20. By 1906, Jesuits staffed nineteen parishes and 121 mission stations in the Southwestern United States and Mexico. One of those isolated outposts was Iglesia de Santa Cruz de la Cañada (Holy Cross Church) at Santa Cruz, a small town in northern New Mexico. In this 1908 photograph, carriages, wagons, and horses await in the street while congregants attend services. Courtesy, Denver Public Library, Western History Collection, H. S. Poley, P-210

ents, protested when a woman was appointed to teach at a public boys' school in Las Vegas. The Jesuits themselves prohibited their men from giving music lessons to female students.[83]

The promotion of literacy drew the Italians into the publishing business. "The daily newspaper is one of those things which are rooted in the necessities of modern civilization," the *North American Review* had announced in 1866. "The steam engine is not more essential to us." This was a declaration with which the Jesuits concurred. Viewing the printed word as they did the classroom and sermon — another means of instructing the masses — the Italians in 1873 founded the Revista Católica Press. One of their aims was to counter inroads made among Catholics by Protestant clergy, such as the Methodist minister who boasted in 1873 that he had "scattered several thousand pages of Spanish tracts," testaments, and Bibles throughout Arizona. Like a thief climbing through the window, the Protestant interloper had to be resisted with his own weapon. Headquartered first in Albuquerque, then in Las Vegas, and finally in El Paso, the press's chief imprint was a Spanish-language newspaper, *La Revista Católica*, which was inspired by similar Jesuit publications in Europe, particularly Rome's *Civiltà Cattolica*. The first periodical of its kind in New Mexico, it became a major vehicle for communicating news between isolated settlements and one of the most potent instruments of Catholic influence.[84]

As its inaugural issue announced, the *Revista* aimed at the promotion of learning and at "maintaining and encouraging the faith and piety of the Mexican population, safeguarding them from dangers of Protestantism." The newspaper "will publish some news, especially religious," Gasparri wrote, "but this will not be its principal task." "We view it as a special means for the instruction of our readers, for the principles of private and public honesty, for debate on important questions." Soon after its inauguration, its editors claimed that the *Revista* enjoyed "a greater number of subscribers than twelve other newspapers in this territory." Imprints from the press circulated not only in New Mexico but also in Colorado, Arizona, Texas, and eventually in Mexico and South America. "Throughout this vast region," a priest reported in 1875, "our books are distributed and the periodical read."[85]

There was a ready market for offprints. Since the United States lacked a Spanish-language publishing house, books and pamphlets — such as they were — came from Mexico or Europe. "The complete absence of a press," a priest reported in 1875, meant that "good books in Spanish were up until now very scarce and very costly for everyone; in several families, an old book is still guarded and cared for like a precious legacy from father to son." Alert to the market, the Jesuits soon began publishing "selected books of piety." "It was a constant necessity to be well provided with prayer books, catechisms, rosaries, etc. in those days," recalled Gabriel Ussel, a circuit-riding priest. The Neapolitans filled another lacuna by publishing textbooks — including an English speller, Spanish grammar, and a 146-page mathematics text.[86] "Already four counties have adopted these books for public schools," Camillo Mazzella reported in 1875. Within a few years, the press was churning out nearly every textbook used in the 138 public and 33 private schools of New Mexico, an outcome that deeply disturbed opponents in the territory. Despite the controversy that ensued, public institutions continued to rely on Jesuit output well into the 1880s.[87]

During its eighty-seven-year history, *La Revista Católica* made its mark in many ways. Directed for decades by Giuseppe Marra — dubbed "the writer who scalps" because of his gifts of argument and satire — the journal riveted its Hispanic readership on issues of interest. As late as 1917, editors boasted theirs was "the only Catholic weekly in the Spanish language in the United States."[88] An unofficial organ of the church in the Southwest, the *Revista* was lauded by Catholics for promoting the faith among its Mexican American readers. The periodical "fought rigorously, unmasking all errors and solving all difficulties against religion," an early historian claimed. "If the people have not been robbed of their faith, it is chiefly the influence of this weekly." The expatriate Neapolitans had learned an essential lesson in America about shaping popular thought. As a writer for the *Revista* observed in 1911, the press is the "absolute owner of the public opinion that in democratic regimes governs the nation."[89]

No controversial topic escaped the *Revista*'s magnifying glass, including shifting gender roles. "Keep in mind the differences placed by nature between men and women," the caveat-laden journal advised. "Public life is for the man, and for the woman there is the domestic and private life." Reflecting the view commonly held in Italian and Hispanic cultures that women were the upholders of traditional values, a writer declared: "Give me good mothers, and I will give you good citizens."[90] As educators, the Jesuits championed schooling for woman ("She should be an intelligent wife and mother") but they bucked against equal educational opportunity. Too much intellectual activity not only confused a woman, they asserted, but kept her from completing her household duties.[91]

When New Mexicans began to debate women's suffrage, the *Revista* joined other Spanish-language journals in opposition. "How absurd it is, now repugnant to the sentiments of respect that we all hold for the gentle sex, to see a woman who abandons household work to present herself before the ballot box!" wrote an indignant Gasparri in 1877. Extension of the franchise would upset accustomed functions. "The merchant will have to leave his store, the lawyer the office, the worker his workshop, the laborer his plower, and go to the house to take care of the crib!" Typically, when neighboring Colorado granted suffrage in 1893, the journal lamented that women had forgotten "the sublime mission that they received from God. . . . They ridiculously affect to become men."[92]

A steady output of imprints reinforcing the Catholic arsenal in the ongoing propaganda war with Protestants also flowed from the press. Our "principal concern is dogmatic controversy with the end of defending our religion against attacks from its enemies, and of instructing our New Mexican Catholics in the truths of their faith," the editors declared in 1894. "If the *Revista* had done nothing more than break the influence of the Protestants, then with this alone would we be satisfied." Pasquale Tomassini described how he used this literary ammunition in his battle with Methodists in southern Colorado. "Our press in Albuquerque can provide us with persuasive booklets with which we can oppose the flood of trash that flows from the offices of the Bible Society of New York and inundates these parts." Thus, the Revista Católica Press contributed to the explosion of devotional literature that was transforming nineteenth-century Catholicism. Devotional manuals, prayer books, hymnals, and pamphlets printed by the Neapolitans served to bridge the gap between the orally transmitted popular devotions of Southwestern villages and the uniform, book-based devotions of the larger church.[93]

As the activity of the Revista Católica Press showed, the Neapolitan Jesuits shared many goals with the French clergy, including their promotion of institutional Catholicism. The Italians' dedication to the Europeanization of spiritual life was not so absolute, however, that they were unable to adapt their consolidating strategy to time and place. Indeed, their Mediterranean heritage led them to bridge the cultures of Rome and Albuquerque and inclined them toward greater tolerance of local customs than was the case with some co-workers.

Nor can one neatly pigeonhole the Italians as Americanizers. According to scholars, the French priests and bishops identified with the American future of the region and their primary goal was to serve "the local elites, mostly Anglo Americans, whether Catholic or non-Catholic, in order to secure permanence for the church." The focus of the Neapolitan ministry shifted toward the end of the century from a tight focus on Spanish speakers to a broader apostolate, but even so, as late as 1906, two-thirds of the population cared for by them were Italian immigrants and Mexican Americans. The only places whose clientele was "purely American," as one priest put it, were Denver and Pueblo, Colorado.[94] Easing the entry of the Spanish-speaking population into the national mainstream was indeed a long-term goal of the Italians, as it was of the French clergy. This they did in the pulpit, classroom, and press. At the same time, however, they resisted Americanization of New Mexico's indigenous society — not only its religion but also its language and culture. So staunchly did the *Revista* fight efforts to erode regional customs that one historian has described it as "sometime anti-American."[95]

If it is true that many early bishops, priests, and sisters cultivated well-to-do Anglo Americans and Hispanic *ricos*, the same exclusivity cannot be ascribed to the Neapolitans, who worked as much with the poor as with the wealthy. Salvatore Personè, who spent half a century in the Southwest, was not untypical of the group. Described by contemporaries as "Italian in his birth and Mexican in his heart," the Neapolitan was widely recognized "for treating rich and poor alike."[96] Consequently, while the heterogeneous Catholic clergy of the nineteenth-century Southwest shared many features, it is impossible to paint them all with the same brush and in the same colors. The religious panorama of the region, like much of the frontier, was too complex for facile characterization.

9 "Who Could Have Done Anything Like This in Italy?"

THE COLLEGES

> These men are establishing their institutions of learning all
> over the West. . . . Of their money there seems to be no end.
>
> — Rev. Nathan S. S. Beman, Philadelphia, 1847[1]

In 1867, Jesuit Giovanni Battista Ponte swept into San Francisco as official visitor to the California Mission. Dispatched from Italy to oversee operations on the West Coast, the fifty-four-year-old *piemontese* was a seasoned administrator whose six years as head of the Turin Province augured well for successful governance. Already familiar with Jesuit educational work in California, he arrived trusting that his past experience would stand him in good stead in guiding his society's fledgling American colleges. What he encountered, however, soon eroded that certainty. Once confident that time-tested protocols could be easily transposed from Italy to the United States, Ponte grew less sure as he encountered the reality of California. Ruminating on his experience two years later, he concluded that there were limits to what schools staffed entirely by Italians could achieve, "even in America."[2]

"It is not infrequent," Ponte recounted to the superior general, "that one hears it said, 'These good fathers don't understand the country; they're all Italians.'" These doubts inevitably inspired little trust in the Jesuits, "particularly in the area of teaching." "What if," he speculated, "a provincial of France wanted to establish in Italy — in Florence, for example — a college comprised of only or nearly only Frenchmen who had learned Italian as far as they could?" And what if these foreigners taught "not French, but Italian — Tuscan Italian — to the Italians?" "A foreign tongue," Ponte concluded, "always reveals a foreigner."[3]

The linguistic challenge faced by the Italian Jesuits illuminated an essential feature of early American higher education. Unable to find sufficient native-born teachers, institutions relied on immigrant academics from Europe. "It is very hard to find competent professors for the University," Harvard's president, Charles W. Eliot, stated in 1869. "Very few Americans of eminent quality are attracted to this profession." Catholic institutions especially depended on foreign faculty. According to one study, nearly 30 percent of the professors in the nation's pre–Civil War colleges run by the church emigrated from Europe.[4]

At Jesuit schools, the number of imported teachers was even higher. Saint Louis University was run by Belgian priests, who emigrated to the United States to do missionary work. French Jesuits, whose schools in their homeland had been closed by governmental decree, staffed Spring Hill College in Alabama and Fordham College in New York. German clerics deported by Bismarck's *Kulturkampf* founded five schools across the Northeast from New York to the Mississippi River, including Canisius College in Buffalo and John Carroll University in Cleveland. The first rector of every Jesuit college started in the United States before 1900, with only two exceptions, was a foreigner. Thus, the institutions founded by Italians in California, New Mexico, Washington, and Colorado reflected a national pattern. The only thing that made them unique, as will be explained, was that they retained their European character longer than their Catholic counterparts in the rest of the country did.

What was the quality of the exiled educators from Italy? Contemporaries believed that Europe had not sent "mediocrity" to the United States.[5] For their day, the Italians possessed impressive academic credentials, the majority of them having accumulated extensive experience in Europe and the eastern United States before taking up classroom work in the West. A few of the exiles, including the polymath Giuseppe Bayma — mathematician, philosopher, and theoretical physicist — were men of exceptional accomplishment. Bayma's scholarly writings, beginning with *Elements of Molecular Mechanics*, published in London in 1866, earned him recognition as a pioneer in stereochemistry and acclaim as "the foremost, intellectually, of the Jesuit body in California." Although few émigrés matched Bayma's brilliance, most of the Italians enjoyed a sound academic background. "It was the ordinary education of the better classes in Europe," wrote one historian, with additional philosophical and theological training. "Although by present standards this education had serious defects, in mid-nineteenth century America, and especially on the frontier, it was impressive."[6]

As Ponte's report from San Francisco attested, however, the Italians' provenance was a mixed blessing. For one thing, their status as outsiders invited hostility from nativists. "Reasoning from the analogy of the Jesuits' history in Europe," a California newspaper cautioned during the Civil War, "it cannot be doubted" that these same "political ecclesiastics" were playing an "important part" in America's national conflict. In the 1870s, another journal warned that the priests' arriving in San Francisco "a baker's dozen weekly from Europe" imperiled the security of the state. Political leaders in New

Mexico too loudly lamented the coming of "Neapolitan adventurers," cautioning that the "Jesuits and their methods are like suppressed measles — fatal if not conquered." Their exotic quality even ruffled feathers within the Catholic fold. The "manners and ideas" of the Piedmontese priests were, an Irish contemporary recorded, sometimes "too Italian to meet the tastes of the young Republicans of the West."[7]

Caught in perpetual ambivalence, the Italian school masters struggled to strike a balance between two dynamics central to their schools' existence. Like other transplanted educators, they sought to bottle the wine of a centuries-old European educational tradition and dispense its riches in America. If they assimilated American culture to excess, they argued, that heritage would be diluted and lost. On the other hand, too much emphasis on the past would isolate the schools from American society and culture. Accordingly, because Catholic establishments existed to prepare young people for roles in that society, they had to accommodate themselves to the norms and requirements of the United States.[8]

This tension between custom and concession roiled Jesuit institutions in the West throughout their long history. Letters between American college presidents and religious superiors in Italy disclose a constant struggle to uphold cherished educational conventions while at the same time adapting customs to the exigencies of American life. Typically, Giuseppe Cataldo assured the Jesuit superior general in 1892 that the course of studies at Gonzaga College was pursued "just like they are done in an established college in the old world." But it was hardly a case of déjà vu. Cataldo and other leaders filled page after page with justifications for tailoring curriculum, student discipline, and even the Jesuit lifestyle itself to the American scene. We will force Catholics to send their children to soulless public schools where they will lose their religion, Nicola Congiato once chided Roman superiors, if we do not compromise. The corollary of this dynamic tension was that the Italian colleges in the West uniquely blended both Italian and American academic traditions.[9]

Missionaries were sometimes asked to justify their admissions policies to European supervisors. Despite admonitions to keep Protestant enrollments to "as few as possible," all of the frontier colleges drew diverse populations. "They were of all ages and nationalities and opposite creeds," a graduate described his classmates. "A great many Protestant families are our best friends," a newly arrived Italian marveled. Few colleges were as ecumenical as Santa Clara, where in 1868 half of the enrollees were Protestant.[10] "Of course, if we had none but Catholics, things would be better," a priest speculated. "But it is yet too early in this country to refuse admittance to Protestants, and we daily see that some good results from their frequenting our colleges; the removal of religious prejudices being followed in many instances by conversions, sometimes during their stay here, and sometimes at home."[11] Even if "they do not all become Catholics," Michele Accolti added, at least they leave the college "without prejudice against Catholics, their priests, and their religion." "This mix of personalities, nationalities, and religious educations ought to result in a continual revolution," wrote a president of the College of the Sacred Heart, but "we live in peace — although it takes patience."[12]

What were the hallmarks of the transplanted legacy that the Italian educators imparted to their variegated clientele? Striving to replicate in the United States a system of schooling that arced back to sixteenth-century Europe, they forged institutions that were explicitly Christian and humanistic. "The end of the Society and of its studies," summarized the Jesuit *Constitutions*, "is to aid our fellow men to the knowledge and love of God and to the salvation of souls." Embodying the ideals of the Renaissance world in which they arose, Jesuit schools had since their inception embraced learning as a means to a double end — the perfection of the human person and the betterment of society. The chief vehicle for achieving that objective was a curriculum grounded in Greco-Latin culture and amplified by the Christian dimension. Believing with Renaissance humanists that "good literature was essentially didactic," the Jesuits embraced the classics, because they seemed the ideal instrument for an education centered on ethical training and the development of effective rhetorical style and leadership skill.[13]

The Jesuit *Ratio Studiorum*, or "Plan of Studies," a practical manual issued in 1599 and revised in 1832, outlined the order's system of pedagogy. Reflecting an educational philosophy that placed a high priority on a pupil's early mental and moral formation, the typical Jesuit *collegium* comprised two departments, the first of which was roughly equivalent to the modern high school and the second to collegiate studies. It offered a graduated and integrated program to which the neophyte was introduced around the age of twelve and from which he graduated seven or eight years later. The ideal scholar exhibited *eloquentia perfecta*, or articulate wisdom. As a commentator has observed, this meant not only the ability to speak, to write, and to express ideas with ease and elegance, but also "the capacity to reason, to feel, to express oneself and to act, harmonizing virtue with learning." In short, the goal was "the integral formation and style of life along the lines of what today we would call 'human excellence.'"[14]

This was the educational formula that the émigrés planted in the American West. Their schools' ambition was not vocational schooling or the "mere accumulation of learning," a California spokesman stated, but the full flowering of the student's faculties and "the training of his character." The end and essence of instruction was the cultivation of the whole person, that is, "the full and harmonious development of those faculties that are distinctive

of man." Believing that the moral and religious culture of youth was an indispensable element of Christian learning, the Neapolitan Jesuits of New
Mexico directed "their utmost attention to the formation of both heart and
mind in training the students committed to their care."[15]

To achieve this lofty end, the preferred course of studies centered on the
humanities, especially classical Greek and Latin, the natural sciences, philosophy, and, to a lesser degree, theology. Training in classical languages and
culture had been the centerpiece of Jesuit formation in Europe, and the expatriates strove mightily to transplant that tradition to the United States, believing it was the optimum vehicle for an education that was both formative
and informative. In a letter sent to the order in 1832, Superior General Jan
Roothaan conceded the merit of teaching modern subjects, especially vernacular languages and literature, but he directed that "the study of Latin and
Greek letters must always remain intact and be the chief object of attention"
in Jesuit schools. "The more one distances oneself from the Greek and Latin
classics and from old Italian," he warned, "the more one withdraws from
the truly beautiful" and the more one undermined the development of *eloquentia perfecta*. The highest legislative body of the Society echoed this view.
If Latin "has fallen into neglect anywhere," the order's Twenty-Second
General Congregation decreed in 1853, "every effort is to be expended to
revive it."[16]

Even when other educators began to abandon classical studies, the Jesuits
clung to that tradition — and they did so for increasingly dubious reasons.
As one scholar has observed, the first Jesuits "stressed Latin as fundamental not for its intrinsic merits, but because it was *the* essential tool for understanding and influencing the culture of the sixteenth century."[17] Living in
vastly different times, nineteenth-century defenders proposed a new rationale for reading Virgil and Homer — intellectual formation. Ancient literature
not only imparted abiding and universal values, apologists argued, it also
provided, "the most efficient instrument of mental discipline." The highly
inflected idioms of Latin and Greek, with their complicated syntax and
grammar distant from the language of students, were ideal instruments for
the maturation of intelligence and laying bare the laws of thought and logic.[18]
A disciple in California who had embraced the educational philosophy of his
Jesuit mentors summed up the rationale: "The object of education is not the
acquirement of a certain amount of information; information is only the
instrument of the educated mind; but it is to develop and train the mind, to
open its hidden stores, to bring into requisition its dormant powers. For this
end we claim that no means is better adapted than the classics."[19]

The ideal college graduate, according to Jesuit lights, was the bright young
man who had mastered Demosthenes and Aeschylus and thus attained the
bachelor of arts degree. The most prominent alumni of the western colleges,

although no longer familiar names, were classical scholars. Delphin Delmas, who achieved national prominence as a criminal lawyer and Democratic Party activist, graduated with honors from Santa Clara College. Latin and Greek launched the careers of Stephen M. White, U.S. senator from California, and James F. Smith, governor general of the Philippines. Recipients of classical degrees from St. Ignatius College included Augustus J. Bowie, who earned an international reputation for his work in hydraulic gold mining, and the two Sullivan brothers, Matthew and Jeremiah, both of whom became justices of the California Supreme Court. James D. Phelan, later mayor of San Francisco and U.S. senator, surely pleased his mentors when he graduated in 1881 after delivering a valedictory address on "The Utility of Classical Study."[20]

Such scholars were, however, a rarity. Of the several thousand young men who attended Santa Clara during the school's first fifty years, only a small percentage enrolled in the classical course. Of these, fewer than one hundred left with the bachelor of arts diploma, which was granted solely to graduates proficient in Latin and Greek. The bachelor of science degree was far more popular. About 60 percent of the undergraduate diplomas bestowed by St. Ignatius College by the turn of the century were for classical studies.[21] Few Westerners, eager to enter the emerging professions, perceived any pragmatic value in the study of the ancient literature. "Ours is eminently a practical age," declared Andrew J. Moulder, California's superintendent of public instruction in the 1850s and a foe of the classics. "For the mere bookworm — for the Latin and Greek antiquarian — this is certainly not the country." "Until California is better organized," a priest sighed, "nothing else can be done."[22] Of the 219 academicians enrolled in Las Vegas College that year, a mere dozen signed up to study Latin metrics and versification. "Think of the consolation we derive from our work," a teacher said, "when we know that the highest ambition of the boys whom we try to educate is to become rancheros or clerks."[23]

Nonetheless, higher superiors enforced compliance. In 1861, Felice Sopranis, former rector of the Roman College, visited California during an inspection of Jesuit operations in the United States. Displeased by the laxity he encountered, the European visitor attempted to implement an exclusively classical curriculum. The results were disastrous. "We still have not recovered from the terrible blow unleashed on the College by the edicts ordering obligatory Latin and Greek," a teacher at St. Ignatius College wrote a year later. Angry parents withdrew their sons from the school and enrollments faltered. "Oh what a waste of time are Latin and Greek, "for so many students that I now see working for a living — as grocer, butcher, and who knows what else!"[24]

Unlike Sopranis, Nicola Congiato, the superior of Jesuits on the Pacific

Coast, was willing to compromise. "The time has not yet come in California to teach Latin and Greek exclusively," he told the superior general in 1866. Jesuit institutions should instead offer two parallel courses of study "as is done in the other colleges of America," one in the classical languages and another in which English was the language of instruction. In making this recommendation, which was accepted, Congiato maintained that adaptation to the exigencies of shifting culture was the hallmark of Jesuit education, not the conservation of an outdated tradition. This compromise, although subject to periodic challenge, prevailed for decades. Latin was offered at all Jesuit schools, but, as their bulletins acknowledged, it was "only an optional branch of study." Few institutions made as liberal a concession to frontier standards as Gonzaga College, where, until the turn of the century, the classic languages were taught conjointly with commercial subjects.[25]

It was the possibility of learning English — not Latin or Greek — that drew numerous Spanish speakers. About 25 percent of the 1,650 scholars who enrolled at Santa Clara during its first twenty-five years were of Hispanic origin. So important was its bond with that group that the college actively recruited them by publishing a Spanish-language edition of its yearly bulletin.[26] Young *californios* and *nuevomexicanos* flocked to Jesuit institutions for a variety of reasons. Not only were California and New Mexico slow to open public schools, they were also reluctant to accommodate to the educational needs of their newly conquered populations. The Treaty of Guadalupe Hidalgo of 1848, which had concluded the Mexican War, contained no provision guaranteeing the preservation of Spanish in the former Mexican territories. Indeed, bilingual instruction, the common goal of Hispanic leaders in the post-conquest era, was explicitly prohibited in California. Instead, the state Bureau of Public Instruction ordered in 1855 that English be used as the teaching language in all public institutions. Alienated by insufficiencies in the public system, many Spanish-speaking parents found Catholic schools an appealing alternative.[27]

There was intense pressure to master English and the expertise needed for survival in the Anglo world that had suddenly burst upon them. "Study, study as much as you can. Don't waste time," the mother of a young *californio* urged her son. The young man's resolve to master English and to adapt to novel customs testified to a determination to find a place in the new dispensation. To accommodate these learners, the Jesuits of Santa Clara offered some bilingual instruction. Classes in Christian doctrine were organized for pupils whose first language was Spanish, and there were courses in reading and spelling for young foreigners who came from Mexico. At the ceremonies concluding the first year of Las Vegas College in 1878, the program was equally divided between English and Spanish presentations.

Students had come to school to learn a new language, however, not to converse in the old. Native Californian José María Estudillo recorded in detail the ups and downs of his linguistic progress. "This evening was the first time I ever composed two lines of poetry," he confided to his diary in 1861. A new level of self-confidence was recorded the day a Dublin-born professor lauded his recitation of a prose assignment — " 'The Land I Long to See' — with the feeling of an Irishman." The proud eighteen-year-old's crowning accomplishment was a long-desired invitation to speak at commencement exercises in 1862, "my first speech in public," he recorded.[28]

The milieu of the Italian establishments eased the cultural transition of Spanish speakers in other ways, too. Mixed student bodies provided opportunities for forging friendships with both Anglo and Hispanic classmates, and enrollees discovered among the European faculty mentors who themselves wrestled with the challenge of acculturation. Life at a rural college reminded pupils of the ranchos from which they came, and its familiar religious practices forged a strong bond with Hispanic culture. It is "the best there is in California," maintained James Alexander Forbes, who enrolled his Anglo-Hispanic sons at Santa Clara. The teachers "are concerned about the religious education of the students, without which there can be no true instruction."[29] New Mexican parents insisted that their sons be taught by priests at Las Vegas College. They "were not pleased" that their offspring "should be placed under seculars," a teacher reported. This "was a Jesuit college," and therefore "Jesuits should have the care of their boys."[30] In sum, by providing continuity with pre-conquest society, the Jesuit college filled much the same function for young *californios* and *nuevomexicanos* that the Catholic parish did for European immigrants. It served as a mediating influence between old and new cultures, offering a familiar experience in a unfamiliar environment and thereby easing accommodation to an altered world.[31]

The immigrant school masters adjusted their curriculum to western interests. Reasoning that even classicists required heavy doses of chemistry, physics, and mathematics, the Italians gave their disciples extensive instruction in the sciences — more, in fact, than was available in Jesuit institutions in the East. In part, this emphasis underscored the Society's long commitment to scientific study. But the promotion of technical learning also reflected the prominence given to scientific instruction in American education, particularly in the West.[32] The Italians' frontier colleges had been founded in the aftermath of mineral strikes. Moreover, they served populations whose economic lifeblood was gold from the Sierra Nevada, silver from the Comstock Lode, and gold from the Coeur d'Alene Mountains of Idaho. "The Fathers recognize the fact that this is a mineral country," a San Francisco journal reported in 1866, "and that many of their pupils may become interested in mining development."[33] Apprentices were trained in assaying, a skill "of highest importance here," a priest told European officials. Indeed, so essen-

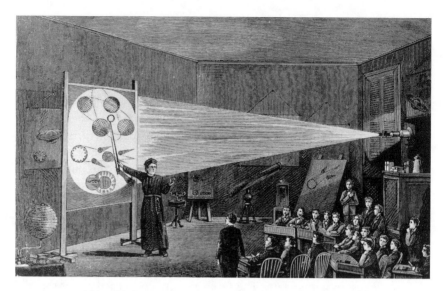

FIGURE 21. Although Jesuit institutions in the West promoted a traditional classical curriculum, they also accommodated to frontier interests by promoting the sciences. In this 1887 lithograph, a priest at Santa Clara College instructs students with the aid of the magic lantern. Courtesy Santa Clara University Archives, CV.7.7

tial was mineral analysis that a course on the subject became obligatory at Gonzaga College in Spokane.[34]

To instruct learners in a wide variety of technical disciplines, the Italians scoured Europe and America for the latest scientific instruments and mineral collections. At a price of nearly ten thousand dollars, the Californians imported from Paris "a complete philosophical [scientific] and chemical apparatus" and other teaching aids to enable their institutions to "keep pace with the progress of science." Santa Clara's array of equipment, some of which was transferred to the Smithsonian Institution in the twentieth century, drew comment from contemporaries. Visitors frequently voiced surprise at finding in a rough frontier college "the most recent inventions from Europe," including a Duboscq telescope, Faraday's electromagnetic machine, electrical instruments made by Rumkhoff, and "the most modern arrangement for producing electric light."[35] In 1863, Congiato informed officials in Europe that the school's physics laboratory was "one of the best in the United States, with a chemistry laboratory that is the best in the State, and also the only one that has what's needed to do chemical analyses. It is to Santa Clara that people have recourse when there is some important chemical analysis to be done. They even come from Mexico for this purpose."[36]

The physics and chemistry laboratories of St. Ignatius College were exceptional. According to a 1880 national survey of science curricula in five hundred American colleges and universities, the San Francisco school, which possessed a "collection of physical apparatus valued at over $50,000," ranked among 120 superior institutions. Offering two years of general chemistry with qualitative and quantitative analysis, its curriculum was exemplary for its day. The course of study at the two California schools was the creation of several priest-scientists, beginning with Carlo Messea, who oversaw the initial purchase of Santa Clara's treasury of minerals and instruments, and Antonio Cichi, whose areas of expertise were chemistry and mineralogy.[37] The Piedmontese priest Giuseppe Neri specialized in spectroscopy and the industrial applications of electricity. His public presentations on spectrum analysis in San Francisco in 1873 were described by San Francisco's *Mining and Scientific Press* as "the most thorough and complete course of scientific lectures every delivered in this city." Neri was the first to introduce electrical lighting — "arc lights of his own invention" — to the city's streets in 1876, a feat that bathed the school in welcome publicity.

Neri and his colleagues engaged in popular experimental lectures, but they gave no heed to published research of the sort that was already gaining national acclaim for faculty at the University of California at Berkeley. Nevertheless, the schools' course of studies did undercut the charge later made by Charles Eliot of Harvard that Jesuit fixation on the classics resulted in a mere "trifling concession made to natural science." While that charge might have been true of eastern colleges, it did not describe the colleges in the West, which, by mid-century standards, offered above-average scientific instruction.[38]

Commercial training constituted another adjustment of the European curriculum to American expectations. Responding to a sharp rise in the number of college graduates entering technical careers, mercantile education emerged as an appealing alternative to the classics throughout the country after the Civil War. As early as 1854, the Jesuit schools in California had begun offering classes in commercial subjects for students who favored "limiting themselves to the common branches of business education." This track, which excluded Latin and Greek, embraced English grammar and rhetoric, bookkeeping, mathematics, algebra, geometry, Spanish, French, political science, and American jurisprudence.[39]

Despite its popularity, Jesuits privately dithered about the worth of vocational education. Many Italians steadfastly opposed the commercial course, because it undermined Latin and Greek and because it seemed a surrender to materialism. Accustomed to a world shaped by tradition, the Jesuits now found themselves in one driven by Mammon, as a visitor to California once observed. "The Americans think only of dollars, talk only of dollars, seek nothing but dollars; they are the men of dollars."[40] Schooling in mercantile subjects might be "greatly suited to the temperament and training of Americans, who from their very cradle are engaged in the accumulation of money," another priest charged, but it is "very foreign to our customs, by which boys are educated in the study of the humanities and natural sciences."[41] They nevertheless held their noses and embraced business instruction because of the tuition revenue that it generated.

Of all the western colleges, Santa Clara offered the most elaborate commercial program in a distinctive hall fabricated expressly for that purpose. Built of wood and brick, the two-story edifice contained classrooms on the first floor; on the second, two large galleries equipped with extensive apparatus were designed to instruct enrollees in the theory and functioning of nineteenth-century capitalism. Replicating the commercial world "in miniature," the hall contained a post office, bank, express office, telegraph office, and other alcoves designed to represent the more important lines of commercial activity. There was a "tribunal of commerce" fashioned as a courtroom for "the adjustment of cases by legal procedure." The ultimate touch of realism was provided by the college press, which printed "commercial currency" that served as cash for student transactions.[42]

Other schools plowed the same path. Gonzaga College offered a modest commercial curriculum as soon as it opened its doors in 1887. In New Mexico, classes in bookkeeping and related subjects dominated the curriculum of Las Vegas College. "Owing to the special requirements of this Territory," the school's prospectus announced, "the course of studies is mainly commercial." Although the classics drew more adherents after the institution relocated in populous Denver, business training continued to flourish because financial exigency prohibited its cessation. The course was equally indispensable at Seattle College, where the city's irregular growth and lack of interest in Latin made it difficult to assemble a full student body. "If we don't open a commercial course," a priest advised, "our college will continue to vegetate." None of the Jesuit institutions conceded collegiate status to the study of business, however. In lieu of a degree, scholars who finished the three- or four-year program were awarded a certificate of completion. Not until the early twentieth century was the commercial course raised to collegiate standing in most American colleges and universities.[43]

Coping with Linguistic Deficiencies

Nowhere was the ethnic character of the Italian school masters more acutely evidenced than in their labor to master the American language. Fluency in English was a must, not only for teaching grammar and literature, but also for the mastery of elocution, which, they discovered, Americans prized highly. "Good speech-making means more to them than rhetoric and philosophy," Giuseppe Marra observed. Eloquent representatives were also essential for the good administration of the colleges and for dealing with the public, upon whom the institutions relied not only for students but for financial support. Additionally, articulate personnel made the best mediators between the college's European tradition and American culture in the on-going process of institutional accommodation. As missionary Carlo Pinto summarized, priests who spoke English fluently possessed an "indispensable quality."[44]

But every Italian enterprise in the West wrestled with linguistic short-comings. Only a few of the Piedmontese in California "know English well," Superior General Pieter Beckx lamented in 1870. An Irish co-worker concurred that in both the classroom and the pulpit, most of the Italians "spoke and taught in a language not altogether English." In some residences, especially during the years of peak immigration, Italian rather than the local language was the common argot. Emanuele Nattini nagged in 1870 that English was "never spoken" at recreation by the Jesuits of St. Ignatius College. Even the president, Giuseppe Bayma, "never speaks English if he can get by without it, although he can speak fairly well." Noting that the faculty relied on Italian and French gazettes for news about the world, Nattini wrote: "we live here as if our house and our interests were a thousand miles away." This "distancing" of ourselves from "the language and customs of the country is a continual mortification to the few American fathers who work indefatigably with us and for us."[45]

The situation was worse in the Southwest. Despite warnings that "the time was not ripe for such a venture," the Neapolitans had opened their modest institution in New Mexico in 1877 without assurance of sufficient man-power. "The little college that we are opening promises to work out well on the condition that one good English teacher, at least, is sent," a superior warned. "If none comes, I am very concerned. It is a matter or life for death for this very poor Mission." Familiarity with the language of America implied familiarity with its culture. When superiors threatened to remove the gifted Giuseppe Marra from the Las Vegas school for assignment elsewhere, the school's head panicked. "Marra is the only one who know how to run these classes," he wailed, because "he is the only one who has spent time in the colleges in the States." If Marra departed, there was no one to replace him.[46]

Lack of suitable personnel led to desperate measures. In 1861, Giacomo Vanzina, freshly landed in San Francisco in 1861, was named prefect of discipline at St. Ignatius College, a job for which he was eminently ill-equipped. Assigned "the task of mastering the difficulties of the character of the American boy," an early chronicler records, Vanzina was himself struggling to master English. No wonder inexperienced teachers balked at the prospect of stepping into the classroom, especially if, like Vanzina, they were tongue-tied and unfamiliar with the culture. "American boys are quite different from Italians," another raw recruit lamented. "When they know that a professor is a foreigner and does not know the language well, they lose all respect for him and all too often the poor teacher becomes their plaything."[47] Want of native speakers hamstrung every undertaking in the Southwest, a priest grieved, thereby creating obstacles that were endlessly "insurmountable." As late as 1902, an official confessed that the faculty of the college in Denver was "not up to the mark" because of its abracadabra English.[48]

Unable to find instructors among their own ranks, the Italians cast their nets widely, gathering helpers wherever they could find them. As an outcome, their communities were international to a degree unusual even for the Society of Jesus. We are "a jumble of Italians, Frenchmen, and Germans," a priest in New Mexico said. A Jesuit Noah's ark, Sacred Heart College in Denver had a staff comprised of "two Frenchmen, an Italian, two American scholastics, one Irish brother, two Mexican brothers, one German novice," observed President Domenico Pantanella, in 1885. "One never knows what language to speak!"[49]

The most prized recruits were native speakers who could "impart a knowledge of higher English" to their pupils. From every corner of the frontier, the Italians appealed to outside Jesuits to "send us helpers who speak English."[50] Not content with letter-writing, the missionaries scrounged Europe in search of volunteers. Of the twenty-three teachers employed by Sacred Heart College in 1888, five were Irish-born. When Patrick Kelly, an Irish Jesuit, died in California in 1887, an Italian associate described his passing as "a serious loss for the Mission, and what's worse, he is irreplaceable." Other draftees hastily ascended up the leadership ladder. Immigrant Edward Allen joined the Californians and soon became president of St. Ignatius College. Charles Mackin, from County Armagh, disregarding taunts from classmates about living "among Dagoes . . . and bears," went West to join the Rocky Mountain Mission, where he served as the second president of Gonzaga College.[51]

Leaders of the western missions toured the Atlantic states in hopes of persuading young Americans to become Jesuits. Several of these highly prized recruits had distinguished careers in the West, including Richard Gleeson of Philadelphia, who, at age seventeen, entered the Society in 1877 after responding to an appeal from Luigi Varsi that netted the California Mission fourteen new members. Gleeson later became president of Santa Clara College, founder of Loyola College in Los Angeles (later Loyola Marymount University), head of the California Jesuit Province, and a leading churchman in San Francisco. A few young Americans, such as John J. Brown, joined the Jesuits after attending one of the western schools. A graduate of Las Vegas

College, Brown became the first American-born president of Sacred Heart College even before he had finished his training, such was the shortage of qualified men in the Neapolitan mission.

Another native-born teacher, a Hugh L. Magevney from Tennessee, was admired by Denver co-workers for his pulpit oratory and "full command and control of the English language." The popular speaker enjoyed such repute among the Denver public that his eventual departure from the Jesuits to join the diocesan priesthood precipitated a crisis. Embarrassed at losing such a valued asset, administrators retained him at the college but tried to conceal the fact that he was no longer a Jesuit. This was done by removing the distinguishing letters "S.J." after the names of *all* of the Jesuit faculty listed in the college bulletin for as long as Magevney remained on the staff. Thus, an unsuspecting public never discovered that the star professor no longer belonged to the Society of Jesus. It was "a real calamity to lose him," Marra observed, because "we do not have others who present themselves so well publicly."[52]

The Italians captured additional workers through trading. From their ranks, they supplied eastern urban parishes and Woodstock College with pastors and professors of philosophy and theology. In return, the westerners acquired coveted native speakers for their schools in San Francisco, Santa Clara, Denver, and Spokane. Like their Irish recruits, American volunteers were pivotal players in the development of the frontier colleges. Edmund Young, a Jesuit from Maine, taught literature, rhetoric, and debate at Santa Clara for thirty years. "The only American among us now," said an appreciative Italian in 1869, the transplanted New Englander had "too much to do." So indelible was his imprint that an early chronicler claimed that "to him in great measure, Santa Clara College owes the reputation it enjoys."[53]

Marylander Michael J. Hughes, the first American teacher at Las Vegas College, filled a similar role in New Mexico. Not every recruit proved satisfactory, however. Californians sent the American priest Florence Boudreaux back to Missouri when he proved "incompetent" to teach physics, chemistry, and mineral analysis "to the high degree which is required here."[54]

Never able to find enough Jesuits, the colleges employed lay persons. Bernard J. Reid, a twenty-six-year-old Pennsylvanian who had failed in the goldfields, worked as teacher and secretary to Santa Clara's first president. Relying on Reid's proficiency in U.S. law and in English, Giovanni Nobili found him indispensable in launching the nascent institution. Attorneys and businessmen aided the foreign clergy with counsel when nativist opposition and financial impecuniousness threatened their institutions, as in California, where disputes over land titles made dexterous legal advice imperative. What a Neapolitan Jesuit said of two instructors at Las Vegas College applied to Reid and other lay faculty: "Without them, we would not have been able to start the school."[55]

The number of lay professors at a typical Jesuit college was never large, however. In 1890, Jesuits outnumbered the half-dozen lay professors on the staff of Santa Clara College by a four-to-one ratio. When Las Vegas College was moved to Denver, only one non-cleric — a violin teacher — was included among the school's twenty-two instructors.[56] Because the colleges were perennially short on cash, if a Jesuit could be found to fill a vacancy, he, rather than a salaried person, was hired. Besides, good teachers were difficult to retain in mining regions that abounded in employment opportunities. Thus, a prospective instructor in California declared in 1854 that "nothing less than $100 a month" — roughly $2,300 today — "would adequately remunerate me for discharging the duties of Mathematical Teacher, etc. in your college." Such persons usually taught courses for which Jesuits were either unavailable or untrained, such as bookkeeping, music, or dancing. St. Ignatius College in San Francisco advertised that its commercial course was "taught exclusively by secular professors."[57]

Other laymen enlisted as maintenance workers, cooks, laundrymen, carpenters, stockmen, and gardeners. Neapolitan immigrants who had come to the United States in search of work occupied these posts at the College of the Sacred Heart in Denver, a convenient arrangement since both employee and employer spoke the same language. Bachelors who lived on campus received religious instruction and joined in the semi-monastic life of the boarding schools, whose moral standards they were expected to uphold. Breaches in conduct led to swift dismissal, as in Denver, where, a priest reported in 1892, the college's "famous first-class cook" had to be let go because "one of his friends was found lying under his . . . bed at 6 A.M."[58]

If the hiring of teachers stretched institutional resourcefulness, locating skilled administrators was equally daunting. What Bishop James Roosevelt Bayley, the founder of Seton Hall, said of East Coast schools was even more true of those in the West. "It is more difficult to find a good college president than to find a good anything else in this world. All that the college needs to insure its permanent prosperity is a president." A Catholic college was confronted with an especially steep challenge because its leader functioned as priest, college administrator, and fundraiser — if done effectively, it was more than a one-man job. He was expected to preside at social gatherings and to visit classes to assure that they were conducted correctly. Since a college was judged by the aptitudes of its director, talent for promoting the good name of the school was a prized presidential quality. Loss of popular esteem had led to the collapse of Jesuit institutions in Europe, and cultivating good public relations was also an ever-present concern in America.[59]

Still more was required of a Jesuit manager, who served not only as head of the college, but also as spiritual leader or rector of both the Jesuit community and the student body. And since a rector's term of office was restricted by the Society's law to six years, colleges were perpetually on the lookout for replacements. Some otherwise-apt candidates were shelved because they were "not very supernatural and not very edifying." For instance, gatekeepers spurned a presidential prospect at Gonzaga College, Francis Dillon, because he was bereft of "the qualities needed to be a rector of a scholasticate," the seminary attached to the college. Likewise, Domenico Pantanella, although skilled at public relations and fundraising, was passed over to head Sacred Heart College in Denver because he was not an effective religious superior. Instead, authorities elevated Salvatore Personè, who, although he lacked "ability in running American colleges," possessed "a likeable manner, respectable presence, good practical judgement, and a conciliatory spirit." Presidents who devoted too much time to their spiritual duties also fell short. Nicola Congiato once complained that Santa Clara's Bouchard Villiger was "not at all made for colleges," because he acted like "a father abbot." "Here you need an active rector and man of affairs."[60]

And then there was the perennial issue of language. Luigi Gentile, writing to Naples in 1881, sounded a cry raised by western superiors, "Oh, if you would send me a man who would be a good rector for the college and who knows English!" Immigrant educators sometimes despaired of successfully completing a presidential search. Finding a candidate at ease with both the language and the culture of the adopted country was fraught with frustration. Giuseppe Sasia, superior of the California Mission, dismissed the nomination of Telesforo Demasini, a capable Latinist, to head St. Ignatius College because he spoke an "almost unintelligible jargon." "It is absolutely necessary" that the head of an American college "know English well," Sasia reminded higher-ups, "and that he be able to speak in public to students and to converse facilely and accurately to lay persons."[61]

Administrative experience gained in Europe was sometimes of limited utility in the United States. As Nicola Congiato once explained to superiors in Rome, the president of an American college "does everything." The head of the Rocky Mountain Mission, Georges de la Motte, insisted during a frustrating search for a president of Seattle College that he must be "a man of action" whose talents suited the needs of a maturing city. During the brick-and-mortar era of nineteenth-century college building, this meant the ability to raise money and cultivate supportive friends for the institution. Seattle College's first president, French-born Victor Garrand, was described by De la Motte as "a hard worker," but his poor management plunged the fledgling institution "deeply into debt." Garrand was smitten with the notion "that we should not care for money matters, but rely only on Providence in building up our places."[62] Nine years and three presidents later, the Jesuits were still looking for "an experienced, prominent rector, one that will command the respect of the bishop, priests, and people" of Seattle. "A true college man is sorely needed at the helm," they told Rome, but we don't have one.[63]

Everyone recognized that the best collegiate leader was an American, or, as

Congiato explained, "at least a well-Americanized Irish president." However, since vocations to the order from native ranks remained low for many years, Europeans — Italians mostly — commanded the western schools. Only four of the first fourteen presidents of St. Ignatius College were non-Italians, and all but three of the priests who governed the College of the Sacred Heart and its predecessor schools were Italian-born. The presidential chair at Santa Clara College was occupied solely by *piemontesi* for thirty-two years, with the exception of the brief, four-year term of a Swiss priest. By contrast, heterogeneity characterized the governance of Jesuit colleges in the Pacific Northwest in consequence of the region's broad appeal as missionary territory. Thus, Gonzaga's first ten presidents included three Germans, three Frenchmen, an Irishman, a Belgian, an American, and only one Italian, Lorenzo Palladino. As elsewhere in the West, however, Italians consistently controlled the governance of the mission itself.[64]

Reliance on Europe for managers produced some near-disasters. Few presidents were less equipped to govern than Enrico Imoda, who led St. Ignatius College for six years. Shy, aloof, and deficient in English, the administrator ducked encounters with both pupils and public. Gatekeepers in Europe sometimes betrayed their ignorance of America through ill-advised meddling in college governance. In 1867, an official visitor from Italy, landing in California, like a muse ex machina gave orders over matters of which he knew little. Displeased with the discipline enforced at the colleges, Giovanni Ponte took matters into his own hands and assumed control — notwithstanding his lack of knowledge about "the country, its customs, and way of doing things." The result, an unhappy Nicola Congiato reported, was a laundry list of "serious mistakes" that damaged the two schools. By unilaterally tightening student discipline at Santa Clara, Ponte angered thirty Hispanic enrollees, who packed their trunks and returned home. Their exodus constituted "a grave loss . . . both for the present and for the future" of the college, Congiato lamented, because it "closes the bridge to Mexico," which customarily boosted enrollment.[65]

The majority of émigrés, however, discharged their duties adequately, some even with distinction. As an Irish associate confirmed, several of the Italians spoke and wrote English "fluently and with precision," as their expressive letters attest. The most effective among them were the most thoroughly Americanized. Luigi Varsi, who headed two California colleges, was well-regarded for his charm and culture and for his skill in winning the support of wealthy benefactors, especially women. Michele Accolti was "one of the most polished gentlemen on this coast," in the estimation of a former student. Giuseppe Marra, "esteemed and loved by the boys and their parents" at Las Vegas College, loomed singularly over his fellow Neapolitans, because he "understands all about American colleges and knows English very well."[66]

FIGURE 22. The founding faculty and students of Gonzaga College
in Spokane, Washington, 1887. Like most Catholic establishments
in the West, the early Jesuit schools enrolled elementary and high
school students as well as collegians. Courtesy Jesuit Oregon Province
Archives, Gonzaga University, CN 233

Several Italians developed entrepreneurial skills that kept institutions
afloat in times of crisis. Alessandro Diomedi was praised as president of Seattle College because he was "a good financial manager." Giovanni Nobili,
although he was not much of a spiritual leader, proved himself excellent in
practical matters. Jesuits winced when plain-speaking Pantanella took command, but they conceded that "when it comes to finding money, he is better than all of us." In his energetic, seat-of-the-pants style, Pantanella trans-

ferred Sacred Heart College to Denver and constructed there an entirely new campus within the space of a year. "He certainly could claim powers of blarney," said an admiring American, "and these he used to good purpose."[67]

Institutional Bridge Building

No chore tested the mettle of a refugee president more than raising money. In Europe, Jesuit institutions had relied for succor on royal patronage, benefactions, and investments, which enabled them to offer instruction gratis. However, neither public funding nor endowments were to be had in America. Most Catholics were lower middle-class immigrants, who, like the Jesuits themselves, had arrived nearly penniless. Consequently, it was in the United States that schools of the Society had begun charging tuition for the first time. In 1833, Pope Gregory XVI, responding to pleas from Saint Louis University — which had been reduced to billing boarders for winter firewood — granted the order a dispensation from its historical commitment to free schooling.

Although fees varied widely, the price of schooling at Jesuit college at mid-century typically ran about $60 a year for a day scholar and $200 for a lodger. Fees in the West, where everything cost more, were usually higher. Institutions in the territories of New Mexico and Washington, which had at first catered solely to juveniles, charged $200 and $250, respectively, for tuition, room, and board. Santa Clara College, one of the most expensive colleges in the country, charged $350, mandated by the high cost of living in Gold Rush California. Later in the century, tuition-free education was briefly attempted at St. Ignatius College, the day school in San Francisco, but the experiment was quickly struck off as financially impractical.[68]

Expensive construction programs sent costs soaring at every frontier college, despite repeated admonitions from European authorities to build modestly. "Our dwellings and colleges must be in accord with poverty and religious simplicity," Superior General Beckx admonished Jesuits in 1860, "adapted, it is true, to our needs and our occupations, but never built with too much expensiveness and elegance of architecture." As events in Europe had demonstrated, drawing public attention was risky, and extravagance "thrusts itself before the eyes of all." When the immigrant school masters began erecting schools in America, poverty and religious simplicity were mandated by circumstance. "Wretched" was the word Archbishop José Alemany used to describe the adobe hovel he handed over to the Piedmontese Jesuits at Santa Clara in 1851. The old mission had been "so plundered and reduced to the condition of a big stable" by years of negligence that Michele Accolti agreed it formed "a poor and ugly school." In New Mexico, "umbrellas would have been very serviceable to keep the Fathers from getting wet in their rooms," a teacher recounted, "but the misery was that they were too poor to afford the luxury of umbrellas."[69]

The exiles soon discovered, however, that looks counted in America. Handsome buildings with "a respectable air" were a necessity, Accolti explained, "especially in the eyes of the Americans," who judge by external appearance. In this country, "you have to 'humbug'" (*bisogna humbuggare*), the Genoese priest Cesare Barchi agreed. "A little show is worth more than a thousand pounds of reality," he advised, as plans for rebuilding St. Ignatius College took impressive form. "We'll be wasting our time if we don't offer the public good rooms that are airy, sunny, ventilated, comfortable and well furnished." Others reprised the refrain. "Appearances count for a lot here," Giuseppe Marra repeatedly told overseas officials. "The American, more than any other nationality is impressed by appearances, and believes in what he sees." They believe "a beautiful building must signify an excellent school," and hence "we must adapt to this weakness of theirs."[70]

When the Neapolitans drew up plans for the College of the Sacred Heart in Denver, Domenico Pantanella insisted that even if he had to borrow heavily from European creditors, the structure would be "as splendid as possible." Public reaction to his architectural soufflé showed Pantanella had been right. Built of pink sandstone, the majestic four-story citadel mirrored his earlier *capo lavoro*, Woodstock College. It contained "magnificent living rooms, general study areas, chemistry labs, an elegant refectory, and a kitchen," reported a dazzled tyro fresh from New Mexico. "The top floor held a spacious dormitory divided into two sections, accommodating 250 boarders in four housing units." "It's not merely beautiful," Pantanella gloated, "it's elegant."[71]

The immigrants labored to transform the western landscape with ornamental foliage *all'italiana*. Investment in gardens, arbors, walkways, and outdoor sculpture not only enhanced the reputation of the school but also contributed to the spiritual and aesthetical uplifting of the academic community. The Piedmontese took advantage of California's Mediterranean climate by introducing a Noah's ark of domestic and foreign foliage into their gardens. Enclosed with verandas and criss-crossed by trellises of grapevines, Santa Clara College's large interior courtyard, with its fountain, flowers, caged song birds, and exotic plants of every type, beckoned visitors from far and wide in a region still lacking floral embellishment. "The whole scene was," one caller chirped, "marvelously like Italy."[72]

With as yet few rivals, the academies of the Italians invariably drew wide public notice. Regardless of religious affiliation, observers recognized that these establishments contributed not a little to the establishment of community and culture on a developing frontier. Santa Clara College "is probably the best literary institution in the state," Horace Greeley decided after a visit in 1859, adding that it "attracts many sons of non-Catholic parents, though a Catholic seminary." San Francisco's St. Ignatius College seemed equally splendid by western standards. Beholding their splendid scientific laboratories, lofty Victorian buildings, crowded classrooms, and lovely gardens, outsiders surmised that the Jesuit colleges were managed, as one San Francisco paper put it, by "far-seeing speculators and the most accomplished of financiers."[73]

In fact, however, the stately structures were weighed down with monumental deficits, sometimes prompting European overseers to suspect fiscal ineptitude. With the completion of each new chapel, theater, or gymnasium, the tally of losses mounted. "We've got enormous debts and nothing else," Luigi Varsi reported from St. Ignatius College, which was over one million dollars in arrears by 1885. In the underdeveloped Southwest, Neapolitans too waged an unrelenting battle with creditors. "These are terrible days for me," grieved Salvatore Personè of Las Vegas College in 1878; "many nights I cannot sleep." The financial health of the College of the Sacred Heart in Denver vacillated with the ebb and flow of Colorado silver production. When its enrollment sank to forty-nine boarders during the depression of the 1890s, the school stood on the brink of closure. "Poor us," mission superior Carlo Pinto sighed in 1897, if we should lose the financial acumen of Fathers Pantanella and Guida. "Who would want to walk along the knife edge as they do?"[74]

All of the western schools took creative steps to balance their books. In New Mexico, students paid their tuition with *oves et boves et pecora campi* ("oxen, cattle, and sheep from the field"), a Bible-quoting priest humorously observed. As a result, mutton became "a rather common dish," and "after awhile there was rather too much of it for comfort." Santa Clara's Giovanni Nobili settled accounts by educating a creditor's several sons at the college free of charge. Taking advantage of the order's internationality, the schools looked abroad for help. The extent to which Jesuit institutions in the United States relied on the south for both students and money is shown by the frequency with which they sent agents to Mexico and Central America.[75]

To sustain the cash flow, the St. Ignatius College treasurer, Antonio Maraschi, invested in real estate. As he reminded the Jesuit superior general, in the United States it was impossible to count on bequests from benefactors as had been the practice in Europe, and hence other ways of sustaining institutions had to be found. However, when the enterprising priest ventured $14,000 in a gold mine in hopes of liquidating the swelling debts of St. Ignatius and Santa Clara colleges, the mission superior threatened to remove him from office. Seven years later, liabilities linked to Maraschi's disastrous mining venture had mounted to $38,000, a "notable sum," which spawned still more burdens for the California Mission.[76] A similar fiasco erupted in Colorado. Two Neapolitan priests, Francesco Gubitosi and Rafael Baldassare, invested in a silver mine that not only failed to return a profit but sank the Southwestern Mission deeply into debt.

The colleges also relied on more conventional sources of income. The contributed services of the Jesuit faculty provided the schools with an unusual form of endowment, but neither this asset nor tuition revenue compensated for high capital outlays. Since most of the schools had churches moored to them, Sunday collections provided a steady income, except in time of recession. As in Italy, agricultural production helped to decrease operational costs. The typical boarding school stuffed its pantry with provisions grown on the campus periphery. The Neapolitans of Denver, for instance, raised pigs and chickens, planted orchards, and harvested fields of alfalfa to fodder their livestock. Gonzaga College ran its own dairy and grew grain and vegetables. The twelve-acre campus of Santa Clara College seemed to visitors "a village more than a mere institution for educational purposes." Hogs and several types of fowl supplied meat. A grove of forty olive trees yielded a sufficiency of oil, a staple of the Italian diet, and nearby orchards and *giardini* stuffed the pantry with fresh fruit and vegetables. The college's image as a self-sustained country village was completed by a tailor shop, a cobbler shop, a machine shop, a carpenter shop, printing office, and blacksmith shop. An apothecary administered by Giovanni Battista Boggio, a Jesuit brother, earned the college as much as $900 a month.[77]

In their pursuit of economic self-sufficiency, the immigrants produced wine in New Mexico, Texas, and California. Having inherited a small vineyard from their Franciscan predecessors, California's *piemontesi* augmented production by planting additional tracts on the western edge of the Santa Clara Valley. Most of the harvest from the college vineyards was used for sacramental purposes or domestic consumption. Older boarders, if their parents consented, were allowed a glass of wine with meals. Offered for sale to the public, wine netted the college an average of several thousand dollars annually. By the late 1880s, the Jesuits regarded their vineyards as one of their main resources.[78]

A staff of Jesuit brothers managed plant operations at each college. Men of varied professional and educational backgrounds, they worked as farmer, carpenter, tailor, sacristan, nurse, cook, milkman, gardener, craftsman, and vintner. Bartolomeo Tortore, an artist before he was a Jesuit, taught painting and drawing at Santa Clara College for twenty-five years. Giuseppe Carignano, who doubled as cook and artist, played a similar role at Gonzaga College. Although few brothers were involved in teaching, they were responsible to no small degree for a school's economic sustenance. Through their varied employments they freed the priests for ministerial and academic work and minimized reliance on salaried employees. Faced with the prospect of losing the services of one brother in Denver in 1895, Marra observed that he was the college's only baker and, if he departed, the institution would have to buy bread; given difficult times, it could not afford to do so.[79]

Despite ups and downs, the transplanted professors adjusted to their adopted country. "It is said that the fathers are not business men," a Jesuit apologist in California observed, but "let us ask any business man to attempt and achieve with the same means at Santa Clara's disposal what Santa Clara has done." Salvatore Personè, proud of the handsome stone edifice the Neapolitans had erected in Denver, paused in 1890 to reflect on that accomplishment. "Who would have thought," he marveled, "that five Italians without a penny in their pocket and unknown in Denver" could have achieved so much? "Who could have done anything like this in Italy?" Confrères in Europe were equally impressed. "All this is not nothing," Turinese provincial Mateo Ciravegna once remarked about Piedmontese attainments in California. Considering that they started on a shoestring and were "not sufficiently versed in the language," their feat was remarkable.[80] Even critics offered occasional kudos. The editor of a usually hostile San Francisco journal declared in 1864, "The Jesuits have the most prosperous and populous educational institutions in California." A few years later, Santa Clara College could claim "the largest number of Professors and Tutors connected with any institution on the Pacific Coast."[81]

One measure of the schools' significance was that they offered educational opportunity in regions that otherwise would not have been served. The 1850 census of New Mexico Territory, for example, revealed 25,089 illiterate persons out of a total population of 61,549. The number of children attending school numbered only 466. It was missionaries, Protestant and Catholic alike, who bridged the educational gap with their pioneer institutions. As one scholar notes, "the first stable plan of formal education" for the inhabitants of the region, the vast majority of whom were Hispanic, was created by the Italian Jesuits.[82] The 1887 founding of Gonzaga College satisfied a similar need in Washington, where for many decades public education remained at tadpole stage. With only half a dozen grade schools in the entire territory and the University of Washington still in its "raw infancy," no uniform system of public education appeared until after the granting of statehood in 1889.[83]

The same was true in California. "With this concourse of people" from all over the world, "the number of families goes on increasing," Accolti observed in 1850, "and so there is a great host of children needing the benefits of an education without anybody being in a position to satisfy this need." But, as contemporaries recognized, "nothing can be expected from the State." Despite the demand for schools, legislators were loath to levy special educational taxes in an era when other costly public services were equally imper-

FIGURE 23. Focused primarily on urban education, the California Jesuits founded St. Ignatius College in San Francisco in 1855. With an enrollment of over 704 students, it was the order's largest day school in the United States by 1884, nearly twice as large as its nearest rival in New York. Courtesy St. Ignatius College Preparatory/University of San Francisco Archives

ative. As a consequence, the responsibility of educating youth, especially on the collegiate level, was left to private institutions, which partly explains why California had no state university until the University of California was founded in 1868. Whatever existed in the form of higher education, observed John Swett, the founder of California's public school system, was provided by Santa Clara, St. Ignatius, and the state's other private institutions.[84]

The schools planted by the émigré educators were also important because they spurred others to action. The potentially destructive power generated by the Know Nothing movement and by sectarian hostility was directed into a constructive educational competition that benefited western communities. The founding of nineteenth-century colleges was a key element in the campaign waged by the various denominations for the spiritual conquest of the American continent. Each church sought to muscle its rivals out of the academic arena. "That power which controls the education of the West," declared Presbyterian minister Albert Barnes, "controls ultimately the western mind." "Vigilance and emulation" were the watchwords with which most Protestants greeted the program of Catholics to open schools on a rapidly expanding frontier. One of the greatest dangers threatening Protestant civilization, Protestant leader E. N. Kirk warned in 1856, "is the calm, shrewd, steady, systematic movement of the Jesuit order now attempting to do in California and in the Mississippi Valley what it once did in Austria. . . .

There, Brethren, there our great battle with the Jesuit, on Western soil, is to be waged. We must build college against college."[85] Protestant promoters, believing that the "wily, tireless" Jesuits were "anxious and ready to educate the youth of the state and endeavor to make their institution popular," pointed to Santa Clara's success as reason for founding in 1855 the College of California, the precursor to the University of California.[86]

Jesuits reciprocated the rivalry. "If we do not move in the matter, the Protestant ministers are there to appropriate all the Catholic youth." One of Giuseppe Cataldo's motives in founding Gonzaga College was to provide competition to Pacific University, a Congregationalist-Presbyterian institution at Forest Grove, Oregon, whose sway among Catholic Native Americans he was determined to foil. Santa Clara's Jesuit founders labored to "counteract the bold influence" of their Methodist neighbors across the street at the College of the Pacific. There are no schools in California "except those of the Protestants," Accolti said when soliciting European support for his own educational project.[87]

In the Southwest, Neapolitan Jesuits were equally alert to the threat posed by rival denominations. Mormons and Protestants "are working to open a school as soon as possible" in Conejos, New Mexico, wrote Rafaelo Baldassare in 1879, and hence it was "absolutely necessary . . . that we establish one ourselves, before they do." Donato Gasparri and his fellow Jesuits sought not only to outdo their opponents by creating their own colleges and parochial schools but also endeavored for decades to control the territory's public school system.[88]

While it may be easy to discount the quality of education provided by these institutions, devaluation misses an essential point. Applying contemporary standards to early religious schools is not only unfair, as one student of American schooling has observed, "but it also blemishes the record of dedicated accomplishments in these colleges." In their own time, they "did good work in educating students along avenues that would otherwise have remained closed, and due credit for this should be acknowledged."[89] The chief focus of the typical college was teaching, not scholarly research or publication. To be sure, the caliber of pedagogy varied. Some teachers labored under the burden of a poor command of English, whereas others excelled despite their foreign origin. But even sectarian naysayers conceded that the Jesuits were superbly trained teachers of both the ancient classics and modern languages. The schools of the Italians shared nineteenth-century America's dedication to science, evidenced by the large numbers of bachelor of science diplomas they bestowed. The colleges of the Society did accommodate to public demand by offering commercial instruction, although they did not grant collegiate status to the business curriculum until far into the twentieth century. No less significant, the colleges remained committed to the moral relevance of education.

What is also clear is that the schools, once among the West's best, drifted from the mainstream as the nineteenth century progressed and higher education took new forms. At the time the colleges were established, their Italian founders had shared contemporary academe's belief in the efficacy of a literary education. After the Civil War, however, American schooling trod a new path. In response to the nation's rapid industrial growth and its expanding frontier, higher education espoused a more diversified course of studies that emphasized professional preparation. In that new world, Caesar and Cicero became increasingly irrelevant. What now made the Jesuit schools idiosyncratic was their adhesion to the old-fashioned ideal of classical schooling long after other institutions had abandoned it. At the colleges of the Society, Latin and Greek, at least theoretically, still reigned supreme. As a result, as the century drew to a close, the schools found themselves in an educational backwater. Faced with cascading enrollments, some Jesuits began to call for a reappraisal of classical training, thus precipitating a sharp new debate among members of the order over the best way to adapt an inherited European tradition to American culture.

10 *"Our Pen Is at Your Service"*

MEDIATING CULTURES

This is a land in which man forgets his native country.
— Giuseppe Garibaldi, visiting the United States[1]

The missionary Urbano Grassi, "very tired and hungry" following a long day of arduous travel, looked forward to rest. After fishing for souls among the tribes of the Columbia River, the fifty-four-year-old Jesuit steered his way amid sighing pine trees to Ellensburg, a small farming settlement in central Washington where his countryman Father Luigi Parodi awaited his arrival. Grassi, a short man with the physique of an oak tree, was a seasoned trekker. This expedition in 1884, however, had been especially grueling. When his pack horse bolted along the trail, Grassi had managed to rein in the runaway, but he was left with a blistered right hand. Exhausted, he limped into Ellensburg "all alone, leading the pack horse after him." Entering the house, the famished traveler's first words were, "Avete di maccheroni?" (Have you macaroni?).[2]

There was paradox in that moment — an Italian feasting on pasta in the middle of Indian country — although the irony was probably lost on the weary traveler. Grassi's experiences that day were emblematic of the striking cultural juxtapositions that defined the lives of hundreds of immigrant Jesuits. They occupied multiple worlds. Grassi moved with equal ease among the Yakima and Okanagan tribes and among the American and immigrant settlers whose white houses and barns dotted a landscape that had been until recently the exclusive domain of Native American hunters.

On the one hand, Grassi and his co-religionists were Americanizers dedicated to the assimilation of the many populations with whom they were linked — Native Americans, Hispanics, and European immigrants. Recognizing the new social realties of the Pacific Northwest, Grassi carried corn seed as well as a Bible when making the rounds of Indian camps. Thus equipped, he tutored his converts in farming and irrigation while imparting the catechism. In the process of facilitating the entry of his hybrid flock into the new American order, Grassi and the other immigrant clergy themselves stepped into the mainstream of American society. Indeed, some became so acculturated that they achieved insider status through their parish schools and urban colleges.

And yet the émigré clerics, like Grassi, the ardent consumer of macaroni, were never so transformed by America that they forgot Europe. Clinging to the traditions of *la patria*, they stood apart insofar as they employed Italian strategies in the running of their colleges, parishes, and Indian missions. Grassi, although intent on religious conversion, did not expect the Yakimas to become white men. Nor did his countrymen who mediated between Anglos and Hispanics in New Mexico encourage Spanish speakers to abandon their language and culture.

Moving in daily contact with ordinary people, the missionaries were sympathetic to American life. But this did not mean that they did not wish to transplant Old World Catholicism — the only form they knew — into American soil. Continuity with their former existence was essential to their self-definition. Like their peers at Woodstock College, the westerners adhered to the legacy of the Roman church and of their own Society by integrating a European heritage into their American classrooms, parishes, and seminaries. Michele Accolti was not merely boasting but expressing a heartfelt desire to replicate the familiar when he told Jesuits in Europe that commencement exercises at Santa Clara College "would have honored the Roman College, to say nothing of any other college of our Italian provinces."[3]

Never inclined toward American self-congratulation, the Italians cast a censorious eye on offensive features of life in the United States. They resisted aspects of Americanization that they found objectionable, including the tendency to banish inferior peoples to the edges of society. As ministers to varied ethnic communities, they generally favored assimilation, not co-option. The nation's religious pluralism, which was unlike anything they had encountered in Italy, provoked curiosity, comment, and condemnation. Americans possessed "many attractive social qualities," a Jesuit in Albuquerque said, but the typical citizen, when asked what church he belongs to, replies "with complete frankness and without the slightest embarrassment, for him all religions are good and he does not belong to any." So corrosive was the national spirit of liberty and materialism that some Europeans feared it would taint the Jesuit order itself. Nicola Cocchi of Washington claimed it was difficult for Americans to become good Jesuits because they were fixated "on making money," and religious obedience was for them "truly a challenging virtue." Additionally, Americans exhibited the "coldness of Catholics" who live in an environment dominated by Protestantism, religious indifference, and unrestrained individual freedom. These challenges demanded of Jesuits in the United States "considerably more virtue than what suffices in the Catholic countries of Europe."[4]

Although associates disputed Cocchi, there was one issue against which they stood in shoulder-to-shoulder opposition. Like Brandi and Mazzella, the Jesuits to a man abhorred "godless" public education. The reason? The American common school — like the secularized academy of liberal Italy that had destroyed the Jesuit pedagogical network — "had no regard for moral education and religious instruction." Just as the suppression of ethical instruction had led to "rampant immorality" in Italy, according to the *Revista Católica*, neglect of spiritual instruction in the United States would produce cultural devastation.[5] "Let the public school system of free religionists do its unwholesome work ten or twelve years longer," Giuseppe Bayma warned in the *American Catholic Quarterly Review* in 1877, "and we venture to predict that the United States of America will become a huge mass of corruption." Even the liberal Michele Accolti decried "the dreadful machinery of the common schools, which is the powerful lever of the century to subvert all morality and religious ideas and introduce indifferentism and infidelity to the very bosom of Christian families."[6]

Cultural Crossroads

Neither the novelty of their new life nor their alienation from secularized Italy lessened the immigrants' *amore di patria*. Familiar food eased the affliction of exile for Urbano Grassi and other immigrant clergy. So too did a flow of news and correspondence from home. Priests in California eagerly awaited the arrival from Rome of copies of *Civiltà Catolica*, which, once read, were relayed on to missionaries in the Rocky Mountain Mission for further perusal until their dog-eared pages frayed from constant usage. Such exchanges enabled the expatriates to follow the progress of the Italian revolution and to keep abreast of happenings in the church around the world. Missionaries tucked away in the American hinterland also relied on European ideas in the exercise of their ministry. "Oh, how much we would like to have some books!," a priest in Colorado sighed to friends in Naples. When decorating churches in the West, the immigrants turned to Italy for copies of traditional paintings and statuary.[7]

Nostalgia for home drove some Jesuits to repatriate, confirming the powerful slingshot effect that Italy had on its citizens, flinging them away and then drawing them back. But the number who engaged in reverse immigration was small. Moreover, those who tried to pick up the pieces of their old life did not regain paradise. Some returnees found anti-clerical Italy oppressive, while others discovered that their hearts tarried in America. When called back to Europe in 1898 to become rector of a new scholasticate at Posilipo, on departing Giovanni Battista Guida confided to a friend that "the call of obedience was the only thing that could ever induce him to leave the United

States." He then opened his trunk to reveal a souvenir neatly folded inside, "an American flag which he was taking with him, and which, he said, would return with him." His duty done, four years later Guida, clutching the Stars and Stripes, sped back to Colorado for eighteen more years of missionary work.[8]

Like Guida, most of the Jesuits evolved beyond the connection to their native land. Possessing one of the immigrant's most valuable skills, they adjusted their values and shed unnecessary beliefs as they set about brokering a new existence in America. In this they were encouraged by the *Constitutions* of their order, which insisted that all Jesuit undertakings "ought to be adapted to places, times, and persons."[9] Despite this dedication to accommodation, however, their higher-ups in Europe expected Jesuits in San Francisco or Santa Fe to replicate the religious lifestyle of Rome or Naples.

Conversely, local leaders reminded distant overseers that customs here "are different than those of the Mother Province." Requiring priests to travel with a Jesuit companion when visiting the sick or traveling the dusty roads of New Mexico on apostolic rounds was absurd, Giuseppe Marra objected. "I don't know what is done in the other American provinces and missions, but it seems impossible to do otherwise when one has the care of souls." Necessity demanded that tradition keep pace with the exigencies of American culture if pews and classrooms were to be filled. Effective missionaries "make themselves Americans so as to be helpful to Americans," wrote the Piedmontese priest G. B. Ponte from San Francisco.[10] Marra agreed. "We Italians are certainly more able to do good in this country to the extent we are like Americans in attitudes, language, and behavior." "Those who get along better with the people here and who do the most good are those who are most like them." He and others groaned when volunteers from Europe proved insufficiently adaptive. Fledglings who bridled at novelty were set right by veteran missionaries like Salvatore Personè, who railed about a fresh recruit from Europe: "He would like to transfer Naples and all its customs" to New Mexico. "The poor fellow is like a chick outside his nest."[11]

While never susceptible of a belief in American exceptionalism, the Italians appreciated the nation's religious freedom, which they inevitably contrasted with the torment they had suffered in Italy. "At least in this country of America," Geronimo D'Aste reported from Montana, "our religion, far from being persecuted, except by a few 'mad dogs,' . . . is honored and is growing prodigiously." In the United States, the sclerosis of the old world seemed to have melted away, offering Catholics an entirely new reality that was awash in possibilities. As a Belgian Jesuit once told Superior General Roothaan, "On the whole and after the experience of recent centuries, liberty as realized in America is better for the church than the protection of absolute monarchies." *La Revista Católica* waxed rhapsodic in praise of "that lovely Providence" that affords our church "so many years of good fortune in this Republic." "The Catholic Church is free in the United States of America, more free than any other country in the world," the editors declared, "and she recognizes this fact, for the great glory of this Republic, and for the confusion and disgrace of all of the countries, large and small, who, the more they yell 'liberty for all,' the more audacious they are in vexing, annoying, and putting the church in chains." "The fullest freedom" is ours, Jesuits told friends in Europe, and "the government does not interfere at all in matters of religion."[12]

Although always wary of what they labeled "the spirit of nationalism," the immigrants were thrilled to be accepted as American. Ridiculed by nativists as aliens unfit for citizenship, they missed no opportunity to wrap the Gospel in the flag and prove their love of country. Few events offered a more baroque blend of patriotism and piety than a celebration at Our Lady of Mount Carmel Church in Pueblo, Colorado, where priests and parishioners gathered in 1919 to honor Our Lady of Guadalupe. "The crowd of people was the greatest we ever had in this church," a Neapolitan Jesuit boasted. Musical uplift for this extraordinary event was provided by a "special orchestra" within the church and a "special band" outside. At the hushed moment during high mass when the priest elevated the host for adoration, the exterior troupe struck up "The Star-Spangled Banner."[13]

Patriotism was expressed in varied forms. Many priests and brothers became U.S. citizens, although it is unclear in individual cases if their motive was love of country or love of the benefits flowing from naturalization.[14] And the immigrants asserted their civil rights. When a reservation agent tried to prevent Prando from ministering to Catholic Blackfeet, the priest confidently disregarded the order, asserting "that the constitution of the United States grants religious liberty to all."[15] To better accommodate to their adopted homeland, some Jesuits anglicized their surnames. Thus "Padre Stefano Bueno" introduced himself as "Father Stephan Good," "Rossi" was simplified to "Ross" and "Tornielli" to "Turnell," "Chiavassa" translated to "Keyes," and "Chiaudano" converted to "Keogh."

In dress, as in name, the Europeans tipped their hat at new mores. When appearing in public in Italy, Jesuits had worn the ankle-length black soutane. But this distinctive outfit drew unwelcome attention and even physical assault in nineteenth-century America. "Neither priests nor monks wear garb that sets them apart from the rest of the people," a traveler in the West observed. "The only distinguishing exterior detail is the clerical collar — and even then, only some of them wear it." When strolling along the street, Jesuits sported nondescript attire or the garb of diocesan clergy. But in church, college, or private residence, the black gown was permitted, moving Nicola Cocchi, a critic of most things American, to gloat that here "we wear the proper ancient garb of the Society, the habit or soutane, with rosary at the cincture, which, as you know, used to be worn in Rome twenty years ago."[16]

Jesuits in New Mexico, however, donned the cassock even in public. "You may see one or another of them, with their long black robes, in the street at any time," nagged a visitor to Albuquerque. Donato Gasparri once presumed to enter the New Mexico House of Representatives in full Jesuit attire. Come to attend a debate on the Society's legal incorporation in the territory, he was censured for his audacity.[17] In the Pacific Northwest, practicality determined the wardrobe of circuit-riders. "Anything goes here," a Montana missionary declared. "In the house generally and also in the neighborhood we wear the soutane in some form or other," but "when we go here and there among the whites, we wear lay clothing" of the type worn by farmers and simple folk. In mufti, Jesuits sometimes could not identify one another. "The first time I met Father Superior," a just-arrived Filippo Rappagliosi wrote, "I took him for one of our rustic brothers and asked, 'Are you the brother that does the farming?' He replied, 'No. I am the superior.'"[18] Without pondering the deeper implications of their casual shedding of custom, the missionaries became pluralists even in attire.

Another novelty of American life was face-to-face encounter with non-Catholics. The refugees "were unprepared by their birth and training for the pluralistic American religious scene," one scholar has written, and hence their stance toward other Christian churches was polemical and adversarial.[19] Ecumenical understanding was the exception rather than the rule in nineteenth-century America, where Protestant and Catholic missionaries could reside for years in the same town and never exchange a word. If religion brought bare-knuckled conflict, however, it also brought fruitful competition. Protestant evangelism invigorated frontier Catholics to improve pastoral care in their parishes and develop better schools. Time and time again, when Jesuits sought permission from European stewards to undertake new projects, their trump card was the threat of Protestant competition. When Cataldo asked the superior general's clearance to found Gonzaga College, for example, he justified his proposal by pointing to a Methodist school in Oregon that was attracting Catholic Indians. Blaming the Protestant bogeyman was also an effective ploy with which to scare cost-conscious European officials into giving an imprimatur to new building projects. It was "absolutely necessary" to erect a parochial school in Conejos, Colorado, Baldassare once argued, because Protestants and Mormons "are working to open a school as soon as possible." "Therefore it is imperative that we establish one ourselves, before they do."[20]

Even so, interdenominational cooperation, unimaginable in Italy, was not uncommon in the West. Americans were religiously deeply divided, one historian wrote, but they "rarely displayed the widespread, uncompromisingly

permanent bitterness that poisoned contemporary Europe."[21] When
Giuseppe Giorda arrived in a Montana village on New Year's Day in 1865
to celebrate mass for a handful of Catholics, he was surprised to discover that
a sympathetic Protestant had anticipated his coming by reserving a ballroom
for the service. After the liturgy concluded, his benefactor "went afterwards
to collect a little money for me, with which I defrayed half the expenses of
my journey." Many priests developed close ties with Protestants who
enrolled children in their schools and attended their churches. "A great many
Protestant families are our best friends," an astonished California Jesuit told
colleagues in England; some even rented pews in Catholic churches.[22]

Jesuits were sometimes Americanized through friendships with Protestant
clergy. Giovanni Nobili praised the kindness of "the excellent Doctor
Whitman," the Presbyterian missionary who offered hospitality to the
Jesuits in the Oregon territory. Episcopalian Bishop Tuttle of Montana, affectionately identifying Antonio Ravalli as "dear friend," rushed to the Jesuit's
bedside to offer prayers and comfort when he lay dying.[23] Accolti, on congenial terms with many non-Catholics, praised the biblical scholarship of his
acquaintances among the Protestant clergy. Their translations and com-
mentaries on scripture, instead of being presented in an "incomprehensible
and abstract fashion, or in an unknown language fit only to decorate some
library [of] a few privileged persons," appeared in the vernacular, an innovation that delighted the Jesuit. My Protestant friends, he told the superior
general, "could pull the wool over the eyes of a Catholic priest who has never
studied anything but a few arcane writings about the sacred book." Accolti,
like other Italians among the *Americanizati* who had melted into the
adopted culture, possessed a keen ability to join the old to the new.[24]

Thus, like a ship driven in one direction by the tide and in another way
by wind, the Italian missionary was propelled by conflicting forces. At times,
deep currents nudged his vessel toward the familiar shore of European tradition; in other instances, the fresh novelty of America steered him on an
entirely new course toward assimilation. But it was a combination of cultural
forces, involving both change and interconnectedness, that most characterized the Italian's American ministry. Jesuit evangelization of Native
Americans, for example, was shaped both by European methodology and by
United States Indian policy. And their parishes in the West introduced congregations to European devotional life while at the same time aiding immigrants' entry into the American mainstream. But the push and pull of these
competing energies was inevitably an uneven affair, and its outcome was
always a hybrid. Thus, the educational style of the Society's frontier colleges,
which braided elements of both European and American practice, was never
exclusively one or the other, but a patchwork of both.

What historians have written about the melting-pot quality of frontier

Catholicism can be applied perforce to the Jesuits. From their earliest days, their undertakings in the West were characterized by cultural pluralism.[25] If most Americans favored a homogeneous nation, the Italians argued for the benefits of amalgamation and cultural variety. Their *modus agendi* was an alloy, however, not merely because it was bicultural but because its was multicultural and because it pursued a varied agenda. The binary paradigm that historians are accustomed to applying to the study of immigrant assimilation is therefore insufficient in explaining the Italian clerics. Rather than narrowly categorizing them either as Romanizers or Americanizers, it is more useful to view them as intermediaries between multiple cultures.

The reasons for this orientation are not hard to discern. In part, their pluralistic approach was inevitable because they belonged to a heterogeneous church. The missionaries daily engaged a farrago of nationalities: Italians, Germans, Slavs, French, Anglo Americans, Hispanics, to cite only a few. Consider also their evangelization of Native Americans, which was shaped by many forces. The Jesuits sometimes advanced an American program (founding industrial schools to facilitate native acculturation), but they also promoted European goals (introducing Italian devotional practices to the tribes). They sometimes even adopted what might be labeled an Indian agenda (encouraging the retention of native languages). Flexibility was further mandated by the fact that the missionaries served as mediators between Native Americans and whites.

Complexity, too, characterized the Italians' undertakings in the Southwest, where they encountered the cultures of traditional Hispanics and Anglo American newcomers. Although they resisted the coercive acculturation of Spanish-speaking Catholics by Anglos, their own schools aimed at preparing young *californios* and *nuevomexicanos* for participation in the Yanqui world. A historian of New Mexico has correctly summarized: "The Jesuit contribution lies in their ambivalence: as Italians they could understand and adapt to both cultures and thus provide a bridge between the two."[26] At the same time, of course, they functioned as agents of ecclesiastical centralization, imparting the theology and devotions of a Rome-rooted Catholicism.

Ministering to immigrants presented the nineteenth-century Society of Jesus with an activity it had long sought to avoid, the staffing of parishes. In addition to being a ministry more appropriate to the diocesan clergy, the parish, with its fixed revenues, compromised the Society's vow of poverty, and the appointment of lifetime pastors limited the religious order's mobility. For this reason, the first Jesuits had aspired not to minister to people who already had pastors, but to populations that were neglected. The restored order soon found reason, however, to relax its prohibition against parish work. Short on diocesan clergy, bishops in the United States frequently turned to the Jesuits and other orders to supply priests for churches, particularly on

FIGURE 24. Circuit-riding Neapolitan Jesuits ministered to a mix of nationalities in mining communities throughout the West, described by one priest as "a real Tower of Babel." In this photograph, Italian mining families pose near a store in a coal camp, probably in Las Animas County, Colorado, sometime after 1890. Courtesy Colorado Historical Society, Trinidad Collection, CHS.X4874

the frontier. As Giuseppe Marra once remarked, "Here the parishes are a necessity" for us.[27]

Although they accepted parishes, Jesuits fretted about the impact on communitarian religious life. Thus, when Marra surrendered one of his priests to work in Arizona Territory in 1888, he did so reluctantly. Our man "works there alone and does well," Marra told the provincial, but we "disapprove of having a fellow out there solely on his own." Superiors continued, nevertheless, to assign personnel to parishes while simultaneously wringing their hands over their action. "All this work of ours in parishes is contrary to the spirit of the Society," an official groused in 1917, "because it is not the proper work of missionaries as the Society understands 'missionary.'"[28] Jesuits were, as a matter of fact, especially well-suited for the work because multi-ethnic and multi-class Catholicism progressively required a polyglot clergy. Priests here "find themselves in charge of mixed congregations of people from the main countries of Europe," a California Jesuit reported. "Since we have studied these languages for over thirty years, there's a lot we can do." What was said of the Italian, Alessandro Mazzetti, master of seven tongues, could be applied to other European Jesuits: "His ability to speak several languages made him especially valuable as a spiritual guide to people of many races."[29]

The typical western church echoed with the chatter of mutually incomprehensible tongues. "The population here is made up of every nationality," wrote Salvatore Personè from Trinidad, Colorado, a coal-mining center serving over 20,000 Catholics. In addition to his American and Irish flock, the Neapolitan shepherded English, Spanish, Slavs, Germans, Bohemians, Russians, Greeks, Poles, and Japanese parishioners. This is, he declared, "a real Tower of Babel."[30] Jesuits in San Jose, California, ministered to Germans, Italians, Mexicans, Portuguese, Irish, and Anglo-American congregations. This potpourri of races, one observer piously noted, "served to remind one very forcibly of that universality which is one of the marks of the church."[31]

Providing liturgies for hybrid congregations taxed the resources of the most creative missionary. Even experienced pastors found it "impossible to satisfy all the various nationalities that frequently make up the same congregation," said the Jesuit preacher Francis X. Weninger. "I sometimes say jestingly to the pastors, that I would like to suggest, as an addition to the litanies, the prayer recited at the finale of a mission: 'From mixed congregations, deliver us O Lord!'" Francesco Tomassini of Trinidad, Colorado, described how he coped with the babel of tongues that infused his district: "In the settlements, where the majority speak the Spanish language, the administration is not very difficult." But variances grew extreme in the hotchpotch coal-mining zone, where every isolated settlement was home to "two dozen Catholics five of different nationalities, who speak their own language."[32]

Complicating matters, impoverished miners who lived in the hinterland were without transportation. In order to facilitate church attendance by the poor, the Neapolitans built dozens of modest chapels (thirty-three of them by 1917) up and down Colorado's Purgatoire River Valley. Under ideal circumstances, mass was celebrated for each ethnic consortium in its own language. But since most assemblies housed a fusion of nationalities, many liturgies were perforce polylingual extravaganzas with sermons delivered in as many as four tongues in a single service.[33] Depending on the makeup of the congregation, a *parroco* had to decide on the spot as he stepped into the sanctuary which idiom to utter. Weninger once described how he thrashed out what language to use when he commenced a mission in British Columbia. Mounting the pulpit of the cathedral in Victoria, "I inquired first, what nationalities were represented in the congregation. The answer was: 'We have here English, Irish, Germans, French, Italians, Spaniards, Indians.'" In this instance, "my resolution was easily taken." Learning that "with the exception of the Indians, all the rest understood English, I determined to use that language in my sermons, reserving the others for use in the confessional."[34] This procedure was common in the linguistic melting pot of the American frontier.

The Jesuits served a constituency that was primarily blue-collar. The

Germans of San Jose were "mostly people who work for a living," California missionaries reported. Colorado's Mexicans were "extremely poor," and Italian miners were so destitute they could not supply their pastor with "even enough to live on."[35] Indigence obliged the clergy to tightly manage resources to a degree unprecedented in Europe, where the state had formerly built and maintained ecclesiastical properties. In America, however, churches had to be raised from scratch. The education of immigrant children brought additional challenges after the Third Plenary Council of Baltimore, in 1884, mandated that every parish in the United States have a school.

To run churches and parochial schools, pastors became, perforce, entrepreneurs. Frontier priests depended on voluntary offerings from the faithful—fees for pews, although that source was quickly passing out of use. "We will send a collector this week to collect pew rent," a Trinidad pastor once told his flock. "If you are not prepared to pay in full, you will pay what you are able to pay." Two months later, his patience had worn thin. "As the pew rent has been so small, we have been obliged to reduce the salary of the teacher," he pleaded. "What can we do with 7 or 8 dollars we receive every Sunday?"[36]

Unable to count on poor immigrants to sustain schools, the priests discovered the American church fair. An elaborate "Grand Bazar for the benefit of the new Catholic school" held in Pueblo, Colorado, in 1885 typified this important fund-raising event. For six consecutive spring evenings, street cars bore party-goers down banner-festooned streets to the Pueblo Opera House, where a gala lasted until midnight, providing "a large amount of money" for the new Catholic school and welcome diversion to a frontier community aching for entertainment.[37]

Italian Jesuits and the Irish

When categorizing national groups, pastors typically viewed Irish and American-born parishioners through a rosy lens. Of the dozens of nationalities with whom we work, a priest in Colorado reported, "those who give us the greatest consolation for attendance at mass and sacraments are the practicing American Catholics. They scrupulously care for the education of their children, [and] . . . are always respectful and help us out." Writing from California in 1870, another Italian declared, "A great deal of the good that is done is due to the Irish who are the main supporters of our work."[38]

American and Irish Catholics not only showed deference to the clergy, they filled the Sunday collection plate and aided indigent congregations. When the Catholic Germans of San Jose sought their own church, for example, it was an Irishman, Miles O'Connor, who provided the funds. American and Irish

Catholics sent their sons to Jesuit schools in high numbers, and they flocked to the order's large temples in urban Denver, Spokane, and San Francisco. "The number of people that come to our church is incredible," marveled Nicola Congiato of San Francisco in 1862. "Last Sunday more than a thousand people left because they could not find a seat." So attractive were these congregations that a German Jesuit accused his Italian confrères of playing favorites and "running after the Irish people."[39]

Packed pews reflected not only piety, but the high priority the Anglo-Irish congregations placed on pulpit performance. "One thing is certain," a visiting cleric from Italy observed in 1860, "the Americans will always go where the preaching is best." In San Francisco, a series of masses in St. Ignatius church drew an estimated eight thousand congregants every Sunday. Stirring oratory drew standing-room-only crowds of Protestants as well as Catholics eager to hear sermons of great length, which were reprinted in the city's newspapers.[40] Of Michele Accolti, a contemporary once said, "It was enough to know that he was preaching and the church was filled with Protestants." Most Italians, however, were by their own admission "not very good preachers" in English, which impelled them to import helpers who were.[41]

The arrival in 1861 of the famed Jesuit preacher and lecturer James Bouchard mapped a turning point in the fortunes of the Society in San Francisco. Son of a Delaware chief and a French woman who was raised by the Comanche, Bouchard was the first Native American ordained a priest in the United States and an orator of premier rank who held forth in the rococo style of his generation. For three decades, California audiences listened in open-mouth amazement to the eloquent Indian, who, according to contemporaries, charmed "by the sound of his silvery voice, by the power of his nervous eloquence." People were, an Italian priest said, "wild to have a preacher like him."[42]

But there were never enough Bouchards to meet the demand. Jesuit inability to provide congregations with magnetic speakers was "the greatest source of troubles, past and present, in this Mission," wrote Giuseppe Marra from the Southwest. Those most inclined to sulk about the shortcomings of Italian pastors were the Irish. In 1891, an exasperated Marra replaced an Italian Jesuit with an Irish one in a Denver parish, because "that is precisely what those people have been asking for ten years — an Irish priest. If, after this, we have not satisfied, pacified, and been reconciled to them, there will be nothing left to do but abandon the place forever."[43] A worse conflict erupted between priest and parishioners in Pueblo, Colorado, where the Neapolitans so alienated Irish Catholics that the congregation rebelled. The ensuing explosion ripped such a hole in the tranquility of the New Mexico–Colorado Mission that worried Jesuits were still tiptoeing around its crater thirty years later.

NOW THE IRISH ROMAN CATHOLICS BLOCKADE THE SIDE WALK EVERY SUNDAY, IN FRONT OF THE JESUITS R.C. CHURCH ON MARKET STREET AFTER LAST MASS.

FIGURE 25. Between Italian Jesuits and Irish Catholics in California there developed a close affinity. In 1874, *Thistleton's Illustrated Jolly Giant*, an anti-Catholic newspaper in San Francisco, ridiculed the Irish who gathered at St. Ignatius Church in that city on Sundays. "This custom of vulgarity is practiced in every Catholic country of the world. But this being a Protestant country, we object to the Irish show, for the sake of decency and civilization." Courtesy Donohue Rare Book Room, University of San Francisco

Troubles began in 1872, when the Jesuits responded to a request from Colorado's bishop, Joseph P. Machebeuf, to build a church in Pueblo. Carlo Pinto, to whom the project was given, discovered that, although the city was "almost entirely Protestant and American," it was a place with a future. "Houses are being built, shops opened, people are arriving, business is booming." Steel and iron production would soon make Pueblo the chief manufacturing center of Colorado and a rival to Denver for state capital. Completion of the city's first Catholic church, St. Ignatius, marked a turning point not only for the local Catholics, but also for the Neapolitan Jesuits. For the first time they had ventured out of Spanish-speaking New Mexico into a region dominated by English language and culture. "Our headquarters should be here and our language English," reported an impressed Pinto.[44]

But the challenge of serving a novel clientele was a trial for the immigrant, who had landed in the United States barely a year earlier. "English is not

Spanish, and the Americans are neither Spaniards nor Mexicans," Pinto reported, upon learning that these new churchgoers were not as easy to please as easy-going *nuevomexicanos*. "The Americans are not very obliging, as far as the language goes." For their part, Pueblans carped that they could not easily attend mass because Pinto's church was too far from the city center. And they were disappointed in Pinto himself, who struggled to communicate with them in the "exceedingly difficult" (his words) English language.[45]

When Pinto was reassigned — surely to his relief — to a Spanish-speaking parish in Trinidad a few years later, he was replaced by a series of Italians equally unfamiliar with the United States. In 1875, Francesco Gubitosi, who had worked briefly (and without success) with African-American and white Catholics in Maryland, became pastor of Pueblo immediately upon arrival in the Southwest. He was assisted by a succession of priests, each of whom proved more problematic than the rest. Antonio Minasi — "stubborn," "eccentric," and lazy, according to fellow Jesuits — was soon sent packing because, his disgusted superior said, he was "doing *absolutely* nothing, . . . under the pretext of learning English, in which he will never succeed." The quarrelsome Francesco Saverio Maffei, ignorant of English and "barely tolerated by the faithful," lasted less than a year.[46] And then there were the Montenarelli brothers: Giuseppe, whose conduct was so inappropriate he could not be left unsupervised, and Luigi, a temperamental hard-head whose imprudence was exceeded only by his brother's boorishness.[47] But the basic problem of all the Jesuits, one of them said, was that they were "ignorant of the language and customs of the Americans." After seven years, superiors were so discouraged at their inability to do a good job that they gave serious thought to withdrawing from Pueblo.[48]

In 1879, however, Rafaelo Baldassare, superior of the Mission, informed European authorities that the situation had taken a turn for the better. "The discovery of Father Gubitosi makes us more hopeful about the place." A few months earlier, Pueblo's leading newspaper, the *Colorado Daily Chieftain*, announced the "wonderful discovery" of silver and gold so rich that "the most obtuse tenderfoot can satisfy himself that the wealth is here in exhaustless quantities." Nearby Silver Cliff, the paper predicted, "is destined to be the grandest mining city in the United States."[49] Trusting in the counsel of a young Italian geologist ("an excellent Catholic"), Francesco Gubitosi confidently predicted that the new strike would be "a real blessing for the poor Mission and for our needy Province." After persuading Baldassare that they should invest, Gubitosi borrowed several thousand dollars to join a partnership in eleven "rich and promising mines." He also bought stock in a $25,000 processing plant auspiciously named for his favorite saint, the St. Joseph Mining and Smelting Company.[50] "Do not worry," Baldassare assured nervous European superiors. We soon will begin to receive profits, debts will disappear, and "we will be able to establish an endowment for opening free parochial schools" and to even undertake new ministries.[51]

Less than a year later, a red-faced Baldassare confessed a fiasco. The mines were not yielding a return, Gubitosi was stuck with a wad of debts he could not pay, and the pastoral situation in Pueblo had become very serious.[52] Among the aggrieved creditors demanding reimbursement was Bishop Machebeuf, who had sunk $1,000 in the venture and now threatened to suspend Gubitosi from his priestly functions. Enmeshed in the investment project, Gubitosi had neglected his pastoral duties, chattering incessantly only about "mines and money, money and mines." When Baldassare made an official visit of the parish in 1880, he discovered "there was not a one [parishioner] who did not bring up some charge against Gubitosi." While Catholics simmered with outrage, Gubitosi scrambled to sell his shares in the mines and smelter, and his superiors frantically sought to borrow money from creditors in St. Louis and California to cover his debts. Meanwhile, the Jesuits desperately searched for an English-speaking priest to minister to their troubled parish.[53]

Peace was temporarily restored in 1881, when the Neapolitans coaxed Father Daniel Haugh, an East Coast Jesuit, to come to their rescue. However, the Irish newcomer and one of his Italian co-workers, Carlo Ferrari, soon developed an intense mutual animosity. When St. Ignatius church, one of Pueblo's two Jesuit establishments, was destroyed by fire, each priest blamed the other's negligence for the disaster. Efforts at reconciliation having proved futile, both men were finally sent packing, and in the emergency the unpopular Carlo Pinto scurried back to Pueblo to reassume administration of the parish. News of the disliked Italian's return and the popular Haugh's hasty exodus occasioned what one Jesuit described as a "revolt of the Irish Catholics of Pueblo."[54]

The first blast in the city's religious war was fired by J. J. Lambert, an Irish parishioner and editor of the *Pueblo Daily Chieftain*. "Father Haugh Supplanted and Another Begins in His Stead," screamed the headlines of Lambert's paper on 14 December 1882. "The Catholics of this city are up in arms" because "Father Haugh was deposed by underhand means." Neither the appointment of an English-speaking replacement of Haugh as assistant pastor nor the removal of the much-scorned Neapolitan Carlo Pinto as head of the parish satisfied the self-proclaimed "Catholic Vigilance Committee." "They do not want and will not have an Italian priest as superior," Lambert declared. "The Italian Jesuits can go . . . where they came from. We want them not!"[55]

Claiming to represent "a very large and influential majority of the Catholics" of Pueblo, Lambert for months lobbied Bishop Machebeuf "to remove the *Italian* Jesuits from here." We know "the tricks of the Organ

Grinders" and "the whole Italian mob," a fellow vigilante declared. But neither the threat of legal action nor the withholding of funds from the diocese budged the stubborn bishop, leading another protestor to conclude, "I don't think you will get much satisfaction from the Bishop in regard to the removal of the dagos."[56] Eighteen months after its eruption, Pueblo's sad little civil war ended. In late 1883, the rebels, ostensibly softened by the reconciliation efforts of an English-speaking priest, James Holland, laid down their arms. In a letter published in the *Pueblo Chieftain*, the Irish Catholics declared that their critique of the Jesuits had been ill-advised, and they apologized for their "hasty act."[57]

But Catholic morale in Pueblo remained low for years, and the distrust of Italians did not evanesce. Gregorio Leggio, one of the few Italian Jesuits who spoke fluent English, recalled his first liturgy in the parish in 1887. "I looked around this place of worship to see but a few" people in the pews, and "the few that congregated looked up to me with a kind of natural suspicion which was keen to mistrust." If parishioners were slow to forget their grievances, the priests, too, were scarred by the racism that once blazed in Pueblo. Carlo Pinto became a popular figure among the Hispanic Catholics of El Paso, but he retained a life-long sensitivity to "anti-dago" prejudice and a cool lack of interest in ministry to *nobili Americani*.[58]

Italian Catholics and Italian Jesuits

Mediation between Italian immigrants and the Catholic clergy proved another challenge. Of all the groups whom we serve, Salvatore Personè once said, "the most disappointing are the Italians." Ministering to them is "a thankless work," Giuseppe Marra agreed, adding that it required priests of extraordinary zeal and dedication. Italians "posed the greatest pastoral problems" for church leaders, wrote one historian, because they "seemed to confirm the anti-Catholic accusations that the church was foreign, anti-American, superstitious and incompatible with the principles of liberty and freedom." Immigrants from Italy, champions of Italian unification and the demise of the temporal power of the papacy, appeared as "an anti-papal heathen [and] to many American ecclesiastics, a headache." The majority were ignorant, poor, and illiterate; speaking neither English nor Italian, their only means of communication was a local dialect unintelligible to anyone but fellow *paisani*.[59]

And then there was the matter of their religious practice. "With rare exceptions," Personè stated, "their brand of Catholicism consists in having their children baptized and in staging elaborate weddings and, especially, funerals that they can ill afford." And "most funerals are reserved for those who do not leave behind superstitious parents or friends."[60] Our country-men are "very indifferent as far as religion is concerned," agreed Father Antonio Cichi, "because they don't know the language and cannot com-municate with a priest even if one should happen to be near" — and "many of them are friends of neither priest nor church." Missionary Giovanni Boschi lamented that the Italians he encountered in Montana were "without reli-gion and some even enemies of religion who vaunt their disbelief and laugh at the priest." "Of the 400 Italians who are here, barely twenty adults reg-ularly come to church."[61]

As their numbers grew, the spiritual and material plight of the *emigranti italiani* attracted international scrutiny. In 1880, the number of persons in the United States who had been born in Italy numbered 44,230. Twenty years later the figure had risen to 484,027 — and it continued to expand at a phe-nomenal rate, reaching over two million in the first decade of the new cen-tury. Alarmed at the "toilsome and disastrous" condition of his countrymen in the United States, Pope Leo XIII in 1888 issued a special appeal to Ameri-can bishops to "render every possible help to them." Among the religious orders that responded to his plea was the Society of Jesus, which began post-ing Italian priests to immigrant enclaves.[62]

The clergy continued to carp, however, about the reception they received. In 1900, after the Italians of Pueblo pleaded for their own *capella*, Palermo-born Salvatore Giglio agreed to raise funds for the construction of Our Lady of Mount Carmel church. After weeks of knocking on doors, the weary Jesuit returned home from a begging tour with a mere $734.90. This was "a very hard and unpleasant task," he confided to his diary. "I received many insults and the Lord only knows how much I suffered A. M. D. G. ['For God's Greater Glory,' the Jesuit motto]." Two years later, F. X. Tomassini met a sim-ilar fog of disappointment when he tried to erect a substantial stone chapel for Trinidad's numerous *italiani*. "For the building of this church," he wrote, "no help was obtained from the people."[63]

Missionaries recognized that immigrants' aloofness stemmed from a variety of factors, not the least important of which was the condition of life in Italy. "I have quite a number of Italians" in my charge, wrote Paulo Ponziglione from Milwaukee, "who strictly speaking are not bad, but have been so neglected, and have been educated in the midst of so many preju-dices against our holy religion, that it is a very hard thing to bring them to attend their duties." Others pointed to the harmful influence of life in the United States.[64] A highly successful New York pastor, Nicola Russo, per-ceptively linked the immigrants' spiritual apathy to their extreme poverty and poorly remunerated labor. "They work like slaves," he said. The church also bore some responsibility for the Italians' condition. "I cannot help believing that things would not be in so bad a shape now, if more care had been bestowed upon them" when they arrived in this country. "Look back to the first years of Italian immigration. Who was there to smooth their first difficulties, to warn them of the danger, to sympathize with their distressed condition, to turn their mind to heaven, and to remind them of the immortal soul? Was it even known how many of them were without a pastor."[65]

So onerous was the Italian apostolate that many priests in Italy spurned pleas to come and minister to their countrymen. It was not that they were unwilling to leave Italy, one scholar said, but "even those Italian clerics who were here shunned rather than sought out their compatriots." The language barrier kept most native-born clergy out of the immigrant enclaves. "An American priest however well he may speak Italian," a pastor said in 1893, "will never be understood by the Italians, who for the most part only speak their many respective dialects, which only after a long practice can be understood." Thus it was that church leaders appealed to the Jesuits and other immigrant clergy to attend, as a priest in Seattle put it, to these "unhappy countrymen of Christopher Columbus."[66]

Some Italians shrank from the prospect. When Filippo Cardella was summoned from New Mexico to work with Italians in New York, his provincial apologized for issuing the unpalatable order. "I know what dreadful news this is, and how it afflicts you," he said, "and I feel like an executioner in announcing it."[67] More typical was the response of Carlo Pinto. When Denver's bishop insisted that the Jesuits assume responsibility for an Italian parish in his city, Pinto endorsed the project "because we Italians have often complained about how neglected these our countrymen are." Nicola Russo gave up a successful academic career at Boston College to work among destitute *contadini* in New York's Lower East Side. The Montana missionary Giovanni Boschi likewise shifted careers with equanimity. "I was for twelve years among the Indians, and it was for them that I came to this country," he reasoned. But the "deplorable condition" of these "poor immigrants" moves me "to dedicate the rest of my life to their salvation."[68] These and other Jesuits from Italy ministered to tens of thousands of their countrymen throughout the West, founding churches in Seattle, Tacoma, Spokane, Butte, Portland, San Francisco, San Jose, Denver, Pueblo, Trinidad, and in countless mining camps. Many others established parishes in urban ghettos on the East Coast.

There was no unique Jesuit system for the pastoral care of Italians, although the methods employed by the enterprising Nicola Russo provided a model of successful ministry across the country. To Jesuits in remote western regions who strove to maintain the protocols of their order in more established centers, the recommendations of this eminent philosopher carried great weight. In a widely distributed essay published in 1896 in the *Woodstock Letters*, the Neapolitan scholar described to co-religionists the program he had launched in New York's Lower East Side. To minister to parishioners at the chapel of Our Lady of Loretto who did not speak standard Italian, he recruited Sicilian Jesuits, who were "better able to understand the dialect and manners of the people who came from that part of Italy." Aware that good preaching was only the first step in productive ministry, Russo and his staff spent more time walking ghetto streets than they did inside the church. "It was necessary to go continually after people and evangelize them at home, family after family," he insisted.[69]

In order to draw "the rising generation" to church and hasten their Americanization, Russo offered catechetical instruction and schooling to nearly five hundred children. The strategy of focusing on youth was not lost on Ludovico Caramello, a freshly ordained priest from Italy who learned parish management from Russo in New York before emigrating west. As the chronicler of Monte Virgine, Caramello's Italian parish in Seattle, observed, "Many parents who had not attended church for years, were induced to return to their religious duties by seeing the children taking part in church processions and school entertainments."[70]

In a well-run parish, no individual was overlooked. "We have distinct sodalities for every class of people," Russo recounted, "for married men, married women, young men, young women and children; and two clubs for boys and young men." Traditional voluntary associations and devotional activities provided a respite from the immigrants' hard lives and eased their transition to American life. All pastors recognized the importance of doings things all'italiana. Thus, the statues that adorned the walls of Our Lady of Loretto represented Italian saints, not Jesuit holy men. Russo and his staff worked closely with the church's mutual aid consortium, the St. Rocco Society, encouraging members to honor their patron saint "in their own way," meaning "banners, music, parades, fireworks [were] essentials of the feast."[71]

Successful parishes such as Our Lady of Loretto or Mount Virgin in Seattle were not just religious institutions, but dynamic community centers. Offering members a variety of social services, pastors functioned as intermediaries between the immigrant and the world beyond Little Italy. They provided legal aid to parishioners in trouble with the police; offered health care to the sick; created cooking and sewing classes for girls; and gave nursery care to the children of working mothers. Special mindfulness was accorded youth, as evidenced by clubs that engaged juveniles in games, crafts, and dramatic productions. Teenagers perfected their English by joining the parish debating club. In Trinidad, Colorado, an energetic priest, Felice Ziccardi, built a two-story brick music hall for the young musicians who played in his much-publicized brass band. Such sympathetic understanding of the immigrants' reality produced results. "We have a regular congregation," Russo reported in 1896, "of over three thousand people at Mass every Sunday."[72]

There were limits, however, to the applicability of Russo's New York par-

FIGURE 26. Conversant in multiple languages, the Jesuits worked with a potpourri of immigrant populations in the West, including fellow Italians, although
their ministry among their countrymen was fraught with tensions. This photo
records an Italian-American funeral, ca. 1928, at Mt. Carmel Church in Pueblo,
Colorado. Courtesy Pueblo City-County Library District, Pueblo, Colorado,
Tsume Manabe photo

adigm. National parishes founded for the exclusive use of Italians — although
they existed in cities such as Trinidad, Seattle, and San Jose — were the exception rather than the norm in the West. Instead of being concentrated in large
urban ghettos, as in the East, immigrants on the frontier were scattered over
great distances in small communities that were visited irregularly by itinerant priests. "I have to go wherever there is a town about or wherever there
is a Catholic family," a Jesuit in Washington described his work. "I always
carry my altar with me, and say Mass, hear confessions, baptize, in any place,
even in the kitchen." In many locales, Italians immigrants joined existing
Catholic parishes, worshiping with the Irish in ethnically mixed congregations. In other places, Italians constituted a sub-congregation for whom separate services were held, either in the church itself or in the basement of the
building, a less popular option.[73]

The rationale for segregation had several justifications, not the least of
which was the obvious benefit of hearing sermons in one's own language.

Separation also conveniently accommodated the fastidiousness of Anglos who were loath to share pews with Italians. As a journalist for the *Catholic World* wrote in 1888, the immigrants' lavish *feste* seemed to non-Italians "the luxuries of religion without its substantials." Italians themselves were sometimes unwilling to mix with other groups. They are embarrassed because they are poorly dressed, illiterate, and ignorant of English, a priest explained, and they know "the American people has little esteem for our fellow Italian immigrants" and "does not always welcome them."[74]

Nor was the atmosphere of Irish and German churches inviting to the Italians, who regarded them as cold and as foreign as Protestant chapels. As one contemporary observed, "the Catholic Church in America is to the mass of Italians almost like a new religion."[75] For this reason, pastors strove to create worship spaces for their Italian congregations that evoked the familiar world of Mediterranean Catholicism. If they have chapels of their own in "their own district," a Jesuit working among railroad workers in Spokane predicted, "they would come in numbers."[76]

"All the Italian priests have the merit of keeping alive the sentiment of *italianità*," an observer reported in 1912. Jesuits such as Nicola Russo, however, did not seek to preserve Italian culture but rather to "capture the Italians' affection for the church in this country." In order to achieve their objective, they did not hesitate to use American methods, including the establishment of parochial schools, to win the loyalty of their countrymen. "We could not . . . consider our work established on a solid basis," Russo argued, "so long as we had no school."[77] Because the Jesuits prized acculturation, pastors insisted that students master English. Seattle's Ludovico Caramello once clashed with Mother Francesca X. Cabrini, the founder of the Missionary Sisters of the Sacred Heart, over this issue when he sought her help for his parish school. "I never liked Mother Cabrini," he stated later. Not only did she refuse to adapt her congregation's strict regimen to life in American culture, Cabrini brushed aside Caramello's insistence on Americanizing Italian children. When the Jesuit asked for a sister who spoke English, she instead "sent for a sister from Italy."[78]

Thus, if immigrants transformed the American church, the church also transformed the immigrant. Even while it temporarily sealed them off in a familiar cocoon, the ethnic parish facilitated re-socialization and nudged immigrants toward integration in the larger, pluralistic society. It was more than symbolic, therefore, that when the Italians of the Marconi-Columbo Society convened in Spokane in 1913 to celebrate the first anniversary of their church of Santa Maria, they blessed two new flags, one Italian and the other American. As one historian summarized, the ethnic parish, while reinforcing solidarity and group identity, "was also an indispensable institution of change."[79]

The church was a less potent instrument of Italian assimilation in the West than in the East. In the absence of large ghettos, where immigrants shopped in stores run by *paisani*, bought newspapers in their native tongue, regularly conversed in Italian, and worshiped in churches founded exclusively for them, immigrants on the frontier were forced by circumstance to adapt more speedily. In a word, the western milieu hastened acculturation. The church assisted that transformation, but so too did other institutions dominant in frontier society, including railroad construction companies, consular offices, lay fraternal organizations, and, most especially, labor unions.[80]

Jesuits and Spanish-speaking Catholics

When ministering to Italians, the Jesuits functioned as intermediaries between the immigrant and the Catholic Church, on the one hand, and the immigrant and American culture, on the other. They played a similar role with Spanish speakers. Their reception by that population was less rocky, but in the eyes of the clergy the stakes were equally high. "Two religions, Catholicism and modern religious indifference" met on common ground in the Southwest, an early chronicler wrote, "to struggle for the mastery of the Mexican population." In that combat, the priest's ultimate objective was to bring neglected Hispanic Catholics into line with the larger ecclesiastical community. Never far from the sound of grinding axes, the Jesuits, as if on a battlefield, saw themselves as "soldiers sent by Almighty God." They were combatants in a "holy war" in which their chief weapon was the popular mission and the devotional tradition of Roman Catholicism.

Every parish, every mission, every station of the Archdiocese of Santa Fe became gradually the scene of religious fervor. Later on the Fathers visited almost every Mexican parish in Colorado and Texas and Arizona. Finally they visited all California and the states of the Mexican frontier. In these latter states they had to teach the rudiments of religion to a large number of people who never before had the opportunity of making their first holy communion.[81]

Thus it was that the Jesuits positioned themselves as intermediaries between Catholicism and the Anglo world, against whose destructive impulses they defended the Mexican faithful. Americans "speak their own language and observe their own customs, rarely, if ever, intermingling with the natives," a priest noted in 1881. "Here, as in some parts of the Orient, two nationalities live side by side, yet keep themselves entirely distinct in language and customs."[82] In the struggle for equality, the Jesuits took the side of voiceless Mexicans.

Much ink was spilled by the *Revista Católica* in defense of Hispanic customs. We seek "to be useful to the population in whose midst we live," a writer declared. "Attention, Mexicans! Our pen is entirely at your service."[83] To critics who accused them of "laziness, dirtiness, and vice," the journal answered that Mexicans simply preferred a less frenetic existence. "If there is a civilization appropriate for businessmen, there is also an appropriate civilization for ranchers and shepherds. If the former is attractive to lively restless people, the latter also has its attractions for more tranquil people."[84] Because Americans "have blue eyes and blonde hair," a priest groused, they "have grown accustomed to looking upon us as an inferior race." In 1882, when the *New York Times* opposed statehood for New Mexico because its "language, religion, and traditions" differed from those in the rest of the United States, the *Revista* shot back: "If this country [New Mexico], with its inhabitants, is as horrible a thing as the New York paper pretends, then why did they annex it, and why don't they give it back to whom it used to belong?"[85]

Muckraking Jesuit journalists delighted in exposing the biases of public officials. When the editors discovered in 1891 that the superintendent of schools in New Mexico had published an article in a Chicago gazette accusing the natives of "still living as if they were in the Middle Ages," the *Revista* reprinted the essay. That same year the journal reproduced a speech delivered by a New Mexican teacher in which he denounced his fellow *nuevomexicanos* as superstitious. "Mexicans," roared the *Revista*, "see how they insult . . . and denigrate you abroad, those same people that here break their backs adulating you, flattering you, and giving you incense. And will you still continue to believe the words and promises of so many liars and charlatans?"[86] Many shots were fired over the use of Spanish. The introduction of a bill into the U.S. Congress in 1890 to keep persons who used interpreters from holding public office or serving on a jury prompted a hot editorial that charged the bill's sponsors with racial discrimination. When the *Revista* itself was chastised for failing to provide articles in English, "the proper language of the United States," the editors retorted, "Was not the *Revista* born for the Mexicans?" "We will thus continue for those for whom we began. Case closed."[87]

While the Jesuits defended their flock from the assaulting wolf of Anglo-American culture, they sought at the same time to win for them access to its benefits. Writers for the *Revista* schooled their readers on the intricacies of U.S. government, the voting system, the significance of the Declaration of Independence, and the meaning of the separation of powers. To citizens accustomed to centuries of self-rule, the newspaper explained that in the U.S. system, the local pueblo was not sovereign.

Few subjects filled as many pages of the *Revista* as education. In the early decades of American rule, Jesuits advocated separate schooling in Spanish, but as the region's native population sought access to public institutions, they pushed for integration and bilingual training. The ongoing segregation of Mexican-American children in separate public schools came under frequent attack. "To this is the famous equality before the law reduced?," the *Revista* queried in 1895.[88] "The Americans treated those poor Mexicans as the black sons of Africa," a Colorado priest reported in 1912, after observing how the citizens of Alamosa shunted Hispanic children to a school of their own "so that the American boys would not have to mingle with the Mexicans."[89] In favor of integrated schools, the *Revista Católica* urged bilingual instruction for the first few years of learning. Spanish-speaking students could not be expected to master English, the journal argued, unless they learned it through comparison with their first language. Instead of segregated schools, the journal called for simultaneous instruction in both English and Spanish— as the Jesuits had done early on in their college in Las Vegas. The *Revista*'s frequent call was: "Give us teachers who know both languages well."[90]

Unlike public schools, most parish schools were both bicultural and bilingual. In order to succeed economically, many Mexican Americans sought the necessary skills to survive in an increasingly Anglo culture. As a New Mexican school official reported in 1912, rural people, especially, realized that "if their children are to compete successfully in the struggle for existence . . . the new generation must be educated and trained according to modern standards."[91] For this reason, girls in El Paso attending Sacred Heart parochial school received instruction in both English and Spanish, and they studied Mexican as well as U.S. history. Institutions such as this served a twofold purpose, according to the historian Mario Garcia. "They helped transmit Mexican ethnicity and, at the same time, provided lessons in English and American culture in order to assist students to adjust and hopefully succeed in the United States." When students of Sacred Heart graduated, their Italian pastor advised them "to adopt the best of other cultures but never to forget who they were: young Catholic Mexican girls, who were obliged to follow Christ and, as Mexicans, to conserve the beautiful customs and traditions of *la raza*."[92]

Although the Jesuits integrated schools, they segregated churches. Our Spanish-speaking parishioners in Colorado "are so thoroughly despised by the Americans that it was necessary in most places to build a church that served them alone," a priest said in 1912. "The Americans refused to come together into the same church, or at least at the same time with the Mexicans." Although most Hispanics lived in rural communities in which time-honored mores survived, others dwelled in cities dominated by Anglo-Americans. "Where Americans do live mixed with the Mexicans," the Jesuit wrote, "it is always necessary that the liturgy be celebrated both in English and in Spanish." In such situations, pastors tried not to alienate one side or the other.

FIGURE 27. The staff of *La Revista Católica*, the Neapolitan Jesuits' Spanish-language newspaper, gathered in El Paso, Texas, with Carlo Pinto seated third from right. Inspired by Jesuit publications in Europe, especially Rome's *Civiltà Cattolica*, the journal shaped Catholic opinion throughout the Southwest for eighty-seven years. Courtesy New Orleans Jesuit Province Archives, Loyola University

"Great prudence and not a little caution is necessary in dealing with the Mexicans," another said. "They know that they are despised by Americans and carefully scrutinized the fathers' way of dealing with them and whether they treat Americans more kindly than the poor Mexicans." "Let me illustrate this with one example. The Mexicans count the candles that father lights when he celebrates the mass for the Americans, and if he does not light as many in his mass for the Mexicans, it bothers them a great deal, and they think that they have been slighted by a great injury."[93]

In many cities, the priests operated two churches, as in Albuquerque. One stood in the old plaza, where the Jesuits and most Mexicans lived, and another was built two miles away in a new plaza for Anglo-Americans. Segregation was also evident in El Paso, especially after the Mexican Revolution, when thousands of fugitives flooded across the border seeking refuge in the United States. "The American part is practically cut off completely from the Mexican," Carlo Pinto observed in 1914. We run two parishes, each with its own school, one for Spanish-speakers and a second for English speakers. The Jesuits justified separation not only out of necessity, but also in order to preserve Mexican culture while they simultaneously promoted Americanization. St. Ignatius Church, for instance, sought to ease the immigrant's adjustment by providing social services and by sponsoring the religious associations that were popular in Mexico, such as the Congregación de las Hijas de María for women and the Congregación de San Luis Gonzaga for youth. At the same time, the parish supplied bilingual schools for both children and adults because its long-term goal was assimilation. As Garcia has written, pastors were convinced that "Mexicans for their own economic benefit should learn the language, customs, and values of the United States as quickly as possible."[94]

Italians All

Although they served as brokers of multiple secular cultures, the Jesuits were single-minded in their religious agenda. They consistently advanced a supranational form of Catholicism among the mélange of populations whom they served. Hispanics and Anglos, Irish and Italians, literate and illiterate, rich and poor — all were introduced to religious customs that drew heavily on an Italian model. The European exiles adapted their methodology to diverse ethnic cultures, but they ultimately sought the integration of all believers into a consolidated, universal church. Wherever they went, the church was more Roman when they left.

The Romanization of American Catholicism, of which the Jesuits were not the only champions, took many shapes. One of the most powerful was standardized devotionalism. Thus the comment made by a prominent French Catholic at the time Americanism was condemned had profound implications for Catholic spiritual practice: "ultramontanism would make Italians out of us all."[95] Italian devotionalism, as practiced by the Jesuits, had several common features. One of these was active and public involvement by the faithful. In parishes and Indian missions, for example, participants in Marian May devotions received *i fioretti spirituali*, paper wish-slips on which intended acts of virtue were offered to an image of the Madonna. Students in Jesuit schools celebrated by reciting in unison the office of the Blessed Virgin Mary every evening during the month of May. And Coeur d'Alene Indians at Sacred Heart Mission scooped up bouquets of wild flowers to create a carpet of blossoms before a reproduction of a Roman painting of Mary.

The Italian Jesuits, recognizing that religion is emotive as well as cognitive, encouraged the expression of devotion through the use of evocative physical objects. By so doing they acknowledged, in the words of the historian Colleen McDannell, that "people use their sight, touch, smell, and voice to stimulate pious feelings." The wearing of scapulars and medals, burning of candles, saying of the rosary, reciting of special prayers from mass-produced manuals, singing of hymns — all served as doorways between the secular and sacred worlds. Consequently, just as pious women in Rome decorated images of the Blessed Mother with votive offerings of gold and silver jewelry, Indian devotees in Montana, too, adorned their Madonna. As a missionary wrote, at St. Ignatius Mission the saint wore on her breast "beautiful necklaces of shells, and many strings of glass beads of various colors with contrasting big wolf tooth, a bear's claw and other niceties" offered by native women.[96]

Few devotional objects received as enthusiastic a reception as the *praesepio*, or Christmas crib, an Italian custom ascribed to St. Francis of Assisi. Wherever the Jesuits went, they introduced the elaborate nativity scenes for which their churches in Italy had been renowned. "The most beautiful crib" in the United States, *The Catholic Family Almanac* claimed in 1875, was fashioned in Rome for St. Ignatius Church in San Francisco. "It cost many thousands of dollars" and was "exhibited privately in the scene room of the Teatro Argentina before being packed for America." Like many Mediterranean pieties, meditation on the manger scene was meant to elicit a lively response from viewers, as in San Francisco, where, reported Nicola Congiato, "people went crazy over [the] beautiful Italian-style creche." While visitors offered prayers and coins of silver and gold to an image of the Christ Child, students did their part by contributing "straws for the manger," slips of paper on which were inscribed the virtuous deeds with which they intended to honor the Child.[97]

Although not opposed to private devotions, the Italians emphasized acts of corporate piety. Catholics everywhere honored the sacrament of the Eucharist on the Feast of Corpus Christi by marching in tandem with a priest who held the host in solemn display through town and countryside. Meanwhile, a throng of onlookers, like sunflowers in a field, reverently focused on the communal tableau that played out before them. Similar displays of corporate devotion marked the feasts of patron saints and Marian celebrations on college campuses, in Indian villages, and in towns spread across the West.

All of these activities fostered the uniformity in Catholic devotional life through the central roles given to priest and parish in their performance. Just as the Corpus Christi procession advanced to its final destination in the church, where participants received a priest's blessing, other ultramontane devotions were also church-based and affirmed clerical authority. Candles used by the faithful for the Feast of the Purification, for example, were not homemade, but purchased at the church and blessed during high mass for proper use by a priest, the church's representative. Through their performance of these prescribed acts of piety, the faithful received assurance that their prayers were efficacious. Thus, Catholics around the world joined sodalities and confraternities approved by Rome, recited prayers of stereotyped text, and wore special medals and scapulars that conferred Roman indulgences. By relocating devotional practices into the parish church under the control of the priest, by distinguishing Catholics from non-Catholics, and by mobilizing the laity to the defense of the church and its hierarchy in the face of perceived threats from without, summarizes the historian Ann Taves, the hierarchy standardized practices within the church internationally.[98]

Devotion to the Sacred Heart of Jesus was emblematic of all these tendencies. This practice, which was extended to the whole church by Pius IX in 1856, so permeated church life after mid-century that it emerged as the trademark of devotional Catholicism. The Society of Jesus became a main propagator of the tradition. A global network of Jesuit churches, chapels, schools, prayer manuals, and pamphlets all bore the name Sacred Heart. Promoted in the United States by Benedetto Sestini's *Messenger of the Sacred Heart*, the devotion focused on the physical heart of Jesus as a symbol of divine love. As Archbishop James Roosevelt Bayley of Baltimore said in 1873, it offered an antidote for "the deadly poison of materialism and sensuality" that menaced the church. Devotion to the Sacred Heart also accentuated reparation for transgressions and atonement "by the hearts of men . . . hardened against . . . the influence of religion." "Never perhaps, was the mass of human misery so great as at the present day," Sestini himself wrote. "The evil has penetrated everywhere. From the revolt against God and His Church . . . [to] a depreciation in the minds of men of all visible authority."[99]

If this devotion gave significance to the suffering of displaced immigrants, it also bestowed meaning to the humiliations endured by the church itself while simultaneously enhancing ecclesiastical authority. As Taves has noted, a reverential attitude toward the Sacred Heart was applied metaphorically to the institutional church and its leadership, especially to the papacy. This extension was a favored theme of the *Messenger of the Sacred Heart*. "What, then, are the tendencies characterizing the Devotion to the Heart of the Incarnate God?" Sestini asked rhetorically. "Before, and above all, *submission*. . . . Submission to those representing His authority, and lastly a spirit of subordination to all legitimately instituted power." By the Jesuit's reckoning, "Peter is, as it were, the brain of this mystical body and for him consequently the Heart of Jesus apportions the requisite abundance of its vivifying spirit, not for Peter's sake alone, but to benefit through him the whole body of the church."[100]

Ardent support of the papacy revealed itself not merely in Sestini's *Messenger*, but in every parish and Indian mission run by Jesuits. After the fall of papal Rome in 1870, thousands of Catholics paraded through the streets of San Francisco the following year in honor of the besieged "pontiff-king." Leaders of the Coeur d'Alene Indians—no doubt urged on by Giuseppe

Cataldo — wrote to the pope to assure him that tribal warriors were willing "to spill their blood and give their lives for our good Father Pius IX." This focusing of devotion on the person of the pope, coupled with the declaration of infallibility, advanced the centralization of the church around Rome and the papacy. In church and school, sermons that centered on papal authority, papal banners, and papal portraits fortified the preacher's message and strengthened the position of the pope to a degree unprecedented in the history of the church.[101] Jesuits were not the only churchmen promoting this important movement, but they played a significant role in its advancement.

Ultramontane pieties advanced by Italian Jesuits also aimed at integrating Americans into a single Catholic culture, a culture that transcended national boundaries. As Sestini explained, devotion to the Sacred Heart, "united all Christian hearts" divided "by race, by country, by condition." "Wide apart as their lots may be cast," all the faithful "should be united as one great family." May devotions, the Christmas crib, Corpus Christi processions, to name only a few — all were equally unitive. They symbolically joined all Catholics, regardless of nationality or class, into a transnational spiritual community. This orientation was not without appeal to a progressively heterogeneous and often divided American church. Nineteenth-century devotionalism, as scholars have pointed out, became a powerful force whereby "Catholics drew boundaries around themselves and imposed upon their badly divided and combative tribe a sense of common identity."[102]

In her engaging study titled *Material Christianity*, the historian Colleen McDannell has analyzed the significance of this religious centralization. Scholars have in the past focused their research almost exclusively on the so-called "American" quality of Catholicism, she has argued. The unfortunate consequence has been that the Romanization of American piety — which appealed not only to the clergy, but to the great mass of churchgoers — has escaped close scrutiny. "While the American environment certainly made an indelible mark on Catholics living in the United States," McDannell argues, "we need not overlook the continuing presence of Europe in shaping American Catholicism." Indeed, many pious practices — devotion to the Sacred Heart, devotion to Our Lady of Lourdes, and the cult of the papacy — testified to "a strong impulse within American Catholic devotional life to reach beyond the ethnic neighborhood and pragmatic American ideology to the transtemporal and transnational." She adds: "Catholics embraced this universalizing trend not merely because it was being forced upon them by a church increasingly directed from Rome. They embraced it because it allowed them to transcend restrictions set up by nature, history, and society. . . . In late nineteenth-century America, Catholics simultaneously enjoyed the familiarity of ethnic traditions, the freedoms of democratic ideology, and the universality of the supernatural."[103]

If transnational religiosity enabled Catholics to belong, it also taught them what it meant to be an outsider. As the *Revista Católica* stated in 1888, "The whole life of a Catholic these days can be summed up in one word: fight." Many devotions symbolized the alienation — from both modernity and from the world — felt by Catholics of that era. The Romanization of Catholic piety intensified the division of Catholic and Protestant into distinct and different communities. Devotion to the Sacred Heart, for instance, sought to protect the church from the corruption of heresy.[104]

Other pieties further alienated Catholics from their fellow citizens and reaffirmed their status as foreigners. Protestants, believing that the Sabbath should be devoted to repose and spiritual edification of one's neighbor, were dismayed by the gaudy processions favored by Mexican Catholics.[105] When a new bishop was appointed in Brownsville, Texas, in 1874, an anonymous letter writer chided Catholics, "if you attempt to have a procession through the public thoroughfares of our city, there is a bullet ready for your worthless carcass and another for your d— Bishop."[106] Catholic emphasis on infallibility and the authority of the pope made them appear still more alien and more cut off from mainstream culture. It was not nativist hostility alone, therefore, that created the ghettoized world of nineteenth-century Catholicism. Indeed, Catholic theology and practice itself nurtured the evolution of an isolated Catholic subculture, which saw itself, in the words of one historian, "as a beleaguered minority banding together to protect itself from the attacks of its enemies." To this characteristically Catholic phenomenon, the immigrant Jesuits from Italy contributed not a little.[107]

As the case of the Jesuits confirms, nineteenth-century American Catholicism was a complicated affair, and it was more complex than historians generally acknowledge. It involved multiple dynamics, paradoxes, and seemingly dichotomous goals. In their brokerage role, the Jesuits fostered an opening up of the immigrant world on several levels. This was accomplished in the cultural dimension through the Americanization of European immigrants, Native Americans, and Latinos by means of education. It was achieved on the religious level through the advancement of transnational devotionalism and ultramontanism. However, by fostering a distinctly Catholic ethos, the émigrés also contributed to the ghettoizing of American Catholics. Their over-arching goal was always the advancement of the Catholic cause. In many instances this objective led to religious uniformity. In others it engendered cultural pluralism. The Italian Jesuits wanted everyone to march toward the same goal, but they also recognized the truth of the old proverb, *A tutti non si adatta una sola scarpa*, "The same shoe does not fit every foot."

11 *"A Delicate State of Transition"*

JESUITS DIVIDED

> Methods that are good and wise for Italy are not so for California.
>
> — Jesuit Robert Kenna, 1893[1]

The Italian Jesuits usually succeeded in adapting European institutions to a multicultural America, as the story of their effective brokering of a range of cultures confirms. But sometimes they faltered, largely because they could not agree on the proper strategy to achieve that goal. Nowhere perhaps were the strains associated with accommodation more intense than in late nineteenth-century California. Not only did the Italians clash with one another over that issue, they also butted heads with their native-born protégés. As progressive numbers of Americans — often graduates of the émigré colleges — joined the order, the ethnic composition of the California Mission shifted. With displacement came impassioned debates between aging Italians and young Americans on how best to minister to the state's increasingly American population. One group revered the past; the other lived for the future.

The row among the Californians left the order's superior general in Europe perplexed. Some Jesuits "cling ferociously to Italian usages and think that it is an abomination to deviate [from] them even a little," Anton Anderledy said. They forget that "times and places are different, as are customs and habits." Equally intolerable were priests in the liberal camp who were infatuated with "novelty" and had "a passion for change and devote all their energies to adopt everything . . . to the American character." So polarized had warring Jesuits become by 1889 that Anderledy dispatched a visitor to San Francisco. Expressing "great anxiety" over the disunion and laxity prevailing in California, he charged trouble-shooter Rudolph J. Meyer, the St. Louis-born former head of the Missouri Jesuit Province, to investigate and, if possible, set things right.[2] As subsequent events demonstrated, however, the seemingly parochial disagreement that unhinged the peace of the Californians was not subject to instant repair. The reason: the roots of their woe were more than local; they were grounded in deep divisions within Catholic culture at large.

The greatest challenge facing American Catholicism in the latter half of the nineteenth century was the assimilation of its exploding foreign population. With a million new members pouring into the country every decade between 1880 and 1920, immigration transformed the church into something entirely new.[3] Since mid-century the nation's largest religious body, the Catholic Church became its most ethnically heterogeneous denomination. By 1916, more than 75 percent of the 15.7 million faithful living in the United States were classified as aliens.[4] This diversity reaped a whirlwind of problems. Beginning in the 1880s, the inrush of millions of destitute outsiders into an overwhelmingly Protestant society generated a new wave of racism and anti-Catholicism. It also unleashed division within the Catholic Church. Bishops strongly disagreed on how best to assimilate their diverse membership into a cohesive body of believers. As a consequence, ethnic differences not only spurred a tendency toward separateness from the dominant culture, they also undermined ecclesiastical unity.

"In this complicated setting," a historian wrote, "the need to situate themselves within the American environment yet safeguard their traditions remained the essential motivating force for Catholics." The great test facing church leaders was to negotiate their complex community's survival in both religious and secular society. This multicultural approach was complicated not merely by the heterogeneity of the participants, but by two additional pitfalls. Leaders somehow had to convey sufficient respect for American conventions to calm non-Catholics (and yet not alarm Rome), while simultaneously maintaining the faith of the immigrant masses and integrating them into the mainstream.[5]

By the 1890s, this dilemma had split the hierarchy into opposing camps. A liberal or progressive consortium, dominated by Irish-Americans eager to enter society, sought to form a more indigenous church by quickly adapting to American ways. "We should live in our age, know it, be in touch with it," said spokesman John Ireland, archbishop of St. Paul, Minnesota. "The church of America must be, of course Catholic as even in Jerusalem or Rome; but as far as her garments assume color from the local atmosphere, she must be America," Ireland argued. "Let no one dare to paint her brow with a foreign taint or pin to her mantle foreign linings." Some of the so-called Americanizers even believed that the United States' unique church-state relationship gleamed as a paradigm of universal applicability. God had given America a mission, proclaimed Bishop John J. Keane. It "was meant to be a teacher through whose lips and in whose life he was to solve the social problems of the Old World."[6]

A rival version of the future was championed by traditionalists and by curia officials in Rome, who, unconvinced by claims of American uniqueness, emphasized the supranational character of the church. Fearful that accommodation would undermine ecclesiastical solidarity and anxious lest the liberal contagion contaminate Europe, they promoted a continental European version of Catholicism. Their program called for greater central-ization of the American church under Roman authority. As early as 1878, the Irish bishop George Conroy, a visitor to the United States, had warned Rome about the growing accommodationist threat. "In order to demonstrate that Catholics are good Americans, some would shape the Church along American lines," he reported. "They affect a kind of ecclesiastical inde-pendence, which, if the faith were to fail among the clergy or the people, would not be without damage to the very unity of the Church."[7]

These disagreements, eventually dubbed the Americanist controversy, were finally resolved by a series of papal interventions in favor of the transnational position. In 1895, Leo XIII issued a letter to the American hierarchy titled *Longinqua oceani*, demanding conformity to Roman guidelines. While praising "the equity of the laws which obtain in America" and "the customs of the well-ordered Republic," he rejected church-state separation as a model for all nations. "It would be very erroneous," the pope warned, "to draw the conclusion that in America is to be sought the type of the most desirable status of the Church, or that it would be universally lawful or expedient for State and Church to be, as in America, dissevered and divorced." Four years later, his encyclical *Testem benevolentiae* dismissed other notions associated with Americanism, including the idea that the church should adapt its teach-ing to the modern age and that U.S. Catholicism could be "different from that which is in the rest of the world." The decrees were concussive in their outcome. With the condemnation of Americanism, experimentation yielded to timidity, debate and discussion within the church waned, and innovation was henceforth regarded with suspicion. "As a distinctive religious idea or pastoral strategy," one scholar writes, Americanism "had been stopped cold."[8]

Jesuits played no small role in the victory over Americanism. Among the most effective proponents of Romanization were two Italians once associ-ated with Woodstock College, Camillo Mazzella, its one-time dean, and his protégé, Salvatore Brandi. By the time the controversy came to a head, both men had returned to Rome, where Mazzella became professor of theology at the Gregorian University and then, in 1886, a cardinal of the church. A strong advocate of centralization, the beetle-browed Neapolitan wielded wide influence through several powerful posts in the Vatican. Brandi, after sixteen years in America, become editor of Rome's authoritative *Civiltà Cattolica*. Citizens of the United States, both Italians were considered experts on American affairs and were frequently consulted by popes and curia officials. Brandi, whom one historian described as "an unofficial agent of the Ameri-can conservative prelates," vigorously piloted the assault against liberalism in the pages of the powerful *Civiltà*. So heated was the cross-fire between the two camps that opponents descended to name-calling. "Brandi is a devil," Ireland once told a confidant. Brandi, brandishing the most derogatory terms available to a nineteenth-century churchman, retorted that Ireland was "a liberal and revolutionary bishop." Brandi and Mazzella not only led the charge against Americanism, they also helped deliver its coup de grâce. Brandi boasted authorship of *Longinqua oceani*, and Mazzella played a major role in the composition of *Testem benevolentiae*.[9]

What position did Italian Jesuits in the United States take in this struggle? Mazzella and Brandi were not the only ones who feared that accommodating American prelates, if left unchecked, would undermine church discipline and erode essential doctrine. Sestini's *Sacred Heart Messenger* was critical of the liberal program, as was *La Revista Católica*, which greeted *Testem benevolentiae* with "immense satisfaction." Some Italian theologians in the United States — Luigi Sabetti, Carlo Piccirillo, Filippo Cardella, and Nicola Russo — sympathized with Roman conservatives and reported to them about the perils threatening Catholicism. In the midst of the Americanist crisis, an agitated Cardella of New York warned a curia official that the United States was in a mode of "full ecclesiastical revolution."[10]

Jesuits in the West, less inclined toward theological speculation and consumed by pastoral work, did not engage in the intellectual debate over Americanism. This did not mean they were untouched by it. Indeed, by century's end, the multiple issues interlaced in the controversy had so suffused the church that most thinking Catholics were affected by it to some degree. While bishops and Vatican officials argued about the limits of divergence from European models of church order, ordinary priests dealt with these questions in concrete ways. Even after Rome snuffed out debate over the separation of church and state, the rank-and-file clergy continued to wrestle with the pastoral challenge of integrating Catholics into American society. Popes Leo XIII and Pius X may have muffled Catholic intellectual speculation, as scholars have suggested, but they could not, even if they had wished to, keep the church and its people from pushing for influence, power, and acceptance. The assimilation process continued, as did the impelling itch to find acceptance as fully American and Catholic.[11] Missionaries debated, indeed fought among themselves, about how best to engage the modern world. As the church in the West became less cosmopolitan and more identifiably American, their disputes intensified, demonstrating that they were as conflicted as the church itself.

Clashing Cultures in California

Fin de siècle California, which had begun as a Spanish colony, marched into the new century speaking English as it embraced an era of rapid modernization and Americanization. During the 1860s, nearly 40 percent of the state's population had been foreign-born, the majority of them Europeans, but by 1900 that ratio had fallen to around 28 percent. Although still immigrant country, California was becoming culturally more like the rest of the nation. In the north, Gilded Age San Franciscans molded their city into the American capital of the Pacific, while Los Angeles, inundated by an influx of Midwesterners, flowered as "the new Eden of the Saxon home-seeker," as one contemporary put it.[12] The eradication of racial differences became a central tenet of the state's progressive movement. Californians agreed with Theodore Roosevelt, who declared: "The foreign-born population of this country must be an Americanized population. It must talk the language of its native-born fellow citizens, it must possess American citizenship and American ideals."[13]

The Catholic Church, dominated by new arrivals, could not remain untouched by the Americanization campaign. The economic depression of the 1890s ignited the first earnest U.S. effort to limit immigration from Europe. National impatience with a hyphenated citizenry, coupled with a revival of anti-Catholicism after the founding of the American Protective Association in 1887, left many Catholics embarrassed by their church's alien aspect. "Priests foreign in disposition and work were not fitted to make favorable impressions upon the non-Catholic population," Archbishop Ireland wrote in 1894, "and the American-born children of Catholic immigrants were likely to escape their action." When the time came to find a successor for José Alemany, California's Spanish-born archbishop, some proponents favored a native son. "In San Francisco is to be found a mixed population composed of many nationalities," Bishop Bernard J. McQuaid of Rochester reported to Rome. "To harmonize all these, no one would be more acceptable than a native American." Americanizers were pleased, therefore, when the Vatican appointed Patrick W. Riordan in 1883. The new bishop was an English-speaking Canadian who had grown up in Chicago and was a churchman of liberal attitudes.[14]

The nationalizing movement reshaped the Italian Jesuit subculture of California. A metaphor of that transformation, Santa Clara College had sprung into existence in 1851 as a crossroads culture. But by century's close, its student body and faculty were dominated by Americans and Irish Americans. As the institution became more mainstream, its European curriculum and strict code of student conduct, which had been readily accepted during California's cosmopolitan era, became difficult to defend. And in their parishes, Jesuits now preached to congregations intolerant of sermons marred by the hiccup of broken language. "We cannot assign certain duties to men who cannot speak English with sufficient correctness," a California superior declared in 1897, citing the case of Giovanni Sardi, an Italian priest who had recently offered a series of Lenten sermons in San Francisco. "What was the result? By the end of Lent, the attendance was dwindled down to less than one hundred people!"[15]

To many Jesuits, Italian hegemony over operations in California had become an anachronism. "The Italian Fathers no longer enjoy the support and following of the people that they once had," declared Edward P. Allen, the Dublin-born president of St. Ignatius College. Since Catholics now preferred native-born or Irish priests, the church should in the future be run by English-speaking clergy.[16] "I am not blind to the immense work done by the older Fathers," echoed Joseph A. Riordan of Santa Clara, "but circumstances have changed . . . and the policy that was admirable years ago may not be admirable now."[17] The period between 1880 and 1910 was, therefore, a major transitional time as middle-class Catholics sought to adapt to American culture. Like the church itself, the Jesuit enterprise in California was no longer entirely European; nor was it fully American. As Riordan summed up, the Jesuits were in a "delicate state of transition."[18]

Riordan's description of the interregnum as "delicate" understated the matter. It was, in fact, bellicose. As more Americans joined the Society in California, a widening divide winnowed natives from Europeans. Italian modes of running schools, parishes, and religious communities came under sharp scrutiny. Jesuits found themselves disagreeing on every aspect of their lives — how they should work, how they should recreate, what they should study, and even what they should eat and drink. As a result, discord and division separated ethnic groups who in an earlier generation had been companionable. So hot had their intramural wrangling become that a Jesuit visitor to San Francisco in 1885 remarked: "There are more politics here than one could possibly conceive. I have never seen such disunion . . . as exists among us here in California."[19]

The challenge of creating community among diverse ethnicities was not new to the Society of Jesus. From its founding in the sixteenth century, Portuguese Jesuits had clashed with Spaniards; Germans disagreed with Poles; and Frenchmen butted heads with everyone. That the order flourished testified not to religion's ability to divide, but to its capacity to forge common ground. But the challenge of remaining peaceably cosmopolitan remained for Jesuits. Despite warnings about the corrosive "spirit of nationalism," disputes between persons from different countries inevitably arose in the nineteenth century. In 1889, Visitor Rudolph J. Meyer had reminded the Californians of the principle that all Jesuit undertakings be adapted to time and place, but a coterie of traditionalists persisted in imposing old world norms on the new.[20]

The Jesuits were one among many religious orders torn by disputes over accommodation in this era. The Christian Brothers of the United States clashed with European members of their congregation when they took their educational work in new directions. Overseas authorities insisted that their brethren restrict their teaching to traditional grammar schools, commercial colleges, and polytechnic institutions. When the Americans took up Latin-based secondary and collegiate education, European gatekeepers threatened to expel them from the congregation. Benedictines, too, differed on the extent to which their monastic tradition should be tailored to the American scene. Pioneering German monks at St. John's Abbey in Minnesota had adjusted their European horarium to the needs of a missionary country, dispersing members far and wide to establish schools, parishes, and Indian missions on an advancing frontier. With time, however, this flight from the cloister was denounced by younger monks, who called for stability and a return to the monastic spirit of their vocation. Throughout the 1880s, the Benedictines debated the nature of that heritage and its adaptation to America, finally resolving differences through the bitter resignation in 1889 of their abbot.[21]

If the Benedictine battle found older and younger monks on opposite flanks, Jesuit partisans were riven by more than age. According to Jérôme Ricard, a French priest working in California, they were "divided into two camps, the Italians on one side and the Americans and Irish on the other." And yet, battles lines did not neatly coincide with nationality, since the Europeans were split among themselves. A Varsi, Sasia, Pinasco, or Calzia made as good a case for adaptation as did a Kenna, Riordan, Allen, or Mahoney. Indeed, Luigi Varsi — hailed by Americans as "the very best man we have" — was skewered by Italian doomsayers as the "ring leader" of the movement to "update and nationalize our Institute," a reference to the Society's *Constitutions* and its key rules and regulations. Compounding offenses, the popular Italian disparaged the conservative journal *Civiltà Cattolica*, critics said, and he embraced "American and modern ideas about our way of living and acting."[22]

Giuseppe Sasia was another Americanized European. Even as a student at Woodstock College, the amiable Italian was known as a witty raconteur and was popular with Europeans and Americans alike.[23] Frequently appointed to positions of authority in California, he was admired by progressives for his intimate knowledge of life in the United States. Although liberal-minded Jesuits placed their hopes in Sasia, traditionalists brushed him aside as "full of American ideas."[24] As the examples of Sasia and Varsi reveal, the abyss separating Jesuits was not limited simply to nationality: they were also deeply split by ideological fissures. At its most basic, their divergence exposed a conflicted self-understanding. Jesuits, like the German Benedictines, could not agree how their Institute should be embodied in the modern era.

Since the high ground was the best place from which to fight, protago-

nists on both sides appealed to the order's rules and *Constitutions* as justification for their position. Assessments of each of the dissonant parties were
summed up by two observers in Europe, one an unnamed official in the Jesuit
curia in Rome and the other Carlo Torti, a Turinese provincial. According
to a memo penned by the curialist, one cluster of Californians championed
strict observance of the Institute; the other advocated a lax approach. The
rigorists — often Italians, but not always — demanded that everything be done
"as it was done years ago in their own province far away." Clinging to the
old Latin maxim *Via trita via tuta*, "the trodden path is the safe path," they
refused "to make any allowance for difference of circumstances." Torti elaborated: The "ancient customs" of the Roman College and other Italian institutions "appear in their eyes to be as important as our rules." Nor could they
concede that some aspects of American culture and American institutions
might be superior to their own.[25]

According to the curia official, advocates of a loose interpretation of the
rules hankered to be "Americans." In their rush to adapt to local mores, they
made light of "religious observances, which wise and prudent men everywhere consider of the greatest moment." While conservatives enforced
"the *letter* of the rules" of the Society, Torti went on, liberals emphasized "the
spirit of the rules." The nationalists agreed with Archbishop Ireland that a
churchman's work was "to bridge the chasm separating the Church from the
age." Thus, if conservatives were concerned about modernity and its excesses,
and preserving discipline, asceticism, and continuity with the past, their
opposite number championed flexibility, adaptation, and preparation for
what a later period would designate as *aggiornamento*.[26]

Disparity of power exacerbated ideological contrasts. So, too, did age, as
Riordan disclosed when he described his cohort as those "who have suffered
so bitterly from the opposition and lack of confidence of older men."[27]
Although an elderly minority, the conservative Italians wielded leverage
beyond their numbers, in part because the Jesuit system of governance gave
disproportionate deference to priests with seniority, the *patres graviores*, as
they were referred to in Latin. The leverage of this rump group, numbering
perhaps only about a half-dozen older men, was heightened by their personal
ties with officials in Italy. Authorities were companions with whom they had
once lived and studied, familiars to whom they could confidently correspond
in Italian. Because overseers in far-away Europe were often clueless about
American reality, their reliance on émigré informants was substantial.

Therefore, it seemed to liberal Americans that higher-ups in Europe sympathized with the opposition. According to Giovanni Mateo Ciravegna, one-
time head of the Turin Province, fathers general Pieter Beckx and Anton
Anderledy did indeed favor the conservative circle.[28] Beckx, a Belgian, and
Anderledy, a Swiss, successively governed the Society of Jesus during a period

FIGURE 28. With the graying of the Italians, European influence over Jesuit operations in the West began to wane. Four elderly Jesuits assemble in the gardens of Santa Clara College at century's end. From left to right: Thomas P. Leonard, Carlo E. Messea, Giovanni Pinasco, and Giuseppe Caredda. Courtesy Santa Clara University Archives, Andrew P. Hill photo, Hill.608

of persecution and at a time when ultramontanism prevailed. "Since our lot is cast amidst these troublous times," Anderledy chided Jesuits, "we must beware of contracting even the slightest taint of liberal opinions."[29] The third superior general during this troubled era was Luis Martín Garcia, a Spaniard. Left inconsolable by his homeland's losses in the Spanish-American War, he privately confessed an "antipathy, not to mention aversion, toward . . . all that was American."[30] Try as he might, Martín was unable to conceal his bias from progressive Californians. "Evidently, His Paternity has little or no confidence in us Americans," a bewildered John Frieden, superior of the California Mission, once told to a friend. "How a man in his exalted position, of his mind, and with the opportunities at his disposal should be so utterly blind to the real state of affairs is startling."[31]

This did not mean that authorities did not strive to understand the bickering Californians, as is evidenced by their appeals for reliable data upon which to make decisions. Although enemies caricatured the Society as a top-down monolith, its governance was in fact highly consultative, requiring frequent reports from the field to higher authorities. With their pens as their weapons, partisans in America let fly with letters whenever the time came to evaluate policy or to select new superiors. But their accounts were so contradictory and lopsided, an exasperated European official said, that "it's really difficult to figure out where the truth lies."[32] To keep the peace, supervisors attempted balance-of-power politics, alternately appointing a liberal superior for one term and then replacing him with a conservative. But since the usual term of office was six years, the quest to find fresh nominees was as unending as it was unsatisfactory.

Meanwhile, the California Mission careened from right to left and back again; and partisans were never appeased. When word of a new appointment arrived from Rome, it occasioned either celebration or lamentation, depending on one's point of view. In 1883, when liberals learned that the strict constructionist Nicola Congiato would be succeeded as mission superior by Giuseppe Sasia, an Italian sympathetic to American ways, they rejoiced. Conversely, conservatives were crestfallen. The "lax and malcontents" are delighted at Sasia's nomination, Congiato said, but men of "regular observance [are] greatly alarmed."[33] The appointment of Rudolph J. Meyer of St. Louis as an official visitor to the fractious mission a few years later evoked similarly polar reactions. "The younger portion" of the mission "was very glad indeed" at his advent, said Jérôme Ricard. "Our liberals" have high hopes in Meyer, confirmed Carlo Pollano, a conservative San Franciscan with a flair for detecting conspiracy scenarios, but "we hope that in the end they will be as surprised by him as the [Italian] liberals of '48 were by Pius IX." Pollano's elation toppled into disappointment, however, when Meyer sympathized with advocates of reform.[34]

Partisans could not agree on what they expected from superiors. Repelled by "excessive observance of little things," younger Jesuits wanted their directors to "trust them and treat them like men."[35] To conservatives, to do so translated into freedom from restraint. Americans, yearning to end their marginalization from California culture, favored an open style of leadership that would reframe how Jesuits viewed the world and how the world viewed them. To progressives, their semi-cloistered European elders seemed monkishly immune to worldly concerns. "They are essentially men who live in the inside of the house and know little or nothing of the outside," an American argued. "They always keep aloof and rule from misty heights," charged another critic.[36] "We are in a new land, all is energy, all is life," still another protested. The church in California is young and growing, but with men unsympathetic to American ways in charge, we Jesuits "have a very little part in shaping the work."[37]

Thus the tempest raged. Because leaders in Europe resisted innovation and because conservatives often occupied positions of authority in California, the Americanization of Jesuit operations was deferred by decades of acrimony. In the process, Jesuits favoring reform chafed increasingly at their dependence upon European oversight. That displeasure contributed not a little to the eventual severance of ties between the three American missions and Italy. In 1909, the California Mission, newly amalgamated with the Rocky Mountain Mission, became an independent province of the Society, thus ending a half-century of cooperation between the Turin Province of Italy and the Far West. Ten years later, in 1919, the New Mexico Mission became independent of Naples. The journey toward autonomy was, however, long and painful, taking nearly three decades to accomplish.

Conflict erupted in the California Mission in the 1890s as Americans began assuming positions of leadership — and Italian traditionalists for the first time saw power beginning to slip from their hands. In accord with the democratic leveling process of the frontier, young Jesuits itched to have a say in decision-making. Prominent among the new breed of leaders was Robert Kenna, president of St. Ignatius College and later of Santa Clara College. The first American to head either institution, Kenna came from a high-profile California family and was skilled in public relations. If some older Europeans fled contact with the world, Kenna dashed to embrace it. He quickly became spokesperson for the liberal side in the domestic squabble between Jesuit defenders of the status quo and aficionados of reform within the mission. In the process, he made himself a moving target for those who thought priests should stay out of secular affairs.

In 1883, Kenna clashed head on with Nicola Congiato, whom Rome had recently returned to the superiorship of the California Mission for an unprecedented third term. Congiato, whose first tenure had taken place thirty years prior, had been progressive and enterprising as a young man. But the sixty-year-old Sardinian now became renowned for trying to turn the clock back. As his run-in with Kenna illustrated, the crossfire over Americanization pitted young against old. Some elderly Jesuits, having lost the flexibility of their salad days when they had creatively adapted to the demands of a missionary country, fought the drift from the safe moorings of tradition. Alarmed by innovations advanced by young "revolutionaries," the old guard, of whom Congiato was a leader, feared the eventual Americanization of the order itself.[38]

As soon as he returned to office, Congiato ordered Kenna to assemble Santa Clara's faculty for a special consultation to review an agenda readied in advance. Unhappy with a recent relaxation of student discipline, the Italian pushed for restoration of the old order. Would it be possible, he posed, "to no longer grant students the freedom of leaving the college without prefects" as had been the custom in the past? Second, could the old custom of having "reading at table for the students" be revived? Third, would it be expedient to require all students to attend Mass daily? Submitted for open debate to "nearly all the fathers," Congiato's proposals were rejected, with faculty arguing that nothing be altered lest the students "think the College is a prison."[39]

In the aftermath, Kenna, emboldened perhaps by this show of support, sought to enlarge student freedom. Boarders were now granted "the privilege of going once a month, and alone, to the city of San Jose, where they may remain the whole day." The only conditions were parental approval and, as one student recalled, that "our conduct had been good." Attendance at weekly mass continued to be left to the individual student's discretion. In the dining hall, conversation (rather than reading) became common practice. Kenna's allowances did not pass unchallenged. Alarmed not only by lax discipline but also by the young president's indifference to the classics, Congiato moved to restore the old order by laying his complaint before the superior general in Europe. In answer, a displeased Pieter Beckx sent word that Kenna's abuse of allowing boarding students to "go out alone" must cease.[40]

Similar retrenchment occurred in San Francisco. In 1887, Congiato appointed Enrico Imoda, a fifty-five-year-old *piemontese*, to the presidency of St. Ignatius College. A strict disciplinarian, he was an unlikely candidate to lead the Society's largest day school in the United States.[41] Not only did Imoda know nothing about running a college, he was paralyzed by fractured English and "crushing timidity." (He seems, for example, never to have permitted himself the vanity of being photographed.) Imoda was a decent fellow, co-workers said, but he could not bring himself to "visit a classroom or say a word to students, much less to lay persons."[42] Ostrich-like, he vanished when benefactors or parents called at the college, an acquaintance reported, because he abhorred their company. The reclusive president limited his public appearances to church services, over which he presided with attention to proper rubrics, his life's sole passion. Absorbed in minutiae, Imoda spent days arranging the books in the library, "himself sewing and binding pamphlets and magazines." Trusting no one, he ran everything from his room, a Jesuit analogue of "L'état c'est moi."[43]

In the eyes of critics, Imoda's worst shortcoming was his ignorance. Like a man living in a borrowed culture, he failed to comprehend either the United States or the Society of Jesus. "Men who do not understand our people, should be slow in forcing their old traditions in a new country and upon a new people," declared Robert Kenna. Nor did Imoda truly grasp the Jesuit Institute. Incapable of adapting religious life to altered circumstance, he failed to perceive that practical application of the Jesuit rules "must always be in the spirit of St. Ignatius and hence vary with times, places and persons." He meant well, cynics supposed, but his literalness made him both anachronistic and dangerous.[44]

Why was such an improbable man elevated? Because, as a contemporary said, he enforced "observance of the rule." Like any Jesuit president, Enrico Imoda wore two hats — one as the school's chief executive and another as superior of the religious community affiliated with the college. Accordingly, the order's legislation prescribed that a rector-president be simultaneously "experienced in matters of business and of the spiritual life" and that he should "endeavor to have the *Constitutions* observed in their entirety." Imoda might know nothing about running a college, a supporter in Turin conceded, but the flinty contrarian was "tough and strong" in enforcing discipline and in applying the brakes to the "tendency toward American laxity." In the era of the papal condemnation of Americanism, such exactitude was applauded.[45]

Transatlantic Debates

If Imoda's "rabbinical interpretation of our rules" (as Sasia put it) offended progressives, supervisors abroad and conservatives at home cheered his rigor. Thus, when the time came to select a new superior for the California Mission in 1891, Imoda emerged as top candidate. That he had "many adversaries" was inconsequential, a backer argued; nor was it necessary that he "be able to speak in public or to the community or to the students in order to be a good superior." What mattered was his unyielding asceticism.[46] When appointing Imoda, Father General Anderledy tellingly borrowed a phrase from the Latin title of Pope Leo XIII's encyclical of that year. Imoda was worthy, he wrote, because the California Jesuits seemed "weakened by an enthusiasm for new things [*rerum novarum*] and for a freer discipline more in keeping with the temper of the times." Echoing Rome's praise, traditionalists acclaimed Imoda's elevation. "Thanks be to God," one exclaimed; "things are improving."[47]

If there was one aspect of Jesuit education that Imoda and other conservatives hoped to upgrade, it was its quality. Even the liberal opposition conceded that admission standards had slipped. For the first time in decades, the California colleges faced stiff competition from public institutions, whose modern campuses, lower tuition, and diverse curricula siphoned off students by the thousands. Faced with an imperative itch to improve, Americanists counseled patience lest the schools drive away their clientele; meanwhile, conservative Europeans demanded immediate reform, which, they reasoned, meant a restoration of the ancient languages. Everyone recognized that Latin and Greek studies had declined. Even at Santa Clara, the order's flagship college in the West, four times as many graduates took the Bachelor of Science degree as the classical Bachelor of Arts. Preference for a more utilitarian course of studies was not confined to the western states. In response to rapid industrial development, American education itself was moving away from Virgil and Homer. Of the nearly six thousand students attending Jesuit colleges across the United States at this time, less than 2 percent graduated with the Bachelor of Arts degree in the classics.[48]

That fewer and fewer westerners esteemed the ancient languages was clear from report after report. "The standard of classical studies is not very high," a priest wrote from Spokane in 1900. He ascribed the deficiency to the students' "natural inconstancy, their dislike of the classics, their insatiable desire to make money, and because they are content with a purely commercial education." Bowing to necessity, the Neapolitans of Sacred Heart College in Denver made no pretense of giving primacy to Latin and Greek. "While appreciating the value of the ancient classical languages as a means of education," they wrote, we "believe that their value may easily be exaggerated and that much of the time commonly devoted to the study of them might with more profit be given to the study of the vernacular." Hence their conclusion: "The language of the school and the one to which most attention is devoted is English."[49]

Some Californians, too, favored a conciliatory approach. Students are not disposed to "receive that education which we are ready and desirous to give," the Jesuit Henry Woods wrote from San Francisco in 1884. Many pupils come from poor Irish working-class families, and seek only sufficient learning to give them a toehold in life. Since they were "anxious to finish their college course when it ought to be only beginning," a lengthy and expensive commitment to classical training was out of the question. We do what we can to promote the study of Latin and Greek, Woods insisted, by discouraging the commercial course "as far as prudence permits." But to impose Caesar and Cicero as strictly as one might wish was "impossible." We must proceed gingerly when trying to raise the standard of education, he warned, for in precipitate action "there is the risk of seeing our classrooms emptied, and our work strangled instead of being strengthened."[50]

Woods's caveats were spurned. Offered an escape from the cul-de-sac created by a rigid curriculum, conservative *piemontesi* refused to budge. In this, they were backed by stewards in Europe. Alarmed at the unraveling of literary studies, they waged a campaign to restore Latin and Greek. Congiato, writing to Rome in 1884, announced that the classics had been "almost abandoned by everyone."[51] In response, Father General Anderledy ordered the Californians to rehabilitate the course. Although Robert Kenna countered that Congiato had exaggerated, the president had no choice but to comply with Rome's mandate.

Stalwarts of the classics achieved their greatest victory three years later. In 1887, the two Piedmontese colleges in California announced they would hereafter grant academic degrees solely to students who enrolled in the classical course and passed examinations in Latin and Greek. Those languages, which before had been optional, were now made mandatory; the study of English was downgraded; and the non-classical Bachelor of Science degree was terminated. To hasten acceptance, President Imoda of St. Ignatius College

spread a coat of sugar over an otherwise bitter reform by offering "an absolutely gratuitous education" to students enrolled in the classical course.[52]
But the experiment was short-lived. Four years later, his successor, Edward
P. Allen, discovering that students could not even be bribed to study the
ancient languages, abandoned the scholarship program. European authorities, however, would not permit Allen to restore the non-classical diploma.
The outcome? Enrollments continued to slip, a direct result, critics maintained, of "the enforcement of the strictly classical course for degrees and the
discouragement of the commercial course."[53]

The imposition of ancient culture from on high unleashed an avalanche
of protest. The next mission superior, Giuseppe Sasia, drawing on his long
experience in the United States, informed Anderledy that "due to special circumstances in this country it is a very difficult thing to persuade students and
their parents of the great importance . . . of classical studies." Kenna echoed
Sasia's argument in a series of sharp appeals to Rome. "Greek keeps many
[students] away and also drives some away after they come here," he wrote
to Luis Martín. "You will never convince Californians" preparing for
careers in business and the professions "that a knowledge of Greek is of any
great importance."[54]

"It is a fact that many of our most successful public men are not *classical* scholars," Kenna continued. Even "the president-elect, Mr. Cleveland, is
not a college graduate." And U.S. Senator Stephen M. White, "the most popular man in California," had earned his Bachelor of Science at Santa Clara
College before the degree was eliminated. "Had he come later, we would not
give him a degree." White "is a power in the land, and there are others like
him who now cannot and will not come to this college," Kenna told an
uncomprehending Martín. "I do not think that Saint Ignatius would refuse
to reach souls unless he could do so by cramming them with Greek." "I realize that my words may sound like heresy to many," he concluded in one of
his many transatlantic appeals, "but they are true all the same."[55]

These laments were disregarded, however. Higher-ups refused to budge,
and enrollments persisted in their downward slide, as predicted. An educational system whose efficacy had been taken for granted for generations was
fast becoming outdated, but too few Jesuits perceived either the need for
change or the way in which change might be accomplished within the context of their tradition. The order's mantra about adapting to times, places,
and persons did not, it seemed, enjoy universal acceptance.

Student discipline further polarized Jesuits. The old European system of
around-the-clock surveillance frustrated teachers and pupils alike. "The only
difference between Santa Clara and any other prison," groused one alumnus, "was that classes instead of a stone quarry brought a student out of his
cell for a considerable period each day." "The college rules prohibited everything but study and, once enrolled, the festive young student might as well

have been waiting for the [electric] chair." Traditionalists nevertheless insisted on adhering to European conventions. During his tenure at St. Ignatius College, Enrico Imoda forbade card playing, smoking, boxing, and similar breaches of discipline. When the Americanizing Luigi Varsi "allowed the boys to be taught round dances" at Santa Clara — "we must adapt ourselves to the ideas of the country," he said — the Jesuit rigorists were scandalized.[56]

Still more ink was spilled over money matters, particularly in San Francisco, where the Jesuits had fallen into a sinkhole of debt in the construction of a new St. Ignatius College. By 1888, the liability had grown to $1,008,511, a figure roughly equivalent to eighteen times that amount today. Americans criticized the bookkeeping of septuagenarian Antonio Maraschi, the college's founder and for decades the treasurer of the California Mission. Even Roman authorities feared the failing priest was embroiled in risky transactions that endangered the security of the entire mission. "If there were a sudden failure," Superior General Anderledy warned, "we would probably be entangled in all manner of law suits."[57]

Conservatives conceded that Maraschi's ledgers were "a real mess," but they were reluctant to dismiss the venerable patriarch and could not agree on a replacement. Knowledgeable observers said Luigi Varsi — because of his "natural talents" and the "esteem and friendship" he enjoyed with many wealthy Californians — was the only person who could "pull the College out of its financial difficulties and manage it well." But defenders of the status quo, offended by Varsi's liberal views, blocked his advancement. In consequence, Maraschi, old and nearly blind, soldiered on. Some priests, disgusted by their superiors' foot-dragging reluctance to retire the elderly treasurer, alleged a double standard. "If an English-speaking Father had been guilty of Fr. Maraschi's doings," said John Frieden, "there would have been a terrible outcry."[58]

The training given to young Jesuits became another lightning rod. Americans charged that California's director of novices, Domenico Giacobbi, was naive, impractical, and incapable of "managing our American novices." They "are shrewder than he is," one man exclaimed. His "uncouth foreign method" of instruction was so offensive that scholastics either left the order in disgust or were "completely broken down, with no manhood left."[59] The only way a young person could receive a solid preparation in California, some Americans maintained, was to leave it. "You must go East to meet those of the Society," visitor Rudolph J. Meyer once told a scholastic preparing for theology studies. "It will never do for you to grow up with the idea you get of [the Society] here." But conservative Europeans, holding "a 'holy horror' of things American," stood in granite opposition. The only thing seminarians learned at Woodstock College, they archly asserted, was "how to dress well."[60]

No aspect of domestic life escaped condemnation by one unhappy faction

FIGURE 29. If older Europeans fled contact with the world, the American Jesuit Robert Kenna typified those who rushed to embrace it. He became spokesperson for the liberal side in the domestic squabble between Jesuit traditionalists and advocates of change within the California Mission. Kenna (fifth from left, with walking stick) is gathered here with conservationist friends dedicated to saving the California redwoods. Courtesy Santa Clara University Archives, Local.24731c

or the other. Antonio Cichi, a priest in his seventies and former professor of Woodstock College, drafted several letters to Rome in 1893 lamenting the fraying of his religious community. "The bond of unity" that formerly prevailed at Santa Clara had dissolved, he wrote. Coming together for meals and recreation, normally a centerpiece of fraternal commonality, had declined because some men — "mostly the young Fathers" — came late or boycotted common exercises. Ignoring the rule mandating travel with a companion, others went to town alone in order "to visit friends and kill time." In Cichi's serio-comic litany of calamities, food topped the list. A few years earlier, visitor Rudolph J. Meyer had reminded Californians of the Jesuit practice of adapting meals to "the manner of the region in which one lives." But that admonition had quickly fallen down the memory hole. Non-Italians still grumbled that the kitchen served too much pasta, and Cichi still claimed there were too many American dishes. To the conventional breakfast (coffee, milk, butter, and meat) an American superior had, for example, added mush — to which another then joined cream. The college, Cichi whined, had become "a house of gluttons."[61]

And then there was the controversy about wine. For Italians who had pioneered viticulture in California, the beverage was an integral part of daily living. *Un giorno senza vino e un giorno senza sole*, an old adage said: "A day without wine is a day without sunshine." But to American Jesuits sympathetic to the temperance movement, alcohol provoked scandal. Robert Kenna frowned on the wine-making that supplied revenue for cash-strapped Santa Clara College. "In this country where drunkenness is so widespread, this way of supporting our college will do us harm," he warned. Although unable to seal the spigot, the president did halt the sale of wine to local customers, arguing that since "we preach on Sunday against drunkenness, it is not becoming to give out by our back gate on Saturday the means of which our hearers may become drunk." Kenna also rationed Jesuit access to the beverage. Denied his daily tipple, old Cichi grumbled that he could enjoy "a glass of good wine" only on "rare occasions."[62]

For exiles like Cichi, a whole way of life was being transformed without possibility of repair. Ancient grapevines, "thick as small trees," that had once flourished in Santa Clara's luxurious *giardino* had been uprooted. "Today all is destroyed," he cried, and the garden "is now planted with potatoes and flowers." Young Jesuits did strange things. Jérôme Ricard, a Frenchman, had begun cultivating lettuce and other vegetables on the edge of the campus. Even more perplexing, an Irishman, Michael A. McKey, tended sweet peas. "A priest in the Society surely had other things to do than garden," the old Italian huffed. Adding insult to injury, McKey did not decorate the church with his blossoms, but instead presented bouquets to female callers who visited the college.[63]

How should celibate Jesuits relate to women? That was another topic that divided young and old, liberal and conservative. According to the gendered conventions of the past, separation had been the rule, but by the end of the century, the bonds of tradition were unraveling. More Catholic women were involved in church work than ever before, and in California women were moving in greater numbers from the domestic to the public realm. Coeducation, for example, had proven so successful at Stanford University by 1904 that alarmed admission officers established a ratio of three males to each female student.[64] In this shifting environment, Jesuits such as Michael McKey or Luigi Varsi favored more relaxed relationships with women in accord with the principle of adapting to changing times. Cichi and others, equating the rules and *Constitutions* of their religious order with the mores of Europe, argued for retention of the old ways, an interpretation shared by overseas gatekeepers. In 1886, Father General Pieter Beckx instructed

Jesuits to avoid conversing with women, because they "are generally speaking, inconstant in their resolutions, and talk so much, that a great deal of time is wasted with them, and very little lasting fruit comes from it." Visitor Rudolph J. Meyer, an American, although progressive in some matters, betrayed the same intolerance. Jesuits should not undertake ministries to women "easily or without sufficient reason," he decreed in 1889. If women approached priests on their own initiative, Jesuits "should not engage in lengthy and useless chatter but should excuse themselves in short order."[65]

If extreme caution was the fruit of a cramped interpretation of Jesuit tradition, it was also the fruit of fear — fear of females and fear of provoking public criticism and scandal. Allegations of illicit relations between priests and nuns was a favorite theme of salacious bestsellers of the day such as *The Escaped Nun; or, Disclosures of Convent Life*. Jesuits "endeavor to make us Americans believe that they are chaste and that nuns are virtuous women," a San Francisco newspaper charged, but we believe "they live lives of sin and profligacy rather than that of virtue and chastity."[66] Dreading false accusations, Jesuits were highly circumspect in dealing with the opposite sex. When earthquake and fire destroyed San Francisco's St. Ignatius College in 1906, the homeless clergy were temporarily offered refuge in a convent of nuns. One elderly Italian priest, Telesforo Demasini, anguished over the invitation. "He thought it was compromising for us," a contemporary said, "and also for the poor sisters."[67]

Consequently, Jesuits wagged fingers at companions judged guilty of "excessive socializing" with women whom they met in their ministry. Luigi Varsi, a magnetic personality with great social facility, became a frequent target of faultfinders who claimed he was "continually occupied with ladies."[68] Giuseppe Sasia defended the popular priest, pointing out that his female associates were not only "persons of outstanding piety" but also generous benefactors of the Society. Such assurances did not assuage the wary, however. Some old-timers, dipping their pens in a kind of all-knowing "I told you so," recalled Jesuits of the past who had fallen in love and left the Society. "So many cases of this kind have I seen in America in the forty or more years that I've been here," Congiato warned, "that I greatly fear the coming of superiors who are not vigilant and don't follow to the letter the wise rules left by our Father St. Ignatius."[69]

Unable to hammer out their differences on multiple issues, turn-of-the-century Jesuits ricocheted from one crisis to the next, their effectiveness blunted by the disparities that divided them. By the time Enrico Imoda's term drew to a close in 1896, the chasm of disagreement had so widened and deepened that even his former cheerleaders conceded that the reclusive superior and his coterie had done "great damage" to operations in California. In a startling about-face, Domenico Giacobbi charged that Imoda's "diffidence and sharp manner" alienated almost everyone; instead of uniting personnel in opposition to himself, he had exacerbated divisions.[70]

So vast was the rift that decision-makers despaired of finding anyone to replace Imoda. Whoever was appointed superior, if he was acceptable to one faction, "would be quite unsatisfactory to the other," Luis Martín observed. Unable to light on an internal candidate, the Society cast its nets widely and in 1896 appointed an outsider, John P. Frieden, to head the California Mission. A native of Luxembourg, he had grown up in the American Midwest. Now fifty-two, Frieden had extensive academic and administrative experience, including a just-completed term as provincial of the Jesuits' Missouri Province. Like a deus ex machina, the newcomer appeared to expectant Californians as "the salvation of the Mission."[71]

Settling into his San Francisco office, Frieden was appalled at what he discovered. The Californians seemed incorrigibly provincial, he told officials in Rome. Their pygmy universe centered on the San Francisco Bay Area, and they had no residence more than fifty-five miles distant from the next. "Narrow and cramped in their ideas, . . . several Fathers of this mission have a strange idea of life in the Society," he wrote, revealing that his sympathies did not lie with defenders of the status quo. These misguided souls "are conceited enough to imagine that the true spirit of the Society is preeminently in California, not in any other part of the United States." They "imagine that they are doing all that is expected of them if they devote full time to their spiritual exercises. For the rest, they shut themselves so completely off from the outside world as if our vocation were monastic, solely contemplative, and not actively apostolic."[72]

The damage resulting from this distorted grasp of Jesuit life was far-reaching, Frieden concluded. Our young men are being "trained on wrong lines," and "we are losing our hold on the people; men especially are drifting away from us." If Imoda and his advisers had "deliberately tried to break down Jesuit work and Jesuit standing in the city of San Francisco and in California," he wrote, "they could not have chosen better means." "We must bestir ourselves to regain the hold which we used to have on the people years ago, and which simply passed away during the past ten or twelve years."[73]

Frieden attempted to chart a new course by appointing progressives to positions of authority. But his cranky personality and sharp reversal of long-standing practices inevitably antagonized the old guard, prompting alarmists like Cichi to declare that "Father Frieden and his Irish consultors had destroyed the Mission." Meanwhile, Americanizers cheered his reforms. And his firm-handed leadership during the San Francisco earthquake and fire of 1906, which destroyed St. Ignatius College, won him many admirers.[74]

But when time came to find a successor for Frieden, the old conundrum reappeared. Whom to appoint? "There is no one in California that could in the near future govern the Mission," Frieden advised Rome. However, if the General was willing to merge the Rocky Mountain and California missions — a plan that had been under consideration for several years — a solution was at hand. There was an experienced administrator in Oregon who could fill the bill.[75] Thus it was that the two jurisdictions were reunited, and Georges de la Motte, a forty-six-year-old *wunderkind* from Alsace, became head of Jesuit operations on the West Coast. A man of uncommon intelligence and culture, this highly respected missionary was well-equipped for his new role. As restrained and diplomatic as Frieden was blunt and imperious, de la Motte integrated the two missionary jurisdictions and calmed the dyspeptic Californians, a task eased by the attrition through death of some of the old guard. At the same time, he tackled a set of challenges unique to the Rocky Mountain Mission.

Regional Differences

De la Motte, his authority extending from Seattle to San Francisco, governed a region quite different from the missionary domain he had known all his life. Although linked economically, the Pacific Northwest and California had followed divergent paths of development. One was rooted in a Hispanic past dominated by ranchos and missions; the other began as a British-Indian trading empire. California, rocketed into overnight urbanization and industrialization, was gripped by a boom mentality from the Gold Rush onward. Until the arrival of the railroad, the Northwest remained for many years an agrarian territory sequestered from larger markets and from the rest of the nation.

Jesuit operations in the two realms were also studies in contrast. "Mostly all nationalities are to be found among us," de la Motte once wrote, and yet "the hateful spirit of nationality has not yet made its appearance among us." This was clearly an overstatement, since de la Motte himself deplored that Jesuits of Irish and German ancestry were often at odds.[76] Nonetheless, the northerners' heterogeneity did guarantee that no one ethnic block permanently dominated the mission's leadership — as it had in California.

What the two missions did share was lukewarm support for fusion, a visceral reaction traceable to the differing historical experiences of the two regions. In California, "there is no interest of uniting with the Rocky Mountain Mission," Frieden had reported to Rome in 1897. What is more, "I doubt very much if such a desire can be created in the near future." From its inception, the work of the Californians had centered on colleges and urban parishes puddled around San Francisco Bay. Their confrères to the north, by contrast, had focused on Native American evangelization over a vast territory. Additionally, the two groups had a contentious history. The missionaries of the mountains harbored grievances against their urban brethren that were traceable to the period when their dominions had been joined earlier in the century. They claimed that California soaked up more than its share of the mission's common resources. From this unequal distribution of helpers and money festered their "near-hatred for California," as Congiato put it. A lotus-land of colleges and big city parishes, California shanghaied men assigned to the Indian missions. Whenever a neophyte paused in San Francisco on his way to the Northwest, missionaries alleged, the Californians sniffed out "some reason like health or something to keep him there."[77]

Jesuits in each region were so narrowly fixated on their own tiny sphere that they were unable to see value in any work but their own. When a Montana missionary learned that Santa Clara College had spent "forty thousand *piastres*" to buy physics equipment for the college, he was irate. "This amount alone would have been enough for run the missions for fifteen years," he snapped. The only reason the Indian missions lacked revenue was "the college in California." Other churchmen in the region shared this view. "I consider that sending to heaven so many infants that usually die among Indian tribes is a work far more important than teaching Latin and mathematics," Idaho bishop Louis Lottens once told Giuseppe Giorda.[78] For their part, Californians accused the missionaries of having an itch for the far horizon, dubbing them "up-the-river boys" for their alleged inability to stay in one place very long. "The Fathers of the Rocky Mountains do only two things," critics joked; "they recite their breviary and milk their cows."[79]

From this niggling mutual incomprehension sprouted a serious objection to merging the two jurisdictions. Union would be "utterly ruinous and destructive" for Jesuit work among Native Americans, northerners maintained. It would "mean the total ruin of the Indian missions," because no Californian "thinks the missions are worthwhile." Italy's provincial, Giacomo Razzini, concurred. Not only were Americans prejudiced against native peoples, he warned, but "even the best of them" could not put up with the privations and uncomfortable traveling of missionary life.[80]

After weighing all the pros and cons, decision-makers in Europe opted for merger, however. With an eye to the future, they concluded that only by pooling resources could the two missions provide a better preparation for Jesuits in training. Equally important, consolidation would make it easier to solve the problem that had crippled each mission from the beginning, namely finding men suited for administration. As for Indian missions, even backers maintained that work was in its twilight years, while work with whites was on the rise. Consequently, protests notwithstanding, in 1907 the two missions were joined, with de la Motte as head.[81]

Merger with California did not slam the door on Indian evangelization.

That enterprise was sapped by forces at work within the Pacific Northwest itself. It is "exceedingly difficult nowadays" to sustain this undertaking, de la Motte glumly acknowledged in 1895. "Our Indian missions are not flourishing," and we "toil without appreciable result." In recent years, "even Fr. Cataldo — our great missionary — has met with nothing but failure" among the Nez Percés. His lack of success "contributes not a little to discourage some of us; for if he fails, who shall succeed?"[82] There are "difficulties of all kinds [to] overcome which our predecessors did not face," de la Motte went on. Most of the challenges resulted from federal legislation that had dismantled reservations, broken up time-honored tribal organization, and snuffed out government support of church-run schools. The outcome was clear: The Catholic Indian missions of the Pacific Northwest, like their antecedents in the eastern United States, were "destined to come to an end before much longer." With a leaden heart, de la Motte predicted in 1909 that within twenty years, "we will no longer have Indian missions." "They will have become American parishes where everything will be done in English." However, it would be tragic, he added, to let them "disappear in a premature fashion, as a result of our negligence."[83]

The Dawes Act of 1887, missionaries agreed, had devastated the tribes and crippled their own efforts. Replacing tribal ownership of land with allotments to individual Indians, the law mandated the sale of the remaining reservation property to white settlers. "I fear very much that our Indians will not be benefitted, materially or spiritually, by this coming change," a Jesuit wrote in 1908, as the government prepared to open the Flatheads' Jocko reservation to settlement. The Coeur d'Alenes, who had run highly successful cooperative farms, fell into economic decline with the imposition of severalty. "The invasion of the whites is increasing more and more; their rapacity is well known," de la Motte said. "The government has already decided to open all of the Indian reservations — all of which sounds the death knell of our Indian missions."[84]

From a Jesuit perspective, allotment had also undermined the relationship between priest and people. It broke up native communities and physically separated them from churches and missionary schools. For this reason, Pietro Bandini, learning that the Crow reservation would be opened to development, lobbied officials in Washington to give the tribe contiguous holdings. "To scatter them all around the country" among white settlers would, he argued, "spoil all the good already done among them" by missionaries. Giuseppe Caruana also urged the Coeur d'Alenes to stick together by selecting adjacent allotments. "I'm doing everything I can to persuade them to occupy all the land around the church and mission," he said, "so they will remain together and thus be better able to persevere their [religious] spirit and keep separate from the whites." "Close contact with the whites may civilize them," de la Motte added, "but it does not christianize them"; in fact, it "cools down their faith."[85]

Missionaries concluded that the dissolution of reservations gave new urgency to educational work. If natives were constrained to live as private property holders, they reasoned, it was more crucial than ever that they be prepared to survive in the Anglo-American world. Because of severalty, one priest said, "I consider our schoolwork of the utmost importance." With the disappearance of federal aid, that work now stood on shaky ground, however. Private fund-raising provided some relief, particularly monies bestowed by the Bureau of Catholic Indian Missions and by Mother Katharine Drexel. But since charitable donations were never enough to keep budgets balanced, missionaries relied more and more on agricultural income, a notoriously unstable source of cash. "There is a good number of boys" attending our school, a Jesuit teacher in Idaho reported in 1909, but our situation "is not very bright." "The crop failed this year on account of the drought," and we now face "the difficulty of feeding and clothing over eighty children." From the Crow mission in Montana, another missionary wrote, "We receive support from our farm [but] very little support it is."[86]

In 1907, de la Motte summed up the economic fix of the Rocky Mountain Mission. "We are living after the manner of the country," he reported, and "our staple food is fish and vegetables" that we procure ourselves. "Every year our boys catch from 8,000 to 15,000 salmon, and this is a godsend. But for that, we could not live." Operational costs were soaring. To replace declining Jesuit personnel, St. Ignatius Mission employed fifteen salaried lay workers, with the consequence that "a large part of the income of the mission goes into wages." In addition, mission schools faced more and more competition from public institutions. For example, by 1913, the region of the former Flathead reservation, which had once been dominated by St. Ignatius Mission, boasted nine public schools.[87]

The era of the contract system had represented a high-water mark against which missionaries would forever measure the efficacy of their schools. Jesuits now became their own loudest critics. "Poor St. Ignatius" Mission, De la Motte exclaimed in atypical near-despair in 1906. "What a fiasco our work has been. 50 years work and this is the result. Superstitious practices on the increase; the Indians lazy, uncivilized, unequipped for the opening of the Reservation, and little inclined to pray."[88] Even more disturbing, he said in painful candor, "our schools alienate the hearts of the Indians." Crow students at Montana's St. Xavier Mission "are the very best we have in our missions," he thought. "They are bright, gentle, kindhearted, wonderfully attached to us," but the tenacity with which they clung to native culture left him mystified. Despite years of schooling, "one or two months of camp life seems to wipe off every vestige of religion." He added: "They will marry and divorce like the others within two or three months; they will take part in the coarse superstitions of the tribe; they will die without calling us to their deathbed; they will refuse to let us baptize their children. This . . . is the sad condition of the Crow Indians. It is a puzzle which no one can solve."[89]

So black was the cloud hanging over the schools by 1907 that de la Motte convoked a special conclave to thrash out their fate. No longer able to count on the Bureau of Catholic Indian Missions for funds, the Jesuits debated whether they should abandon the work entirely. After much soul-searching, they decided that "closing of the schools would mean the closing and ruin of the Indian missions." They opted instead for reform, but industrial training would be discontinued because it cost so much. In order to balance accounts, the schools would admit more tuition-paying white students, "so long as their parents consent to their being treated no better than our Indian pupils." In hopes of making their institutions self-sustaining, the Jesuits also resolved to "improve the farms connected to the schools and thereby diminish the amount needed for the running of the schools." Finally, the missionaries proposed a series of pedagogical and curricular reforms to make them "more efficient, attractive, and interesting."[90]

Americanization was changing church work in other ways. Finding English-speaking priests was becoming more and more indispensable not only for white parishes but also for Indian congregations. By the turn of the century, missionaries and natives alike regretted the disappearance of native languages. "Oh, it used to sound good, wonderful, when all the people in church said their prayers in Indian," a Blackfoot woman reminisced, "but that's no more. Time has changed everything." English became so common that Europeans who volunteered for missionary work in the United States were no longer welcome if they could not speak it. "Knowledge of English, real knowledge, not just mediocre, is absolutely necessary in our Indian missions today," de la Motte wrote in 1909. "A good half of our European fathers, especially Italian, speak very poor English, and cannot even present a mediocre catechism" to children. "In the majority of our missions," he went on, "the young Indians know English — better than the majority of our Italian, German, or European missionaries." Priests not fluent in the now-dominant language were "almost completely useless."[91]

Clergy who made hash of the English language were equally unacceptable to whites. In Seattle, Archbishop Alexander Christie chastised de la Motte for assigning too many German priests to the city's parishes. And Montana's Bishop John P. Carroll angered European clergymen by declaring publicly: "only American-born, or Irish priests, would work in this country for the glory of God." The Jesuits were adding Americans to their ranks at a rapid rate — but not fast enough. By 1895, nearly half of the mission's sixty scholastics were native speakers, thanks to successful recruiting by Giuseppe

FIGURE 30. At first committed primarily to ministry among Native Americans, Jesuits of the Rocky Mountain Mission shifted to whites toward the end of the nineteenth century. Work with Indians continued, however, exemplified by the dedication of a new St. Louis Church near Monse, Washington, in 1918. Courtesy Jesuit Oregon Province Archives, Gonzaga University, 505-9-22

Cataldo, but they were still in training and unprepared to step into the linguistic breach.[92]

Shifting demographics forced a reevaluation of parish work. As thousands of settlers poured into the region after completion of the Northern Pacific Railroad in 1883, bishops looked to the Jesuits to supply priests for mushrooming dioceses. By the time Washington received statehood in 1889, its population had leapt in one decade from 75,000 to 300,000.[93] The discovery of gold in the Klondike had transformed Seattle into a major shipping and supply center, making it, as one Jesuit said, a city with "a bright future." With new towns rising up like spring grass, missionaries recognized that the time was not far distant when they would be laboring "mostly, if not altogether among these whites."[94] "All at once our work has been doubled, without our number of priests receiving any addition," one said. "Before, we could hardly take care of our old missions among the Indians. But now it has become impossible to attend both the Indians and the whites scattered in the territories of Montana, Idaho, and Washington." Men who had spent most of their lives in the company of natives now celebrated mass, delivered sermons, and baptized babies for white communities, although they recognized that "we are too few in numbers to attend to all as ought to be done."[95]

The Pacific Northwest was becoming more like the rest of the United

States. A larger percentage of people in the West now dwelled in cities, a scholar at Columbia University reported in 1899, "than in any other part of the nation except the North Atlantic states."[96] In response to changing demographics, the Catholic Church was directing more of its resources to the founding of urban parishes and ministering to immigrants. Bishops and clergy who had once concentrated on the conversion of Indians now shifted focus, seeking to find ways of making their faith compatible with dominant Protestantism and integrating new populations from abroad. Jesuits, partly in response to pressure from Rome, began shifting priests from marooned rural parishes to urban centers. "It behooves us to try to secure new desirable places on the Pacific Slope," missionaries in Oregon said, "if we wish to have a future."[97]

No single event more profoundly signaled — indeed propelled — this switch than the decision to open colleges. With the founding of Gonzaga College in 1887 and of Seattle College four years later, the Rocky Mountain missionaries committed themselves irrevocably to the white man. Under Cataldo's leadership, the mission's motto had long been *Sumus primo pro Indianis* ("We are here primarily for the Indians").[98] Drummed into every missionary who stepped off the boat, this principle was also proclaimed by authorities in Europe. Except in the case of men "worn down by the ministry and age," Superior General Beckx told Jesuits in 1873, they were "completely prohibited from undertaking the care of white men." The Society's sole concern was the native population. The care of white people was the responsibility of bishops and diocesan clergy. As late as 1895, de la Motte reiterated, "the principal ministry of the Rocky Mountain Mission always has been and still is evangelization of the Indians."[99]

Even as he uttered those words, however, de la Motte was assigning more men to non-native congregations. Did this mean the Jesuits had jumped off their own bandwagon? Despite his pro-Indian reflex, Giuseppe Cataldo, the most ardent of missionaries, asserted they had not. Work with white people was entirely consistent with the commitment to native evangelization, he argued, because the two undertakings were essentially and inextricably linked. Cataldo believed what John McLoughlin, head factor of the Hudson Bay Company, had said many years before: "The Indians will form themselves on what they see done by the whites." Put another way by de la Motte, the example of white persons "be it good or bad, can be either extremely helpful or extremely injurious to Catholic Indians." So convinced was he of the interconnectedness of the two races that he once asserted, "if kind Providence sends us some good Catholic whites, their example will accomplish even more than our sermons." By persuading whites to treat natives justly, the priests reasoned, both would benefit. The Jesuits' policy shift was further grounded in a sober appraisal of new regional realities. If Indians had been obliged to adapt to the white invasion of the Pacific Northwest, Jesuits "too must change our ways," an aged Joseph Joset asserted in 1888. "We came for the Indian and until now our relations were only with him," but today, "if we want to keep our missions, we must see to have the good will of the new masters."[100]

Rome gave its imprimatur to the reorientation of ministries. "Whites are neglected in certain places," Superior General Anderledy told the missionaries in 1890, and so "our care will have to be moderated to as to be accessible to all." Cataldo agreed that whites had as great a claim on his charity as did natives. "The spiritual needs of the greater part of the white population in Montana are much greater than those of the Indians," he advised. "And the population increases daily, and the Catholic youngsters grow up [without religion] because there is no one to care for them."[101]

Some missionaries, however, believing they had been asked to preside at their own funeral, resisted the reversal. One German flatly refused to work in a white parish. "I would under no condition be the bishop's pastor, but gladly a Jesuit missionary," he insisted. The depth of feeling suffusing the transition was disclosed when the Rocky Mountain Mission moved its scholasticate from St. Ignatius Mission to Gonzaga College. Persuaded that reservation life worked "mischief, both intellectually and spiritually" on the formation of potential priests, De la Motte had decided in 1899 that scholastics would receive a better preparation in Spokane. But to seventy-year-old Geronimo D'Aste, who had spent most of his life among the Flatheads, the departure of the young tolled the death knell of his beloved mission. Sent from Spokane to oversee the transport of books and luggage to the College, the old man wailed in his diary, "I started for St. Ignatius where I am destined again to bury the Mission!" A few weeks later he recorded a final obsequy. "Today they packed 12 wagons of stuff to Spokane, emptying almost the house of everything that *might* be useful to the *grand College*." Even the herds were sold. "They are gathering the cattle," he thundered, "sold for Spokane!!"[102]

The passage from the rustic existence on an Indian mission to city living was traumatic for old missionaries. "By degrees we tried to introduced the customs of civilized people" into the Jesuit community at Gonzaga College, President James Rebmann recalled, beginning with cloth napkins at meals. "When they appeared the first time at dinner laid on the soup plates, our old patriarch Father Joset, failed to understand why in our Indian mission contrivances of the white people should be introduced. He crumpled his napkin like a handkerchief and put it in his pocket."[103] The substitution of rough woolen blankets with bed sheets provoked another crisis. Joset, who had spent half a century living in tent and cabin, ripped off the linens "and stuck them into the remotest corner under his bed." " 'Indian missionaries,' he said the following morning to me, 'should not sleep in bed sheets.'" Fed up with modern living, the old war horse stomped out of town and took up residence at nearby St. Michael's Mission, leaving only his shaving outfit at the college. "Every Saturday morning," Rebmann recorded, "he walked the five miles from St. Michael's to Gonzaga to take his shave and go to confession; he wanted exercise."[104]

Younger men, however, applauded the transition. Cataldo's axiom about giving priority to Indians was "perhaps good" twenty year ago, observed Victor Garrand, the founder of Seattle College, in 1893, but today that principle is a "source of much dissatisfaction," because "Indians are few and whites are many." In 1901, Georges de la Motte conceded that Jesuits were voting with their feet in favor of the new order. "I find more zeal displayed in the ministries among the whites than in the Indian mission," he noted with evident dissatisfaction. Less than a decade later, only 20 percent of the 417 Jesuits on the West Coast remained among native peoples. Thus, despite many real differences, the Rocky Mountain and California missions had become progressively similar. As Santa Clara's Richard A. Gleeson observed in 1902, "The Rocky Mountains are doing the identical work in many lines which is being done in California."[105]

Triangular Government

With augmented Americanization in both regions, the European phase of Jesuit missionary work was passing. In 1880, 158 Jesuits, half of the work force of the Turin Province, had been stationed in the West. That number dwindled steadily in the decade that followed as old-timers passed from the scene and as fewer young Italians replaced them. The slowing of emigration to America was traceable to the restoration of the Society of Jesus in Italy. After thirty years in exile, the Jesuits of Piedmont-Sardinia were in 1878 permitted by the Italian government to reopen their novitiate in Chieri, closed since the revolution of 1848.[106]

With the subsequent resumption of work in Genoa, Niza, and Bastia, and the expansion of schools in the principality of Monaco, the flow of Piedmontese Jesuits to the United States slowed and then ceased entirely. "We presently find ourselves with such scarcity of men," an official wrote in 1892, that we don't even have enough to run our houses in Europe. By 1910, only thirty-eight Italians, most of them aged and infirm, remained in the American missions. That small cohort represented only 9 percent of the province's total membership of 416 men, proof that Italian manpower resources were now centered almost entirely in Europe.[107]

As the tide of volunteers ebbed, American missionaries began to cast a critical eye on their relationship with Europe. This was not the first time that the idea of separating the missions in the United States from Italian jurisdiction had been raised. Italians themselves had posed the question as early as 1870 to Giovanni Battista Ponte, former provincial of Turin and official visitor to the American outposts. Several leading missionaries — Accolti, Bayma, Varsi, and Raffo — proposed that California be severed from dependence on Turin and grafted into an American province. Ponte, who relayed the request to Rome, thought it made sense. "Even in America," he told the general, there were limits to what institutions staffed entirely by Italians might hope to accomplish. As long as they are dependent on Italy, our men in America "will always remain Italians in every sense," and our colleges will be "little or not at all American." Could Americans and Europeans ever really comprehend one another?, he wondered. Looking back on his own experience as provincial, Ponte candidly conceded, "I confess to having understood nothing" about California before I came here. Authorities in Italy, however, displeased at the proposal, rebuffed it as premature.[108]

Eighteen years later, Giuseppe Cataldo again tried to cut the knot by proposing that the Rocky Mountain Mission be bound to an American jurisdiction. Because Italy had ceased supplying *personali*, he argued, "it would be better to join this Mission to another province." Once again, European stewards rejected the notion, claiming it would deliver a death blow to operations both at home and abroad. "Deprived of the attractive mission of the Rocky Mountains," the Turin Province would be crippled in its ability to recruit new members. And the mission, dependent on a province in the United States, would suffer, because Americans, with their "very strong prejudices against Indians," would never give missionary work the support it needed.[109]

When the issue resurfaced at the end of the century, it received a more favorable reception. In the intervening years, circumstances in both Europe and the United States made division more likely. John Frieden's persistent filibustering for autonomy during his term as superior of the California Mission in 1896–1907 had advanced the cause, as did the appointment in Rome of Rudolph J. Meyer as the superior general's assistant for the English-speaking Jesuit provinces. Meyer offered a sympathetic ear to Frieden's proposition and promoted it within the Jesuit curia. Central to Frieden's argument was that reliance on Italy made governance in America impossible. Within a year of his arrival in San Francisco, Frieden discovered that his authority was constantly being undercut by the old guard, who deluged Europe with fervid letters of complaint. When they disagree with my decisions, he reported, they lobby directly with the Italian provincial, who, "not knowing much of the situation in California," received a distorted view of our situation. "I fairly dread a change of provincials in Turin," he once told Meyer; "it is like a nightmare." He added: "When the new provincial enters upon office, I will be helpless indeed. He won't know anything about our doings here; some people will surely give him a colored version of things, and I will get into a big mess. . . . My position will become untenable. . . . This 'triangular' form of government does not work."[110]

As bickering between factions heated up in California, Frieden grew daily more vexed by Europe's failure to comprehend his plight. More than miles separated Turin and San Francisco, he charged, since higher-ups abroad knew "nothing of the missions or the country and its customs." Writing to Meyer, he asked rhetorically: What if I, an American, were charged with the governance of an Italian province? "Surely you wouldn't for a moment imagine that I could direct any superior in Milan or in Genoa. I've been in both cities, but cannot measure the spirit of that part of the world." Similarly, officials in Italy "do not and cannot appreciate the true nature of affairs in the United States, and particularly in California." The truth is, "our being united to the Province of Turin is no help to this Mission. On the contrary, it proves an impediment — it hampers us."[111]

In an earlier era, aid flowed freely to America, but that lifeline had long since dried to a trickle. "The Province of Turin for the past twenty years has been either unable or unwilling to help the Mission and to encourage its development," Frieden charged. "And much less is it able to do so at the present time." Because the European provinces could not subsist by themselves, "they draw on the missions instead of helping them." To pretend that Italy still sustained operations in America was "humbug and fraud."[112]

As tension between center and periphery mounted, fresh voices joined the chorus calling for autonomy. The prominent Californian Richard A. Gleeson reminded the superior general that other European missions in the United States had already won independence. Why, he asked, was California kept in a subordinate condition? There was only one thing standing in the way of independence, he suggested. "Our Mother Province is loath to lose her oldest daughter, especially in the financial straits in which she finds herself." His point was well-taken, as the accustomed assessments that a Jesuit province levied on its individual houses made clear. In 1898, 70 percent of the revenue for the common operating expenses of the province derived from taxes on its colleges in America. Inevitably, therefore, Turin bucked at separation, arguing that the dissolution of the historic tie between Italy and the United States was "premature."[113]

While Turin and San Francisco dithered, outside forces gave the final nudge to severance. In 1892, the Jesuit order elevated the Maryland–New York and Missouri provinces to full equality with those of Europe, an advance that enabled American Jesuits to wield more leverage over the governance of their own operations. The next year, a newly elected superior general, Franz Wernz, created the province of New Orleans with an American at its head, and in 1907, Rome dissolved the Buffalo Mission, a missionary enclave in western New York that had been governed since 1848 by the order's German Province.[114]

This redrawing of the Jesuit map reflected a reconfiguration of authority in the Catholic Church itself. With the suppression of Americanism and modernism, American Catholicism had come ever more firmly under Vatican control. Assured of its fidelity, Rome was now ready to grant autonomy to the American church by abolishing its historic dependence upon the Congregation for the Propagation of the Faith. In 1908, therefore, Pope Pius X issued *Sapienti consilio*, a document that terminated oversight by the Congregation, thereby ending the nation's missionary status. American Catholicism had at last come of age. If practical confirmation of the new status was needed, it came in economic guise. Within sixteen years, Rome found itself dependent upon the Catholics in the United States for 50 percent of the funds it expended on missionary work worldwide.[115]

Sapienti consilio also set the stage for terminating European surveillance of Jesuit operations in the United States. A few months after the promulgation of the document, the Society of Jesus severed ties between the Turin Province and its American missions by lifting the latter to the status of a province, an ecclesiastical action comparable to the secular process of promoting a U.S. territory to statehood.[116] In 1909, the order announced the establishment of the new jurisdiction. Dubbed the California Province, it embraced the former missions of California, the Rocky Mountains, and Alaska. The name disappointed some missionaries in the Pacific Northwest, because, as one priest put it, "hereafter there will be no more Rocky Mountain Mission"; but the superior general, trusting Jesuits would "not dwell on such petty matters," insisted on the designation.[117] Despite the cavil, missionaries up and down the West Coast greeted the general's decree with rejoicing. "Today, precisely at noon," de la Motte recorded on 8 September 1909, "the good news of the creation of the California Province [was] promulgated."[118]

Self-government did not put an end to dissonance, but it did inaugurate an era of innovation in which Jesuits moved closer to the American mainstream. Just as independence from the Congregation of the Propagation of the Faith had imbued the hierarchy of the United States with uncharacteristic assertiveness, so too sovereignty gave members of the Society of Jesus the assurances they needed to examine their self-described isolation from American society. Self-confident new leaders among that cautious body now began to act on the ideal championed by Archbishop John Ireland two decades earlier: "We should live in our age, know it, be in touch with it."[119]

12 *"Sic Transit Gloria Mundi"*

FOREIGN NO MORE

> The clergy is mostly European, yet we are all in America
> and in time must all be Americanized . . .
> — Bishop Joseph P. Machebeuf of Colorado, 1887[1]

Although the West Coast fell swiftly to Americanization, the South-west submitted more slowly. In both places, however, that transformation gave new direction to church work. Just as the order's ministry to Native Americans declined in the face of shifting demographics in the Pacific Northwest, so too Jesuit activity among Hispanics in the Southwest moved into a transitional phase as white congregations swallowed up more re-sources. In both regions, as in California, Americanization polarized the clergy, often pitting Europeans and Americans against one another. Thus, an accelerating Anglo presence in the West, coupled with restoration of the Society of Jesus in Europe, loosened the missionaries' historic ties with Italy. Within a decade, all Jesuit operations would end their jurisdictional depend-ence upon Italy and emerge as independent American jurisdictions.

In the Pacific Northwest and the Southwest, the coming of the transcon-tinental railroad hastened Americanization. By 1875, the Atchison, Topeka, and Santa Fe was barreling across the southern plains at the rate of a mile a day. When the first engine rolled into Pueblo at the foot of the Rockies the next year, it uncorked what a Colorado newspaper described as "the biggest drunk of the present century." On 22 April 1880, Albuquerque greeted the track's debut more soberly, with a celebration marked by "peace, order, and tranquility," according to the Jesuit bystander Donato Gasparri. But it was "the day of all days in Albuquerque," a local gazette chirped, "a day long expected and anxiously looked forward to by the friends of progress and advancement." Within months, the long-awaited "monster engine" made its mountainous ascent to neighboring Santa Fe. No sooner had the train shoul-dered its way into the territorial capital than an excited Governor Lew Wallace telegrammed Washington, D.C., to announce that "a large immi-gration is pouring in under inducement of rich mineral discoveries and in-creased railroad facilities." In 1881, the appearance of the Southern Pacific sparked similar expectations in El Paso, where one jubilant official announced "We have sprung into a city."[2]

With the coming of the rails, sleepy Southwestern towns overnight became home to business districts, military garrisons, and universities. "Stores and factories, schools and churches, banks and hotels, hospitals and courthouses, theaters and saloons" served an expanding urban populace and adjacent hinterlands. The archdiocese of Santa Fe jumped from a population of 50,000 in 1890 to 133,000 a decade later. Quiet hamlets exploded in size. Albuquerque, occupied by about 2,000 people in 1880, was home to 20,750 inhabitants fifty years later. Quickly surpassing Santa Fe in importance, the city underwent an unprecedented building boom that split it into two sections. Old Town, an area surrounding the community's original plaza and the adobe church of San Felipe de Neri, became home to a largely Hispanic population, while Americans flocked to stylish shops and elegant wooden homes in New Town, a freshly developed site that sprouted up along the rail line. Once content to serve a largely homogeneous clientele, the Neapolitan Jesuits were now pressed to care for more diverse populations. What had once been a rural ministry became progressively city-centered.[3]

The physical division of Albuquerque symbolized the cultural transformation of the Southwest. As urban and rural realms blended into one another, New Mexico became dominated by settlers from Missouri, Pennsylvania, Ohio, and Illinois, who poured in to take advantage of fresh opportunities. Until the 1880s, American pioneers had found it worthwhile to embrace local customs, learn Spanish, and take Mexican wives. For the new immigrants, however, neither Hispanic nor indigenous Indian culture held much charm; indeed, their expanding community quickly made an anachronism of earlier Anglo assimilation of Hispanic ways. By monopolizing economic and political power, they established hegemony over local agriculture and business. As a consequence, native villages lost their communal farm lands and previous shareholders became salaried day laborers.[4]

Within the Catholic Church, the newcomers exerted power beyond their numbers. Religious leaders struggled to build bigger churches and schools and to recruit more English-speaking priests and sisters. In 1887, an uneasy Bishop Joseph P. Machebeuf speculated about who might succeed him as head of the diocese of Denver, "where there are so many Americans and a mixed clergy." "I feared that Rome might send me an outside man, either a German or an Irishman," he said, but he was relieved when word arrived of the appointment of Nicholas C. Matz. Although French-born, the multilingual new bishop had been "identified with America since his early years," and hence, in Machebeuf's eyes, he was acceptable. In "this far west — in New Mexico, Arizona, and Colorado — the population is an amalgamation of all nations, with the Mexican predominant," Machebeuf concluded. "The clergy is mostly European, yet we are in America and in time must all be Americanized."[5]

The Jesuits, too, scrambled to adjust. Not only did priests distance themselves from the *penitentes* — "especially now that the trains come as far as the frontiers of New Mexico," the *Revista Católica* noted — they also began to accommodate American parishioners in ways that sometimes rankled older congregations. Jesuits in Albuquerque's Old Town announced in 1880 that the parish's customary Corpus Christi celebration would be transferred from its usual feast day to an ordinary Sunday, "because of the large number of American residents in the piazza." For the same reason, it was decreed that the statue of the Virgin Mary, which normally made the rounds of the parish, "would not appear in Albuquerque." In New Town, the Jesuits erected a church of brick masonry for the city's newest residents.[6]

Spanish speakers were, nonetheless, still the central focus of Jesuit activity. "Presently, our ministry is easier among Mexicans than among Americans," Giuseppe Marra explained in 1888, because our culture and linguistic training best prepare us to operate with that population. By 1906, the mission operated nineteen parochial or quasi-parochial churches in the Southwest. Three of them were in New Mexico, eight in Colorado, seven in Texas, and one in Juarez, Mexico, which was joined to El Paso by a bridge across the Rio Grande. In addition, circuit-riders staffed 121 missions or stations serving a population of 78,420. Two-thirds of the population in these places were either Spanish speakers or Italian immigrants.[7]

After 1910, the number of Hispanic parishioners soared even higher as refugees flooded into the United States from neighboring Mexico in the wake of revolution and civil war. From a population of 736 in 1880, El Paso blossomed to nearly 100,000 forty years later. By 1918, the Neapolitans were caring for nearly 40,000 immigrants in that city alone, an impossible task without the aid of the numerous Mexican Jesuits who sought refuge in Texas after their expulsion by an anti-clerical government.[8] So central had work with Mexicans become that when officials in Naples offered to send a fresh volunteer to the Southwest in 1913, they were told that unless he spoke Spanish, he would be "totally useless."[9]

But the Neapolitans also preached in churches packed with *Americanos*. Spanish was still their primary language, Marra said in 1888, but "in the *future*, it won't be like this." "The Mission is changing as is the country itself," and is "becoming Americanized day by day." The Jesuits themselves were changing. Twenty-five of the Mission's thirty scholastics were English speakers, an encouraging augury of the order's ministerial prospects. The number of Italians working in the Southwest stayed steady (hovering at about forty), but they were no longer the ethnic majority. In 1880, Italians had constituted a dominant 77 percent of the mission's membership. By 1915, the

Neapolitans had shrunk to an aging minority of 27 percent that was speedily being supplanted by other nationalities. Meanwhile, Anglo-American
churches absorbed more and more priests — so much so that leaders like
Pinto began to worry about the "lack of men for the Mexican part of our
Mission." As in the Pacific Northwest, Jesuits in the Southwest were incrementally forsaking scattered rural missions for urban parishes and classrooms. With the unfolding of the new century, Pinto summarized, "we have
only two places of importance, Denver and El Paso."[10]

How to cope with Americanization divided the Southwestern Jesuits just
as it had their brethren on the West Coast. Most Neapolitans, believing that
Mexicans and Italian immigrants still had the greatest claim to their services,
worried when the balance of manpower and money shifted to the care of
Americans. Few missionaries were as dedicated to the care of the Mexican
population as the Tomassini brothers, Pasquale and Francesco. Alarmed that
"the attention of all our men here is now turned toward the great college in
Denver," Pasquale wondered who would be left to serve the *Mexicanos*. In
1913, his brother Francesco unhappily contrasted the run-down condition
of his mud-brick school in Albuquerque's Old Town with "the sum that was
loaned to the college in Denver to build a gymnasium for the boarders that
cost $15,000." To the dismay of champions of Hispanic ministry, many
younger Jesuits — including even "a few of our Italians" — were drawn to the
new clientele. "The trouble is that our young men are beguiled by the desire
to be with the Americans rather than with the Mexicans," an Italian
lamented in 1914. Those who shared his passion regretted the division of
resources that the mission's commitment to both Spanish and English
speakers made inevitable.[11]

No one anguished more about the future than Carlo Pinto, whose fealty
to Spanish-speaking congregations was absolute. His drumbeat insistence on
their priority riled co-workers who detected an anti-Anglo bias in his preference. "He thinks of nothing but El Paso," gripped John J. Brown, a prominent American Jesuit, "and little or nothing else attracts his attention."
Scarred by the rough treatment he had once been given by the English speakers of Pueblo, Colorado, Pinto had not survived hardship without becoming hard himself. For ambitious priests who sought to "amount to anything
in the *Impero* American," he once sarcastically observed, English was an
"indispensable quality."[12] Miffed that his companions shunned Italian
immigrants, he claimed that some Jesuits were infected with "anti-dago
fever" and wanted "nothing to do with dagos." Many of these "gentlemen,"
he acerbically observed, were associated with the college in Denver, a project for which he had little sympathy. It comes as no surprise that Pinto and
his compatriots sometimes alienated colleagues. "One's first impression is
that there is a great compatibility among the different nationalities" in our

mission, he once wrote, but "we Italians, are, in fact, more tolerated than loved by the others."[13]

Another fallout of Americanization was an eruption of fresh doubts about alliance with Italy. As one Alsatian priest clumsily expressed it, our mission has a "foreign aspect" that is not "persona grata" as far as colleges and American parishes are concerned. Giuseppe Marra defined the problem more bluntly: "Very few of our Italians are acceptable to the people." Parishioners incessantly ask, "Why can we not have Irish priests?" No one expected Italy to magically supply English-speaking clergy, but the missionaries did look to Naples to provide more Italians to staff expanding projects. "Can you not send us some men for this Mission?" was the refrain that scored every letter from New Mexico. "Other provinces support more than one mission," an unhappy Neapolitan told his provincial; "Cannot ours sustain one?" The response was as clear as it was disappointing. In times to come, Naples would post fewer men to the United States because new opportunities were opening up in Europe.[14]

But the restoration of the Society of Jesus in Italy did not come suddenly. Twenty years after Garibaldi had driven them from the Kingdom of the Two Sicilies, Jesuits in Naples were still walking on tiptoes, engaged in unobtrusive ministries and living in small residences strewn about the city. A crucial step toward normalcy occurred in 1877, with the covert establishment of a novitiate at Villa Melecrinis on a secluded hillside overlooking the bay. "There is lots of work here," Ferdinando Canger wrote from Naples in 1880. "I am continuing my career as parish priest" and have "a thousand other things to do." He had even managed to publish a six-volume work of sermons, and two other priests had opened a school that was prospering. Still, Canger lived at home with his sister, and lack of resources hobbled all his efforts to do more.[15]

Legal impediments to fuller activity remained for years. "I would like to send you some news about us here in Naples," a priest told confrères in the United States in 1883, "but there is nothing but misery to be told." It is "mostly pecuniary misery," but also "misery of the mind and of the spirit, in the religious sense, a result, almost necessary of the first." "How were we to support ourselves," Marra wondered, "having no parish revenues or fees, as in the U.S., and no hope of alms or donations from the people, who are generally very poor and unaccustomed to support their priests?" Without stable income, the Neapolitans scaled back the number of men admitted to their novitiate, because they could not feed and clothe all those who asked to join. At one point, they considered limiting themselves to two meals a day in order to save money.[16] As late as 1897, Jesuits in Naples were still without a church of their own, and in Sicily they were prohibited from possessing schools or teaching without government certification, a barrier they managed to bypass by offering instruction in buildings owned by friends and by hiring lay teachers. The Jesuits were once "in a flourishing condition" on this island, a visitor summed up in 1890, but "now they have next to nothing."[17]

Shortly thereafter, Italy's locked doors began slowly to reopen. Intermittent periods of governmental leniency brought greater freedom, thus beginning a process of wary rapprochement between church and state. When Anton Anderledy, the Society's exiled superior general, died in exile in Fiesole in 1892, skittish Jesuits avoided bringing his body to Rome for burial lest they provoke public outcry. Similar apprehension led them to meet outside of Italy to elect his successor. The general congregation that convened in Loyola, Spain, to chose Luis Martín, the new leader, did recommend, however, that he transfer the order's headquarters back to Rome as soon as possible. A potent symbol of the order's resurrection occurred the following year. The Italian government ended the Society's thirty-year exile by allowing the Jesuits to reoccupy the church of the Gesù in Rome. That Baroque temple, from which Jan Roothaan had fled in disguise in 1848, thus once again became the center of Jesuit ceremonial life. Two years later, in 1895, the superior general himself returned, taking up residence in the order's German College. With nearly a thousand students enrolled in the newly established Gregorian University, a jubilant *Woodstock Letters* reported, "the Society is doing glorious work at Rome."[18]

With the reestablishment of the order, "the anti-religious agitation so violent in the first formation of United Italy gradually began to give way," Marra recounted, and "a period of comparative toleration commenced." With restoration, the Italian Jesuit provinces scrubbed the qualifier *diaspora* from their official catalogues and reckoned the future. Led by Marra, who had been summoned back to Europe to serve as provincial, the Neapolitans opened a theologate for twenty-one scholastics on the periphery of Naples in 1898. But because powerful pockets of anti-Jesuit resistance remained, the site, which was discreetly situated in a sequestered setting, was purchased through a lay intermediary to avoid arousing suspicion.[19]

Believing themselves on the cusp of a new era, some exiled Neapolitans gazed homeward. To aid in rebuilding the Society in Italy, key personnel in America — Marra was the most high-profile — were recalled to Europe. Although Marra went reluctantly, other missionaries jumped at the chance to go, their resettlement provoking lamentation in New Mexico, where the *cri de coeur* about a "depressing lack" of workers grew steadily louder. By 1912, so many coadjutor brothers had requested leave that the superior of the Mission issued an ultimatum to Naples. "If things continue this way, we will soon be forced to hire women to take the jobs of the brothers because it's very difficult and almost impossible to find men."[20]

Although calculated to set off alarms in Europe, this time the threat turned

Congregazione Del S. Cuore Di Gesu. July 16 1936

FIGURE 31. After the dissolution of Italian hegemony over the American missions and Europe, few Jesuits repatriated to Italy. The Sicilian priest Salvatore Giglio, pictured here with members of the Congregation of the Sacred Heart of Jesus in Pueblo, Colorado, in 1936, typified those who remained, many of whom worked with immigrants from their homeland. Courtesy Pueblo City-County Library District, Pueblo, Colorado, Mutamoto photo

toothless. Short on writers, the *Revista Católica* lurched from one staffing crisis to the next. Eager to save the journal "whatever the sacrifice it takes," authorities in Italy released Marra from duty in Naples in 1908 so that he could rush back to New Mexico to edit the publication. More often, however, the struggling province found it "absolutely impossible" to satisfy America's repeated and lively requests for workers. "It is a shame that in the Province so few can be found who want to come work here," Marra reported upon his return to the States. "When we old fellows who are still on our feet pass on — and we cannot hang on much longer — I don't know who will take our place."[21]

As impatience at Europe's seeming indifference rose, missionaries in the United States pleaded that headquarters send an emissary to gain first-hand knowledge of their plight. But at every request, Naples balked. Although the Piedmontese had dispatched no less than three visitors to their American mission in the space of eleven years, only once during the half-century of

Neapolitan jurisdiction over the Southwest — and that on the eve of separation — did Naples send an official representative to New Mexico from Europe.

It was with justifiable disappointment, therefore, that Salvatore Personè concluded in 1915, "for many years now it seems like the Province has had no interest in us."[22] To compound the grievances, he brushed aside the few men that Naples did release for work in America as lightweights. The last two missionaries who landed in Albuquerque "seemed like dogs tied to their chains," Personè growled. Unsuited for missionary life, they were immediately sent packing back across the Atlantic. When Naples offered the services of a disruptive brother — a troublemaker, it was said, who had alienated everyone with whom he lived — Marra refused to accept him. "For goodness sake!," he admonished the provincial, "Have mercy on us." Marra found a way to relieve his frustration when the controversial topic of money arose. In 1894, the province announced plans to up its annual assessment of the Mission from a 10 percent tax on income to a flat $60 charge for every able man. Marra howled in protest. If the old charge had been a burden on the indigent mission, he charged, the new one would be far more onerous. The Neapolitans, like their Piedmontese countrymen on the West Coast, grew more and more convinced that far-away superiors did not understand them and that their dependency upon Europe had become more burden than benefit.[23]

Like a drowning man, Marra reached for a rope — but one not tied to Europe. "Dependency implies the right to be nourished, kept alive, and sustained," he told the provincial in 1912, but since we "cannot expect anything from Naples when we have the greatest need of help," we should either affiliate with an American province that can help us or become an independent mission. The possibility of cutting the cord had been considered before but was for several reasons abandoned. First, the mission was too small to stay afloat as an autonomous region; second, no American province wanted to take charge of such a secluded backwater; and third, influential Jesuits in both Naples and the States were sentimentally opposed to loosening their historic bond.[24]

A final reason why Europeans clung to their American dependency was economic. Cash from New Mexico, descending like manna on the struggling province, was Naples' lifeline to survival. Aid appeared in a variety of forms: taxes paid annually to the home province, stipends offered by lay people for masses said in Italy, *per diem* fees paid by missionaries who returned to Naples for study, and outright donations. In 1884, for example, the nephew of a New Mexican Jesuit was accepted as a candidate for the Society in Europe, "on the condition that he be supported in the novitiate by the New Mexico Mission." In return for this subsidy, the Americans hoped that the young man would later come to America as a missionary.[25] In 1917, the mission sent 2,308.90 lire for three hundred masses to be said by priests in Italy, an amount so large that it that enabled the Neapolitans to acquire a building in which to start a day school.[26]

Authorities in Naples, like their confrères in Turin, inevitably viewed the loss of their American outpost as a potential disaster. Peeling away the reasons for preserving the status quo, they concluded that partition would leave them financially destitute. Even more damaging, it would hurt their recruitment of new members, because the loss of Naples' sole foreign mission would remove an incentive that drew young men to the Society. Jesuits on both continents further worried that separation would undermine the ministry to Italian immigrants and Spanish speakers in the United States. "What would become of this work?," Carlo Pinto demanded. Not only was it clear that no American Jesuit province could supply priests fluent in the languages of those neglected populations, the "aversion of those who call themselves Americans toward Italians and Mexicans [was] well known." Pinto made a bleak forecast: "Annexation to an American province would herald the dissolution of an undertaking" that had taken years of toil and sacrifice to sustain.[27]

Separationists countered that the mission had outgrown its European roots. John J. Brown, an American who became mission superior in 1912, agreed with Pinto that the Hispanic ministry was "still our greatest work," but he predicted it would come to an end "sooner or later." Regardless, the status quo was no longer tenable. The mission's vast and numerous undertakings — which by now extended into the Republic of Mexico — had become "too large for its number of priests." Vastly overextended, the Jesuits could no longer maintain "well and completely" their present commitments; nor could they plan for tomorrow. Because the Mission was understaffed, there was "no chance" of realizing the dream of establishing a college in El Paso.[28]

Instead, the Jesuits were yoked for an indefinite time to come to staffing scattered rural parishes. This was, Brown insisted, an undertaking "contrary to the spirit of the Society" because it was not "the proper work of missionaries as the Society understands 'missionary.'" Hence he sympathized with priests holed up in out-of-the-way places, such as the unhappy missionary in southern Colorado who had recently signed a letter identifying himself as "that supposed Jesuit who is living all alone at the end of the world." The time had come, Brown declared, to begin transferring to bishops and to the secular clergy the dozens of Jesuit missions strung out across the Southwest. "Our apostolic work as pioneers is almost over," he declared in 1918. As municipalities multiply, "we should retire in favor of the diocesan clergy" from these rural stations, and "concentrate our efforts in a few large cities."[29]

After sifting the pros and cons, in 1919 Wlodmir Ledochowski, new superior general of the Society, solved the crisis in Solomonic fashion. Drawing on an idea floated by Giuseppe Marra some years earlier, he decreed the dissolution of the Neapolitan Mission and a division of its assets between new proprietors. The Jesuit residences in Colorado would be absorbed by the Jesuit Missouri Province. Those in New Mexico and Texas would join the recently formed province of New Orleans. The Society's long-term goal would be to focus its resources on the bustling cities of Denver and El Paso. Missionaries would therefore withdraw from scores of small towns that they had served throughout the region because none of them could support an eventual college. For a brief time, Albuquerque and Trinidad would be retained for the sake of "the fifteen old men . . . who have spent most of their lives working there."[30]

Thus, the dismemberment dreaded by Carlo Pinto came to pass. Unlike the California Mission, which had evolved into a province, the Southwestern enterprise was marked for dissolution. No one was pleased with the outcome. But, as the consultors of the Neapolitan Province observed, "given the diversity of the two races that made up the Mission, its division could almost have been predicted." John Brown's dream of an urban ministry became the Jesuits' new reality. On 15 August 1919, the decree winnowing the Southwest Mission from the Naples Province was officially read to the Jesuits gathered for dinner in the refectory of Sacred Heart College in Denver and in every residence of the Society in three states. In Holy Trinity Parish in Trinidad, Colorado, a place slated for eventual surrender, eighty-six-year-old Salvatore Personè recorded his reaction to the unraveling of the mission that he had helped to found. A veteran of nearly a half-century of missionary work, the white-haired old priest scribbled a simple line of poignant surrender, "sic transit gloria mundi."[31]

Authorities did what they could to ease the transition. To sweeten the bitter pill forced upon Naples, the dissolving mission bestowed upon the impoverished province a parting gift of $100,000, money earned through the liquidation of properties in Albuquerque, which were, in Brown's words, "the greater part of the assets established by the Mission."[32] To lessen the pain felt by men whose life's project had been liquidated, the forty Neapolitans still working in the Southwest were offered a ticket home; that is, they were given the option of returning to Europe or remaining in the United States. The leathery old warrior Carlo Pinto, furious at the anticipated "dismemberment" of the mission and the surrender of Jesuit properties in Texas to the bishop, had left for California in 1917 to nurse his wounds. But he was disappointed to discover that the *californios* had "renounced their origin and language" and did not require a Spanish-speaking priest. "Here nobody needs me," he sadly wrote from Santa Barbara. He was soon back in his beloved El Paso working with "real and pure Mexicans."[33]

Despite Brown's fear that "everyone will leave," only nine Neapolitans packed their bags and departed. A few adventurous souls moved on to a new mission in Ceylon, and the others booked passage for Italy. But some of these repatriates, after living for years in America, found their homeland was no longer home. From Naples, a former missionary discovered his body was in one place, but his heart was in another. "I am homesick for America," he said to a colleague. "I thought I had outgrown the disease, but it has got hold of me worse than ever. Sometimes I feel ashamed of myself; a man of my age shouldn't feel lonesome," he confessed. "The spell is only second to the one I had in my first year in Poughkeepsie," in New York, he added.

Some days I feel actually miserable; I loathe this wretched old place and would go to anywhere in the world to leave it. Often I stand in the garden overlooking the Bay [of Naples] and gaze longingly on the steamers headed toward the western shores. The word homesick is well chosen. . . . Oh, for a little American speed, and efficiency, and bigness, and cleanliness! Oh, for the lofty American mountains, the broad rivers, and endless plains, the wild woods and bushes![34]

The Naples of the repatriates was not the Naples they had cherished in their youth. Nor was the America for which some now pined the same wilderness they had encountered many years earlier. The "speed, efficiency, and cleanliness" of 1919 had been missing in the Far West of the first generation of émigrés. "The railroads have almost transformed the country and certainly have benefitted us," a priest wrote from New Mexico in 1883. "Our Mission does not present only difficulties, as it once did."[35]

An Urban Frontier

Primitive discomforts were yielding to modern conveniences that transformed the lives of missionaries throughout the West. By the time Italy's dependencies shed their European connection, the napkins and bed linens that had disgusted Joseph Joset in Spokane were common in the remotest missionary outposts. Pioneers who had once penned sermons by candlelight now read by electric illumination, received summons to minister over the telephone, and drove automobiles to anoint the sick and dying. In former times, it had taken years for news from the outside world to reach the missions of Montana. When earthquake and fire struck San Francisco in 1906, news of the disaster reached the Jesuits of St. Ignatius Mission the next day.

But not all was gain. The installation of a telephone enabled parishioners to summon a priest to a sickbed instantaneously — whether the visit was necessary or not. When phones commenced ringing day and night, rural missionaries scrambled to find ways of coping with unwarranted excursions. The passing of the horse-and-buggy evoked special mention in the annals of many country parishes. When circuit-rider Celestino Caldi of Washington received his first car in 1909, he insisted on calling the new vehicle an "autobuggy." Our Chevrolet "has been brought to our stable changed into a garage," said a priest in Colorado in 1917. "During these days, Fr. Riezi is learning how to drive the automobile." Horses were not instantly put to pasture, because they still proved useful in emergencies. Seventy-seven-year-old D'Aste of St. Ignatius took perverse delight on learning that a young priest was having a hard time with his "unhappy automobile." He "fell into a mud hole," the old man chuckled, "and had to be pulled out by a team."[36]

By the time the western missions split from Europe, Jesuit work was profoundly altered. As opponents of autonomy had forecast, the severance of ties with Italy was followed by a declining ministry among Native Americans. And Americans were not interested in evangelizing Indians. As J. A. Stephan, head of the Bureau of Catholic Indian Missions, had observed in 1899, priests in the United States were "very loath to say a good word, as a general rule, for the Indians either in private or from the pulpit. . . . Nearly everyone is afraid to raise his voice in their behalf. " According to the bureau, by 1909, there were 147 Catholic priests engaged in missionary work nationwide. Of these, only forty-four (about a third) were born in the United States. Among Jesuits, the percentage of native-born priests was even smaller — only nine out of thirty-eight. "All of the priests of other orders and a large majority of secular priests engaged in work for Indians," the report concluded, "are foreign born." The implication was clear. Without the influx of clergy from abroad, the Catholic commitment to Indian ministry would continue to shrink.[37]

Among Jesuits, however, there was another factor that accounted for the drop-off. European interest in missionary work had already begun to shift, even before the severance of ties with America. By century's end, the preferred destination of Jesuits in Italy was no longer the Rocky Mountain Mission, but a new field of endeavor that had opened in 1886. Of the twenty-six men in the Turin Province who petitioned Rome for a missionary posting at the end of the century, half listed Alaska as their first choice. This novel arena appealed to young Jesuits for the same reasons that the siren call of the Rocky Mountains had charmed idealists of an earlier time. As volunteers put it, Alaska seemed to have greatest need for workers, it was "the hardest mission of the Society," and it seemed a "paradise of poverty and humility."[38]

Replete with sweet challenges, Alaska also enticed experienced missionaries for whom the Pacific Northwest had become too tame. Descriptions of life among the Aleuts and Eskimos stirred up rosy memories of early days among the Flatheads and the Coeur d'Alenes. Recruitment literature abounded with appealing accounts, as did a report sent from Alaska in 1907. "Our Indians are so perfectly nomadic in their habits and disposition that we have to be always on the move, if we wish to be with them." Jesuits were

FIGURE 32. A turn-of-the-century street scene in Taos, New Mexico, during
a festival. Well-dressed shoppers, including a nun, share the street with cars and
wagons. Signs advertising "the Ideal Hat" and "Dupont Red Cross Dynamite"
mark the growing U.S. presence. Courtesy Denver Public Library, Western History
Collection, George Bean, GB-7397

drawn to such possibilities. They "wanted to go where the glamour was,"
a chronicler wrote, "and where the danger could be found." For the more
adventurous, that place was no longer Washington or Oregon or Montana,
but Alaska.[39]

As interest ebbed, so too did the number of Jesuit establishments in the
rural Pacific Northwest. Indian missions that had once been major hubs of
activity devolved into more modest operations staffed by fewer priests who
spent fewer hours with fewer Indians. According to one estimate, between
1800 and 1900 the nation's Native American population plummeted from
roughly 600,00 to 250,000. "You may see by our reports that the number
of deaths among our people is enormous," a priest wrote from Montana in
1911. "Doubtless the Indians are disappearing."[40]

Missionaries seemed to be fading, too. About forty-five priests and
brothers still resided in the native communities of the former Rocky Mountain Mission, but they were now aged and unable to sustain the travels of
yesteryear. Fifty-six-year-old Giuseppe Guidi recorded in 1898 that he was
the only priest to preside at Christmas services at St. Francis Regis Mission,

whose far-reaching realm embraced nearly seven thousand square miles. "At noon the train from the south did not bring any helper as in past years." But I managed to carry on alone because, he concluded whimsically, "I was born a good mule." At St. Ignatius Mission, Geronimo D'Aste penned a similar note in his journal on Sunday, 15 August 1909. "Fr. Sullivan preached for the first time in English," he said, but there was "no Indian sermon because no Father could do it."[41]

In 1918, Jesuits still ran schools—eight in their ten remaining missions—but decades of penury and governmental discouragement of Indian attendance had muffled their impact. St. Ignatius Mission could describe its school as flourishing—thanks in part to a 1908 decision of the U.S. Supreme Court that endorsed the right of Native Americans to use tribal funds on a pro rata basis to attend mission schools. But most establishments struggled even to stay afloat from one year to the next. Opposition to mission schools by the U.S. Bureau of Indian Affairs accelerated the drift of students to government classrooms.

In the new century, St. Xavier's Mission in Montana typified the Jesuits' scaled-down school system. By 1902, it remained open to sixty children, the resident priest reported, but "every week I also go to the government school 20 miles distant to teach boys and girls catechism."[42] Indian missions more and more resembled regular parishes than the multi-task institutions of thirty years prior. By 1948, the Jesuits had withdrawn from Montana's Holy Family Mission, although a circuit-rider from nearby Heart Butte still visited Catholics there. His routine typified the scenario at many shrunken outposts.

I live in an extension to the old church. . . . My territory covers 1,500 squares miles, and I have about 1,500 Catholic Indians and four whites. I say Mass at Heart Butte one Sunday, Holy Family the second, Little Badger the third, and Old Agency the fourth. . . . I have no schools but teach catechism in 11 country schools once a week. . . . But the people are good, God bless them; and honestly glad to have a priest.[43]

A similar retrenchment occurred in the Southwest, where the Jesuits transferred men and resources from rural parishes to urban schools and churches. Prior to the dissolution of the New Mexico–Colorado Mission, Visitor Alexander J. Burrowes had recommended that the Society "withdraw gradually from all the small missions and residences . . . until we shall have retired from every place except Denver and El Paso." Thus, churches once run by Neapolitan Jesuits were transferred to the diocesan clergy or to priests of other religious congregations. That process began almost immediately upon the severance of ties with Europe, beginning with Conejos in 1920 and Pueblo three years later. In places where replacements could not be found, the Jesuits stayed on, reluctantly. Strategies for exiting the parish of San Felipe de Neri in Albuquerque's Old Town were discussed for several years but finally abandoned in 1928, after a scowling Vatican official accused the Jesuits of being "more anxious to withdraw from the field than to develop it."[44]

The New Orleans Province struggled to extract itself from the several parishes it had inherited in El Paso, including Sacred Heart Church, once a hub of Jesuit activity. "If we cannot get the Mexican Province to accept some of this work," the general's assistant in Rome told the New Orleans provincial in 1924, "I see no other way but to prepare a certain number of willing men and make them look forward to it during their scholastic years. They will be our missionaries later on." That the official felt obliged to "make them" do the work was telling since it implied that most Americans were no more keen on ministering to Hispanics than they were to Native Americans.[45]

In El Paso and many other cities, clergy from Mexico did come to the rescue. Priests and nuns who had been expelled by the revolution reestablished themselves in the United States, inaugurating a variety of ministries to fellow-refugees in Texas. Included were Jesuits, who began arriving in El Paso in 1929. Aided by the Sisters of Loretto, they assumed care for the thousands of immigrants pouring into the city from across the Rio Grande. By 1932, Sacred Heart was feeding 1,400 persons — more than 300 families — daily in its soup kitchen. To the founding of additional churches, however, American Jesuits remained adamantly opposed. "It is something most horrible," an alarmed official wrote in 1927, when asked to staff a new station in New Mexico. "We shall not open another parish under any circumstances at all," he adamantly declared. "We are strictly forbidden" to do so by Father General.[46]

Education, from the start the centerpiece of Jesuit activity in California, received renewed emphasis everywhere as the twentieth century unfolded. As a spokesman for the new thinking declared in 1921, "There is, perhaps, no work of the Society, especially in our day, where greater advantage to souls may be gained" than in running schools. Breaking out of their limited ambit in the northern part of the state, the California Jesuits launched a new educational program in Los Angeles, opening in 1911 the institution that became Loyola Marymount University. With the severance of European bonds, the Society entered a fresh phase of development that was more American in its orientation. A general congregation of the Jesuits meeting in Rome in 1906 had once again proclaimed the classics as "the most suitable instrument for the development of abilities and the most conformable to our institute." In response to pressure from the United States, however, the congregation broke with the past by recognizing that non-classical studies were not contrary to the Jesuit way. They "may laudably be set up," the conclave declared, provided Latin and Greek "do not thereby suffer any harm."[47]

Given a green light, feeble as it was, modernizers in the United States rejoiced. In 1907, curricular reform made inroads at Santa Clara and St. Ignatius colleges, as specialized undergraduate courses in journalism, elementary law, architecture, civil engineering, and pre-medicine appeared for the first time. Within a few years, both institutions reintroduced the bachelor of science degree that had been suppressed in 1887 by European traditionalists.

The inauguration of modest graduate programs in law and engineering prompted the colleges to assume titles reflecting their new status. When Santa Clara College announced in 1912 that it would become a university, St. Ignatius and Gonzaga colleges followed suit. Further name changes testified to the Jesuits' desire to integrate their institutions into the American mainstream. Just as the founders of Seattle College had chosen to identify their school with a city instead of with a saint or Jesuit hero, the directors of St. Ignatius College retitled their institution the University of San Francisco. And in 1921, Denver's College of the Sacred Heart in Denver switched its name to Regis College — much to the dismay of its Neapolitan founder, Domenico Pantanella. The new label, which honored St. John Francis Regis, a seventeenth-century French Jesuit, was less apt to provoke religious prejudice, since the designation Regis was not as patently Catholic as Sacred Heart.[48]

A relaxation of European norms of student discipline accompanied curriculum reform. As a Jesuit in Colorado said, "With the change of administration, the conservative policy of Sacred Heart College gave way to the progressive policy of Regis College."[49] Wooden fences that had confined students to the Santa Clara campus came down in 1911 — a move that chagrined aged Italians still in residence — and soon afterward, students were allowed to leave the campus for the first time "even at night." Another novelty, a formal dance, was held on the campus that year. Similar transformations occurred in Spokane. For twenty-two years "an isolated educational island" dominated by "European parochialism," in the words of the institution's historian, Gonzaga College opened its doors to the outside world during the presidency of Louis Taelman in 1909–13. The Belgian priest was one of the few European Jesuits able to bridge the gap between the old and the new educational cultures.[50]

In 1912, Santa Clara's President James P. Morrissey, a protégé of Americanizer Robert Kenna, summarized the rationale for his institution's reform: "The past in no human life, however brilliant it may have been, is provocative of man's best energies." Santa Clara "is not conducted on the ideas prevailing fifty years, or even ten years ago," he insisted. A progressive institution had to give its students "whatever is best in modern methods and facilities."[51] Reforms favoring an entirely American-styled education, however, would be slow in coming at all Jesuit institutions, in part because of resistance from the overseas leadership of the religious order. Despite concessions to the new academic outlook, student discipline on the campuses remained rigorous; the faculty still stood in loco parentis; and the classical languages maintained a place of honor in the curriculum until the middle of the new century.[52]

Although the umbilical to Italy had been cut, most Jesuits remained in the United States, where they sustained the accustomed ministries of their order. In the Southwest, Neapolitans continued to make their rounds from one small village to the next, saying mass for Spanish-speaking congregations until replacement clergy could be found. After the tide of immigrants into the United States spiked in the early twentieth century, Italian priests ministered to even larger numbers of their countrymen in the nation's great urban centers. In the Pacific Northwest, their knowledge of Native American languages made European missionaries more valuable than ever, since most younger priests spoke only English. Italians still occupied important teaching and administrative posts in the colleges, as in San Francisco, where Giuseppe Sasia served as president of St. Ignatius College until 1911. He was succeeded by another Italian, forty-eight-year-old Alberto Trivelli, who laid the cornerstone of the new campus after the earthquake and fire of 1906 and introduced reforms that advanced the college's modernization.

Many missionaries remained active into old age. With typical good humor, Pietro Folchi responded to a parishioner who had inquired about his health. "I'm sliding down life's hill, and the farther down, the stronger is the momentum," he wrote from Spokane in 1909. "Holding to the brakes is no longer of much avail." Some individuals, worn out by years of hard travel and hard living, slid into senescence. Parishioners in Pueblo deplored the preaching of seventy-four-year-old Francesco Tomassini. "He is childish, does not prepare his sermons, says always the same things and lasts very long."[53] By contrast, Giuseppe Cataldo remained sharp into his ninety-second year, a celebrity who was regularly consulted by linguists, anthropologists, and historians until his death in 1928. Also still in the saddle until the last moment was the gentle *Genovese* Geronimo D'Aste, whose passing at age eighty-one was affectionately described by a nun at St. Ignatius Mission. "He was found dead, seated in his arm chair, holding his little notebook of 'particular examen' but a few moments before entering into the presence of the Supreme Judge." Eduardo Griva, born in Turin in 1864 and the builder of twelve churches in the Pacific Northwest, lived until 1948. As the last of the old Italians slipped away, the young men assigned to write their death notices discovered they knew nothing of their early years. Moreover, the circle of Europeans who might be consulted for details was fast shrinking, thus prompting in obituaries the melancholy reflection: "Of his early life, little has been preserved to us."[54]

Some Neapolitans who had immigrated to the New Mexico–Colorado

FIGURE 33. Italian missionaries Giuseppe Damiani and Geronimo D'Aste pose for a photograph in 1909. By this time, about forty-five priests and brothers still resided with Native Americans in the Pacific North-west, but many were elderly and unable to sustain the travels of yesteryear. Courtesy Jesuit Oregon Province Archives, Gonzaga University, 1047-01

Mission on the eve of its dissolution lived far into the twentieth century. Carmelo Tranchese, who had come to the United States in 1911, served for twenty-two years as pastor of Guadalupe Church in San Antonio, Texas, until his death in 1956 at the age of seventy-six. His work with the poor in the city's slums drew nationwide notice during the Great Depression. His appeal to Eleanor Roosevelt for improved housing had eventually resulted in the founding of a housing project, the Guadalupe Community Center and Clinic. Following the example of the pioneering Neapolitans who had established *La Revista Católica*, the enterprising Tranchese had launched his own Spanish-language Catholic newspaper, *La Voz*. Another late arrival, Felice Ziccardi, the fiery bandmaster of Trinidad, lasted until 1964, dying at the age of seventy-six. With the passing of Ziccardi, the Neapolitans of the New Mexico–Colorado Mission had all fallen away.[55]

By the time the last remnant of the Italian missionaries had passed from the scene, the Jesuit presence in the West was mainly urban. Like other clergy on the frontier, the members of the Society of Jesus had calibrated their work to the shifting needs of the region. Arriving at mid-century in the wake of American acquisition, they had encountered a highly diverse population — Native Americans, Hispanics, Anglo Americans, and immigrants from every nook and cranny of polyglot Europe. In that cosmopolitan frontier society, the Italian Jesuit missionaries found themselves in the cockpit. As the West became more Americanized at the turn of the century, however, the spotlight shifted. Europeans now found themselves on the periphery as native-born priests and brothers, at home with the language and culture of the United States, assumed control of the order's universities, high schools, seminaries, and parishes. Although the Italian immigrants soon became forgotten pioneers of the West, they did leave traces of their passing on the cultural landscapes of both America and Europe.

Transnational Ties

During their ascendancy, Italian Jesuits not only transmitted novel ideas and practices to the United States, they also shaped the course of life back home in Italy. Thus their saga demonstrates a phenomenon often ignored by historians — the impact of the United States on Europe. As students of contemporary migration have noted, when "immigrants adapt to their new environment and both they and their religious institutions acquire more financial stability, flows of monetary resources, religious personnel, and influence often reverse or become two way." However, as one student of immigration history, Frank Thistlethwaite, has said, scholarly analysis of this counter-impulse remains thin, revealing how traditional ways of looking at the past often blinker the historical imagination. The passage of some fifty-five million Europeans to the United States was one of the most striking phenomena of the modern era. But that movement seems to have made slight impact on writers of European history. "It has been the consequences and not the causes of migration which have received most attention,"

Thistlethwaite has concluded; "moreover, the consequences in the receiving, not the sending country."[56]

One of the commodities that regularly emanated from the United States to Italy was cash. From the empire of the dollar, missionaries routinely forwarded funds to impoverished confrères abroad. So significant were those remittances, often sent in the form of mass stipends or taxes, that authorities in Naples long deferred severing their lifeline to the New Mexico–Colorado Mission. The specter of dispossession loomed over them as a potentially "painful loss" and "catastrophe."[57] Missionaries in America were not ignorant of the weight their contributions carried in Europe. As Joseph Riordan of California once said, "the only real benefit that the province [Turin] derives from possessing us is our payment of the provincial tax." For this reason — and as an inducement to separation — the Californians had suggested that they continue to "contribute for a number of years both out of charity to our distressed province and out of justice for the help given in past years." Although Turin declined the offer when the break came, Naples did accept aid from American Jesuits for several years.[58]

Benefits more important than money also flowed back across the Atlantic. In the era before the 1929 signing of the Concordat between the Italian state and the church, the ownership of property by religious in Italy was legally precarious. For this reason, the Jesuits of Piedmont, wishing to secure ownership of their college in Genoa, the Istituto Arecco, in 1909 transferred legal title of the property to a California priest studying in Florence. By making a non-Italian sole proprietor, they assured the destiny of the institution.[59]

Information exchange constituted another important transnational tie. Emigration afforded the refugees their first encounter with the Anglo-Saxon world, and in some cases, that exposure moved their scholarship in new directions. It was during his exile in London, for example, that the Roman College theologian Giovanni Perrone began writing about Protestantism. Missions in America also served as conduits for the dissemination of new ideas from abroad. During his restricted ministry in Naples in 1880, Ferdinando Canger developed a correspondence with the Missouri Jesuit Florence Boudreaux, whose popular devotional writings he translated into Italian. From America, Benedetto Sestini's *Messenger of the Sacred Heart* circulated throughout Europe, particularly in France, during the nineteenth century. And from their vantage point in America, transplanted theologians such as Luigi Sabetti, Carlo Piccirillo, Filippo Cardella, and Nicola Russo shaped Vatican opinion about the church in the United States through their reports and advising of American bishops.[60]

Few asylum seekers had more leverage in Rome than did Camillo Mazzella and Salvatore Brandi of Woodstock College. Both theologians returned to Italy as putative experts on the United States, which expertise catapulted them to the front lines during the battle over Americanism. As scholars have shown, in the minds of many churchmen the ultimate stake in that struggle was not the United States, but Europe. Fearing the diffusion of liberal views from the United States, this consortium, which included the two Jesuit theologians, used the American tug-of-war to halt the advance of a contaminated ideology to Europe. Brandi's influence was not limited to combating Americanism; nor was he unremittingly antagonistic toward his former asylum. Jesuits at Rome's *Civiltà Cattolica* claimed that the only thing Brandi salvaged from his America experience was a taste for steak at breakfast, so scant was his appreciation of the country.

But the jest was unfair. According to a biographer, Brandi's staunchly orthodox views became more moderate and conciliatory, as shown by his sympathetic reporting on the United States after he assumed editorship of *Civiltà*. While Brandi was in charge, it was the constructive aspects of American Catholic life that predominated. Indeed, the United States was "held up to Europe as a shining example of respectful treatment of the church in a country where Catholics were a minority." Thus, a 1909 article from the journal's American correspondent declared: "We have truly a separation of Church and State; religion loves our government and our government loves religion." It was only after Brandi's retirement that *Civiltá* began to publish extended criticism of the United States.[61]

European understanding of America was shaped by a steady flow of missionary letters from the Far West. Chief among these were field reports, known as *lettere edificanti*, that circulated throughout the Society of Jesus worldwide. Created to provide spiritual uplift and news about the order's global activities, they cannot be taken at face value, and yet these bulletins filled a significant public relations function. From an American vantage point, the *lettere* helped correct distorted European images of the United States. "They have a general but a poor opinion" of us, an American living in France told associates in 1849. "They do not think that the Americans are capable of religious *élan*." "The greater part of this apprehension is owing to our Fathers in America not being communicative enough," he explained. "We of the American side do not brag and blarney enough."[62]

Europeans were wild for news from far-off locales. Send us letters, "even if written in English," a writer for *Civiltà Cattolica* pleaded with a Jesuit in Alaska in 1895, and "we will publish them." As incentive, the journalist reminded prospective correspondents that *Civiltà* "is read in Rome by the Holy Father and by Cardinals and is distributed throughout the world with a *réclame* that has no equal." Later the missionary received assurances from Italy that his letters had indeed been published "and are now being read publicly" throughout Europe. They will "produce much good," he predicted, "especially among our young men." Like the famous Jesuit *Relations* of the seventeenth century, these reports from America, embraced as bulletins from the front lines of a battlefield, were widely disseminated among students attending Jesuit colleges in Europe. A correspondent informed missionary Lorenzo Palladino in 1864: Your three latest epistles from Paris, New York, and Santa Clara "were read by all the fathers and students" at our school in Monaco. Not only were missionary reports proclaimed aloud in the refectory during meals, copies were distributed to students enrolled in language classes as exercises in translation and composition.[63]

One reason why European Jesuits solicited letters from America was to draw new members into the Society. Send us missives that "tell an interesting story," a Neapolitan once urged New Mexico's Donato Gasparri. Write something that offers instruction about "geography, science, politics," and will "stir up in the heart of the reader a desire to become a missionary." Enthusiastic reports from friends and relatives settled abroad had moved millions of Europeans to emigrate to the United States as settlers in the nineteenth century. As a well-traveled German pastor once observed, "The name of America has now become as familiar to every peasant and laborer; yea to every child in the street, as that of the nearest neighboring country, whilst to thousand and hundreds of thousands, it is a goal of their warmest wishes and boldest hopes."[64] So, too, Europeans became missionaries after reading compelling tales of travel and spiritual derring-do that were described in *lettere edificanti* from America.

European views of America were further shaped by exiles who returned home to tout feats accomplished abroad. All of the Italian missions in the West sent representatives back to Europe to enlist volunteers, imitating the methods of the Society's most effective nineteenth-century salesman, the Belgian Pierre-Jean De Smet. Although less famous than De Smet (his writings and lecture tours made him a well-known figure in nineteenth-century Europe), later missionaries' visits publicized Jesuit operations across the Continent and generated scores of recruits for America. The Southwest returned Marra and Pantanella to Europe for this purpose; Varsi revisited in search of conscripts for California; Grassi, de la Motte, and Cataldo toured on behalf of the Indian missions of the Pacific Northwest.

Cataldo, who possessed De Smet's knack for promotion, made a memorable trip in 1885 that he aptly described as "the jump that saved the Rocky Mountain Mission." Upon his arrival in his native Sicily, specially printed flyers announced: "He is here in Palermo, the zealous apostle of the Rocky Mountains, . . . Father Cataldo, Sicilian." European response to his appearance was electric. To audiences whose only contact with the American West were popular novels and Wild West shows, Cataldo's explanation of the daily life, food, clothing, language, and material cultures of Indians was fascinating. Like De Smet, who dressed members of his audience in Indian moccasins, leggings, and headdress "amid storms of applause," Cataldo was remarkably effective, eventually drawing thirty-one young men from various European countries for work in the Rocky Mountains. But it was not only to America that idealistic volunteers were drawn. Other candidates, attracted to religious life by their encounter with visiting missionaries, joined the Society to pursue careers in Europe. How many were drafted in this manner is impossible to determine, but their number was sufficiently large that it compelled the Italian provinces to resist surrendering their American missions lest they lose a potent incentive for enlisting new members.[65]

A final outcome of persecution in Europe was that it introduced salutary, fresh features into Jesuit life. "Adaptability," one historian argued, "became almost as important as the maintenance of tradition."[66] In early centuries, a readiness to accommodate to changing times and places had been an identifying feature of the order that had enabled Jesuits to insert Christianity into diverse cultures around the world. In the cautious and fearful Society of the nineteenth century, however, adaptability was by no means a consistent hallmark. The experience of diaspora nevertheless led some Jesuits to recover their historic flexibility. Contact with the larger world through emigration reshaped the way Jesuits perceived both themselves and their environment, sometimes yanking them forcibly into modern times.

Men who spent time in the United States returned to Europe with a more catholic grasp of the world. Some of the ideas they brought home were of minor significance, but in a religious order fixated on lockstep uniformity, even small innovations loomed large. Before their dispersal, for example, Jesuits not only dressed similarly but arranged their private rooms "all alike and in a fixed fashion." Refugees who returned to Naples from abroad after the upheaval of 1848 refashioned their living quarters — dubbed the "United States of America" — in the American manner.[67] Other insights acquired through travel were more substantial. So transformed was Giovanni Battista Ponte by his five years as visitor and superior in California that he returned to Italy in 1872 not only an advocate of independence for the California Mission, but critical of both his own and his successor's governance of the Turin Province.

Italians who were recalled to Europe to fill administrative jobs favored a nimble approach to problem-solving, which reflected lessons learned in America. In 1894, Giuseppe Sasia was summoned from San Francisco to Turin to serve as provincial. When his term ended and he returned to California, Sasia left behind a reputation for such extraordinary leniency that the Piedmontese honored the indulgent American with a witticism. Whenever challenged by subsequent superiors to justify a questionable action, their defense was: "Father Sasia gave me permission."[68]

While he occupied the same post in Naples, Giuseppe Marra employed practical skills perfected as a missionary in New Mexico. Under challenging conditions, he advanced the restoration of the order and personally negotiated the return of the historic church of the Gesù Nuovo in the heart of Naples to the Society. Despite court battles over property, he founded a theologate at Posilipo in 1898. ("I have never suffered so much mental anguish" as in this project, the normally stoic priest declared later.) Bucking custom, he inaugurated new guidelines for trainee Jesuits. Recognizing that education solely along familiar lines no longer sufficed, Marra created a program enabling scholastics to pass state examinations and acquire teaching certificates from the Italian government. This able executive was as influential in shaping Jesuit operations in Europe as he had been in the United States.[69]

As Marra's career made plain, the expulsion of the Society of Jesus had in the long term yielded an unexpected harvest. In the dark days of 1848, not even the most optimistic deportee could have anticipated that fifty years hence the order's institutions in Italy would be overseen by an Americanized expatriate. Nor could any Jesuit who stepped into exile have imagined the other subtle ways in which their leave-taking would someday benefit comrades in Italy. If missions in America provided a haven for expatriates, they also boosted the morale of those who stayed at home. Success abroad enabled Europeans to muster new members in Europe, and it also helped them find meaning in the hardships they endured during decades of dispersal and emigration. What the Piedmontese had accomplished in California, Rocky Mountains, and Alaska seemed a "collection of wonders," an Italian author wrote in 1898. Although rebuffed at home as outsiders, the immigrant clergy had been paradoxically transformed abroad into insiders.[70]

In interesting ways, banishment had backfired. Although still subject to legal restrictions, Jesuits emerged as popular as ever in Italy in the new century. By directing its rampage so fiercely and ostentatiously against them, a hostile regime fed the notion that Loyola's disciples were, in the words of one writer, "the backbone of real Catholicism." This impression was reinforced by the Jesuits' dispersal to far-off corners of America, where their accomplishments won wide recognition. Visiting missionaries were greeted as conquering heroes, their exploits trumpeted among the faithful throughout the Italian peninsula. Photographs of San Francisco's elegant St. Ignatius College, of the massive, pink-stoned College of the Sacred Heart in Denver, and of rural churches in Montana, jammed with Native American congregants—all these sustained the reputation of the suppressed order, even in Italy. As a scriptural adage had it, "The stone rejected by the builders has become the cornerstone."[71]

13 *Conclusion*

> The Catholic may travel from one end of the world to the
> other; . . . and everywhere he will recognize the same time-
> honored ceremonial, kneel at the same altars, and feel that
> he is completely at home.
>
> — Bishop Martin J. Spalding, 1857[1]

The role played by religious denominations and clergy in the development of the United States is difficult to ignore. "The religious aspect of
the country was the first thing that caught my attention," Alexis de
Tocqueville wrote when he toured the United States in 1831. "There is no
country in the whole world in which the Christian religion retains a greater
influence over the souls of men than in America." Religion, the French visitor concluded, "is the foremost of the institutions of the country."[2]

De Tocqueville's judgment about the place of faith in American life was
borne out by the national story's unfolding. Slave owners found justification
for servitude in the Bible; bondsmen turned to Christianity as a source of
strength against oppression; abolitionists cited Scripture in their campaign
to overthrow human servitude. Competition between churches transformed
America into the land of colleges in the nineteenth century. Insights drawn
from belief were used to rationalize the worst excesses of capitalism and to
motivate resistance to the abuse of industrial workers. Nor did religion take
a back seat in twentieth-century history. Churches provided leadership to the
civil rights uprising, marched in anti-war protests, and led boycotts during
the anti-apartheid movement. Even in our own day, the re-emergence of religion into the secular realm stirs the caldron of public debate. Like a tune that
stubbornly lingers on the edge of memory, religion has been an ever-present
refrain in American public life.[3]

The persistence of religion has been due, in part, to the uninterrupted flow
of emigration into the country. What the historian Oscar Handlin said over
a half-century ago in *The Uprooted* has remained true. "Once I thought to
write a history of the immigrants in America," he declared in 1951. "Then
I discovered that the immigrants *were* American history."[4] But what of migration's relationship with religion? Despite notable exceptions, as the historian
Jay Dolan has argued, American religious scholars have not paid much heed

to immigration, and students of migration have been reluctant, with some notable exceptions, to cast their eyes on religion.[5]

And yet the correlation between the two phenomena has been central in American history. Of the nearly 36 million people who emigrated to the United States between 1821 and 1924, many were fleeing religious persecution; and once they arrived, faith provided an identity marker assisting survival and adaptation.[6] The clergy of many denominations functioned as cultural intermediaries for immigrant congregations. When displacement threatened newcomers with a loss of roots, churches, mosques, and synagogues preserved ethnic and cultural identity while easing the immigrants' adjustment to a new life in a new environment.

The reverse was also true: immigration anchored faith. That religion, in all its many and varied guises, has consistently occupied a central place in the nation's social, political, and cultural life was due not simply to an interest in things spiritual but also to the repeated waves of immigration that renewed and diversified the country's array of faiths.[7] The nineteenth-century bishop of Indian Territory, John Baptist Miege, a Piedmontese Jesuit, believed there was a vital link between religion and migration, noting that the success of Catholicism in America was due in large part to immigration.[8]

In the Italian Jesuit saga, immigration and religion were conjoined. Cast from Italy for largely religious reasons, the Jesuits' status as emissaries from Rome, the *caput mundi* of Catholicism, gave them repute among co-religionists in the United States. Add to this their linguistic skills and propensity to adapt, and some of the reasons for the refugees' success in maneuvering among multiple races and cultures become clear. Hence, too, the enthusiasm that greeted the fugitives when they stepped ashore in America. With the nation's Catholic population doubling every decade, church leaders competed to acquire the services of the displaced Italians as they began arriving in 1848 in the wake of the *Risorgimento*.

What did the Jesuits bring to the United States as a consequence of the anti-Jesuitism they experienced in Europe? As fallible men of their time, many bore an antipathy toward the modern democratic state and liberalism, which had brought them so much grief. Even more of them burned with antipathy toward public education, as did most nineteenth-century Catholic clergy. But the scarring experience of anti-clericalism in Italy also prompted in the banished Jesuits a profound appreciation of the religious liberty that they discovered in America. As Rudolph J. Meyer once said of the *piemontesi* in California, they "cherish freedom more than water."[9]

The exiles also carried an ideology that simultaneously eased and complicated cultural bridge-building. Once they had found employment in Jesuit institutions in the East Coast, the Italians began the process of assimilating the language and customs of their adopted country. The majority of them, taking the world as it was, not as they wished it to be, embraced the chance to draw upon a fresh slate. They sketched a new life for themselves, establishing personal contacts and acquiring experience that proved advantageous when they founded their own institutions in the West. Others, however, measuring the lifestyle of their American confrères against a Roman yardstick, found much to lament. The fruit of their disappointment was a series of far-reaching reforms — highlighted by the founding of a national seminary at Woodstock College — that recast the way that American Jesuits lived, studied, and worked. The tension between custom and concession, which surfaced first in the East, would be an on-going theme of Italian Jesuit experience as the group extended into the West.

Arriving on the frontier at a time when multiple cultures fused and fired, the Jesuits became a potent force among diverse ethnic groups, confirming the claim of the historian Henry Louis Gates, Jr., that some of the most intriguing developments in history and culture occur when cultures interface. Differences notwithstanding, the points of convergence between Catholic culture and Native American spirituality facilitated early evangelization: belief in an activist deity, confidence in the possibility of miracles, and reliance on communication with the spiritual world. Indian converts were, however, never passive recipients of the Jesuit message, but reshaped and redirected it in ways that profoundly determined missionary outcomes. Nor were the Jesuits untouched by native culture. Indeed, the meeting of European Jesuits and Native Americans showed that the brokering of cultures was invariably a reciprocal affair in which no one emerged unaltered. If Jesuits remolded Indian society through years of familiar interchange, natives also reshaped the missionaries. A lifetime of daily contact with tribal people even led some Europeans to favor the Native American lifestyle to their own.[10]

Armed with a rich panoply of evangelical tactics, the European clergy attained leverage among the tribes. Their facility in mastering native tongues and their ambiguous national status as immigrants eased their reception. Within a short time, Jesuit missions and schools reached from the Yakimas, Umatillas, Nez Percés and beyond to the Cheyenne, Assiniboins, and Crows. By 1890, in Montana alone, there were over 7,000 Catholic Indians out of a federal census count of 10,000.[11]

For all their effectiveness, however, the Jesuits left a tangled legacy. If less ethnocentric than their Protestant rivals, the Europeans' understanding of the Indian world was nonetheless filtered through their own limits and strengths. They opposed the liquidation of communal land ownership and the imposition of severalty, but cooperated with the government in forcing so-called civilization upon the tribes. Despite the best of intentions, the missionaries furthered the eradication of native culture through programs of religious and educational assimilation. Paradoxically, however, they helped preserve other aspects of ethnicity through research that conserved languages that might otherwise have been lost. And reservation boarding schools run by missionaries, despite their patent inadequacies and ethnocentrism, enabled some tribal people to survive economically in the white world.

In the uneducated portions of the West, colleges rather than Indian missions paved the way to Jesuit influence. Despite nativist opposition, the Italians' foreign birth and religion did not deter settlers from enrolling in their schools. Indeed, the clergy's status as outsiders initially proved an asset in recruiting students from among the West's cosmopolitan population. In the years after the Mexican War, Jesuit institutions in California and the Southwest drew not only Anglo Americans, but also large numbers of Hispanics and immigrant foreigners to their classrooms. The Jesuit clergy, along with other Catholic religious orders, provided the only schooling to many ethnic children. By offering familiar religious experiences in an unfamiliar environment, the Italians supplied a vital need of western crossroads culture. To populations sapped by dislocation and loss, their hybridizing schools smoothed the transition from an old to a new society and fostered the cultivation of new fealties.

But the cosmopolitan West also demanded innovation. The transplanted school masters discovered that patterns of education acceptable in the old world had to be recut to fit new world conditions. Students in California or New Mexico were more inclined to study bookkeeping and mineralogy than Latin hexameters. Although reform was difficult to justify to European authorities, missionary teachers supplemented their conventional classical curriculum with courses in practical subjects that appealed to young men of the West. The result of their accommodation were melting-pot institutions that were neither fully American nor fully European, but a casserole blend of both.

In the Southwest, the brokering of cultures was shaped by the Jesuits' national origin from the very start. The Neapolitan missionary Donato Gasparri and his countrymen — like Bishop Lamy and his French contemporaries — brought with them the traditions of their homeland, which they mingled with local Hispanic American notions. For a half-century, the missionaries criss-crossed the countryside, scattering the seeds of Italian influence through their parishes, schools, and publications. They were not inclined, however, to sweep aside indigenous customs entirely. That temptation was tempered by the Mediterranean cultural matrix that the foreign clergy shared with the native population, as well as by the sympathetic grasp of Hispanic culture that many of them had gained during early exile in Spain. By sometimes integrating Italian and Mexican traditions, the Neapolitans legitimized themselves in the eyes of New Mexican Catholics. In turn, their give-and-take approach helped make more acceptable their Romanizing ecclesiastical reforms.

It is not possible, therefore, to fit the Neapolitans into any one single cultural box. On the one hand, they brought novelty to the Southwest through parish missions and religious devotions imported from abroad. On the other, they provided continuity with the New Mexican past by defending traditional village life, supporting folk religion, and championing bilingual schools. Additionally, they furthered the assimilation of their Hispanic congregations into Anglo American culture by laboring to bring them the economic and political advantages of U.S. citizenship. And yet, as the pumped-up editorials of the *Revista Católica* made clear, the Jesuits were not unmitigated Americanizers. Instead, their achievement in the Southwest — as in the Pacific Northwest — lay in ambivalence. While there was much in the dominant culture that they admired, there was also much that they deplored. As Italians, they were able to accommodate what they considered the best of both Anglo American and Hispanic cultures and to build bridges between the two.[12]

Wherever they were posted, the Italians aimed at reconciling religious differences among multicultural congregations. Their objective was to bind American Catholicism more closely to Rome, to advance a European-style institutional church in the United States, and to forge a community in which, as Bishop Martin J. Spalding of Kentucky once said, all races and cultures would find themselves "completely at home."[13] This they accomplished by importing old world religious devotions, by enhancing the role of the priest in church affairs, and by promoting the centralization of Catholicism under papal authority. The standardized practices championed by them far and wide — May devotions, Corpus Christi processions, homage to the Sacred Heart — had a universalist and centralizing purpose. A unified ecclesiastical community was their goal. They therefore promoted the integration of diversified Americans — Italians and Indians, Anglos and Hispanics — into a single Catholic culture that transcended national boundaries. In short, the expatriates advanced what the historian Peter D'Agostino has called the "transnational dynamics built into the very structure of Roman Catholicism."[14] Thus, Jesuits attending the Council of Baltimore in 1885 would have nodded in agreement when Bishop J. F. Shanahan of Pennsylvania declared: "The very expression, national or sectional Church, implies a contradiction in terms. In its very nature the Church rises above nationality."[15]

During most of their history in the West, the Italian missionaries managed to keep their several objectives in equipoise as they engaged in cultural bridge-building. And yet, the paradoxical principles undergirding all their activities — the promotion of ecclesiastical uniformity as well as toleration of local difference; a commitment to universalism, on the one hand, and to malleability, on the other — contained the potential for sharp conflict. Impelled by the conservative and transnational stance of the newly restored Society of Jesus, they resisted aspects of American life that they deemed objectionable. Conversely, their religious heritage, which valued adjustment to times,

places, and persons, drove them to a modus operandi that was often malleable, creative, and fluid. The net result was that Jesuit practice sometimes
collided with Jesuit spirituality, a tension that metastasized into painful dissonance in turn-of-the-century California.

Contradictory impulses surged within the Jesuits of the San Francisco Bay
Area. In their effort to establish commonality amid apartness, some émigrés
favored accommodation while others could not shake imported notions of
orthodoxy. During the so-called Americanist controversy, Jesuits joined battle with other churchmen over the extent to which Catholicism should be tailored to American realities. Veteran missionaries who had once been creative
in adjusting their heritage to California's cosmopolitan culture now manifested a growing disenchantment with the Americanization of their own society. Thus they fiercely resisted deviations championed by confrères of the next
generation. In their troubled encounters, young American Jesuits and aging
Italians differed on just about every topic that surfaced in daily colloquia:
how best to minister to the state's increasingly American population, how
schools should be run, how they themselves should live.

And so the battle raged. Appealing to the principle of accommodation,
American Jesuits sought to jettison notions that impeded a full engagement
with secular culture. Aging nostalgists from Italy, finding the past more fruitful than the future, appealed to overseas superiors for support in imposing
a European-style uniformity. Although the struggle was prolonged, the
advocates of reform partially succeeded in implementing the time-honored
Jesuit strategy of adapting operations to times, places, and persons. But the
metamorphosis was unhurried and never complete, because the Californians
could never entirely dissolve their divisions and because European gatekeepers remained vigilantly suspicious of American innovations.

Turn-of-the-century California was, however, in many respects, exceptional. Even there, it was impossible to categorize the European clergy as
reactionaries and the Americans as progressives; in fact, Italians found themselves on both sides of the conservative-liberal divide. In most frontier
regions, the refugees demonstrated a disposition to overcome the dislocation
of foreignness and to move into the language of a new land. Their inclination to mediate differing traditions during their long sojourn in the West had
several explanations. In part, facility at shifting between linguistic and ethnic communities was a prerequisite for successful ministry on a heterogeneous
frontier. But that was not the only reason why the Jesuit émigré was as
equally at home on Indian reservations in Montana, immigrant mining camps
in Colorado, and classrooms of urban California. It made a difference that
the missionaries came from an Italian culture that valued an ad hoc approach
to problems and prized cooperation over confrontation. As contemporary
Americans pointed out, refugees from Italy were differentiated from other

immigrants by their resilience. Even when choosing employment, observers said, "the Italian immigrant is perhaps the most adaptable of all."[16] The fact that most of Italian Jesuits emigrated as malleable young men also contributed to their openness to novelty and experimentation.

If predisposed toward flexibility by secular culture, the Jesuits were further inclined to harmonize disparities by religious training. Since its founding, the Society of Jesus had identified "a ministry of reconciliation" as one of its central undertakings; and "reconciling the estranged" remained central to its self-understanding in the nineteenth century. The order's ruling ideology placed a high priority on accommodation and on operating amid a "great diversity of persons throughout a variety of regions." Although religious principle and religious practice sometimes clashed, the fundamental Jesuit instinct to mediate between diverse social groups shaped the mentality of the nineteenth-century missionaries.[17]

The Italians' success in spanning cultures was also attributable to their profession. The Jesuits were accorded deference by lay people — many of whom were themselves immigrants — because they were priests, a distinction that often trumped even ethnic differences. As scholars have suggested, wherever he exercised his ministry, the priest was "the charismatic, central figure in his Catholic community." Regardless of how Protestant critics and others might view him, the pastor was to his own people "nothing short of an intellectual giant" worthy of unique respectability. Adept as a theologian, his educational superiority empowered him to give advice on "politics, law, education, mechanics, pharmacy, banking, and social reform" — all activities that engaged missionary Jesuits. This esteem was fortified by many beneficial experiences in this country where priests usually met the expectations people had of them.[18]

To achieve this elevated status, however, they had to ascend the narrow, twisting stairs of prejudice. Despised by American nativists because they bore the double stigma of the Catholic priesthood and Italian birth, these unfashionable men began their careers as aliens in a borrowed culture. Their views on many issues of the day were controversial, including how best to assimilate Native Americans, European immigrants, and Hispanic Americans into mainstream society. Thus, William G. Ritch, territorial secretary of New Mexico, declared that the "Neapolitan adventurers" were not fit to teach in the United States, because they favored "the retention of the Spanish language in preference to the language of the country."[19]

Nevertheless, the Italians followed a path that led them from the obscurity of outsiders to the accomplishment associated with insiders. The founding of colleges was a significant step in their journey to acceptance in the unschooled West, especially in metropolitan California, where their institutions enjoyed their greatest success. Disdained by some Americans in New

Mexico as interlopers because of their power over public education, they were admired by Hispanics with whom they allied themselves. In the Pacific Northwest, the Jesuits' role in maintaining peace between the races and in working with government during periods of crisis won them the admiration of native and white alike. Originally denied federal funding, the priests and their allies eventually emerged as the ultimate insiders when they won government financing for their Native American boarding schools. Even those who nowadays lament their role in altering tribal identities concur that the Jesuits were effective missionaries.[20]

In the process of transforming themselves from outsiders to insiders, the Italians hastened the maturation of the Society of Jesus in the United States. Contemporaries early on anticipated that the infusion of European clergy into the American branch of the order would reshape its history. "The present state of the Society is a very painful one," wrote John Larkin, a New York priest, in 1848 as he pondered the expulsion of Jesuits from country after country in Europe. Larkin was confident that the exodus of clerical refugees from abroad boded well, however, for the future of American Catholicism. Their shining example would end the cramped provincialism of the Jesuit order in the States, he forecast, and its members would learn "there are more ways of doing a thing, and doing it well." The missionary Michele Accolti, who almost single-handedly persuaded the Piedmontese Jesuits to emigrate to the West Coast, concurred. "As the sea in receding from the shores of one country proceeds to enrich with its waters the littoral of another," he announced in typically florid language, "so in like manner the Society, in losing its provinces in Europe through the adversities of the times, will come to pour out its blessings on American soil."[21]

While not all Americans interpreted the coming of Jesuits as benediction, the outcome of their immigration was far-reaching. As one historian has observed, Italian revolutionaries like Garibaldi, Cavour, Mazzini and others "were the unwitting sowers of the seed from which sprang the Society's most plentiful harvest."[22] For this reason, too, the story of the Italian Jesuits of the West warrants examination. It is a part of a larger saga that continues to resonate in a nation that constantly incorporates, albeit with varying degrees of acceptance and resistance, a dazzling array of peoples and religions.

Once high-profile figures in western communities, the Italian Jesuits slipped into the shadow of obscurity, becoming mere footnotes to their own history. And yet ripples of their passage lingered in the varied institutions they forged in the multi-layered West. *La Revista Católica* remained in publication until 1962, although by then it had morphed into a tame version of its once-fiery self. Even today, dozens of churches and mission stations founded by the émigrés are peppered throughout the rural counties of New Mexico,

Colorado, and Texas. Some remain in operation, but more stand abandoned — primitive if picturesque reminders of the thousands of Hispanics and European immigrants who once packed the pews at Sunday morning services. In the larger cities of the Southwest, including El Paso, Albuquerque, Trinidad, and Denver, parishes formerly operated by Neapolitans continue in lively operation. The claim made by a chronicler in 1948 holds true. Without the foundation laid by the immigrant clergy from Naples, "the remarkable development of the church in the states of New Mexico and Colorado, and in the city and environs of El Paso would have been impossible."[23]

On the Pacific Coast, dozens of institutions attest to the clergy's role in community-building and in raising the West from a rural to an urban frontier. Parishes and schools founded by the Italians and their co-workers prosper still in the cities of Seattle, Tacoma, Spokane, Missoula, San Francisco, San Jose, and Santa Clara and in dozens of rural parishes and missions. Their still-flourishing churches on Indian reservations in the Pacific Northwest testify to what one historian has described as the "the tangible results of a far-flung missionary system rivaling the Spanish California mission chain of adobe and brick."[24] Perhaps the most lasting legacy of the Italians lies in the numerous preparatory schools and the five universities founded by them, including Santa Clara University and the University of San Francisco in California; Gonzaga University and Seattle University in Washington; and Regis University in Colorado.

Although the Italian clergy have been an under-researched population, in the eyes of their nineteenth-century contemporaries they were central figures in the evolution of a multicultural American West. "If it was not for the restraining influence of the Jesuit fathers, there would have been serious trouble in this section long ago," said federal agent John Sims from Washington in 1874, speaking about missionary efforts to prevent hostilities between whites and Native Americans during the so-called Nez Percé War. To Blandina Segale, a Sister of Charity who worked with the clergy of New Mexico for nearly twenty years, the Neapolitans were without equals. "Out here," she declared, "we call the Jesuits, 'the vanguard of the church.'" Even the Jesuit John Frieden, who fought reactionaries among the Italians, acknowledged their success as pastors, educators, and community builders in a remarkably heterogeneous frontier. What he said in 1897 of the émigrés in California was also expressed by other contemporaries about Italian Jesuits in the West: "They were remarkable men."[25]

Abbreviations

CHS	Colorado Historical Society, The Stephan B. Hart Library, The Colorado History Museum, Denver, Col.
CSL	California State Library, Sacramento, Calif.
HL	Huntington Library, San Marino, Calif.
IJS	Institute of Jesuit Sources, Saint Louis University, St. Louis, Missouri.
JCRU	Jesuitica Collection, Regis University Archives, Regis University, Denver, Col.
JMPA	Jesuit Missouri Province Archives, Jesuit Provincial Office, St. Louis, Missouri.
JOPA	Jesuit Oregon Province Archives, Foley Center, Gonzaga University, Spokane, Wash.
MUDD	Mudd Library, Yale University, New Haven, Conn.
NA	National Archives, Washington, D.C.
WCA	Woodstock College Archives, University Library, Georgetown University, Washington, D.C.
WTCL	Woodstock Theological Center Library, Georgetown University, Washington, D.C.

PERIODICALS

LEPN	*Lettere Edificanti della Provincia Napoletana della Compagnia di Gesù*
LEPT	*Lettere Edificanti della Provincia Torinese della Compagnia di Gesù*
RC	*Revista Católica*
WL	*Woodstock Letters*

Notes

PREFACE

1. Howard R. Lamar, "Much to Celebrate: The Western Historical Association's Twenty-Fifth Birthday," *The Western Historical Quarterly* (1986): 406–13.

2. As the historian Peggy Pascoe has written, some of the most promising recent research on the West as a cultural crossroads has focused on western women, including Christian missionaries, who "were cultural brokers, mediators between two or more very different cultural groups." See Peggy Pascoe, "Western Women at the Cultural Crossroads," in *Trails: Toward a New Western History*, ed. Patricia Nelson Limerick, Clyde A. Milner II, and Charles F. Rankin (Lawrence: Univ. Press of Kansas, 1991), 55. See also Helen Rose Ebaugh and Janet Saltzman, eds., *Religion Across Borders: Transnational Immigrant Networks* (Walnut Creek, Calif.: Altamira Press, 2002), 1–2; Lamar, "Much to Celebrate," 406–13.

3. Jeremy Eichler, Review of Michael B. Beckerman, *New Worlds of Dvorak: Searching in America for the Composer's Inner Life*, in *New York Times*, 10 Jan. 2003.

4. Colleen McDannell, *Material Christianity: Religion and Popular Culture in America* (New Haven: Yale Univ. Press, 1995), 162.

5. Coleman J. Barry, *Worship and Work: Saint John's Abbey and University, 1856–1980* (Collegeville, Minn.: Liturgical Press, 1980), 41. The reference was to Jesuit Francis Weninger, who worked among divided German Catholics.

6. John T. McGreevy, "Productivity and Promise: American Catholic History Since 1993," *U.S. Catholic Historian* 21 (Spring 2003): 124; see also Madeline Duntley, "Identity and Marginalization," *U.S. Catholic Historian* 21 (Spring 2003): 102–3.

7. Laurie F. Maffly-Kipp, "Eastward Ho! American Religion from the Perspective of the Pacific Rim," *Retelling U.S. Religious History*, ed. Thomas A. Tweed (Berkeley: Univ. of California Press, 1997), 130.

8. John W. O'Malley, *The First Jesuits* (Cambridge: Harvard Univ. Press, 1993); John W. O'Malley, "How the Jesuits Changed: 1540–56," *America*, 27 July 1991, 32. See also Dauril Alden, *The Making of an Enterprise: The Society of Jesus in Portugal, Its Empire, and Beyond 1540–1715* (Palo Alto: Stanford Univ. Press, 1996).

9. Geoffrey Cubitt, *The Jesuit Myth: Conspiracy Theory and Politics in Nineteenth-Century France* (Oxford: Clarendon Press, 1993); David G. Shultenover, *A View from Rome on the Eve of the Modernist Crisis* (New York: Fordham Univ. Press, 1993); Thomas Morrissey, *As One Sent: Peter Kenney, S.J.* (Dublin: Four Courts Press, 1996).

10. Frances Trollope, *Father Eustace: A Tale of the Jesuits* (London: Colburn, 1847), 1:152; Luigi Barzini, *The Italians* (New York: Atheneum, 1983), 318; David O'Brien, Review of Peter McDonough, *Men Astutely Trained: A History of the*

Jesuits in the American Century (New York: Free Press, 1992), in *Boston Globe*, 22 Dec. 1991.

11. Andrew F. Rolle, *The Immigrant Upraised: Italian Adventurers and Colonists in an Expanding America* (Norman: Univ. of Oklahoma Press, 1968), 197; Frederick G. Bohme, "A History of the Italians in New Mexico" (Ph.D. diss., Univ. of New Mexico, 1958); Robert C. Carriker, "Joseph M. Cataldo, S.J.: Courier of Catholicism to the Nez Percés," in *Churchmen and the Western Indians, 1820–1920*, ed. Clyde A. Milner II and Floyd A. O'Neil (Norman: Univ. of Oklahoma Press, 1985), 109–39; M. Lillian Owens, *Reverend Carlos M. Pinto, S.J., Apostle of El Paso, 1892–1919* (El Paso: Revista Catolica, 1951); Herman J. Muller, *Bishop East of the Rockies: The Life and Letters of John Baptist Miege, S.J.* (Chicago: Loyola Univ. Press, 1994); Lucylle H. Evans, *Good Samaritan of the Northwest: Anthony Ravalli, S.J., 1812–1884* (Missoula: Univ. of Montana Press, 1981); Giuseppe Lovecchio, *Alla Scoperta della Storia Ignota di Padre Michele Accolti Gil* (Conversano/Bari, Italy: Arti Grafiche SCISCI, 2001); Lucia Ahern, "The Long Harvest: The Life of Joseph M. Cataldo, S.J." (M.A. thesis, Nebraska State Teachers College at Peru, 1958); Louis Brioni, "Father John Nobili, Founder of Santa Clara College" (M.A. thesis, Santa Clara Univ., 1968); Michael E. Engh, "A True Gentleman and a Crow: Peter Paul Prando, S.J." (M.A. thesis, Gonzaga Univ., Spokane, Wash., 1978).

12. Robert Bigart, *Letters from the Rocky Mountain Missions: Father Philip Rappagliosi* (Lincoln: Univ. of Nebraska Press, 2003); Gregory Mengarini, *Recollections of the Flathead Mission, Containing Brief Observations Both Ancient and Contemporary Concerning This Particular Nation*, ed. and trans. Gloria Ricci Lothrop (Glendale, Calif.: Arthur H. Clark, 1977); "St. Ignatius Montana: Reports from Two Jesuit Missionaries, 1885 and 1900–1901" (Parts I and II), ed. Robert Bigart and Clarence Woodcock, *Arizona and the West* 23 (Summer 1981): 149–71 and (Autumn 1981): 267–78.

Analyses of the work of the Neapolitan Jesuits of the Southwest include M. Lilliana Owens, *Jesuit Beginnings in New Mexico, 1867–1882* (El Paso, Tex.: Revista Catolica, 1950); Giuseppe M. Sorrentino, *Dalle Montagne Rocciose al Rio Bravo* (Naples: Federico & Ardia, ca. 1948); Thomas J. Steele, *Works and Days: A History of San Felipe Neri Church, 1867–1895* (Albuquerque, N.Mex.: Albuquerque Museum, 1983); idem, *Diary of the Jesuit Residence of Our Lady of Guadalupe Parish, Consejos, Colorado, December 1871–December 1875*, ed. Marianne L. Stoller and Thomas J. Steele (Colorado Springs, Colo.: Colorado College, 1982); Gerald McKevitt, "Italian Jesuits in New Mexico: A Report by Donato M. Gasparri, 1867–1869," *New Mexico Historical Review* 67 (1992): 357–92.

For the Northwest, see Robert Ignatius Burns, *The Jesuits and the Indian Wars of the Northwest* (New Haven, Conn.: Yale Univ. Press, 1966); Wilfred P. Schoenberg, *Paths to the Northwest: A Jesuit History of the Oregon Province* (Chicago: Loyola Univ. Press, 1982); Howard L. Harrod, *Mission Among the Blackfeet* (Norman: Univ. of Oklahoma Press, 1971).

CHAPTER I

1. "The Jesuits," *The Southern Quarterly Review* 12 (July 1855): 12.
2. A. D. Splivalo, "Corpus Christi at Santa Clara in 1853," *The Redwood* (Oct.

1908), 4, Archives of Santa Clara Univ., Santa Clara, Calif. (hereafter ASCU); David Hornbeck, *California Patterns: A Geographical and Historical Atlas* (Palo Alto: Mayfield Publishing, 1983), 70.

3. W. J. Howlett, *Life of the Right Reverend Joseph P. Machebeuf*, ed. Thomas J. Steele and Ronald S. Brockway (Denver, Colo.: Regis College, 1987), 400–401.

4. For an analysis of the rich research possibilities of the topic of Christian women as cultural mediators, see Pascoe, "Western Women at the Cultural Crossroads," 40–58.

5. Anne M. Butler, "Sacred Contests in the West," *Frontiers and Catholic Identities*, 53, 107–8. For an examination of the evolving meanings of the term "cultural broker" in recent scholarship, see Margaret Connell Szasz, ed., *Between Indian and White Worlds: The Cultural Broker* (Norman: Univ. Oklahoma Press, 1994), 1–20, 294–300.

6. O'Malley, *The First Jesuits*, 348; Jean Lacouture, *Jesuits: A Multibiography* (Washington, D.C.: Counterpoint, 1995), 70; George E. Ganns, trans. and ed., *The Constitutions of the Society of Jesus* (St. Louis, Mo.: Institute of Jesuit Sources, 1970), 69, 164–65.

7. John Henry Newman, *The Letters and Diaries of John Henry Newman*, ed. Charles Stephen Dessain (London: Thomas Nelson & Sons, 1961–62), 12:26.

8. Ganns, *Constitutions of the Society of Jesus*, 245.

9. *Constitutions of the Society of Jesus*, 245–49; Lacouture, *Jesuits: A Multibiography*, 84–87; Trollope, *Father Eustace*, 3:291.

10. Ganns, *Constitutions of the Society of Jesus*, 185; George E. Ganns, *Saint Ignatius' Idea of a Jesuit University* (Milwaukee, Wis.: Marquette Univ. Press, 1956), 79–80.

11. Ganns, *Constitutions of the Society of Jesus*, 262, 78–80.

12. Ibid., 204.

13. "Brother Bartholomew Tortore," *Woodstock Letters* (hereafter WL) 35 (1906): 289; "Obituary: Brother William Lakebrink," WL 17 (1888): 383.

14. Accolti testimonial, in "Informationes Novitiorum S.J., 1825–1841," Archives of the Roman Province of the Society of Jesus, Via degli Astalli 16, Rome, Italy (hereafter ARPSJ); Michael O'Malley, "Notes on the Jesuit Brothers who served generously in the work of the Jesuit Rocky Mountain Mission (some in Alaska) from 1841 to 1907," Michael O'Malley Papers, Jesuit Oregon Province Archives, Foley Center, Gonzaga University, Spokane, Wash. (hereafter JOPA).

15. James Axtell, *The Invasion Within: The Contest of Cultures in Colonial North America* (New York: Oxford Univ. Press, 1985).

16. [Marra], "Missionis Nov. Mexici et Coloradi, Provinciae Nap.; Catalogus Rerum, Ann. 1902," Archives of the Naples Province of the Society of Jesus (Archivo della Provincia Neapolitana della Compagnia del Gesù), Naples, Italy (hereafter ANPSJ).

17. N. Porter, *The Educational Systems of the Puritans and Jesuits Compared* (New York: 1851), 78–80, copy in Mudd Library, Yale University, New Haven, Conn. (hereafter MUDD).

18. E. N. Kirk, *Dr. Kirk's Discourse before the Society for the Promotion of Collegiate and Theological Education in the West, November 11, 1856*, 29, MUDD;

Porter, *Educational Systems*, 78–80, MUDD; Albert Barnes, *Plea in Behalf of Western Colleges* (Philadelphia, Pa.: William Sloanaker, 1846), 23, MUDD.

19. Donald G. Tewksbury, *The Founding of American Colleges and Universities Before the Civil War* (New York: Archon, 1965), 8, 31, 21l.

20. Louis B. Wright, *Culture on the Moving Frontier* (New York: Harper & Row, 1961), 144.

21. Barry, *Worship and Work*, 17–18; Sister Mary Dominica McNamee, *Willamette Interlude* (Palo Alto, Calif.: Pacific Books, 1959), 32.

22. Joseph W. Riordan, *The First Half Century of St. Ignatius Church and College* (San Francisco, Calif.: H. S. Crocker Co., 1905), 45–46. Named from their house on Rue Picpus in Paris, the Picpus Fathers were formally called the Congregation of the Sacred Hearts of Jesus and Mary and the Perpetual Adoration of the Blessed Sacrament of the Altar.

23. *Diary of the Jesuit Residence*, ed. Stoller and Steele, 70n112.

24. *Constitutions of the Society of Jesus*, 262–63.

25. R. Laurence Moore, *Religious Outsiders and the Making of Americans* (New York: Oxford University Press, 1986), 67–69.

26. Peter R. D'Agostino, *Rome in America: Transnational Catholic Ideology from the Risorgimento to Fascism* (Chapel Hill: Univ. of North Carolina Press, 2004), 313.

27. McDannell, *Material Christianity*, 162.

CHAPTER 2

1. Michelet lecture in Lacouture, *Jesuits: A Multibiography*, 366.

2. "Ultimi avventimenti in Roma in marzo 1848," in Pietro Pirri, *P. Giovanni Roothaan, XXI Generale della Compagnia di Gesù* (Isola del Liri, ca. 1930), 406–18. This document describing the Jesuit dispersion of 1848 was edited and perhaps written by Roothaan.

3. Roothaan (Rome) to Monsignor Billet, 25 Mar. 1848, in C. J. Ligthart, *The Return of the Jesuits: The Life of Jan Philip Roothaan*, trans. Jan J. Slijkerman (London: T. Shand, 1978), 301.

4. Pirri, *Roothaan*, 422; Ligthart, *Return of the Jesuits*, 302–3.

5. Roothaan, "A Letter of Very Reverend Father John Roothaan, on the Tercentenary of the Society," 1839, in *Renovation Reading* (Woodstock, Md.: Woodstock College Press, 1886), 279; Roothaan (Rome) to Cardinal Cadolini, 25 Mar. 1848, in Ligthart, *Return of the Jesuits*, 301.

6. Roothaan, "A Letter of Very Reverend Fr. Roothaan on the Calamities of our Times and on Zeal for the Acquirement of Perfection," in *Select Letters of Our Very Reverend Fathers General to the Fathers and Brothers of the Society of Jesus* (Woodstock, Md.: Woodstock College Press, 1900), 270–71; and idem, "A Letter of Very Reverend Father John Roothaan on Devotion to the Sacred Heart of Jesus," in *Renovation Reading*, 293; Ligthart, *Return of the Jesuits*, 113–19.

7. Roger Aubert et al., *The Church in the Age of Liberalism*, trans. Peter Becker (New York: Crossroad, 1981), 11, 210; Carlton J. H. Hayes, *A Generation of Materialism, 1871–1900* (New York: Harper & Row, 1941), 85.

8. Newman, *Letters and Diaries*, 2:103-4, 117.

9. Clara Lovett, *The Democratic Movement in Italy, 1830-1876* (Cambridge: Harvard Univ. Press, 1982), 10-11, 24-27.

10. Antonio Gallenga, *History of Piedmont* (London: Chapman & Hall, 1855), 3:400.

11. William Bangert, *History of the Society of Jesus* (St. Louis, Mo.: St. Louis Institute, 1972), 432-33.

12. Roger Aubert, *Il Pontificato di Pio IX (1846-1878)*, 2nd ed., trans. Giacomo Martina (Torino: Editrice AAIE, 1976), 1:44; Friedrich Curtius, ed., *Memoirs of Prince Chlodwig of Hohenlohe Schillingsfuerst*, trans. George W. Chrystal (London: William Heinemann, 1906), 2:75.

13. Bangert, *History of the Society*, 41, 431-33, 497; Thomas Bokenkotter, *A Concise History of the Catholic Church* (New York: Doubleday, 1979), 256. For a thorough analysis of the origins and early history of the order, see O'Malley, *First Jesuits*. A surprisingly candid description of the suppression by a contemporary Jesuit can be found in Giulio Cesare Cordara, *On the Suppression of the Society of Jesus: A Contemporary Account*, trans. John P. Murphy (Chicago: Loyola Press, 1999).

14. Bangert, *History of the Society*, 431-33, 497.

15. Aldo Scaglione, *The Liberal Arts and the Jesuit College System* (Philadelphia: John Benjamins, 1986), 1-2.

16. Bangert, *History of the Society*, 54, 215, 309.

17. Friedrich Heyer, *The Catholic Church from 1648 to 1870*, trans. D. W. D. Shaw (London: Adam & Charles Black, 1969), 61-62.

18. Survey of 1871, found in John Roach, "Education and the Press," *The New Cambridge Modern History*, vol. 10, *The Zenith of European Power, 1830-70*, ed. J. P. T. Bury (Cambridge: Cambridge Univ. Press, 1960), 106-11, 117; Paul F. Grendler, Review of Guerrino Pelliccia, *La scuola primaria a Roma dal secolo XVI al XIX. L'istruzione popolare e la catechesi ai fanciulli, nell'ambito della parrocchia e dello 'Studium Urbis,' da Leone X a Leone XII, 1513-1829*, in *Catholic Historical Review* 74 (1988): 604; Gallenga, *Piedmont*, 442. For an analysis of the educational conflict in Piedmont, see Scaglione, *The Liberal Arts*.

19. Martin Clark, *Modern Italy 1871-1982* (London: Longman, 1984), 37-38.

20. William Roscoe Thayer, *The Life and Times of Cavour* (Boston: Houghton & Mifflin, 1914), 2:78.

21. Michele Volpe, *I Gesuiti nel Napoletano: note ed appunti di storia contemporanea da documenti inediti e con larghe illustrazioni, 1814-1914* (Naples: Tipografia Editrice Pontificia M. D'Auria, 1914-15), 2:296, 3:192-93.

22. Roger Aubert et al., *The Church Between Revolution and Restoration* (New York: Crossroad, 1981), 129; Volpe, *I Gesuiti*, 3:113, 143, 204.

23. Ligthart, *Return of the Jesuits*, 113. See also John Padberg, *Colleges in Controversy: The Jesuit Schools in France from Revival to Suppression, 1815-1880* (Cambridge, Mass.: Harvard Univ. Press, 1969).

24. Denis Mack Smith, "Italy," in *The New Cambridge Modern History, Volume 10, The Zenith of European Power, 1830-70*, ed. J.T.P. Bury (Cambridge: Cambridge Univ. Press, 1960), 553; Aubert, *Church Between Revolution*, 310-14.

25. Newman, *Letters*, 12:118; Gioberti in Ligthart, *Return of the Jesuits*, 283. For a discussion of whether or not Gioberti once taught in a Jesuit college in Turin, see Ilario Rinieri, *Il P. Francesco Pellico e I suoi tempi: vol. III, la vita e le opere* (Genoa: Derelitti, 1933), 56; and Alessandro Monti, *La Compagnia di Gesù nel territorio della Provincia Torinese* (Chieri: M. Ghirardi, 1920), 5:4.

26. J. C. H. Aveling, *The Jesuits* (New York: Stein & Day, 1982), 310. See also Scaglione, *The Liberal Arts*, 158; and David Mitchell, *The Jesuits: A History* (New York: Franklin Watts, 1981), 220.

27. Antonio Bresciani to Jan Roothaan, 22 Nov. [1843], in Rinieri, *Pellico*, 49; Monti, *Compagnia di Gesù*, 4:461, 5:94. See also Stuart Woolf, *A History of Italy, 1700–1860: The Social Constraints of Political Change* (London: Methuen, 1979), 435.

28. Bresciani to Roothaan, 2 Jan. 1846, in Rinieri, *Pellico*, 103; Monti, *Compagnia di Gesù*, 5:96, 168.

29. Bresciani to Roothaan, 2 Jan. 1846, in Rinieri, *Pellico*, 103–4.

30. Rinieri, *Pellico*, 113, 116–17.

31. "Father Joseph Bayma: A Sketch," *WL* 21 (1892): 320; Monti, *Compagnia di Gesù*, 5:180; Rinieri, *Pellico*, 116–17.

32. Francesco Pellico, "1848, Secolarazzione. Elenco dei 75 che chiesero la secolarizz. e osservazioni del P. Pellico," [ms. dated 27 Apr. 1849], Archives of the Turin Province of the Society of Jesus, Villa San Maurizio, Strada comunale di Superga, 70, Turin, Italy (hereafter ATPSJ); Monti, *Compagnia di Gesù*, 5:180–88; Rinieri, *Pellico*, 166.

33. Paul M. Ponziglione, "Reminiscences of Half a Century: A Last Letter from Father Ponziglione," *WL* 29 (1900): 267–72.

34. Smith, "Italy," *New Cambridge*, 559.

35. A. C. Jemolo, *Church and State in Italy, 1850–1950*, trans. David Moore (Oxford: Basil Blackwell, 1960), 6.

36. Aubert, *Church in the Age of Liberalism*, 62.

37. Patrick Murray, "Father Roothaan's Visit to Maynooth College, 1848," *Letters and Notices* [Newsletter of the British Jesuit Province] 20 (1890): 352, Archives of the British Province of the Society of Jesus, 114 Mount St., London (hereafter ABPSJ). See also "The Church of the Gesù, Rome: An Historical and Descriptive Sketch," *Letters and Notices* 28 (1905): 166, ABPSJ; and Patrick J. Dooley, *Woodstock and Its Makers* (Woodstock, Md.: Woodstock College Press, 1927), 126.

38. Rinieri, *Pellico*, 117; "Catalogus Sociorum et Officiorum Provinciae Taurinensis Societatis Iesu Ineunte Anno 1848," copy, Archives of the California Province of the Society of Jesus, Jesuit Provincial Office, Los Gatos, Calif. (hereafter ACPSJ); Pietro Galletti, *Memorie storiche intorno al P. Ugo Molza e alla Compagnia di Gesù in Roma durante il secolo XIX* (Rome: Fratelli Tempesta, 1912), 15.

39. "Father Sanctus Traverso," *WL* 36 (1907): 364; "Father Anthony Maraschi," *WL* 26 (1897): 490–91.

40. Note by John McElroy attached to J. Grassi (Rome) to John McElroy, 8 June 1848, Archives of the Maryland Province of the Society of Jesus, University Library, Georgetown Univ., Washington, D.C. (hereafter AMPSJ).

41. Walter Tempest (Rome) to Father Jenkins, 13 May 1849, "Foreign Correspondence" Volume, ABPSJ.

42. Ligthart, *Return of the Jesuits*, 294, 310.

43. Jemolo, *Church and State*, 12.

44. James Sheerin (Frederick, Md.) to Samuel Barber, [8 Dec] 1851, Catholic Historical Manuscripts Collection (219K5), University Library, Special Collections Division, Georgetown Univ., Washington, D.C. (hereafter AGU). Sheerin-related information received from Father Felice Sopranis in Rome; Carmelo Papalo (Naples) to Mr. Ardia, 20 Sept. 1851, Woodstock College Archives, (219P10.a), University Archives, Georgetown Univ., Washington, D.C. (hereafter WCA).

45. Frederic De Travers (Georgetown) to Ignace Brocard, 24 Apr. 1850, AMPSJ. The account drew upon reports that De Travers, a Swiss Jesuit, received from Naples.

46. Aubert, *Church in the Age of Liberalism*, 10. See also E. E. Y. Hales, *Pio Nono: A Study in European Politics and Religion in the Nineteenth Century* (New York: P. J. Kennedy & Sons, 1954), 178; and Jemolo, *Church and State*, 8-11.

47. Newman, *Letters*, 11:268, 290.

48. John Etheridge (Rome) to Joseph Johnson, 17 Feb. 1854, ABPSJ; papal biographer Hales rejected the popular notion that the pope was manipulated and controlled by the Society. "Pio Nono returned from his Neapolitan exile a sadder and wiser man, no doubt, but not a changed man, not the tool of the Jesuits," he wrote. "It is altogether too easy to father upon the Jesuits the conservative policies which experience had taught Pio Nono to accept." See Hales, *Pio Nono*, 150-51, 283.

49. Jemolo, *Church and State*, 5.

50. Lorenzo Tognetti, *Memorie storiche intorno alla Provincia Romana della Compagnia di Gesù dall'anno 1814 all'anno 1870 raccolte dal P. Pietro Galletti*, vol. 2, *1849-1870* (Rome: Tipografia Agostiniana, 1939), 28-32; Hales, *Pio Nono*, 284. Curci was dismissed from the Society in 1877 after he wrote about the possibility of entente between the Holy See and the Italian kingdom, and his books were condemned. See Ligthart, *Return of the Jesuits*, 444.

51. Bangert, *History of the Society*, 442.

52. Smith, "Italy," *New Cambridge*, 565.

53. Jemolo, *Church and State*, 11-12, 30; Hales, *Pio Nono*, 179-80.

54. "Dispersion of the Neapolitan Province," *Letters and Notices* 4 (1867): 101; Tognetti, *Memorie storiche intorno alla Provincia Romana*, 2:423-24.

55. Philip Caraman, *University of the Nations: The Story of the Gregorian University with Its Associated Institutes, the Biblical and Oriental, 1551-1962* (New York: Paulist Press, 1981), 104; *New York Times*, 30 July 1872, p. 4.

56. "Memories of San Girolamo, Fiesole, from 1873 to 1893," *Letters and Notices* 10 (1873): 248 and 24 (1898): 508-12, both in ABPSJ; Clark, *Modern Italy*, 82.

57. P. Gonella (Monaco) to Beckx, 26 Feb. 1868, Tuar. 1010 — II-11, Archivum Romanum Societatis Iesu (Roman Archive of the Society of Jesus), Rome, Italy (hereafter ARSI); *Catalogus Provinciae Taurinensis Dispersae Societatis Iesu* (Nicaea, 1878), ARSI.

58. *Catalogus Provinciae Siculae Dispersae Societatis Iesu Ineunte Anno 1879*

(Naples, 1879), 22–26; *Catalogus Dispersae Provinciae Neapolitanae Societatis Iesu Ineunte Anno 1868* (Rome, 1868), 6, ARSI; "Dispersion of the Neapolitan Province," *Letters and Notices* 4 (1867): 114, ABPSJ.

59. Palomba (Naples) to Gasparri, 28 May 1871, ANPSJ; Minutes of May meeting, "Consulte, 1871–1900," ANPSJ.

60. G. Perrone (Stonyhurst) to Finotti, 10 June 1848, AMPSJ.

61. "Bayma," *WL* 21 (1892): 320.

62. L. B. Palladino, *Indian and White in the Northwest; or, a History of Catholicity in Montana* (Baltimore: John Murphy, 1894), 57–58.

63. Letter of Pietro Fontana cited in P. A. Leanza, *I Gesuiti di Sicilia nel Secolo XIX* (Palermo: Tip. Francesco Lugaro, 1914), 212.

CHAPTER 3

1. Santo Schiffini, "Dispersion of the College of Laval," *WL* 10 (1881): 67.

2. Fontana quoted in Leanza, *I Gesuiti in Sicilia*, 204–5.

3. "Laval: Letter from Mr. J. Hayes," *Letters and Notices* 9 (1873–74): 158.

4. "In Memoriam: A Short Account of Fr. Vito Carrozzini, S.J.," *WL* 6 (1877): 125–26; Santo Schiffini, "Dispersion of the College of Laval," *WL* 10 (1881): 67.

5. "Father Carmelus Polino," *WL* 17 (1888): 385–86.

6. Pietro Galletti, *Memorie storiche intorno alla Provincia Romana della Compagnia di Gesù dall'anno 1814 all'anno 1914* (Prato: Tipografia Giachetti, 1914), 558.

7. Data are drawn from the annual catalogues of the various Italian provinces for the years indicated. Copies are preserved in ARSI. The dramatic drop in Jesuit numbers was due not solely or even principally to departures, but also to a sharp drop-off in new admissions.

8. Percentages are based on membership figures found in the catalogues of the Turin and Naples provinces and on biographical data from the *Catalogus Defunctorum in renata Societate Iesu ab a. 1814 ad a. 1970*, ed. Rufo Mendizábal (Rome: Curia of the Society of Jesus, 1972). See also "Catalogus Sociorum et Officiorum Provinciae Taurinensis Societatis Iesu, Ineunte Anno 1848," ms. copy at ACPSJ.

9. "F. Cherubino Ansalone," *Lettere Edificanti della Provincia Napoletana* (1911): 247–78 (hereafter *LEPN*); "Br. Raphael Vezza," *WL* 18 (1889): 249; Michael O'Malley, "Northwest Blackrobe: Missionary Career of Father Joseph Cataldo, S.J., 1837–1928," O'Malley Papers, JOPA.

10. Minutes of meetings, 1871, "Consulte, 1871–1900," ANPSJ.

11. Galletti, *Molza*, 18–19.

12. Padberg, *Colleges in Controversy*, 18–19, provides a good summary of the controversy and places it in its larger context. The most detailed account of the battle over ontologism at Vals is found in Joseph Burnichon, *La Compagnie de Jésus en France: Histoire d'un Siècle, 1814–1914* (Paris: Gabriel Beauchesne, 1919), 3:140–61. See also Pirri, *Giovanni Roothaan*; and Galletti, *Memorie storiche intorno alla Provincia Romana*.

13. "Father Aloysius Sabetti," *WL* 29 (1900): 212.

14. Leanza, *I Gesuiti in Sicilia*, 205–6; Davide Palomba (Naples) to Donato Gas-

parri, 22 May 1873, ANPSJ; Minutes of meetings, 1875, "Consulte, 1871–1900," ANPSJ.

15. Descriptions of the Italians' stay in England are found in Galletti, *Molza*, 21–22; and G. Perrone (Stonyhurst) to Fr. Ryder, 10 June 1848, AGU. Their arrival at the Jesuit school of Stonyhurst is mentioned in Christie (Rome) to James Etheridge, 8 May 1853, "Foreign Correspondence," ABPSJ. Careers of prominent members of the group are briefly summarized in Caraman, *University of the Nations*, 87–89, 101.

16. Margaret M. Maison, *The Victorian Vision: Studies in the Religious Novel* (New York: Sheed & Ward, 1962), 170; Bernard Basset, *The English Jesuits from Campion to Martindale* (London: Burns & Oates, 1967), 392.

17. E. W. Grinfield, *The Jesuits: An Historical Sketch* (London: Seelys, 1853), 342, 359, 386, 321; Sinclair in Maison, *The Victorian Vision*, 171–73.

18. William Cobb (London) to Roothaan, 27 Jan. 1848, Anglia 1004-I-6, ARSI; John Early (Holy Cross) to Maryland Provincial [Ignace Brocard], 27 Nov. 1848, AMPSJ. Early's assessment was based on conversations with the former rector of the Roman College, Felice Sopranis. By contrast, an English Jesuit claimed the Italians were well received by their English colleagues. "The charity of Ours at Stonyhurst was praised" by the Italian exiles, wrote James Christie (Rome) to James Etheridge, 8 May 1853, "Foreign Correspondence," ABPSJ.

19. Galletti, *Molza*, 26–27. Passaglia, who later left the order after a clash with superiors, accepted a chair of moral theology at Turin in 1859, then joined in the movement for Italian unification, and served for a year in the Italian parliament. See Bangert, *History of the Society*, 444–45. During the following decades, additional Jesuits sought refuge in England. A group of Piedmontese clerics, which included the philosopher and mathematician Giuseppe Bayma, arrived in 1858. Bayma remained for ten years as professor at Stonyhurst before re-emigrating to California. After the fall of Rome in 1870, nearly fifty novices and scholastics emigrated there, although the majority of them soon transferred elsewhere. See Francis Edwards, *The Jesuits in England from 1580 to the Present Day* (London: Burns & Oates, 1985), 191.

20. The Turin Province reported that 158 of its 308 members were serving in its two missions in the Far West. The Neapolitans, who numbered 305 men, had one person in California, three in the Rocky Mountain Mission, sixteen at Woodstock College, and fifty-one in New Mexico. See *Catalogus Sociorum et Officiorum Provinciae Taurinensis Societatis Iesu Ineunte Anno 1880* (Monaco, 1880), 52–53; and *Catalogus Provinciae Neapolitanae Societatis Iesu Ineunte Anno 1880* (Naples, 1880), 31–32, 39, ARSI.

21. Silvio Pellico to Giuseppino, 2 Mar. 1848, in Rinieri, *Pellico*, 126–27.

22. Heyer, *Catholic Church*, 207–8; Jay P. Dolan, *The American Catholic Experience: A History from Colonial Times to the Present* (Garden City, N.Y.: Doubleday & Co., 1985), 170; "Bishop Bruté's Report to Rome in 1836," *Catholic Historical Review* 29 (1943): 224; Augustus Langcake, "North America: Letter from Mr. Langcake," *Letters and Notices* 2 (1864): 65.

23. Larkin (New York) to F. W. Gockeln, 10 July 1848, John Larkin Correspondence, Archives of the New York Province of the Society of Jesus, Fordham Uni-

versity, Bronx, New York (hereafter ANYPSJ); Brocard (Georgetown) to Roothaan, 24 Aug. 1848, Marylandia 1008-II-7, ARSI; Keller (Maryland) to [Robert Whitty?], Oct. 1870, in a note appended to "Circular Letter and Decree" [regarding the founding of Woodstock College], Marylandia 1010-XXV-7, ARSI.

24. Gilbert J. Garraghan, "John Anthony Grassi, S.J., 1775–1849," *Catholic Historical Review* 23 (1937): 273–72; Paul Horgan, *A Certain Climate: Essays in History, Arts, and Letters* (Middletown, Conn.: Wesleyan Univ. Press, 1988), 97–105.

25. Information on Mazzella is found in "Gesuiti Napoletani nelle Missioni dell'America Settentionale," n.d., ms., ANPSJ. Gabaria, who served for a while as superior of scholastics at Georgetown, died in Pennsylvania in 1847. Ryder's recruits also included Giuseppe Finotti, later editor of the *Boston Pilot*; Antonio Ciampi, president of three Jesuit colleges in America; and New Mexican missionary Livio Vigilante. Finotti's career is described in Vincent A. Lapomarda, *The Jesuit Heritage of New England* (Worcester: Holy Cross, 1977), 83. Two enlistees, Eugenio Vetromile and Almerico Zappone, subsequently left the order. See "Father Basil Pacciarini," *WL* 13 (1884): 409–12.; "Father Paresce," *WL* 33 (1904): 145.

26. Francesco De Vico (New York) to Ignazio Cugnoni, 5 Sept. 1848, Archives of the Pontifical Gregorian University, Rome, Italy. See also G. Stein, "Francesco de Vico e I suoi contributi alle scienze astronomiche," *Civiltà Cattolica* 2 (1949): 314–24.

27. Bernard McGuire, "Quaedam Verba Salutatoria ad Patres Fratresque Italos," ms., Georgetown, Nov. 1848, Marylandia 1009 – XIV-4, ARSI.

28. William L. Hamilton, "At Home with Robert Edison Fulton, Jr.," *New York Times*, 9 Mar. 2000; Antonio M. de Aldama, *An Introductory Commentary on the Constitutions*, trans. Aloysius J. Owen (St. Louis: Institute of Jesuit Sources, 1989), 249–51.

29. *Constitutions of the Society of Jesus*, 104, 172, 262, 278; John W. O'Malley, "To Travel to Any Part of the World: Jerónimo Nadal and the Jesuit Vocation," *Studies in the Spirituality of the Jesuits* 16 (Mar. 1984): 6–7, 14.

30. "Rules for Those on Missions" (1582) and "Rules for Pilgrims" (1582). English translations of these documents and their Latin originals are preserved in the Institute of the Society and were provided by the Institute of Jesuit Sources, St. Louis Univ., St. Louis, Mo. (hereafter IJS). For a nineteenth-century variant of these guidelines, see *Constitutiones Societatis Jesus, cum earum Declarationibus* (Avenione: Ex Typographia Francisci Seguin, 1827), 181–84 and 254–62.

31. *Consuetudines Provinciae Marylandiae Societatis Jesu* (Baltimore, Md.: Joannis Murphy, 1873), Woodstock Theological Center Library, Georgetown Univ., Washington, D.C. (hereafter WTCL).

32. Bangert, *History of the Society of Jesus*, 28; John W. Donohue, *Jesuit Education: An Essay on the Foundations of Its Idea* (New York: Fordham Univ. Press, 1963), 4.

33. Robert Bernard Martin, *Gerard Manley Hopkins: A Very Private Life* (London: Flamingo, 1992), 199.

34. Gerard M. Hopkins (St. Bueno's, St. Asaph, North Wales) to Mother, 23 Sept. 1876, in *Further Letters of Gerard Manley Hopkins, Including His Correspondence with Coventry Patmore*, ed. C. C. Abbot, 2nd ed. (London: Oxford Univ. Press, 1956), 142.

35. Rule 4, "Rules for Those on Missions," trans. from IJS.

36. Gazzoli (Paris) to Roothaan, 15 Oct. 1846, Mont. Sax. 1001-I-28, ARSI.

37. Rule 7, "Rules for Pilgrims," trans. from IJS; Gazzoli (Marseilles) to Roothaan, 21 Sept. 1846, Mont. Sax. 1001-I-27, ARSI; Gazzoli (Paris) to Roothaan, n.d. Oct. 1846, Mont. Sax. 1001-I-29, ARSI.

38. Efrén Sandoval, "Catholicism and Transnational Networks: Three Cases from the Monterrey-Houston Connection," in *Religion Across Borders*, 95.

39. Rules 1, 4, "Rules for Pilgrims," and Rules 5, 6, "Rules for Those on Missions," trans. from IJS.

40. Filippo Rappagliosi, *Memorie del P. Filippo Rappagliosi D.C.D.G. missionario apostolico nelle Montagne Rocciose*, ed. Victor Garrand (Rome: Bernardo Morini, 1879), 59–61, JOPA.

41. Palomba (Naples) to Gasparri, 15 July 1872; Palomba (Rome) to Gasparri, 17 Sept. 1869; Palomba (Naples) to Gasparri, 4 Feb. 1871; Palomba (Naples) to Gasparri, 6 Dec. 1871, ANPSJ.

42. Ferdinando Troyanek (New York) to Nicasio Mola, 24 Sept. 1889, ANPSJ.

43. Sanctes Lattanzi (Anagni, Italy) to Rappagliosi, 26 May 1877, JOPA.

44. Carmelo Giordano, "Memoirs: Dictated to Father A. D. Spearman, 1934–35," Giordano Papers, JOPA; Sebastiano [Palladino] to Lorenzo Palladino, 30 Aug. 1863, Palladino Papers, JOPA.

45. Francis Barnum, "Memoir of Fr. Giorda," Barnum Papers, AGU.

46. Francesco Maestro [?] (Padova) to Palladino, 30 Aug. 1863, Palladino Papers, JOP; Pieter Beckx, "A Letter of Very Reverend Peter Beckx on the Fruit to be Gathered from the Example of Blessed Peter Canisius and John Berchmans," in *Renovation Reading*, 386.

47. Roothaan, "On the Desire of Foreign Missions," in *Renovation Reading*, 239–42, 245.

48. Leon and Rebecca Grinberg, *Psychoanalytic Perspectives on Migration and Exile*, trans. Nancy Festinger (New Haven: Yale Univ. Press, 1989), 127.

49. Gazzoli (Paris) to Roothaan, 15 Oct. 1846, Mont. Sax. 1001-I-28, ARSI.

50. Antonio Goetz (Paris) to Roothaan, 17 Jan. 1847, Mont. Sax. 1001-I-31, ARSI.

51. Sanctus Lattanzi (Anagni, Italy) to Filippo Rappagliosi, 26 May 1877, JOPA.

52. Robert Lewis Stevenson, *The Amateur Emigrant*, intro. by Jonathan Raban (London: Hogarth Press, 1984), ii–iv.

53. Harold L. Stansell, *Regis on the Crest of the West* (Denver: Regis Educational Corporation, 1977), 35.

54. Joseph Keller (Baltimore, Md.) to Palomba, 29 Mar. 1871, ANPSJ.

55. Thomas J. Archdeacon, *Becoming American: An Ethnic History* (New York: Free Press, 1983) 35–36; Hayes, *Generation of Materialism*, 90.

56. Giacomo Diamare (New York) to Palomba, 31 Aug. 1873, ANPSJ.

57. Gregorio Mengarini, "Rocky Mountains," WL 17 (1888): 299; Mengarini (Georgetown) to Roothaan, 21 Sept. 1840, Mont. Sax. 1001-II-2, ARSI.

58. Salvatore Personè (Woodstock) to Davide Palomba, 26 Mar. 1871, ANPSJ.

59. Keller's account is found in Dooley, *Woodstock*, 15; Vincenzo Novelli (Woodstock) to Palomba, 17 Sept. 1874, ANPSJ.

60. Zerbinatti (St. Louis) to Roothaan, 18 May 1843, Mont. Sax. 1001-IV-9, ARSI; the account of the Carrozzini brothers is found in *WL* 6 (1877): 125–26.

61. Barnum, "Memoir of Fr. Giorda," Barnum Papers, AGU.

62. Paresce (New York) to Ferrante, 27 May 1867, ANPSJ. The scrupulous Jesuit Iovane [Jovino?] taught for a while at Woodstock, but was not successful, and hence he returned to Europe.

63. August Coemans, *Commentary on the Rules of the Society of Jesus: The Summary of the Constitutions, the Common Rules, the Rules of Modesty* (El Paso: Revista Católica Press, 1942), 80; Accolti (Italy?) to Beckx, June 1854, Californiana 1001-I-43, ARSI. Even though the trip was shortened thereby, the final leg through rough seas from Panama to San Francisco remained an ordeal. Pinto (El Paso) to Marra, 16 Apr. 1902, ANPSJ.

64. Rules 2, 3 and 5, "Rules for Pilgrims," trans. from ISJ; Zerbinatti (Marseilles) to Roothaan, 13 Feb. 1843, Mont. Sax. 1001-IV-3, ARSI; Mengarini (Georgetown) to Roothaan, 21 Sept. 1840, Mont. Sax. 1001-II-2, ARSI.

65. McNamee, *Willamette Interlude*, 94.

66. G. B. Ponte (Monaco) to Lorenzo Palladino, 18 Sept. 1863, Palladino Papers, JOPA; Rappagliosi, *Memorie*, 68, JOPA.

67. "Letter from Father Diomedi," *Letters and Notices* 10 (1875): 232.

68. Rappagliosi, *Memorie*, 68–69, JOPA; Donato Gasparri, "Versione della relazione scritta dal R.P. D. Gasparri in ispangnuolo del suo viaggio alla Missione del Nuovo Messico," [1867], 8, ANPSJ.

69. Marra (New York) to Antonio Stravino, 11 Nov. 1910, ANPSJ; Francesco Tomassini (Woodstock) to G. Mascalchi, 5 Sept. 1875, ANPSJ.

70. Rappagliosi, *Memorie*, 67, JOPA; "Father John Pinasco," *WL* 26 (1897): 487.

71. Ponziglione, "Reminiscences," *WL* 29 (1900): 272.

72. Diamare (New York) to Palomba, 31 Aug. 1873, ANPSJ; Mengarini (Georgetown) to Roothaan, 21 Sept. 1840, Mont. Sax. 1001-II-2, ARSI; Roothaan (Rome) to Accolti, 14 Nov. 1843, "Missiones [Summary of Father General's outgoing letters]: 25 Aug. 1840–14 Aug. 1850," ARSI.

73. Francis Barnum, "Incidents in the Lives of Our Saints," Francis Barnum, S.J., Papers, AGU; Francesco De Vico (New York) to Ignazio Cugnoni, 5 Sept. 1848, Archives of the Pontifical Gregorian University, Rome, Italy. See also G. Stein, "Francesco de Vico e I suoi contributi alle scienze astronomiche," *Civiltà Cattolica*, 2 (1949): 314–24.

74. G. B. Pianciani (Georgetown) to Roothaan, Mar. 1849, Marylandia, 1009-XIV-10, ARSI; Pianciani postscript to B. Sestini (Georgetown) to Roothaan, 15 Dec. 1848, Marylandia 1009-XIV-5a, ARSI; Michele S. Tomei (Georgetown) to Roothaan, 12 Mar. 1849, Marylandia, 1009-XIV-9, ARSI; Francesco de Maria (St. Louis) to Roothaan, 12 Aug. 1842, Mont. Sax. 1001-III-4, ARSI.

75. Donato Gasparri, "Versione della relazione scritta dal R.P. D. Gasparri in ispangnuolo del suo viaggio alla Missione del Nuovo Messico," [1867], 8, 10, ANPSJ; Ferdinando Troyanek (New York) to Carlo Torti, 24 Sept. 1889, ANPSJ; Galletti, *Molza*, 32.

76. Torquatus Armellini (Georgetown) to Charles Brooke, 8 Dec. 1848, "Foreign Correspondence," ABPSJ. Unhappy because the religious were scattered about in sev-

eral buildings and because the rules of cloister were frequently ignored, a French Jesuit told Roothaan that the Georgetown Jesuits should build a single structure that would house the entire religious community. See Antoine Rey (Georgetown) to Roothaan, 22 July 1842, Marylandia 1007-I-51, ARSI.

77. Galletti, *Molza*, 34.

78. Galletti, *Molza*, 40–41.

79. Galletti, *Molza*, 39–40; Charles C. Lancaster (Georgetown) to Maryland Provincial, 6 Mar. 1849, AMPSJ.

80. Gasparri, "Versione della relazione," 20–21, ANPSJ.

CHAPTER 4

1. "Calamo" [Sestini] (Georgetown) to Sopranis, 1859, Marylandia, 1008-VI-11, 20 to 21, ARSI.

2. Joseph Keller (Baltimore) to Davide Palomba, 30 Sept. 1873, ANPSJ. For an analysis of the importance of work for immigrants, see Grinberg, *Psychological Perspectives*, 96.

3. John Larkin (New York) to F. W. Gockeln, 10 July 1848, Larkin Correspondence, ANYPSJ.

4. Angelo Paresce (Frederick, Md.) to Charles Stonestreet, 25, 30 Aug. 1855, AMPSJ; Paresce (Frederick, Md.) to Stonestreet, 17 Mar. 1856, 224N8, AGU.

5. William S. Murphy [St. Louis?] to Stonestreet, 12 Dec. 1855, AMPSJ.

6. Robert Emmett Curran, *Georgetown University, Volume 1: From Academy to University, 1789–1889* (Washington, D.C.: Georgetown Univ. Press, 1993), 1:143. According to Joseph T. Durkin, *Georgetown University: First in the Nation's Capital* (Garden City, N.J.: Doubleday, 1964), 27, the impetus given to Georgetown College by the immigration of Italians and other professors from abroad "can scarcely be over stressed."

7. Curran, *Georgetown University*, 1:133, 397–98; "Catalogues [of Georgetown College], 1835–1836 to 1849–1850, Incl.," AGU; Joseph Havens Richards, S.J., "An Explanation in Reply to Some Recent Strictures," *WL* 26 (1897): 153.

8. Early (Worcester, Mass.) to Brocard, 15 Jan. 1849, "Maryland Letters 1810s–50s," ANYPSJ.

9. One of Russo's students at Boston College was William H. O'Connell, future cardinal of the American Catholic Church. See David R. Dunigan, *History of Boston College* (Milwaukee: Bruce Publishing, 1947), 128–29, 142–43.

10. Barnum, [Statement regarding Ciampi Papers, n.d.], A. Ciampi Papers, Catholic Historical Manuscript Collection, AGU; Ciampi's role at Holy Cross is described in Anthony J. Kuzniewski, *Thy Honored Name: A History of The College of the Holy Cross, 1843–1994* (Washington, D.C.: Catholic Univ. of America Press, 1999). The Piedmontese Jesuit John Francis Miege became the founding president of Detroit College after he retired as bishop of Indian Territory.

11. Nicholas Varga, *Baltimore's Loyola, Loyola's Baltimore, 1851–1986* (Baltimore: Maryland Historical Society, 1990), 71.

12. John J. Ryan, S.J., "Our Scholasticate: An Account of Its Growth and History to the Opening of Woodstock, 1805–1869," *WL* 33 (1904): 141.

13. Paresce (Baltimore) to Beckx, 12 Jan. 1869, Marylandia 1010-I-33, ARSI.

14. Dolan, *American Catholic Experience*, 79–82, 87–90; Lapomarda, *Jesuit Heritage*, 18. For a thorough analysis of Jesuit racism and African American slavery, see Thomas Murphy, *Jesuit Slaveholding in Maryland, 1717–1838* (New York: Routledge, 2001),187–88 , 216–19.

15. Brocard (Georgetown) to Roothaan, 12 Apr. 1850, Marylandia 1008-II-24, ARSI.

16. Brocard (Georgetown) to Roothaan, 17 Sept. 1849 Marylandia 1008-II-16; Ward (Baltimore) to Beckx, 17 Nov. 1854, Marylandia 1008-III-9, ARSI.

17. Pianciani (Georgetown) to Roothaan, n.d., Sept. 1849, Marylandia 1009-XIV-11; and Pianciani (Georgetown) to Roothaan, 4 Oct. 1849, Marylandia 1009-XIV-14, ARSI.

18. Brocard (Georgetown) to Roothaan, 12 Apr. 1850, Marylandia 1008-II-24, ARSI; Ignazio Ciampi (Georgetown) to Roothaan, 18 Feb. 1850, Marylandia 1009-XIV-16, ARSI; Benedetto Sestini (Georgetown) to Roothaan, 17 Sept. 1849, Marylandia 1009-XIV-12, ARSI.

19. *Catalogus Provinciae Marylandiae 1846* and following years.

20. Sixteenth-century Jesuit praises of Rome are found in Martin, *Mentality*, 19; E. I. Pubrick, S.J., "Triduum in Honour of B. John Berchmans at the Roman College: Letter from Father Pubrick," *Letters and Notices* 3 (1865–66): 84.

21. Robert F. McNamara, *The American College in Rome, 1855–1955* (Rochester, N.Y.: Christopher Press, 1956), 16–17.

22. J. B. Shaw (Boston) to Ryder, 5 Oct. 1848, Ryder Papers, AGU.

23. *Catalogus Provinciae Marylandiae Anno 1848* and *Catalogus Provinciae Marylandiae Anno 1849*, AMPSJ.

24. Frederick William Gockeln (La Val, France) to John Larkin, 7 Sept. 1848, Larkin Collection, ANYPSJ. Gockeln responded to complaints he had received about French Jesuits in New York.

25. Brocard (Georgetown) to Roothaan, 27 Feb. 1849, Marylandia 1008-II-11; 10 Nov. 1849, Marylandia 1008-II-19; and 6 Oct. 1849, Marylandia 1008-II-17, ARSI.

26. [Barnum], "The Catalogue of 1852," [one page insert in] *Catalogus Provinciae Marylandiae Societatis Iesu, Ineunte Anno 1853* (Baltimore, 1853), GTWN; and Curran, *Georgetown University*, 137.

27. James A. Ward (Baltimore) to Beckx, 17 Nov. 1854, Marylandia 1008-III-9, ARSI.

28. Filippo Sacchi (Georgetown) to Roothaan, 23 Jan. 1839, Marylandia 1007-III-4, ARSI.

29. Molza in Brocard (Georgetown) to Sopranis, 19 Feb. 1850, Marylandia, 1009-XI-32, ARSI.

30. "Calamo" [Sestini] (Georgetown) to Sopranis, 1859, Marylandia, 1008-VI-9 to 21, ARSI.

31. Grassi, "Catholic Religion," *WL* 11 (1882): 241–42; Jean François Abbadie (Grand Couteau) to Roothaan, 23 Mar. 1839, in Cornelius M. Buckley, *Nicholas Point, S.J.: His Life and Northwest Indian Chronicles* (Chicago: Loyola Univ. Press, 1989), 155; Roothaan (Rome) to Sopranis, 9 Jan. 1851, Marylandia 1009-XI-17, ARSI; Galletti, *Molza*, 44, 46.

32. Complaints about Gubitosi in John Gaffney (Worcester, Mass.) to Paresce, 30 Apr. 1863; and John Clark (Worcester, Mass.) to Paresce, 17 Nov. 1863, AMPSJ.

33. Vetromile's antics described in John Bapst (Bangor, Maine) to Maryland Provincial, 20 July 1855, AMPSJ; Mazzella (Woodstock, Md.) to Palomba, 25 June 1876, ANPSJ.

34. Verhagen (Georgetown) to McElroy, 4 Feb. 1847, AMPSJ; Volpe, *I Gesuiti*, 3:286.

35. Statistics from *Catalogus Sociorum et Officiorum Provinciae Neapolitanae Societatis Iesu Ineunte Anno 1860* (Naples, 1860) and *Catalogus Provinciae Romanae Societatis Iesu Ineunte Anno 1847*, ARSI.

36. "Calamo" [Sestini] (Georgetown) to Sopranis, 1859, Marylandia, 1008-VI-9 to 21, ARSI.

37. Hughes cited in Larkin (New York) to Gockeln, 15 May 1849, Larkin Correspondence, ANYPSJ.

38. Dolan, *American Catholic Experience*, 123.

39. McElroy, Ryder, and Vespri (Frederick, Md.) to Grassi, 17 June 1843, Marylandia 1007-II-14, ARSI. One of the reasons for ending Jesuit slaveholding in 1838 had been to shift the Marylanders' ministry to the care of urban whites, but that transition was slow in coming. On the link between the termination of chattel slavery and new ministries, see Murphy, *Jesuit Slaveholding*, 187–92.

40. McElroy (Boston) to Beckx, 27 Sept. 1854, Marylandia 1009-XIX-14, ARSI.

41. Beckx (Rome) to Sopranis, 8 Oct. 1859, Marylandia 1008-Sopranis 1-V-1, ARSI.

42. Gilbert Joseph Garraghan, *Jesuits of the Middle United States* (New York: America Press, 1938), 1:591n. His initial experience as tertian master had persuaded Sopranis that Americans "will not adjust themselves, unlike the Italians," to the challenges of a thirty-day retreat and tertianship. Unused to discipline, they "always look upon themselves as missionaries," and hence seek exceptions to any and all regulations. See Sopranis (Frederick, Md.) to Roothaan, 27 Dec. 1849, Marylandia 1009-XI-6, ARSI. On the other hand, Sopranis believed that a properly trained native-born priest could better inculcate the spirit of the Society in novices than could a foreigner. Thus, in 1850 he promoted, albeit unsuccessfully, James Ward, an American, to become Maryland novice master rather than the Neapolitan Angelo Paresce. See Sopranis (Frederick, Md.) to Roothaan, 14 Jan. 1850, Marylandia 1009-XI-9, ARSI.

43. "Calamo" [Sestini] (Georgetown) to Sopranis, 1859, Marylandia, 1008-VI-11, 20 to 21, ARSI.

44. "Calamo" [Sestini] (Georgetown) to Sopranis, 1859, Marylandia 1008-VI-13 to 17, ARSI.

45. "Calamo" [Sestini] (Georgetown) to Sopranis, 1859, Marylandia, 1008-VI-9 to 10, and 1008-VI-14 to 17, ARSI.

46. Robert Emmett Curran, *American Jesuit Spirituality: The Maryland Tradition, 1634–1900* (New York: Paulist Press, 1988), 24.

47. Francis X. Talbot, S.J., *Jesuit Education in Philadelphia: St. Joseph's College, 1851–1926* (Philadelphia: Saint Joseph's College, 1927), 65–66.

48. Curran, *American Jesuit Spirituality*, 21; Dooley, *Woodstock and Its Makers*, 74.

49. Villiger (Worcester, Mass.) to Beckx, 21 May 1859, Marylandia 1008-IV-8; see also Curran, *American Jesuit Spirituality*, 32; Calamo [Sestini] (Georgetown) to Sopranis, 1859, Marylandia 1008-VI-9 to 21, ARSI.

50. Antonio Wiesend (Georgetown) to Jean Muller, 13 Mar. 1848, Thomas F. Mulledy Papers, Catholic Historical Manuscripts Collection, AGU.

51. Murphy [St. Louis?] to Stonestreet, 12 Dec. 1855, AMPSJ; Curran, *American Jesuit Spirituality*, 25.

52. Eliot and Bedini in John Tracy Ellis, "Short History of Seminary Education: II — Trent to Today," in *Seminary Education in a Time of Change*, ed. James Michael Lee and Louis J. Putz (Notre Dame: Fides, 1965), 58–59, 65n62; Sydney E. Ahlstrom, *A Religious History of the American People* (New Haven: Yale Univ. Press, 1972), 735–38.

53. Antoine Rey (Georgetown) to Roothaan, 22 July 1842, Marylandia 1007-I-51, ARSI.

54. Francis Vespre (Georgetown) to Roothaan, 16 Jan. 1841, Marylandia 1007-I-33, ARSI; Curran, *Georgetown University*, 141.

55. Sestini (Georgetown) to Roothaan, 6 July 1852, Marylandia 1008-II-53, ARSI.

56. McElroy to Stonestreet, 21 July 1847, in "The Novitiate in Maryland," *WL* 44 (1915): 9–10.

57. Dooley, *Woodstock and Its Makers*, 151.

58. Maréchal in John Tracy Ellis, "The Formation of the American Priest: An Historical Perspective," in *The Catholic Priest in the United States: Historical Investigations*, ed. John Tracy Ellis (Collegeville, Minn.: Saint John's Univ. Press, 1971), 19, 32.

59. Augustus Langcake, "Letter from Mr. Langcake, St. John's College, Fordham, 1 Dec. 1863," *Letters and Notices* 2 (1864): 65–66.

60. John T. McGreevy, *Catholicism and American Freedom: A History* (New York: W. W. Norton, 2003), 107.

61. Dunigan, *History of Boston College*, 57–58; Beckx to Sopranis, 25 Sept. 1861, [Summary of Father General's Correspondence: Missions of the English Assistancy, 1 Nov. 1861–6 Oct. 1891], ARSI; G. J. Garraghan, "The Project of a Common Scholasticate for the Society of Jesus in North America," *Archivum Historicum Societatis Iesu* 2 (1933): 1–10.

62. Paresce (Baltimore) to Beckx, 27 Dec. 1861, Marylandia 1009-XX-5, ARSI.

63. An additional 177 acres were annexed to the original tract in 1880. See [Ryan], "Woodstock College," 9, AGU. For an account of the opening of the college, see "North America," *Letters and Notices* 7 (1870): 50–58.

64. Paresce (Baltimore) to Beckx, n.d. May 1865, Marylandia 1010-XXV-1.

65. Roothaan, "A Letter Upon Prosperity and the Dangers that Attend it," in *Select Letters*, 265.

66. "P. Giovanni Battista Guida," in *LEPN, 1914–1920*, 152–53. See also *WL* 49 (1920): 122–26; on Catholics and the Civil War, see McGreevy, *Catholicism and American Freedom*, 66–75.

67. Paresce (Baltimore) to Beckx, 27 Dec. 1861, Marylandia 1009-XX-5; and Paresce (Baltimore) to Beckx, n.d. May 1865, Marylandia 1010-XXV-1, ARSI.

68. Joseph M. White, "The Diocesan Seminary and the Community of Faith," *U.S. Catholic Historian* 11 (1993): 1–20; Joseph M. White, *The Diocesan Seminary in the United States: A History from the 1870s to the Present* (Notre Dame: Univ. of Notre Dame Press, 1989), 67–85.

69. John L. Ciani, "Across a Wide Ocean: Salvatore Maria Brandi, S.J., and the 'Civiltà Cattolica,' from Americanism to Modernism, 1891–1914" (Ph.D. diss., Univ. of Virginia, 1992), 66–67. In the pages that follow, I rely heavily upon Ciani's dissertation for my analysis of early Woodstock College.

70. F. X. Tomassini (Las Vegas, N.Mex.) to Piccirillo, 1 Feb 1880, Piccirillo Papers, WCA. See also "Father Charles Piccirillo; a Sketch," *WL* 17 (1888): 339–50.

71. Dooley, *Woodstock and Its Makers*, 23, 47.

72. "North America," *Letters and Notices* 7 (1870): 55.

73. Robert I. Gannon, *Up to the Present: The Story of Fordham* (Garden City, N.J.: Doubleday, 1967), 95.

74. Dooley, *Woodstock and Its Makers*, 48; Domenico Pantanella (Woodstock) to Palomba, 8 Oct. 1872, ANPSJ, in Ciani, "Across a Wide Ocean," 57.

75. Camillo Mazzella (Woodstock) to Palomba, 25 June 1876, ANPSJ. The college was relocated to New York City in 1969.

76. "Maryland: Letter from Brother Van Rensselaer," *Letters and Notices* 15 (1882): 200–203; Dooley, *Woodstock and Its Makers*, 8, 52. "Many poor Italians have arrived in New York, peasants who were dying of starvation," wrote Joseph Keller. "Fr. Paresce went there and brought several back to work at Woodstock and they are happy there." See Keller (Baltimore) to Palomba, 2 Jan. 1873, ANPSJ.

77. Sopranis (Rome) to Beckx, 25 Sept. 1861, Marylandia 1008-Sopranis 1-IV-2, ARSI; Paresce (Baltimore) to Francisco Ferrante, 8 Jan. 1867, ANPSJ; Paresce (Baltimore) to Beckx, n.d., May 1865, Marylandia 1010-XXV-1, ARSI.

78. Dooley, *Woodstock and Its Makers*, 11.

79. Pantanella (Woodstock) to Palomba, 8 Dec. 1873, ANPSJ.

80. Ciani, "Across a Wide Ocean," 55; Dooley, *Woodstock and Its Makers*, 85, 137–38; "Father Aloysius Sabetti," *WL* 29 (1900): 216–23.

81. Mazzella (Woodstock) to Beckx, 21 May 1870, Marylandia 1010-XXV-6, ARSI; Mazzella (Woodstock) to Palomba, 25 June 1876, ANPSJ.

82. "Archbishop Satolli at Woodstock," *WL* 19 (1890): 5.

83. Dunigan, *History of Boston College*, 54; Wilfred P. Schoenberg, *Jesuit Mission Presses in the Pacific Northwest: A History and Bibliography of Imprints, 1876–1899* (Portland, Ore.: Champoeg Press, 1957) 42–43; Schoenberg, *Paths to the Northwest*, 200.

84. Ciani, "Across a Wide Ocean," 65. See also Gerald McCool, *Catholic Theology in the Nineteenth Century: The Quest for a Unitary Method* (New York: Seabury Press, 1967), 27.

85. McCool, *Catholic Theology*, 238; "Father Aloysius Sabetti; An Autobiography with Reminiscences of His Former Pupils," *WL* 29 (1900): 216, 227.

86. Dooley, *Woodstock and Its Makers*, 140–41.

87. Ibid., 29; "Cardinal Mazzella," *WL* 15 (1866): 289–90.

88. Camillo Mazzella, *Praelectiones scholastico-dogmaticae de virtutibus infusis in genere et de virtutibus theologicis in specie, quas in Seminario Soc. Jesu ad Woodstock habuit an. 1870–71* (Woodstock, Md.: Woodstock College Press, 1870), i; John L. Morrison, "A History of American Catholic Opinion on the Theory of Evolution, 1859–1950" (Ph.D. diss., Univ. of Missouri, 1951), 92–93.

89. Camillo Mazzella, *De religione et ecclesia: praelectiones scholastico-dogmaticae quas in collegio SS. Cordis ad Woodstock habuit Ann. 1875–6* (Woodstock, Md.: Woodstock College Press, 1876), in Ciani, "Across a Wide Ocean," 90–93.

90. Maguire in John Gilmary Shea, *Memorial of the First Centenary of Georgetown College, D.C., Comprising a History of Georgetown University by John Gilmary Shea, LL.D., and an Account of the Centennial Celebration by a Member of the Faculty* (Washington, D.C.: P. F. Collier, 1891), 231.

91. Ciani, "Across a Wide Ocean," 108–9.

92. Ibid.

93. Piccirillo (Woodstock) to Canger, 11 Mar. 1884, ANPSJ; Congiato (San Jose) to Robert Fulton, 28 Nov. 1886, Marylandia 1010-XXV-17, ARSI. Mazzella cautioned Italian officials not to promote or "to publicize what our Neapolitan Jesuits have done in this province," because "what would cause satisfaction in Naples would cause dissatisfaction here." See Mazzella (Philadelphia) to Palomba, 12 Apr. 1876, ANPSJ.

94. Piccirillo (Woodstock) to Canger, 4 Apr. 1887, ANPSJ, in Ciani, "Across a Wide Ocean," 65. That Americans were ostracized from teaching was confirmed by the Maryland provincial. It has been the policy that "we would have no American professors in Woodstock," wrote Robert Fulton, "unless we were compelled to get them by the withdrawal of the European professors." See Fulton (Baltimore) to Anderledy, 11 Mar 1886, Marylandia 1010-IV-10, ARSI.

95. Dooley, *Woodstock and Its Makers*, 152; [Ryan], "Woodstock College," 2, AGU.

96. [Ryan], "Woodstock College," 3, AGU; Sabetti (Woodstock) to Anderledy, 14 Oct. 1884, Marylandia 1010-XXV-12, ARSI.

97. Curran, *American Jesuit Spirituality*, 35; Sabetti (Woodstock) to Vioni, 14 Dec. 1884, ANPSJ.

98. Keller (Baltimore) to Palomba, 3 Aug. 1872, and 20 Sept. 1872, ANPSJ. On American Jesuit observance of the rules, see also Fulton (New York) to Anderledy, 1 June 1884, Marylandia 1010-IV-3, ARSI.

99. A. T. Tisdall (Frederick, Md.) to Piccirillo, 22 Feb. 1883, Piccirillo Papers, WCA.

100. Garraghan, *Jesuits*, 1:645.

101. McDonough, *Men Astutely Trained*, 153–56; McGreevy, *Catholicism and American Freedom*, 107.

102. Maguire, "Notes," AGU; Richards, "An Explanation," *WL* 26 (1897): 149, 153.

103. Ellis, "Formation," 28, 32–33, 40–44.

104. McCool, *Catholic Theology*, 239–40.

105. Sabetti (Woodstock) to Vioni, 13 Sept. 1882, ANPSJ; *WL* 25 (1896): 332.

106. Ciravegna (Monaco) to Beckx, 18 Apr. 1870, Taur. 1010-III-11, ARSI; Weckx (Santa Clara) to Mola, n.d. June 1888, ANPSJ.

CHAPTER 5

1. William S. Murphy (St. Louis?) to Stonestreet, 12 Dec. 1855, AMPSJ.

2. W. H. Brands, *The Age of Gold: The California Gold Rush and the New American Dream* (New York: Doubleday, 2002), 22.

3. Mary McDougall Gordon, ed., *Overland to California with the Pioneer Line: The Gold Rush Diary of Bernard J. Reid* (Palo Alto: Stanford Univ. Press, 1983), 24, 170, and passim.

4. J. S. Holliday, *The World Rushed In: The California Gold Rush Experience* (New York: Simon & Schuster, 1981).

5. On the early missions, see Burns, *Jesuits and the Indian Wars*, 42–60.

6. De Smet (St. Louis) to Roothaan, 7 Feb. 1841, Mont. Sax. 1001-II-4, ARSI; Hiram Martin Chittenden and Alfred Talbot Richardson, *Life, Letters and Travels of Father De Smet* (New York: Arno Press and the New York Times, 1969), 1:306.

7. De Smet (St. Louis) to Roothaan, 7 Feb. 1841, Mont. Sax. 1001-II-4, ARSI; Chittenden and Richardson, *De Smet*, 1:306, 329. See also Harrod, *Mission Among the Blackfeet*, 34.

8. Chittenden and Richardson, *De Smet*, 1:327. De Smet's equally ingenuous co-worker, Gregorio Mengarini, reported the people's "ancient superstitions" had faded, "so much so that I can say without fear of exaggeration that some of them are approaching religious perfection." See Mengarini (Vancouver) to Roothaan, 26 Sept. 1844, Mont. Sax. 1001-VII-2, ARSI.

9. Roothaan to De Smet, 15 Apr. 1852, in Garraghan, *Jesuits*, 2:248.

10. Nobili (Santa Clara) to Roothaan, 20 July 1851, Calif. 1001-I-7, ARSI; Roothaan to De Smet, 15 Apr. 1852, in Garraghan, *Jesuits*, 2:438.

11. American Home Missionary Society, *Annual Report* (New York, 1850), 92; Nobili (Santa Clara) to Roothaan, 20 July 1851, Calif. 1001-I-7, ARSI.

12. Accolti (n.p.) to Roothaan, 24 May 1849, in Garraghan, *Jesuits*, 2:396–97.

13. John B. McGloin, "The California Catholic Church in Transition, 1846–1850," *California Historical Society Quarterly* 42 (March 1963): 46; Alemany to the "President of the Central Council of the Work for the Propagation of the Faith," San Francisco, 19 July 1851, in John B. McGloin, *California's First Archbishop: The Life of Joseph Sadoc Alemany, O.P., 1814–1888* (New York: Herder & Herder, 1966), 125.

14. James Alexander Forbes (Santa Clara, Calif.) to Accolti, 16 May 1852, and 14 Sept. 1852, "Letter Book," vol. 1, California State Library, Sacramento, Calif. (hereafter CSL).

15. Accolti (Santa Clara) to Pascal Richard, 18 May 1853, Archives Deschatelets, Scholasticat St. Joseph, Ottawa, Canada; and Accolti, "Osservazioni sopra una lettera dall'Arcivo. di San Francisco, Cal., al Rdo. P. Felice, S.J., Visitatore in data del 23 Dicembre 1863," ACPSJ.

16. Beckx announced the Piedmontese decision to assume responsibility for the California and Rocky Mountain missions in a letter sent to William Stack Murphy, provincial of the Missouri Jesuits, on 30 June 1854. See John B. McGloin, "Michael Accolti, Gold Rush Padre and Founder of the California Jesuits," *Archivum Historicum Societatis Iesu* 20 (1951): 314.

17. "The Dispersed Province of Turin," *Letters and Notices* 1 (1862–63): 296–97, ARSI.

18. Dolores Liptak, *Immigrants and Their Church* (New York: Macmillan, 1989), 186.

19. Statistics found in *Catalogus Dispersae Provinciae Neapolitanae Societatis Iesu Ineunte Anno 1868* (Rome: Typis Bernardi Morini), ARSI.

20. Donato M. Gasparri, "Versione della relazione scritta dal R. P. D. Gasparri in ispagnuolo del suo viaggio alla Missione del Nuovo-Messico," ANPSJ. Gasparri's account of the expedition has been translated and published by J. Manuel Espinosa in "Account of the First Jesuit Missionary Journey Across the Plains to New Mexico," *Mid-America* 20 (1938): 51–62.

21. "St. Joseph's College, Bardstown, Ky.," *WL* 26 (1897): 102; Congiato (Santa Clara) to Stonestreet, 18 Aug. 1856, AMPSJ. See also Congiato (Bardstown, Ky.) to Stonestreet, 27 Sept. 1854, AMPSJ. When Sestini, teaching at Georgetown, heard of the deal, he was furious. Stonestreet had effected a "deception" and "fraud" worthy of the "Turks and savages," he complained to Sopranis, and Cicaterri had been "tossed out like a dog." See "Calamo" [Sestini] (Georgetown) to Sopranis, ca. 1859, Marylandia 1008-VI-9 to 21, ARSI. A year earlier, however, Angelo Paresce, Cicaterri's superior at the Maryland novitiate, indicated he would "rejoice" at the prospect of surrendering the troublesome Cicaterri to another assignment. See Paresce (Frederick, Md.) to Stonestreet, 30 Aug. 1855, AMPSJ.

22. John Bapst (Boston) to Paresce, 3 Aug. 1863, AMPSJ.

23. William S. Murphy (St. Louis?) to Stonestreet, 12 Dec. 1855, AMPSJ.

24. De Smet (St. Louis, Mo.) to George Carrell, 14 May 1850, De Smetiana IX-D-1, Jesuit Missouri Province Archives, Jesuit Provincial Office, St. Louis, Mo. (hereafter JMPA).

25. Keller (Baltimore) to Palomba, 11 Aug. 1874, ANPSJ.

26. Mazzella (Woodstock) to Palomba, 30 Oct. 1875, ANPSJ; Gentile (Las Vegas) to Michele Musto, 9 Nov. 1881, ANPSJ.

27. Palomba (Naples) to Gasparri, 26 July 1872, ANPSJ.

28. Pantanella (Woodstock) to Mascalchi, 26 Sept. 1879, ANPSJ.

29. Keller (Baltimore) to Palomba, 18 Nov. 1871, ANPSJ; Mazzella (Woodstock) to Mascalchi, 11 May 1877, ANPSJ.

30. Francis Barnum, "Concerning Fr. Tosi," Barnum Papers, AGU.

31. Congiato (Bardstown, Ky.) to Stonestreet, 27 Sept. 1854 (222B12), AMPSJ; Villiger (Santa Clara) to Maryland Provincial, 22 Aug. 1861, ACPSJ.

32. Paresce in P. P. Gonella (Monaco) to Beckx, 23 Feb. 1867, Taur. 1010-II-9, ARSI.

33. Baldassare (Woodstock) to Mascalchi, 16 July and 21 Sept. 1877, ANPSJ; Pantanella (Woodstock) to Mascalchi, 26 Sept. 1879, ANPSJ.

34. Murphy (St. Louis) to Beckx, 25 Feb. 1855, Missouriana 1005-II-35, ARSI; G. M. Ciravegna (Torino) to Beckx, 20 Aug. 1870, Taur. 1010-III-15, ARSI. Barbero sought readmission to the order many years later.

35. Paresce (Baltimore) to Palomba, 20 Apr. 1869, ANPSJ; Keller (Baltimore) to Palomba, 17 July 1870, ANPSJ. Although Keller advised that both Guida and

Gubitosi be allowed to remain in the East, in fact, the pair ended up in the Southwest; Carlo Ferrari (Woodstock) to Mascalchi, 24 Aug. 1879, ANPSJ.

36. Sabetti (Woodstock) to Giovanni Vioni, 16 Oct. 1882; and Sabetti (Woodstock) to Giovanni Vioni, 13 Sept. 1882, ANPSJ.

37. Palomba (Naples) to Gasparri, 3 July 1873, ANPSJ.

38. Marra (New York) to Stravino, 12 Nov. 1910, ANPSJ; Lopinto (Fordham) to Palomba, 5 Mar. 1875, ANPSJ.

39. Marigliano (Woodstock) to Palomba, 23 Sept. 1874, ANPSJ; Capilupi (Baltimore) to Palomba, 18 Dec. 1874, ANPSJ.

40. Sabetti (Woodstock) to Giovanni Vioni, 13 Sept. 1882, ANPSJ; Sabetti (Woodstock) to Degni, n.d., ca. 1884, ANPSJ.

41. [Michael Hughes?], "New Mexico," *WL* 12 (1883): 299; F. X. Maffei (Conejos, N.Mex.) to Palomba, 10 Mar. 1873, ANPSJ.

42. Palomba (Tarragon) to Gasparri, 14 Mar. [1867?], ANPSJ; Mazzella (Woodstock) to Gaietano Mascalchi, 25 Apr. 1878, ANPSJ; Baldassare (Albuquerque) to Mascalchi, 11 Sept. 1877, ANPSJ; Gentile (Las Vegas) to Vioni, 8 Oct. 1883, ANPSJ.

43. Mazzella (Woodstock) to Mascalchi, 25 May 1878, ANPSJ. Mazella (Rome) to Vioni, 6 June 1882, and M. M. Musto addendum to Mazzella letter, ANPSJ; "Consulte, 1871–1900," meeting minutes for Apr. 28, 1879, ANPSJ.

44. Ferrari (Woodstock) to Mascalchi, 24 Aug. 1879, ANPSJ.

45. Paresce (Woodstock) to Palomba, 12 July 1872, ANPSJ; Keller (Baltimore) to Palomba, 11 Aug. 1874, ANPSJ; Paresce (Woodstock) to Palomba, 11 Dec. 1872, ANPSJ.

46. O'Malley, "Northwest Blackrobe," JOPA. The remark about Methodist applicants is found in Robert J. Loewenberg, *Equality on the Oregon Frontier: Jason Lee and the Methodist Mission, 1834–43* (Seattle: Univ. of Washington, 1976), 126.

47. Ponza (Genoa) to Beckx, 10 Mar. 1859, Calif. 1001-III-2, ARSI. Affranchino taught at both St. Ignatius and Santa Clara colleges, and published a Mass in G for organ and piano. He died at an early age at Santa Clara in 1879.

48. Parodi, "Memoirs," JOPA; Schoenberg, *Paths to the Northwest*, 144.

49. Mengarini, "Rocky Mountains," *WL* 17 (1888): 298; "Sketch of St. Peter's Mission," JOPA.

50. Joseph Treca to Cataldo, 11 Apr. 1887, Treca Papers, JOPA. See also "Epistolae Missiones Petentium" Prov. Taur. 1012-XIII-1 to 36, ARSI; Aloysius Soer, "Good Done and to Be Done in the Far West," JOPA; Joseph Brucker (Littlehampton, England) to Cataldo, 11 May 1889, JOPA; Palomba (Naples) to Gasparri, 12 Nov. 1870, ANPSJ.

51. Carmelo Giordano, "Memoirs: Dictation to Spearman," Giordano Papers, JOPA; Aloysius Roccati, "Interview by Wilfred Schoenberg, S.J.," JOPA.

52. Grassi (San Francisco) to Beckx, 3 Apr. 1860, Mont. Sax. 1002-III-7a, ARSI; Mengarini (St. Louis) to Roothaan, Mont. Sax. 1001-II-7, ARSI; Palomba (Naples) to Gasparri, 12 Mar. 1872, ANPSJ.

53. Palladino, *Indian and White*, 218–29; Schoenberg, *Paths to the Northwest*, 115.

54. P. Gonella (Monaco) to Beckx, 20 Feb. 1869, Taur. 1010-II-13, ARSI;

Gonella (Monaco) to Beckx, 19 June 1869, Taur. 1010-II-15, ARSI; Mackin, "Wanderings," JOPA. Parodi, who traveled to America with Canestrelli, claimed that the latter was also inspired by the death of Rappagliosi. See Parodi, "Memoirs," JOPA.

55. Paresce (Baltimore) to Palomba, 30 July 1869; Paresce (New York) to Palomba, 12 Feb. 1869, ANPSJ; Paresce (Woodstock) to Palomba, 5 Sept. 1871, ANPSJ.

56. Paresce (Baltimore) to Palomba, 30 July 1869; Paresce (New York) to Palomba, 12 Feb. 1869, ANPSJ; Paresce (Woodstock) to Palomba, 5 Sept. 1871, ANPSJ.

57. Cataldo (n.p.) to Tosi, 1 Mar. 1893, Miss. Mon. Sax. 1003-I-47, ARSI; Caruana (De Smet, Idaho) to Luis Martín, 22 July 1897, "Historia Missionis Yakima," 1897, 1003-VIII, ARSI; Congiato (San Francisco) to Sopranis, n.d. Apr. 1866, Calif. 1001-VI-6, ARSI.

58. Regarding Leggio, see Marra (Pueblo, Colo.) to Canger, 4 Nov. 1889, ANPSJ; Schiffini is described in Marra (Pueblo, Colo.) to Canger, 25 Mar. 1890, ANPSJ; the assessment of Ferrari is in Marra (Las Vegas) to Mola, 18 Aug. 1888, ANPSJ.

59. Gerald McKevitt, " 'The Jump That Saved the Rocky Mountain Mission': Jesuit Recruitment and the Pacific Northwest," *Pacific Historical Review* 55 (Aug. 1986): 449. Statistics comparing dropout rates are based on the mission's membership as recorded in "Catalogus Primus, 1892–1895," JOPA.

60. For a comparison of gender differences during travel, see Lillian Schlissel, *Women's Diaries of the Westward Journey* (New York: Schocken Books, 1992).

61. Ponziglione, "Reminiscences," WL 29 (1900): 272; Keller (Baltimore) to Palomba, 29 Mar. 1871, ANPSJ.

62. Schoenberg, *Paths to the Northwest*, 29.

63. James M. C. Beshor [Bouchard] (Santa Clara) to Maryland provincial, 23 Aug. 1861 (228M11), AMPSJ; Antonio Cichi (Santa Clara) to Paresce, 10 Sept. 1862 (228M15), AMPSJ.

64. Cataldo, "Notes for Lectures," ca. 1900, Cataldo Papers, JOPA; O'Malley, "Brief Biography of Cataldo," Cataldo Papers, JOPA.

65. "[Dictation] from Fr. Caruana through Fr. J. Post, Feb. 1, 1912," Caruana Papers, JOPA.

66. "Extract from a Letter of Father Bayma," *Letters and Notices* 7 (1870): 58.

67. Rappagliosi, *Memorie*, 74–75, JOPA.

68. Ibid., 75, JOPA.

69. Ibid., 77, JOPA.

70. Francesco Saverio Maffei (Woodstock) to Palomba, 9 Jan. 1873, and Maffei (Conejos, Colo.) to Palomba, 10 Mar. 1873, ANPSJ.

71. "New Mexico," WL 12 (1883): 301–2; "New Mexico," WL 13 (1884): 42.

72. Rolle, *Immigrant Upraised*, 149; Mengarini, "Memoirs," WL 17 (1888): 304–6; "Extract from a Letter of Father Bayma," *Letters and Notices* 7 (1870): 58.

73. Mengarini, "Memoirs," WL 17 (1888): 304–6; Rappagliosi, *Memorie*, 89.

74. Mackin, "Wanderings," 2, JOPA.

75. Personè (Albuquerque) to Palomba, 21 Nov. 1869, ANPSJ; Congiato (Santa Clara) to Roothaan, 18 Apr. 1856, Calif. 1001-II-4, ARSI.

76. Benham in Sarah Deutsch, *No Separate Refuge: Culture, Class, and Gender of an Anglo-Hispanic Frontier in the American Southwest, 1880–1940* (New York: Oxford Univ. Press, 1987), 63; Paresce (Baltimore) to Beckx, 29 June 1869, ANPSJ; F. X. Maffei (Conejos, Colo.) to Palomba, 10 Mar. 1873, ANPSJ; "New Mexico," *WL* 12 (1883): 301.

77. Accolti, "Osservazioni," 1863, ACPSJ; Accolti to Roothaan, 28 Mar. 1850, in Garraghan, *Jesuits*, 2:407.

78. "Extract from a Letter of Father Bayma, *Letters and Notices* 7 (1870): 59–60.

79. Michael O'Malley, "English translation of Victor Garrand, *Le Père Augustine Laure* (1895)," JOPA; Giordano, "Memoirs; Dictation to Spearman," Giordano Papers, JOPA.

80. Cataldo, "Spokane Mission," Cataldo Papers, JOPA; and Crosby, "Kuailks," JOPA; Rappagliosi, *Memorie*, 8, JOPA.

81. Cataldo, "Spokane Mission," Cataldo Papers, JOPA.

82. Ibid.

83. Rappagliosi, *Memorie*, 94–95, JOPA.

84. Rolle, *Immigrant Upraised*, 336–37.

85. Paresce (New York) to Palomba, 12 Feb. 1869, ANPSJ.

CHAPTER 6

1. Barcelò (Helena) to Brouillet, 14 Sept. 1881, Bureau of Catholic Indian Missions Records, Archives, Marquette University, Milwaukee, Wis. (hereafter BCIM), 10/9.

2. Buckley, *Point*, 86; Eleanor C. Donnelly, *A Memoir of Father Felix Joseph Barbelin, S.J., that Great and Good Son of St. Ignatius Loyola, who lived and labored for more than Thirty-one Years at Old St. Joseph's Church, Philadelphia* (Philadelphia: St. Joseph's Church, 1886), 23.

3. From the 1841 founding of the mission until the severance of its ties with Italy in 1909, all but four of its eleven superiors were Italian. The Jesuits' urban California Mission consistently drew larger numbers of missionaries, but their national origins were more homogeneous. The first ten presidents of Santa Clara College, for example, were all, save one, Italians. By contrast, their counterparts at Gonzaga College were much more diverse, three having come from Germany, three from France, and one each from Belgium, Canada, Italy, and the United States. Membership statistics found in "Catalogus Primus, Anno 1892–95, Missio Mont. Saxos.," Provincial Papers: Histories, JOPA.

4. Burns, *Jesuits and the Indian Wars*, 54–57; Carriker, "Cataldo," in *Churchmen and the Western Indians*, 137; Francis Paul Prucha, *American Indian Policy in Crisis: Christian Reformers and the Indian 1865–1900* (Norman: Univ. of Oklahoma Press, 1976), 158–59; Loewenberg, *Equality on the Oregon Frontier*, 96–97; McKevitt, " 'The Jump that Saved the Rocky Mountain Mission,' " *Pacific Historical Review* 55 (1986): 447.

5. Congiato (Champoeg, Ore.) to Wernz, 10 Dec. 1858, Mont. Sax. 1002-III-1, ARSI.

6. Grassi (Colville) to Beckx, 14 Nov. 1868, Mont. Sax. 1002-VI-3, ARSI; Schoenberg, *Paths to the Northwest*, 75.

7. Giorda (Stevensville, Mont.) to Beckx, 6 Jan. 1870, Mont. Sax. 1002-VII-5b, ARSI; Beckx (Rome) to Giorda, 21 Nov. 1869, Excerpts from Letters of Father General, etc., Joset Papers, JOPA; Van Gorp (Spokane) to Martín, 30 Aug. 1893, Mont. Sax. 1003-II-4, ARSI.

8. Alexander Diomedi, *Sketches of Indian Life in the Pacific Northwest* (Fairfield, Wash.: Ye Galleon Press, 1978), 60, 81.

9. Dolan, *American Catholic Experience*, 173–74; for a fuller analysis of conversion strategies, see Gerald McKevitt, "The Art of Conversion: Jesuits and Flatheads in Nineteenth-Century Montana," *U.S. Catholic Historian* 12 (1994): 49–64; Szasz, ed., *Between Indian and White Worlds*, 16–17.

10. Axtell, *Invasion Within*, 14.

11. [Joseph Joset], "Women in the Different Tribes," Joset Papers, JOPA; Lillian A. Ackerman, *A Necessary Balance: Gender and Power Among Indians of the Columbia Plateau* (Norman: Univ. of Oklahoma Press, 2003).

12. [Joset], "Women in the Different Tribes," Joset Papers, JOPA; Prando (Crow Camp) to Cataldo, 26 Sept. 1883, Prando Papers, OPA.

13. [Joset], "Histoire de la Mission de Colville, d'après les notes du P. Joset"; Joset, "Colville Mission," Joset Papers, JOPA.

14. Le Jeune's reference to Romans 10:17 is found in Reuben Gold Thwaites, ed., *The Jesuit Relations and Allied Documents: Travels and Explorations of the Jesuit Missionaries in New France, 1620–1719* (New York, 1959), 5:191; Gerald McKevitt, "Missionary Linguistics in the Pacific Northwest: A Comparative Study," *Western Historical Quarterly* 21 (1990): 281–304.

15. Robert H. Ruby and John A. Brown, *Indians of the Pacific Northwest: A History* (Norman: Univ. of Oklahoma Press, 1981), 71; Milner and O'Neil, *Churchmen and the Western Indians*, 57–62; Stephen R. Riggs, *Mary and I: Forty Years with the Sioux* (Chicago: W. G. Holmes, ca. 1880), 38.

16. De Smet cited in Chittenden and Richardson, *De Smet*, 1:329; [Camillus Imoda?], draft of letter to Mission Superior, n.d., JOPA.

17. Joset's remarks are found in *Letters and Notices* [English Jesuit Province Newsletter], 7 (n.p., 1871), 322–23, ARSI; Harrod, *Mission Among the Blackfeet*, 58–59; *Helena* (Montana) *Daily Herald*, 12 Aug. 1882, news clipping in Giorda Papers, JOPA; data regarding Cataldo are found in Eleanor and Robert C. Carriker et al., *Guide to Microfilm Collection of the Oregon Province Archives of the Society of Jesus Indian Language Collection: The Pacific Northwest Tribes* (Spokane, 1976), 10, 13.

18. Cataldo's opinion recorded in Aloysius Parodi, "Reminiscences," JOPA.

19. Mengarini (Vancouver) to Roothaan, 26 Sept. 1844, Mont. Sax. 1001-VI-2, ARSI.

20. Hans Vogt, *The Kalispel Language: An Outline of the Grammar with Texts, Translations, and Dictionary* (Oslo, 1940), 9; Gladys Reichard, *Coeur d'Alene: Handbook of American Indian Languages* (Washington, D.C., 1938), 3:517–707; Herman K. Haeberlin, "Types of Reduplication in the Salish Dialects," *International Journal of American Linguistics* (hereafter *IJAL*) 1 (1917–20): 161; Franz Boas and Haeberlin, "Sound Shifts in Salishan Dialects," *IJAL* 4 (1927): 121; Mengarini, *Rec-*

ollections, 132–3; Philip Canestrelli, "Grammar of the Kutenai Language by Pater Philippo Canestrelli, S.J., Annotated by Franz Boas," *IJAL* 4 (1927): 1.

21. Carriker, *Guide to Microfilm*.

22. Parodi, "Reminiscences," JOPA; Rappagliosi, *Memorie*, 86, JOPA; William Claessens [n.p.] to unnamed Belgian woman, [n.d.], Claessens Papers, JOPA; regarding Canestrelli see Mackin, "Wanderings of Fifty Years," Mackin Papers, JOPA. See also Carriker, *Guide to Microfilm*, 9. According to another missionary, Canestrelli himself refused to learn English "to be sure that he would be assigned to work only with Indians." See Pietro Bandini (Torino) to Anderledy, [ca. May 1889], Taur. 1011-II-37a, ARSI.

23. Gregory Mengarini, "The Rocky Mountains: Memoirs of Fr. Gregory Mengarini," *WL* 17 (1888): 307–8; 18 (1889): 26; Crosby, "Kuailks," 11–13, JOPA.

24. Chittenden and Richardson, *De Smet*, 1:324 and 240; Mengarini, "Rocky Mountains," *WL* 18 (1889): 29; Mengarini (Vancouver) to Roothaan, 26 Sept. 1844, Mont. Sax. 1001-VI-2, ARSI.

25. Crosby, "Kuailks," 11–13, JOPA.

26. Palladino, *Indian and White*, 37; De Smet in Cornelius M. Buckley, *Nicolas Point, S.J.: His Life and Northwestern Indian Chronicles* (Chicago: Loyola Univ. Press, 1989), 207.

27. Chittenden and Richardson, *De Smet*, 1:324; Buckley, *Nicholas Point*, 295; Caruana (De Smet, Idaho) to Martin, 22 July 1897, "Historia Missionis Yakima, 1897," Mont. Sax. 1003-VIII, ARSI.

28. Mengarini, "Rocky Mountains," *WL* 18 (1889):34.

29. Chittenden and Richardson, *De Smet*, 1:336–37; Mengarini, *Recollections*, 31.

30. Mengarini, *Recollections*, 203.

31. Prando (St. Peter's Mission) to Cataldo, ca. 1881, *WL* 12 (1883): 307–10; "Minister's Diary, 1891–92," entry for 3 Aug. 1891, JOPA.

32. Frederick Eberschweiler, "An Indian Clergy Impossible," *Catholic World* (Sept. 1897): 815–24, JOPA.

33. M. I. Raufer, *Black Robes and Indians on the Last Frontier: A Story of Heroism* (Milwaukee, Wis.: Bruce Publishing, 1966), 155, 345.

34. Inscription found on back of photograph of Alexander Aimaita, church chief (tribal religious leader) at St. Ignatius Mission, Montana, n.d., St. Ignatius Mission Photograph Collection, Box 2, JOPA.

35. Crosby, "Kuailks," 13, JOPA; Deward E. Walker, Jr., *Conflict and Schism in Nez Perce Acculturation: A Study of Religion and Politics* (Pullman: Washington State Univ. Press, 1968), 65.

36. Maurice Vaussard, *Daily Life in Eighteenth Century Italy*, trans. Michael Heron (New York: Macmillan, 1963), 159; Mengarini (Vancouver) to Roothaan, 26 Sept. 1844, Mont. Sax. 1001-V-2, ARSI; Mengarini, *Recollections*, 201, 162; Alan P. Merriam, *Ethnomusicology of the Flathead Indians* (Chicago: Aldine Publishing, 1967), 3, 127–31.

37. Rappagliosi, *Memorie*, 122, JOPA; Prando (St. Peter's Mission) to Cataldo, ca. 1881, in *WL* 12 (1883): 311.

38. Palladino, *Indian and White*, 76; Mengarini, "Rocky Mountains," *WL* 18 (1889): 33-34; Rappagliosi, *Memorie*, 81, 91, JOPA; Merriam, *Ethnomusicology of the Flathead Indians*, 131.

39. Myron Eells, *Father Eells, or the Results of 55 Years of Missionary Labors in Washington and Oregon* (Boston, 1894), 103.

40. Prando (Crow Camp) to Cataldo, 26 Sept. 1883, Prando Papers, JOPA; Prando, *WL* 12 (1883): 326; see also Harrod, *Mission Among the Blackfeet*, 59.

41. [Joset], "Missions Catholiques. . . ." Mont. Sax. 1001-VIII-2, ARSI; Prando (St. Xavier Mission, Mont.) to Ketchum, 17 Feb. 1904, BCIM, 47/14. On Jesuit use of art, see Jane ten Brink Goldsmith, "Jesuit Iconography: The Evolution of the Visual Idiom," 17, and J. Patrick Donnelly, "Art and the Early Jesuits: The Historical Context," both in *Jesuit Art in North American Collections* (Dobbs Ferry, N.Y.: Patrick and Beatrice Haggerty Museum of Art, Marquette Univ., 1991), 13-14.

42. Chittenden and Richardson, *De Smet*, 1:334, 337.

43. Harrod, *Mission Among the Blackfeet*, 32; Nicolas Point, *Wilderness Kingdom: Indian Life in the Rocky Mountains: 1840-1847: The Journals and Paintings of Nicolas Point, S.J.*, ed. and trans. Joseph Donnelly (New York: Holt, Rinehart, & Winston, 1967), 12-13.

44. Louis Rossi, *Six Years on the West Coast of America, 1856-1862*, trans. W. Victor Wortley (Fairfield, Wash.: Ye Galleon Press, 1983), 321.

45. "De Smet [Sacred Heart Mission] Diary, 1878-1939," entry for 21 June 1895, JOPA.

46. Harold Allen, *Father Ravalli's Missions* (Chicago: School of the Art Institute, 1972), 27.

47. James Axtell, "The European Failure to Convert the Indians: An Autopsy," *Papers of the Sixth Algonquian Conference, 1974* (Ottawa: National Museum of Canada, 1975), 280; Mengarini (Vancouver) to Roothaan, 26 Sept. 1844, Mont. Sax. 1001-VI-2, ARSI.

48. Harrod, *Mission Among the Blackfeet*, 188.

49. Vaussard, *Daily Life*, 142-43; O'Malley, "Cataldo ms.," JOPA.

50. Donald Weinstein, *Saints and Society: The Two Worlds of Western Christendom* (Chicago: Univ. of Chicago Press, 1982), 183-5.

51. "De Smet [Sacred Heart Mission] Diary, 1878-1939," entry, 18 Mar. 1889, JOPA.

52. "De Smet [Sacred Heart Mission] Diary, 1878-1939," entry for 25 Dec. 1895, JOPA; Cataldo, [Dictation re Nez Percés to O'Malley], JOPA.

53. "De Smet [Sacred Heart Mission] Diary, 1878-1939," entries for 24 Dec. 1889, 25 Dec. 1897, JOPA.

54. "De Smet [Sacred Heart Mission] Diary, 1878-1939," entry for 1 Jan. 1898, JOPA.

55. Bandini letter, 1885, in Bigart and Woodcock, "St. Ignatius Mission," *Arizona and the West* 23 (Summer 1981): 170.

56. "House Diary, St. Ignatius Mission, 1901-09," entries for 26 May 1903 and 15 May 1906, JOPA.

57. "De Smet [Sacred Heart] Mission Diary, 1878-1939," entry, 18 and 19 Mar. 1889, JOPA; Barnum, "Joset," *WL* 30 (1901): 211.

58. Alfonso Muzzarelli, *Il Mese di Maggio Consecrato a Maria Santissima* (Rome, 1856 ed.); Giuseppe Mellinato, "Maggio, Mese Mariano e I Gesuiti," *Ai Nostri Amici* [Monthly Review of the Jesuits of Sicily] 29 (1958): 103-8.

59. *Letters and Notices* 6 (1869): 226-33, ARSI; Rappagliosi, *Memorie*, 115, JOPA.

60. The most complete analysis of the feast is Miri Rubin, *Corpus Christi: The Eucharist in Late Medieval Culture* (Cambridge: Cambridge Univ. Press, 1991); John Fahey, *The Kalispel Indians* (Norman: Univ. of Oklahoma Press, 1986), 32.

61. Sisters of Providence (Colville) to Brouillet, 1 Feb. 1877, BCIM 12/3; Parodi, "Memoirs," JOPA; Cataldo, "Dictation" [to O'Malley], Cataldo Papers, JOPA; Parodi, "Memoirs," JOPA.

62. "St. Francis Regis House Diary, 1892-1900," entry, 8 May 1893, JOPA; "Hist. of St. Peter's Mission" [fragment], JOPA.

63. Cataldo (De Smet) to Torti, 25 Jan. 1890, ATPSJ; Mengarini, *Recollections*, 165-66; Buckley, *Nicholas Point*, 309, 316. Mengarini was picked for missionary work because of his medical training. Ravalli, too, was "skilled in medicine," according to De Smet, *Oregon Missions and Travels over the Rocky Mountains in 1845-46* (Fairfield, Wash.: Ye Galleon Press, 1978), 97.

64. Mengarini (St. Mary's Mission) to Roothaan, 10 Mar. 1842, Mont. Sax. 1001-III-2, ARSI; Chittenden and Richardson, *De Smet*, 1:336; Gazzoli (Sacred Heart Mission) to General, 7 Mar. 1850, Mont. Sax. 1001-IX-6, ARSI; on Ravalli, see Rolle, *Immigrant Upraised*, 192.

65. Engh, "True Gentleman and Crow," 47-48.

66. Prando (Holy Family Mission) to R. Freddi, 23 May 1896, Mont. Sax. 1003-V-29, ARSI; S. Filippi (Colville, Wash.) to Stephan, 10 Jan. 1889, BCIM, 24/23; Van Gorp (Spokane) to J. A. Stephan, 17 May 1890, BCIM, 27/22; Chief Joseph in Bigart and Woodcock, "St. Ignatius Mission," *Arizona and the West* 23 (Summer 1981): 156.

67. "St. Regis House Diary, 1904-1908," JOPA; Rappagliosi, *Memorie*, 84, 86, 120-3, JOPA.

68. A. J. Splawn, *Ka-mi-akin: The Last Hero of the Yakimas* (Portland, Ore.: Binford & Mort, 1944), 360.

69. Cataldo, "Notes for Lectures, ca. 1900," Cataldo Papers, JOPA; Splawn, *Ka-mi-akin*, 359-60.

70. "Fr. Urban Grassi," WL 19 (1890): 268.

71. O'Malley, "English translation of Garrand, *Le Père Laure*," JOPA.

72. Carriker, "Cataldo," in *Churchmen and Western Indians*, 138; Prando (Mission of St. Peter) to Cataldo, 28 July 1881, in WL 12 (1883): 306-7.

73. Walker, *Conflict and Schism*, 64.

74. Bandini letter, 1885, in Bigart and Woodcock, "St. Ignatius Mission," *Arizona and the West* 23 (Summer 1981): 165; Cataldo (Lapwai, Idaho) to S. S. Fenn, 25 Jan. 1876, BCIM, 9/1. On codependent relationships between priest and Natives Americans, see Marie Therese Archambault, "Native Americans and Evangelization," *Native and Christian: Indigenous Voices on Religious Identity in the United States and Canada*, ed. James Treat (New York: Routledge, 1996), 145-49.

75. Giorda (Lapwai) to Palladino, 10 Feb. 1882, Provincial Correspondence, 1862-77, JOPA; "Father Adrian Hoecken," WL 26 (1897): 364-68; Cataldo

(Slickpoo, Idaho) to Ketcham, 4 Nov. 1907, BCIM, 56/4; Caruana (Colville, Wash.) to Cataldo, 21 Jan. 1882, *WL* 12 (1883): 48; Caruana (Sacred Heart Mission) to Giorda, 27 Dec. 1869, Helena Diocese Papers, JOPA.

76. Cataldo (De Smet, Idaho) to Torti, 3 Jan. 1888, ATPSJ; Ravalli (Sacred Heart Mission?) to Congiato, ca. 1857, Mont. Sax. 1002-XII-8, ARSI; Boschi, "Indians of the West," Boschi Papers, JOPA; Cataldo (Slickpoo, Idaho) to H. J. Cook, 4 Feb. 1920, draft, Cataldo Papers, JOPA.

77. Giovanni Boschi, "Indians of West," 14–23, Boschi Papers, JOPA; Cataldo (Slickpoo, Idaho) to H. J. Cook, 4 Feb. 1920, draft, Cataldo Papers, JOPA; Giovanni Boschi, "Indians of West," 14–23, Boschi Papers, JOPA.

78. Mary Morgan Trombley, [Recollections of Holy Family Mission in 1908], Ursuline Collection, JOPA; Chief Joseph in Carriker, "Cataldo," in *Churchmen and Western Indians*, 139; Axtell, *Invasion Within*, 83–84.

79. Rappagliosi, *Memorie*, 124, JOPA; Sullivan, "Information About Fr. D'Aste," D'Aste Papers, JOPA; O'Malley, "Northwest Blackrobe: Cataldo," O'Malley Papers, JOPA.

80. Caruana (De Smet, Idaho) to Martín, 22 July 1897, [History], Mont. Sax. 1003-VIII, ARSI; reference to D'Aste in "House Diary, St. Ignatius Mission, 1895–1901," entry for 17 Sept. 1897, JOPA; Sifton mentioned in Goller (Missoula, Mont.) to W. Ketcham, 31 Oct. 1909, BCIM, 66/7.

81. Barcelò (Helena) to Brouillet, 14 Sept. 1881, BCIM, 10/9; Bigart and Woodcock, "St. Ignatius Mission," *Arizona and the West* 23 (Autumn 1981): 268n58; *Bureau of Catholic Indian Missions, Report, 1907*, BCIM.

82. Van Gorp (Spokane) to Martín, 19 July 1897, Mont. Sax. 1003-II-27, ARSI; Harrod, *Mission Among the Blackfeet*, 65.

83. Barcelò (Miles City, Mont.) to Brouillet, 29 Nov. 1889, BCIM, 10/9; [Van der Velden], "The Cheyenne Indians," St. Labre's Mission Collection, JOPA.

84. D'Aste (St. Ignatius, Idaho) to Martín, 30 Jan. 1902, Mont. Sax. 1003-VI-17, ARSI; Damiani (Holy Family Mission, Mont.) to Martín, 12 Jan. 1903, Mont. Sax. 1003-VI-24, ARSI.

85. Damiani (Holy Family Mission, Mont.) to Martín, 12 Jan. 1903, Mont. Sax. 1003-VI-24, ARSI.

CHAPTER 7

An early version of this chapter appeared in *Spirit, Style, Story: Essays Honoring John W. Padberg, S.J.* (Chicago: Loyola Press, 2002), 365–401.

1. D'Arcy McNickle, "Going to School," *The Hawk Is Hungry and Other Stories*, ed. Birgit Hans (Tucson: Univ. of Arizona Press, 1992), 112.

2. Edward J. Power, *A History of Catholic Higher Education in the United States* (Milwaukee, Wis.: Bruce Publishing, 1958), 55, 77.

3. Statistics in "Mission des Montagnes Rocheuses de la Compagnie de Jesus, Anneé 1897–98," Provincial Papers, Box 6, JOPA; Ross Alexander Enochs, *The Jesuit Mission to the Lakota Sioux: Pastoral Theology and Ministry, 1886–1945* (Kansas City, Mo.: Sheed & Ward, 1996); Robert H. Keller, Jr., *American Protestantism and United States Indian Policy, 1869–82* (Lincoln: Univ. of Nebraska Press, 1883).

4. Joset (Spokane) to Ruellan, 13 Feb. 1883, Ruellan Papers, JOPA; Joset (Spokane Bridge, Wash.) to Charles Ewing, 19 July 1876, BCIM, 9/1; Chief Michael in Burns, *Jesuits and Indian Wars*, 316.

5. Palladino, *Indian and White*, 93; F. Digmann (Rosebud Agency, S.Dak.) to William H. Ketchum, 12 Nov. 1902, BCIM, 43/2.

6. C. Imoda (St. Peter's Mission, Mont.) to Brouillet, 21 June 1880, BCIM, 11/4; Giorda (St. Ignatius Mission) to G. B. Baroni, 28 Jan. 1879, ATPSJ.

7. Joset (Spokane) to Ewing, 19 July 1876, BCIM, 9/1.

8. Joset (Spokane) to Ewing, 19 July 1876, BCIM, 9/1; Joset, "Old Mission Church," Joset Papers, JOPA.

9. C. Imoda (St. Peter's Mission, Mont.) to Brouillet, 5 Jan. 1878, BCIM,11/4; Cataldo (Lapwai) to Ewing, 30 Nov. 1875, BCIM, 9/1.

10. Beckx (Rome) to Giorda, 10 Jan. 1863, "Extracts of Letters," Joset Papers, JOPA; John Fahey, *Flathead Indians* (Norman: Univ. of Oklahoma Press, 1974), 119–20; Edmund Robinson, "History of St. Ignatius Mission," *Mission Valley News*, 1 July 1976, St. Ignatius Collection, Centennial Album, JOPA.

11. Joset (Spokane) to Ruellan, 13 Feb. 1883, Ruellan Papers, JOPA; Palladino, *Indian and White*, 94; Prando, "Sketch of St. Xavier's Mission," 8 Sept. 1890, JOPA.

12. Prando (St. Peter's Mission) to Cataldo, 28 July 1881, in *WL* 2 (1883): 37.

13. Cataldo (Fort Show, Mont.) to Brouillet, 3 June 1878, BCIM, 12/1; Joset (Spokane) to Charles Ewing, 19 July 1876, BCIM, 9/1; Andrew Seltice, Petition to President of U.S., 28 July 1873, Correspondence, BCIM.

14. Painted Red cited in Bigart and Woodcock, "St. Ignatius Mission, Montana: Reports from Two Jesuit Missionaries, 1885 and 1900–1901," *Arizona and the West* 23 (Summer 1981): 156–57.

15. Keller, *American Protestantism and United States Indian Policy*, 2.

16. Francis Paul Prucha, *The Churches and the Indian Schools, 1888–1912* (Lincoln: Univ. of Nebraska Press, 1979), 1–2; Peter J. Rahill, *Catholic Indian Missions and Grant's Peace Policy, 1870–1884* (Washington, D.C.: Catholic Univ. of America Press, 1953), 60.

17. Anne M. Butler, "Mother Katharine Drexel: Spiritual Visionary for the West," in *By Grit and Grace: Eleven Women Who Shaped the West*, ed. Glenda Riley and Richard W. Etulain (Golden, Colo.: Fulcrum, 1997), 198–220; Consuela Marie Duffy, *Katherine Drexel: A Biography* (Cornwells Heights, Pa.: Drexel Guild, 1966), 267; Drexel addendum in Cataldo (Farmington, Wash.) to Drexel, 9 Jan. 1889, and Bandini (Fort Custer, Mont.) to Drexel, 21 Oct. 1888, Archives of the Sisters of the Blessed Sacrament, Bensalem, Pa. (hereafter ASBS).

18. Prucha, *Churches and Indian Schools*, 3–4, 6–8.

19. Burns, *Jesuits and the Indian Wars*, 56; Caruana (Colville Mission, Wash.) to R. Freddi, Italian Assistant, 9 Apr. 1895, Mont. Sax. 1003-V-22, ARSI; *Bureau of Catholic Indian Missions, 1874–1895* (Washington, D.C., 1895), 20–25, BCIM.

20. J. D. Bevier (Flathead Agency) to E. P. Smith, 14 July 1874, BCIM; Palladino (St. Ignatius Mission) to Brouillet, 29 Oct. 1873, BCIM; Palladino, *Indian and White*, 242–43.

21. John Mullan (Washington, D.C.) to Palladino and Van Gorp, 11 Apr. 1885; Palladino (St. Ignatius Mission) to Mullan, 23 Apr. 1885, BCIM, 15/7.

22. *Report of the Commissioner of Indian Affairs for 1889*, 228; Markham, "St. Ignatius Mission," *Sacred Heart Messenger*, July 1892, 521–22, JOPA.

23. Schurz in David Wallace Adams, *Education for Extinction: American Indians and the Boarding School Experience, 1875–1928* (Lawrence: Univ. of Kansas Press, 1995), 30; Cataldo (Lewiston) to Brouillet, 13 Jan. 1878, BCIM, 12/1; Palladino, *Indian and White*, 94–95.

24. Van Gorp (St. Ignatius) to Charles Ewing, 13 Nov. 1873, BCIM; Prando, "St. Xavier's Mission," 1887, Prando Papers, JOPA; Palladino, *Indian and White*, 103.

25. Thomas J. Morgan, "The Education of American Indians," *Proceedings of the Seventh Annual Meeting of the Lake Mohonk Conference of Friends of the Indian, 1889*, 22; Robert A. Trennert, Jr., *The Phoenix Indian School: Forced Assimilation in Arizona, 1891–1935* (Norman: Univ. of Oklahoma Press, 1988), 7–8; Adams, *Education for Extinction*, 58–59.

26. Feusi (St. Stephen's, Wyo.) to J. A. Stephan, 26 Jan. 1898, BCIM, 37/25; Cataldo (Spokane) to Stephan, 28 July 1890, BCIM, 27/9.

27. Palladino, *Indian and White*, 83, 96–100, 147; Van Gorp (St. Ignatius) to Ewing, 13 Nov. 1873, BCIM.

28. Prando, "St. Xavier's Mission," 1887, Prando Papers, JOPA; agent's reports in *Report of the Commissioner of Indian Affairs for 1889*, 228.

29. "The Holy Family Mission school in the Blackfoot Reservation," Holy Family Mission Collection, n.d., JOPA; P. Ronan, "Report of the U.S. Indian Agent to the Hon. Commissioner of Indian Affairs [extract]," 1890, BCIM, 27/8.

30. Andrew Seltice, Petition to President of the U.S., 28 July 1873, Correspondence, BCIM; Palladino, *Indian and White*, 151.

31. Celestin Tregret, *Seven Years Among the Western Indians*, (n.p., n.d.), 108–9, 118, JOPA.

32. Student recollections in Jackie Parsons, *Educational Movement of the Blackfeet Indians, 1840–1979* (Browning, Mont.: Blackfeet Heritage Program, Browning Public Schools, 1980), 9–10; T. J. Morgan (Washington, D.C.) to J. Rebmann, 22 Mar. 1892, St. Ignatius Mission Collection: Outgoing Correspondence, JOPA; Sister M. Imela Hanratty, "I Remember" [Recollections of St. Labre's Mission, Ashland, Mont., 1922], St. Labre's Mission Collection, JOPA.

33. O'Malley, "Northwest Blackrobe: Cataldo," O'Malley Papers, JOPA.

34. Michael O'Malley, "Notes on the Jesuit Brothers," O'Malley Papers, JOPA.

35. O'Malley, "Notes on the Jesuit Brothers," O'Malley Papers, JOPA; Stephen DeRouge, [Account of St. Mary's Mission, Omak, Wash.], n.d., St. Mary's Mission Collection, JOPA; Mullan (Washington, D.C.) to Bureau of Catholic Indian Missions, 2 Dec. 1886, St. Regis Mission Collection, JOPA.

36. P. Bandini (St. Xavier Mission, Mont.) to K. M. Drexel, 9 Mar. 1888, ASBS.

37. Bandini (St. Francis Xavier) to Stephan, 20 May 1890, BCIM, 27/7; Cataldo (De Smet, Idaho) to Father Willard, 24 Apr. 1889, BCIM, 23/1; Damiani (St. Paul's, Mont.) to Anderledy, 7 Feb. 1891, Mont. Sax. 1003-IV-23, ARSI.

38. D'Aste (St. Ignatius) to Stephan, 29 Nov. 1890, BCIM, 27/8.

39. Eberschweiler (St. Paul's) to Stephan, 12 July 1889, BCIM, 24/6.

40. D'Aste, "Diary, 1902–1903," entry, 12 July 1902, JOPA.

41. Palladino, *Indian and White*, 234–35.

42. Giorda (Attanam, Wash.) to Charles Ewing, 13 May 1874, BCIM; C. Imoda (St. Peter's Mission) to Brouillet, 5 Jan. 1878, BCIM, 11/4; Sister Genevieve McBride, *The Bird Trail* (New York: Vantage, 1984), 104; "Chronicles of the Convent of Mary Immaculate, De Smet, Idaho," 56, 89a, JOPA.

43. Giorda (Attanam, Wash.) to Tosi, 21 May 1874, Giuseppe Giorda Papers, JOPA; Jesuit comment on Ursulines found on unsigned note on reverse of photograph no. 50 (Ursuline nuns and kindergarten students), St. Ignatius Mission Collection, Photographs, JOPA; Sisters Holy Angels, Angela, and Ignatia (St. Labre's Mission, Mont.) to Mother Superior, 23 Dec. 1884, Folder 7, St. Labre's Mission Letters: 1884–85, Archives, Ursuline Convent, Toledo, Ohio.

44. Mother Amadeus (St. Peter's Mission, Mont.), 19 Dec. 1884, Folder 12B, St. Peter's Mission Letters: 1884–1906, Archives, Ursuline Convent, Toledo, Ohio.

45. Sister Mary Amadeus (St. Peter's, Mont.) to Stephan, 15 July 1900; and Stephan (Washington, D.C.) to Mother Mary Amadeus, 19 July 1900, BCIM, 40/23; Amadeus (St. Peter's Mission, Mont.) to Stephan, 24 July 1900, BCIM, 40/23.

46. Van Gorp (Spokane, Wash.) to Drexel, 28 July 1892, ASBS; De la Motte, "Diary," entry, 7 Dec. 1903, JOPA. On relations between men and women religious, see Carol K. Coburn and Martha Smith, *Spirited Lives: How Nuns Shaped Catholic Culture and American Life, 1836–1920* (Chapel Hill: Univ. of North Carolina Press, 1999), 118–22.

47. E. Boll (Slickpoo, Idaho) to Ketchum, 30 Nov. 1908, BCIM, 60/5.

48. P. Tosi (De Smet Mission) to Brouillet, 5 Dec. 1883, BCIM, 9/1; Palladino, *Indian and White*, 93–94; "A Few Facts Concerning St. Xavier's Mission," ca. 1895, BCIM, 33/56; for a case study of the contradictions inherent in the missionaries' agricultural program, see Suzanne H. Schrems, "The Northern Cheyenne and the Fight for Cultural Sovereignty: The Notes of Father Aloysius Van Der Velden, S.J.," *Montana: The Magazine of Western History* 45 (1995): 18–33.

49. E. D. Bannister (Helena, Mont.) to Secretary of the Interior, 22 Oct. 1888, BCIM, 21/19; Ronan's account in *Report of the Commissioner of Indian Affairs for 1886*, 180.

50. "De Smet [Sacred Heart] Indian School, De Smet, Idaho," Report, ca. 1895, BCIM, 33/48.

51. Ibid; *Fruit of Her Hands; Sketches from the History of the Institute of Providence During the First Century of Its Existence, 1843–1943* (Montreal, 1943), JOPA; Sister M. Amedee (De Smet) to Stephan, 12 May 1890, BCIM, 26/4.

52. Fahey, *Flathead Indians*, 183, 224; Bureau of Catholic Indian Missions, *School Report*, "Holy Family Mission, Mont., 1909," 53, BCIM.

53. Schurz account in clipping from *Allgemeinen Zeitung* (Munich, Germany), 1883 (no. 287), copy and translation in St. Ignatius Mission Collection, JOPA; P. Bandini (St. Francis Xavier Mission) to Stephan, 20 Mar. 1888, BCIM, 21/19.

54. "De Smet [Sacred Heart Mission] Diary, 1878–1939," JOPA; Thomas J. Morgan, "The Education of American Indians," *Proceedings of the Seventh Annual Meeting of the Lake Mohonk Conference of Friends of the Indian, 1889*, 27; Jon Reyhner, ed., *Teaching American Indian Students* (Norman: Univ. of Oklahoma Press, 1992), 199; chief cited in Sister Providencia Tolan, *A Shining from the Mountains* (n.p.: Sisters of Providence, 1980), 94.

55. *Allgemeinen Zeitung* (Munich, Germany) clipping, 1883 (no. 287), translation in St. Ignatius Mission Collection, JOPA; Stephan to Van Gorp, 13 Feb. 1891, BCIM, 30/10.

56. J. A. Simms (Colville Agency, Wash.) to J. B. A. Brouillet, 16 Nov. 1879, BCIM, 12/4; Brouillet (Washington, D.C.) to J. A. Simms, 13 Dec. 1879, BCIM, 12/4; Cataldo (De Smet, Idaho) to Giudice, 3 Jan. 1888 and 23 May 1888, ATPSJ; D'Aste, "Diary, 1903–04," entry, 7 Sept. 1903, JOPA.

57. Fahey, *Flathead Indians*, 273; C. Lusk (Washington, D.C.) to Vest, 26 Jan. 1885, BCIM, 15/7; Cataldo (Spokane) to Eberschweiler, 30 Oct. 1888, St. Paul's Mission Collection, JOPA.

58. Damiani (St. Peter's Mission) to Stephan, 12 Mar. 1886, BCIM, 17/10; Dimier letter, 1901, in Bigart and Woodcock, "St. Ignatius Mission," *Arizona and the West* 23 (Autumn 1981): 277–78; McNickle, *The Hawk Is Hungry*, x.

59. Agent Jay Lynch in Margaret Szasz, *Education and the American Indian: The Road to Self-Determination, 1928–1973* (Albuquerque: Univ. of New Mexico Press, 1974), 368–69; Caruana (De Smet, Idaho) to Stephan, 21 Feb. 1890, BCIM, 26/4.

60. Caruana (St. Joseph's Mission, Attanam, Wash.) to Brouillet, 7 Nov. 1876, BCIM, 13/4; Tosi (De Smet, Idaho) to Lusk, 12 June 1884, BCIM, 9/1.

61. Caruana (De Smet, Idaho) to Morgan, 8 Sept. 1890, BCIM, 26/4.

62. Damiani (St. Peter's, Mont.) to Anderledy, 21 Feb. 1889, Mont. Sax. 1003-IV-15, ARSI; Cataldo (St. Xavier Mission) to Anderledy, 27 Jan. 1891, Mont. Sax. 1003-I-34, ARSI.

63. Tregret, *Seven Years Among Western Indians*, 71, JOPA; "House Diary, St. Ignatius Mission, 1895–1901," entry, 30 Apr. 1898, JOPA; "Minute Book of the B.V.M. Sodality, 1884–1910," entries for 1884, Sacred Heart Mission Collection, JOPA.

64. *Report of the Commissioner of Indian Affairs for 1891*, 69; Adams, *Education for Extinction*, 196–99; "House Diary, St. Ignatius Mission, 1895–1901," entries, 25 Nov. 1897 and 22 Feb. 1898, JOPA.

65. De la Motte (St. Xavier) to Martín, 19 Jan. 1901, Mont. Sax. 1003-III-3, ARSI.

66. "Notes," St. Ignatius Mission, 1902, St. Ignatius Mission Collection, JOPA.

67. Turnell (De Smet) to Brouillet, 21 Dec. 1883, BCIM, 9/1; "De Smet [Sacred Heart] Indian School, De Smet, Idaho," Report, ca. 1895, BCIM, 33/48.

68. "House Diary," St. Ignatius Mission, 1901–2, entry, 22 June 1902, JOPA; John Merlin Tripp, "Music at St. Ignatius Mission, 1854–1900" (M.A. thesis, Univ. of Montana, 1966), 35.

69. Student recollections in "Notes on Sister Josephine," n.p., n.d., Ursuline Collection, JOPA; D'Arcy McNickle, *The Surrounded* (Albuquerque: Univ. of New Mexico Press, 1978), 99–100, 106.

70. Fahey, *Flathead Indians*, 266.

71. Sister St. Ignatius (St. Labre's) to Stephan, 8 Jan. 1888, BCIM, 21/22; Van der Velden (St. Labre's) to Bureau of Catholic Indian Missions, 31 Dec. 1889, BCIM, 24/8; "De Smet [Sacred Heart] Indian School, De Smet, Idaho," Report, ca. 1895, BCIM, 33/48.

72. Sister St. Ignatius (St. Labre's) to Stephan, 8 Jan. 1888, BCIM; "Chronicles of Convent of Mary Immaculate, De Smet," JOPA.

73. Palladino (St. Ignatius Mission) to Lusk, 3 July 1886, BCIM, 17/9.

74. Lusk (Washington, D.C.) to Palladino, 5 Aug. 1886, BCIM, 17/9.

75. Sister St. Ignatius (St. Labre's) to Stephan, 8 Jan. 1888, BCIM, 21/22; "Chronicles of the Convent of Mary Immaculate, De Smet," entries for 1910, JOPA.

76. D'Aste (St. Ignatius Mission) to W. H. Ketchum, 13 Feb. 1902, BCIM, 43/21; Mackin (St. Paul's Mission, Mont.) to Ketchum, 6 Jan. 1902, BCIM, 43/22.

77. Prando (Holy Family Mission, Mont.) to Stephan, 1 Dec. 1897, BCIM, 36/1; "St. Francis Regis House Diary, 1892–1900," entry, 13 Sept. 1892, JOPA.

78. Interviews with Mary Ground, Mary Little Bull, George Bremer, and James Little Dog in Parsons, *Educational Movement of Blackfeet*, 6–11; Michael C. Coleman, "Motivations of Indian Children at Missionary and U.S. Government Schools," *Montana: The Magazine of Western History* 40 (Winter 1990): 30–45.

79. Parsons, *Educational Movement of Blackfeet*, 6–11; Grassi (St. Joseph's Church, Providence) to Stephan 23 July 1887, BCIM, 18/22.

80. Flathead agent report in Bigart and Woodcock, "St. Ignatius Mission," *Arizona and the West* 23 (Autumn 1981): 272n73; Raufer, *Black Robes and Indians*, 379–80; J. C. Gordon, "Report of Catholic Indian Missions for 1906," St. Xavier Mission, Mont., Indian Mission Reports, BCIM.

81. Treat, *Native and Christian*, 9–10.

82. John Schuyler Crosby and others (Helena, Mont.) to Erwin Price, 1 Oct. 1883, Letter 1883.18080, Office of Indian Affairs, Letters Received 1881–1907, Record Group 75, National Archives (hereafter NA).

83. E. D. Bannister (Helena, Mont.) to Secretary of the Interior, 22 Oct. 1888, BCIM, 21/19.

84. Keller, *American Protestantism and U. S. Indian Policy*, 208–9. Morgan in Prucha, *American Indian Policy in Crisis*, 305–9, 317–19.

85. Augustine Dimier (St. Ignatius Mission) to Father Provincial, Apr. 1901, in Bigart and Woodcock, "St. Ignatius Mission," *Arizona and the West* 23 (Autumn 1981): 277. See also McKevitt, "'The Jump That Saved the Rocky Mountain Mission,'" *Pacific Historical Review* 55 (Aug. 1986): 450.

86. Prando (Holy Family Mission) to Martín, 4 Nov. 1897, Mont. Sax. 1003-V-49, ARSI.

87. De la Motte (Spokane) to Martín, 18 Jan. 1902, Mont. Sax. 1003-III-11, ARSI.

88. Damiani (St. Peter's Mission, Mont.) to Anderledy, 20 Feb. 1888, Mont. Sax. 1003-IV-6, ARSI; Damiani (St. Peter's Mission) to Anderledy, 14 Jan. 1890, Mont. Sax. 1003-IV-18, ARSI; Damiani (St. Paul's, Mont.) to Anderledy, 7 Feb. 1891, Mont. Sax. 1003-IV-23, ARSI.

89. Taelman (St. Xavier, Mont.) to F. Dillon, 22 Sept. 1921, JOPA.

90. Szasz, *Assimilation and Federal Indian Education*, 12; John Post, "De Smet [Sacred Heart] Mission and School" Report, 25 Sept. 1912, BCIM, 80/7.

CHAPTER 8

1. F. Tomassini, "Lettera XLIX, Collegio di Las Vegas, 31 Ottobre 1880," *LEPN*, 3 (1879–80):118, ANPSJ.

2. Report of Rev. Thomas Harwood, 1874, in *Annual Report* (New York: Methodist Episcopal Church Board of Foreign Missions, 1875), 171.

3. Paul Horgan, *Lamy of Santa Fe: His Life and Times* (New York: Farrar, Straus & Giroux, 1975), 387.

4. Persons of Spanish-Mexican culture in the Southwest, California, and Texas are referred to in the text as *Hispanos* or Hispanics, although the terms *nuevomexicans*, *californios*, and *tejanos* are sometimes used to identify people of specific provinces or states. The term Anglo or Anglo American refers to citizens of the United States who are neither Hispanic nor Native American.

5. Liptak, *Immigrants and Their Church*, 31; *Mexican Americans and the Catholic Church, 1900–1965*, ed. Jay P. Dolan and Gilberto M. Hinojosa (Notre Dame: Univ. of Notre Dame Press, 1994), 19–21.

6. Frances Margaret Campbell, "American Catholicism in Northern New Mexico: A Kaleidoscope of Development, 1840–1885" (Ph.D. diss., Graduate Theological Union, Berkeley, Calif., 1986), 285.

7. See Leslie Woodcock Tentler, "On the Margins: The State of American Catholic History," *U.S. Catholic Historian* 21 (Spring 2003): 92.

8. Donato Gasparri, "Historia de la Misión de la Compañia de Jesús en Nuevo Méjico, Norte America, Desde El Principio 15 Agosto 1867," 1, 4–5, 8–9, ANPSJ. An analysis of the "Historia" is found in McKevitt, "Italian Jesuits in New Mexico," *New Mexico Historical Review* 67 (1992): 357–92.

9. S. Personè, "Lettera III, Conejos, Feb. 1874," *LEPN*, 1 (1874–75): 4; P. Tomassini (Socorro) to Palomba, 6 Feb. 1871 ANPSJ; S. Personè (Conejos) to Palomba, n.d. Oct. 1872, ANPSJ.

10. Gentile (Pueblo, Colo.) to Vioni, 1 Feb. 1881, ANPSJ; Palomba (Naples) to Gasparri, 15 July 1872, ANPSJ.

11. Erna Fergusson, *Our Southwest* (New York: Alfred A. Knopf, 1952), 18–19.

12. C. Personè [Albuquerque] to Palomba, 21 Nov. 1869, ANPSJ; "New Mexico," *WL* 12 (1883): 301; extracts from Gasparri letter in Paresce (Baltimore) to Beckx, 29 June 1869, ANPSJ; Gasparri described in Sister Blandina Segale, *At the End of the Santa Fe Trail*, foreword by Marc Simmons, afterword by Anne M. Butler (Albuquerque: Univ. of New Mexico Press, 1999), 214–15, 233–36.

13. Gentile (Pueblo, Colo.) to Vioni, 1 Feb. 1881, ANPSJ; Gentile (Las Vegas, N.Mex.) to Vioni, 15 Dec. 1883, ANPSJ; "Consulte, 1901–1920," entry, 8 Aug. 1909, ANPSJ.

14. "Consulta, 1871–1900," minutes for 1–2 May 1884, ANPSJ; "Consulte, 1901–1920," entries, 28 Sept. and 4 Oct. 1904, ANPSJ; Gentile (Trinidad, Colo.) to Vioni, 28 Aug. 1883, ANPSJ; Marra (Denver) to Mola, 1 June 1889, ANPSJ; Marra (Las Vegas?) to Canger, 9 Feb. 1887, ANPSJ.

15. Wade C. Barclay, *History of Methodist Missions* (New York: Board of Missions and Church Extension of the Methodist Church, 1949), 3:237–39; Report of Rev. Thomas Harwood in *Annual Report* (New York: Episcopal Church Board of Foreign Missions, 1892), 310; *Report, 1910* (New York: Congregational Home Missionary Society, 1910), 44.

16. W. Eugene Hollon, *The Southwest: Old and New* (Lincoln: Univ. of Nebraska Press, 1968), 187.

17. Martínez in David Lavender, *The Southwest* (Albuquerque: Univ. of New Mexico Press, 1984), 127; Engh, "The Southwest," *Frontiers and Catholic Identities*, 179–80; Dolan, *American Catholic Experience*, 76.

18. Lamy in Horgan, *Lamy of Santa Fe*, 126, 148; Lavender, *The Southwest*, 127–28; Marta Weigle, *Brothers of Light, Brothers of Blood: The Penitentes of the Southwest* (Albuquerque: Univ. of New Mexico Press, 1976), xvii–xix, 5–6; A. Leone, "Lettera XIX, Santa Fe, Agosto 1874," *LEPN*, 1 (1874–75):45, ANPSJ.

19. Fede, "Lettera XL, Las Vegas, N.M., 31 marzo 1878," *LEPN*, 2 (1878–79):126, ANPSJ; Baldassare, "Lettera XXX, Conejos, Col., dicembre 1874," *LEPN*, 1 (1874–75):84, ANPSJ.

20. Vito M. Tromby (Albuquerque) to Vioni, 29 Mar. 1883, ANPSJ. The second and longer characterization, although included in Tromby's letter, is penned in an unidentified hand.

21. [Marra], "Stato della Missione del Nueva Messico e Colorado nell 'agosto del 1891," ANPSJ; "Father Weninger on the Pacific Coast," *WL* 3 (1874): 116.

22. Weigle, *Brothers of Light*, 97; Rufus B. Sage in David J. Weber, ed., *Foreigners in Their Native Land: Historical Roots of the Mexican Americans* (Albuquerque: Univ. of New Mexico Press, 1973), 73; Jacob Miles Ashley, in Randi Jones Walker, "Protestantism in the Sangre de Cristos: Factors in the Growth and Decline of the Hispanic Protestant Churches in Northern New Mexico and Southern Colorado, 1850–1920" (Ph.D. diss., Claremont Graduate School, 1983), 73.

23. Vito M. Tromby (Albuquerque) to Vioni, 29 Mar. 1883, ANPSJ; S. Personè, "Lettera L, Albuquerque, 20 gennaio 1884," *LEPN*, 4 (1882–83):117, ANPSJ; F. Tomassini, "Lettera LXXVIII, Tiptonville, Mora Co. N.M., 3 maggio 1882," *LEPN*, 3 (1880–81):187, ANPSJ.

24. Salpointe, *Soldiers of the Cross*, 258; Gasparri, "Historia," 12–23, ANPSJ.

25. Baldassare (Albuquerque) to Palomba, 28 May 1876, ANPSJ; *Catalogus Provinciae Neapolitanae Societatis Iesus Ineunte Anno MDCCCLX* (Naples, 1860), 6–14, ANPSJ.

26. See Barry, *Worship and Work*, 39, 85.

27. Anon. (Old Albuquerque) to J. Brown, 14 Aug. 1900, ANPSJ; Baldassare (Conejos) to Palomba, 29 Mar. 1875, ANPSJ.

28. Marra (Pueblo) to Mola, 30 Jan. 1890, ANPSJ; G. Marra (Pueblo) to Machebeuf, 14 June 1888, Archives of the Archdiocese of Denver, Denver, Colo. (hereafter AADC).

29. Harwood, *Annual Report*, 171; *Catalogus Dispersae Provinciae Neapolitanae Societatis Iesu Ineunte Anno MDCCCLXXV* (Naples: Ex Typis Marchesianis, 1875), 22–3, ANPSJ.

30. "An Historical Sketch of the Mission of New Mexico," 1906, Archives of the New Orleans Province of the Society of Jesus, Loyola Univ., New Orleans, La. (hereafter ANOPSJ).

31. S. Personè, "Lettera III, Conejos, Feb. 1874," *LEPN*, 1 (1874–75):3, ANPSJ; Pinto, "Lettera IV, Pueblo, Feb. 1874," *LEPN* 1 (1874–75):6, ANPSJ.

32. Robert Gafford, S.J., interview by author, 21 Nov. 1981, Sacred Heart Church Rectory, El Paso, Tex.

33. Gasparri, "Historia," 14–16, ANPSJ.

34. S. Personè, "Lettera III, Conejos, Colo., Feb. 1874," *LEPN*, 1 (1874–75):4, ANPSJ; P. Tomassini (Socorro) to Palomba, 6 Feb. 1871; and P. Tomassini (La Junta) to Palomba, 15 Apr. 1874, ANPSJ.

35. See Jay P. Dolan, *Catholic Revivalism: The American Experience, 1830–1900* (Notre Dame: Univ. of Notre Dame Press, 1978), 12–16.

36. Armando Guidetti, *Le missioni popolari: I grandi Gesuiti italiani, disegno storico-biografico delle missioni popolari dei gesuiti d'Italia dalle origini al Concilio Vaticano II* (Milan: Rusconi, 1988), 216; P. Tomassini, "Lettera X, Albuquerque, N. M., 8 Maggio 1879," *LEPN*, 3 (1879–80):24, ANPSJ.

37. M. J. Hughes, "Lenten Missions in Old Mexico," *WL* 27 (1898): 218.

38. Gasparri, "Historia," 17, 21–22, ANPSJ. See also Owens, *Jesuit Beginnings*, 49.

39. Bohme, "A History of the Italians in New Mexico," 36; Dolan, *Catholic Revivalism*, 54, 19; Gabino Rendón, *Hand on My Shoulder* (New Mexico, 1953), 31.

40. Giovanni d'Aponte, "Lettera VII, Las Vegas, Aprile 1874," *LEPN*, 1 (1874–75):12, ANPSJ; Jay P. Dolan, *The Immigrant Church: New York's Irish and German Catholics, 1815–1865* (Notre Dame: Univ. of Notre Dame Press, 1983), 159–69.

41. Gasparri, "Historia," 16–8, 21–2, ANPSJ.

42. Ibid., 25–35. Gasparri, hoping perhaps to impress European superiors, exaggerated the impact of the Taos mission, even asserting later that it had "destroyed the schism." Other sources indicate that reconciliation did not come as quickly to the divided village as he claimed. Nevertheless, Gasparri's preaching did mark a turning point in the religious life of the Taos community, as it did elsewhere. Lamy claimed this in a letter to Archbishop John B. Purcell of Cincinnati on 3 Feb. 1869. "Most of the people, except some of his nearest relations, are coming back to obedience," he wrote, "and the mission which is producing a great change will leave very few remains, if any, of that sad event." See McKevitt, "Italian Jesuits in New Mexico," *New Mexico Historical Review* 67 (1992): 382–88; and Fray Angelico Chavez, *But Time and Chance: The Story of Padre Martinez of Taos, 1793–1867* (Santa Fe, N.Mex.: Sunstone, 1981), 108–13.

43. After a mission in Conejos given by Gasparri and Minasi, for example, the missionaries proposed that as a memorial of the event the parishioners enlarge the convent of the Sisters of Loretto. The resulting ten-room structure prompted a chronicler to proclaim: "It can truly be said that Father Gasparri's sermons got results." "If a girls' school run by the sisters appears next to the church in a few months," Minasi noted, "one can say that the mission was exceedingly fruitful." By the summer of the next year, the sisters' Guadalupe Academy had opened its doors. See Patrick C. Stauter, *100 Years in Colorado's Oldest Parish* (Denver: St. Cajetan's Press, 1958), 18–20; Minasi, "Lettera XVIII, Conejos, dicembre, 1876," *LEPN*, 2 (1876–77):78, ANPSJ.

44. Dolan, *Catholic Revivalism*, 32–33.

45. Gasparri, "Historia," 20, ANPSJ. Aloysius Gonzaga, a sixteenth-century Jesuit scholastic (d. 1591), was held up as a paragon of virtue for boys and young men. Also closely associated with the Jesuits, Mariana de Jesús Paredes y Flores (1618–45) of Quito, Peru, was known for her life of prayer, fasting, and penance and

her care for Indian children. Gasparri probably presented her as a model for Catholic girls and young women.

46. Gasparri, "Historia," 24–25; S. Personè (Las Vegas, N.Mex.) to Palomba, 9 May 1876, ANPSJ.

47. Curran, *American Jesuit Spirituality*, 272, 296. See also Michael P. Carroll, *Catholic Cults and Devotions: A Psychological Inquiry* (Kingston: McGill-Queen's Univ. Press, 1989), 146–51.

48. Steele, *Works and Days*, 50.

49. F. S. Tomassini, "Lettera XLIX, Collegio di Las Vegas, 31 ottobre 1880," *LEPN*, 3 (1879–80):116–17, ANPSJ. A description of the enactment known as "Verónica y las tres caídas" is found in John A. Chester, "Holy Week at San Miguel," *WL* 10 (1881): 278. On the enhanced role of the priest in nineteenth-century devotionalism, see Ann Taves, *Household of Faith: Roman Catholic Devotions in Mid-Nineteenth-Century America* (Notre Dame: Univ. of Notre Dame Press, 1986), 111.

50. P. Tomassini, "Lettera XXIV, La Junta, N.Mex., ottobre 1874," *LEPN*, 1 (1874–75):68; "Lettera XXII, Conejos, Colorado, 25 Febbraio 1885," *LEPN*, 4 (1882–83):58–60, ANPSJ.

51. Diarist cited in Stoller and Steele, *Diary of Conejos*, 24 and 70n112.

52. F. S. Tomassini, "Lettera XLIX, Collegio di Las Vegas, 31 Ottobre 1880," *LEPN*, 3 (1879–80):118, ANPSJ; "Father Salvatore Personè," *WL* 53 (1924): 389.

53. S. Personè, "Lettera XV, Conejos, Agosto, 1874," *LEPN*, 1 (1874–75):38, ANPSJ. For a study of popular Hispano Catholicism, see Jay P. Dolan and Allan Figueroa Deck, eds., *Hispanic Catholic Culture in the U.S.: Issues and Concerns* (Notre Dame: Univ. of Notre Dame Press, 1994); and Allan Figueroa Deck, ed., *Frontiers of Hispanic Theology in the United States* (Maryknoll, N.Y.: Orbis Books, 1992).

54. G. Diamare (Guadalupe, Colo.) to [Gaffredo?], 3 June 1877, ANPSJ.

55. Carroll, *Catholic Cults and Devotions*, 161; see also Michael P. Carroll, *Veiled Threats: The Logic of Popular Catholicism in Italy* (Baltimore: Johns Hopkins Univ. Press, 1996).

56. Carroll, *Catholic Cults and Devotions*, 161; Thomas J. Steele, *Santos and Saints: The Religious Folk Art of Hispanic New Mexico* (Santa Fe, N.Mex.: Ancient City Press, 1982), 174–79.

57. S. Personè, "Lettera XV, Conejos, Agosto, 1874," *LEPN*, 1 (1874–75):38, ANPSJ; regarding Arizona, see P. Tomassini, "Lettera X, Albuquerque, N. M. 8 Maggio 1879," *LEPN*, 3 (1879–80):24, 114, ANPSJ. Tomassini insisted that the practice of the sung rosary was introduced by Personè, but other evidence suggested it was a modification of an earlier Spanish custom. See Steele, *Works and Days*, 105.

58. S. Personè (Conejos, Colo.) to Palomba, 27 Dec. 1872, ANPSJ; regarding Arizona, see Nattini, "Letter from Father C. M. Nattini, Santa Clara College, Aug. 29th, 1864," *Letters and Notices* 3 (1865–66): 25.

59. "Bertram Manuscript," 3–4, Jesuitica Collection, Regis Univ. Archives, Denver, Colo. (hereafter JCRU), in Steele, *Works and Days*, 104; Steele, *Santos and Saints*, 19.

60. Guidetti, *Missioni Populari*, 220ff; Michael P. Carroll, *The Penitente Brotherhood: Patriarchy and Hispano-Catholicism in New Mexico* (Baltimore: Johns Hopkins Univ. Press, 2002), 81–83, 173–77. Carroll, while not claiming that the *penitentes* were modeled on the Jesuits, noted that the two groups showed organizational similarities. Other scholars have observed that members of the brotherhood were devoted to St. Ignatius, founder of the Jesuits. On flagellant processions in Italy, see Michael P. Carroll, *Madonnas That Maim: Popular Catholicism in Italy Since the Fifteenth Century* (Baltimore: Johns Hopkins Univ. Press, 1992), 131–33.

61. Thomas J. Steele and Rowena A. Rivera, *Penitente Self-Government: Brotherhoods and Councils, 1797–1947* (Santa Fe, N.Mex.: Ancient City Press, 1985), 35–6; Stoller and Steele, *Diary of Conejos*, xxvii–xxxiii. See also Thomas J. Steele, "Italian Jesuits and Hispano Penitentes," *Il Giornalino* (Albuquerque, N.Mex.) 5 (Feb. 1978): 11–17; S. Personè, "Lettera XV, Conejos, Agosto, 1874," *LEPN*, 1 (1874–75):40, ANPSJ.

62. Pinto, "Lettera L, Trinidad, Colorado, 7 Maggio 1878," *LEPN*, 2 (1878–79):140, ANPSJ. Stoller and Steele, *Diary of Conejos*, 111–12.

63. *Revista Católica* (hereafter *RC*), 28 July 1877, 354, in Weigle, *Brothers of Light*, 79.

64. *Morning Journal* cited in Steele, *Works and Days*, 106–7; Personè in *RC*, 25 May 1890.

65. F. M. Troy (Albuquerque) draft of letter to J. B. Lux, 6 Oct. 1936; and Troy, "Chap. XVII. The American Passion Play," ms. copy, ANOPSJ. Another Jesuit, Giuseppe Sorrentino, described his work with the *penitentes* of southern Colorado in 1919 in *Dalle Montagne Rocciose al Rio Bravo*, 282–85.

66. For an analysis of Hispanic popular religion, see Allan Figueroa Deck, *The Second Wave: Hispanic Ministry and the Evangelization of Cultures* (New York: Paulist Press, 1989).

67. Gasparri, "Historia," 17, ANPSJ; nicknames found in Segale, *At the End of the Santa Fe Trail*, 178, 180; "Father Alexander Leone," *WL* 43 (1914): 99.

68. Romero in *Frontiers and Catholic Identities*, 202–3.

69. Steele, *Diary of Conejos*, 6n.

70. Orlando O. Espín, "Popular Catholicism Among Latinos," in *Hispanic Culture in the U.S.*, ed. Dolan and Deck, 313; Leonard Pitt, *The Decline of the Californios: A Social History of the Spanish-Speaking Californians, 1846–1890* (Berkeley: Univ. of California Press, 1966), 228; Emmet Larkin, "The Devotional Revolution in Ireland, 1850–1875," *American Historical Review* 77 (1972): 625–52.

71. Hughes, "New Mexico," *WL* 9 (1880): 137; Diamare (Conejos, Colo.) to Mascalchi, 6 June 1878, ANPSJ; "Estratto dalla Revista Catolica di Las Vegas, N.M., 29 luglio 1882," *LEPN*, 4 (1882–83):10, ANPSJ.

72. Baldassare (Conejos) to Palomba, 29 Mar. 1875, ANPSJ; Baldassare, "Lettera XXX, Conejos, Colorado, dicembre 1874," *LEPN*, 1 (1874–75):83, ANPSJ.

73. Dianna Everett, "The Public School Debate in New Mexico, 1850–1891," *Arizona and the West* 26 (1984): 109–10; Lavender, *The Southwest*, 283.

74. *The Old Faith and Glory: Story of the Church in New Mexico Since the American Occupation* (Santa Fe, N.Mex., 1946), 13, cited in Weigle, *Brothers of Light*, 13.

75. Vito Tromby, "La Escuela Nueva de San Felipe Neri," in *New Mexican Spanish Religious Oratory, 1800–1900*, ed. Thomas J. Steele (Albuquerque: Univ. of New Mexico Press, 1997), 167; Everett, "Public School Debate," *Arizona and the West* 26 (1984): 108–10; Lavender, *The Southwest*, 281–83.

76. Raffaele Baldasssare, "Lettera XXX, Conejos, Col., Dec. 1874," *LEPN*, 1 (1874–75):83, ANPSJ.

77. Segale, *At the End of the Santa Fe Trail*, 202, 322.

78. Lamar, *Far Southwest*, 167–68; *RC*, 5 Oct. 1890; William G. Ritch, "Whitch! [sic] Stagnation or Progress," [1878], William Gillet Ritch Papers, Huntington Library, San Marino, Calif. (hereafter HL).

79. Everett, "Public School Debate," *Arizona and the West* 26 (1984): 134; Bohme, "Italians in New Mexico," 67–68, 79–82.

80. Gasparri, "Historia," 15–16, ANPSJ; Report From the Las Vegas Residence, Las Vegas, N.Mex., 1875, ANPSJ; *RC*, 11 Aug. 1877.

81. Minasi, "Lettera LXIX, Las Vegas, N.M., 5 gennaio 1879," *LEPN*, 2(1878–79): 180, ANPSJ; Fede, "Lettera XL, Las Vegas, Nuevo Messico, 31 marzo 1878," *LEPN*, 2 (1878–79):126, ANPSJ; Personè, "Lettera LI, Las Vegas, 24 maggio 1878," *LEPN*, 2 (1878–79):143, ANPSJ.

82. Regarding Madero, see Bohme, "Italians in New Mexico," 84; Vito Tromby, "Lettera XVII, Albuquerque, Agosto 1874," *LEPN*, 1 (1874–75):43–44; "Una breve relazione di questa nostra scuoletta di Albuquerque," Hist. Domus San Felipe, Albuquerque, ANOPSJ; A. Mescia, "Lettera LVII, Las Vegas, 17 agosto 1881," *LEPN*, 3 (1880–81):133, ANPSJ.

83. Mazzella, "Memoriale," 15 Sept. 1875, ANPSJ; *RC*, 7 and 10 June 1876; *RC*, 25 Mar. 1876; Richard Griswold del Castillo, *La Familia: Chicano Families in the Urban Southwest, 1848 to the Present* (Notre Dame: Univ. Notre Dame Press, 1984), 83.

84. *North American Review* (Apr. 1866); *Annual Report, 1873* (Methodist Episcopal Church Board of Foreign Missions), 172–75, Library of the Graduate Theological Union, Berkeley, Calif.

85. One Neapolitan Jesuit described the *Revista* as "the *Civiltà cattolica* of this Mission." See Report from the Las Vegas, New Mexico, Residence, 1875, ANPSJ; Gasparri cited in *RC*, 2 Jan. 1875; Mazzella (La Junta) to Palomba, 19 Sept. 1875, ANPSJ.

86. Report from Las Vegas Residence, New Mexico, 1875, ANPSJ; Marra (Denver) to Galucci, 30 Apr. 1896, ANPSJ; Gabriel Ussel, "Memoirs," (80203–82137), 71–72, Colorado Historical Society, The Stephan B. Hart Library, The Colorado History Museum, Denver, Colo. (hereafter CHS).

87. Bohme, "Italians in New Mexico," 67; Mazzella (La Junta) to Palomba, 19 Sept. 1875, ANPSJ; Everett, "Public School Debate," *Arizona and the West* 26 (1984): 126; Lamar, *The Far Southwest*, 167.

88. Marra in Segale, *End of the Santa Fe Trail*, 180; *RC*, 10 Dec. 1911; Everett, "Public School Debate," *Arizona and the West* 26 (1984): 112.

89. Benjamin M. Read, *Illustrated History of New Mexico* (Santa Fe: Santa Fe Weekly New Mexican Publishing, 1912; repr., New York: Arno Press, 1986), 526; *RC*, 10 Dec. 1911.

90. *RC*, 20 Feb. 1887, 23 June 1907, 7 Dec. 1902.

91. *RC*, 21 Sept. 1878 and 20 Feb. 1887.

92. *RC*, 24 Mar. 1877, 10 Dec. 1893; Griswold del Castillo, *La Familia*, 80–81.

93. *RC*, 7 Jan. 1894 and 25 Aug. 1895; Pasquale Tomassini, "Lettera VI, La Junta, N.M., Aprile 1874," *LEPN*, 1 (1874–75):10, ANPSJ. On the development of book-based devotionalism, see Campbell, "Kaleidoscope," 281; and Taves, *Household of Faith*, 1–10.

94. Dolan and Hinojosa, *Mexican Americans and the Catholic Church*, 30; A. Brunner (Trinidad, Colo.) to Scarcella, 16 Feb. 1906, ANPSJ.

95. Mario García, *Desert Immigrants: The Mexicans of El Paso, 1880–1920* (New Haven: Yale Univ. Press, 1981), 218.

96. Dolan and Hinojosa, *Mexican Americans and the Catholic Church*, 20–21, 29–30.

CHAPTER 9

1. Rev. Nathan S. S. Beman, *Collegiate and Theological Education at the West: A Discourse Delivered before the Society for the Promotion of Collegiate and Theological Education at the West, at its Annual Meeting at Springfield, Mass., 28 Oct 1848* (New York: S. W. Benedict, 1847), 15, MUDD.

2. Ponte (San Francisco) to Beckx, 27 Mar. 1870, Calif. 1001-VII-21, ARSI.

3. Ibid.

4. Eliot in Laurence R. Veysey, *The Emergence of the American University* (Chicago: Univ. of Chicago Press, 1965), 6–7; Power, *History of Catholic Higher Education*, 90.

5. John P. Frieden, "The Society of Jesus in California," in *Echoes of the Golden Jubilee* (Santa Clara, Calif., 1901), 66; Gerald McKevitt, *The University of Santa Clara, a History, 1851–1977* (Stanford: Stanford Univ. Press, 1979), 52–53.

6. Bryan J. Clinch, "The Jesuits in American California," *Records of the American Catholic Historical Society* 17 (1906): 447; Mel Gorman, "Stereochemical Concepts in the Molecular System of Joseph Bayma," *Proceedings of the Tenth International Congress of the History of Science* (1962): 899–901; *Dictionary of American Biography* (New York, 1929), 2:79–80; Burns, *Jesuits and the Indian Wars*, 55.

7. *San Francisco Weekly American Flag*, 10 July 1864; and *Thistleton's Illustrated Jolly Giant* (San Francisco), 1 Nov. 1873 and 1 Dec. 1873, in John B. McGloin, *Eloquent Indian: The Life of James Bouchard, California Jesuit* (Stanford: Stanford Univ. Press, 1950), 145; governors Samuel B. Axtell and William Ritch, quoted in Everett, "Public School Debate," *Arizona and the West* 26 (1984): 121–22; Michael O'Ferrall, "Five Years at the Golden Gate," *San Francisco Monitor*, 29 Mar. 1872.

8. Philip Gleason, "American Catholic Higher Education: A Historical Perspective," in *The Shape of American Higher Education*, ed. Robert Hassenger (Chicago: Univ. of Chicago Press, 1967), 15.

9. Cataldo (Spokane) to Anderledy, 17 Jan. 1892, Mont. Sax. 1003-I-43, ARSI; Congiato (San Francisco?) to Sopranis, Apr. 1866, Calif. 1001-VI, 6, ARSI.

10. Beckx to Sopranis, 15 Sept. 1861, Summary, Mission. Asst. Angl. 1 Nov.

1861–6 Oct. 1891, ARSI; *Redwood* (Oct. 1908), 4; "From Father Prelato," *WL* 1 (1862–63):202; "Catalogus Alumnorum Coll. Stae Clarae, Soc. Iesu, Cal., 1868–1890," ASCU.

11. "Letter from Father C. M. Nattini," *Letters and Notices*, 3 (1865–66):23, ABPSJ.

12. Accolti, "Osservazioni," 26 May 1863, Calif. 1002-I-30, ARSI; S. Personè (Denver) to Canger, 6 May 1889, ANPSJ.

13. *Constitutions of the Society of Jesus*, trans. Ganss, 213; O'Malley, *First Jesuits*, 256.

14. Gabriel Codina, "'Our Way of Proceeding' in Education: The Ratio Studiorum," *Educatio SJ* (May 1999): 11–12.

15. John J. Barrett, "Address," *Echoes of the Golden Jubilee*, 46; *Santa Clara College Catalog, 1910–1911*; *Catalogue of Las Vegas College, 1877–1878*, JCRU.

16. Roothaan's circular letter in Allen P. Farrell, *The Jesuit Code of Liberal Education: Development and Scope of the Ratio Studiorum* (Milwaukee, 1938), 390; Roothaan (Rome) to Ulbaldini, 14 Jan. 1832, Prov. Rom. [Summary of the General's Outgoing Letters], 1 Apr. 1830–30 July 1833," ARSI; John W. Padberg et al., "Decree 31, General Congregation 22," in *For Matters of Greater Moment: The First Thirty Jesuit General Congregations: A Brief History and a Translation of the Decrees* (St. Louis, 1994), 454.

17. Arthur McGovern, "Jesuit Education," *Studies in Jesuit Spirituality* (1988): 7. For a full examination of the evolving approach to the study of Latin, see Ganns, *Saint Ignatius's Idea of a Jesuit University*, 218–40.

18. *Catalogue of Las Vegas College, 1887–1888, to be known henceforward as College of the Sacred Heart, Denver, Colo.*, JCRU; *Santa Clara College Catalog, 1910–1911*. A later exposition of this argument is found in Joseph A. Walsh, "Jesuit College Education After the War," *Jesuit Educational Quarterly* 6 (1944): 168.

19. *Owl*, May 1871, ASCU.

20. McKevitt, *University of Santa Clara*, 102–3; Mel Gorman, "German Influence on American Mining: A. J. Bowie and the Freiberg Connection," Archives of the University of San Francisco; Eric Abrahamson, *The University of San Francisco School of Law: A History, 1912–1987* (San Francisco: USF School of Law, 1987), 17; James P. Walsh and Timothy J. O'Keefe, *Legacy of a Native Son: James David Phelan and Villa Montalvo* (Saratoga, Calif.: Montalvo Association, 1993), 16–17.

21. McKevitt, *University of Santa Clara*, 55–58; John B. McGloin, *Jesuits by the Golden Gate* (San Francisco: Univ. of San Francisco Press, 1972), 64–65.

22. Moulder in William Warren Ferrier, *Origin and Development of the University of California* (Berkeley: Univ. of California Press, 1930), 34; Cicaterri (Santa Clara) to Beckx, 1 Jan. 1858, Calif. 1001-III-1, ARSI.

23. Hughes, "New Mexico," *WL* 9 (1880): 135; Mascia, "Lettera LVII, Las Vegas, 17 agosto 1881," *LEPN*, 3 (1881–82):133, ANPSJ.

24. Sasia (San Francisco) to Anderledy, 20 Feb. 1890, Calif. 1003-II-4, ARSI, quotes from letter of Beckx to Villiger, 26 Mar. 1866; C. Barchi (San Francisco) to Sopranis, 1 Sept. 1866, Calif. 1001-XI-13, ARSI.

25. Congiato (San Francisco) to Beckx, 1 June 1866, Calif. 1001-VI-7, ARSI; George F. Weibel, *Gonzaga's Silver Jubilee: A Memoir* (Spokane, 1912), 192.

26. McKevitt, *University of Santa Clara*, 39–40.

27. David Frederic Ferris, *Judge Marvin and the Founding of the California Public School System* (Berkeley and Los Angeles: Univ. of California Press, 1962), 53.

28. Vallejo quoted in Madie Brown Emparan, *The Vallejos of California* (San Francisco: Gleeson Library Associates, 1968), 366–67; José María Estudillo, "Diary," entries for 25 Apr. 1861; 25 May 1861; 25 June 1862; Bancroft Library, University of California, Berkeley, Calif. (hereafter BL); Baldassare (Albuquerque) to Palomba, 28 May 1876, ANPSJ.

29. Gerald McKevitt, "Hispanic Californians and Catholic Higher Education: The Diary of Jesús María Estudillo, 1857–1864," *California History* 64 (1991): 320–403; James Alexander Forbes to José Antonio Aguirre, 13 Dec. 1852, "Letter Book of James Alexander Forbes," vol. 1, CSL.

30. "New Mexico," *WL* 13 (1884): 42.

31. McKevitt, "Hispanic Californians and Catholic Higher Education," *California History* 64 (1991): 325–26; Dolan, *The Immigrant Church*, 162.

32. Richard Hofstadter and C. Dewitt Hardy, *Development and Scope of Higher Education in the United States* (New York: Columbia Univ. Press, 1954), 26.

33. "St. Ignatius College, San Francisco, Cal.," *WL* 15 (1886): 217; article reprinted from San Francisco's *Journal of Commerce*.

34. Bayma (San Francisco) to Beckx, July 29, 1869, Calif. 1001-X-22, ARSI; Weibel, *Gonzaga's Silver Jubilee*, 192. Santa Clara College had gained "credit and renown" in this field early in its history, as newly appointed President Bouchard Villiger discovered when he arrived at the college in 1861. See Villiger, "Autobiography," 78.

35. *Prospectus of Santa Clara College*, 1855–56, 1857–58, and 1879–80, ASCU; "Father Messea's Life Work Ended," *San Jose Mercury* (?), 12 Aug. 1897, Messea File, ASCU. An account of a visit by a Mr. Anderson from Scotland, originally published in the Philadelphia *Argus*, in Clinch, "Jesuits in American California," *Records of the American Catholic Historical Society* 17 (1906): 316–17.

36. Congiato (San Francisco) to Roothaan, 19 Mar. 1863, Calif. 1002-I-26, ARSI.

37. "Report of the Teaching of Chemistry and Physics in the United States," *Circulars of Information of the U.S. Bureau of Education, No. 6, 1880* (Washington, D.C.: Government Printing Office, 1881).

38. *Mining and Scientific Press*, 3 May 1873, 281; Mel Gorman, "Chemistry at the University of San Francisco, 1863–1906," *Journal of Chemical Education* 41 (1964): 628; Charles W. Eliot, "Recent Changes in Secondary Education," *Atlantic Monthly* 84 (Oct. 1899): 443.

39. *Prospectus of Santa Clara College, 1858–1859*.

40. The visitor, a Catholic priest, quoted in William Francis Hanchett, "Religion in the California Gold Rush, 1849–1854: The Christian Churches and the California Mines" (Ph.D. diss., Univ. of California, Berkeley, 1952), 54. In 1861, the order's superior general authorized the commercial course in places where it was "absolutely necessary," and its inauguration did not trigger a mass exodus of students from Latin and Greek studies. The following year, a uniform national policy was adopted for Jesuit institutions in the United States that had either introduced the course or

intended to do so. See Roothaan (Rome) to Sopranis, 25 Sept. 1861, Mission. Asst. Angl., 1 Nov. 1861–6 Oct. 1891 [Summary of Father General's Correspondence], ARSI.

41. "Historia Domus, 1877," ACPSJ. One of the reasons why authorities in Italy had initially withheld permission to found a Jesuit college in Spokane was their fear that its curriculum would be "more commercial than strictly scientific." See Carlo Torti (Chieri, Italy) to General, 8 Jan. 1889, Prov. Taur. 1011-II-30, ARSI.

42. *Prospectus of Santa Clara College, 1877–1878*; *San Jose Daily News*, 15 May 1892.

43. Las Vegas prospectus in Stansell, *Regis*, 18; de la Motte (Spokane) to General, 12 May 1907, Mont. Sax. 1003-III-42, ARSI.

44. Marra (Pueblo, Colo.) to Mola, 30 Jan. 1890, ANPSJ; Pinto (El Paso, Texas) to Marra, 16 Apr. 1902, ANPSJ.

45. Beckx to Ciravegna, 18 Apr. 1870, Prov. Taur. 1010-III-11, ARSI; O'Ferrall, "Five Years at the Golden Gate, " *San Francisco Monitor*, 29 Mar 1872; Nattini (San Francisco) to Beckx, 30 Jan. 1870, Calif. 1001-XI-28, ARSI.

46. Baldassare (Albuquerque) to P. Gaffredo [?], 4 Sept. 1877, ANPSJ; S. Personè (Las Vegas) to Vioni, 26 June 1885, ANPSJ.

47. Vanzia described in Riordan, *First Half Century*, 102; "Consulte, 1901–1920," entry for 23 Nov. 1906; and Federico Lupi [?] (St. Louis) to Stravino?, 26 Apr. 1907, ANPSJ.

48. Baldassare (Conejos, Colo.) to Mascalchi, 17 Dec. 1878, ANPSJ; A. Brunner (Pueblo, Colo.) to Marra, 21 Jan. 1902, ANPSJ.

49. Marra [Las Vegas?] to Canger, 9 Feb. 1887, and Marra [Denver] to Canger, 8 June 1889, ANPSJ; Pantanella (Morrison, Colo.) to Canger, 28 Jan. 1885, ANPSJ.

50. Waddell, "Some Memories," ASCU; C. A. Barchi (San Francisco) to Sopranis, 7 July 1865, Calif. 1001-XI-10, ARSI.

51. Stansell, *Regis*, 50; "Patrick Kelly" file, ATPSJ; Charles Mackin, "The Wanderings of Fifty Years," JOPA. Mackin spent most of his career as a missionary in Alaska.

52. Stansell, *Regis*, 33, 51; F. X. Koward, "Sacred Heart College, Morrison, Colorado, 1884–1888," 53–65, JCRU; Marra (Las Vegas) to Mola, 18 Aug. 1888, ANPSJ.

53. Varsi (Santa Clara) to Beckx, 4 Aug. 1869, Calif. 1001-X-22, ARSI; "Rev. Father Young, S.J.," *Souvenir, Golden Jubilee, Santa Clara College 1851–1901* (Santa Clara, Calif., 1901), 22.

54. Villiger (Santa Clara) to Angelo Paresce, 22 Aug. 1861?, AMPSJ.

55. Baldassare (Las Vegas) to Mascalchi, 11 Jan. 1878, ANPSJ.

56. Stansell, *Regis*, 50.

57. *WL* 22 (1893): 336; Joseph O'Halloran (San Francisco) to Nobili, 6 Aug. 1852, ASCU; Congiato (San Francisco) to Beckx, Mar. 1983, Calif. 1002-I-26, ARSI.

58. "Diarium Coll. Denver, 1888–1894," JCRU.

59. Power, *History of Catholic Higher Education*, 105, 151–2.

60. De la Motte (Pendleton, Ore.) to Martín, 26 Jan. 1905, Mont. Sax. 1003-III-31, ARSI; Francis Dillon, Gonzaga's acting president in 1904–05, was rejected as permanent holder of the office; regarding Pantanella, see Marra (Denver) to Mola,

8 Sept. 1888, ANPSJ; Congiato (San Francisco) to Sopranis, 20 Aug. 1866, Calif. 1001-VI-9, ARSI.

61. Gentile (Albuquerque) to Vioni, 16 July 1881, ANPSJ; Sasia (Torino) to Martín, 21 Mar. 1896, Taur. 1011-IV-60, ARSI.

62. Congiato (San Jose, Calif.) to Anderledy, 1 Sept. 1888, Calif. 1004-III-1, ARSI; de la Motte (Pendleton, Ore.) to Wernz, 26 Jan. 1905, Mont. Sax. 1003-III-31, ARSI; Van Gorp (Spokane) to Martín, 30 Aug. 1897, Mont. Sax. 1003-II-29, ARSI.

63. Robert J. Smith (Seattle) to Wernz, 29 July 1909, Mont. Sax. 1003-VI-82, ARSI; de la Motte (St. Xavier) to Martín, 19 Jan. 1901, Mont. Sax. 1003-III-3, ARSI.

64. Congiato (Santa Clara) to Charles Stonestreet, 18 Aug. 1856, AMPSJ.

65. Congiato (San Francisco) to Beckx, 21 Feb. 1868, Calif. 1001-VII-3, ARSI.

66. O'Ferrall, "Five Years at the Golden Gate," *San Francisco Monitor*, 29 Mar. 1872; Ryan, "Our Scholasticate," *WL* 33 (1904): 141. Appraisals of Accolti are found in Jesús María Estudillo, "Diary," entry for 10 May 1867, BL; and O. P. Fitzgerald, *California Sketches* (Nashville, Tenn., 1880), 145. Regarding Marra, see S. Personè (Las Vegas) to Vioni, 26 June 1885, ANPSJ; Gentile (Las Vegas) to Carlo Gallucci, 24 Oct. 1891, ANPSJ.

67. On Diomedi, see Van Gorp (Spokane) to Martín, 14 Jan. 1896, Mont. Sax. 1003-II-15, ARSI; Nobili is evaluated in Congiato (Santa Clara) to Roothaan, 18 Oct. 1855, Calif. 1001-II-3, ARSI; data on Pantanella in Marra (Denver) to Mola, 8 Sept. 1888, ANPSJ; Dooley, *Woodstock and Its Makers*, 63–64.

68. Stansell, *Regis*, 11; Schoenberg, *Paths to the Northwest*, 154; McKevitt, *University of Santa Clara*, 75–77. By 1870, room, board, and tuition had increased to $325 at Georgetown; $300 at Fordham; and $250 at Holy Cross and St. Louis. Non-Catholic colleges with endowments charged much less; for example, in 1870 fees at Yale totaled merely $90 and at Columbia, $100. (See Power, *History of Catholic Higher Education*, 166–67.)

69. Beckx, "Letter of . . . the Safety . . . ," *Select Letters*, 313; Hughes, "New Mexico," *WL* 9 (1880): 134; Accolti (Oregon City, Ore.) to W. S. Murphy, 8 Nov. 1852, De Smetiana, JMPA.

70. Accolti, "Osservazione . . . [1863], Calif. 1002-I-30, ARSI; Barchi (San Francisco) to Sopranis, 1 Sept. 1866, Calif. 1001-XI-13, ARSI; Marra (Denver) to Canger, 22 Nov. 1887, and Marra (Pueblo, Colo.) to Mola, 30 Jan. 1890, ANPSJ.

71. Pantanella, "Lettera LV, College of the Sacred Heart, Morrison, Colo., 10 Ottobre 1884" and "College of the Sacred Heart Conducted by the Jesuit Fathers, Colorado, N. M., 3 Ottobre 1885," *LEPN*, 4 (1882–83): 127, 168, ANPSJ; Pantanella (Morrison, Colo.) to Canger, 28 Jan. 1885, ANPSJ; student description in Pablo C. DeBaca, "Pastimes in the Life of Pablo Cabeza de Baca," in *La Gente: Hispano History and Life in Colorado*, ed. Vincent C. de Baca (Denver: Colorado Historical Society, 1998), 58–59.

72. Sara Lippincott in Kevin Starr, *Americans and the California Dream, 1850–1915* (New York: Oxford Univ. Press, 1973), 376.

73. Horace Greeley, *An Overland Journey, From New York to San Francisco in the Summer of 1859* (New York: Saxton, Barker, 1860); *San Francisco Weekly American Flag* (10 July 1864), in McGloin, *Eloquent Indian*, 144.

74. Varsi (San Francisco) to Piccirillo, 28 Apr. 1880, Piccirillo Papers, AMPSJ;

Sasia (San Francisco) to Vicar General, 12 Mar. 1885, Calif. 1004-II-10, ARSI; Personè (Las Vegas) to Mascalchi, 6 Nov. 1878, and 8 Dec. 1878, ANPSJ; Pinto (El Paso) to Marra, 27 Jan. 1897, ANPSJ.

75. "New Mexico," *WL* 13 (1884): 43; Hughes, "New Mexico," *WL* 9 (1880): 135. In 1859, resources were so low at Santa Clara that two Jesuits were sent begging to Mexico and Central America; two years later, they returned with $1,000. See *Souvenir of Santa Clara College, 1851–1901,* 44.

76. [Maraschi?], "Collegio di St. Ignazio, San Francisco, Cal., 25 Genn 1868, Memoria," Calif. 1001-XI-16, ARSI; Congiato (San Francisco) to Beckx, 10 Feb. 1866, Calif. 1001-VI-5, ARSI; Varsi (Santa Clara) to Beckx, 28 Sept. 1873, Calif. 1001-X-25, ARSI.

77. *Alta California* (San Francisco), 11 Aug. 1870.

78. McKevitt, *University of Santa Clara,* 97–98.

79. Stansell, *Regis,* 20; McKevitt, *University of Santa Clara,* 97–99; Marra (Denver) to Gallucci, 2 June 1895, ANPSJ.

80. *Souvenir of Santa Clara College,* 51; S. Personè (Denver) to Canger, 27 Aug. 1890, ANPSJ; Ciravegna (Monaco) to Beckx, 18 Apr. 1870, Taur. 1010-III-11, ARSI.

81. *San Francisco Weekly American Flag,* 10 July 1864, in McGloin, *Eloquent Indian,* 144; *Owl* (Santa Clara College), 2 (Apr. 1871).

82. Campbell, "Kaleidoscope," 133–34.

83. Robert George Raymer, "Educational Development in the Territory and State of Washington, 1853–1908," *Washington Historical Quarterly* 18 (1927): 165–67, 176; John C. Lawrence, "Pioneer Experiences," *Washington Historical Quarterly* 16 (1925): 257; Eric F. Goldman, "J. Allen Smith: The Reformer and His Dilemma," *Pacific Northwest Quarterly* 35 (1944): 195.

84. Accolti (San Francisco) to Roothaan, 28 Mar. 1850, in Garraghan, *Jesuits,* 2:407; *A Statement on Behalf of the College of California* (1860), BL; John Swett, *Public Education in California* (New York, 1969), 264.

85. Barnes, *Plea in Behalf of Western Colleges,* 22, MUDD: Kirk, *Dr. Kirk's Discourse,* 29, MUDD.

86. Ferrier, *Ninety Years of Education,* 206; Ferrier, *Origin and Development of the University of California,* 149; *A Statement in Behalf of the College of California* (1860), 13, BL; McKevitt, *University of Santa Clara,* 38–41.

87. Cataldo's letter to the superior general in Schoenberg, *Gonzaga University,* 46; Accolti to Roothaan, 28 Mar. 1850, Garraghan, *Jesuits,* 2:407.

88. Baldassare (Pueblo, Colo.) to Mascalchi, 25 Apr. 1879, ANPSJ.

89. Power, *History of Catholic Higher Education,* 109; Barnes, *Plea in Behalf of Western Colleges,* 26, MUDD.

CHAPTER 10

1. Garibaldi in Andrew F. Rolle, *The Italian Americans: Troubled Roots* (New York: Free Press, 1980), 10.

2. Parodi, "Memoirs," JOPA.

3. Michele Accolti, "Osservazioni," [1863], Calif. 1002-I-30, ARSI.

4. Tromby (Albuquerque) to Vioni, 29 Mar. 1883, ANPSJ; Cocchi, "Lettera," *LEPN,* 1 (1892):93–95.

5. *RC,* 23 Aug. 1879.

6. Bayma, "The Liberalistic View of the Public School Question," *American Catholic Quarterly Review* 2 (Jan. 1877): 11–12; Accolti (Oregon City, Ore.) to Murphy, 8 Nov. 1852, JMPA.

7. Diamare (Guadalupe, Colo.) to Mascalchi, 2 Oct. 1877, ANPSJ.

8. "Rev. John B. Guida," *WL* 49 (1920): 125; Burkhart Bilger, Review of Chris Offutt, *No Heroes: A Memoir of Coming Home,* in *New York Times,* 7 July 2002.

9. *Constitutions of the Society of Jesus,* 215.

10. Marra (Pueblo) to Mola, 7 Jan. 1891, ANPSJ; Ponte (San Francisco) to Beckx, 27 Mar. 1870, Calif. 1001-VII-21, ARSI.

11. Marra (Las Vegas) to De Francesco, 29 Nov. 1911, ANPSJ; S. Personè (Trinidad, Colo.) to Stravino, 14 Dec. 1909, ANPSJ.

12. D'Aste (St. Mary's Mission) to Razzini, 16 Jan. 1884, ATPSJ; *RC,* 25 Jan. 1885; *RC,* 1 Mar. 1885; F. I. Prelato, "Extracts of Letters from California: From Father Prelato," *Letters and Notices* 1 (1862–63): 201–3.

13. "Historia Domus, 1919–1920," entry for 11 Jan. 1919, Archives of Mt. Carmel Church, Pueblo, Colo. On Catholic patriotism, see Liptak, *Immigrants and Their Church,* 59.

14. Ciani suggested that Mazzella and Brandi sought U.S. citizenship "because of the protection that status might provide them if they returned to Italy." See John L. Ciani, "Metal Statue, Granite Base: The Jesuits' Woodstock College, Maryland, 1869–1891" (University of Notre Dame: Cushwa Center for the Study of American Catholicism, Working Papers Series) ser. 25, no. 4 (Fall 1993): 13n.

15. Palladino (St. Peter's Mission) to Cataldo, ca. 1881, *WL* 12 (1883): 318–19.

16. Rossi, *Six Years on the West Coast,* 94; Cocchi, "Lettera," *Lettere Edificanti della Provincia Torinese della Compagnia di Gesù* (hereafter *LEPT*), 1 (1892):93–95.

17. Ashley in Steele, *Works and Days,* 38; *RC,* 15 Jan. 1876. In the 1870s, Archbishop Lamy repeatedly ordered priests of his diocese to wear an overcoat when on call — "It must be black and extend below the knees" — to differentiate them from lay persons, but his mandates were often ignored. Juan B. Lamy (Santa Fe), circular letters to clergy, 10 Oct. 1870, AR-882-JBL-#15, and 1 Feb. 1876, AR-882-JBL-no. 30, ANOPSJ.

18. Rappagliosi, *Memorie,* 107–9, JOPA. It was not until after 1884, when the American bishops of the Third Plenary Council of Baltimore standardized clerical dress, that the Roman collar became mandatory for all priests.

19. Steele, *Diary of Conejos,* xxxiv.

20. Baldassare (Pueblo, Colo.) to Mascalchi, 25 Apr. 1879, ANPSJ.

21. Burns, *Jesuits,* 35.

22. "Extract from a Letter of Fr. Giorda," *Letters and Notices* 3 (1865–66): 293; Prelato, "Extracts of Letters from California: From Father Prelato," *Letters and Notices* 1 (1862–63): 20–23.

23. Burns, *Jesuits,* 35.

24. Accolti (Santa Clara) to Beckx, 15 Feb. 1865, Calif. 1001-V-5, ARSI.

25. Michael E. Engh, "The Pacific Slope — 'When Others Rushed In,'" *The Frontiers and Catholic Identities,* ed. Anne M. Butler, Michael E. Engh, and Thomas W. Spalding (Maryknoll, N.Y.: Orbis Books, 1999), 143.

26. Bohme, "Italians in New Mexico," 145.

27. O'Malley, *First Jesuits*, 74; Marra (Pueblo, Colo.) to Mola, 25 Mar. 1890, ANPSJ.

28. Marra (Las Vegas) to Mola, 18 Aug. 1888, ANPSJ; Brown (Denver) to De Francesco, 13 Oct. 1917, ANPSJ.

29. B. Piccardo (San Jose) to G. B. Barone, 18 Nov. 1880, ATPSJ; "Father Alexander Mazzetti," *WL* 53 (1924): 91; see also Dolan, *American Catholic Experience*, 19–20.

30. S. Personè (Trinidad, Colo.) to A. Stravino, 14 Dec. 1909, ANPSJ. Statistics found in Personè (Trinidad, Colo.) to Superior, 18 July 1912, B2/E5/Z1.X1, ANOPSJ.

31. "Saints Patrick and Ignatius Diary, 1888–1889," undated clipping insert regarding the dedication of St. Joseph's Church, JCRU.

32. "Father Weninger on the Pacific Coast," *WL* 2 (1873): 222; F. X. Tomassini, "History of Trinidad Parish," Holy Trinity Rectory, Trinidad, Colo.

33. Father Shuleck [?] "said Mass at 9 and preached in four languages" according to "Saints Patrick and Ignatius Diary, 1888–1889," entry for June 1, 1890, JCRU.

34. "Father Weninger on the Pacific Coast," *WL* 3 (1874): 203. Weninger did not dazzle all congregations. In 1869, the Jesuits of San Francisco asked the famed Austrian Jesuit give a mission in English in St. Ignatius Church. "We cannot say much in commendation" of his English, a chronicler writes, "for we think that but few of his hearers grasped any great part of what he said." See Riordan, *First Half Century*, 160.

35. Congiato (San Jose?) to Martín, 18 June 1893, Calif. 1004-III-5, ARSI; "Litterae Annuae Residenciae Delnortensis, 1911–12," ANPSJ; Marra (Las Vegas) to Stravino, 31 Jan. 1911, ANPSJ.

36. ["Announcements, Holy Trinity Church, Trinidad, Colo.], Jan. 1893–March 1896," entries 17 Nov. 1895, 19 Jan. 1896, 8 Mar. 1896, Holy Trinity Rectory Archive, Trinidad, Colo.

37. "Saints Patrick and Ignatius Diary, 1872–1885," entries, 18–23 May 1885, JCRU.

38. S. Personè (Trinidad, Colo.) to Stravino, 14 Dec. 1909, ANPSJ; G. B. Ponte (San Francisco) to Beckx, 21 Mar. 1870, Calif. 1001-VII-21, ARSI.

39. Congiato (San Francisco) to Anderledy, 12 Dec. 1862, Calif. 1002-I-19, ARSI; Muller (San Jose) to R. Meyer, 19 May 1893, Calif. 1004-III-8, ARSI; see also Vecoli, "Priests and Prelates," *Journal of Social History* 2: 242.

40. Rossi, *Six Years on the West Coast*, 218; Henry Woods, "California Mission of the Soc. of Jesus," *WL* 13 (1884): 161.

41. Regarding Accolti, see Congiato (Champoeg, Oregon Territory) to Beckx, 15 Jan. 1856, Mont. Sax. 1002-I-11, ARSI; regarding Italian preachers, see Richard A. Gleeson quoted in McGloin, *Eloquent Indian*, 103.

42. Riordan, *First Half Century*, 105–6; Antonio Cichi (San Francisco) to Paresce, 10 Sept. 1862 (228M15), AMPSJ.

43. Marra (Pueblo) to Mola, 16 Oct. 1888, ANPSJ; Marra (Denver) to Gallucci, 30 Dec. 1891, ANPSJ.

44. Pinto (Pueblo, Colo.) to Palomba, 9 Dec. 1872, ANPSJ; P. Tomassini (La Junta) to Mascalchi, 25 Jan. 1878, ANPSJ.

45. Palomba (Naples) to Gasparri, 23 Aug. 1872, ANPSJ; Pinto (Santa Fe) to Palomba, 14 Sept. 1872, ANPSJ; Pinto (Pueblo, Colo.) to Palomba, 9 Dec. 1872, ANPSJ; Pinto (Pueblo) to Palomba, 29 Aug. 1873, ANPSJ.

46. Baldassare (Albuquerque) to Palomba, 20 Sept. 1876 and 12 Jan. 1877, ANPSJ; Marra (Pueblo) to Mola, 25 Mar. 1890, ANPSJ.

47. Critques of the Montenarelli brothers, found in Pinto (Trinidad, Colo.) to Canger, 12 Oct. 1885, ANPSJ.

48. Leggio (Pueblo) to Canger, 29 Jan. 1888, ANPSJ.

49. Baldassare (Pueblo) to Mascalchi, 10 Jan. 1879, ANPSJ; *Colorado Daily Chieftain* (Pueblo, Colo.,) 19 Oct. 1878 and 1 May 1879.

50. Baldassare (Pueblo) to Mascalchi, 10 Jan. 1879, ANPSJ; Baldassare (Pueblo) to Mascalchi, 26 May 1879, ANPSJ. Gubitosi placed the value of the smelter at $25,000. See Gubitosi (Pueblo) to Mascalchi, 22 Dec. 1879, ANPSJ.

51. Baldassare (Pueblo) to Mascalchi, 26 May 1879, ANPSJ.

52. Baldassare (Trinidad) to Mascalchi, 6 May 1880, ANPSJ.

53. S. Personè (Las Vegas) to Mascalchi, 24 May 1880, ANPSJ; Baldassare (Trinidad) to Mascalchi, 6 May 1880. Nearly a quarter of a century after the financial imbroglio of 1879, the Neapolitans discovered that they might actually turn a profit on one of Gubitosi's mines. They had been offered $8,000 to $10,000, wrote Pinto in 1901, for twenty shares in "one of those holes that Gubitosi opened to our renown in Silver Cliff." See Pinto (El Paso, Tex.) to Marra, 7 Nov. 1901, ANPSJ.

54. The fullest account of the impasse is found in a report of the mission superior to the Naples provincial: Gentile (Albuquerque) to Vioni, 23 Nov. 1882, ANPSJ. See also "Saints Patrick and Ignatius Diary, 1872–1885," entries for 1882–1883, JCRU; and Gentile (Las Vegas, N.Mex.) to Vioni, 13 Jan 1883, ANPSJ.

55. *Pueblo Chieftain* (Pueblo, Colo.) 14 Dec. 1882; clipping from *Daily Chieftain*, 22 Jan. 1883, ANPSJ.

56. Lambert (Pueblo) to Machebeuf, 27 Sept. 1883; Lambert et al. (Pueblo) 23 Nov. 1883, AADC. One irate parishioner claimed that when his infant son was baptized in Pueblo, the priest "could not speak one word of English. If he could, he took good care not to for some reason, and I will remember the stink of his breath I think while I live." See Hugh Smith (Denver) to Machebeuf, 9 Aug. 1884; and also Thomas Smith (Pueblo?) to Hugh Smith, ca. Aug. 1884, AADC.

57. *Daily Chieftain* (Pueblo, Colo.), 3 Oct. 1884.

58. "Saints Patrick and Ignatius Diary, 1884–89," Leggio entry, 1889, JCRU; Marra (Pueblo) to Canger, 9 Nov. 1887, ANPSJ; Pinto (El Paso) to Marra, 16 Feb. 1900 and 20 Aug. 1903, ANPSJ.

59. Personè (Trinidad, Colo.) to Stravino, 14 Dec. 1909, ANPSJ; Marra (El Paso, Tex.) to Mola, 6 Feb. 1889, ANPSJ; Stephen M. DiGiovanni, "Michael Augustine Corrigan and the Italian Immigrants: The Relationship Between the Church and the Italians in the Archdiocese of New York, 1885–1902," in *Italian Americans: New Perspectives in Italian Immigration and Ethnicity*, ed. Lydio F. Tomasi (New York: Center for Migration Studies of New York, 1985), 302–19.

60. Personè (Trinidad, Colo.) to Stravino, 14 Dec. 1909, ANPSJ.

61. Cichi (Santa Clara) to (Ponte?), 20 Feb. 1889, ATPSJ; Boschi (Meaderville, Mont.) to Martín, 24 Jan. 1906, Mont. Sax. 1003-VI-56, ARSI.

62. *Documents of American Catholic History*, 2: 46-48.

63. "Expenses [for Building Our Lady of Mt. Carmel Church, Pueblo, Colo.]," four-page manuscript inserted into "Historia Domus, S.J. Beatae Virg. Mont. Carmel [1915-1921], vol. 1, Mt. Carmel Church Rectory, Pueblo, Colo.; F. X. Tomassini, "History of Trinidad Parish," Holy Trinity Rectory, Trinidad, Colo.

64. Ponziglione (Milwaukee) to Mother Mary Bridget Hayden, 10 Dec. 1889, Archives, Sisters of Loretto at the Foot of the Cross, Loretto Mother House, Nerinx, Ky.

65. N. Russo, "The Origin and Progress of Our Italian Mission in New York," *WL* 25 (1896): 138-43.

66. Vecoli, "Peasants and Prelates," *Journal of Social History* 2 (1969): 235-36; R. P. Moretti (New York) to J. B. Guida, 28 Aug. 1893, Our Lady of Mt. Carmel file (AADC); Antonio Luchetti (Seattle) to Italian Assistant, Jesuit Curia, Rome, 24 Oct. 1908, Mont. Sax. 1003-VI-76, ARSI.

67. Provincial quoted in Cardella (Leon, Mexico) to Anderledy, 12 Mar. 1891, Marylandia 1011-VI-1, ARSI.

68. Pinto (Pueblo, Colo.) to Marra, 6 Jan. 1897, ANPSJ; Boschi (Meaderville, Mont.) to Martín, 24 Jan. 1906, Mont. Sax. 1003-VI-56, ARSI.

69. Russo, "Origin and Progress," *WL* 25 (1896): 141-43.

70. Russo, "Origin and Progress," *WL* 25 (1896): 141-43; "Silver Jubilee, Rev. Ludovico Caramello, S.J.," Seattle, Wash. [pamphlet], JOPA.

71. Russo, "Origin and Progress," *WL* 25 (1896): 137-43.

72. Russo, "Origin and Progress," *WL* 25 (1896): 143. For an analysis of the role of the Catholic parish, see Dolan, *American Catholic Experience*, 159.

73. "Letter from Father Robaut to Mr. Bougis," *WL* 13 (1884): 154.

74. Bernard Lynch, "The Italians in New York," *Catholic World* 67 (1888): 67-73, quoted in Mary Elizabeth Brown, "The Making of Italian-American Catholics: Jesuit Work on the Lower East Side, New York, 1890's-1950's," *Catholic Historical Review* 73 (1987): 197; N. Cocchi and G. Chianale, "Opera della S. Famiglia per gli emigranti Italiani stabiliti in Spokane," 1 May 1903, Mont. Sax. 1003-VI-37, ARSI.

75. Writer quoted in Richard N. Juliani, "The Interaction of Irish and Italians: From Conflict to Integration," in *Italians and Irish in America: Proceedings of the Sixth Annual Conference of the American Italian Historical Association*, ed. Francis X. Femminella (Staten Island, N.Y.: American Italian Historical Association, 1985), 28.

76. R. J. Crimont (Spokane) to Franz Wernz, 30 Jan. 1904, Mont. Sax. 1003-VI-43, ARSI; see also Rudolph Vecoli, "Prelates and Priests," *Journal of Social History* 2 (1969): 230.

77. Luigi Villari (1912) in Silvano M. Tomasi, *Piety and Power: The Role of Italian Parishes in the New York Metropolitan Area, 1880-1930* (New York: Center for Migration Studies, 1975), 181; Brown, "Making of Italian-American Catholics,"

Catholic Historical Review 73 (1987): 210; Russo, "Origin and Progress," *WL* 25 (1896):137.

78. Caramello reference in Aloysius A. Roccati, interview by Wilfred Schoenberg, 1963, typed transcript, JOPA.

79. *Spokesman Review* (Spokane, Wash.), 12 May 1913, clipping, Aloysius Roccati, S.J., File, JOPA; Tomasi, *Piety and Power*, 1-30.

80. For an analysis of the role played by institutions other than the national parish in Italian assimilation, see Peter R. D'Agostino, "Orthodoxy or Decorum?: Missionary Discourse, Religious Representations, and Historical Knowledge," *Church History* 72 (2003): 703-35; Rolle, *Immigrant Upraised*, 39.

81. "An Historical Sketch of the Mission of New Mexico," 1906, ANOPSJ.

82. John A. Chester, "Holy Week in San Miguel," *WL* 10 (1881): 275.

83. *RC*, 6 Jan. 1889; 1 Jan. 1899; 17 Aug. 1878.

84. *RC*, 28 July 1877; 21 Apr. 1889; 18 June 1891.

85. *RC*, 17 Aug. 1878; 11 Mar. 1882.

86. *RC*, 10 May 1891; 16 Aug. 1891.

87. *RC*, 21 Oct. 1876; 19 Oct. 1890; 1 Jan. 1888.

88. *RC*, 10 Mar. 1895.

89. Author unnamed, "Litterae Annuae Residenciae Delnortensis, 1910-1912," ANPSJ.

90. *RC*, 26 July 1914; 20 Dec. 1914; 14 Nov. 1915.

91. New Mexico Superintendent of Public Instruction, *Report*, 1910-1912, 44, in Deutsch, *No Separate Refuge*, 27.

92. García, *Desert Immigrants*, 214.

93. Author unnamed, "Litterae Annuae Residenciae Delnortensis, 1910-1912," ANPSJ.

94. Pinto (El Paso) to De Francesco, 24 Jan. 1914, ANPSJ; Garcia, *Desert Immigrants*, 218.

95. Count Guillaume de Chabrol, quoted in Thomas T. McAvoy, *The Americanist Heresy in Roman Catholicism, 1895-1900* (Notre Dame: Univ. of Notre Dame Press, 1963), 244.

96. McDannell, *Material Christianity*, 14; Rappagliosi, *Memorie*, 107-9, JOPA.

97. Almanac quoted in *Catholic Sentinel* (Portland, Ore.), 25 Dec. 1874, JOPA; Congiato (San Francisco) to Sopranis, 28 Dec. 1863, Calif. 1002-III-5, ARSI.

98. McDannell, *Material Christianity*, 24; Taves, *Household of Faith*, 110-11.

99. John W. Padberg, "Notes on the History of the Devotion to the Heart of Jesus," *Studies in Jesuit Spirituality*, 20 (May 1988): 20-21; Bayley quoted in Taves, *Household of Faith*, 110-11; Sestini, "The Sacred Heart the Salvation of Nations (1873)," in Curran, *American Jesuit Spirituality*, 294.

100. Taves, *Household of Faith*, 110-11; Sestini, "The Heart of Jesus and the Vicar of Christ (1869)" and "The Sacred Heart the Salvation of Nations (1873)," in Curran, *American Jesuit Spirituality*, 287, 292.

101. Parade described in *Owl* (Santa Clara), 3 (June 1871): 401-16; Riordan, *First Half Century*, 210; Coeur d'Alene letter quoted in E. Laveille, *Life of Father De Smet: Apostle of the Rocky Mountains, 1801-1873* (New York: Century Co., 1928),

367–68; Riordan, *First Half Century*, 168–70; Dolan, *American Catholic Experience*, 222–24.

102. Sestini, "The Sacred Heart the Salvation of Nations," in Curran, *American Jesuit Spirituality*, 297; Tentler, "On the Margins," *U.S. Catholic Historian* 21 (Spring 2003): 89.

103. McDannell, *Material Christianity*, 162.

104. *RC*, 8 Jan. 1882; Taves, *Household of Faith*, 127.

105. Winton U. Solberg, "The Sabbath on the Overland Trail to California," *Church History* 59 (1990): 355.

106. The letter is in James Talmadge Moore, *Through Fire and Flood: The Catholic Church in Frontier Texas, 1836–1900* (College Station: Texas A&M University Press, 1992), 184.

107. Taves, *Household of Faith*, 128.

CHAPTER 11

1. Kenna (Santa Clara) to Martín, 23 Feb. 1893, Calif. 1004-1-8, ARSI.

2. [Anderledy], "Capita quaedam Patri Visitatori Missionis Californiae prae ceteris commendanda 1889," Calif. 1003-II-3; Anderledy (Fiesole) to Meyer, 15 May 1889, Calif. 1003-III-1, ARSI.

3. James J. Hennesey, *American Catholics: A History of the Roman Catholic Community in the United States* (New York: Oxford Univ. Press, 1983), 173.

4. Dolan, *American Catholic Experience*, 124, 135.

5. Liptak, *Immigrants and Their Church*, 59–60, 65; Marvin R. O'Connell, *John Ireland and the American Catholic Church* (St. Paul: Minnesota Historical Society, 1988), 165–73.

6. Ireland and Keane in Winthrop S. Hudson, *Religion in America: A Historical Account of the Development of American Religious Life* 2nd ed. (New York: Charles Scribner's Sons, 1973), 252–53. See also O'Connell, *John Ireland*, 168. Moore, in *Religious Outsiders and the Making of Americans*, argued that the conservatives were not opposed to Americanization, but they favored ethnic and cultural pluralism.

7. Conroy in Gerald P. Fogarty, *The Vatican and the American Hierarchy from 1870 to 1965* (Wilmington, Del.: Michael Glazier, 1985), 18.

8. Papal documents in *Documents of American Catholic History, Volume 2, 1866 to 1966* , ed. John Tracy Ellis (Wilmington, Del.: Michael Glazier, 1987), 502, 546; Hudson, *Religion in America*, 259; Philip Gleason, *Contending with Modernity: Catholic Higher Education in the Twentieth Century* (New York: Oxford Univ. Press, 1995), 11–12. On "Americanism" and "Americanization," see Philip Gleason, "Coming to Terms with American Catholic History," *Societas: A Review of Social History* 3 (1973): 283–312.

9. Ciani, "Across a Wide Ocean," 184–85, 206; O'Connell, *John Ireland*, 235; Fogarty, *Vatican and American Hierarchy*, 171–75.

10. *RC*, 21 May 1899; Cardella in McAvoy, *The Americanist Heresy*, 35–36; Ciani, "Across a Wide Ocean," 191.

11. David J. O'Brien, *The Renewal of American Catholicism* (New York: Oxford Univ. Press, 1972), 63–64, 110–111.

12. Hornbeck, *California Patterns*, 70; Kevin Starr, *Inventing the Dream: California Through the Progressive Era* (New York: Oxford Univ. Press, 1985), 89, 180.

13. Roosevelt cited in Frank Van Nuys, *Americanizing the West: Race, Immigrants, and Citizenship, 1890–1930* (Lawrence: Univ. of Kansas Press, 2002), 1–6.

14. Ireland in Michael Gannon, "Before and After Modernism: The Intellectual Isolation of the American Priest," in *Catholic Priest in the United States*, 308; McQuaid to Simeoni, 5 Aug. 1882, in McGloin, *California's First Archbishop*, 307.

15. Frieden (San Francisco) to Meyer, 29 Apr. 1897, Calif. 1003-V-6, ARSI.

16. Edward Allen (San Francisco) to Martín, 28 Jan. 1896, Calif. 1004-II-28, ARSI.

17. Riordan (Santa Clara) to Meyer, 16 Apr. 1895, Calif. 1003-IV-15a, ARSI.

18. Riordan (Santa Clara) to Meyer, 6 May 1895, Calif. 1003-IV-15b, ARSI. See Jay P. Dolan, *In Search of an American Catholicism: A History of Religion and Culture in Transition* (New York: Oxford Univ. Press, 2002), 125.

19. John W. Barry (San Francisco) to Beckx, 17 Oct. 1885, Taur. 1012-XIII-1, ARSI.

20. Meyer, "Memoriale de Visitata California Missione, anno 1889," Archivo Istituto Sociale, Turin, Italy (hereafter AIST).

21. Ronald Eugene Isetti, *Called to the Pacific: A History of the Christian Brothers of the San Francisco District, 1868–1944* (Moraga, Calif.: St. Mary's College, 1979), passim; Barry, *Worship and Work*, 39, 85, 163–93.

22. Ricard (Santa Clara) to Anderledy, 24 Apr. 1888, Calif. 1003-VIII-1, ARSI; Kenna (Santa Clara) to Anderledy, [7 July 1888], Calif. 1004-I-5, ARSI; Congiato (San Jose) to Fr. Vicar General, 12 May 1886, Calif. 1003-I-1, ARSI.

23. Sasia described in Dooley, *Woodstock and Its Makers*, 188.

24. Riordan (Santa Clara) to Meyer, 16 Apr. 1895, Calif. 1003-IV-15a, ARSI; Henry D. Whittle (San Francisco) to Martín, 26 Sept. 1893, Calif. 1003-IV-17, ARSI. Young Whittle was one of the few Americans who sided with the Italian conservatives.

25. Anon., "Some Hints for the new Superior of the California Mission," [ca. 1896?], Calif. 1003-V-25, ARSI; Torti (Torino) to Anderledy, 28 Feb. 1889, Taur. 1011-II-33, ARSI.

26. Anon., "Some Hints for the new Superior of the California Mission," [ca. 1896?], Calif. 1003-V-25, ARSI; Torti (Torino) to Anderledy, 28 Feb. 1889, Taur. 1011-II-33, ARSI; Ireland in Ellis, *The Catholic Priest in the United States*, 324.

27. Riordan (San Francisco) to Martín, 30 Sept. 1903, Calif. 1004-II-38, ARSI.

28. Ciravegna (Chieri) to Martín, 14 May 1895, Taur. 1011-IV-37a, ARSI.

29. Anderledy, "Letter on . . . Our Unbloody Martyrdom," *Select Letters*, 351.

30. Martín in David G. Schultenover, *A View from Rome on the Eve of the Modernist Crisis* (New York: Fordham Univ. Press, 1993), 202.

31. Frieden (San Francisco) to Meyer, 19 Nov. 1902, Calif. 1003-V-62, ARSI.

32. Torti (Chieri) to Anderledy, 8 Feb. 1888, Prov. Taur. 1011-II-19, ARSI.

33. Congiato (San Jose) to Anderledy, 24 Apr. 1889, Calif. 1004-III-3, ARSI.

34. Ricard (Santa Clara) to Meyer, 25 May 1893, Calif. 1004-I-10, ARSI; Pollano (San Francisco) to Torti, 27 May 1889, Taur. 1011-11-47, ARSI. See also Pollano (San Francisco) to Martín, 21 Oct. 1893, Calif. 1003-IV-18, ARSI.

35. Pollano (San Francisco) to Torti, 27 May 1889, Taur. 1011-11-47, ARSI.

36. Riordan (Santa Clara) to Meyer, 16 Apr. 1895, Calif. 1003-IV-15a, ARSI; Ricard (Santa Clara) to Meyer, 25 May 1893, Calif. 1004-I-10, ARSI.

37. Kenna (Santa Clara) to Anderledy, 18 Jan. 1886, Calif. 1004-I-1, ARSI. When Kenna addressed the student body of the Methodists' University of the Pacific in 1903, the press hailed it as an unprecedented "era of good feelings" between Catholics and Protestants. See the *San Jose Mercury* (San Jose, Calif.), 22 Feb. 1903. But when he endorsed a non-Catholic candidate for public office, even some Americans concluded he was "too much occupied with external matters." See Frieden (San Francisco) to Martín, 13 Mar. 1905, Calif. 1003-V-85, ARSI.

38. Frieden (Santa Clara) to Meyer, 16 Apr. 1897, ARSI; Fortunato Giudice (Turin?) to Martín, 18 Sept. 1893, Prov. Taur. 1011, ARSI; Giacobbi (Los Gatos, Calif.?) to Sasia, 11 Nov. 1894, Prov. Taur. 1011, ARSI.

39. "Liber Consultationum Domesticarum, 1855–1894," entry, 1 Aug. 1883, ASCU.

40. "Permission Slip" [1880s], ASCU; *The Monthly Santa Claran* 5 (May–June 1937); Beckx (Rome?) to Congiato, 7 Mar. 1884, ACPSJ.

41. With an enrollment of over 704 students, St. Ignatius College was nearly twice as large as its nearest rival, St. Xavier College in New York, which had a student body of 382. Enrollment figures for all Jesuit institutions in the United States are listed in "Our Colleges in the United States, 1883–4," *WL* 13 (1884): 425.

42. Giacobbi (Los Gatos) to Martín, 7 Mar. 1896, Calif. 1004-IV-10, ARSI; Sasia (Turin) to Martín, 21 Mar. 1896, Taur. 1011-IV-60, ARSI. "All display was distasteful to him outside the sanctuary," the author of his obituary wrote, and "to popularity he was utterly indifferent." See "Father Henry Imoda," *WL* 31 (1902): 286–87.

43. Sardi (San Francisco) to Fr. General, ca. 1891, Calif. 1004-II-22, ARSI; Whittle (San Francisco) to Anderledy, 28 Mar. 1891, Calif. 1004-II-20, ARSI.

44. Kenna (Santa Clara) to Martín, 23 Feb. 1893, Calif. 1004-I-8, ARSI; Kenna (Santa Clara) to Anderledy, 18 Jan. 1886, Calif. 1004-I-1, ARSI.

45. Whittle (San Francisco) to Anderledy, 28 Mar. 1891, Calif. 1004-II-20, ARSI; Ganns, *Constitutions of the Society of Jesus,* 424–25; Razzini (Torino) to Anderledy, 11 Jan. 1887, Taur. 1011-I-8, ARSI.

46. Sasia (Monaco) to Martín, 23 June 1894, Prov. Taur. 1011-IV-13, ARSI; Pollano (San Francisco) to Anderledy, 3 Apr. 1891, Calif. 1004-II-19, ARSI.

47. A. M. Anderledy (Fiesole) to F. Giudice, 1 May 1891, AIST; J. Minotti (San Francisco) to Galucci, 29 Oct. 1893, ANPSJ.

48. Statistics on U.S. Jesuits in *WL* 13 (1884): 425. Between 1857 and 1891, Santa Clara conferred 171 bachelor of science degrees and 44 bachelor of arts degrees. See McKevitt, *University of Santa Clara,* 123.

49. De la Motte (Spokane) to Martín, 12 Jan. 1900, Mont. Sax. 1003-V-64, ARSI; and de la Motte (Pendleton, Ore.) to Martín, 26 Jan. 1905, Mont. Sax. 1003-

III-31, ARSI; *College of the Sacred Heart, Morrison, Colo., 1885–86*, 3–4; *Catalogue of Las Vegas College, 1887–88, to be known henceforward as College of the Sacred Heart, Denver, Col.*, 81, JCRU.

50. Henry Woods, "California Mission of the Society of Jesus," WL 13 (1884): 162–63.

51. Beckx (Fiesole) to Congiato, 7 Mar. 1884, ACPSJ. See also Razzini (Fiesole, Italy) to Beckx, 28 Feb. 1884, AIST.

52. Caredda (Santa Clara) to Anderledy, 16 Mar. 1888, Calif. 1004-I-2, ARSI; McGloin, *Jesuits by the Golden Gate*, 58, 61–62, 283. Not until 1913 was the bachelor of science degree restored at St. Ignatius College.

53. Kenna (Santa Clara) to Martín, 23 Feb. 1893, Calif. 1004-I-8, ARSI.

54. Sasia (San Francisco) to Anderledy, 30 Apr. 1891, Calif. 1003-II-7, ARSI; Kenna (Santa Clara) to Martín, 23 Feb. 1893, Calif. 1004-I-8, ARSI; Kenna (Santa Clara) to Martín, 13 Sept. 1900, Calif. 1004-I-18, ARSI; McKevitt, *University of Santa Clara*, 123–25.

55. Kenna (Santa Clara) to Martín, 23 Feb. 1893, Calif. 1004-I-8, ARSI; Kenna (Santa Clara) to Martín, 13 Sept. 1900, Calif. 1004-I-18, ARSI; McKevitt, *University of Santa Clara*, 123–25.

56. Alumnus cited in Edward D. Sullivan, *The Fabulous Wilson Mizner*, 67; Whittle (San Francisco) to Anderledy, 28 Mar. 1891, Calif. 1004-II-20, ARSI.

57. Anderledy, "Excerpta ex litteris Consultorum in Prov. Tauriensi, anno 1888," AIST. Visitor Rudolph J. Meyer, too, had urged more diligent bookkeeping during his inspection tour in 1889; see Meyer, "Memoriale, 1889," AIST.

58. Riordan, *First Half Century*, 266; Riordan (Santa Clara) to Meyer, 16 Apr. 1895, Calif. 1003-IV-15a, ARSI; Pollano (San Francisco) to Freddi, 30 Jan. 1895, Calif. 1003-VIII-4, ARSI; Frieden (San Francisco) to Martín, 29 Apr. 1897, Calif. 1003-V-6, ARSI.

59. Kenna (Santa Clara) to Martín, 20 Feb. 1902, Calif. 1004-I-25, ARSI; Ricard (Santa Clara) to Meyer, 25 May 1893, Calif. 1004-I-10, ARSI.

60. Hugh Gallagher (Santa Clara) to Meyer, 11 June 1895, Taur. 1011-IV-79a, ARSI; Ricard (Santa Clara) to Meyer, 25 May 1893, Calif. 1004-I-10, ARSI.

61. Meyer, "Memoriale, 1889," AIST; Cichi (Santa Clara) to [Meyer?], 25 May 1893, Calif. 1003-IV-16, ARSI; Cichi (Santa Clara) to Martín, 12 Apr. 1901, Calif. 1004-I-22, ARSI.

62. Kenna (Santa Clara) to Anderledy, 18 Jan. 1886, Calif. 1004-I-1, ARSI. The wine proverb is recorded in Rolle, *Italian Americans*, 165; Cichi (Santa Clara) to [Meyer?], 25 May 1893, Calif. 1003-IV-16, ARSI.

63. Cichi (Santa Clara) to Martín, 12 Apr. 1901, Calif. 1004-I-22, ARSI. In fact, the Jesuits continued to make wine, although the main vineyards were moved off campus to a place called Villa Maria. "Our vineyard has been ruined by philoxera," wrote Kenna in 1901, "but we are replanting with resistant vines and in a few years this source of revenue will again be fruitful." See Kenna (Santa Clara) to Martín, Jan. 1901, Calif. 1004-I-20, ARSI.

64. Barbara Miller Solomon, *In the Company of Educated Women: A History of Women and Higher Education in America* (New Haven: Yale Univ. Press, 1985), 58–59.

65. Beckx, "Zeal for Souls," *Renovation Reading*, 406–7; Meyer, "Memoriale, 1889," AIST.

66. *Jolly Giant* (San Francisco), 1874, in McGloin, *Eloquent Indian*, 148; Jenny Franchot, *Roads to Rome: The Antebellum Protestant Encounter with Catholicism* (Berkeley: Univ. of California Press, 1994).

67. Gregorio Leggio, "Diary, 1906," entry for 12 May 1906, Leggio Papers, JOPA.

68. Whittle (San Francisco) to Anderledy, 28 Mar. 1891, Calif. 1004-II-20, ARSI.

69. Sasia (San Francisco) to Anderledy, 30 Apr. 1891, Calif. 1003-II-7, ARSI; Pollano (San Francisco) to Martín, 21 Oct. 1893, Calif. 1003-IV-18, ARSI. Varsi's defense of his work with women is outlined in Varsi (Baltimore) to Beckx, 26 Nov. 1884, ARSI; Congiato (San Jose) to Anderledy, 24 Apr. 1889, Calif. 1004-III-3, ARSI.

70. Giacobbi (Los Gatos) to Martín, 23 Feb. 1897, Calif. 1004-IV-11, ARSI; Sasia (Monaco) to Martín, 23 June 1894, Taur. 1011-IV-13, ARSI.

71. Martín (Rome) to Sasia, 20 June 1895, AIST; Giacobbi (Los Gatos) to Martín, 23 Feb. 1897, Calif. 1004-IV-11, ARSI.

72. Frieden (San Francisco) to Meyer, 12 Aug. 1897, Calif. 1003-V-11, ARSI; Frieden (Santa Clara) to [Meyer], 12 Feb. 1897, Calif. 1003-V-3, ARSI; Frieden (Santa Clara) to Martín, 11 Feb. 1897, Calif. 1003-V-2, ARSI.

73. Frieden (San Francisco) to Martín, 9 Aug. 1901, Calif. 1003-V-49, ARSI; Frieden (San Francisco) to Meyer, 18 Mar. 1898, Calif. 1003-V-18, ARSI.

74. Cichi (Santa Clara) to Martín, 12 Apr. 1901, Calif. 1004-I-22, ARSI. When Frieden's unprecedented eleven-year term of office ended the following year, his departure evoked regret from some Jesuits. "I have met no man in my life, for whom I had a profounder esteem," one man wrote. "It is altogether unlikely that I shall ever have another superior like him." See Leggio, "Diary, 1907," entries for 8 and 9 Oct. 1907, Leggio Papers, JOPA.

75. Frieden (San Francisco) to Martín, 9 July 1901, Calif. 1003-V-46, ARSI.

76. De la Motte (St. Xavier Mission) to Martín, 19 Jan. 1901, Mont. Sax. 1003-III-3, ARSI.

77. Frieden (Santa Clara) to Martín, 11 Feb. 1897, Calif. 1003-V-2, ARSI; Congiato (Champoeg) to Beckx, 10 Dec. 1858, Mont. Sax. 1002-III-1, ARSI; Caruana (Sacred Heart Mission) to Sopranis, 28 Apr. 1866, Mont. Sax. 1002-XII-11, ARSI.

78. Gazzoli (St. Ignatius Mission, Mont.) to Beckx, 24 Aug. 1857, Mont. Sax. 1002-XI-3, ARSI; Lootens (Idaho City, Idaho) to Giuseppe Giorda, 24 May 1871, Provincial Correspondence, 1862–77, JOPA.

79. Austin F. Fagothey, interview by author, Santa Clara, Calif., Dec. 1971; de la Motte (Spokane) to R. Friedl, 19 July 1895, Calif. 1003-VII-6, ARSI.

80. Diomedi (Spokane) to Beckx, 17 Jan. 1887, Mont. Sax. 1003-IV-1, ARSI; de la Motte (Spokane) to Sasia, 19 July 1895, Calif. 1003-VII-6, ARSI; Razzini (Turin) to Martín, 20 May 1889, Taur. 1011-II-37b, ARSI.

81. "Summary of consultations regarding the proposal to unite the California and Rocky Mountain missions, 1902," Calif. 1003-VII-23, ARSI.

82. De la Motte (Spokane) to Sasia, 19 July 1895, Calif. 1003-VII-6, ARSI; de la Motte (St. Xavier's Mission, Wash.) to Martín, 19 Jan. 1901, Mont. Sax. 1003-

III-3, ARSI; de la Motte (St. Francis Mission, Wash.) to Wernz, 3 May 1909, Calif. 1005-I-10, ARSI.

83. De la Motte (St. Francis Regis) to Wernz, 3 May 1909, Calif. 1005-I-10, ARSI.

84. Taelman (St. Ignatius Mission) to Ketcham, 9 Oct. 1908, BCIM, 60/16; de la Motte (St. Francis Regis) to Wernz, 3 May 1909, Calif. 1005-I-10, ARSI.

85. P. Bandini (R.M.S. *Adriatic*) to J. A. Stephen, 17 Apr. 1889, BCIM, 24/8; G. Caruana (De Smet, Idaho) to F. Wernz, 26 Jan. 1907, Mont. Sax. 1003-VI-60, ARSI; and Caruana (De Smet, Idaho) to Wernz, 19 Jan. 1908, Mont. Sax. 1003-VI-71, ARSI; de la Motte (St. Xavier's Mission) to Martín, 19 Jan. 1901, Mont. Sax. 1003-III-3, ARSI.

86. L. Taelman (St. Ignatius Mission) to Ketcham, 9 Oct. 1908, BCIM, 60/16; Diomedi (De Smet, Idaho) to Ketcham, 11 Jan. 1909, BCIM, 54/5; *Report of Catholic Indian Missions for 1906*, St. Xavier Mission, Mont., BCIM.

87. De la Motte (Spokane) to W. H. Ketcham, 10 Feb. 1907, BCIM, 57/33; Van Gorp (St. Ignatius, Mont.) to Louis Martín, 24 Jan. 1903, Mont. Sax. 1003-VI-27, ARSI; Fahey, *Flathead Indians*, 276.

88. De la Motte, "Mission Superior's Diary, 1901–1908," entry for 17 Feb. 1906, JOPA.

89. De la Motte (St. Xavier) to Martín, 19 Jan. 1901, Mont. Sax. 1003-III-3, ARSI.

90. "Minutes of the Consultation . . . St. Ignatius Mission, 9 and 10 Jan. 1907," St. Ignatius Collection, JOPA; de la Motte (Spokane) to W. H. Ketcham, 23 Jan. 1907, BCIM, 57/33.

91. Trombley, Mary Morgan, [Recollections of Holy Family Mission in 1908,] Ursuline Collection, JOPA; Bigart and Woodcock, "St. Ignatius Mission," *Arizona and the West* 23 (Autumn 1981): 272, 73; de la Motte (St. Francis Regis Mission) to Wernz, 3 May 1909, Calif. 1005-I-10, ARSI.

92. De la Motte, "Diary," entry, 23 Sept. 1904, JOPA; Carroll in J. D. D'Aste (St. Ignatius Mission) to de la Motte, 30 Aug. 1908, D'Aste Papers, JOPA; statistics in "Catalogus Primus, Anno 1892–95, Missio Mont. Saxos.," Provincial Papers: Histories, JOPA.

93. John M. McClelland, Jr., "Our Pleasant Condition, Surrounded by Fewer Acres of Clams," *Regionalism and the Pacific Northwest*, ed. William G. Robbins, Frank J. Ross, and Richard E. Ross (Corvallis: Oregon State Univ. Press, 1983), 209–10.

94. Van Gorp (Spokane) to Martín, 6 Jan. 1898, Mont. Sax. 1003-II-30, ARSI; Van Gorp (Spokane) to Martín, 10 Jan. 1898, Mont. Sax. 1003-II-34, ARSI.

95. Anon., "The Rocky Mountain Missions . . . ," n.d., Provincial Papers, Box 8, JOPA; Van der Velden (St. Francis Regis, Wash.) to Wernz, Mont. Sax. 1003-VI-67, ARSI.

96. Adna F. Weber, *The Growth of Cities: A Study in Statistics* (New York: Columbia Univ. Press, 1899), 20, 27.

97. Liptak, *Immigrants and Their Church*, 34; Van Gorp (Spokane) to Sasia, 19 Dec. 1897, Taur. 1011-IV-124a, ARSI.

98. Cataldo in Garrand (Seattle) to Wernz, 10 Jan. 1893, Mont. Sax. 1003-IV-34, ARSI. See also Schoenberg, *Gonzaga University*, 48n7. Cataldo said that that principle had been established by the Jesuit Father General. See Cataldo (St. Ignatius Mission) to Carlo Torti, 3 Jan. 1888, ATPSJ. Even the colleges "had been founded and should continue to exist," Cataldo insisted, "*primarily* for the well-being of the Indians." See Cataldo, "Osservazioni private del P. Cataldo" (De Smet, Idaho) to Anderledy, 31 Jan. 1890, ATPSJ.

99. Beckx (Fiesole) to Giorda, 24 Nov. 1873, Provincial Letters, Box 1, JOPA; de la Motte (Spokane) to Sasia, 19 July 1895, Calif. 1003-VII-6, ARSI.

100. McLoughlin in Chittenden and Richardson, *De Smet*, 4:1555; de la Motte (St. Ignatius, Mont.) to Ketcham, 15 Dec. 1909, BCIM, 65/3; de la Motte (Spokane) to Martín, 16 July 1904, Mont. Sax. 1003-III-30, ARSI; Joset (Spokane Falls) to unnamed Jesuit, 24 June 1883, Joset Papers, JOPA.

101. Anderledy (Fiesole) to Torti, 10 Apr. 1890, AIST; Cataldo (De Smet Mission) to Anderledy [?], 29 Jan. 1890, ATPSJ.

102. Eberschweiler (Fort Belknap) to Cataldo, 28 July 1885, St. Paul's Mission Collection, JOPA; de la Motte (St. Xavier Mission) to Martín, 19 Jan. 1901, Mont. Sax. 1003-III-3, ARSI; D'Aste, "Diary, 1898–1901," entries, 24 July 1899, 7 Aug. 1899, 18 Jan. 1900, JOPA.

103. Rebmann, "Reminiscences of 40 Years," JOPA.

104. Ibid.

105. Garrand (Seattle) to Martín, 10 Jan. 1893, Mont. Sax. 1003-IV-34, ARSI; de la Motte (St. Xavier's Mission) to Martín, 19 Jan. 1901, Mont. Sax. 1003-III-3, ARSI; Gleeson (Santa Clara) to Martín, [ca. 1902], Calif. 1003-VII-7, ARSI.

106. *Catalogus Sociorum e Officiorum Prov. Taurinensis*, 1880, 52–53.

107. F. Giudice (Chieri) to Anderledy, 29 July 1892, Taur. 1011-III-34, ARSI; de la Motte (Santa Clara) to Wernz, 19 Mar. 1909, Calif. 1005-I-7, ARSI.

108. G. B. Ponte (San Francisco) to Beckx, 27 Mar. 1870, Calif. 1001-VII-21, ARSI.

109. Cataldo (De Smet Mission) to Torti, 10 Apr. 1889, ATPSJ; Torti (Chieri) to Anderledy, 8 Jan. 1889, Taur. 1011-II-30, ARSI; Pietro Bandini (Torino) to Anderledy, [ca. May 1880] Taur. 1011-II-37a, ARSI; R. Fumagalli (Chieri) to Anderledy, 19 May 1889, Taur. 1011-II-37f, ARSI.

110. Frieden (San Francisco) to Meyer, 8 June 1897 and 4 Jan. 1898, Calif. 1003-V-7, ARSI.

111. Frieden (San Francisco) to Meyer, 18 Mar. 1898; 29 Apr. and 29 Aug. 1897, Calif. 1003-V-6 to 12, ARSI; Frieden (San Francisco) to Martín, 3 July 1898, AIST.

112. Frieden (San Francisco) to Meyer, 18 Mar. 1898; 29 Apr. and 29 Aug. 1897, Calif. 1003-V-6 to 12, ARSI; Frieden (San Francisco) to Martín, 3 July 1898, AIST. Frieden, with his chin-out approach, never grasped that Italian authorities labored under similar restraints. From Turin, provincial Carlo Torti told the superior general in 1889 that he could "no longer make decisions based on written information they send from there." Reports from California were so tendentious and contradictory on every issue that it was impossible to make prudent decisions. I have little power to control what happens in America, Torti confessed, and "I know they quite often

laugh over there at the instructions I send them." See Torti (Torino) to Anderledy, 28 Feb. 1889, Taur. 1011-II-33, ARSI.

113. Gleeson et al. (Spokane) to Wernz, 24 Nov. 1908, Calif. 1005-I-2, ARSI; G. Chiaudano (Torino) to Wernz, 18 Dec 1908, Calif. 1005-I-1, ARSI. Some 5,400 of 7,668 lire spent on common expenses came from the mission. See "[Turin Province Accounts], Anno 1898," Taur. 1011-IV-157. ARSI.

114. *Matters of Greater Moment*, 482.

115. Edward R. Kantowicz, *Corporation Sole: Cardinal Mundelein and Chicago Catholicism* (Notre Dame: Univ. of Notre Dame Press, 1983), 44.

116. Murphy, *Jesuit Slaveholding*, 187.

117. "House Diary, St. Ignatius Mission, 1909–14," entry for 8 Sept. 1909, JOPA; Wernz (Rome) to Chiaudano, 18 May 1909, AIST. Gleeson had urged retention of the original name of the united missions, namely "Oregon Province." De la Motte proposed either "Pacific Province" or "Oregon." But Wernz decided that "Oregon" was "too little known in the rest of the Society and throughout the world" and that "Pacific Coast" implied too broad a region. See Gleeson et al. (Spokane) to Wernz, 24. Nov 1908, Calif. 1005-I-2, ARSI; and de la Motte (Spokane) to Wernz, 8 Sept. 1909, Calif. 1005-II-1bis, ARSI.

118. De la Motte (Spokane) to Wernz, 8 Sept. 1909, Calif. 1005-II-1bis, ARSI. By granting autonomy to its American missions, the Society of Jesus took a different path from the majority of immigrant Italian clergy in the United States. At the turn of the century, when Jesuit émigrés were severing their bonds with *la patria*, other immigrant religious congregations were tightening ties with Italy by separating from their American provinces and forming independent national vice-provinces within the United States. Thus, while the Jesuits were moving toward the melting pot, most immigrant Italian priests were becoming increasingly segregated from the mainstream American church and more closely affiliated with Italy. Consequently, despite all their self-criticism, the Jesuits were, in fact, more fluid than they themselves realized. The diocesan clergy from Italy, by contrast, were more ghettoized than the religious clergy. In 1917–18, 80 percent of the Italian secular priests in the United States (about 330) were not full members of American dioceses (that is, they were not "incardinated," to use the canonical term), but instead remained under the authority of bishops in Italy. See D'Agostino, *Rome in America*, 135, 282–85.

119. Hudson, *Religion in America*, 252–53; Leahy, *Adapting to America*, 34–35.

CHAPTER 12

1. Machebeuf in William H. Jones, *The History of Catholic Education in the State of Colorado* (Washington, D.C.: Catholic Univ. of America Press, 1955), 129–30.

2. Bradford Luckingham, "The American Southwest: An Urban View," *Western Historical Quarterly* 40 (1984): 265; Gasparri in Steele, *Works and Days* 114–15; Wallace in Horan, *Lamy of Santa Fe*, 384–86.

3. Population figures may be found in *Mexican Americans and the Catholic Church*, 38; Nicholas P. Ciotola, "From Agriculturalists to Entrepreneurs: Economic Success and Mobility Among Albuquerque's Italian Immigrants, 1900–1930," *New Mexico Historical Review* 74 (1999): 18; Luckingham, "American Southwest," *Western Historical Quarterly* 40 (1984): 266.

4. Weigle, *Brothers of Light*, 96–97; Deutsch, *No Separate Refuge*, 13, 19–21; *Mexican Americans and the Church*, 20.

5. Jones, *Catholic Education in Colorado*, 129–30.

6. *RC*, 28 July 1877, 354, in Weigle, *Brothers of Light*, 79; "Consulte domestiche, San Felipe, Albuquerque, 1875–1913," entry, 7 Apr. 1880, ANOPSJ.

7. Marra (Denver) to Mola, 12 Sept. 1888, ANPSJ; Marra (Denver) to Vioni, 11 Nov. 1888, ANPSJ; "An Historical Sketch of the Mission of New Mexico," 1906, ANOPSJ; Brunner (Trinidad, Colo.) to Scarcella, 16 Feb. 1906, ANPSJ.

8. Pinto (El Paso) to De Francesco, 14 Feb. 1916, ANPSJ; statistics in Garcia, *Desert Immigrants*, 31.

9. *Catalogus Provinciae Neapolitanae*, 1918, ANSPJ; Brown (Trinidad, Colo.) to De Francesco, 8 June 1913, ANPSJ.

10. Marra (Denver) to Vioni, 11 Nov. 1888, ANPSJ; statistics in *Catalogus Dispersae Provinciae Neapolitanae Societatis Iesu*, 1880, and *Catalogus Provinciae Neapolitanae Societatis Iesu*, 1915, ANPSJ; Pinto (El Paso) to De Francesco, 30 July 1912, ANPSJ; Pinto (El Paso) to Stravino, 15 Feb. 1907, ANPSJ.

11. P. Tomassini (Conejos) to Canger, 5 May 1890, ANPSJ; F. Tomassini (Albuquerque) to De Francesco, 28 Jan. 1913, ANPSJ; Di Pietro (Albuquerque) to De Francesco, 28 Jan. 1914, ANPSJ.

12. Brown (Denver) to De Francesco, 19 Apr. 1915, ANPSJ; Pinto (El Paso) to Marra, 16 Apr. 1902, ANPSJ.

13. Pinto (El Paso) to Marra, 18 June 1900; Pinto (El Paso) to Marra, 27 Feb. 1901, ANPSJ; Pinto (El Paso) to Stravino, 9 Jan. 1907, ANPSJ; Owens, *Carlos M. Pinto*, 160–63, 175–77.

14. Brunner (Trinidad, Colo.) to Scarcella, 16 Feb. 1906, ANPSJ; [Marra], "Stato della Missione del Nueva Messico e Colorado nell'agosto del 1891," NAP; Gentile (Pueblo) to Vioni, 1 Feb. 1881, ANPSJ.

15. F. Canger (Naples) to Piccirillo, 6 July 1880, Carlo Piccirillo Papers, IIA 4b-1, WCA. On the Society's restoration, see *Diccionario Histórico de la Compañía de Jesús*, 3: 2105–6.

16. A. X. Valente (Naples) to Piccirillo, 9 Jan. 1883, Carlo Piccirillo Papers, IIA 4b-2, WCA; Marra, "A New Residence at the Birthplace of St. Francis Hieronymo," *WL* 26 (1897): 442.

17. E. Carroll, "Sixteen Days in Sicily," *Letters and Notices* 20 (1889–90): 275–83.

18. "Various Items," *WL* 24 (1895): 342.

19. Marra, "The Story of the 'Gesu Nuovo' at Naples," *WL* 27 (1898): 9; M. Errichetti, "S. Brigida a Posillip e Villa S. Luigi," *Societatis* (Naples) 28 (Jan.–Apr. 1979): 11–16, ANPSJ.

20. "Consulte, 1901–1920," minutes, 8 Aug. 1909, ANPSJ; Brown (Denver) to De Francesco, 27 Feb. 1912, ANPSJ.

21. "Consulte, 1901–1920," minutes, 9–10 Oct. 1908, 1 May 1912, ANPSJ; Marra (Las Vegas, N.Mex.) to Stravino, 2 Jan. 1909, ANPSJ.

22. S. Personè (Trinidad, Colo.) to De Francesco, 17 Feb. 1915, ANPSJ.

23. Marra (Las Vegas) to De Francesco, 5 Mar. 1912, ANPSJ; Marra (Denver) to Gallucci, 23 May 1894 and 31 Mar. 1895, ANPSJ. From a European perspective,

America seemed to gobble up money. Pressed with loan requests from San Francisco, Razzini, provincial of Turin, complained about "the general fever" of American Jesuits to load themselves up with debts and then ask Europe for the dollars to pay them. See Razzini (Genoa) to Tosi, 6 Nov. 1881, Tosi Papers, JOPA.

24. Marra (Las Vegas) to De Francesco, 3 Feb. 1912, ANPSJ.

25. E. M. Cappelletti (Las Vegas, N.Mex.) to Vioni, 31 Jan. 1884, ANPSJ.

26. Brown (Denver) to De Francesco, 13 Oct. 1917, ANPSJ. A few years earlier, the Neapolitans paid 2,800 lire for the former Dominican villa at Posilipo in which they established a scholasticate. Sold at auction, it was worth 125,000 lire, Marra stated, so "we got it for a song." See Marra, "The New Theologate at Naples," WL 27 (1898): 364.

27. The pros and cons of separation reported in Di Pietro (Albuquerque) to De Francesco, 21 Dec. 1915, ANPSJ; "Consulte, 1901–1920," minutes of meetings, 23 Oct. 1905 and 23 Sept. 1908, in ANPSJ; Pinto (El Paso) to Stravino, 8 Feb. 1906; and Pinto (El Paso) to De Francesco, 1 May 1917, ANPSJ.

28. Brown (Denver) to De Giovanni, 26 Feb. 1918, 18 Apr. 1918, ANPSJ.

29. Brown (Denver) to De Giovanni, 11 Aug. 1919, ANPSJ; A. J. Lebeau (Del Norte, Colo.) to Mission Superior, 14 May 1917, Del Norte File, JCRU.

30. Brown (Denver) to De Giovanni, 16 Feb. 1918, ANPSJ. "This is an old idea of Fr. Meyer's, who mentioned it to me in Rome in 1896," Marra wrote of the division plan. "It is certain that Missouri would gain if it took the splendid city of Denver with our magnificent college, . . . and Pueblo. New Orleans would not do badly picking up El Paso, with its five churches and three schools, and Albuquerque with three churches and three schools and investments worth $30,000 or $40,000." See Marra (Las Vegas) to De Francesco, 24 Mar. 1912, ANPSJ.

31. "P. Carlo Pinto," LEPN (1914–20): 3, ARSI; "Consulte, 1901–1920," entry, 26 Jan. 1918, ANPSJ; Personè in "House Diary, 1911–1920," entry, 15 Aug. 1919, Holy Trinity Parish, Trinidad, Colo.

32. Brown (Denver) to De Giovanni, 29 Apr. 1919, ANPSJ. It is unclear who suggested the subsidy. Writing to the Neapolitan provincial, Brown claimed that "it was I who originally and of my own accord proposed giving you a sum of money outright and it was I who urge the matter with Father General and got him to consent to this," after Naples first proposed borrowing a sum from the mission. See Brown (Denver) to De Giovanni, 18 Sept. 1919, ANPSJ. Another source quotes Brown as having said that the superior general ordered the donation. See McMenamy (St. Louis) to Emile Mattern, 21 Mar. 1921, "Litt. a Prov. Acceptae," APNO. By 31 May 1920, Naples had already received $84,813.74 of the promised donation. See "Statement, 31 May 1920," ANPSJ.

33. Pinto's request to leave the Southwest and go to California is described in Pinto (El Paso) to De Francesco, 18 Mar. and 1 May 1917, ANPSJ; Owens, Carlos M. Pinto, 136–41.

34. Brown (Denver) to De Giovanni, 29 Apr. 1919, ANPSJ; unidentified author, "Return from the States," typescript ca. 1919, ANPSJ.

35. Gentile (Las Vegas, N.Mex.) to Vioni, 15 Dec. 1883, ANPSJ.

36. Caldi in "St. Regis Mission Diary, 1908–12," entries, 19 and 23 July 1909,

JOPA; "Historia Domus" [Our Lady of Mount Carmel], 1915–1921," entries, 16 and 18 Aug. 1917, Mount Carmel Rectory, Pueblo, Colo.; D'Aste, "Diary, 1908–10," entries, 14 and 31 May 1909, JOPA.

37. Stephan in *Frontiers and Catholic Identities*, 67–69; Bureau of Catholic Indian Missions, *Report for 1909* (Washington, D.C., 1910), 46–47, BCIM.

38. "Epistolae Missiones Petentium," Tuar. 1012-XIII-1–36, ARSI; "Obituary of Crispino Rossi," Rossi file, JOPA.

39. Julius Jette, "Alaska: An Autumn Trip," *WL* 36 (1907): 277; Schoenberg, *Paths to the Northwest*, 183.

40. Statistics reported in Clifford E. Trafzer, *As Long as the Grass Shall Grow and Rivers Flow: A History of Native Americans* (Fort Worth: Harcourt College Publishers, 2000), 322; de la Motte (St. Ignatius, Mont.) to Ketcham, 8 Jan. 1911, BCIM, 75/8.

41. Guidi entry in "St. Regis Mission Diary, 1892–1900," entry, 24 Dec. 1898, JOPA; D'Aste entry in "House Diary, St. Ignatius Mission, 1909–14," entry, 15 Aug. 1909, JOPA.

42. Taelman (St. Xavier's Mission, Mont.) to Martín, 16 Jan. 1902, Mont. Sax. 1003-VI-14, ARSI.

43. Egon Mallman, *Jesuit Missions* 22 (1948): 3, cited in Schoenberg, *Paths to the Northwest*, 409.

44. Burrowes (St. Louis) to Ledochowski, 22 Apr. 1918, draft, Denver Collection, III, JMPA; Mattern (Rome) to John M. Salter, 12 Sept. 1928, "Litteras a Prov. Acceptae," ANOPSJ. The Jesuits did not leave the parish until 1966, when the diocesan clergy assumed responsibility for it.

45. Emile Mattern (Rome) to Edward Cummings, 22 May 1924, "Litterae a Provincialibus Acceptae," ANOPSJ.

46. Owens, *Carlos M. Pinto*, 167. In 1944, Sacred Heart reverted to the Jesuits of the New Orleans Province, who still retain the parish. Cummings (New Orleans) to Giglio, 23 Aug. 1927, "Closed Houses File, 1927–60," Archives of St. Francis Xavier Church, Albuquerque, N.Mex.

47. Everard J. Beukus, *Circular Letter to the [Missouri] Province* (Chicago: Loyola Univ. Press, 1921), 27; Decree 12 of General Congregation 25, *Matters of Greater Moment*, 497.

48. Walt Crowley, *Seattle University: A Century of Jesuit Education* (Seattle: Seattle Univ. Press, 1991), 31; Thomas J. Noel, *Colorado Catholicism and the Archdiocese of Denver, 1857–1889* (Boulder: Univ. Press of Colorado, 1989), 63.

49. Edward R. Vollmar, "History of the Jesuit Colleges of New Mexico and Colorado, 1867–1919" (M.A. thesis, St. Louis University, 1938), v.

50. McKevitt, *University of Santa Clara*, 70; Schoenberg, *Gonzaga University*, 213–14.

51. Morrissey in *Morning Times* (San Jose), 1 Apr. 1912.

52. Kathleen A. Mahoney, *Catholic Higher Education in Protestant America: The Jesuits and Harvard in the Age of the University* (Baltimore: Johns Hopkins, 2003), 236–37.

53. Folchi (Spokane) to Viola Mihm, 29 Oct. 1909, Folchi Papers, JOPA; A. M.

Valentino (Pueblo) to F. X. McMenamy, 23 June 1922, Section III, Pueblo, Colo., JMPA (SLU film 1042).

54. On D'Aste, see M. Imelda Hanratty, "Taken from Quarterly Review, 1 February 1911," Ursuline Collection, JOPA; "Father Francis J. Prelato," *WL* 37 (1908): 255.

55. James Talmadge Moore, *Acts of Faith: The Catholic Church in Texas, 1900–1950* (College Station: Texas A&M Univ. Press, 2002), 126–27; George St. Paul, "Menology of the New Orleans Province," 242–44, A1.A3/HH1/Z1.0, APNO.

56. Ebaugh and Chafetz, *Religion Across Borders*, xi–xii; Thistlethwaite, "Migration," *A Century of European Migrations*, 21, 19; for a study of America's impact on European thought, see Germán Arciniegas, *America in Europe: A History of the New World in Reverse* (San Diego: Harcourt Brace Jovanovich, 1986), 240.

57. Di Pietro (Albuquerque) to De Francesco, 21 Dec. 1915, ANPSJ.

58. Riordan (Santa Clara) to Meyer, 16 Apr. 1895, Calif. 1003-IV-15a, ARSI; The Neapolitan provincial "begs of me to let him have as many mass intentions as I can spare," the head of the New Orleans Province wrote in 1921, and he asks me to "continue to send him masses as before." See E. Mattern (New Orleans) to Mandalari, 7 Mar. 1921, Albuquerque-San Felipe Correspondence, B2/E5/Z1.ZI, APNO. When separation came between the West and Turin, the latter, apparently less dependent on foreign funds than Naples, turned down a subsidy, claiming: "it does not seem just to us to be demanding support of this sort from a new province." See Chiaudano [Turin] to Wernz, 6 May 1909, Calif. 1005-II-11, ARSI. Whether support actually continued after separation, despite Chiaudano's protestation, is unclear.

59. Documentation about the transfer of title to the California Jesuit James P. Morrissey is in the Morrissey file at ACPSJ; see also Monti, *Compagnia di Gesù*, 5:498–99, 512–51.

60. Curran, *American Jesuit Spirituality*, 272.

61. Ciani, "Across a Wide Ocean," 236–46, 379–83.

62. F. W. Gockeln (La Val, France) to John Larkin, 4 Aug. 1849, ANYPSJ.

63. Angelo De Santi (Rome) to Tosi, 7 May 1895, Tosi Papers, JOPA; Giudice (Chieri) to Tosi, 2 Apr. 1892, Tosi Papers, JOPA; Ponte (Monaco) to Palladino, n.d. 1864, Palladino Papers, JOPA.

64. Palomba (Naples) to Gasparri, 12 May 1873, ANPSJ; the German pastor is cited in Bruce Levine, *Spirit of 1848: German Immigrants, Labor Conflict, and the Coming of the Civil War* (Urbana: Univ. of Illinois Press, 1922), 53.

65. Gerald McKevitt, "'The Jump That Saved Rocky Mountain Mission': Jesuit Recruitment," *Pacific Historical Review* 55 (1986): 427–53. According to province catalogues, by 1914, the Italian provinces boasted a total membership of 1,400, which was nearly as great as in 1870.

66. Aveling, *Jesuits*, 322.

67. Tognetti, *Memorie Storiche intorno alla Provincia Romana*, 682–83; C. Papalo (Naples) to Ardia, 20 Sept. 1851, 219P10.a, AMPSJ.

68. Interview by author with Luigi Camolese, S.J., Apr. 1982, Villa San Maurizio, Turin, Italy. Similar influence was wielded by Catholic nuns from the West who were recalled to their mother house to assume high office. "Influenced by the reali-

ties of a western world that had forced them to choose between an exact adherence to the rule or a necessary act of charity of survival, the western mission sisters . . . prodded and encouraged their companion sisters to promote a progressive style of religious life, one that adapted to the demands at hand." See Butler, "Afterword," *End of the Santa Fe Trail*, 368–69.

69. Alfredo Mezza, "Breve Memoria del P. Giuseppe Marra S.I.," *LEPN* (1914–20): 120–29, ANPSJ.

70. *Notizie Storiche de Descrittive delle Missioni della Provincia Torinese della Compagnia di Gesù nell'America del Nord* (Torino: Derossi, 1898), 3, ACPSJ.

71. Aveling, *Jesuits*, 321–22; Matthew 21:12.

CHAPTER 13

1. M. J. Spalding, *The Evidences of Catholicity: A Series of Lectures, Delivered in the Cathedral of Louisville*, 6th ed. (Baltimore: 1857; reprint, 1882), 188.

2. Alexis de Tocqueville, *Democracy in America* (New York: 1899) 1:309–10, 313.

3. Kenneth D. Wald, *Religion and Politics in the United States*, 3rd ed., (Washington, D.C.: Congressional Quarterly Press, 1997), 8–9, 20–21; Felicia R. Lee, "The Secular Society Gets Religion," *New York Times*, 24 Aug. 2002.

4. Oscar Handlin, *The Uprooted: The Epic Story of the Great Migrations That Made the American People* (New York: Grosset & Dunlap, 1951), 3.

5. Jay P. Dolan, "The Immigrants and Their Gods: A New Perspective in American Religious History," *Church History* 57 (1988): 65–66. Religion's role in Italian emigration to the United States has received ample attention in the path-breaking work of Rudolph J. Vecoli, Lydio F. Tomasi, Silvano M. Tomasi, and Robert A. Orsi. Peter R. D'Agostino has contended recently, however, that earlier scholars gave too much emphasis to religion in the assimilation of Italian Americans. See D'Agostino, "Orthodoxy or Decorum?," *Church History* 72 (2003): 703–35.

6. Archdeacon, *Becoming American*, xii, 114; see also Roger Daniels, *Coming to America: A History of Immigration and Ethnicity in American Life* (Princeton, N.J.: Harper Perennial, 1991).

7. Wald, *Religion and Politics in the United States*, 20; 7–8; Stewart M. Hoover, *Religion in the News: Faith and Journalism in American Public Discourse* (Thousand Oaks, Calif.: Sage, 1998), 67.

8. Muller, *Bishop East of the Rockies*, 158.

9. R. Meyer (San Francisco) to Anton Anderledy, 24 May 1889, Calif. 1003-III-8, ARSI.

10. Henry Louis Gates, Jr., Review of *Cultures of Complaint*, by Robert Hughes, *New Yorker*, 19 Apr. 1993, 115; Wright, *The Jesuits*, 116–24.

11. Burns, *Jesuits and the Indian Wars*, 56.

12. Bohme, "Italians in New Mexico," 145.

13. Spalding, *The Evidences of Catholicity*, 188.

14. D'Agostino, *Rome in America*, 283.

15. Bishop J. F. Shanahan, "The Unity of the Church," *Memorial Volume of the Third Plenary Council of Baltimore* (Baltimore: Baltimore Publishing, 1885), 67.

16. "Italians in the United States," *The Catholic Encyclopedia* (Robert Appleton, 1910), 8:n.p. Reproduced online at http://www.newadvent.org/cathen/08202a.htm.

17. O'Malley, *First Jesuits*, 169–70; *Constitutions of the Society of Jesus*, 262.

18. Gannon, "Before and After Modernism," 306–7.

19. William G. Ritch, "Whitch! [sic] Stagnation or Progress," [1878], William Gillet Rich Papers, HL.

20. Jacqueline Peterson, review of *Churchmen and the Western Indians*, ed. Clyde A. Milner II and Floyd A. O'Neil, in *Pacific Northwest Quarterly* 78 (1987): 110.

21. John Larkin (New York) to F. W. Gockeln, 10 July 1848, Larkin Correspondence, ANYPSJ; Accolti (n.p.) to Roothaan, 28 Mar. 1850, ARSI, in Garraghan, *Jesuits*, 2:407–8.

22. Bangert, *History of the Society of Jesus*, 480.

23. Sorrentino, *Dalle Montagne Rocciose al Rio Bravo*, 307.

24. Rolle, *Immigrant Upraised*, 336–37.

25. John Sims (Colville) to Brouillet, 26 Apr. 1874, BCIM; Segale, *At the End of the Santa Fe Trail*, 294; Frieden (San Francisco) to R. J. Meyer, 12 Aug. 1897, Calif. 1003-V-11, ARSI.

Glossary

BROTHER a Jesuit who is not a priest and yet is a full member of the Society of Jesus; brothers usually joined the Jesuits with the expectation of doing the order's manual and menial work.

FORMATION term used by religious orders to describe the period of training and the program of education given to its recruits or seminarians.

INSTITUTE a synonym for the Society of Jesus that refers particularly to its foundational documents such as the Formula of the Institute and its *Constitutions*.

JESUIT common description of a member of the Society of Jesus, a Catholic religious order of men founded in 1540 by Ignatius of Loyola, a Spaniard, and a small band of multinational students from the University of Paris.

MISSION a religious outpost in missionary country (for example, St. Ignatius Mission, Montana); also an administrative unit of the Society of Jesus reflecting national or geographic conditions (for example, the Rocky Mountain Mission), and whose operations are subject to oversight from a Jesuit province and its provincial.

MISSION, POPULAR a type of Catholic religious revivalism originating in the sixteenth century; usually spread over several days, consisting of devotional exercises, catechesis, penance, inspirational sermons, and meditations aimed at quickening the spiritual life of the faithful.

NOVICE in the Society of Jesus, candidates who seek admission to the order by undergoing a two-year program of testing and spiritual formation, at the end of which they pronounce vows of poverty, chastity, and obedience.

NOVITIATE the initial two-year program of Jesuit training; also the building or place in which that training occurs.

NUN member of a women's religious community who takes solemn vows of poverty, chastity, and obedience and lives in cloister; the term is also used as a synonym for "sister."

PROVINCE an administrative unit within the Society of Jesus that is based on national and geographic considerations, for example, the Maryland Province or the Turin Province.

PROVINCIAL the priest appointed by the father general in Rome to head a Jesuit province, usually for a six-year term.

RELIGIOUS a noun referring to members of religious congregations and orders who live in community, as contrasted with secular or diocesan clergy, who do not belong to religious orders.

SCHOLASTIC a Jesuit seminarian who has completed the two-year novitiate, made vows of poverty, chastity, and obedience, and is in training to become a priest.

SCHOLASTICATE a house of studies or seminary for Jesuits-in-training who have completed their novitiate program.

SISTER religious woman who pronounces simple vows of poverty, chastity, and obedience and engages in ministering to the needs of society.

SODALITY an association of lay Catholics formed by Jesuits in parishes and schools to promote the spiritual life of its members, to undertake apostolic activities, and to aid persons in need.

SUPERIOR GENERAL the head of the Society of Jesus, who is elected for life by a general congregation of the order. Popularly called "Father General," he normally resides in Rome.

THEOLOGIAN a Jesuit student of theology; the term can also refer to a professor of theology.

VISITOR an administrative inspector, usually of provinces, missions, and regions, who acts as the personal emissary of the father general in Rome. He is empowered not merely to examine, but also to implement reforms.

Index

academics. *See* colleges and universities

Accolti, Michele: in California, 94–96, 116, 226–27, 232, 245; life and legacy, 6, 10, 57, 224, 327; and Protestants, 211, 240; Rocky Mountain Mission, 92, 121. Views on: education, 205, 226–27, 230–32

accommodation/cultural reconciliation: art/architecture, 4–5, 80–81, 89–90, *135*, *136*, 140, 226–28, 236; dress, 238–39; Jesuit principle of, 1–5, 7, 10–11, 63, 119, 123–25, 324–27; Jesuits as culture brokers, 2–3, 240–44, 263, 322, 333n5; music and visual arts, 54, 132–36, 189; native customs and languages, 2, 10–11, 117–19, 123–28, 132–33, 142–49; travel, 36–37. *See also* adaptation; transcultural expressions

acculturation: cultural insertion, 142–49; education, 88, 158–59, 171–77, 203, 214–15, 226–33, 241; immigrant communities, 244–55, 259–63, 269–71, 380n80, 393n5; importance of, 101, 115–16; Jesuit émigrés, 7–8, 55–60, 62–63, 70, 236–40, 259, 283; Native American resistance to, 171–77; pluralism, 236–44, 381n6; religion, 199, 255; in Southwest, 178–79, 183–84, 207; Spanish-speaking Catholics, 2 41, 255–59. *See also* accommodation/cultural reconciliation; Americanism/Americanist controversy

adaptation: to American way of life, 7, 63, 66–67, 101–102, 112, 210, 316, 321, 344n24; California Mission, 270–71, 276–85, 324–25; and Jesuit *Constitutions*, 3, 5, 270, 281; to native cultures, 143–49; religious customs, 298; in travel, 47, 115–16; in various aspects of Jesuit life, 188, 237–40, 318–19. *See also* accommodation/cultural reconciliation; Americanism/Americanist controversy

Advent, 137

Affranchino, Angelo, 106–107, 351n47

African Americans, 115, 182, 247, 257

aggiornamento, 271

agriculture/farming, 4–6, 63, 71, 141; in colleges, 229, 281; Native Americans, 125, 148, 151–53, 156–59, 165, 173–76, 234, 286–88, 359n48

Aimaita, Alexander, 355n34

Alamosa, Colo., 257

Alaska/Alaska Mission: achievements and expectations, 101, 123, 319; California Province, 295; interest in, 41, 89, 107, 307–308, 316, 319, 373n51; veneration of St. Joseph, 139

Albania, 41

Albuquerque/Albuquerque Mission, 90, 105, 115, 196, 235, 239, 303; dissolution of Southwest Mission, 305, 310, 390n30; education, 201–202, 203; ethnic segregation, 258, 297–98; founding and growth, 184, 185, *186*, 187, 188, 192, 204, 296–97, 299; Jesuit legacy, 328; *Morning Journal*, 198. *See also penitentes; Revista Católica*

alcohol, 115, 281. *See also* wine

Alemany, José Sadoc, 95, 226, 268,

alienation: American Catholicism, 88, 199, 263, 388n118; immigrant communities, 250, 263. *See also* isolation

Allen, Edward P., 220, 269–70, 278

allotment: Anglo settlers on reservations, 137, 148, 168, 286–87; for education, 155. *See also* Dawes Act

America: European views on, 317–18; importance of external appearances, 227; Jesuit impressions of, 57–60, 113–17, 315

American Catholicism: acculturation, 267, 269–71; alienation and isolation, 88, 263, 388n118; Anglo American hegemony, 297–98; demographics, 265; European model, 74, 178–79, 191–200, 207, 235–36, 262, 264–67, 295;

religious garb. *See* clothing
religious orders, dissolution of, 5, 17–18,
33–35
Renaissance, 4, 18
Repetti, Giuseppe, 3
repatriation, xv, 29–30, 65, 86, 110–11,
236–37, 300–306, 317–18, 388n118
Rerum novarum, 276
Revista Católica: Americanist controversy, 267; content/circulation, 11,
205–207; defense of Hispanic culture,
255–57; founding of, 204–205, 314;
legacy, 327–28; staff, 9, 258, 302;
women's suffrage debate, 206. Views
on: adaptation of religious customs,
298; anti-Spanish language legislation,
256, 323; education, 256–57; government and citizenship, 256, 324; Las
Vegas College, 203; *penitentes*, 198;
public education, 236; religious free-
dom, 237 .
Revista Católica Press, 187, 205–207
revivals/revivalism, 189–91. *See also*
missions, popular
Revolution of 1848, 1,14–18, 23–29,
34–35; 36–45; 189
Rey, Antoine, 342–43n76
rhetoric, 1, 4, 211, 217, 219, 221
Ricard, Jérôme, 270, 273, 281
Richards, Joseph Havens, 88
Riel, Louis, 162
Riezi (Jesuit priest), 307
Riggs, Stephen R., 125
Rinieri, Ilario, 336n25
Rio Grande River, 310
Rio Grande Valley, 185–88, 201–202
Riordan, Joseph W., 269, 271, 315,
334n22
Riordan, Patrick W., 268
Risorgimento, 17–18, 23, 30–33, 41, 82,
321
Ritch, William G., 202, 326
Roach, John, 335n18
Roccati, Luigi, 108–109
Rocky Mountain Mission:
achievements/success, 148, 175, 319,
349n8; Americanization, 284, 288;
Anglo population growth, 289–92;
autonomy, 292–95, 388nn117,118;
and California Mission, 284–92, 295;
contract school program, 154–60, 170,
174–75, 177, 287; decline, 307–309,

312; establishment and growth, 92–96,
120–23, 122, 144, 155, 322, 349n16;
evangelism and religious instruction,
123–25, 148, 177, 284, 286, 290–91,
349n8; financial crisis, 94; living conditions, 117–19, 143; motivation for
serving, 108, 110, 120–21, 181; Native
American education, 150–60, 287–
88; personnel, 110–11, 120–21, 162,
181, 312, 339n20, 353n3; seminaries/
seminary training, 144, 291; travel to,
48, 285; Ursulines, 162–63. *See also*
boarding schools
Rogation Days, 141–42, 169
role models: in pedagogy, 130, 192,
366–67n45; in Indian ministry, 93,
130, 149, 170; Rome as, 65–66, 80–
81, 321
Rolle, Andrew F., xvii
Roman College: adaptation debates, 271;
closure, 27–28; descriptions of
missionary life, 108, 316–18; Forty
Hours devotion, 136; replication of,
80–90, 235; *Risorgimento*, 33; stature
of, 66, 71. *See also* Gregorian
University
Rome, Italy, 3, 4, 6, 12, 14–15, 19, 20,
24, 26, 27, 29, 30, 32, 33, 36, 40, 42,
44, 45, 49, 54, 55, 58, 59, 76, 78, 82,
84, 96, 97, 109, 110, 113, 115, 119,
130, 139, 207, 239, 241, 258, 260,
271, 273, 274, 276, 293, 301, 307,
310, 315, 316, 324, 337n44, 339n19;
anti-Jesuitism, 22, 24–29, 28, 33–34;
curricula mandates, 277–78; Gesù,
church of, 15, 33, 66, 134, 135, 140,
301; Jesuit return to, 44, 64–65, 68,
72, 86, 266; stature, 65–66, 75, 321
Roman Province, 88, 108, 152, 205, 223,
236, 237, 261–62, 265, 266, 267, 268,
280, 283–84, 290, 291, 295, 297,
390n30; anti-Jesuitism, 14–16, 21, 26–
33; emigration from Italy, 38, 40–45,
59–60; personnel in U.S., 61–65, 65–
70, 71–72
Romero, Rafael, 199
Ronan, Peter, 165
Roosevelt, Eleanor, 314
Roosevelt, Theodore, 268
Roothaan, Jan: anti-clericalism, 31; death
of, 33; exile, 27, 42, 301; expulsion of
Jesuits, 14–16, 334n2; return to Rome,